RUNNING

Microsoft®
FrontPage® 2000

Jim Buyens

PUBLISHED BY
Microsoft Press
A Division of Microsoft Corporation
One Microsoft Way
Redmond, Washington 98052-6399

Library of Congress Cataloging-in-Publication Data
Buyens, Jim.
    Running Microsoft FrontPage 2000 / Jim Buyens.
        p. cm.
    Includes index.
    ISBN 1-57231-947-X
    1. Microsoft FrontPage. 2. Web sites--Design. 3. Web publishing.
    I. Title.
    TK5105.8885.M53B89   1999
    005.7'2--dc21   98-43585
                                            CIP

Printed and bound in the United States of America.

6 7 8 9 WCWC   4 3 2 1 0

Distributed in Canada by Penguin Books Canada Limited.

A CIP catalogue record for this book is available from the British Library.

Microsoft Press books are available through booksellers and distributors worldwide. For further information about international editions, contact your local Microsoft Corporation office or contact Microsoft Press International directly at fax (425) 936-7329. Visit our Web site at mspress.microsoft.com.

For TIPS Technical Publishing:
Project Manager: Robert Kern
Copy Editor: Ellen Fussell
Technical Editor: Russ Mullen
Compositor: Lorraine Elder
Proofreader: Jessica Ryan
Indexer: Tim Griffin

For Microsoft Press:
Acquisitions Editor: Christey Bahn
Project Editor: Laura Sackerman
CD-ROM Editor: Kim Fryer
Editorial Assistant: Kristen Weatherby

Chapters at a Glance

Table of Contents

Acknowledgments

Many thanks to my wife, Connie, and my children, Lorrill, Justin, and Lynessa, for their support and for putting up with all the time I spent writing this book. Thanks as well to my parents, my brothers, and their families: Harold, Marcella, Ruth, Dave, Connie, Michael, Steven, Rick, Jenny, Matt, and Claire. What a bunch we are.

At Microsoft, thanks to Kim Fryer, who set up the business details, and to Laura Sackerman, the project editor.

Thanks as well to the people at **TIPS** Technical Publishing for transforming a draft manuscript into the book you're holding today: Robert Kern, Ellen Fussell, Russ Mullen, Jessica Ryan, Tim Griffin, and Lorraine Elder.

Thanks to Interland, Inc., and in particular to Ken Gavranovic and Jason Peoples, for their assistance in providing the *www.interlacken.com* Web site.

Most of all, thanks to you, the readers, who make an effort such as this both possible and worthwhile. I hope the book meets your expectations and that we meet again.

Introduction

Welcome to *Running Microsoft FrontPage 2000*. I'm glad you decided to create Web pages with Microsoft FrontPage, and I'm doubly glad you chose this book to learn about it. I hope both the software and the book live up to your expectations.

For most of the brief history of the World Wide Web, text editors have been the tool of choice for creating Web pages. The inventors of Hyper-Text Markup Language (HTML), the *lingua franca* of the Web, designed it so that anyone could produce Web pages with tools already at hand—that is, with text editors.

As Web page design approaches commercial art in its goals and audience, however, the original simplicity of HTML has become a hindrance. Not only has HTML grown continually more complex and difficult, but so have the techniques for living within its limitations. Meanwhile, as the Web penetrates mainstream society, more and more people seek ways to produce their own Web pages with less and less technical background. And organizations and businesses, both large and small, seek to avoid the high cost of hand-crafted Web pages, often priced at $1,000 each and more.

The solution to producing more complex output from simple input is a classic one: high-function software. This is the position that Front-Page occupies. FrontPage lets *you* concentrate on design while *it* writes the HTML.

The PostScript language, used for producing the pages of this book, consists of plain text—as does HTML. No one in their right mind uses a text editor to produce PostScript documents, though; instead, we use sophisticated word processing, drawing, and desktop-publishing software that creates PostScript for us. PostScript, though, lacks hyperlinks and is built around the concept of a fixed page size. That, along with many historical factors, is why the Web uses HTML rather than PostScript—and why you need a program like FrontPage, rather than a word processor or a spreadsheet, to create your Web pages.

Still, for many of the pioneers of Web authoring, coding HTML by hand remains the time-honored method. Its adherents disdain other approaches as artless, but these purists might better criticize artists for not weaving their own canvas, not gathering their own pigments, and not plucking the animal hairs for their brushes. After all, art resides in the original concept and the finished product—*not* in the means of production.

Objectives of This Book

This book is primarily about using software and much less about planning, designing, and implementing Web sites. Like all books in the Running series, *Running Microsoft FrontPage 2000* aspires to describe every feature of the subject software—FrontPage, in this case. Of course, the amount of coverage varies depending on each feature's importance, complexity, and expected frequency of use. If I've forgotten something, I'm sure you'll let me know.

Continuing in its family resemblance, *Running Microsoft FrontPage 2000* additionally covers topics related to the software but not a part of it. For FrontPage, this includes introductory material on:

- Planning and managing Web content.

- Principles of style.

- Designing page layouts.

- Choosing fonts and colors.

- The technical workings of the World Wide Web.

- Managing Web servers.

- The Web capabilities of other Office 2000 applications.

The reason for including these topics is twofold. First, you can't use FrontPage—or any other publishing program—to its fullest potential without understanding the target environment. Second, making the best use of software requires knowing the difference between good results and bad.

This book won't teach you about specific elements of HTML, its syntax, or its techniques; that's what you bought FrontPage to avoid. Neither will it tell you how to design a specific Web page you have in mind; a book can no more design your Web page than arrange your living room, office, or computer niche.

Still, the primary emphasis—and the greatest amount of writing—is on using FrontPage to transform your designs into working Web pages.

How This Book Is Organized

There are five main parts to *Running Microsoft FrontPage 2000.*

I. Web Publishing with FrontPage 2000

The two chapters in this part provide a high-level overview of the features in FrontPage 2000. Chapter 1 primarily describes features you can use to edit individual Web pages stored on your disk, while Chapter 2 explains the additional features available if you organize your work into groups of Web pages, that is, into FrontPage Webs.

II. Creating Web Pages

This is the core of the book: the part that describes in detail how to create Web pages. Ten chapters describe how to create, save, and open Web pages; how to add and format text; how to add, manage, and modify images and hyperlinks; how to choose page layouts, colors, and themes; and how to use the FrontPage components that don't require the use of FrontPage Webs. It concludes with two chapters that explain how FrontPage lets you work with raw HTML and how you can customize FrontPage to reflect your own preferences.

Where appropriate, these chapters also describe related features in other Office 2000 applications and provide guidelines for effective and attractive page design.

III. Managing a Personal Web Server

In previous versions of FrontPage, the normal mode of operation was to install a Web server on each Web author's PC, and then run FrontPage in concert with that Web server. The result was a difficult setup process and a complex working environment for new software users.

FrontPage 2000 takes a different approach. Its normal operating mode *doesn't* require the presence of a Personal Web Server, but this mode thereby sacrifices a number of high-end features: primarily the ability to interface Web pages with databases, and to test server-side components like Hit Counter and Search. If you need these features, you still need a Personal Web Server, and the two chapters in this part will describe how to set one up. Chapter 16 describes generally how Web servers operate, and Chapter 17 describes how to choose, install, and configure a Web server on your own PC.

IV. Using FrontPage Webs

If you're accustomed to creating Web pages by using conventional tools, you probably think of Web sites as collections of individual yet interrelated files. Furthermore, you're probably accustomed to managing these relationships by hand.

FrontPage can also work with collections of Web files, and it can manage their interrelationships for you. FrontPage calls these collections FrontPage Webs, and chapters 17 through 22 explain how they work.

Chapter 17 explains the FrontPage Server Extensions. This software needs to be on any Web server that hosts a FrontPage Web or that delivers pages using browse-time components configured through the FrontPage desktop software.

Chapter 18 explains how to create and manage a FrontPage Web residing either on a Web server or in an ordinary folder on your disk.

Chapter 19 explains how to work with files in a FrontPage Web: how to organize files in folders; how to add, copy, move, and delete files in a Web; how to create and view reports; and so forth.

Chapter 20 describes the FrontPage components that require using a FrontPage Web when you create pages, but don't require the FrontPage Server Extensions on the Web server that delivers the resulting pages to your Web visitors.

Chapter 21 describes the FrontPage components that require the FrontPage Server Extensions on the Web server your Web visitors access.

Chapter 22 explains how to create two kinds of database applications with FrontPage. First, it explains how you can receive data from an HTML form and save it in a Microsoft Access database. Then, it explains how to query such a database and present the results to Web visitors. Because it deals with Access databases, this chapter briefly describes the Web features present in Access itself.

V. Maintaining Your Site

The last part of the book covers two main topics: Web maintenance and Web publishing. The chapter on Web maintenance explains how FrontPage keeps hyperlinks updated, how to find and correct any hyperlink errors that do occur, how to search an entire Web for text, and how to correct the FrontPage indexes for a site.

Web publishing refers to the process of copying Webs from one location to another: from the machine where you run FrontPage to the Web server your visitors access, for example. After all, you *do* want other people looking at your pages, don't you?

What's New in FrontPage 2000

FrontPage 2000 provides a wealth of new and useful features. By category, these are as follows:

Tools for Creating Great-Looking Web Sites

New

- **Integrated FrontPage Editor and FrontPage Explorer.** It's easier than ever to get started using FrontPage because all of the Web-page creation and site-management tools you need are in one easy-to-use application. FrontPage Explorer and FrontPage Editor are no longer separate applications.

- **Theme Designer.** Without leaving FrontPage, you can customize theme elements like colors, logos, graphics, backgrounds, and bullets to create just the right look for your site.

- **Pixel Precise Positioning and Layering.** Place page elements like graphics and text anywhere on the page—and even layer content—through absolute and relative positioning.

- **Format Painter.** You can quickly copy the formatting of styles and Dynamic HTML effects from one piece of text to another by selecting some text that has the format you want, clicking the Format Painter button, and then highlighting any text you want similarly formatted.

- **Category Component.** Assign your Web pages to categories, and then automatically create lists of hyperlinks to all pages in a category. These lists remain up-to-date even as you add, remove, or recategorize pages anywhere in your Web.

Improved

- **Predesigned Themes.** You can choose from over 50 new pre-designed business-ready themes to provide a consistent look across a single page, multiple pages, or an entire Web site.

- **Shared Web Themes.** Office 2000 and FrontPage 2000 share themes so that pages created in Word or Access or FrontPage can share the same look and feel.

- **Enhanced Color Tools.** Choose custom colors from a color picker or color wheel, pick a specific color from a graphic to add to the available custom colors, or choose from a number of coordinating, Web-safe color schemes. Custom colors are available everywhere colors are available, and across editing sessions.

- **Cascading Style Sheets.** Use Cascading Style Sheets (CSS) to provide customized and consistent typography to a page, to several pages, or to an entire site.

- **Background Spell Checking.** FrontPage 2000 displays the familiar red, squiggly lines to show misspelled or unrecognized words. Right-clicking these words displays suggestions for the correct spelling.

- **Automatic Hyperlink Fix-Up.** Hyperlinks are automatically fixed when pages or graphics are renamed or moved in a FrontPage-based Web site.

- **Cross-Browser DHTML Animation Effects.** Add Dynamic HTML effects, including animation and collapsible outlines, to pages with the click of a button. Effects work seamlessly with Netscape Navigator 4.0 and Microsoft Internet Explorer 4.0, and appear statically across version 3 browsers.

Easy Database Integration

New

- **Access Database Connectivity.** Easily incorporate Access databases and Data Access Pages into FrontPage-based Web pages. Web visitors can then view or add records to the database.

- **Save Results to Database.** This feature makes creating and updating a database as easy as creating a form. You can create a new Access database or modify an existing one based on form data on a page.

Improved

- **Database Results Wizard.** Even without prior database experience, you can easily and automatically incorporate database queries directly into your pages. The data is dynamic, where current data is returned from the database each time the page is loaded.

HTML Editing

New

- **100% HTML Source Preservation.** Edit existing HTML and scripts (including ASP) worry-free in FrontPage. Bring HTML created in other tools into FrontPage, and FrontPage won't modify the code. Tag and comment order, capitalization, and even white space are preserved.

- **Quickly Insert Code in HTML View.** Use simple buttons or drop-down menus to insert code directly in HTML view (that is, when viewing the raw HTML).

- **Personalized HTML Formatting.** You can decide how you want your code indented, in what color tags should appear in HTML view, when to capitalize, and when to use optional tags. In addition, when pages are imported or new content is created, FrontPage automatically applies those preferences to the new code.

- **Reveal HTML Tags in WYSIWYG View.** You can quickly see which tags create specific effects on your pages by using Reveal HTML Tags while still in Normal view (WYSIWYG mode).

- **Target Specific Browsers, Features, and Servers.** Preselect which environments to target (browser, server, FrontPage Server Extensions, ASP, DHTML, CSS, Javascript), and FrontPage automatically restricts features that won't work on the targeted systems.

■ **Microsoft Script Editor.** Edit and debug scripts, including Java-Script and VBScript, more quickly with the built-in script editor.

Improved

■ **Edit HTML, DHTML, script, ASP, and XML.** Use the HTML tab to view pages and scripts, and edit them directly. Includes HTML, DHTML, script, ASP, and XML.

Site Management Reports and Views

 ### New

■ **Reports View.** You can quickly see a summary report of the pages, graphics, and files in your Web. With ease, you can also run reports listing slow pages; unlinked, recently added, or changed files; broken hyperlinks; and component errors, and you can review status, name assigned to, categories, publish status, or checkout status for any of the files.

Improved

■ **Folders View.** Show all the Web pages, graphics, and files in your Web.

■ **Navigation View.** Easily manage site navigation structure by quickly creating navigation bars, easily viewing the navigational layout of the site, persisting settings across editing sessions, and zooming into specific nodes for a close-up view.

■ **Hyperlinks View.** Graphically see all of the items that link to or from a specific page or Microsoft Office document, and visually see if any links are broken.

■ **Tasks View.** Track what tasks need to be done, who the tasks are assigned to, and quickly see the status, description, and the priority of the tasks.

Flexible Collaboration Features

 ### New

■ **Nested Subwebs.** Create Webs within other Webs, nested to any level. This provides separate control over any part of your total site.

■ **Page-Level Check In/Check Out.** Reserve files in a FrontPage Web so that no one else can edit them. This prevents one Web author from changing files another is working on. You can also revert quickly to the pervious version of a file.

- **Workflow Reports.** You can assign responsibility for a page to a team member when pages are saved, and you can even set up and assign approval levels or stages in your own publishing process.

Improved

- **Multi-User and Remote Authoring and Management.** Multiple Web authors can author and add content to FrontPage-based Web sites at the same time, allowing teams to work together easily. Web authors can author content directly to a server running the FrontPage Server Extensions, save environment preferences across editing sessions, and administer FrontPage Webs remotely.

Flexible Publishing Features

Improved

- **Create Webs Anywhere.** You no longer need a Web server to create Web content with FrontPage. You can create a complete Web site right on your hard drive and then publish to a server when you're ready. Of course, creating pages on a Web server is still fully supported, including Personal Web Servers.

- **Page-Level Control Over Publishing.** You decide exactly which pages to upload to the server by setting specific pages as "do not publish" or by publishing only pages that have changed.

- **Publish Anywhere.** Easily publish to an ISP with or without the FrontPage Server Extensions installed using FrontPage's built-in FTP. ISPs can choose from Windows NT or a broad variety of Unix platforms and operating systems.

- **Progress Indicator When Publishing.** The progress indicator makes it more clear what's happening during the publishing process.

Supports Your Way of Working

New

- **Personalized Menus.** Normally only the most used commands will be visible on menus. However, you can easily expand any menu to reveal all its commands.

- **Personalized Toolbars.** To reduce screen clutter, toolbars intelligently share space on the screen based on usage. Multiple toolbars are displayed in a single row on the screen. As a part of a toolbar is used, it's "promoted" and displayed in a hierarchical fashion.

- **Customizable Toolbars.** Toolbars are quicker and easier than ever to customize with Yes/No customization and drag-and-drop toolbar configuration.

- **HTML Help.** HTML Help appears on the screen while you continue to work within FrontPage. This means you can follow the help steps more closely and get questions answered more quickly.

- **Answer Wizard.** The Answer Wizard provides answers faster because it responds to questions posed in natural language. FrontPage infers from the way the question was phrased what you need help with.

Extensibility and Programmability

New

- **Visual Basic for Applications.** Build powerful FrontPage-based solutions using VBA. Leverage existing expertise to extend these solutions across Office applications.

Improved

- **Integration with Design-Time Controls and Visual InterDev.** Extend FrontPage's functionality by using Design-Time Controls delivered with Microsoft Visual InterDev and third-party products.

Works Great with Microsoft Office

New

- **Microsoft Office 2000 Save To Web.** You can lighten your workload because every team member can open and save Office 2000 documents directly to your FrontPage-based Web.

- **Open and Save Office 2000 Documents to FrontPage-Based Webs.** You can save Office documents and Web pages directly to FrontPage-based Web sites as easily as saving a file to a hard drive.

- **Integrated HTML Editing with Office applications.** When you edit an Office 2000 file that resides in a FrontPage-based Web, the Office application that created the file is its default editor. This works for files saved as HTML as well as for regular Office files.

Improved

- **Looks and Feels Like Microsoft Office.** Office 2000 and Front-Page 2000 share common themes, toolbars, menus, and short-cuts. In addition, tools like the Format Painter, HTML Help, and background spell-checking work alike.

- **Works Great with Other Widely Used Microsoft Products.** Personal Web Server uses the same management console as Windows NT Server, Internet Information Server, and other Back-Office applications.

Designed for Worldwide Use

New

- **Set Language by Page.** FrontPage 2000 can control the language its proofing tools use for each page, making it easier than ever for one Web author to create Web content in multiple languages. You can use search products like Microsoft Index Server to search for pages that were created in a specific language.

Improved

- **Available in 15 Languages.** The FrontPage 2000 Web author interface is available in English, French, German, Italian, Japanese, Spanish, and most recently, Norwegian, Dutch, Swedish, Korean, Traditional Chinese, Brazilian, Simplified Chinese, Danish, and Finnish. Additionally, with any language FrontPage product, you can create and manage Web content in the language of your Windows operating system.

- **Single Worldwide Executable.** One worldwide executable means that companies can standardize the base Office 2000 or FrontPage installation around the globe and then add support for appropriate languages when required.

- **Global User Interface and Multilingual Editing.** When additional languages are required, you simply install from the appropriate language pack. You can also have the FrontPage user interface in one language but create content in other languages.

Get Up and Running Quickly and Easily

 New

- **Windows Installer Technology.** FrontPage 2000 uses Microsoft's new Windows Installer Technology—the same installation program used by the rest of Microsoft Office 2000. This means you can install FrontPage 2000 and Office 2000 together on one computer or thousands.

- **Install on Demand.** Components such as clip art and language packs are installed as needed, saving space on a hard drive until you need the functionality. When you first use an uninstalled feature, FrontPage installs it on the fly.

- **Self-Repairing Application.** FrontPage 2000 determines at launch if essential files are missing and where they can be found. It then reinstalls the missing files with little or no Web author intervention.

- **Microsoft Office Custom Installation Wizard (CIW).** Administrators can deploy customized versions of Microsoft Office 2000 and FrontPage 2000 containing preselected configuration options at the individual feature, menu, and toolbar level.

Improved

- **Easier Web Server Administration.** FrontPage 2000 uses the same management console as Windows NT and Internet Information Server, and you can manage FrontPage-based Webs remotely. Administration of Unix Web servers is also easier with FrontPage 2000.

Using the *Running Microsoft FrontPage 2000* Companion CD

There are three kinds of content on the CD accompanying this book:

- The rfp2000 Web, which contains most of the Web pages shown as samples throughout the book.

- Various Microsoft utilities related to FrontPage.

- A selection of third-party software related to FrontPage.

Inserting the CD displays a Web page with three corresponding links under the heading "What's on the Companion Disc?"

Using the rfp2000 Web

The CD that accompanies this book contains most of the sample Web pages that appear in the book's figures. This provides a way to view the pages in color on your own monitor, to examine how they're constructed, and to experiment. While not a complete, well-integrated Web site, the rfp2000 Web illustrates many FrontPage features and gives you a starting point for your own work.

 **ON THE WEB**

You can avoid the hassle of installing the rfp2000 Web by viewing it on the Internet. The URL is http://www.interlacken.com/rfp2000.

The files for the rfp2000 Web are located in the rfp2000 folder on the CD. There are three ways to use these files:

 SEE ALSO

For an explanation of disk-based Webs and server-based Webs, see Chapter 18, "Creating and Managing FrontPage Webs."

■ For casual browsing, you can open files simply by pointing your browser to this folder on your CD-ROM drive.

■ To savor the full FrontPage experience, including modifying the pages and seeing active components in action, you should copy the rfp2000 folder to your hard disk and make it a *disk-based Web*.

SEE ALSO

For information about publishing FrontPage Webs, see Chapter 24, "Publishing Your FrontPage Web."

■ To see *all* the components in action, you'll need to publish the disk-based Web to a *server-based Web*.

To copy the rfp2000 folder to your hard disk and make it a disk-based Web, proceed as follows:

CAUTION

FrontPage cannot open the rfp2000 Web directly from the CD. Whenever it opens a Web, FrontPage writes information to certain internal files. On CD, of course, these files aren't writable.

1 Open an MS-DOS window and copy the rfp2000 folder from the accompanying CD to a folder on your local hard disk. Assuming your hard disk is drive C and your CD-ROM is drive D, the necessary command would be

- On Windows 95 or Windows 98:

```
xcopy32 d:\rfp2000\*.* "c:\My Documents\
My Webs\rfp2000\" /s
```

- On Windows NT:

```
xcopy d:\rfp2000\*.* "c:\My Documents\
My Webs\rfp2000\" /s
```

2 Close the MS-DOS window.

3 Start FrontPage, and then choose Open Web from the File menu.

4 When the Open Web dialog box appears, locate the text box titled Folder Name and enter the location you specified in step 1.

5 Click the Open button to open the rfp2000 Web.

To use the rfp2000 Web as a disk-based Web only, stop here. To install the rfp2000 Web on your Personal Web Server (or any other Web server), continue with these steps:

6 Choose Publish Web from the File menu.

7 Enter the desired Web location in the text box titled Specify The Location To Publish Your Web To. Typically this would be:

```
http://<<server>>/rfp2000
```

where <server> is the network address of the destination Web server.

8 Verify that the following options are in effect. If they aren't visible in the Publish Web dialog box, click the Options button.

- Publish Changed Pages Only (selected).

- Include Child Webs (turned off).

- Secure Connection Required (turned off unless required by your Web server).

9 Click the Publish button.

10 If prompted, enter the destination server's root Web administrator password.

Once publishing is complete, you should be able to open the rfp2000 Web on the destination server. To do so, choose Open Web from the File menu, specify the Web's location, and then click the Open button.

Please note the following restrictions:

- The rfp2000 Web isn't a fully functioning, integrated Web site. It's only a collection of exercises and sample pages constructed primarily for figures in this book.

- Various hyperlinks and form handlers may be incorrect or missing if they aren't relevant to the point at hand.

- Some functions may use facilities that were present in the author's lab but located outside the rfp2000 Web.

- The rfp2000 Web has been tested with the FrontPage Server Extensions running on a Windows NT 4 server running IIS 4, and on a Windows 98 machine running Microsoft Personal Web Server. The browser was Microsoft Internet Explorer releases 4 and 5. Results may vary with other configurations.

Installing the Microsoft FrontPage 2000 Trial Version

If you haven't yet purchased FrontPage 2000 but would like to try it for 45 days, you can install a trial version from the companion CD. The trial version has these restrictions:

■ The trial version will cease to function 45 days after you install it.

■ Removing and reinstalling the trial version won't extend the trial period.

■ If you install the trial version over an earlier version of FrontPage, the following will happen:

• The trial version will nevertheless cease to function after 45 days.

• If you later buy an upgrade version of FrontPage 2000, you'll have to reinstall your old software before you can install the upgrade.

For more information and support concerning the FrontPage 2000 trial version, browse the following location on Microsoft's Web site:

    http://www.Microsoft.com/frontpage/trial

To install the FrontPage 2000 trial version from the companion CD, follow the instructions on the CD's startup page or follow this procedure:

1 Click the Start button on the Windows taskbar.

2 Select Run from the Start menu.

3 Type *d*:\trial\setup (where *d* is your CD-ROM drive letter).

4 Follow the setup instructions that appear on your screen.

Using the Supplied Microsoft Utilities

The \fonts directory contains a selection of fonts and utilities from the Microsoft Typography group. To install them, browse the Web page at \fonts\default.htm and click the following links:

■ **Font Properties Extension.** This utility enhances your Control Panel Fonts applet to display each font's copyright, embedding permissions, hinting, multi-language support, and additional properties.

- **TrueType Core Fonts for the Web.** This is a collection of fonts epecially designed for clarity on Web pages (despite the low resolution of most computer monitors).

- **Microsoft Web Embedding Fonts Tool.** This utility packages fonts so that Internet Explorer can download them. This ensures that your Web visitors see text as you intended.

To install any utility or font, click its link and then click the CD-ROM link on the resulting page.

To learn more about any utility or font, or to check for a newer version, browse:

http://www.microsoft.com/typography/

Using the Third-Party Software

The CD folders listed below contain third-party software designed to work with FrontPage. These are copyrighted programs, each provided for your convenience, with the permission of the respective supplier.

- These items are supported by their respective suppliers—not by Microsoft and not by the author. For additional information or assistance, consult the product's Web site or contact the supplier directly.

- In many cases, newer versions of the same software will be available on the listed Web sites. This is because, simply stated, it's much faster to update a Web site than to produce a new edition of a book.

- Purchasing this book doesn't provide a permanent license to use this software. If an item is listed as a trial or demo version and you want to keep using it, you'll need to purchase a license through normal channels.

(W) ON THE WEB For updated links to these and additional products, consult http://www.microsoft.com/frontpage/

\1stJava   1st JAVA Navigator

Set of JAVA applets that provide tabbed selection lists, expandable tree selection lists, and both types combined.

14-day evaluation version.

Auscomp
P.O. Box 75
Patterson Lakes
Victoria, 3197
Australia

Voice:	+61 3 9776 2060
Fax:	+61 3 9776 2060
Web:	http://www.auscomp.com
E-mail:	team@auscomp.com.au

\1stTheme 1st Theme Factory (Series 1)
1st Theme Factory (Sport)

Professionally designed FrontPage themes.

Free evaluation version.

Auscomp
P.O. Box 75
Patterson Lakes
Victoria, 3197
Australia

Voice:	+61 3 9776 2060
Fax:	+61 3 9776 2060
Web:	http://www.auscomp.com
E-mail:	team@auscomp.com.au

\3Space 3D Space Publisher Interactive
3D Suite

Creates two- and three-dimensional graphics for the Web. Includes a drag-and-drop design interface, an animated GIF editor, an automatic HTML code generator, clip-art objects and textures, and a collection of image-related Java applets.

Fully functional trial version.

Template Graphics Software Inc.
9920 Pacific Heights Blvd. Suite 200
San Diego, CA 92121

Voice:	619-457-5359
Fax:	619-452-2547

Web: http://www.tgs.com
E-mail: hotline@tgs.com

\AudioCafe   L&H Audio Cafe Lite

Adds Java-based audio streaming to a FrontPage Web.

Limited function evaluation version: works only with pre-selected audio clips. Full version works with your own audio files.

Lernout & Hauspie
Speech Products N.V.
Sint-Krispijnstraat 7 8900
Ieper, Belgium

Voice: +32 57.22.88.88
Fax: 781-238-0986
Web: http://www.lhs.com
E-mail: sales@lhs.com

\Crystal3D   Crystal 3D IMPACT! Pro

Creates three-dimensional and animated graphics.

Trial version stops working 10 days after installation.

Crystal Graphics, Inc.
3350 Scott Blvd. Bldg. 14
Santa Clara, CA 95054

Voice: 800-394-0700
           408-496-6175 (outside contiguous U.S.)
Fax: 408-496-0970
Web: http://www.crystalgraphics.com
E-mail: cgimktg@crystalgraphics.com

\JustAdd   JustAddCommerce

FrontPage component that adds a shopping cart system to your Web site.

Demo version.

Rich Media Technologies, Inc.
7338 S. Alton Way Suite G
Englewood, CO 80112

Voice: 303-221-3023
Fax: 303-221-3274
Web: http://www.richmediatech.com
E-mail: support@richmediatech.com

\SPGWEB   SPG Web Tools for PhotoShop

A wide assortment of image-processing tools for the Web. Work with any program that accepts PhotoShop Plug-Ins.

Demo version good for 10 starts.

SPG Incorporated

Voice: 305-362-6602
Web: http://www.spg-net.com
E-mail: info@spg-net.com

\ThemeMart   Theme Collection 2000

A special collection of 12 self-installing themes for FrontPage 2000.

Fully functional trial version.

Theme Mart
My Computer Service
P. O. Box 2607
Eaton Park, FL 33840

Voice: 941-619-8190
Web: http://www.thememart.com
E-mail: info@thememart.com

\WebSpice   WebSpice Sampler

Clip-art pictures.

Samples for individual use.

DeMorgan Industries Corporation
37 Danbury Road
Ridgefield, CT 06877

Voice: 203-431-6661
Fax: 203-794-0008
Web: http://www.webspice.com

Contacting the Author

Hearing from happy readers is always a welcome and pleasant experience, and hearing from the less-than-satisfied is important as well. Please write in English. My e-mail address is:

buyensj@primenet.com

I'm most interested in your impressions of this book: what you liked or disliked about it, what questions it did or didn't answer, what you found superfluous and what you'd like to see added in the next edition. (I'm not privy to any inside information, but FrontPage 2000 hardly seems the last of its kind.) I'll post errors, omissions, and corrections on my Web site at:

http://www.interlacken.com/rfp2k/errata.htm

I can accept enhancement requests only for this book, and *not* for the FrontPage software itself. The e-mail address for suggesting product enhancements is:

mswish@microsoft.com

Please understand that I'm just one person and I can't provide FrontPage technical support, installation assistance, or Web page repair service— not even for readers. Please try other channels, including the following newsgroups:

microsoft.public.frontpage.client
microsoft.public.frontpage.extensions.windowsnt

Also try the following Microsoft Web locations:

http://www.microsoft.com/frontpage/
http://support.microsoft.com/support/

If all else fails, please write. While I can't promise to answer each message, I'll try to provide at least a useful suggestion. Even when I can't answer your e-mail messages directly, I find it instructive to learn what problems users like you are experiencing—and therefore how I can make this book more useful to everyone in its next edition.

Thirteen Desperate Measures for Building a Web Site

Many new Web authors (and FrontPage users) seem to have trouble getting started with their first site. There are literally so many things to do that they can't decide where to begin. If you find yourself in this position, consider the following approach.

1 Decide what you want to say.

This step determines the information you want your site to convey. This can be as simple as, "What I did last summer," or as complex as the vast collection of topics presented by a major corporation. The larger the body of content, the more you'll need to plan by categories rather than by specifics.

2 Organize what you want to say.

For the most part, this is the job of consolidating your content into high-level categories and designing a menu structure. Be sure to organize this according to the Web visitor's mindset and expectations.

3   Decide whether to use any special features or active elements.

If your Web content and services require only static Web pages or browser-side programming, almost any Web server will do. If, however, you require programmed or interactive responses from the Web server, you'll need to verify that the necessary programs are present and accessible on the Web server. The server-side programs FrontPage expects to be present are called the FrontPage Server Extensions.

4   Choose a visual appearance.

Decide how you want the site to look. This includes factors such as color scheme, font style, standard page layout, stock images, button and icon appearance, and so forth. Consider using a FrontPage theme.

5   Define your working environment.

In general, this involves the following decisions.

- The machine on which you'll run FrontPage.

- How and where you'll store work in progress. Typically, this will be on your own computer or a departmental file server, either in a disk-based Web or a server-based Web. (See Chapter 18 for more information about these terms.) If several people are going to work together on the same Web, you should probably locate it on a file server or Web server.

- The machine that will store finished Web pages and deliver them to people who visit your site.

6   Install FrontPage in your authoring environment.

If you decided in step 5 to use a server-based Web running on your own PC, install a Personal Web Server and *then* install FrontPage 2000. Otherwise, just install FrontPage 2000.

7   Create a FrontPage Web.

FrontPage Setup creates one Web, called the *root Web*, as part of the installation process. Nevertheless, you should create a new FrontPage Web for each project or major body of content. (Choose New from the File menu, and then choose Web.)

8   Decide whether to use Navigation view.

If you want to maintain your Web's menu structure by dragging and dropping nodes on a diagram resembling an organization chart, open the new Web, click the Navigation button in the Views bar, click the New Page button on the Standard toolbar, give the new page a title, and then drag it under the home page or wherever it belongs in overall hierarchy. The first time you edit these pages (by double-clicking them), add Page Banner and Navigation Bar components. (See Chapters 19 and 20.)

If you'd rather maintain your site's structure by hand, create new pages by choosing New from the File menu and then choosing Page. Enter page titles and menu bars (that is, hyperlinks among high-level pages) manually.

9   Create the first few pages.

Try creating a few pages. Review their operation and appearance. If possible, get outside opinions from the sort of people you want to attract as Web visitors. If you're building the site for someone else, get their feedback.

10   Refine your content and visual presentation.

Revise the site based on feedback from step 9. Repeat steps 9 and 10 until everything seems acceptable. Be satisfied with something less than perfection, though; no matter how much work you do up front, the site is going to keep changing.

11   Continue adding content.

Fully develop an initial set of pages. Strive to get all pages ready for public consumption—at least in minimal form—or leave them out. Don't use any of those trite Under Construction icons.

12   Publish to your production Web server.

Make the site available to its intended audience by publishing it (that is, copying it) to the production server identified in step 5. Test, then publicize.

13   Refine and repeat.

Web sites are never finished. There's always existing content to revise, new content to add, and outdated content to remove. Visual designs get stale or outdated and need to be redone. Congratulations on your new career and don't worry, you can always quit or line up a successor.

Of course, no project is ever this straightforward. And, as you may have noticed, making decisions in the early steps requires experience performing the later steps. That's why no two people go about developing Web sites the same way, and why it's an iterative process.

A common mistake is performing steps 6, 9, and 4, then attempting step 1, and then giving up. Don't let this happen to you! Decide what your site is about *before* trying to build it.

Now, let's look at FrontPage 2000 in detail.

PART I

Web Publishing with FrontPage 2000

The FrontPage Approach to Creating Web Pages

The World Wide Web has become the predominant electronic publishing medium on the planet. Once considered an obscure technical resource, the Internet now receives prominent publicity at sporting events, in presidential debates, in television commercials, and in print advertising and marketing materials everywhere. Every type of organization you can imagine is using Web technology to locate customers, disseminate information, and develop interactive applications.

As the Web itself has moved from obscurity into the mainstream, so has its authoring community. Many new Web authors have neither interest nor aptitude for coding HyperText Markup Language—the stuff of which Web pages are actually made—but nevertheless they expect to create Web pages with high-level tools as sophisticated and easy to use as their favorite word processing, spreadsheet, or desktop publishing applications. This facility is exactly what Microsoft FrontPage provides.

At some fundamental level, word-processed documents, spreadsheets, slide-show presentations, and database reports are all documents. Nevertheless, each of these document types represents a different mindset and requires a different program to handle its unique requirements. So it is with Web pages. Concept divisions, and not the physical dimensions of paper, govern breaks from one Web page to another. Because Web pages have no fixed width or length, they reformat automatically with changes to the display window. Web pages change automatically depending on the current date, the capabilities of your Web visitor's computer, visitor input, or other factors. For all these reasons and more, producing Web pages is a task with unique requirements and challenges. As you will discover from this book, FrontPage 2000 provides a corresponding set of features uniquely suited to the task at hand.

This chapter and the next introduce the major components of FrontPage 2000, explain their purpose, and provide an overview of how they work. Chapter 1 is primarily about creating individual Web pages, while Chapter 2 addresses the management of multi-page sites. Together, these chapters provide an overview not only of the software, but of the book as well. Once you understand FrontPage conceptually, you'll be ready for the details, presented in later chapters, that will give you mastery over Web development.

Welcome to the Web

The operation of the World Wide Web is quite simple. It involves the exchange of information between a computer that requests information, often called a *client,* and one that delivers the information, usually called a *server.* The client's software, called a *browser,* requests Web pages from a server located somewhere on a network, whether it's a corporate intranet or the global World Wide Web. The browser identifies the requested file by its name in the server's file system and requests that the server send it. After receiving the requested file, the browser displays it to the Web visitor. If the Web page calls for additional files as components—graphics, sound, and video files, for example—the browser requests them, using the same mechanism.

The creator of a Web page can designate areas of text, images, and other objects as *hyperlinks.* Each hyperlink specifies the network address and file name of another Web page. Clicking a hyperlink in the current Web page instructs the browser to retrieve and display the associated page or file.

HTML and Text Editors

A key decision in the invention of the World Wide Web was to throw away ten years of progress in word processing. Instead, browsers expect Web pages to be in a format called HyperText Markup Language (HTML). HTML consists of plain ASCII text "marked up" with tags such as <P> for new paragraph, <UL> for unnumbered list, and <LI> for list item. This is a format anyone can produce using a simple ASCII editor, such as the Microsoft Notepad accessory that comes with Windows.

NOTE

> In HTML, formatting commands are enclosed in <angle brackets> while ordinary text is not.

There was no way to know what size screen or what fonts each Web visitor would have, so these details were left to the discretion of each visitor's browser and system configuration, and not to the page designer. Text would flow within whatever document window the visitor chose. The designer could assign style codes such as <H1> through <H6> for progressively smaller headings, for example, but every computer in the world could theoretically display these styles in a different font, size, and color.

Objectively, HTML is one of the worst page description languages around. Its greatest strength and its greatest weakness are one and the same: simplicity. Its simplicity allows anyone with a plain text editor (such as Notepad) to create Web pages and lets anyone with a browser on any computer system read those pages—but at the same time, it constrains page designers so harshly that they spend huge amounts of time trying to overcome its limitations. Page designers should be designers, stylists, and artists, not technicians required to create intricate program code.

To be charitable, early versions of HTML were designed for publishing scholarly and technical papers—and simple ones at that. There was no provision for publishing equations, charts, or tables, for example. Nevertheless, the HTML specification developed in those days still provides the basis for the most complicated Web pages we see today. In fact, plain text editors remain among the most common tools for creating Web pages, no matter how complex the page or how cryptic the HTML codes might be.

The ability to produce Web pages using only simple, universally available tools has been a key factor in the growth of the Web itself and remains a common practice. For many people, though, coding Web pages by hand presents serious obstacles:

- Coding Web pages manually requires intimate knowledge of a variety of markup commands such as <H1> to denote a heading typeface, <B> and </B> to start and stop boldface, and <IMG SRC="/images/logo.gif"> to insert a specific graphic file.

- Lack of a graphical interface provides no visual feedback of what the Web page will look like to the Web visitor and offers no visual cues regarding commands and options.

- The relationships among text, images, and other kinds of files in a typical collection of Web pages are highly detailed and complex. Errors result if a single file is misnamed or misplaced. Initially creating such a structure is difficult, but maintaining it over time can be daunting.

FrontPage provides a rich variety of features to relieve Web page creators of problems like these, and many others. The rest of this chapter will introduce them briefly. As you review each feature, consider how much more difficult it would be to achieve the same results with only a simple text editor.

WYSIWYG Editing in FrontPage

Web designers working with a text editor typically keep a browser running in the background and displaying the page they're working on. To preview the appearance of a page, the author first saves it from the editor to disk, and then clicks the browser's Refresh button to load the disk file into the browser. "But this is crazy," you say. "Why doesn't someone invent a Web page editor that displays what the Web visitor will see—in true what-you-see-is-what-you-get (WYSIWYG) fashion—and not a bunch of HTML gibberish?"

To a large extent, FrontPage 2000 provides an answer to this question: someone has done just that. Figure 1-1 and Figure 1-2 show how Internet Explorer and FrontPage display the same page with remarkable similarity.

There are, of course, limits to the extent that any HTML editor can provide a WYSIWYG view. Your Web visitor's system still controls the screen resolution, color depth, page width, typeface, font size, and other visual aspects, according to its operating system, browser software, installed fonts, and so forth. No HTML editor can predict what these settings will be at display time, so no HTML editor can accurately preview them. FrontPage, however, does provide a reasonable preview of what a visitor with similar browser settings would see.

FIGURE 1-1.

Internet Explorer displays a reasonably complex Web page that belongs to the author.

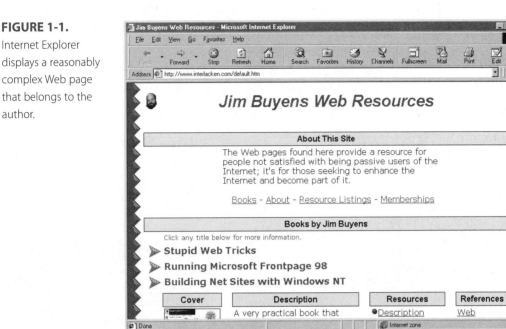

FIGURE 1-2.

FrontPage closely matches Internet Explorer's display of a Web page (Figure 1-1) and also provides a great assortment of editing commands and tools. Note that the Normal view tab is selected at the bottom of the screen.

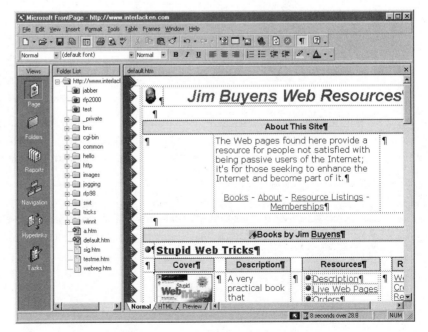

If you compare Figure 1-1 and Figure 1-2, it's apparent that FrontPage also displays certain structural elements that the browser doesn't. FrontPage, by design, displays invisible table borders, invisible line breaks, and in some cases even invisible colors, all as aids to editing. Even though the Web visitor won't see these elements, *you* need to, in order to edit them.

Figure 1-3 shows FrontPage displaying the HTML code that actually creates the Web page shown above. As you can see, for the vast majority of Web page creators, editing with FrontPage will offer tremendous advantages over editing raw HTML code with an ordinary text editor.

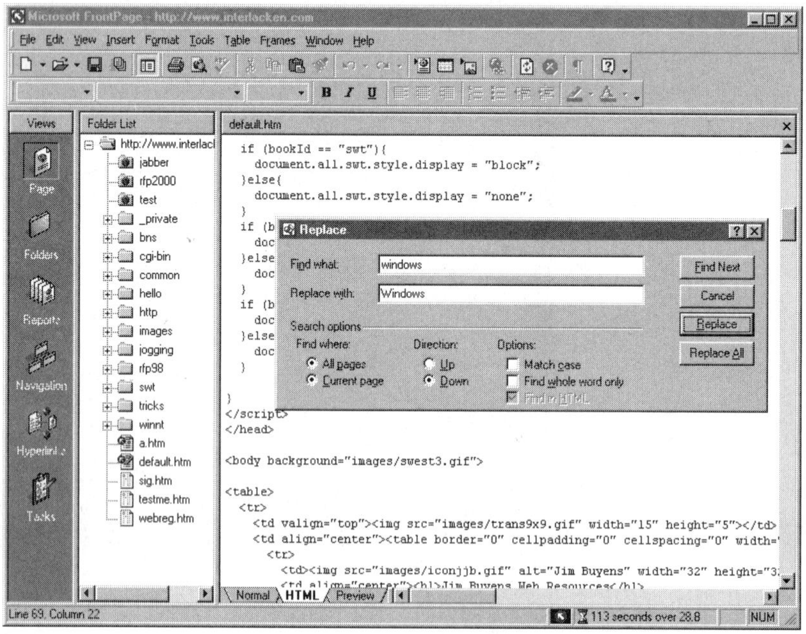

FIGURE 1-3.

Select the HTML tab at the bottom of the Editor screen to view the HTML behind the current page. You can edit the code directly and then return to Normal view to see the results.

SEE ALSO

For more information about editing Web pages with FrontPage, see Part II, "Creating Web Pages."

FrontPage also provides extensive support for dragging and dropping objects from one location on a page to another, from one Web page to another, and from Windows Explorer onto Web pages.

The FrontPage 2000 user interface follows all the style and organizational conventions of other Office 2000 applications. If you're familiar with other Office applications, most of FrontPage 2000's commands and toolbar icons will be just as you expect them to be.

Special FrontPage Features

In addition to expected Office 2000 similarities like overall appearance, menu organization, icon assignment, dialog box similarity, keyboard shortcuts, and drag and drop, FrontPage supports:

- **File format conversion to and from Microsoft Office formats and HTML**. This includes inserting entire Microsoft Office files into Web pages as well as copying content from an Office application and pasting it into FrontPage. For example, if you copy a Microsoft Word table, a range of Excel cells, or a block of Access records, FrontPage will paste it as an HTML table.

- **Uniform table commands.** The FrontPage procedures for creating and editing tables are, to the maximum extent possible, the same as in other Office applications. This single feature alone provides an order of magnitude improvement over editing HTML with a text editor.

- **Uniform layout commands.** Wherever possible, FrontPage uses familiar Office commands and dialog boxes for aligning objects, setting fonts, and controlling bullets and other paragraph properties.

- **Creation of HTML forms.** HTML supports a variety of user interface objects such as text boxes, drop-down lists, option buttons, and push buttons. A grouping of such drag-and-drop elements is called an *HTML form*. FrontPage provides a WYSIWYG, drag-and-drop environment for designing HTML forms, form Wizards, and menu-driven configuration of all form elements.

Styling Your Content

FrontPage provides a full complement of intuitive dialog boxes for applying colors, fonts, alignment, and other properties to the content of your Web pages. Virtually every feature of HTML is available for making your pages look their best, all accessed through the familiar Office 2000 user interface.

Despite all this flexibility—and rock bands notwithstanding—members of a group should generally be united by a common appearance. This is just as true for Web pages as it is for marching bands, store clerks, armies, executives, and Girl Scouts. FrontPage offers a number of tools with which you can create a unified and attractive style for all your pages. And anyway, why format Web pages one at a time when you can do them all together in bunches?

? SEE ALSO

For more information about FrontPage Webs, consult "FrontPage Webs," page 36.

FrontPage Webs—A Sneak Preview

Many of FrontPage's most powerful features work not just on single Web pages, but on all Web pages in a given set. This begs the question of what constitutes a set, and the answer is a FrontPage Web.

A FrontPage Web consists of all the individual pages and folders that reside within a specially designated folder on your hard disk or Web server. The only exception is that no one file or folder can be a member of two Webs. You can physically locate one Web inside another, but operations on the "outer" Web won't affect the "inner" Web (as they would if the "inner" Web were an ordinary folder).

Themes

Its collection of themes is the most pervasive, all-encompassing style facility FrontPage has to offer. Themes control overall page properties like colors, fonts, bullet styles, graphical buttons, and backgrounds. Applying a theme to a page or Web locks in a professionally designed appearance and disables any command that could override it. If you want to guarantee that your site has consistent style and colors, nothing else has the force of FrontPage themes.

You can apply themes a page at a time or throughout an entire Web. Figure 1-4 shows the Blueprint theme being previewed just before applying it to a Web page.

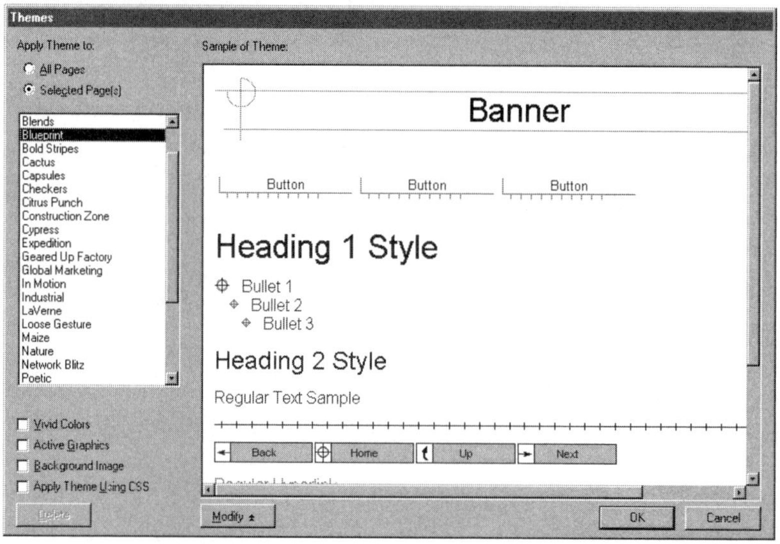

FIGURE 1-4.

Choosing a theme in FrontPage applies it, at your option, to either a single Web page or to every page in the current Web.

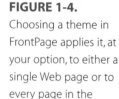

? SEE ALSO

For more information about themes, consult Chapter 9, "Using FrontPage Themes."

? SEE ALSO

For more information about templates, see Chapter 20, "Using Web-Based FrontPage Components."

Unlike FrontPage 98, FrontPage 2000 can create and modify themes directly within the FrontPage application. What's more, any themes you create or modify are available automatically in Word 2000, ready and waiting for whatever use you desire.

We'll discuss themes again, in more detail, later in this chapter.

Templates

Another way FrontPage helps provide a consistent Web appearance is with its *templates* feature. Using a template is simple.

1 Use FrontPage to create a Web page with the color scheme, background, and other standard features you want in the template.

2 Use FrontPage's Save As feature to save the page as a template. Figure 1-5 illustrates this function in progress.

3 When creating a new Web page that should have the given template features, select that template in the New dialog box shown in Figure 1-6, on the next page.

As you can see in Figure 1-6, FrontPage also provides its own assortment of standard templates.

FIGURE 1-5.

FrontPage can save draft Web pages as templates, which then serve as models for other pages.

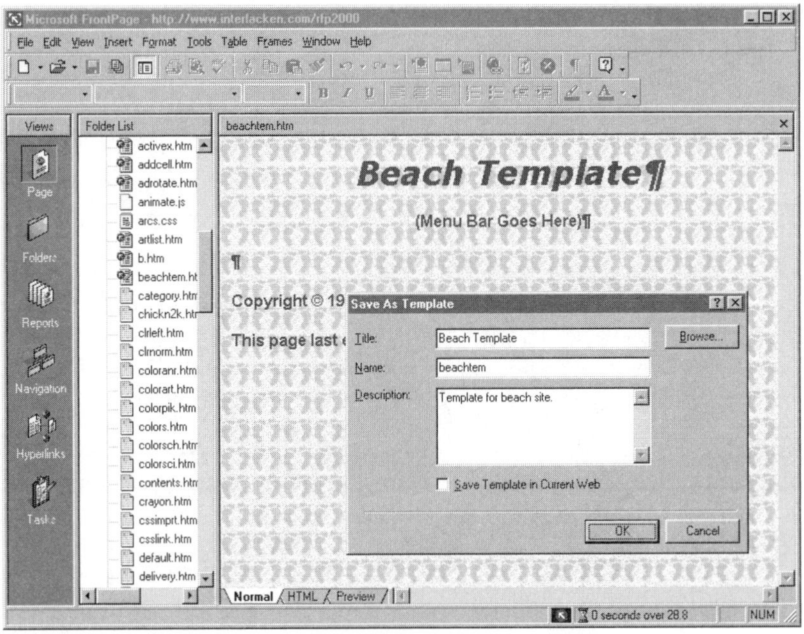

FIGURE 1-6.

The New dialog box contains templates you can use to create a Web page.

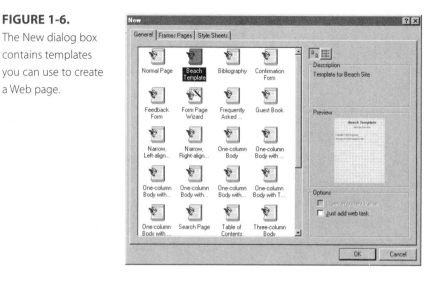

Cascading Style Sheets

To overcome the many stylistic limitations of HTML, the World Wide Web Consortium recently devised a new specification that fills in most of HTML's gaps. This specification, as you may have guessed from the heading, is called Cascading Style Sheets. There are two levels.

 NOTE

> The World Wide Web Consortium (W3C) is the international standards body that controls the definition of HTML.

- **CSS Level 1** is primarily concerned with typography. Compared to HTML, CSS provides powerful control over typefaces, colors, and paragraph formatting.

- **CSS Level 2** is primarily concerned with positioning.

  - CSS2 provides statements that position Web page elements precisely on the page.

  - CSS2 offers a wide variety of measurement systems, such as pixels, points, ems, inches, centimeters, and percent of available space.

  - There are two positioning strategies: *absolute* and *relative*. Absolute positioning displays page content a specified distance from the top left corner of its container. (The topic of containers is complex, but the default container is the space the document occupies in the visitor's browser.) Relative positioning displays content a specified distance from its normal position, that is, from where it would appear if no positioning were in effect.

You can apply either set of CSS features—or both—to individual Web page elements, to portions of Web pages, to whole Web pages, or to groups of pages. FrontPage supports all these options. In Figure 1-7, for example, FrontPage is creating a CSS style named ".punk." Once this style exists, it'll appear in the drop-down list of styles on FrontPage's Format toolbar, and you can apply it to anything on the Web page.

? SEE ALSO

For more information on CSS2 positioning, see "Positioning Content with CSS," page 273.

The dialog box for CSS Positioning (that is, CSS2) appears in Figure 1-8. Positioning a block of content can be as easy as this:

1   Open the Web page in Page view.

2   Select the elements you want to position.

3   Choose Position from the Format menu.

4   Enter the position setting you want.

5   Click OK.

What's in a Name (CSS-wise)?

The official term for the name of a CSS style is a *selector*. There are three kinds of selectors:

- **Type Selectors** have the same names as (and control the appearance of) HTML tags. You can control the appearance of all list items in a Web page, for example, by defining a selector named LI and giving it the properties you want.

- **Class Selectors** begin with a period, and using them involves a two-step process. First you define the class, then you apply it to each HTML element you want.

- **ID Selectors** begin with a pound sign, and using them involves a slightly different two-step process. First you give the desired HTML element an ID, and then you define a corresponding ID selector that specifies the CSS properties you want that element to have.

In practice, type and class selectors are by far the most used.

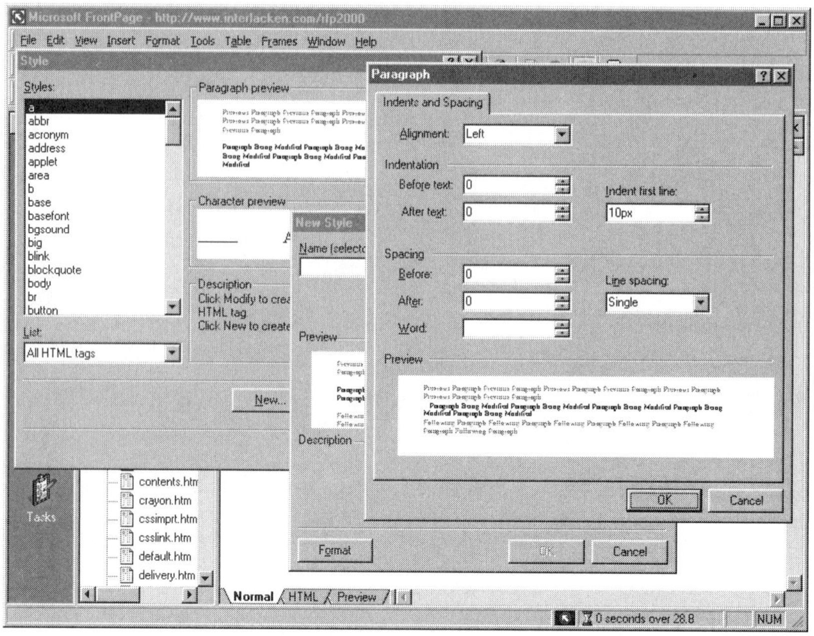

FIGURE 1-7.

These dialog boxes are building a new style named .punk. Once created, it appears in the Styles list on the Format toolbar.

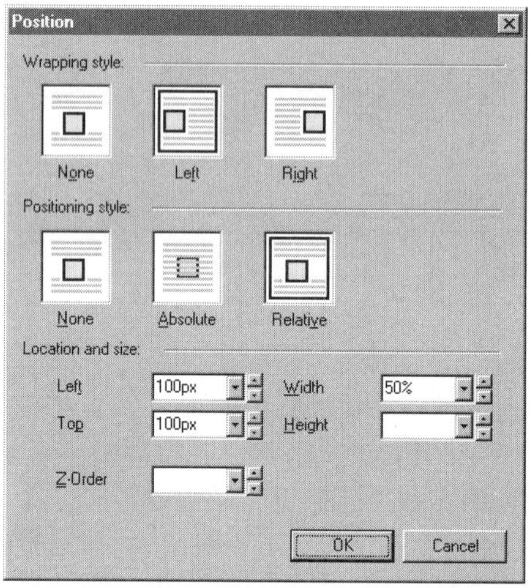

FIGURE 1-8.

This FrontPage 2000 dialog box specifies CSS2 positioning for the currently selected content.

? SEE ALSO

For more information on FrontPage's support of Cascading Style Sheets, refer to Chapter 5, "Adding and Formatting Text."

If you've been spending a major portion of your life fighting HTML, trying to control fonts and page layout, CSS can be a dream come true. There are just two catches:

- Specifying a font doesn't make it available on the remote visitor's system.

- If parts of your Web page are positioned and parts aren't, the parts that aren't may not flow properly around the ones that are.

Absolute Positioning and the Z-Index

Absolute positioning is a feature of browsers that support the Cascading Style Sheet (CSS) Level 2 specification. CSS2 provides a way to locate elements at specific locations, measured either from their normal location or from the upper left corner of their container. (The default CSS container is the space inside the document's margins. However, marked subsections of a Web page can also be containers. Table cells, divisions, and spans can all be CSS containers.)

A new CSS property called *z-index* governs the visibility of overlapping page elements. When several page elements on the same Web page overlap, the element with the highest z-index appears on top (that is, unobstructed), and those with lesser z-indexes appear in order behind it.

Normal page elements have the default z-index, which is zero. Elements with positive z-index values appear superimposed over normal page content, and those with a negative z-index appear behind it.

Framesets

A frameset is a special Web page whose sole purpose is to divide the browser window into several rectangular areas called *frames*. Each frame has a *name* and a *target*; the *name* identifies the frame and the *target* identifies the Web page within it.

FIGURE 1-9.
FrontPage 2000 provides full WYSIWYG editing of framesets. Four HTML files are open in this example: the frameset itself, plus one ordinary HTML page for each of its three frames.

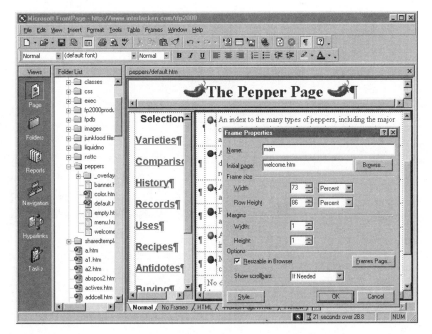

SEE ALSO

For more information about framesets, refer to "Creating and Editing Frames," page 261.

Hyperlinks clicked in one frame can load pages into another frame. A common application is therefore to define a menu as the target of one frame and corresponding content as the target of another. Clicking a hyperlink in the menu frame changes the target in the content frame. This avoids the need to keep menus up to date on each content page. Of course, many other applications are possible as well. Anytime you wish to replace only portions of the browser window, framesets are an option worth considering.

Figure 1-9 shows a frameset open in FrontPage. Framesets and default targets appear in fully editable, WYSIWYG view. Note the title frame at the top of the page, the menu bar at the lower left, and the large content frame at the lower right. This is a fairly typical arrangement.

Shared Borders

This feature applies any combination of top, bottom, left, and right borders—including the content within them—to selected pages or to an entire Web. Shared borders are very handy for applying standard heading styles, standard footers, and standard margin content to an entire Web.

SEE ALSO

For more information about shared borders, refer to "Shared Borders," page 677.

The following dialog box in FrontPage activates shared borders for a single page or an entire FrontPage Web. The Borders To Include graphic shows the approximate position for each border.

The borders themselves are actually table cells. FrontPage surrounds the normal page content with an all-encompassing table; if all four borders are used, this would be a 3x3 table, with all three columns in rows 1 and 3 merged. Figure 1-10 shows a page with four shared borders open in FrontPage.

You can edit the shared border areas within any page that uses them, but remember that changes may affect every page in your Web.

The contents of each shared border are contained in four files, named

_borders/bottom.htm

_borders/left.htm

_borders/right.htm

_borders/top.htm

By default, top.htm contains a page banner component and a horizontal Navigation Bar component. The left.htm file contains a vertical navigation bar component, and the other two files contain only comments.

? SEE ALSO

For more information about Navigation view, see "Navigation View," page 55.

The section, "Automatic Content with FrontPage Components," later in this chapter discusses Page banners more fully, but for now it's enough to know that they display the current page's Title (as configured in Navigation view) as text. The page banner component allows top.htm to show the correct Title for every page in the Web, even with a single copy of top.htm that doesn't change.

FIGURE 1-10.

The rectangular areas at the top, bottom, left, and right of this page are shared borders and will be applied to all pages in the Web.

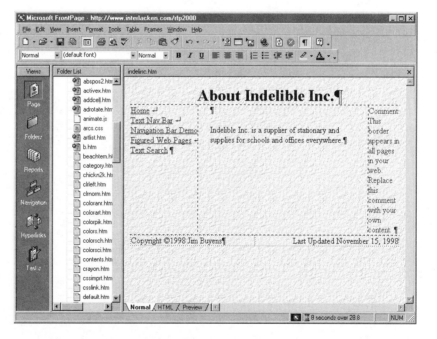

Briefly, Navigation Bars are FrontPage components that automatically create links among the pages in a FrontPage Web. The links on any

given page reflect a structure you define by dragging Web pages onto a hierarchical diagram that looks like an organization chart. For more detail, consult the "Automatic Content with FrontPage Components" section later in this chapter or Chapter 20, "Using Web-Based FrontPage Components."

Color Masters

Somewhat less drastic than themes, color masters provide a way for one page in a Web to inherit the text colors and background of another. Any page can be the source (or master) of colors and background for another, though the best approach is usually to create a special page for each shared color combination in your Web.

? SEE ALSO

For more information on Color Masters, see "Color Masters," page 669.

To create a color master, simply create a new page, assign the colors and background you want, and save it. This page may or may not actually appear in your Web, but its properties can be used for pages that do appear.

To assign colors to a Web page from a color master

1   Open the Web page in FrontPage.

2   Choose Properties from the File menu.

3   Click the Background tab. The following dialog box will result.

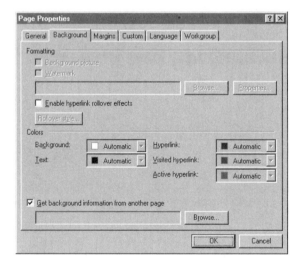

4   Click the button titled Get Background Information From Another Page.

5   Click the active Browse button and locate the page whose colors you want to assign to the current page.

6 Click OK to select the color master page, and then click OK again to close the Page Properties dialog box.

Changing the colors or background on a color master will automatically change the same attributes of any page set up this way to inherit its colors.

Working with Images in FrontPage

Graphics (also called images or pictures) are among the most important components of any Web page—so important that it's rare to see a page without them. Therefore, in addition to providing tools to edit and manage HTML files, FrontPage provides a rich assortment of tools for editing images.

SEE ALSO
For more information about working with images, refer to Chapter 6, "Incorporating Graphics."

Inserting Images

FrontPage can insert images from any file location on your computer, from the Clipboard, from the current FrontPage Web, or from any location on the Web.

Once an image is present in a Web page, FrontPage provides full access to its HTML properties through easy-to-use dialog boxes. FrontPage also provides a variety of tools (described below in the section titled, "Image Editing in FrontPage") for modifying existing images.

No matter where the image comes from, FrontPage will, if necessary, prompt you for a Save As location the next time you save the Web page.

Clip Art

FrontPage provides an extensive library of buttons, horizontal rules, backgrounds, images, and other figures you can use to enhance your Web pages. This collection is shared with the rest of the Microsoft Office 2000 suite, making clip art you install for any other Office applications (such as Publisher) automatically available to FrontPage as well.

For ease of use, FrontPage lists clip art by category in the Clip Gallery and provides the graphical clip-art selection dialog box shown in Figure 1-11.

Image Editing in FrontPage

FrontPage provides a number of tools for directly modifying images in open Web pages. You can find these on the Picture toolbar.

- **Insert Picture** displays a file dialog box for adding a new image to your Web page. You can select images from your local hard disk, the Office 2000 Clip Art library, or any location on the Web.

- **Text On GIF** allows entry of text superimposed over an image.

- **Auto Thumbnail** replaces a large image with a smaller version, and creates a hyperlink so that clicking the small image displays the original, larger one.

? SEE ALSO

For more information about z-indexes, refer to "Absolute Position-ing and the Z-Index," page 15.

- **Absolutely Positioned** indicates that the currently selected image, rather than appearing in flow with the rest of the Web page, should appear at specific x-y coordinates. To set the coordinates, drag the image into place after clicking this button.

- **Bring Forward** increases the z-index of a selected image by one.

- **Send Back** decreases the z-index of a selected image by one.

FIGURE 1-11.

To insert clip art, set the insertion point, choose Picture from FrontPage's Insert menu and then click the Clip Art tab.

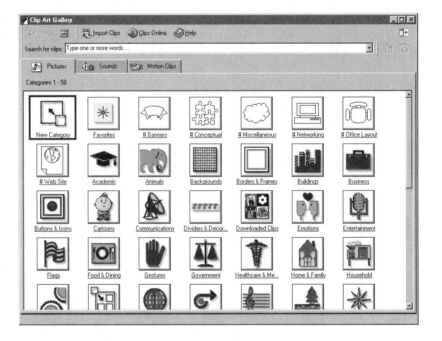

- **Rotate Left / Rotate Right** rotates the selected image 90 degrees counterclockwise or clockwise.

- **Flip Horizontal / Vertical** reverses the selected image left to right or top to bottom.

- **More Contrast / Less Contrast** increases or decreases the con-trast in an image. Increasing contrast means light colors get lighter and dark colors get darker; decreasing contrast means the reverse.

- **More Brightness / Less Brightness** increases or decreases the brightness of an image. Increasing brightness means that dark colors get brighter; decreasing brightness means that light colors get darker.

- **Crop** provides a way to display only a rectangular subset of an image. You can adjust the rectangular area using the mouse.

- **Set Transparent Color** converts any single color in an image to transparency by clicking a pixel of that color.

- **Black And White** converts an image to monochrome.

- **Washout** adds whiteness to all the colors in an image, making it look washed out. This is frequently desirable for images used as backgrounds.

- **Bevel** adds a three-dimensional border around the image. FrontPage will lighten the top and left edges while darkening the bottom and right edges.

- **Resample** converts a visual image to one with the actual desired size. Suppose, for example, you used the Image properties dialog box or dragged the mouse to display a 200x100 pixel image as 100x50. This would download the original, 200x100 image to the browser and tell the browser to resize it. The Resample command would create a new image whose actual size is 100x50, and it would download in 1/4 the time of the original.

- **Select** tells FrontPage that clicking an image selects it. This is the default; all remaining tools require that an image first be selected.

Imposing Text on GIF

This is quite a unique feature. When you overtype a graphic with text, FrontPage remembers the file name of the original image, the text string you enter, and the font characteristics you specify. It then formats the text onto the image, saves the results using an internally generated file name, and displays the combined text-and-graphics image rather than the original.

This feature is useful not only for labeling images, but also for creating headings and titles that use special fonts or colors. To create headings and titles, you would typically choose a textured surface, solid color, or completely transparent image as the background.

- **Rectangular Hotspot** marks a rectangular area within an image as a *hotspot*. At browse time, clicking any pixel within a hotspot activates an associated hyperlink.

- **Circular Hotspot** marks a circular area within an image as a hotspot.

- **Polygonal Hotspot** marks an irregular, straight-sided area as a hotspot.

- **Highlight Hotspots** displays all current hotspots within an image.

- **Restore** returns an image to its original appearance. However, this may not be possible after the image is saved.

In addition, FrontPage lets you copy, cut, and paste graphics (using the traditional Windows commands or shortcut keys), move them around the page by dragging and dropping, and resize selected graphics with the mouse.

Microsoft PhotoDraw

Office 2000 Premier includes Microsoft PhotoDraw, a feature-laden image editor. PhotoDraw accepts images in a wide variety of formats or directly from your scanner, and it offers more than 500 transformation functions. Among the things PhotoDraw can do:

- Adjust color, tint, and brightness

- Apply hundreds of different and configurable transformations such as drop shadow, bas relief, spattering, texturing, and smudging

- Convert image file formats

- Create text images using any font on the system

- Fill, paint, and replace colors using a variety of brush shapes

- Optimize the palette and palette depth

- Rotate, flip, crop, shrink, and enlarge images

SEE ALSO
For more information about image file format, see "Graphic File Formats," page 204.

PhotoDraw's major strength, however, lies in assembling pictures from several elements (such as a button background, an icon, and some text), saving them in its native format, and then opening that file with the original elements preserved. This is great if, for example, you created a set of buttons some time ago and you've forgotten exactly how you created the originals. If you saved the originals in PhotoDraw's native format—.mic—as well as exporting them as GIF or JPG images, PhotoDraw remembers the font and other details for you. What's more, the original objects remain fully editable.

Microsoft GIF Animator

Animated GIF files have become a popular feature on the Web. Unlike ordinary GIF files, the animated type contains a series of images and instructions on how long to display each one. Displaying an ordered set of images fast enough produces the illusion of continuous motion.

FrontPage 2000 comes with a simple program called Microsoft GIF Animator that, as you might expect, creates animated GIFs. GIF Animator, shown in Figure 1-12, is neither an image editor nor an animation studio; you must create each image in the series using some other program, paste them one-by-one into GIF Animator, and then set all the timing parameters. This is animation at its most elemental level, but at least in simple cases, it gets the job done.

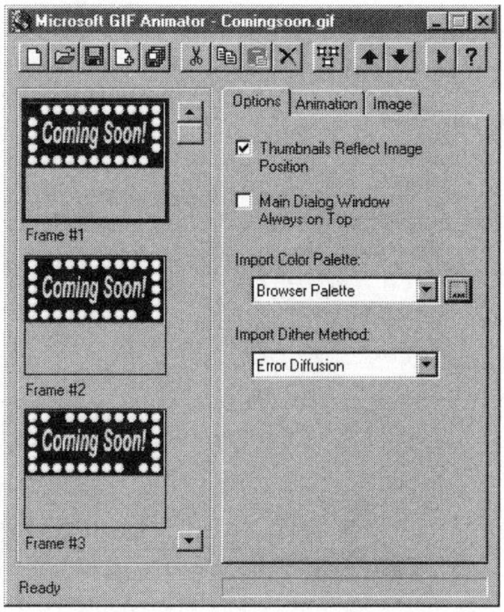

FIGURE 1-12.
This is Microsoft GIF Animator displaying a 13-frame animation, three frames at a time. The animation mimics the moving lights of a theater's marquee.

> **NOTE**
>
> Microsoft GIF Animator comes only with the full single-product version of FrontPage 2000. Installing Microsoft Image Composer from that CD also installs GIF Animator. If you buy a FrontPage 2000 upgrade, you can still install Image Composer and GIF Animator from your old FrontPage 98 CD. Neither program has been upgraded.

Automatic Content with FrontPage Components

To help you produce advanced Web pages quickly, FrontPage includes a powerful set of intelligent features called FrontPage Components. FrontPage inserts these wherever you specify, prompts you for any variable information, and then generates the corresponding HTML

SEE ALSO

For more information about any FrontPage Component, refer to Chapter 11, "Using Page-Level FrontPage Components," or Chapter 20, "Using Web-Based FrontPage Components."

codes when it saves the page. Along with the HTML, FrontPage saves the dialog box fields you specified so it can redisplay them in future editing sessions or re-create the HTML if some other factor has changed.

In almost every case, FrontPage components provide active output; that is, their content or appearance will change automatically based on events beyond the Web page that contains them. This may occur because

- The generated HTML includes a browser-side or server-side script that produces variable output.

- The generated HTML invokes a program on the server, such as a database query or full text search.

- The generated HTML reflects information located elsewhere within the FrontPage Web. If you change the information located elsewhere, FrontPage will automatically correct all the Web pages that reference it.

FrontPage 2000 provides 18 FrontPage Components. Of these, the 14 described next operate totally within the FrontPage authoring environment or the remote user's browser. Because they involve no components on the server, they don't require any FrontPage software installed on the Web server.

- **Categories.** Given one or more category codes, this feature builds a list of hyperlinks to pages in those categories. You can categorize Web pages either as you edit them or from FrontPage's Folder list. (Right-click the file, choose Properties, and then choose Workgroup.)

SEE ALSO

For more information about Java applets, refer to "Industry Standard Active Components," page 27.

- **Banner Ad Manager.** This component displays a series of images, each for a specified number of seconds. Whenever remote users load the page, their browsers load a FrontPage Java applet that continuously retrieves and displays the specified images.

- **Comment.** This component displays text that's visible only in FrontPage. The same text doesn't appear when viewing the Web page with a browser.

- **Hover Button.** HTML provides a built-in button object commonly used to submit forms or trigger other actions, but such buttons have become boring and mundane. FrontPage hover buttons provide much more flexibility in appearance, and they allow buttons to change appearance in various ways when the remote user passes the mouse pointer over them.

- **Include Page.** FrontPage replaces this component with the contents of another page in the same site. Whenever you have the same features appearing in many Web pages and might need to change them in the future, you should consider using the Include Page component.

- **Insert HTML.** If you know how to code HTML and wish to insert some special code directly into a Web page, this component provides the method. FrontPage will insert any HTML you provide directly into the Web page without interpretation, validation, or correction.

TIP

To fully integrate your HTML with the HTML generated by FrontPage, insert the new HTML lines after switching FrontPage into HTML view. This will permit subsequent WYSIWYG viewing and editing. Use the Insert HTML component only for HTML that you don't want FrontPage to process in any way.

- **Marquee.** This component creates an area of text that moves across the Web page. FrontPage provides a rich assortment of colors, effects, and timing options that control the marquee's appearance at browse time.

    Some browsers, such as Netscape Navigator, don't display marquees actively. In these cases, the marquee text will appear but remain stationary.

SEE ALSO

For more information about Navigation View, refer to "Navigation View," page 55; "Working with Navigation View," page 639; and "Navigation Bars," page 671.

- **Navigation Bar.** FrontPage's Navigation view (described elsewhere) records the hierarchical structure of the pages in your Web but, for various reasons, it can't automatically add the corresponding hyperlinks to each page. FrontPage simply can't guess how you want the links formatted or positioned on each Web page.

    The navigation bar component builds a set of text or graphic hyperlinks—usually consisting of the current page's children—and inserts them wherever you want on the current Web page. Changing the structure in FrontPage's Navigation view then updates the navigation bars—automatically—in any relevant pages.

    Navigation bars can provide links not only to child pages, but also to the current page's parent, to all pages at the parent level, to all other pages at the same level, to the previous and next pages, to the Web's home page, and to all pages at the top level. A single Web page may contain any number of navigation bars.

- **Page Banner.** This component inserts a text or graphic object containing the current page's title, as specified in Navigation view. This is particularly useful when constructing page templates or standard page headings. Each time the template or heading is used, the page banner component will display the title of the current page.

- **Scheduled Picture.** FrontPage replaces this component with a specified image every time the page is saved during a specified time period. After the time expires, FrontPage no longer displays the image. Figure 1-13 shows the dialog box that controls the Scheduled Picture component. In this example it labels an element on the Web page as *New!* for a period of one month.

- **Scheduled Include Page.** This component works like a Scheduled Image except that the FrontPage component replaces itself with a Web page (or page segment) rather than an image.

? SEE ALSO

For an explanation of Web configuration variables, see "Controlling Web Parameters," page 588.

- **Substitution.** This component replaces itself with a page-level or Web-level configuration variable.

- **Table of Contents.** This FrontPage component creates an outline with hyperlinks to each page in your FrontPage Web. It also updates the outline whenever the Web changes.

- **Timestamp.** FrontPage replaces this component with the date and time of your last update to the page.

FIGURE 1-13.

The Scheduled Image component starts and stops displaying an image based on date.

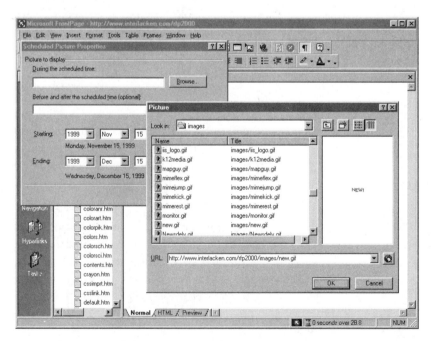

The four FrontPage components listed below operate at least partially on the Web server. Be sure your Web server has the FrontPage Server Extensions installed before using them.

- **Confirmation Field.** When providing feedback to a Web visitor who's submitted an HTML form, FrontPage replaces this component with the submitted contents of a form field. For example, if a visitor fills out a name-and-address form, this component can redisplay the information for the visitor to verify what's been filed away on the server.

- **Hit Counter.** This FrontPage component increments and displays a counter every time a visitor accesses the page that contains it.

- **Save Results.** You won't find this component on any of the standard FrontPage toolbars; it's an option on the Properties dialog box for an HTML form. The Save Results component processes data submitted from an HTML form by (1) writing it to a file on the server, (2) sending the data to a designated e-mail address, or (3) adding the data to a database.

- **Search Form.** The Search Form component creates a form for full-text searching of a FrontPage Web. The visitor submits a form containing words to locate, and the Search Form component returns a list of hyperlinks to relevant pages.

All FrontPage components depend on the FrontPage's invoking them whenever a page is saved. If you make changes to your Web with *another* editor, the FrontPage component won't be invoked at save time and might not function correctly. Scheduled FrontPage components will take effect only when you save the affected pages on or after the specified start and stop dates.

Industry Standard Active Components

? SEE ALSO
For more information, see "FrontPage Server Extensions," page 39, and Chapter 17, "Understanding the FrontPage Server Extensions."

The fact that computers deliver Web pages on demand and display them interactively means that computer programming instructions can be inserted at any step of the process: storing pages to the server, processing Web visitor requests, delivering requested pages, and displaying the pages. This is a significant difference between the Web and other mass media. Newspapers, magazines, books, radio, and television all provide very little interactivity or customization.

Developers have invented a wide range of technologies for adding programmed intelligence to the Web experience. These include:

- **CGI, WinCGI, and ISAPI programs.** These are programs that run on the Web server and produce Web pages as output. Visitors on the Web invoke these programs by submitting a special Web page request, and the server returns the generated page to the visitor who submitted the request. Creating such programs is beyond the objectives of FrontPage, but FrontPage does provide a useful, prewritten set of them—the FrontPage Server Extensions.

- **Script languages.** Scripts are short sections of program code inserted directly into Web pages and set off by special tags so that the source code doesn't appear on the displayed page. Scripts can run on either the browser or the Web server, subject to the design of the script and the capabilities of the environment.

Two common uses for scripts are inserting variable information, such as the current date or the date a page was saved, and responding to visitor events, such as resizing the browser window or clicking a button. Script languages can also interact with ActiveX controls and Java applets on the same page, and with the browser or server itself.

FrontPage supports script languages by (1) providing a way to insert visitor-written scripts into FrontPage Web pages and (2) automatically generating script code for common functions such as field validation. FrontPage supports both VBScript (Microsoft Visual Basic Scripting Edition) and JavaScript, the two most popular browser script languages. Figure 1-14 shows a JavaScript function inserted into a Web page.

FIGURE 1-14.

FrontPage can insert JavaScript or VBScript code at any position on a Web page.

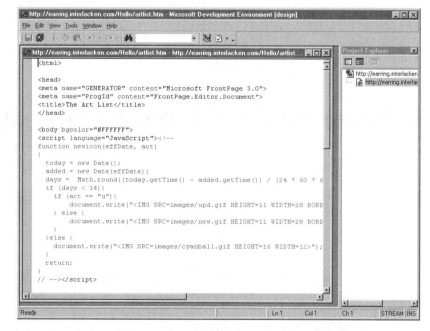

- **Java applets.** Java is a programming language capable of running on almost any computer. Programmers convert their Java programs to a format called bytecode, which then runs on any computer that has another piece of software called a Java bytecode interpreter. The interpreter creates an environment called the Java Virtual Machine that, in theory at least, can run any Java program written. This frees programmers from having to write different versions of their software for each type of computer. The interpreter must be matched to the type of computer, but the Java program need not be matched.

  A Java applet is a Java program designed to run as part of a Web page. The applet usually occupies a portion of the browser window, controls its contents, and responds to any visitor events that occur there. For security reasons, applets can't access files and other resources on the local computer, and they can initiate network connections only to the machine from which the applet was downloaded. (These restrictions are frequently compared to a sandbox, inside which Java applets must play.) FrontPage isn't a development environment for Java applets, though it does support placing existing applets onto a page and displaying them in their initial state.

- **ActiveX controls.** Like Java applets, ActiveX controls are programmed objects capable of providing a given function in a variety of contexts. Unlike Java applets, however, ActiveX controls are based on the OLE approach developed for Microsoft Windows. ActiveX is a very flexible specification that defines not only Web page objects, but objects that run on the Web server, operating system, and non-Web applications as well.

  Controls designed to run within a browser window occupy a portion of the Web page and accept input from the HTML, the Web visitor, or other controls. In response, they change their appearance and make results available for transmission back to the Web server. ActiveX controls running on a Web server don't create visual output directly, but they perform server-side functions such as writing and retrieving data in files and databases. They typically get their input from requests originating from a browser client or from a script that invokes them. To express output, they return values to the script that invoked them or write HTML for transmission to the Web visitor.

  ActiveX controls are compiled for a specific computer type and operating system, and a separate version is therefore required for each environment. There's no "sandbox" limiting what an ActiveX control can do, but each control is digitally signed so that the Web visitor can verify that it arrived both intact and from a trusted source. While FrontPage isn't a development environment for ActiveX controls, it supports placing such controls on a page and displaying them in their initial state.

- **Plug-ins.** This is another category of software module, first developed by Netscape Communications, that integrates into the display of a Web browser. Plug-ins typically provide interactive and multimedia capability.

TIP

Unlike Java applets and ActiveX controls, plug-in programs don't integrate automatically with the Web visitor's browser when a Web page needs them. When using plug-ins, be considerate and provide links to the plug-in vendor's download site.

- **Design-time controls.** The purpose of design-time controls is to preview Web functions and create the required HTML. As such, design-time controls run in the authoring environment only. The HTML or other created objects can run either on the server when a request is received, or at the browser when it receives a response. However, servers and browsers use the output of a design-time control and not the control itself.

Eventually, design-time controls might permit visitors to seamlessly add new functions at will to Web editors like FrontPage. For now, FrontPage will accommodate them—but not seamlessly.

Wizards

Like other Microsoft Office applications, FrontPage provides wizards to perform complex operations. Wizards prompt you for options in a structured way, first prompting for options with a series of dialog boxes like the one shown below and then completing their work uninterrupted. This avoids prompts for unnecessary options and minimizes the chance of a partially completed update.

These are some of the Wizards that FrontPage provides:

- **Corporate Presence Wizard** creates a typical set of Web pages for representing a company on the Internet. The wizard contains generic pages you can use as a starting point, and leaves comments indicating what you should update and what kinds of information to include.

- **Customer Support Web** creates a set of Web pages for a company offering customer support on the Internet. It's particularly designed for computer software companies.

- **Discussion Web Wizard** creates a special FrontPage Web designed for interactive discussions. Web visitors can submit topics by entering text in a form, review existing articles listed in a table of contents, or locate articles by word searching.

- **Import Web Wizard** adds an existing set of Web pages to a new or existing FrontPage Web.

- **Personal Web Wizard** creates a Web that represents an individual, with pages for interests, favorite sites, and photos.

The following wizards help you to create a Web page.

- **Form Page Wizard** creates an HTML form based on the type of information you need to collect.

- **Data Access Pages** created by Access 2000 incorporate Access databases into a Web page so that other visitors can update the database from their browsers. FrontPage 2000 can edit such pages and change their page layout.

- The **Database Results Wizard,** based on responses from the Web designer, adds database queries into Web pages automatically. These queries are dynamic, meaning the page displays current database data each time it's loaded. The database can be from any ODBC (Open Database Connectivity)-compliant database, but the Web server must be compatible with Microsoft Internet Information Server.

- **One-Button Database Publishing** creates an Access database with fields for each element on an HTML form, adds it to a FrontPage Web, and modifies the form so that each submission saves its data in the database.

Built-In Upload/Download

While developing your Web pages, you have a choice of four places for storing them.

❓ SEE ALSO

For more information about publishing Front-Page Webs, see Chapter 24, "Publishing Your FrontPage Web."

- As individual files on your local disk.

- As a FrontPage Web on your local disk.

- As a FrontPage Web on a Web server running on your computer. (Remember, this requires the FrontPage Server Extensions as well as the Web server itself.)

- As a FrontPage Web on a Web server that runs on some other computer. (Again, the FrontPage Server Extensions are required.)

In the latter two cases, it's certainly possible that the Web server is accessible to all your intended Web visitors; if so, your pages are ready and waiting for access the moment you finish them. It's more likely, though, that you'll need to copy your finished work to some other location for public consumption. FrontPage calls this function *publishing*.

If the *target* of your publishing—that is, the publicly accessible Web server that delivers your pages—has the FrontPage Server Extensions installed, then FrontPage 2000 can intelligently upload your finished pages either a page at a time or a FrontPage Web at a time.

If the target doesn't have the FrontPage Server Extensions, FrontPage 2000 can still upload your page for you via FTP, the Internet's File Transfer Protocol. However, being less intelligent, such transfers might take a little longer and of course, any FrontPage features (such as Hit Counter) that require the extensions won't work.

You can start FrontPage's built-in Publishing function either by choosing Publish Web from the File menu or by clicking the Publish Web button on the Standard toolbar. Either way, the dialog box shown in Figure 1-15 will appear. Type or select the URL of the other site's home folder, click the Publish button, and you're running.

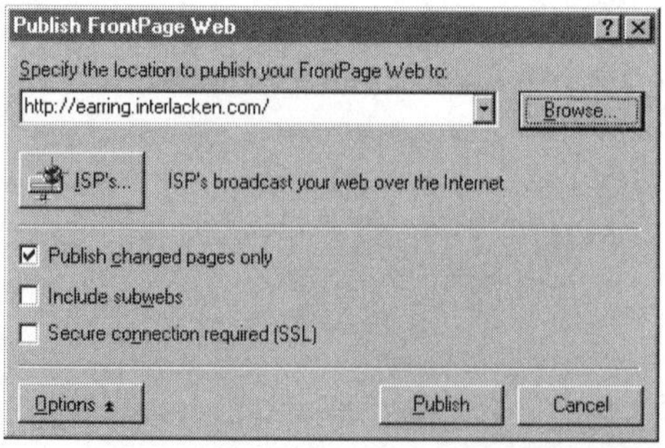

FIGURE 1-15.

This dialog box starts FrontPage's built-in Publishing feature, which copies Webs from one location to another.

Once you've published your Web, clicking the Publish Web toolbar no longer displays the Publish FrontPage Web dialog box. Instead, it uses saved settings to publish the Web directly. To once again display the dialog box and change the saved settings, choose Publish Web from the File menu.

Like all Office 2000 applications, FrontPage also supports Web publishing through a new facility called Web Folders. This is a new icon that Office 2000 applications add to the My Computer window. The Web Folders feature works like this:

1 Open My Computer.

2 Double-click Web Folders.

3 If the Web location you want is already listed, double-click it. If not, add the location by choosing New from the File menu. Then choose Web Folder.

4 The Web Folders window will now resemble Figure 1-16. Note that instead of folder locations on your local disk or file server, this window shows Internet addresses.

5 To transfer files and folders to and from the remote Web server, drag them in and out just as you would in Windows.

⊗ CAUTION

Any locations you add to Web Folders must be Web servers running the FrontPage Server Extensions. Otherwise, the Web Folders software can't communicate with them.

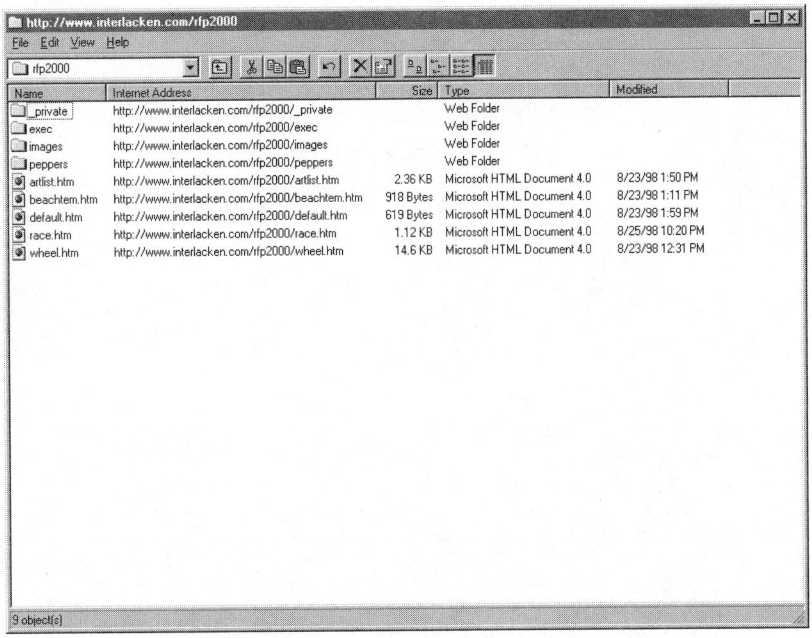

FIGURE 1-16.

Office 2000's Web Folders feature handles files on remote FrontPage Web servers as easily as it handles those on a local disk.

In Summary...

FrontPage 2000 provides a well-integrated, advanced set of tools for creating high-function Web pages quickly and easily. Not only through WYSIWYG editing, but also through comprehensive dialog boxes and automated tools, FrontPage opens exciting possibilities in Web design—possibilities difficult or impossible for many people to achieve using text editors alone.

The next chapter will describe FrontPage 2000's features for processing and managing groups of Web pages together—Web pages organized into FrontPage Webs.

CHAPTER 2

The FrontPage Approach to Organizing Web Sites

Most electronic documents reside in a single file regardless of the number of pages they contain. Web documents, by contrast, store each page in a separate file. There are several reasons for this practice.

- Storing each page in a separate file provides small, easily downloaded units of content.

- Using a separate file for each page provides a convenient means of hypertext addressing. Links to a given Web page simply point to the corresponding file name.

- Web pages scroll and have no fixed length, so there's no need to set page breaks every 11 inches.

Web pages, then, are like ducks, buffalo, and barracuda; they usually occur in groups. For all but the smallest or most unusual publishing projects, you should produce a set of interrelated Web pages rather than a single, large document file. Creating a one-page Web site is like producing a one-slide presentation or a one-chapter book—not only boring, but also a poor use of the medium.

This chapter provides a high-level overview of the ways FrontPage 2000 organizes, manages, and updates groups of Web pages as a set.

FrontPage Webs

To facilitate content management and administration, FrontPage organizes Web pages into units called FrontPage Webs. The first Web on a particular server or folder tree is called a root Web, and may contain any number of additional Webs. These are called user Webs or subwebs. If security is in effect, whoever creates the root Web usually retains control of it and delegates administration of user Webs to individual owners.

There are no concrete rules or technical requirements that dictate how many subwebs a root Web should have, or what they should contain. Certain principles apply, however:

- Pages with many hyperlinks among themselves usually belong in the same FrontPage Web. That is, distinct bodies of content should generally reside in a single Web.

- Groups of pages administered by different people should generally be in different Webs.

- The larger the Web, the longer it will take to upload and update. For purposes of both performance and content management, FrontPage Webs generally shouldn't exceed a few thousand files.

On a Web server, the root Web gets created as part of installing the FrontPage Server Extensions. Initially, the root Web consists of the server's entire existing content, and its owner is the Web server's administrator. The root Web administrator can then create subwebs—either new, empty subwebs or subwebs covering existing content—and grant appropriate permissions for administration, authoring, and browsing.

Personal Web Servers

Ignoring minor variations, there are basically four places you can keep Web pages you're developing:

- **As individual files on your own computer.**

  This is the simplest approach for beginners because you just start FrontPage, add the text and images for a Web page, apply formatting, and save it just as you would in any other Office 2000 application. As the number of such pages grows, however, managing all of them one by one becomes increasingly difficult. This typically leads to one of the remaining alternatives.

> **NOTE**
>
> For purposes of this discussion, files on a network file server are equivalent to files on your local hard disk.

- **As a FrontPage Web on your own computer.**

  With this approach, you designate a folder on your hard disk as a FrontPage Web. This can be a new folder with nothing in it, a new folder FrontPage will populate with sample pages, or an existing folder full of Web pages, images, and other files you've created. The result, in FrontPage terminology, is a *disk-based Web*.

  Once you've defined a disk-based Web, FrontPage can perform global operations on it. This includes things like spell-checking the entire Web, checking all the hyperlinks within the Web, and uploading the entire Web to another computer.

  What a disk-based Web *can't* do is emulate active processes designed to run on a Web server. This includes things like hit counters, content searching, processing data from HTML forms, and database processing. The programs that do these things on the World Wide Web are designed to run as part of a Web server and not as part of your disk; it's as simple as that. If you want these functions to work in your development environment, read on.

- **As a FrontPage Web, hosted on a Web server accessible via your network connection.**

  In this scenario, you put Web pages and associated files on a real Web server: one you can access via your network connection, of course. This could be a dial-up network connection, a Local Area Network at your office, or a Home Area Network that connects the computers in your house. (Trust me, this is going the be the next big thing.)

  For two reasons, a Web server used this way needs to have the FrontPage Server Extensions installed. First, when you tell FrontPage to create the HTML for, say, a hit counter, FrontPage generates code that tries to run the *FrontPage* hit counter program. And to install that program, the Webmaster needs to install the FrontPage Extensions. Second, the Web server needs the FrontPage Extensions so you can upload files.

  Reading files from a Web server is no problem for FrontPage 2000; it just reads them in the same way as any browser. The tricky part comes in *writing* files to a Web server, and FrontPage does this by packing up the file and submitting it like data coming from an HTML form. This requires a program on the other end of the connection—on the Web server—that can unpack the file and write it into the server's file system. And that program is part of the FrontPage Server Extensions.

Fortunately, you don't need to deal with all this complexity if you already have a FrontPage-enabled Web server on your network. Just ask the administrator for a FrontPage Web, specify its location in FrontPage, and away you go. Unfortunately, not everyone is in this position and so, for full functionality, they need to become their own Webmaster. Read on.

■ **As a FrontPage Web, hosted on a Web server running on your own computer.**

As it turns out, you can enjoy full-bore, server-based FrontPage functionality even if you create Web pages on a single, stand-alone computer. All you need to do is install network software, Web-server software, and the FrontPage Server Extensions, all on that one machine. Figure 2-1 illustrates this arrangement. This isn't as hard as it sounds, but it does mean you need to become your own Webmaster.

FIGURE 2-1.

The FrontPage 2000 client and a Web server used for authoring can reside either on separate computers or on the same computer.

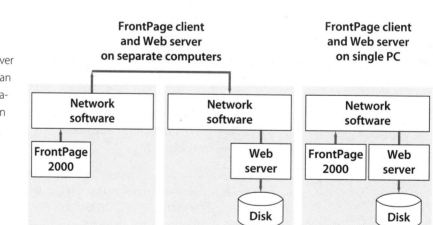

If you already connect to a TCP/IP network, either on a Local Area Network or by dialing into an Internet service provider, then the network software is already installed. If not, go to Control Panel, Network, and add the TCP/IP protocol.

You can use any Web server software that both runs on your computer and has a version of the FrontPage Server Extensions available. For most computers running Windows, this will be the Microsoft Web server software that corresponds to your operating system.

There are four ways to install the FrontPage Server Extensions. First, they may come with—and install with, perhaps as an option—the Web server software. Second, if you install FrontPage 2000 on a computer with a supported Web server already installed, FrontPage 2000 setup will install the server extensions automatically. Third, you can download the extensions from Microsoft's Web site. Fourth and finally, you can install the Office Server Extensions, which include the FrontPage Extensions plus some additional Office 2000 collaboration features. In general, you should choose the method that provides the most current software available at the time.

? SEE ALSO
For more information about setting up and managing a personal Web server, see Chapter 16, "Installing and Configuring a Web Server."

Microsoft's premier Web server is Internet Information Server (IIS), which runs only on Windows NT Server. Microsoft also provides scaled-down versions of IIS—called Personal Web servers—for Windows NT Workstation, Windows 98, and Windows 95. You can install any of these servers by obtaining and installing the Windows NT 4.0 Option Pack. (Yes, that's right; to install a personal Web server for Windows 98 or Windows 95, you install the Windows NT Option Pack. The setup program installs the proper software for your operating system.)

FrontPage Server Extensions

FrontPage achieves its maximum potential when the FrontPage Server Extensions are installed both on the Web author's machine and on the server that eventually delivers those pages to the remote users. The extensions are a set of programs that:

- Work with FrontPage 2000 to provide file upload via HTTP (HyperText Transfer Protocol).

? SEE ALSO
For more information about setting up the FrontPage Server Extensions on your own Web server, refer to Chapter 17, "Understanding the FrontPage Server Extensions."

- Maintain cross-reference indexes and other site-management information.

- Provide various centralized services—such as data collection, mailing, and search—for remote users when they visit your site.

Server extensions are available for a variety of popular Web servers and computing platforms including Windows 95, Windows 98, Windows NT, and Unix. If you're a server administrator planning to support Web authors running FrontPage, you should definitely install the extensions and keep them up to date. If you're a FrontPage Web author, you should definitely encourage your Web server administrator to do the same. If you have a Web site hosted by an Internet service provider (ISP), check to see if the provider has installed (or will install) the latest FrontPage Extensions.

Graphical Tools for Organizing Your Site

Keeping all but the smallest Web-page collections organized would be difficult without a graphical organizer like FrontPage. To suit various needs, FrontPage provides six distinct views of a FrontPage Web site. To select a particular view, click its icon at the left of the FrontPage window or choose its name from the View menu.

- **Page view** provides three views of a Web page:

  - An editable, WYSIWYG view.

  - An editable view of the HTML source code.

  - A preview of the finished page, displayed by Internet Explorer.

  If a FrontPage Web is open (as opposed to one or more single Web pages being open), then Page view also displays a list of folders and files in the current Web. This permits editing, creating, deleting, moving, and renaming files just as in Windows Explorer, even if the FrontPage Web is located on another computer.

  The following views also require that a FrontPage Web be open.

- **Folders view** displays a more complete list of a Web's files and folders than Page view's simple Folder List.

- **Reports view** displays 14 reports to help you manage your site.

- **Navigation view** accepts and then displays a hierarchical view of the pages in your site. You input the hierarchy by dragging rectangles, each representing a Web page, into a diagram that resembles an organization chart. Adding a Navigation Bar component to any Web page then creates a menu corresponding to your hierarchy.

- **Hyperlinks view** is, in some ways, the reverse of Navigation view. With Navigation view, you input the structure, and the Navigation Bar component creates the hyperlinks. With Hyperlinks view,

FrontPage analyzes your existing hyperlinks and graphically displays links to and from any page.

■ **Tasks view** displays a list of tasks you've created for the current Web page. In essence, it's an electronic, multi-user to-do list.

Later topics within this section discuss each view in detail. Regardless of the view in effect, though, FrontPage's menu bar and toolbar provide rich options to:

■ Create, modify globally, or delete Web sites.

■ Import pages from existing sites not controlled by FrontPage.

■ Run spelling checks and text searches throughout a site.

■ Copy sites from one server to another.

■ Control security.

Page View

In all probability, the main reason you bought FrontPage was to create Web pages visually, that is, by working through a WYSIWYG view instead of HTML code. It's therefore only logical that Page view be the first and default view FrontPage provides. Page view, shown in Figure 2-2, presents FrontPage's WYSIWYG editor.

FIGURE 2-2.
Page view displays Web pages for editing in near-WYSIWYG mode. The folder list at the left shows the current FrontPage Web if one is open.

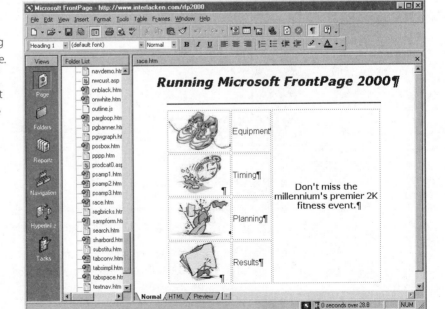

Ignoring the usual title bar, menu bar, and toolbars at the top of the window—and the status bar at the bottom—the Page View window consists of three panes:

- The Views bar at the far left provides access to all the views in FrontPage 2000 including, of course, Page view itself.

⑦ SEE ALSO

For more information on using Page view to manage the files in your Web site, refer to Chapter 19, "Working with FrontPage Webs."

- The Folder List, second from the left, is active only if you've opened a FrontPage Web. In that case, it shows the files and folders in that Web. All the usual Windows Explorer functions work here, even if the FrontPage Web resides on a Web server on another computer. Double-clicking a file opens it with the default editor—FrontPage's WYSIWYG editor in the case of .htm or .html files.

⑦ SEE ALSO

For detailed instructions on the use of Page view for editing Web pages, refer to Part II, "Creating Web Pages."

- The editing pane, which is usually the largest area in Page view, is where you edit your Web pages. Here you can enter text, import images, paste content from the Clipboard, and apply a rich variety of formatting options.

To open a Web page in Page view, choose Open from the File menu. This displays the dialog box in Figure 2-3.

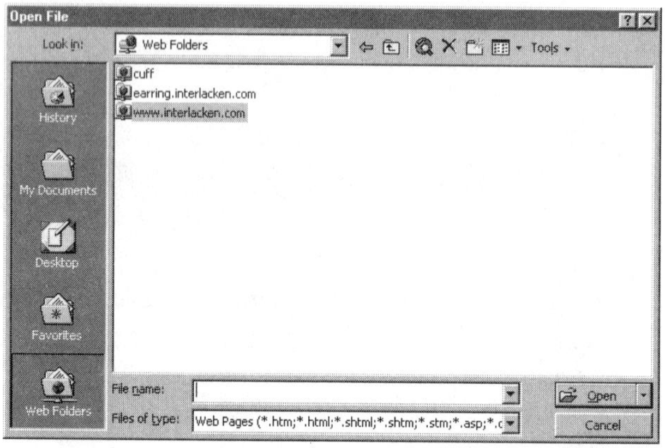

FIGURE 2-3.

FrontPage uses the standard Office 2000 file dialog box for opening files and Webs in Page view. It can open not only files from your local disk or file server but also, acting like a browser, files from the Web.

- The History icon displays a list of Web pages you've recently opened.

- The My Documents icon displays the contents of the same My Documents folder that Office 2000 and other applications use.

- The Desktop icon displays a list of items on your Windows desktop: My Computer, My Documents, Network Neighborhood, My Briefcase, and so forth.

- The Favorites icon displays the same list of Web pages as the Favorites menu in your copy of Internet Explorer.

■ The Web Folders icon displays a list of FrontPage Web locations you've used in the past.

To open a folder displayed by any of these icons, double-click the folder. Drill down through as many folders as needed to locate your file, then double-click the file to open it.

You can also open any file or folder by typing its name in the File Name box and clicking Open. You can type either file locations, such as C:\MyDocuments\WebDocs\mypage.htm, or URLs, such as http://www.anysite.com. When you enter a URL, FrontPage reads the HTML file, its images, and any other components from the Web, as if FrontPage were a browser.

If you open a file that's contained within a FrontPage Web, FrontPage opens both the Web and the file. To open a FrontPage Web without opening any particular file, choose Open Web from the File menu.

If you open more than one file in the same Web, only one file at a time is normally visible in Page view. To view a list of currently open files and switch among them, pull down the Window menu.

TIP

> To view two pages in the same Web at the same time, choose New Window from the Window menu, and then use each window to display a different page.

If you open more than one Web at the same time, each Web appears in a separate FrontPage window. You can switch among them in typical Windows fashion, that is, by clicking buttons on the Windows taskbar or by pressing Alt+Tab.

Folders View

This view provides a representation, strongly resembling Windows Explorer, that displays the files and folders in a FrontPage Web. Figure 2-4 shows an example of Folders view.

Folders view works very much like Explorer in Windows 95, Windows 98, and Windows NT. Note the extra column for Title, however. As in Windows Explorer, double-clicking folders navigates through them. Double-clicking Web pages opens them in Page view, and double-clicking an image file invokes either Microsoft PhotoDraw or another image editor of your choice.

TIP

> You can maintain the list of available editors by choosing FrontPage's Tools menu, selecting Options, and clicking the Configure Editors tab.

FIGURE 2-4.

FrontPage's Folders view gives a graphical view of the files and folders that make up a FrontPage Web site.

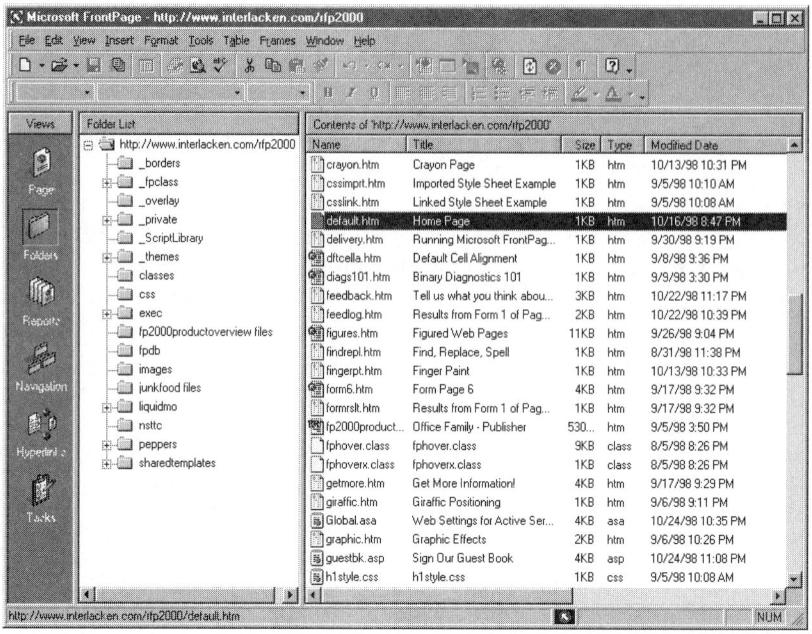

Right-clicking an item in Folders view results in this menu.

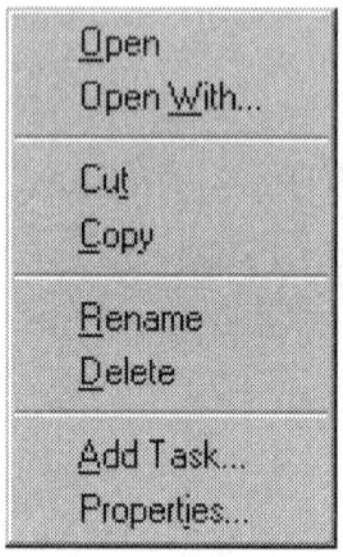

- **Open** opens the file in Page view, PhotoDraw, or another program appropriate to the type of file.

- **Open With** opens the file with another editor of your choice.

- **Cut** puts the clicked file in the Clipboard and adds a Paste option for storing the file elsewhere. After pasting, the original file is deleted.

- **Copy**, like Cut, puts the clicked file in the Clipboard and adds a Paste option. However, the original file is retained after pasting.

TIP

> When you move or rename a file by any means in FrontPage, FrontPage updates references from other files in the same Web.

- **Rename** opens the file name to editing.

- **Delete** permanently removes the file. (There is no Undelete.)

- **Add Task** creates a Task view reminder regarding this page.

- **Properties** displays a dialog box showing the object's characteristics and settings.

? SEE ALSO

For more information on using Folders view, refer to "Working with Folders View," page 626.

FrontPage's Folders view supports all the drag-and-drop operations you've grown accustomed to in Windows. The difference is that if you move or rename files in Windows, you have to (1) manually locate each hypertext link from other pages in your site to the moved or renamed one and (2) update each of these pages manually. When you move or rename a file in FrontPage, FrontPage updates the other pages in your Web.

Reports View

FrontPage 2000 provides 14 highly useful, interactive reports for managing your site. To view a specific report, choose Reports from the View menu, then the report you want from the resulting submenu. Clicking the Reports icon in the Views bar also invokes Reports view, showing either the last report you requested or, by default, the Site Summary report (described later in the this section).

As usual in Windows, you can sort any FrontPage report on any column simply by clicking its heading. Clicking the same heading repeatedly alternates between ascending and descending sequence.

Double-clicking any line of a report opens the corresponding file. Double-clicking an HTML file opens it in Page view; double-clicking an image opens it in the default image editor; double-clicking a task opens that task; and so forth. Right-clicking any line of any report produces a pop-up menu showing everything you can do with that line.

? SEE ALSO

For more information on using Reports view, see "Working with Reports View," page 629.

By their nature, reports pertain to collections of objects; one-line reports just aren't very interesting. For this reason, Reports view pertains only to FrontPage Webs. If you're just using FrontPage to edit a single page and haven't opened a FrontPage Web, Reports view won't be available. If you *have* opened a Web, the reports pertain to that Web.

The rest of this section presents an overview of each report.

The Site Summary Report

This report displays a series of statistics for the current FrontPage Web: the number and total size of all files, the number and size of all image files, the number of files unreachable from any hyperlink in the current Web, and so forth. Figure 2-5 shows a typical Site Summary report.

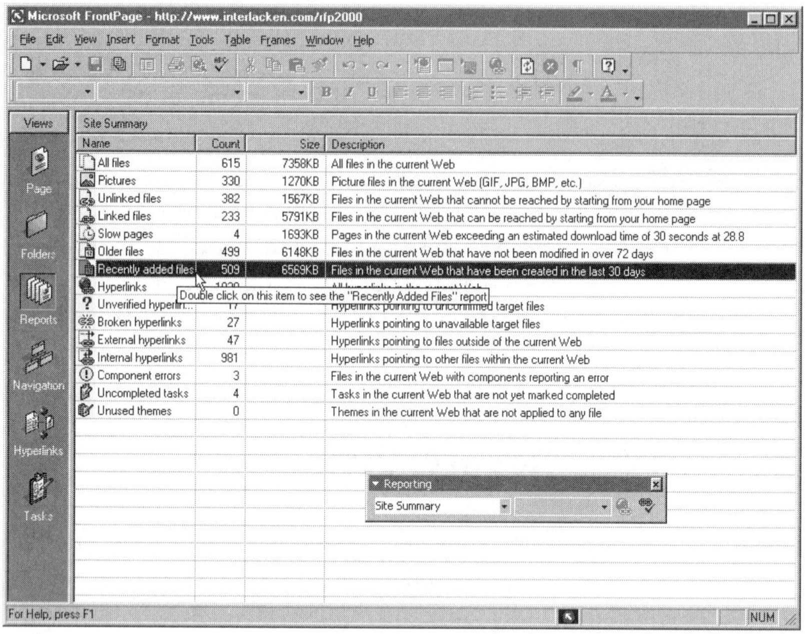

FIGURE 2-5.

The Site Summary report displays site-wide statistics for the current FrontPage Web.

Note the entries for recent, older, and slow files. The dialog box shown in Figure 2-6 determines which files fall into these categories. To display it, choose Options from the Tools menu, then click the Reports View tab.

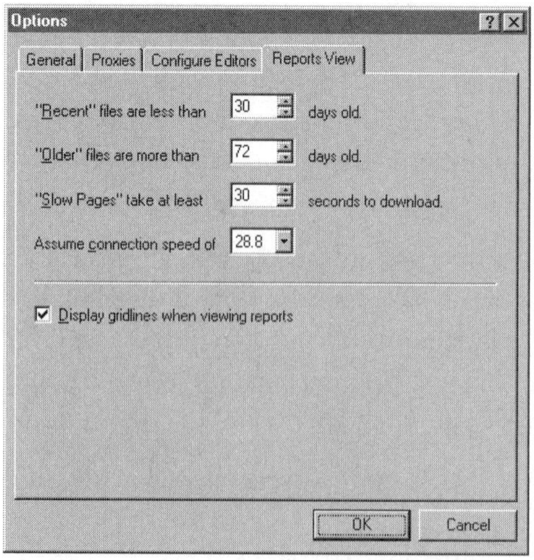

FIGURE 2-6.

This dialog box determines what constitutes a recent, an older, and a slow Web page for Site Summary statistics and the corresponding detail reports.

Web Publishing
with FrontPage 2000

The All Files Report

This report provides a list of all files in a FrontPage Web, regardless of the folder in which they reside. Figure 2-7 provides an example. Having a single list of all files in your Web can be convenient for locating files with a particular attribute. Clicking Modified Date, for example, makes it easy to identify all files—in any folder—changed within a certain time span. The All Files report provides all the capabilities of Folders view except for the ability to move files among folders.

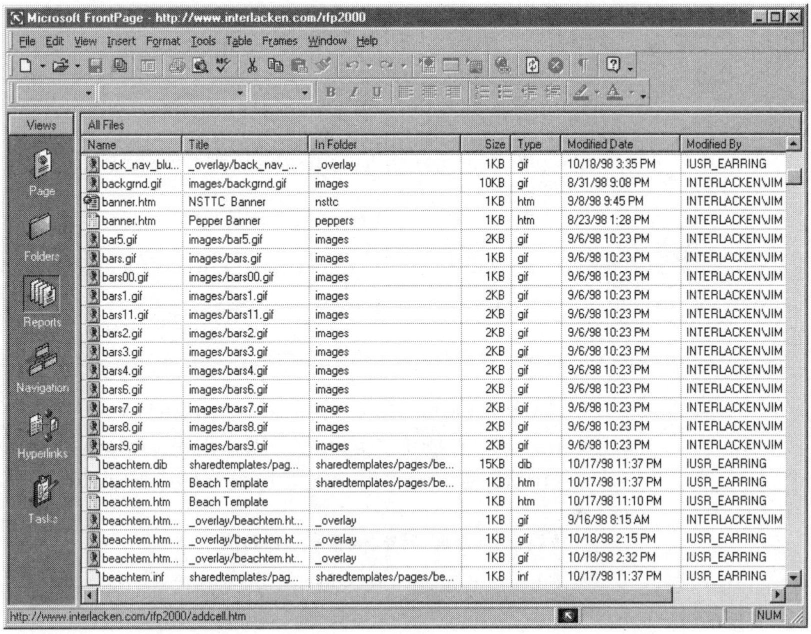

FIGURE 2-7.
FrontPage's All Files report shows all files in the current Web, with folder location as an attribute.

The Recently Added Files Report

This report has the same layout as the All Files report, but it only includes files added to the current Web within the Recent interval specified in Figure 2-6. This is very handy if you've forgotten where you put something or otherwise need to review recent changes.

The Recently Changed Files Report

Again using the format of the All Files report (Figure 2-7), this choice displays files changed within the specified Recent interval. This includes everything in the Recently Added Files report, plus existing files that someone updated during the Recent interval.

The Older Files Report

This is yet another cousin of the All Files report. It includes any files in the current Web whose most recent change was beyond the Older interval specified in the dialog box in Figure 2-6. This is useful for locating pages that might be stale or outdated.

The Unlinked Files Report

Any files that appear in this report have no apparent hyperlinks from other files within the current Web. Again, this report closely resembles the format shown in Figure 2-7.

The fact that a file shows up as unlinked doesn't necessarily mean it's safe to delete it. Files can be unlinked for any of these reasons:

- The hyperlinks to the page are missing.

- All hyperlinks to the file are from outside the current Web.

SEE ALSO
For more information about scripts, see "Working with Script Code," page 418.

- All hyperlinks to the file are built by script code too complicated for FrontPage to interpret.

- The file is obsolete and can safely be deleted.

Nevertheless, it's usually worthwhile to review the Unlinked Files report from time to time. Although some listed files may have links FrontPage can't detect, others may be legitimate technological waste.

The Slow Pages Report

Files in this report, shown in Figure 2-8, simply take a long time to download. The estimated time required appears in the Download Time column.

FrontPage computes the download time by adding up the size of the base file and all its components (such as images), then dividing by the download speed specified in the Reports View Options tab (Figure 2-6). If the download time is greater than or equal to the Slow Pages limit, the base page appears in the Slow Pages report.

You should generally consider changing any page that appears on this report, especially if you expect Web visitors to visit it very often. You might consider using fewer or smaller images, for example, or converting large pages into several smaller ones. No one enjoys slow-loading Web pages.

The Broken Hyperlinks Report

The Broken Hyperlinks report shown in Figure 2-9 displays each questionable hyperlink in a FrontPage Web, tells where it occurs, and indicates whether the link's status is Broken or Unknown.

FrontPage uses its own internal indexes to verify the status of hyperlinks among pages in the current FrontPage Web. As long as these indexes are correct, FrontPage will provide instant, always-up-to-date information on these links.

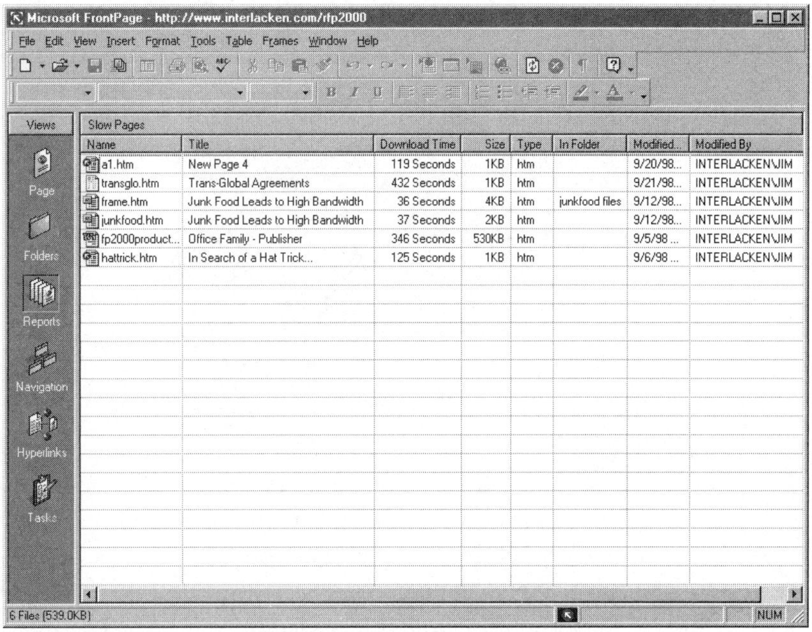

FIGURE 2-8.
Files in this listing exceed site guidelines for browser download time. Note the Download Time column.

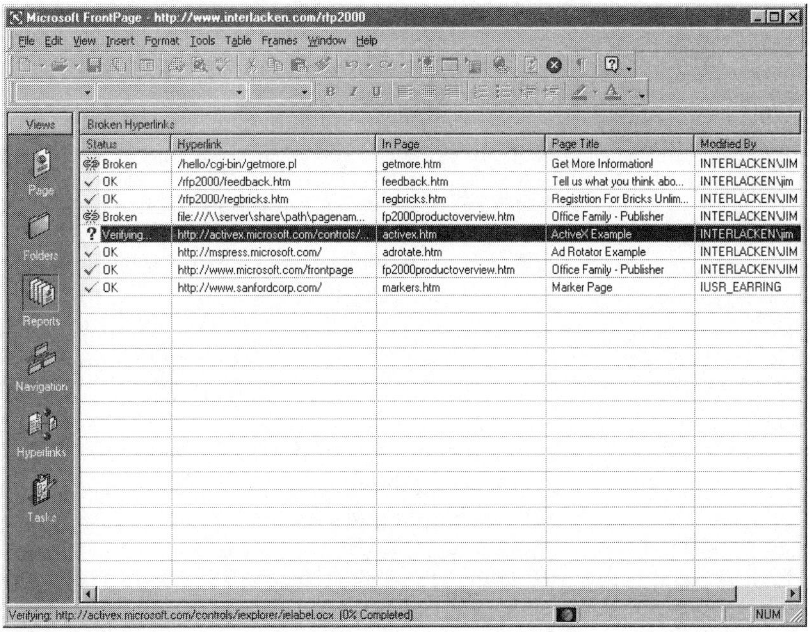

FIGURE 2-9.
The Broken Hyperlinks report displays the status of all internal hyperlinks. To verify hyperlinks pointing outside the current Web, first select them, then right-click the selected group, and then choose Verify Hyperlinks from the pop-up menu.

Checking links outside the current Web requires attempting actual connections. This can be a time-consuming operation, especially when connections time out, so FrontPage doesn't verify these links automatically. To verify one or more external hyperlinks, select them, right-click them, and choose Verify Hyperlinks from the pop-up menu.

To fix a broken link, double-click it to display the Edit Hyperlink dialog box:

If you know the correct hyperlink address, you can type it directly into the Replace Hyperlink With text box. If not, click Browse to start your Web browser and locate the desired page. When you return to the Edit Hyperlink dialog box, FrontPage will get the current page location from the browser and insert it for you.

The Component Errors Report

This report displays a list of errors and inconsistencies involving FrontPage components in the current Web. In Figure 2-10, for example:

SEE ALSO

For more information about the FrontPage Substitution component, see Chapter 21, "Using Server-Side Front-Page Components."

- Three pages contain a FrontPage Substitution component that references a site parameter that doesn't exist.

- One page has an error in its Internet Database Connector (IDC) code.

- Three pages have warnings regarding HTML forms. Their designer has configured these forms so that when visitors submit them, the Web server will send e-mail containing the submitted data. The warning is a reminder that this technique requires configuration on the Web server as well as within the HTML form.

If an error message appears truncated, you can view the entire text by right-clicking the message, choosing Properties from the pop-up menu, then clicking the Errors tab.

To open a Web page and correct an error, double-click the corresponding line in the report.

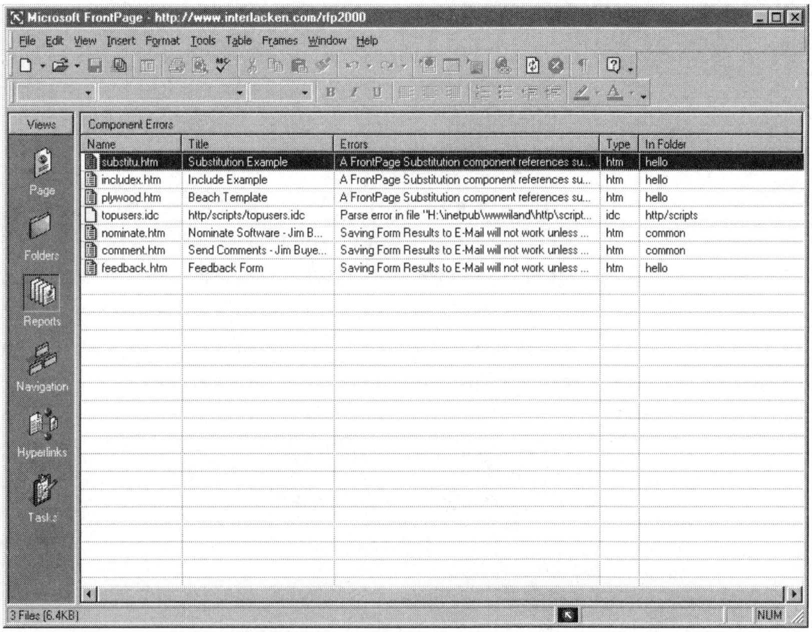

FIGURE 2-10.

Web pages listed in this report have FrontPage components that are improperly configured or that otherwise merit caution.

The Review Status Report

FrontPage 2000 includes new features for managing the work of several people creating a single FrontPage Web. For example, FrontPage can remember who's assigned to work on a particular page, when each page was last reviewed, by whom, and the result. This information is then available for viewing in the Review Status report.

The dialog box for entering Assigned To and Review Status information appears in Figure 2-11. To display this dialog box, right-click the corresponding file in any view or report, choose Properties from the pop-up menu, and then click the Workgroup tab.

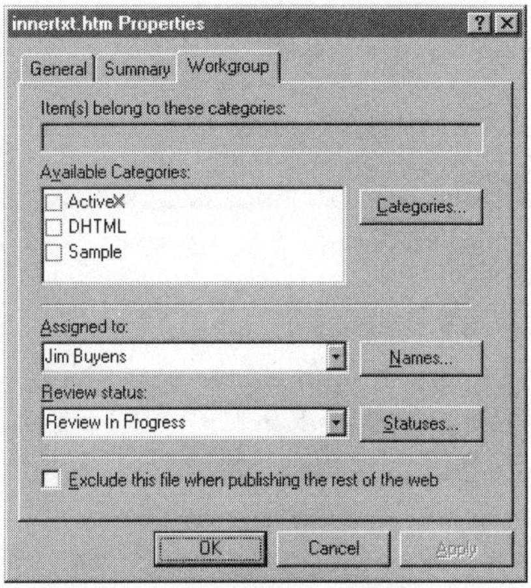

FIGURE 2-11.

Use this dialog box to assign Web files to individuals and to indicate the status of reviews.

You can enter both Assigned To and Review Status information either directly, by typing, or by selecting from the drop-down lists. Initially the drop-down lists will be empty, but you can populate them by clicking the Names and Statuses buttons. To save your entries, click either the OK button or the Apply button.

The Review Status report, illustrated in Figure 2-12, shows the current Review Status and Assigned To fields described just above. In addition, it shows when the status last changed (Review Date) and the login ID of the person who changed it (Reviewed By). Whenever someone changes the Review Status field, FrontPage updates the Review Date and Reviewed By fields.

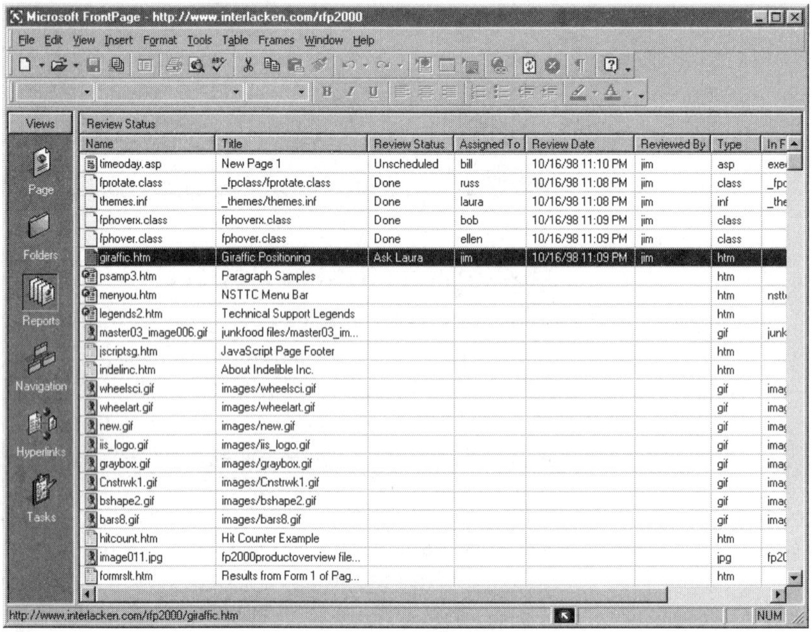

FIGURE 2-12.

The Review Status report shows the person assigned to each page, and the current status of all reviews.

The Assigned To Report

This report, shown in Figure 2-13, primarily lists the Assigned To data entered in the dialog box shown in Figure 2-11. FrontPage records the accompanying Assigned Date and Assigned By fields whenever someone updates Assigned To.

The Categories Report

At the top of Figure 2-11 you may have noticed a selection list called Available Categories. (If you didn't, it's OK to look back.) In that dialog box, you can assign any Web file to one or more categories by clicking the box in front of the category name. To create new categories, click the Categories button in the same dialog box.

Once you've assigned categories to one or more Web pages, you can use the FrontPage Categories Component to build a hyperlinked list of all files in a category. This is a very cool feature, but as described so far, it doesn't provide a way to review all the category codes in your Web. This is the purpose of the Categories report shown in Figure 2-14.

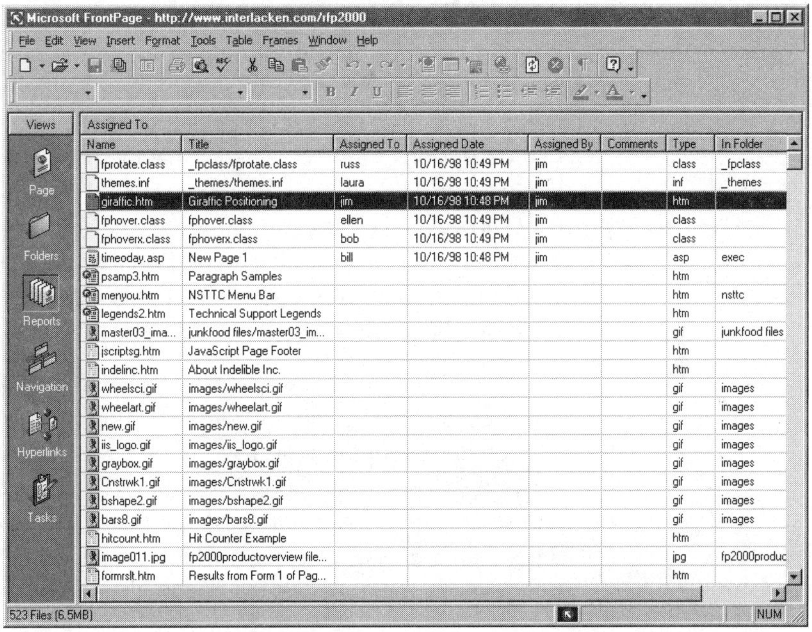

FIGURE 2-13.

The Assigned To column in this report comes from the Assigned To field in the dialog box in Figure 2-11. FrontPage records the Assigned Date and Assigned By fields.

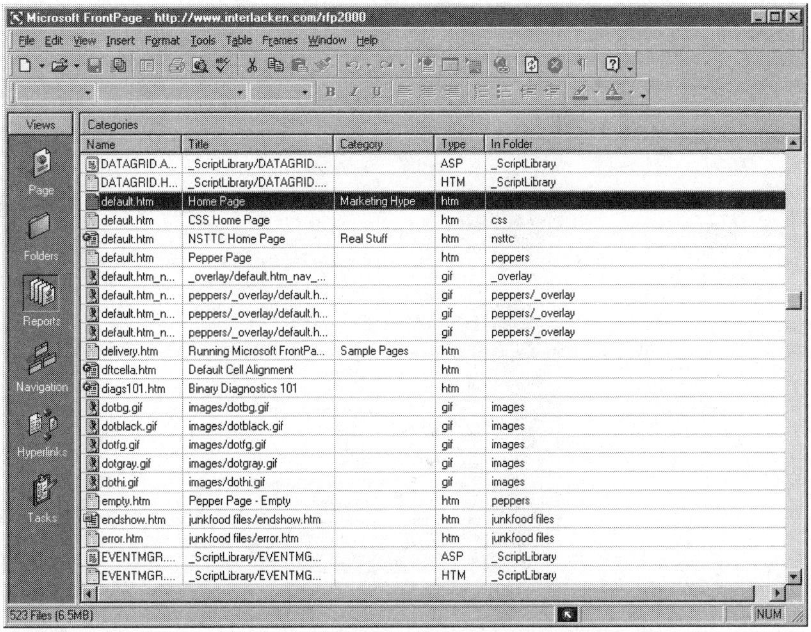

FIGURE 2-14.

The Categories report shows the categories assigned—via the dialog box in Figure 2-11 —to each page in a FrontPage Web.

To modify the categories for any page, right-click the page, choose Properties from the pop-up menu, click the Workgroup tab, and modify—you guessed it—the dialog box shown in Figure 2-11. Changing the categories for any file in your Web updates any applicable Categories Components in the same Web.

The Publish Status Report

When publishing files from one Web to another (as when uploading files from your development site to your public Web server), FrontPage normally assumes it should copy every file in your Web. (There are a few exceptions, such as files that haven't changed and files related to system configuration, but we'll ignore those for now.) For various reasons, however, you might occasionally wish to hold back certain pages. Perhaps the file is a database you don't want overwritten every time you upload your Web, or perhaps the development copy simply isn't ready for prime time.

The check box titled Exclude This File When Publishing The Rest Of The Web, located on the ubiquitous Workgroup tab shown in Figure 2-11, supports this requirement. If you don't want a certain file uploaded, open the Workgroup dialog box, check the box, click OK or Apply, and rest securely. The only nagging detail is figuring out, from time to time, which files are cleared for upload and which are not. This is the function of the Publish Status report shown in Figure 2-15.

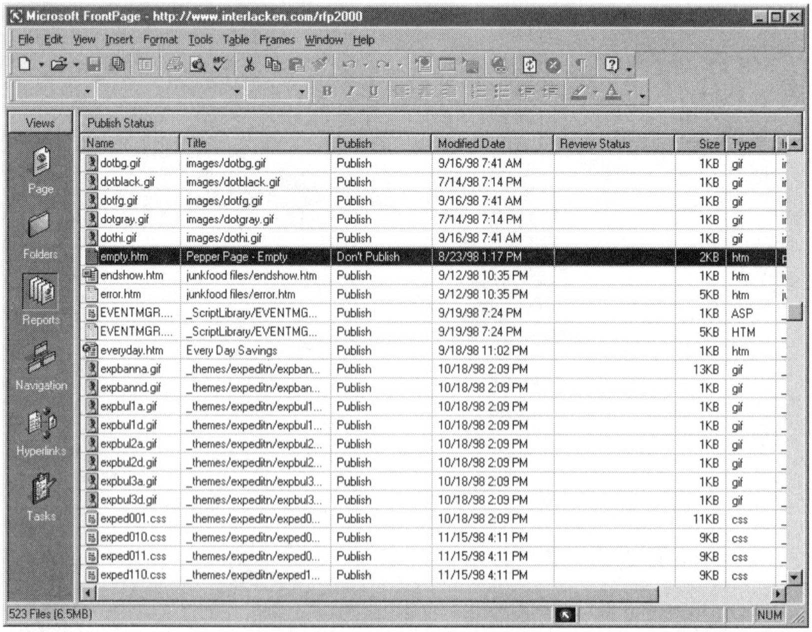

FIGURE 2-15.

In the Publish Status report, files marked Don't Publish are blocked from transfer whenever you publish from the current Web to another.

If a file's workgroup properties indicate Exclude This File…, its value in the Publish column will be Don't Publish. Otherwise, its Publish value will be Publish. As always, you can click the column heading to sort on this field.

The Checkout Status Report

Using FrontPage's new Page-Level Check-In/Check-Out feature, Web designers can now take ownership of files in a FrontPage Web. This guarantees no one else can edit or overwrite the file until the owner relinquishes it. Checking out a file also provides a measure of version control because the owner can undo the check-out and automatically revert to the prior version of the file.

The Checkout Status Report shows which files are checked out to which users, plus the current status of each such file.

Navigation View

Most Web authors organize their content hierarchically—that is, much like an organization chart. The Web begins at the top level with a home page and continues downward with a child page for each primary choice on the home-page menu. Children at the second level might be parents to other groups of children at a third level, and so forth.

FrontPage's Navigation view provides a way to enter, view, and print just such an organization chart for any Web. Figure 2-16 provides a typical example.

For new Webs, FrontPage will create a home page named default.htm or index.htm and place it in the center of the upper Navigation View window. For existing Webs, FrontPage will identify the home page if possible. If FrontPage can't identify a Web's home page, clicking the New Page toolbar icon will create one.

? SEE ALSO
For more information on Navigation view, see "Working with Navigation View," page 639.

Once Navigation view knows the home page, you can identify its children by dragging their file names out of the folder pane and dropping them just below the home page. The pages will remain ordered left to right, depending on where you drop or subsequently drag them. If a page's parent is other than the home page, drop it under its parent. As you drag a page around the Navigation View window, FrontPage draws shaded lines to indicate its parentage if dropped at the current location.

> NOTE

> As the diagram becomes larger and more complex, you might want to zoom in, zoom out, collapse branches, and then expand them. Navigation view provides all these commands.

FIGURE 2-16.

Navigation view provides a way to designate and view the logical organization of a Web.

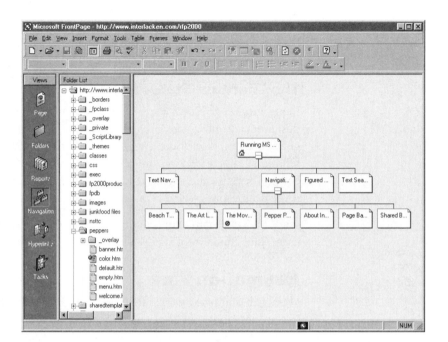

Storyboard Your Site with Navigation View

Once you have a basic structure drawn—even if it consists of nothing but a home page—you might find it convenient to always create new pages in Navigation view. Then you can title the new pages, add them to your Navigation view structure, and update Tasks view with a reminder to supply the actual content. This process is similar to storyboarding your Web site with index cards and pushpins, though much more flexible.

Documenting the structure of your Web might at first seem like redundant work; you might think FrontPage should infer your site's structure automatically, by analyzing hyperlinks or folder structures. On reflection, however, you'll find that neither of these methods will produce the same results as good human judgment.

- Hyperlink analysis fails because most Web pages contain hyperlinks that are convenient for the reader but extraneous to the Web's primary content structure. Also, if a page is the target of hyperlinks on several other pages, there's no way to determine via hyperlinks which is the true parent in terms of the Web's content.

- Folder analysis fails because most sites become disorganized over time and because utility pages are often added beyond the Web's main structure.

For these reasons, FrontPage takes an opposite approach to eliminating double work: Rather than inducing the Web's structure from its HTML, FrontPage generates HTML from information you provide about your Web's structure.

Figure 2-17 shows the FrontPage dialog box for automatically building a navigation bar—what most people call a menu bar—from the information in FrontPage's Navigation view. To display this dialog box, open the page in Page view and choose Navigation Bar from the Insert menu.

FIGURE 2-17.

This dialog box in FrontPage adds a navigation bar to the current Web page. Items on the bar will show the structure and page names as they were entered in Navigation view.

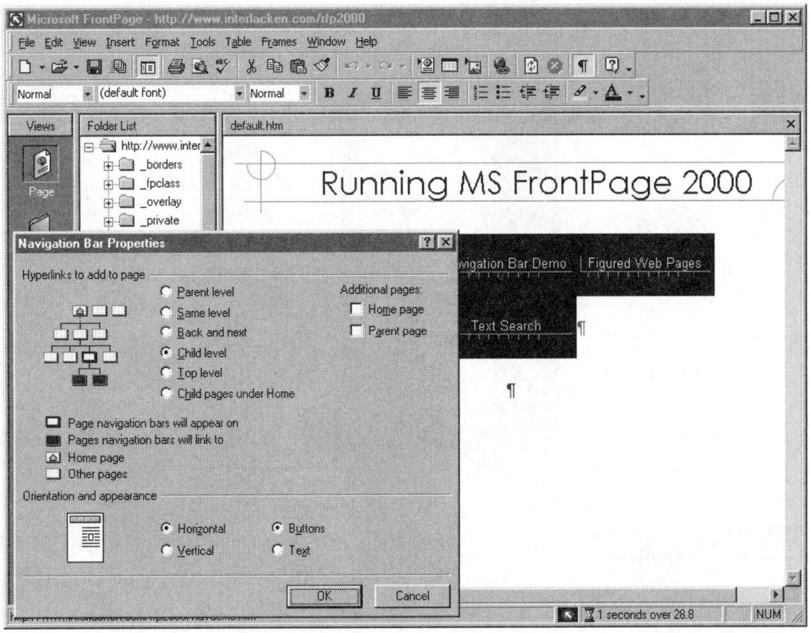

A navigation bar inserted in Page view reflects the current structure in Navigation view. You can change the bar's options and appearance in Page view, but not its content. To change the bar's content, update Navigation view, and FrontPage will propagate the changes to each applicable navigation bar in the Web.

Hyperlinks View

This view provides the hyperlink-based structure analysis you may have expected in Navigation view. It provides a display, centered on any page in the FrontPage Web, that illustrates graphically which other pages are related by hyperlink. Figure 2-18 illustrates this view.

In Hyperlinks view, selecting a page in the left pane moves it to the center position in the right pane. Lines connecting one page to another indicate hyperlinked pages; the arrowhead points *from* the page containing the hyperlink *to* the page being linked.

FIGURE 2-18.

FrontPage's Hyperlink view provides a graphical view of the hyperlink relationships within a Web site.

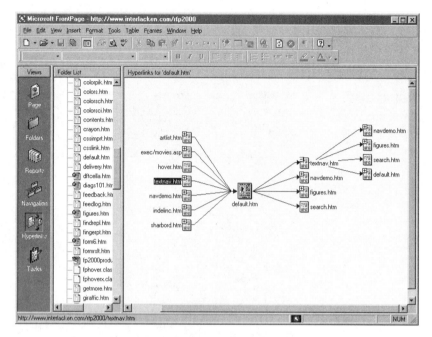

? SEE ALSO

For more information on Hyperlinks view, see "Working with Hyperlinks View," page 647.

Pages marked with plus-sign icons contain hyperlinks to still more pages; you can display these hyperlinks by clicking the plus sign on the icon (which then changes to a minus sign). Clicking the minus sign restores the original view. Resting the mouse pointer over the central page icon in the right pane displays that page's file name, while pausing the mouse pointer over its links displays the pages' file names and information about the type of link.

Double-clicking the body of a Web page icon opens the page in Page view. To move a linked page to the center of the view, right-click it and then choose Move To Center.

Tasks View

This view displays a list of pending tasks for the current FrontPage Web. You can create tasks either manually as you think of them or automatically as a result of other processes.

There are several ways to create a new task. From Tasks view, shown in Figure 2-19, you can simply right-click any blank space in the main window and choose New Task from the pop-up window. Also, from any view, you can choose New from the File menu and select Task.

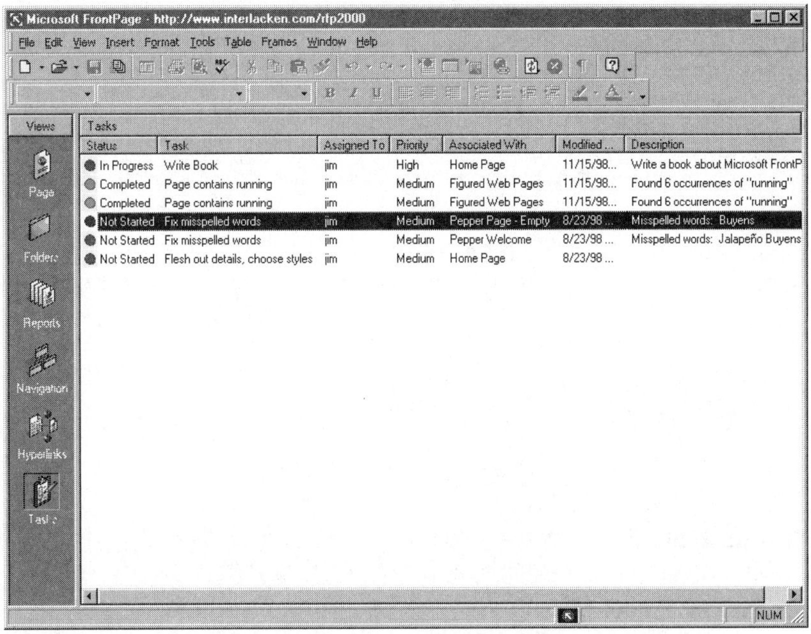

FIGURE 2-19.

Tasks view displays a listing of all known pending issues with your Web. As you resolve each issue, you can mark the task complete.

To create tasks associated with a specific file, right-click the file in any folder view and choose Add Task. In Page view, you can create tasks for the current page by choosing Task from the Edit menu. Finally, in some New Page dialog boxes, you can create a New Page task rather than the new page itself.

Certain global FrontPage operations also create tasks. For example, you can check the spelling on your entire Web and, rather than stopping at each error, simply create tasks pointing to any pages that contain errors.

Right-clicking an entry in Tasks view produces this contextual menu:

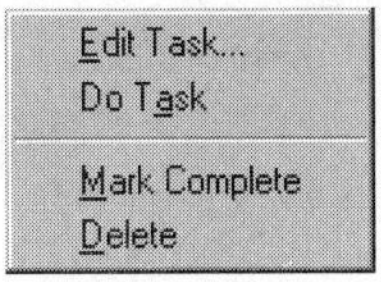

(?) SEE ALSO

For more information on Task view, see "Working with Task View," page 650.

Global Site Parameters

FrontPage provides a facility whereby you can save frequently used data once, in a central location, and then reference it by name in any Web pages you create.

? SEE ALSO

For more information about site parameters, see "Controlling Web Parameters," page 588.

Suppose, for example, that the names of key people at your site change from time to time. You could set up a site parameter for each position in your organization chart and assign each incumbent's name as a value. At this point, you could have each page in the site reference the parameter name (say, *vprad* for your Vice President of Research and Development) rather than the explicit name (say, "Frank P. Jones"). When someone new takes over a position, you can then change the one site parameter rather than having to find and update each affected page by hand, possibly missing some in the process.

Figure 2-20 shows the FrontPage Web Settings dialog box for adding and maintaining site parameters. You can display this dialog box by choosing Web Settings from the Tools menu and then clicking the Parameters tab.

FIGURE 2-20.

FrontPage can accommodate any number of global parameters for a site.

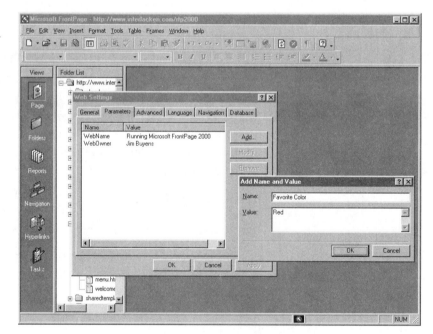

In Summary...

Organizing your Web files into FrontPage Webs imposes extra software and extra discipline on your working environment. In return, it provides powerful tools for managing and manipulating entire Web sites as a unit. If you work on multiple sites or on sites with many pages, you should seriously consider treating them as FrontPage Webs.

PART II

Creating
Web Pages

CHAPTER 3

Planning and Organizing a FrontPage Web

Whatever your site's size and purpose, proper advance planning will produce a better appearance, more organized content, faster construction, and easier ongoing maintenance. More importantly, a well-planned site will attract more visitors, better meet its original goals, and be cheaper to run.

Every site should have a consistency suited to its purpose. Pages should be unified by a common theme, a common organization, and a common style. The words, images, colors, and layout should lead the visitor to the messages—both overt and subtle—that justify the site's existence.

This chapter addresses the core aspects of planning and producing a Web site. These aspects are highly interrelated; you can't plan without understanding the work to be done, and without a sound plan, you can't properly do the work. That's why learning to organize and produce Web sites is an iterative process that considers increasing levels of detail.

Defining Your Site's Content

All successful Web sites start out with a well-defined mission. This leads to a well-organized, well-defined body of content and ultimately to effective communication. Taking the time to get organized up front will certainly pay off in timely, effective results later.

Identifying Your Message

Step one in building or maintaining a Web site is understanding the message its sponsors want to send. Whether your site describes yourself, an area of interest, your organization, your client, or a large multinational corporation, the message you want to send probably isn't, "I'm just learning HTML," "I'm scatterbrained," or "I'm trying to increase ugliness and confusion in the world."

"Establishing a presence" is probably the most common reason for starting a Web site, but this is terribly vague. It usually means following a perceived trend, keeping up with competitors, or responding to requests from others. More focused (and more useful) reasons for starting a Web site include:

- Increasing knowledge and awareness of a person, a topic, or an organization.

- Releasing information in accordance with the law or an organization's charter.

- Promoting a desired public image.

- Advertising products and services.

- Selling products or services directly to Web visitors.

- Providing post-sale product-support information.

You'll almost certainly need to drill through several levels of detail to fully understand your site's mission. Investigating each level generally leads to questions for the next. The end result should be a mission statement, even if informal, that describes the site's purpose and objective.

Understanding the Audience

As important as knowing your site's message is knowing its audience. "Everyone on the Web" is too vague an audience to be useful; you should have some particular *kinds* of people in mind—perhaps even specific people to use as models. Some typical audiences are:

- Everyone in a certain industry.

- Practitioners of a certain skill.

- Purchasers of a certain type of product or service.

- Users of a specific product or service.

Once you know who's in your audience, you should learn whatever you can about them. Are they technical, artistic, or people-oriented? What are their skills and interests? What's their level of vocabulary and education? Do they respond more to detailed text or to color, style, and visual metaphors?

You hope, of course, that your audience will find your site's message inherently interesting and attractive. Often, however, some other enticement is needed. Perhaps you can entice visitors with a free clip-art library and then, while they browse, sell them your graphics program. Perhaps you can sell art supplies as people browse a library of works or techniques. If they come for information about a product they already own, perhaps you can sell them another.

The ultimate enticement, according to recent thinking, is to make your site the meeting place for a community of some kind—presumably a community with an interest in your product or message. The goal is then to make your site such a valuable resource—such a compelling place for people in your target audience to find each other and interact—that the site becomes a "must visit." This generally requires some sort of added content that's updated frequently and not available anywhere else. It also requires a means for visitors to enhance the site themselves and to find other visitors without invading anyone's privacy. Achieving this sort of community is more often talked about than achieved in practice, though it remains a lofty goal. It also illustrates the importance of providing a magnet to attract targeted visitors.

Addressing the Politics of Organizations

Anything involving two or more persons involves politics. Unless you're building a personal Web site or a site for your own entrepreneurial business, you'll probably need to discuss your ideas with someone else, get their approval, or reach consensus. This might seem like an extra task up front, but it generally results in improved content and fewer problems when it's time to go online. In a large organization that's putting up a new external Web site, for example, it's generally best to get input and approval from higher-ups in outer-directed departments such as Public Affairs and Marketing.

II

Creating Web Pages

A greater problem arises when key authorities are asked to render decisions on something they don't understand. Education into the intricacies of Web publishing is obviously critical in such situations, especially when it includes review of established and successful sites with a similar mission. Unfortunately, it's often difficult to get enough time with the right people.

A related problem occurs when key decision makers lack empathy with the intended audience. Some principals from Manufacturing or Engineering, for example, might insist on content with internal rather than external relevance—even for an external Web site. Perhaps you can get customer profiles from Marketing or Public Affairs and discuss them with the inner-directed departments.

These general tips might help you deal with organizational conflict or obstructionism:

- If two key people disagree, try shuttle diplomacy. Speak to them both privately, try to formulate a compromise, and then speak to them privately again.

- If two key groups disagree, identify the opinion leaders and revert to the bullet point immediately above. Remember, the key opinion leaders aren't necessarily the highest-ranking individuals.

- Play the expert. Use long technical explanations of why poor decisions won't work. Bore them until they break.

- Don't assume that a person's view won't change. Asking the same question a different way on a different day frequently produces a different answer—quite possibly a more workable one and even a more effective solution.

- The best way to get action from bureaucrats is to let them know you've found a way around them.

- The second best way to get action from bureaucrats is to make a deal.

- The hardest way to get action from bureaucrats is to figure out their agenda and attack it. A folksy old saying warns, "Don't ever fight with pigs; you both get dirty and the pig likes it."

- Use your boss, project sponsor, or contract authority to the hilt when necessary. They probably occupy their positions because they're better at organizational dealings than you are.

Identifying Content Categories

If your site is typical, the home page will be the most time-consuming of all to construct. There are several reasons for this:

- The home page presents the site's first impression, and therefore it's usually the site's most elaborate page. Remember another old saying: "You get only one chance to make a first impression."

- Despite being the site's most elaborate page, the home page must download quickly. Otherwise, visitors will give up after a minute or two and go elsewhere.

- The home page often serves as the prototype for the entire site's visual appearance. It sets the tone and image for every page that follows.

- If you're new to creating Web pages, a home page will probably be your initial learning experience.

- The options on the home page intrinsically represent the site's primary structure.

The first four points usually work themselves out, but the last is critical. If you can identify the top few options in your site, you probably have a good understanding of its message and audience. If you can't get your home page organized, your content plan probably isn't organized either.

FrontPage provides built-in templates and wizards that create typical pages for many kinds of sites, but at best they produce only starting points. No two sites are exactly alike; your site's content and organization are ultimately your unique creation.

Some terrible ways to organize a site include:

- An option for each member of the design committee.

- An option for each person who reports to the top executive.

- An option for each category someone thought of, in chronological order.

- The same options you used at a previous site.

All of the above share the same problem: they ignore the target visitor's likely interests and mindset. They indicate a lack of defined message, defined audience, or both.

Defining Your Site's Style

Artists and computer specialists usually embody completely different mind-sets. Nevertheless, both design and computer skills are needed to produce an effective Web site. To reduce the gap between art and science—at least in a small way—this section introduces a few topics regarding pleasing and effective visual design.

Elements of Design

Artistic design isn't an exact science, so many technically inclined people conclude it's beyond them—or at least something that gives them a headache. Even if you lack the talent to become a professional artist, though, you can use certain principles of good design to enhance your work and communicate your message more effectively. Contrast and symmetry are two such principles that appear in a variety of contexts.

Contrast vs. Clash

The polar bear at the north pole and the black cat in the coal bin figure in two old jokes involving contrast. In both cases, lack of contrast makes the key element indistinguishable from its surroundings. Graphic contrast serves two important purposes in Web pages or, for that matter, any other document.

- Contrast enhances legibility. For example, the black type and white background in this book make it easier to read than if one color were gray.

- Contrast visually communicates distinctions among various page elements. In this book, for example, contrasting typography makes it easy to distinguish headings from body type.

The contrast knob on your monitor or TV set controls the difference in brightness between the lightest and darkest parts of an image. Contrast, however, occurs in many other dimensions as well: contrast between adjacent colors, contrast between differently sized or shaped fonts, contrasting position on a page, and many more. The total contrast between two page elements thus involves the number of contrasting attributes as well as their individual extents.

The need for contrast is generally intuitive; document creators ordinarily realize that items such as titles, headings, body text, and captions are intrinsically different and that a unique appearance should identify each such element. They run into greater problems deciding what kind of contrast to provide and how much. Too much or too little contrast can be illegible, confusing, or just irritating to the eye. Consider the four samples below.

Contrast enhances appearance.

Contrast enhances appearance.

Contrast enhances appearance.

Contrast enhances appearance.

In the first sample, the word Contrast is presented in the Bookman font and the rest of the sentence in Garamond. These are both *old style* fonts: they both have slanted serifs and nonuniform line widths, while the thinnest top and bottom portions of each circular or elliptical shape align at an angle. In short, there's very little contrast between text set in Bookman and Garamond. This sentence looks like a typesetting error and bothers the eye. The reader's concentration is diverted to figuring out "What's wrong with this picture?" and thus misses the information being conveyed.

The second sample has more contrast. The word Contrast appears in Myriad Bold, which lacks serifs, has uniform line widths, and is much thicker than Garamond. The font size is larger as well. In brief, there's considerable contrast in appearance between the first word and the rest of the sentence. This example works.

The third example uses a decorative font called Kabel Ultra. Like Myriad, Kabel Ultra lacks serifs and is much thicker than Garamond, but this font is very gimmicky and just doesn't look right with the relatively formal Garamond. This example clashes like a clown on a concert stage.

The last example simply italicizes the emphasized word. There's only one kind of contrast between italicized Garamond and normal (roman), namely the overall slant. Nevertheless, this technique catches the eye and provides nearly as much emphasis as examples two and three.

Real life offers—as does Web design—a countless variety of potential contrasts. Contrasts of color, size, alignment, and motion immediately come to mind. If something doesn't look right, consider increasing or reducing the number of contrasts as well as varying their intensities. And remember, the visual equivalent of screaming in someone's face isn't necessarily the best way to communicate your message. When contrast is required:

- Don't be a wimp.

- Don't be a screamer.

- Don't mix signals.

II

Creating Web Pages

Symmetry vs. Monotony

In any page layout, like elements should have a like appearance, and elements that differ should have a different appearance. Neither contrast nor uniformity should be random. This is the principle of symmetry.

All the chapter headings in this book are set in the same font, color, size, and position on the page. When you encounter some text that visually resembles all the other chapter headings, you assume that text is a chapter heading as well. You also assume that any text with a different appearance is *not* a chapter heading.

Note that chapter headings are similar to each other, but not to body text. Because chapter headings and body text are quite different elements, there's much contrast between them. There's essentially no contrast (other than distance) between one chapter head and another, because all chapter headings are alike.

The same reasoning applies to this book's figures, tables, and side notes such as See Also, Caution, and Tip. These elements each have their own unique style that helps identify them and generally makes the book appear cohesive. It would be confusing if See Also notes in this chapter and the next appeared differently.

The principle of symmetry (or parallelism) is equally applicable to Web pages. Make all your top-level headings look the same, for example, not just within each page but within an entire Web site or major section. Use the same color scheme, the same typography, the same alignment (left-aligned, centered, right-aligned, or justified), the same menu appearance, the same title conventions, and so forth. Avoid monotony by adopting (and testing on your eyes and the eyes of others) an attractive set of designs up front and not by making each page look completely different.

An overall site design should be a guide, never a straitjacket. Certainly you'll have several types of pages, and each type of page should have unique elements that visually alert the Web visitor. The number of page types and their corresponding appearances are strictly your decision, but each page type should have:

- Symmetry that unifies it with all other pages in the same site.

- Distinctive contrasts that visually identify each unique type of page or content.

- Symmetry among like types of pages or content.

In short, similar types of content call for fewer contrasting elements having a narrower range of contrast. Dissimilar types call for a greater variety and degree of contrast.

Choosing a Visual Concept

Visual appearance plays a critical role in the way visitors perceive your site and receive its message. No matter how interesting and well-organized your site's content may be, a drab presentation will provide a poor viewing experience for your Web visitors and indicate a lack of interest on your part. Because most Web sites devote the best visual presentation to the most important content, many Web visitors now associate drab presentation with boring, outdated information.

Visual presentation is no substitute for well-organized and useful content; both are necessary to produce an effective site. Except for a few highly specialized sites, content doesn't *consist* of presentation; instead, presentation is a means to *convey* content. HTML is such a weak page-description language that the challenge of achieving visual appeal frequently overshadows that of developing content; don't let this happen to you.

Your site's graphic design should complement its message and appeal to its audience. An abstract, garish design patterned after an album cover might be appropriate for a rock group, but certainly not for a bank or a brokerage house. A site's overall graphic design conveys messages just as surely as its text and images, and you should strive to have those messages reinforce each other rather than clash.

If it happens that you're not an experienced graphic-design professional, don't despair. In many cases, the site's organization will already have logos, colors, and style guidelines designed by professionals for use in other media. If so, these can be adapted for Web use as well. This might even be a requirement of the Legal department.

In the absence of other guidelines, choose a theme related to some aspect of the site's content. For a school, consider the school colors, emblem, and mascot. For an athletic league, consider the colors and textures of the playing field or equipment. For a restaurant, consider the scenes and colors related to the cuisine, locale, fixtures, and objects from the restaurant's decor, the style of the restaurant's menu, or ingredients and cooking utensils.

Beyond these relatively obvious approaches, consider a theme based not on the product itself, but rather on settings where the product is used, cities or sites where it's manufactured or sold, or aspects of the organization's history or technology. Your site's theme should suggest colors, images, and icons you can use throughout the site or its principal sections. If a particular theme doesn't suggest a set of workable colors and images, move on to another. You'll probably get an "aha!" feeling when you've found it.

? **SEE ALSO**

For help in choosing colors that appear correctly on Web pages, see "Achieving Accurate Rendition—Safe Colors," page 102.

The default colors on most browsers are black on gray or black on white. This is every bit as interesting as black-and-white slides projected on a basement wall. Black, white, and gray aren't necessarily colors to avoid, but they *do* deserve augmentation with adjacent frames, images, and borders. When choosing text and background colors, choose dark text on a light background. Bright text on a dark background is harder to read, especially for small type sizes. It's usually a good idea to maintain color contrast as well as brightness contrast between text and background.

Planning Your Pages

Given a mission, an audience, a content plan, management go-ahead, a visual concept, and knowledge of what HTML can and cannot do, you're finally ready to design pages in detail. To at least some extent, this will probably involve storyboards and sketches.

The classic storyboard consists of index cards pinned to a wall. You write up an index card for each Web page, annotate it to indicate planned content, and then arrange all the cards in some kind of hierarchy or sequence. Web visitors will traverse the site along these sequences and hierarchies. Team members and your project sponsor will review the chart, suggest revisions, and someday pronounce it worthy of prime time.

Such archetypical storyboards are rare—but the concept is sound. Your storyboard might be notes on a yellow pad, an outline in a word processor, a draft set of menu pages, or even a Navigator view in FrontPage. No matter: the key result is a well-organized set of pages and not the method used to achieve it.

It's easy to go wild with menus. Visitors are unlikely to find pages more than two or three clicks away from the main page, however, so don't nest menus too deeply. Avoid long pages of hypertext links by using drop-down lists, option buttons, check boxes, and other HTML form elements. A drop-down list of 10 product names and another with 4 kinds of information efficiently supports 40 menu choices.

You should also start sketching or drafting pages at this point. Identify each type of page you plan to use, and then make up a draft or template for each type. Identify changeable components that will exist on multiple pages—menu bars, signature blocks, contact names, and the like—then plan site parameters and include blocks to support them. Accumulate stock images, too. These are logos, icons, buttons, bars, and theme images that, if standardized, will help the site achieve a unified appearance.

SEE ALSO

For more information about managing download time, see Chapter 6, "Incorporating Graphics."

Lengthy text, either as content or HTML commands, is seldom the cause of excessive download times. Images, Java applets, and ActiveX controls are far more often the culprits. As you plan your pages and accumulate your images, keep a rough total of download bytes for each type of page. There are no hard-and-fast rules on the size of Web pages, and this is less a consideration on high-bandwidth intranets than on public Internet sites accessed by dial-in visitors. Pages having more than 25,000 to 30,000 download bytes are generally considered too large for dial-in visitors. This is equivalent to 15 to 20 pages of double-spaced plain text or one uncompressed image 170 pixels on a side.

A final bit of planning advice: you *can* have too much of a good thing. All Web sites are always under construction, so trying in advance to nail down every nit for every page is probably a futile exercise. If you try to plan too much detail, the site's rate of change will exceed the rate of planning. Don't let "Paralysis by Analysis" happen to you.

Achieving Effective Page Layout

The normal progression of topics on a page, whether on the Web or in the morning newspaper, depends on the expectations of your audience. For most written languages, this means top to bottom and left to right. Furthermore, every Web page should have both a meaningful title and a meaningful heading. As Figure 3-1 illustrates, the title appears in the browser's title bar and the heading appears somewhere near the top of the page. The title serves to identify the page externally to programs like FrontPage and search engines like Yahoo, Lycos, AltaVista, and InfoSeek. The heading immediately informs the Web visitor what sort of content appears on the page. If visitors choose a wrong link, they can immediately jump back to the previous page. Otherwise, they should find confirmation that they've arrived at the correct page. If the page is long, bookmark links should provide pathways to each major subsection to avoid extensive scrolling (at least on the home page).

Experienced page designers often find HTML's weak page-layout features extremely frustrating. This reflects a fundamental conflict between the HTML goal of device independence and the artistic desire for precise control. This conflict isn't likely to subside any time soon, though FrontPage does support a number of recent HTML page layout facilities.

II

Creating Web Pages

FIGURE 3-1.

The title of this page is "Microsoft FrontPage Home Page," and its heading is "Microsoft FrontPage, Professional Web Sites Without Programming."

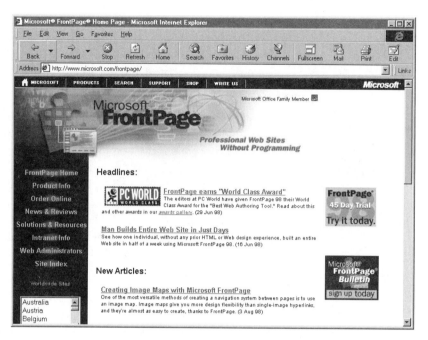

■ **Alignment tags.** The normal flow of HTML text is down the left margin, wrapping lines automatically when they reach the right margin, with a hard-coded line break and an explicit or implied paragraph ending. Images, Java applets, and ActiveX controls retain their relative positions within the HTML text.

Implied paragraph endings occur in several situations:

- Before and after tables.

- At transitions in paragraph style.

- Before and after numbered and bulleted lists.

 **SEE ALSO**

For more information about using alignment tags to control page placement, see "Aligning Text," page 138.

Recent versions of HTML support tags to left-align or right-align images and other objects, flowing text around them. A centering tag centers the same kinds of objects, but no text flows to the right or left of the centered image. Additional tags align nontext objects vertically with the surrounding text flow. FrontPage supports all these tags.

SEE ALSO

For information about using FrontPage to create HTML tables, see "Creating and Editing Tables," page 230.

■ **HTML tables.** Originally designed to display tabular data, HTML tables have become one of the premier means to arrange items spatially on a page. Anytime you'd like to draw an imaginary grid on a page and align items within it, an HTML table should be your choice.

2000

- **CSS Positioning.** This technology finally gives Web designers pixel-precise positioning and layering control over their work. FrontPage provides access to CSS Positioning through the Position choice on its Format menu.

? SEE ALSO

For more information about frames, see "Creating and Editing Frames," page 261.

- **Frames.** This feature provides a way to divide a Web page into tiled rectangles and to independently control the content of each rectangle. One Web page defines a *frameset*—an object that controls the number, sizes, and placement of the frames—while additional Web pages provide the content for each frame. Standard frames have visible borders between them and scroll bars for moving up, down, left, and right within each frame. Borderless frames have no visible borders and are simply page layout areas that corral your text where you want it.

Good page layout always involves balance: use of the right margin as well as the left, size and impact proportional to importance, heading and other navigational aids more prominent than normal text, and so forth. It's a yin and yang thing.

Organizing Your Web Server Environment

Even more than you might expect, the workings of FrontPage are rooted deeply in the Web.

- The FrontPage Server Extensions, which FrontPage relies on for some of its most advanced functions, are designed to run not as ordinary Windows programs, but rather as processes within a Web server.

- When FrontPage loads a file from a fully configured FrontPage Web, it does so using a Web request—as a browser would do—and not by reading a file off your disk as other applications do.

- When FrontPage updates such a file—or any related information—it issues an HTTP POST and asks the Web server to update the data. This is the same mechanism used to process HTML forms.

For most projects, it makes perfect sense to have two FrontPage environments: one where you develop and test new or updated pages, and another that delivers finished pages to remote users. When new content is ready for world consumption, you transfer it from your development environment to your production server.

II

Creating Web Pages

Initially, your development environment could be a small collection of free-standing Web pages and associated images, located in some folder on your hard disk. For sites of any size, however, you'll benefit greatly from using a FrontPage Web. This could be a disk-based Web not involving a Web server, a server-based Web administered by someone else, or a personal Web server administered by you.

In general, the more alike your development and production environments, the more effective your testing will be and the fewer problems you'll encounter. This argues strongly for two Web servers, both running the same software, both running on Windows, and both running the FrontPage Server Extensions. But other considerations frequently apply. Having two FrontPage Web servers certainly isn't a hard-and-fast requirement.

If your needs are simple, and control over content changes isn't critical, a single server may suffice. If your needs are complex, a battery of servers might be needed. Your development environment might be disk-based or Web-server-based. Your production server may be Windows NT or Unix, and in either case it may or may not have the FrontPage Server Extensions installed. If your production server doesn't have the server extensions, publishing your Web won't be quite as smooth, and FrontPage services that run at browse time—like Search, Save Results, and Database Access—won't be available. This may present a crisis or not, depending on your requirements. All in all, these are decisions only you, your organization, or your client can make.

Here are some common scenarios.

- You create Web pages in your home or small office, and you connect only periodically to the network where your production Web server resides. Your development Web is disk-based.

  An Internet service provider, a Web presence provider, or your corporate MIS department operates the production server. It doesn't have the FrontPage Server Extensions installed. You have to publish using either an external FTP program or FrontPage's built-in FTP. Neither your development nor your production environment supports server-based FrontPage components like Hit Counter, Search, and Save Results.

- You create Web pages in an office or campus having a permanent network connection. Your development and production Webs both reside on Windows NT servers running the FrontPage Server Extensions. To get a FrontPage Web created on either machine, you submit paperwork to a system administrator. All FrontPage functions work on both machines.

- Your development environment consists of a personal Web server running on your home PC. The FrontPage Server Extensions are installed on your personal Web server.

Your production environment is a Unix server operated by your ISP, and it doesn't have the FrontPage Server Extensions. This means that while all FrontPage components work perfectly in your development environment, they fail in production. However, if your ISP supplies sample HTML for hit counters, forms processors, or other components supported on the Unix Web server, you can paste it onto FrontPage's HTML view.

If you've decided you need a personal Web server and you're working remotely or, like the author, are cursed to *be* the network administrator, skip ahead to Chapter 15, "Choosing and Configuring Your Web Server." This explains in more detail how to choose the proper Web server for your platform and how to coordinate installation of the Web server, the FrontPage Server Extensions, and the FrontPage client.

In Summary...

Content, style, and platform are three seemingly separate but, in fact, highly related aspects of every Web site. Unless all three components mesh smoothly, your site is almost certainly doomed to chaos. Whatever up-front planning is necessary to develop an effective strategy is certainly worth the effort.

CHAPTER 4

Getting Started with Web Pages

A t some point, the planning and overview discussions stop and the actual work begins. That point is now. This chapter addresses the basics of creating, opening, saving, and deleting Web pages, plus the essentials of overall page properties. Subsequent chapters explain how to enter and format text, insert images, create hyperlinks, format tables, and so forth.

Developing Web pages is, of course, an iterative process. No Web page is ever really finished; pages on the Web are either under construction or stale and outdated. Your proficiency as an author will no doubt progress as well, not only in content but also in style, appearance, tools, and technique. Despite all that, initializing, opening, and saving Web files inevitably remain essential skills.

Creating a New Web Page

If you can start FrontPage, you can create a new Web page. When FrontPage starts up, it displays a blank Web page ready to receive text, images, or anything else you care to toss in. Figure 4-1 illustrates the default, blank Web page, ready for input.

FIGURE 4-1.

Whenever FrontPage starts up, it presents a new, blank Web page ready for development.

Entering text, inserting images, creating hyperlinks, and other tasks are the topics of subsequent chapters. If you feel the need to learn about these things right away, feel free to skip ahead and return here later. Regardless, starting FrontPage is far from the only way to create new Web pages. In any view except Tasks view, you can create a new Web page by:

? SEE ALSO

For more information about all the buttons on the FrontPage Standard toolbar, see Table 4-2 on pages 88–89.

- **Using the Standard toolbar.** New Page is the very first icon on the left side of the Standard toolbar. It looks like a blank, white sheet of paper. Not surprisingly, clicking this icon creates a new Web page.

- **Using the File menu.** Choose New from the File menu, then choose Page.

- **Using the keyboard.** Press Ctrl+N.

■ **Using the right mouse button.** In all views except Tasks view, you can create a new page by right-clicking either a folder icon or a blank space in any folder or file list, then choosing New Page from the pop-up menu.

TIP

When several pages are open in Page view, you can switch among them by pressing Ctrl+Tab, by pressing Ctrl+Shift+Tab, or by choosing the page you want from the Windows menu.

In all views except Page view (discussed in the next paragraph) and Tasks view (where you create new tasks rather than new Web pages), creating a new Web page means creating an HTML file in the current folder, giving the file a default name, and leaving the file name ready for renaming. FrontPage *doesn't* switch to Page view and open the new file; for that, you have to double-click or otherwise open the new file yourself.

TIP

Remember: if you haven't opened a FrontPage Web, Folders View, Reports View, Navigation View, Hyperlinks View, and Tasks View won't be available.

In Page view, clicking the New Page toolbar icon immediately creates and displays a new blank page. The other three methods also display the new page ready for editing but only after presenting the opportunity (or nuisance, depending on your mood) to select a choice of starting points—a choice of templates. The dialog box offering this choice appears in Figure 4-2.

FIGURE 4-2.
This dialog box offers a choice of types and formats for initializing new Web pages.

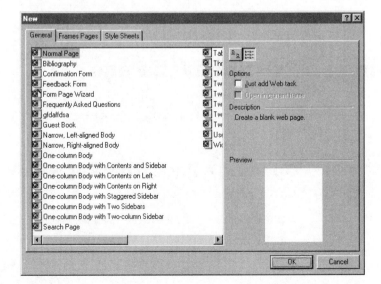

II

Creating Web Pages

- The **General** tab provides a list of currently available page templates. Single-clicking any template selects it, displays its description in the Description frame at the right of the dialog box, and displays a visual preview in the Preview frame.

TIP

If you don't know what template or wizard to choose, select Normal Page. This produces a blank page with no special features or attributes.

SEE ALSO

For information about framesets, see "Creating and Editing Frames," page 261. For more information about Cascading Style Sheets, see "A Quick Course in Cascading Style Sheets," page 138.

- The **Frames Pages** tab works much like the General tab, except that the listed templates create framesets.

- The **Style Sheets** tab initializes a Cascading Style Sheet file, based on a selection of choices, which are based on FrontPage Themes. This is a specially coded text file with a CSS extension. You can reference this file, and thus inherit its format specifications, from as many other pages as you want.

- The **Large Icons** and **List** buttons, located above the Description frame, change the format of the main selection window.

CAUTION

If you create a new page in Page view and then close it without making any changes, FrontPage won't ask whether you want to save it. To save a new empty page, choose either Save or Save As from the File menu.

- The **Open In Current Frame** option will be available only if the active document in FrontPage is a frameset. Ignore this for now.

- The **Just Add Web Task** button adds a task to the Task List rather than initializing a new page in Page view.

It's important to note that creating a new page in Page view *doesn't* create an actual Web file. It only creates an unsaved file, open for editing. To create the actual file, you must save it.

Editing an Existing Web Page

There are many ways to open a Web page for editing, and they vary somewhat depending on the current view. The following sections detail your options for each view.

Opening a Page from Page View

If you're starting from Page view, there are four ways to open a Web page:

- Choose Recent Files from the File menu. This will display a list of your most recently opened files. To open a specific file, just choose it from the menu.

- Right-click a hyperlink in a page that's already open, then choose Follow Hyperlink from the pop-up menu. This opens the hyperlinked page in Page view.

- Locate the file in Page view's Folder List, then double-click it. (Remember, though, that the Folder List won't be available if you're editing single files directly from your hard disk. The Folder List is available only if you've opened a FrontPage Web.)

- Use the Open File dialog box shown in Figure 4-3.

FIGURE 4-3.

The FrontPage Open File dialog box accepts either a local file location or the URL of a page on the Web.

There are three ways to display Page view's Open File dialog box: You can choose Open from the File menu, press Ctrl+O, or click the Open button on the Standard toolbar. The icons along the left of the dialog box offer five ways to locate a Web page:

- **History** displays a list of recently opened Microsoft Office documents. By dropping down the Look In list, you can browse various categories of recent documents.

- **My Documents** displays files in your My Documents folder.

- **Desktop** displays files visible from your Windows desktop. This includes files located within My Computer, My Documents, Network Neighborhood, My Briefcase, and so forth.

- **Favorites** displays the same choices you've configured Internet Explorer's Favorites menu to display.

- **Web Folders** displays files located in a FrontPage Web. FrontPage builds up a list of known FrontPage Webs as you access them. These can be hosted on FrontPage-enabled Web servers or they can be disk-based Webs on your local disk or file server.

II

Creating Web Pages

⊗ CAUTION

You can't open a Web page by dragging it out of FrontPage and dropping it onto an open Web page in Page view. That operation does something else: it modifies the open page by adding a hyperlink to the page you dragged.

No matter which icon you choose and then browse, selecting a file name enters it in the File Name box at the bottom center of the dialog box. That can be either a file location, such as C:\My Documents\mypage.htm, or a Web location, such as http://www.interlacken.com/default.htm. FrontPage opens file locations as Windows applications have been doing for years. It opens Web locations by reading the necessary files as a browser would.

If convenient, you can also enter file locations and Web locations by hand—that is, by typing or pasting them into the File Name box. In any event, once the file name isn't blank, the Open button becomes active, and clicking it tells FrontPage to open the file.

The Files Of Type drop-down menu works as in most Windows File dialog boxes; it controls which file name extensions appear in the file listing. Table 4-1 explains the remaining icons in the Open File toolbar.

TABLE 4-1.   Open File Dialog Box Toolbar

Icon	Description	Function
⇐	Favorites	Displays a list of recently opened locations.
⬆	Up One Level	Shifts the file listing location to its parent folder.
🔍	Search The Web	Uses your browser to find a Web file to open. When you return to FrontPage, the browser's current URL appears in the File Name box.
✕	Delete	Deletes the currently selected file or folder.
📁	Create New Folder	Creates a new folder inside the current Look In location.
▦ ▾	Views	Selects the type of listing displayed: List, Details, Property, or Preview.
Tools ▾	Tools	Applies any of seven utility functions against the currently selected item: Find, Delete, Rename, Print, Add To Favorites, Map Network Drive, and Properties.

When you open a Web page created by another Office 2000 application, FrontPage may surprise you by opening the file in its native application rather than Page view. To avoid this behavior temporarily, click the drop-down button just to the right of the Open button, and then choose Open In Microsoft FrontPage. To avoid it permanently, choose Options from the Tools menu, select the Configure Editors tab, and turn off the check box titled Open Web Pages In The Office Application That Created Them.

Opening a Page from Tasks View

Because Tasks view displays tasks, not Web files, the procedure for opening a file is unique. Do *either* of the following:

- Right-click a task referencing the page, then choose Start Task from the pop-up menu.

- Select a task referencing the page, choose Task from the Edit menu, then choose Start.

NOTE

Tasks view is an electronic to-do list stored within a FrontPage Web. Tasks can be stand-alone or linked to specific Web pages.

Opening a Page from Other Views

If you're starting from FrontPage in Folders view, Reports view, Navigation view, or Hyperlinks view, do *any* of the following:

- Double-click the file name or icon.

- Right-click the file name or icon, and then choose Open from the resulting pop-up menu.

- Select the file name or icon and press Enter, press Ctrl+O, or choose Open from the Edit menu.

Using the FrontPage Standard Toolbar

In addition to commands for opening and creating Web pages, several other commands can be invoked directly from FrontPage's Standard toolbar, as described in Table 4-2. Use the View menu to display or hide this and any other toolbars.

TIP

Like other Office 2000 applications, FrontPage toolbars are floating. This means you can drag them to any edge of the window or, by dragging them away from any edge, you can leave them floating over your work. To avoid clicking toolbar buttons by mistake, try dragging toolbars from their separator bars.

Creating Web Pages

TABLE 4-2.   FrontPage Standard Toolbar

Icon	Description	Function	Menu Command
	New	Creates a new page, task, folder, or Web.	File/New
	Open	Opens a page or a FrontPage Web.	File/Open
	Save	Saves the current page in HTML format.	File/Save
	Publish Web	Copies the current Web to another location.	File/Publish Web
	Folder List	Toggles Page view's Folder List between visible and hidden.	View/Folder List
	Print	Prints the current selection.	File/Print
	Preview in Browser	Launches a browser and sends it a command to open the current page.	File/Preview in Browser
	Check Spelling	Checks spelling of words in the current page.	Tools/Spelling
	Cut	Removes selected items from the page and stores them in the Clipboard.	Edit/Cut
	Copy	Copies selected items from the page and stores them in the Clipboard.	Edit/Copy
	Paste	Copies the contents of the Clipboard to the insertion point.	Edit/Paste
	Format Painter	Copies formatting from one selection within a Web page to another.	none
	Undo	Reverses previous changes to a page. Click the drop-down arrow to undo more than one change.	Edit/Undo

(continued)

TABLE 4-2. *continued*

Icon	Description	Function	Menu Command
	Redo	Reverses the last Undo command. Click the drop-down arrow to undo more than one reversal.	Edit/Redo
	Insert Component	Opens the Insert FrontPage Component dialog box.	Insert/FrontPage Component
	Insert Table	Creates a new table at the insertion point. Select the table's dimensions from the drop-down grid.	Table/Insert Table
	Insert Picture	Inserts a picture at the insertion point.	Insert/Picture
	Hyperlink	Creates or modifies a hyperlink from the currently selected text or image.	Edit/Hyperlink
	Refresh	Reloads the current page from its source. If there are pending changes, FrontPage will prompt whether to save them.	View/Refresh
	Stop	Stops loading of files accessed via a hyperlink.	none
	Show All	Shows or hides invisible items like paragraph endings, hard line returns, bookmarks, and form outlines.	none
	Help	Displays Help on the next element clicked.	Help/Microsoft FrontPage Help

II

Creating Web Pages

Saving Pages

If you fail to regularly save your files, all your hard work will be for naught. To save a file open in Page view, choose the File menu and select Save. If the Web page or any of its components weren't previously saved, FrontPage will generate Save As dialog boxes for them.

To save a page using another name, choose Save As from the File menu. Figure 4-4 shows the resulting dialog box; it's almost the same dialog box used for opening Web pages, with all the same options plus two.

FIGURE 4-4.

This is FrontPage's Save As dialog box.

- **Page Title.** Displays the name of the page in words. Although this is an optional field, for optimal user-friendliness, don't omit it. A page's title appears whenever a remote user browses the page and in many FrontPage contexts.

- **Change.** Clicking this button displays the page title in a small dialog box so you can change it. Figure 4-4 shows this facility in action.

As when opening files, the File Name location can be either on a local disk or file server, or within a FrontPage Web. If the FrontPage Web isn't already open, FrontPage will open it.

Occasionally, when you save a Web page, FrontPage will display a dialog box like Figure 4-5. This means Page view has an object in memory—in this case an image pasted from the Clipboard—and FrontPage doesn't know where to save it. This also happens after using some of FrontPage's image processing tools (described in Chapter 5). The original image may reside on disk but the modified version doesn't; FrontPage therefore has to ask where the modified version should go.

FIGURE 4-5.

When Page view receives or creates a Web-page element only in memory, this dialog box prompts for the element's Save location.

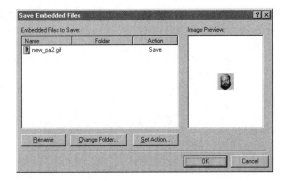

To change the proposed Save properties for any file listed, first select the file and then:

- To change the name of the saved file, click the Rename button and edit the proposed name.

- To change the folder, click the Change Folder button and select a folder from the resulting dialog box.

TIP

If a file's Folder column is blank, FrontPage will save the file in the same folder as the Web page itself.

- To change the action, click the Action button and select either Save or Don't Save from the resulting dialog box.

Deleting an Existing Web Page

Along with the pages you create and add to your Web site will be the inevitable failures and pages that become obsolete over time. There are four ways to delete a page. You must be in Folders view, Reports view, Navigation view, or Hyperlinks view.

1 Select the file name or icon by single-clicking it, and then press the Delete key.

2 Select the file name or icon, and then choose Delete from the Edit menu.

3 Right-click the file name or icon, and then select Delete from the pop-up menu.

II

Creating Web Pages

4 Select the file name and click the Delete button on the Standard toolbar.

In each case you'll be asked to confirm the deletion before the page is permanently erased.

Specifying Page-Level Attributes

Whether you start from a blank page, an existing page, or a page generated by a template or wizard, you no doubt have further changes in mind. These changes might affect not only content, but also the page's title, color scheme, or other general characteristics. Even for existing files, you may decide this is the time to standardize pages and apply uniform page attributes.

FrontPage provides the Page Properties dialog box to control the overall appearance of a page. To open the Page Properties dialog box, choose Properties from the File menu or right-click anywhere on the Page view editing window and choose Page Properties from the pop-up menu.

General Page Properties

There are six tabs on the Page Properties dialog box: General, Background, Margins, Custom, Language, and Workgroup. The General tab appears in Figure 4-6.

The data fields on the Page Properties General tab control the following characteristics. You should always specify a meaningful title, but use of the remaining fields is optional.

- **Location.** This is normally the Uniform Resource Locator of the page: the URL a browser would use to retrieve it. If FrontPage opened the page from a file, a URL beginning with file:/// will appear. For new pages not yet saved, the location will be (New Page). You can't edit this field—it's for information only.

- **Title.** This is the name of the page in words. This is an often-overlooked but important attribute; it appears in many FrontPage windows and dialog boxes, as a page description in search results, and in the title bars of your visitors' browsers. Be certain that every page you maintain has a meaningful title suitable for public display.

- **Base Location.** Use of this field is rare; see the sidebar, "Relative Addressing and Base URLs," on page 98, for an explanation of its use. You will usually leave this field blank.

FIGURE 4-6.

The General tab in FrontPage's Page Properties dialog box.

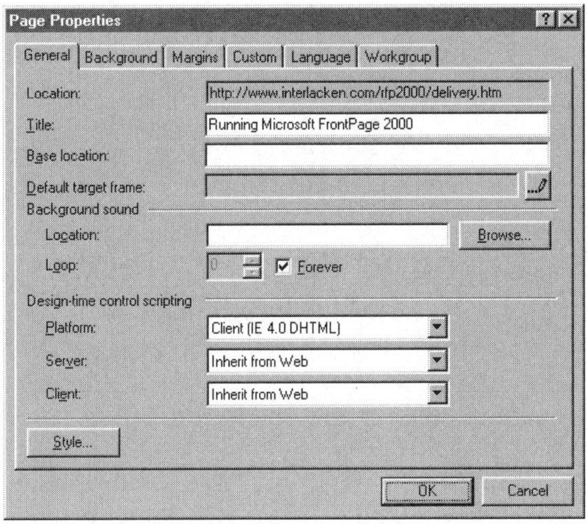

? SEE ALSO

For information on using frames, see "Creating and Editing Frames," page 261.

- **Default Target Frame.** If you've divided the browser window into frames, this field specifies in which frame, by default, hyperlinks from the current page will appear.

- **Background Sound.** These three fields select and control a sound file that the visitor's browser will play when it displays your page.

  - **Location.** Enter the name of the sound file. This can be a local file location or a URL. To browse the local file system or current FrontPage Web, click the Browse button.

  - **Loop.** Enter the number of times the specified file should play.

  - **Forever.** Turn on this box to have the sound file play indefinitely. This overrides the Loop setting.

★ TIP

Avoid specifying large sound files or files in platform-specific formats. In general, MIDI files are the smallest and most widely supported.

- **Design-Time Control Scripting.** These fields control the actions of design-time controls, a type of ActiveX control that can extend FrontPage with additional editing and HTML-generation features.

  - **Platform.** Specifies where scripting should occur—Browser or Server.

  - **Server.** Specifies the language design-time controls should use for server-side scripting: JavaScript, VBScript, or the default setting for the Web.

- **Client.** Specifies the language design-time controls should use for browser-side scripting: JavaScript, VBScript, or the default setting for the Web.

- **Style.** This button opens a dialog box that specifies cascading style-sheet information for the body of the current page.

Background Page Properties

Figure 4-7 illustrates the Background tab of the Page Properties dialog box. It controls most aspects of the page's overall color scheme.

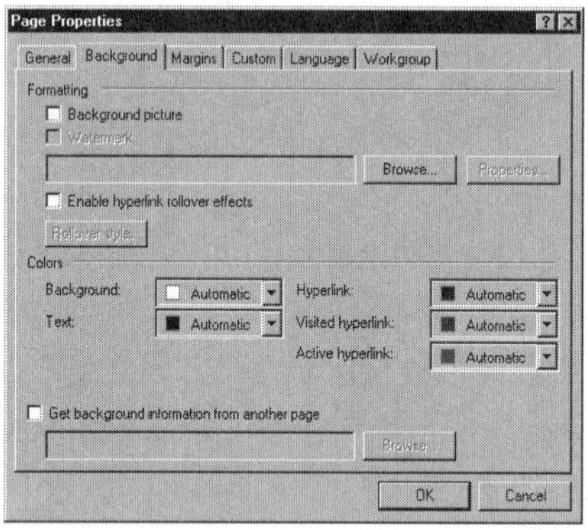

FIGURE 4-7.
The Background tab of the Page Properties dialog box controls a page's overall color scheme.

The Background tab will be absent on any page controlled by a theme. The theme takes over these attributes.

You can also access the Background tab by choosing Background from the Format menu in Page view.

Specify Background and Colors

SEE ALSO
For more information about FrontPage Themes, see Chapter 9, "Using FrontPage Themes."

Checking this option button indicates that you'll specify the color scheme for this page explicitly, rather than getting the information from a theme or another page. It also activates the following controls:

- **Background Image.** Turning on this box specifies that the page has a background image. The associated text box specifies the image-file location. Rather than typing the file location, you can click the Browse button to locate it quickly.

Using Background Images in Your Pages

A background image appears behind any other images or text on the page. If the image is smaller than the page, the browser repeats it (called *tiling*) left to right and top to bottom. This allows a small image, which is fast to download, to fill the entire screen.

To keep the background image from repeating left to right, make it wider than any typical computer screen display. A width of 1,200 pixels is usually sufficient. Most image editors have features called Add Margin or Extend Canvas that can widen images this way. Fill the added pixels with your background color, or make them transparent. Repeating pixels of the same color compress very well and add little to file size and download time.

Wide images of this kind are often used to create border designs along the left margin. The design occupies the first 20 or 30 pixels at the left, and the rest of the image is a solid background color or is transparent.

Avoid strong colors or patterns in background images. These can easily obscure your text.

■ **Watermark.** Turning on this box indicates that when the Web visitor operates the browser's scroll bars, the background image is to remain fixed and not scroll with other content on the page. This feature is supported by Internet Explorer but might not be supported by other browsers. FrontPage itself doesn't exhibit the watermark behavior; it scrolls the background image even though watermarking is in effect. To see watermarking in action, browse the page with Internet Explorer.

SEE ALSO

For an explanation of the Image Properties dialog box, see "Modifying Image Properties," page 183.

■ **Properties.** Clicking this button takes you to a dialog box that displays or alters the properties of the specified background image.

■ **Background.** This setting controls the background color of the page. This color appears if there's no background image, if any part of the background image is transparent, or if the browser is ready to start displaying the page before the background image arrives.

■ **Text.** This setting controls the color of ordinary text.

■ **Hyperlink.** This setting controls the color of hyperlinked text.

■ **Visited Hyperlink.** This setting controls the color of hyperlinked text whose target has recently been visited. The text reverts to named hyperlink color when the remote user fails to visit the hyperlink target within the browser's cache timeout setting.

Creating Web Pages

■ **Active Hyperlink.** This setting controls the color of hyperlinked text the remote user has just clicked.

■ **Enable Hyperlink Rollover Effects.** Turning on this check box specifies that hyperlinked text will change appearance when the mouse pointer passes over it. Clicking the associated Rollover Style button displays a Font dialog box; this specifies how you want hyperlinked text to look when the mouse pointer passes over it.

Get Background and Colors from Page

Turning on this button deactivates the settings in the Specify Background And Colors area and obtains instead the color scheme of another page. Having groups of related pages obtain the same color scheme ensures uniformity and reduces maintenance. To obtain colors from another page, enter its location in the text box or use the Browse button to locate it.

Margin Page Properties

The Margins tab of the Page Properties dialog box appears in Figure 4-8. This tab controls the *x-y* coordinates of the first object displayed on the page, measured from the upper-left corner.

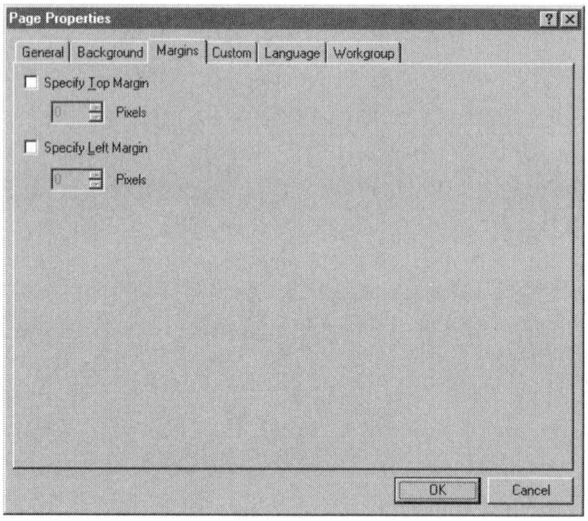

FIGURE 4-8.

The Page Properties tab controls the top and left margins of a Web page.

```
Page Properties                                          [?][X]
General | Background | Margins | Custom | Language | Workgroup |
  ☐ Specify Top Margin
      [0   ]  Pixels
  ☐ Specify Left Margin
      [0   ]  Pixels




                                      [   OK   ]  [ Cancel ]
```

■ To specify the top margin for a Web page, turn on the box captioned Specify Top Margin and enter the number of pixels.

■ To specify the left margin for a Web page, turn on the box captioned Specify Left Margin and enter the number of pixels.

Figure 4-9 shows how a Web page set to zero top and left margins appears in three different applications. Note the amount of space between the window border and the corner graphics. FrontPage and Internet Explorer 4 illustrate a zero margin in effect. Netscape Navigator 4, which sets margins using different commands, ignores these settings and applies its default margins.

FIGURE 4-9.

FrontPage 2000 and Internet Explorer 4 display a page with zero top and left margins. Netscape Navigator 4 ignores this method of setting margins.

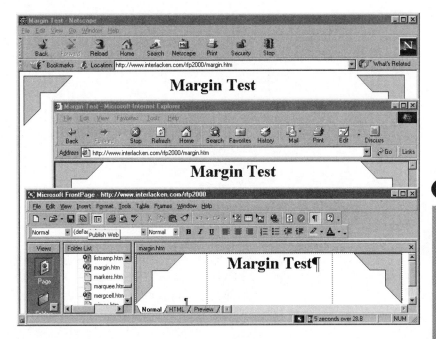

II

Creating Web Pages

Custom Page Properties

Figure 4-10 displays the Custom tab of the Page Properties dialog box, which maintains two categories of variables.

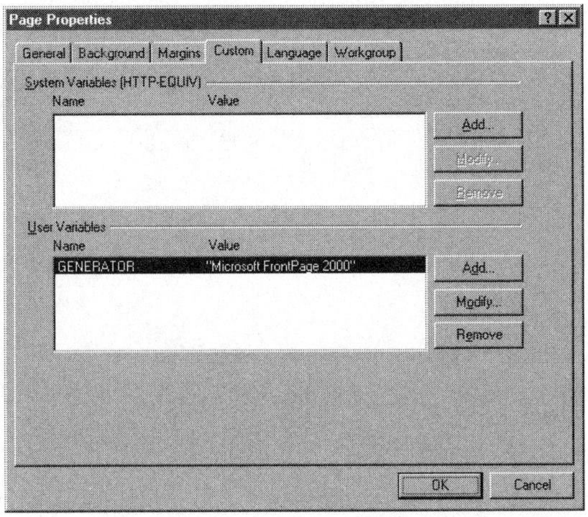

FIGURE 4-10.

The Custom tab specifies HTTP header field equivalents and user variables. These appear in the HEAD section of the HTML.

System variables are those defined as official HTTP headers, while user variables are any others you wish to specify. To add a variable, click the appropriate Add button and then type the variable name and its initial value into the dialog box shown in Figure 4-11.

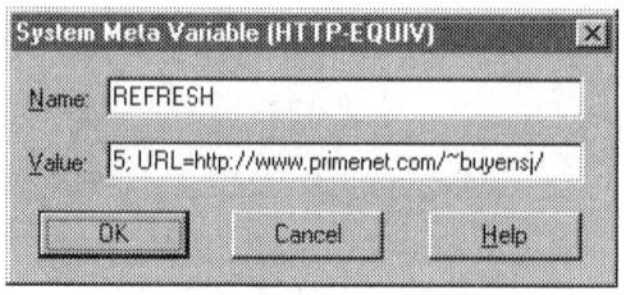

FIGURE 4-11.

This dialog box adds a variable to the System Variables list shown in Figure 4-10.

To change the value of a variable, select the variable, click the Modify button, and replace the value. To delete a variable, select it and then click Delete. The sidebar on page 100 provides more information on the use of system variables.

Relative Addressing and Base URLs

Hyperlinks on Web pages needn't reference complete URLs. If a hyperlink doesn't include a host name, a browser uses the host that delivered the current page. If a hyperlink also contains no folder location, the browser uses the same folder as the current page. This is called relative addressing because hyperlink locations are relative to the current page unless a full and explicit path is included. Below are two examples:

```
Current Page:    http://www.pfew.com/info/default.htm
Hyperlink:                        /products/toasters.htm
Jump Location:   http://www.pfew.com/products/toasters.htm

Current Page:    http://www.pfew.com/info/default.htm
Hyperlink:                              contact.htm
Jump Location:   http://www.pfew.com/info/contact.htm
```

In general, it's best to use relative addressing wherever possible. This makes it very easy to move groups of pages from one Web server or folder to another. By contrast, specifying complete URLs means updating them whenever you move pages from one computer or Web to another.

Occasionally, you may find it convenient to base relative URLs not on the current page but on some other location. Specifying a base URL accomplishes this as follows:

```
Current Page:    http://www.pfew.com/info/default.htm
Base URL:        http://www.w!x!y!z!.com/info/
Hyperlink:                              contact.htm
Jump Location:   http://www.w!x!y!z!.com/info/contact.htm
```

Language Page Properties

Figure 4-12 displays the Language tab, which controls the HTML character encoding for the current page: that is, the international character set. The choices available depend on the languages installed with your copy of FrontPage. The default is US/Western European.

- **Language for Spell Checking.** Specify the language FrontPage should use for spell checking. The default is <Automatic>, which means FrontPage will use whatever spelling dictionary produces the greatest number of correct spellings.

- **HTML Encoding for Saving This Page.** Select the character set FrontPage should use for saving the current page. The default is <none>, which defaults in turn to your system's default language.

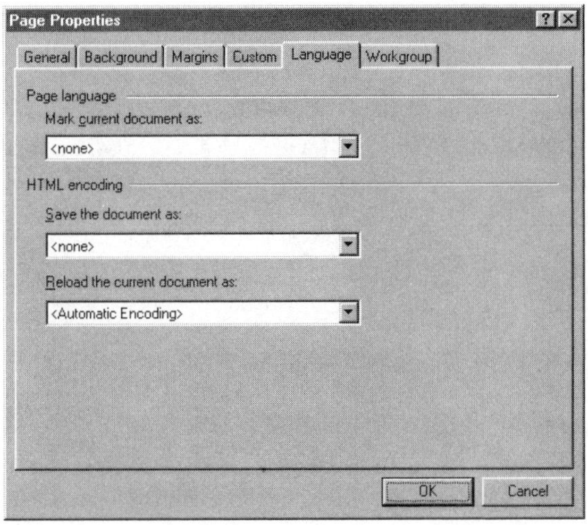

FIGURE 4-12.

The Language tab of the Page Properties dialog box controls the international character set used for saving and loading a specific page.

II

Creating Web Pages

- **HTML Encoding for Displaying This Page.** Select the character set a browser should use to display the current page. The default is <Automatic Encoding>.

Workgroup Page Properties

This group of settings records and controls workgroup progress for developing the current page. The dialog box tab that maintains them appears in Figure 4-13.

- **Available Categories.** Check each listed category applicable to the curent page. The Categories button modifies the list of categories.

Taking Advantage of HTTP System Variables

The Refresh system variable illustrated in Figure 4-11 on page 98 is a useful one. It instructs the browser to wait a specified number of seconds—5 in the example—and then automatically jump to the specified URL. This is how some sites introduce themselves with a timed series of pages. If you move a page to another location, you may wish to leave in its old location a blank or informative page with a Refresh system variable. This will automatically jump visitors to the page's new location. An informative page should appear long enough that the visitor can read at least the most important parts. If you decide to use a blank page, set the delay to a second or two. Setting the delay to zero interferes with the Back button on your Web visitor's browser; the instant the visitor clicks the Back button, your refresh page kicks the view forward again.

Some additional system variables appear below. If present in your pages, they're used by the large Internet search engines (such as Yahoo, Lycos, AltaVista, and InfoSeek) to narrow the search and improve the accuracy of their search results.

- **Copyright.** Any copyright statement.

- **Description**. A sentence that describes the page's content.

- **Distribution.** One of two words: global or local. Local indicates pages of little or no interest to visitors outside a Web site's own organization.

- **Expires.** A date after which the page will no longer be relevant. Use this format:
  Tue, 02 Dec 1997 21:29:02 GMT

- **Keywords.** Likely search terms a prospective visitor might enter. Separate multiple keywords with commas.

- **Robots.** Instructions to control the actions of Web search "robots" such as the large search engines. Compliance is voluntary; some searching robots honor these commands, and some don't. Defined values are:

  - **None.** Tells robots to ignore this page. This is equivalent to Noindex, Nofollow.

  - **All.** Indicates that there are no restrictions on indexing this page or pages referenced in its hyperlinks. This is equivalent to Index, Follow.

  - **Index.** Welcomes all robots to include this page in search results.

  - **Noindex.** Indicates that this page might not be indexed by search engines.

  - **Follow.** Allows robots to follow hyperlinks from this page to other pages.

  - **Nofollow.** Asks robots not to follow hyperlinks from this page.

(W) ON THE WEB

For more information about the Robot Exclusion Standard, browse *http://www.kollar.com/ robots.html.*

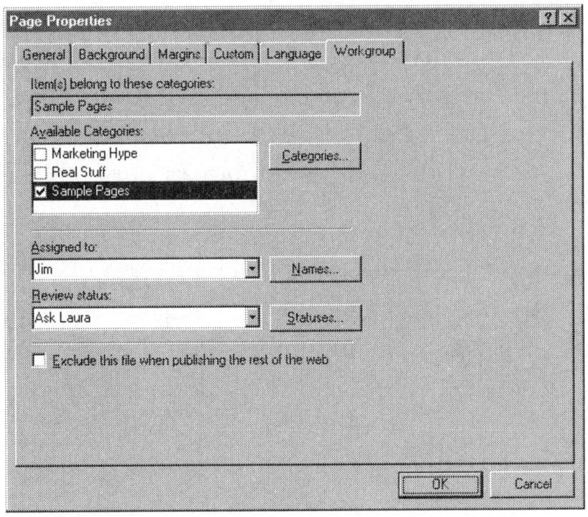

FIGURE 4-13.

The Workgroup tab provides access to fields that track a page's progress within a shared development environment.

This setting works in concert with Categories components to group like pages in the same FrontPage Web. For more information about the Categories component, refer to the section titled "Categories," page 685.

- **Assigned To.** Type or select the name of the person who's assigned to this page. To update the selection list, click the Names button.

- **Review Status.** Type or select the current review status for this page. To update the selection list, click the Statuses button.

- **Exclude This File When Publishing the Rest of the Web.** When you publish the current FrontPage Web to another location, any pages with this check box turned on won't be transferred. This might be desirable for work in progress.

Design Tips—Choosing Colors

Choosing color schemes is one of the most important aspects of creating new Web pages. It's no less important for maintaining existing pages and keeping your site looking fresh. For these reasons, the rest of this chapter introduces some elementary color concepts you should consider when picking colors for page backgrounds, text, and other elements on your pages.

Understanding the RGB Color Model

Despite the infinite number of colors that exist in nature, the human eye perceives only three of them: red, green, and blue. When the eye perceives yellow light, for example, it actually detects a close-to-red condition and a close-to-green condition. The brain interprets these combined signals as yellow. An interesting and useful by-product of this behavior is that humans perceive true yellow light and a mixture of red and green light as being identical. In fact, the proper combination of red, green, and blue light can perfectly simulate any color humans can perceive.

Computer video equipment leverages this effect to display color images. For each pixel (picture element) on the monitor screen, the application specifies, as a number from 0 to 255, the desired amount of red, green, and blue light. The video equipment provides 256 intensities of red light, 256 of green, and 256 of blue: 16,777,216 combinations in all.

? SEE ALSO

For more information about color models, see "Technical Models of Color," page 302, and "The Artistic Color Wheel," page 312.

The so-called RGB color model describes colors just as video cards and monitors do: as three color intensities 0 through 255. The RGB color 255-0-0, for example, means pure, maximum-intensity red. Along the same lines, 0-0-255 means pure, maximum-intensity blue; 0-0-0 means black; and 255-255-255 means white.

Achieving Accurate Rendition—Safe Colors

A large percentage of Web users have video cards with only 8 bits—256 possible values—per pixel. Such systems can display 16,777,216 different colors, but only 256 at once. This isn't a problem when displaying a single GIF image, because most graphics programs adjust the video hardware to display the same 256 colors that appear in the image. However, three problems arise when displaying images on a Web page:

- On most computers with 256-color displays, not all 256 colors are programmable. On Windows-based computers, for example, 20 colors are reserved for use by Windows so that window borders, menu bars, button faces, and other elements of the user interface maintain a consistent appearance. This leaves only 236 colors that can be adjusted to match those in an image.

- Web pages can contain any number of GIF images. Each GIF image can contain only 256 colors, but two images on the same page—if they have no colors in common—can require a total of 512. Three images can require 768 colors, and so forth. This presents a problem if the display hardware can only accommodate 256 colors in total.

- A single JPEG picture can contain far more than 256 colors: up to 16,777,216 (assuming the image has that many pixels). A 256-color system has no hope of rendering such an image accurately.

Most browsers solve this dilemma by programming 256-color displays with a fixed 216-color palette. The 216 colors are all combinations of six evenly spaced levels of red, the same six levels of green, and the same six levels of blue. Table 4-3 shows the six levels. These are the only colors you can be sure browsers will display as you intended, and for this reason those 216 are commonly called *the browser-safe colors*.

To display colors with RGB intensities other than 0, 51, 102, 153, 204, or 255, the browser either *dithers* or *substitutes*. When dithering, the browser displays nonstandard colors as a mixed pattern of standard-color pixels. In theory, the viewer's eye perceives the mixed pattern as a smooth area, but in practice the perception is often grainy. Dithering usually works better on continuous-scale images, such as photographs. It's most objectionable on elements with large solid areas, such as text, flood fills, and line art.

TABLE 4-3. **Safe Palette Color Intensities for 256-Color Video Systems**

Intensity	Decimal	Hex
Minimum	0	00
	51	33
	102	66
	153	99
	204	CC
Maximum	255	FF

When substituting, the browser simply replaces nonstandard colors with its idea of the closest standard color. Browsers normally apply substitution rather than dithering for background colors, because dithering a background can seriously affect the readability of text.

Why should you care about all this? Well, both dithering and substitution result in Web visitors seeing something other than you intended. To avoid this, take one of these steps:

- Specify only the following RGB values for text, backgrounds, and solid images: 0, 51, 102, 153, 204, or 255.

- If you must supply RGB color values in hexadecimal, specify only values 00, 33, 66, 99, CC, or FF.

Using the safe color palette significantly reduces the choice of colors in a harmonious scheme. This presents a dilemma that won't be solved

II

Creating Web Pages

until all Web visitors have 24-bit color displays. For now, you must decide whether to optimize colors for 8-bit displays or 24-bit displays, and at this time, 8-bit displays predominate.

Using FrontPage Color Dialog Boxes

Most color settings in FrontPage are controllable in three levels of detail:

- A drop-down box with 18 choices: Automatic, the 16 original VGA colors, and Custom.

- A second dialog box with 127 color swatches, 15 grayscale swatches, a black swatch, a white swatch, and a button for "picking up" any color currently displayed on screen.

- The standard Windows color picker with 48 basic color swatches, 16 configurable color swatches, and controls for specifying exact colors two different ways: via the Hue, Saturation, Luminance color model, and via the Red, Green, Blue color model.

To fully exploit the use of color in your Web pages, you need to understand all three levels.

Figure 4-14 shows the first level of detail, the drop-down box. The Automatic choice normally means a color configured in the remote user's browser. Clicking any of the 16 color swatches arranged in two rows selects that color. To see the name of any color, let the mouse pointer rest over it.

FIGURE 4-14.

Most color choices in FrontPage begin by offering this drop-down color picker.

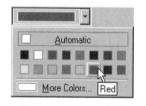

As explained in the previous section, it's always best to choose Web colors with RGB components of 0, 51, 102, 153, 204, and 255. Unfortunately, as illustrated in Table 4-4, only 8 of the 16 drop-down swatches comply with this advice.

Even the eight compliant colors are rather boring: black, white, the three primaries, and their complements. These are wonderful colors and, used properly, they provide plenty of contrast. However, they're hardly intriguing. You'll produce more subtle and interesting Web pages by choosing custom colors with RGB components using combinations of 0, 51, 102, 153, 204, and 255. To do so, click the More Colors choice and receive the Colors dialog box shown in Figure 4-15.

The large hexagon in Figure 4-15 is actually a color wheel with red at five o'clock, green at nine o'clock, and blue at one o'clock. Dark shades occupy the edges, light tints occupy the center, and saturated colors lie between. Below the color wheel are a white swatch, a black swatch, and, between them, 6 grayscale swatches.

FIGURE 4-15.

You can select any color shown in this dialog box simply by clicking the corresponding swatch. In addition, after clicking the Select button, you can use the mouse to pick up any color currently displayed on your screen.

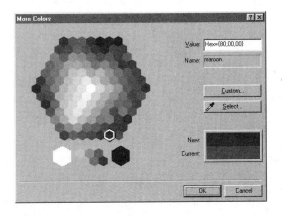

TABLE 4-4. Compliant and Noncompliant Colors

Compliant Colors			Noncompliant Colors		
Standard Name	**FrontPage Name**	**RGB Values**	**Standard Name**	**FrontPage Name**	**RGB Values**
Black	Black	0-0-0	Gray	Gray	128-128-128
White	White	255-255-255	Light Gray	Silver	192-192-192
Red	Red	255-0-0	Dark Red	Maroon	128-0-0
Green	Lime	0-255-0	Dark Green	Green	0-128-0
Blue	Blue	0-0-255	Dark Blue	Navy	0-0-128
Cyan	Aqua	0-255-255	Dark Cyan	Teal	0-128-128
Magenta	Fuchsia	255-0-255	Dark Magenta	Purple	128-0-128
Yellow	Yellow	255-255-0	Dark Yellow	Olive	128-128-0

II

Creating Web Pages

The 216 browser-safe colors include black, white, and four shades of gray: 51-51-51, 102-102-102, 153-153-153, and 204-204-204. A browser-safe version of the Colors dialog box would therefore have black, white, four shades of gray, and 210 colors. In fact, it has 6 shades of gray and 127 colors, and some of each are browser-unsafe. To preserve an Office 2000 family resemblance, FrontPage designers made this dialog box resemble the same one in PowerPoint rather than optimizing it with browser-safe colors.

Fortunately, most of the 127 color swatches *are* browser-safe. To verify the browser safety of any color, hold the mouse pointer over it and check the value displayed in the Value box. If any of the two-digit Hex values aren't 00, 33, 66, 99, CC, or FF, the color isn't browser-safe. The color selected in Figure 4-15, for example, fails the test.

To pick up a color already displayed on your screen, first click the Select button, causing the mouse pointer to become an eyedropper. Move the eyedropper over the color you want, anywhere on the screen, then click the mouse button.

Clicking Color dialog box's Custom button displays the third FrontPage color picker, also displayed in Figure 4-16.

SEE ALSO

For more information about the Hue, Saturation, Luminance color model, see "HSL—The Hue, Saturation, Luminance Color Model," page 320.

This dialog box presents 48 standard color swatches (mostly unsafe), 16 configurable color swatches, and text boxes for specifying exact colors two different ways: using the Hue, Saturation, Luminance color model—which we'll ignore for now—or the Red, Green, Blue color model—which we'll pounce on like a ton of bricks. Entering values of 0, 51, 102, 153, 204, and 255—and no others—into the Red, Green, and Blue boxes at last provides access to all 216 browser-safe colors.

FIGURE 4-16.
FrontPage's third color picker is the standard Windows Color dialog box.

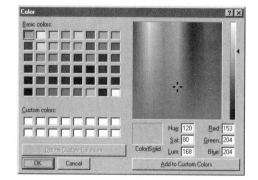

? SEE ALSO

For more information on choosing color schemes for the Web see "Design Tips— Color," page 301.

Choosing Page Colors

Even a short course in color appreciation exceeds the scope of this chapter. Nevertheless, here are some quick guidelines:

- Choose complementary colors: earth tones, sky tones, ocean colors, and so forth. Colors that appear together in beautiful natural settings are likely to look good in other settings as well.

- Coordinate colors with those in any Web-page images you plan to use.

- Ensure there's sufficient contrast between the various text colors and the background.

- Use dark text on a light background, which is easier to read than light text on a dark background.

- Strive for colors that contrast but don't clash.

- Avoid using background images that overpower normal text. The best background images are very light with low contrast.

In Summary...

FrontPage provides a powerful set of commands and dialog boxes that help you create, open, save, and delete Web pages. In addition, it provides great flexibility in configuring a Web page's overall attributes. Shared Cascading Style Sheets, discussed in Chapter 5, and themes, discussed in Chapter 9, provide additional control over page appearance.

II

Creating Web Pages

CHAPTER 5

Adding and Formatting Text

The origin of the World Wide Web was text-based, and text still predominates today. As much as graphics, moving images, sounds, and interactive controls can enhance a Web page, natural language text remains the workhorse for presenting information. This chapter describes the FrontPage commands for entering, modifying, cutting, pasting, moving, and formatting text.

Wherever possible, FrontPage follows the same text entry conventions as other Microsoft Office applications, especially Microsoft Word. This is hardly unexpected, considering Front-Page's status as a member of the Office family, and indeed it's very likely a major reason you or your company bought FrontPage. Despite its family resemblance to Word, though, FrontPage necessarily remains bound to the unique eccentricities and limitations of HTML.

It's critical to remember that the remote user's browser, not FrontPage, controls the final appearance of text and other objects on a Web page. FrontPage saves text with rather imprecise formatting instructions that the remote user's browser will interpret—or ignore—as it chooses. Therefore, the final display differs for each remote user, depending on the capabilities and settings of their browser. Differences in the browser software itself, its version, the size of the remote user's browser window, the availability of fonts on the remote user's system, monitor resolution and color depth, and other factors will *all* cause variations in output. Keep this in mind as you design your page: what you see is only approximately what the remote user will get.

Word Processing Conventions Used by FrontPage

Entering text in FrontPage is very much like typing into a word processor. Follow these steps in Page view:

1　Set an insertion point on the page by clicking the desired spot. The insertion point will jump to the nearest location where text can be entered.

 **TIP**

> FrontPage accepts input like a word processor, and not like some graphics and publishing programs. You can't just click in the middle of some white space and locate objects there.

2　Start typing.

You cut, copy, paste, and clear work in standard fashion, as shown in Table 5-1. In addition, you can drag selected text anywhere on the page that text can normally appear. Simply dragging text moves it, and holding down the Ctrl key and dragging copies it.

The Paste Special command provides choices to paste text as one paragraph or several, and to preserve or ignore the formatting in the pasted text. Paste Special is particularly useful when bringing in text from other applications like databases and spreadsheets.

> **NOTE**
>
> The Paste Special command can also paste HTML code directly into your page. This is quite useful if someone sends you a piece of HTML that does some special job. Just use the Paste Special command and choose Treat As HTML.

Table 5-2 lists the commands for selecting text.

Table 5-3 lists the keyboard commands for changing the insertion point. Again, these are much the same as those in any word processor. Holding down Shift while changing the insertion point extends the current selection.

To end a paragraph and start another, press the Enter key. To begin a new line within the same paragraph, press Shift+Enter.

TABLE 5-1.   Copying, Moving, and Deleting Text

Operation	Preparation	Menu Command	Drag and Drop	Keystroke
Cut	Select source text	Edit/Cut	N/A	Press Ctrl+X or Shift+Del
Move	Select source text	Edit/Cut/Edit/Paste	Drag to new location	(Cut and Paste)
Copy	Select source text	Edit/Copy	Hold down Ctrl and drag to additional location	Press Ctrl+C or Shift+Ins
Paste	Set insertion point	Edit/Paste	N/A	Press Ctrl+V or Ctrl+Ins
Paste Special	Set insertion point	Edit/Paste Special	N/A	N/A
Delete	Select source text	Edit/Delete	N/A	Press Del

TABLE 5-2.   Text Selection Commands

Operation	Command
Select range	Drag mouse across range, or From insertion point, hold down Shift and click at end of range, or Hold down Shift and use arrow keys to highlight desired selection.
Select word	Double-click word.
Select paragraph	Hold down Alt and click anywhere in paragraph.
Select entire document	Choose Select All from the Edit menu, or Press Ctrl+A.

II

Creating Web Pages

TABLE 5-3. Keyboard Commands for Changing the Insertion Point

Operation	Keystroke
Move one character right or left	Right Arrow or Left Arrow
Move one word right or left	Ctrl+Right Arrow or Ctrl+Left Arrow
Move to start of line	Home
Move to end of line	End
Move up or down one line	Up Arrow or Down Arrow
Move up or down one paragraph	Ctrl+Up Arrow or Ctrl+Down Arrow
Move to top of page	Ctrl+Home
Move to bottom of page	Ctrl+End

Importing Text

FrontPage is remarkably capable of accepting whole files or selected portions—in almost any format—and converting them to reasonably effective HTML. To add such content to a Web page, open the page in FrontPage and take the following steps:

- To insert an entire file using the drag-and-drop method:

    1 Locate the file's icon in Windows Explorer.

    2 Drag the icon to the desired location in FrontPage.

    3 Drop it in place.

- To insert an entire file using commands:

    1 Place the insertion point where you want the file to appear in FrontPage.

    2 Choose File from the Insert menu and locate the file you want to insert.

    3 Double-click the file name or select it and click the Open button.

- To insert less than an entire file using drag and drop:

    1 Open the file in its normal application.

    2 Select the desired content.

    3 Drag the selection to the desired location in FrontPage.

    4 Drop it in place.

- To insert part of a file using commands:

    1 Open the file in its normal application.

    2 Select the desired content.

    3 Copy the selection to the Clipboard.

    4 In FrontPage, set the insertion point where you want the content to appear.

    5 Choose Paste from the Edit menu, or press Ctrl+V.

How FrontPage Interprets Text and Graphics

When asked to incorporate content that isn't in HTML format, FrontPage first determines whether the data is character-based or graphic.

If the data is character-based:

- FrontPage consults the table of standard file translators installed on the local machine.

- FrontPage translates the data to Rich Text Format (RTF).

- FrontPage translates the RTF to HTML.

Tabular data such as a spreadsheet becomes an HTML table. Other data becomes free-flowing text. FrontPage attempts to retain formatting instructions in the original data.

If the data is graphic:

- FrontPage converts the data to a Windows bitmap for display.

- When you save your Web page, FrontPage identifies images that originated outside the current Web and displays a Save As dialog box for each one.

- If an image uses transparency or contains no more than 256 colors, FrontPage saves it, by default, as a GIF file. If the image contains more than 256 colors and no transparency, it's saved in JPEG format.

SEE ALSO
For more information on HTML tables, see "Creating and Editing Tables," page 230.

SEE ALSO
For more information on using graphics in Web pages, see Chapter 6, "Incorporating Graphics."

II

Creating Web Pages

Text Conventions Unique to HTML

The preceding section may have convinced you that entering text in FrontPage is no different than using virtually any word processor. This is no accident, and in fact it's a unique strength of FrontPage. Nevertheless, the nature of HTML introduces a number of unique restrictions.

- HTML considers tab characters the same as word spaces. There's no facility for setting tab stops to line up text in columns.

- HTML treats all strings of white-space characters as a single space. White-space characters are spaces, tabs, line feeds, carriage returns, and so forth. FrontPage counteracts this behavior by detecting any repeating spaces you enter and replacing all but the last with nonbreaking spaces—that is, spaces neither FrontPage nor the browser will suppress.

- HTML provides no direct control over first-line indentation, paragraph indentation, line length, or line spacing.

When You Really Want Extra Spaces

By design, browsers compress all strings of white-space characters down to a single space before displaying them. This means there's no way, in HTML, to provide extra word spacing by adding extra spaces. If you really want to insert extra spaces—for instance, to align program code or to provide extra word spacing—you have several options:

- Use the Formatted paragraph style, which provides an exception to HTML's normal handling of white space. FrontPage uses the HTML *<pre>* tag to format paragraphs assigned this style. The *<pre>* tag displays content in an unattractive monospaced font but with all spaces and carriage returns honored, as if you were using a typewriter. You can't, however, use heading levels or other elements within a formatted paragraph; and you should avoid tabs because different browsers might assign different numbers of spaces to them. But if you don't mind the monospaced font, if you stick to using spaces rather than tabs, and if you want to control the alignment of each character on a line, the Formatted style may be acceptable.

- HTML provides a special *nonbreaking space* character that browsers don't compress. A nonbreaking space appears in HTML code as the string * * and every time a browser sees this code, it displays a space, no matter how many appear consecutively. There are three ways to enter nonbreaking spaces in FrontPage.

When You Really Want Extra Spaces *continued*

- When you type multiple spaces in FrontPage, FrontPage inserts nonbreaking spaces rather than ordinary spaces for all but the last space.

- When you're entering text, FrontPage treats pressing the Tab key the same as pressing Spacebar four times.

- To insert nonbreaking spaces one at a time, press Ctrl+Shift+Spacebar.

Despite the presence of these features, spacing text or other objects by using multiple space characters still constitutes bad style. Repeating spaces will seldom produce the results you want, given HTML's use of proportional fonts, variable page width, and automatic line wrapping.

The practice of inserting two spaces between each pair of sentences is a carryover from the days of typewriters when, because of monospaced fonts, letter spacing within words tended to be wide. Nowadays, with proportional fonts, letter spacing is narrower and one space provides plenty of separation between sentences.

Inserting Special Text Elements

The Insert menu in FrontPage can add four kinds of special text elements: line breaks, horizontal lines, symbols, and comments.

Inserting a Line Break

Choosing Break from the Insert menu displays the dialog box shown in Figure 5-1. This dialog box inserts four different kinds of line breaks.

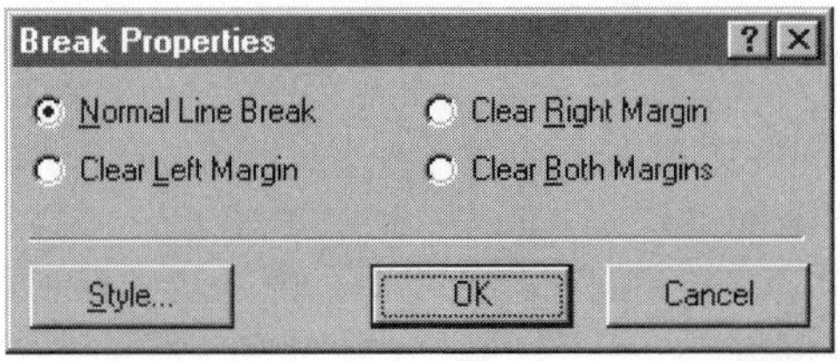

FIGURE 5-1.

The Break Properties dialog box inserts a line break at the current insertion point. Clearing a margin means resuming text flow just below any non-text objects aligned at that margin.

Break Properties

- ⊙ Normal Line Break
- ○ Clear Left Margin
- ○ Clear Right Margin
- ○ Clear Both Margins

Style... | OK | Cancel

- ■ **Normal Line Break.** This is an ordinary line break, just as you would create by pressing Shift+Enter. Text resumes flowing normally exactly one line below the line containing the break.

SEE ALSO

For information on inserting and aligning images, see Chapter 6, "Incorporating Graphics."

- **Clear Left Margin.** If this break occurs in text flowing around an image or other object aligned at the left margin, text following the break will start flowing immediately below that object.

- **Clear Right Margin.** If this break occurs in text flowing around an object aligned at the right margin, text following the break will start flowing immediately below that object.

- **Clear Both Margins.** If this break occurs in text flowing around objects aligned at either or both margins, text following the break will start flowing immediately below them.

SEE ALSO

For a discussion of cascading style sheets, see "A Quick Course in Cascading Style Sheets," page 138.

Clicking the Style button in the lower-left corner of the dialog box displays FrontPage's Modify Style dialog box, seen later in this chapter as Figure 5-22. Any cascading style-sheet properties you specify will apply to the current line break.

Figure 5-2 shows a normal line break. Figure 5-3 shows a Clear Left Margin break for clearing an object on the left margin.

Inserting Horizontal Lines

Choosing Horizontal Line from the Insert menu places a variable-width horizontal line at the current insertion point. The horizontal line normally occupies the entire width of the browser window and forces line breaks before and after itself. Figure 5-2 and Figure 5-3 each contain a horizontal line; it appears just above the graphic and extends across the entire page.

If you right-click a horizontal line and choose Horizontal Line Properties from the pop-up menu, you can set the properties of the horizontal line. See Figure 5-4.

- **Width** specifies the width of the horizontal line in pixels or as a percentage of available display width.

- **Height** specifies the height or thickness of the line in pixels.

- **Alignment** sets the line's alignment to the left, to the right, or in the center.

- **Color** selects the line's color. A drop-down list displays 18 possibilities: Default, the 16 original VGA colors, and Custom.

TIP

For advice on choosing text colors, see "Choosing Page Colors," page 107.

- **Solid Line (No Shading)** eliminates the normal three-dimensional effect along the edges of the line.

- **Style** opens the Modify Style dialog box where you can select any applicable cascading style-sheet (CSS) properties for the horizontal line.

Inserting a Normal line break here…

FIGURE 5-2.
This page illustrates a normal line break.

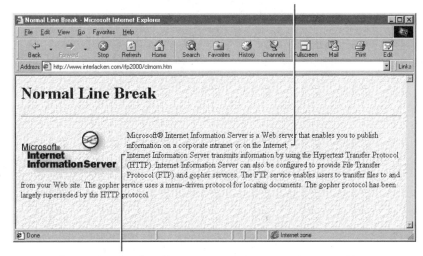

…forces a new line, but allows text to continue wrapping around image.

Inserting a Clear Left Margin line break here…

FIGURE 5-3.
Text following a Clear Left Margin line break jumps around any object on its left and resumes flowing at the true left margin below the object.

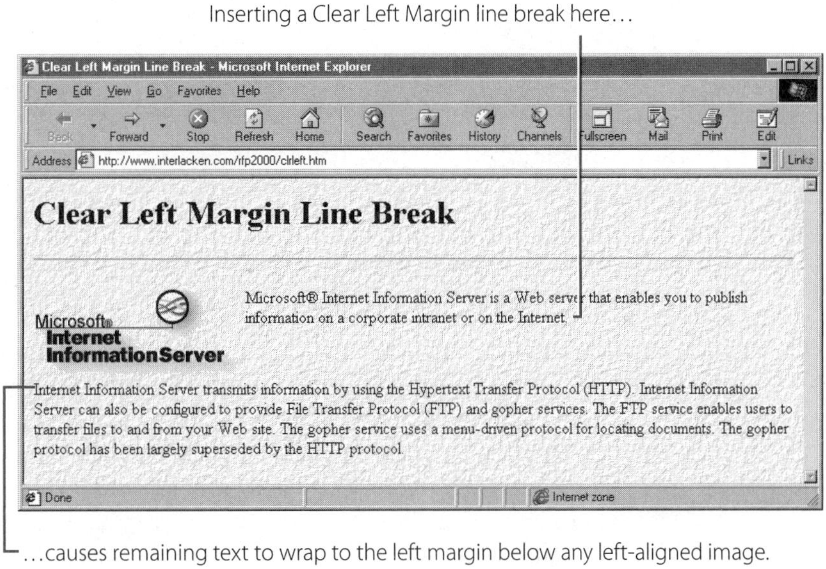

…causes remaining text to wrap to the left margin below any left-aligned image.

II

Creating Web Pages

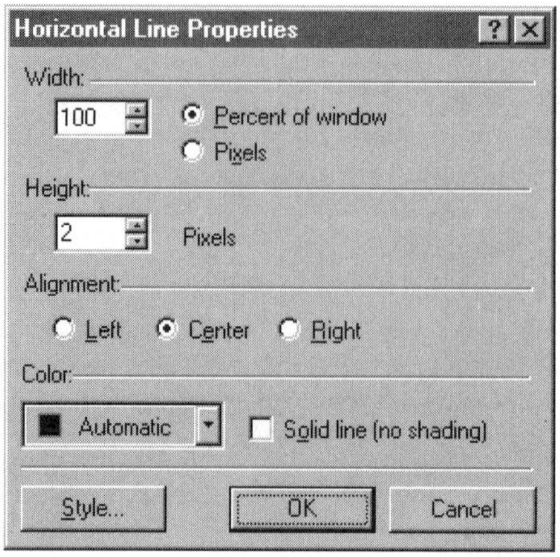

FIGURE 5-4.

This dialog box sets the properties of a horizontal line.

Inserting Symbols

You can easily insert special characters—those that don't appear on your keyboard—using the Symbol dialog box shown in Figure 5-5. To insert a special character:

1 Place the insertion point where you want to insert the symbol.

2 Choose Symbol from the Insert menu.

3 Double-click the desired character, or select the desired character and click Insert.

4 Close the dialog box.

FIGURE 5-5.

To insert characters not on the keyboard, choose Symbol from the Insert dialog box.

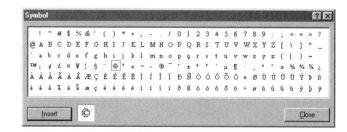

Inserting Comments

Comments include text that appears in FrontPage but that won't be seen by viewers of your Web pages. As shown in Figure 5-6, comments typically contain notes (preferably the scrutable kind) about the page for yourself or others on your team. To add comments to a Web page:

1 Set the insertion point where you want the comment to appear.

2 Choose Comment from the Insert menu.

3 Enter your comments in the Comment dialog box and click OK when done.

FIGURE 5-6.
Comments inserted here won't be visible to viewers of your Web site.

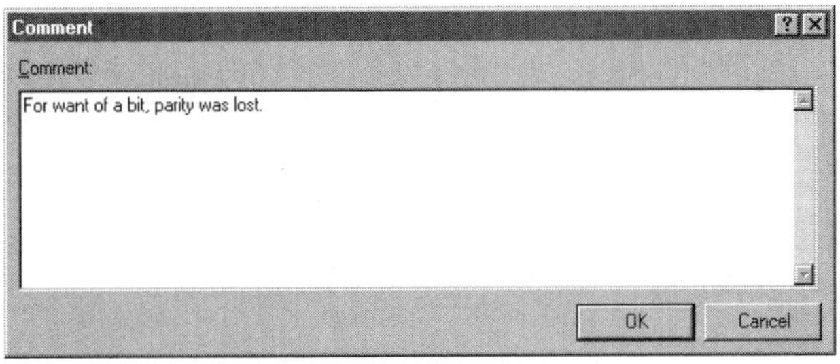

In FrontPage, comments appear as purple text. To modify a comment, either double-click it or right-click it and select Comment Properties. To delete a comment, click it and then press the Delete key.

Searching, Replacing, and Spell Checking

? SEE ALSO
For information about using the Find, Replace, and Spelling functions on groups of selected Web pages or on entire FrontPage Webs, see "Finding and Replacing Text," page 789, and "Spell Checking Your Web," page 795.

FrontPage can search, replace, and check the spelling of text in your Web page.

Searching for Text

To search for text in an open page:

1 Set the insertion point where you want the search to begin. Pressing Ctrl+Home, for example, sets the insertion point at the start of the Web page.

2 Choose Find from the Edit menu. The dialog box shown in Figure 5-7 will appear.

3 In the box marked Find What, enter the text you hope to find.

4 Review the following settings:

  ■ **Find Where.** Choose Selected Pages to search the current page.

  ■ **Direction.** Choose Up to search from the insertion point to the top of the document. To search from the insertion point to the end of the document, choose Down.

- **Find Whole Words Only.** If you turn this box on, Front-Page will ignore partial word matches. A search for the word *walk*, for example, wouldn't stop at the word *walking*.

- **Match Case.** Turning this box on means the search will be case sensitive. A search for *walker* wouldn't stop at *Walker*.

- **Find In HTML.** If this box is on, FrontPage will search for your string not only in ordinary page text, but within the HTML code. However, for this to work, you must click the HTML tab at the bottom of the editing window before choosing Find from the Edit menu.

5 Click the Find Next button.

To search for additional occurrences of the Find text, keep clicking the Find Next button. To edit the page, you don't need to close the Find window; just move it out of the way.

Replacing Text

Choosing Replace from the Edit menu displays the window that appears in Figure 5-8. This dialog box works just the same as the Find function, except that after finding a match, you can click the Replace button to replace it (with the contents of the Replace With box, of course). Clicking Replace All replaces all occurrences of the Find Where string.

FIGURE 5-7.

This dialog box searches your Web page for a specified text string.

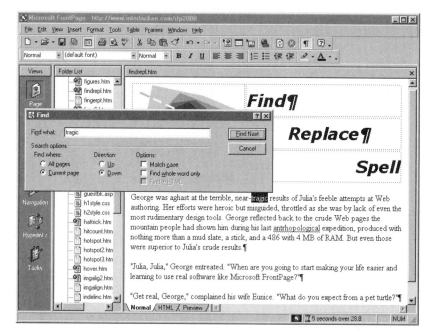

Checking Spelling

FrontPage 2000 supports two kinds of spell checking. First, it can check the spelling of words as you type them and second, it can scan an entire Web page for errors.

Spell checking as you type is the feature that displays squiggly lines under each misspelled word in your document. In Figure 5-7, for example, the word *anthropological* is misspelled and therefore underlined. To configure this feature, choose Page Options from the Tools menu, then click the General tab. This presents two check boxes:

- **Check Spelling As You Type** controls whether or not FrontPage will immediately check the spelling of each word you type. You might elect to turn this off because it slows down your system, or because your page content contains so many nonstandard words. This option is turned on by default.

- **Hide Spelling Errors In All Documents** controls whether FrontPage displays squiggly lines under the misspelled words. Why check spelling as you type and not display the squiggly lines? Well, maybe you don't like squiggly lines but you do like very rapid spell checks later.

When you right-click a misspelled word—one with a squiggly underline—FrontPage displays a pop-up menu containing suggested correct spellings, an Ignore All choice that temporarily accepts the questionable word as correct, and an Add choice that adds the questionable word to the spelling dictionary.

> ⭐ TIP
>
> The misspelled word pop-up menu appears in place of any normal pop-up menus. For example, you can't change paragraph properties by right-clicking a misspelled word and choosing Paragraph properties because all you'll get is the spelling correction pop-up. The solution is to right-click some other part of the paragraph that lacks squiggly underlining.

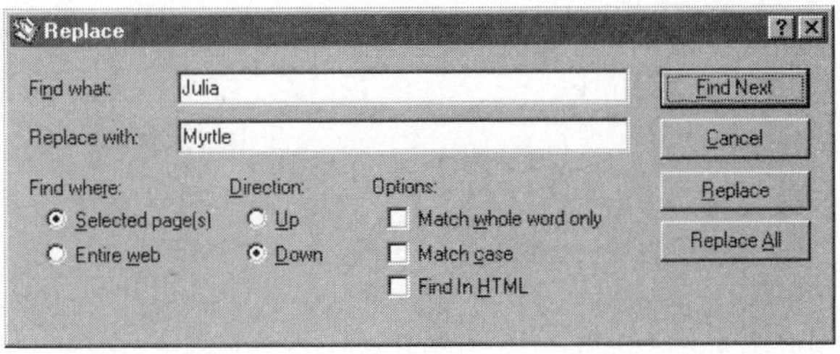

FIGURE 5-8.
The Replace function works much like Find, except that clicking either the Replace or Replace All button modifies the original text.

Creating Web Pages

The actual spell checking dialog box appears in Figure 5-9. To display it, choose Spelling from the Tools menu or press F7. Whenever the spell checker finds a word that's not in its dictionary, it offers these choices:

- **Ignore** makes no change to the questionable word and continues the spell check.

- **Ignore All** works the same as Ignore, except that the spell checker won't stop if it finds more occurrences of the same questionable word during the current spell check.

- **Change** replaces the questionable word with the word in the Change To box. You can accept the spell checker's initial suggestion, select another word from the Suggestions list, or hand-type a word yourself.

- **Change All** works like Change, except that for the remainder of the spell check, it makes the same replacement whenever it finds the same questionable word.

- **Add** adds the questionable word to the spell-checking dictionary.

- **Suggest** checks the spelling of the word in the Change To box and, if it can't be verified, offers suggestions.

- **Cancel** terminates the spell check.

FIGURE 5-9.
FrontPage uses the same spell checker as the rest of the Office 2000 family.

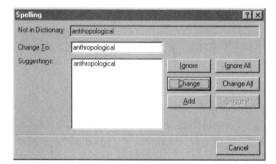

Using the Thesaurus

As you're thinking great thoughts and pounding out text, finding just the right word is frequently a problem. Trust me on this. Or perhaps you need the opposite of a word. To resolve both dilemmas, FrontPage 2000 has a built-in thesaurus. Neither prehistoric nor reptilian, a thesaurus is a dictionary of words with like and opposite meanings. FrontPage uses the same thesaurus as the rest of the Office 2000 suite.

To use the thesaurus, choose Thesaurus from the Tools menu, producing the dialog box that appears in Figure 5-10. If you selected a word before invoking the dialog box, FrontPage will automatically display the selected word's synonyms (words with like meanings) and antonyms (words with opposite meanings). When the original word has several meanings, the Meanings box will have an entry for each. In the example, clicking the *weak* meaning at the left displays a different list of synonyms at the right than clicking the *pathetic* meaning.

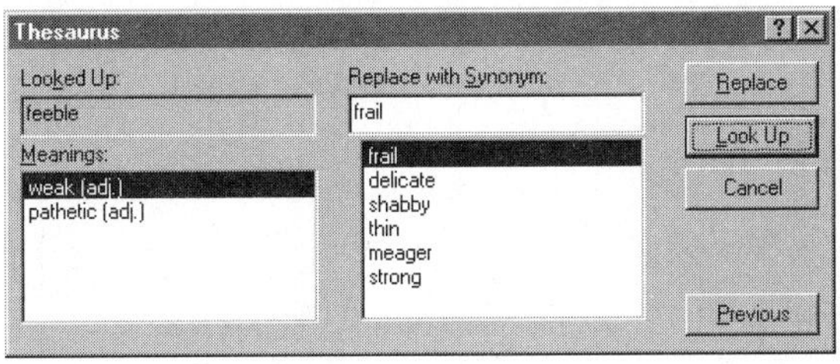

FIGURE 5-10.

The thesaurus searches for words with like and unlike meanings.

If a synonym is closer to what you want but still not exact, double-click it. This tells the thesaurus to look up the double-clicked word and display *its* synonyms. If this takes you farther from your goal rather than closer, click the Previous button.

Once you find the best word, click the Replace button to use it in place of the word you originally selected in the text.

Formatting Paragraphs

The arrangement and layout of paragraphs—or any blocks of text—are a key element of page layout and visual communication. FrontPage therefore provides a rich assortment of tools that control paragraph appearance.

Using HTML's Basic Paragraph Styles

FrontPage supports the 15 basic HTML paragraph styles shown in Figure 5-11. These are paragraph styles and not font styles; they modify the appearance of an entire paragraph and not of any specific text. HTML was designed to specify the structure of a document's elements, not the explicit formatting of a given element; therefore, each browser will display these according to its own settings and the system configuration on which it's running.

Heading 1 through Heading 6 are for successively lower-level titles. In practice, any page with six levels of titles is probably too long and an excellent candidate for separation into multiple pages. Nevertheless, the availability of six styles provides more flexibility in selecting sizes (you might, for example, choose to use Headings 1 through 3, or 4 through 6). Heading 1 generally uses the largest font and Heading 6 the smallest.

FIGURE 5-11.
FrontPage supports these standard HTML paragraph styles.

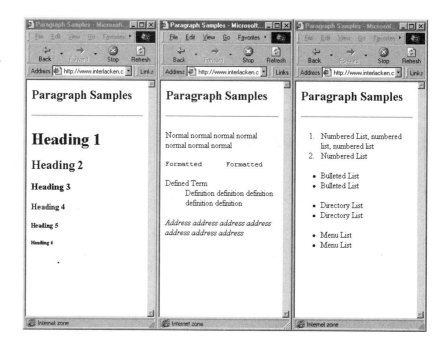

The Normal style is designated for most ordinary text. Like the heading styles and most of the others, it specifies no fixed line width but instead wraps within the current browser window.

The Formatted style is unique in three respects: it uses a monospaced font; it preserves and displays multiple spaces; and it doesn't wrap within the browser window. Because of these characteristics, the Formatted style is useful for applications like tabular data and program-code listings, where preservation of columns and letter spaces is vital.

The Address style is designated to identify Web addresses. Its most common use is making e-mail hyperlinks stand out from ordinary text. Web address paragraphs frequently, though not always, appear in an italic font.

To assign one of the 15 default styles to a paragraph, set the insertion point in the paragraph or select any part of it, then select the desired style from the Change Style list in the Formatting toolbar. Table 5-4 explains the Formatting toolbar. In addition, there are two shortcut keys:

- **Ctrl+Shift+N** applies the Normal style.

- **Ctrl+Shift+L** applies the Bulleted List style.

The formatting toolbar also has buttons to left-align, center, and right-align paragraphs, to apply the bulleted-list style, to apply the numbered-list style, and to shift the indentation of items in a bulleted or numbered list.

Fine-Tuning Paragraph Properties

The Paragraph Properties dialog box appears in Figure 5-12. You can display it by right-clicking the paragraph and choosing Paragraph Properties from the pop-up menu. Or, if you prefer, select all or part of the paragraph, and then choose Paragraph from the Format menu.

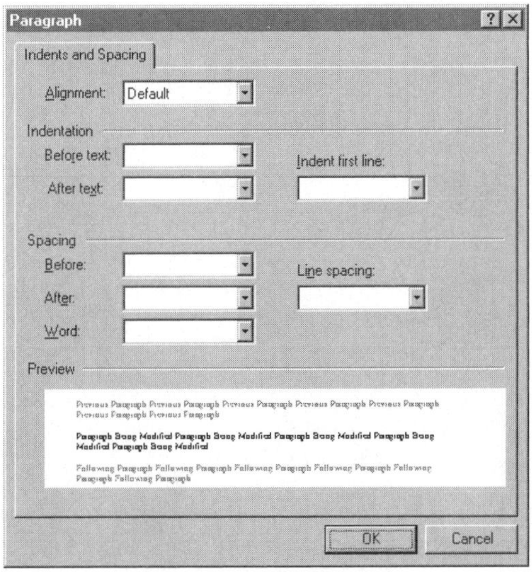

FIGURE 5-12.

Use the Paragraph Properties dialog box to choose paragraph styles.

TABLE 5-4.   Using FrontPage's Formatting Toolbar

Icon	Description	Function	Menu Command
Heading 1	Change Style	Modifies the HTML style of selected paragraphs	Format/Paragraph
(default font)	Change Font	Modifies the font of selected text	Format/Font/Font tab/ Font List
Normal	Font Size	Modifies the font size of selected text	Format/Font/Font tab/ Size

(continued)

TABLE 5-4. *continued*

Icon	Description	Function	Menu Command
B	Bold	Toggles bold attribute of selected text	Format/Font/Font tab/ Font Style
I	Italic	Toggles italic attribute of selected text	Format/Font/Font tab/ Font Style
U	Underline	Toggles underline attribute of selected text	Format/Font/Font tab/ Font Style
	Align Left	Left-aligns text in selected paragraphs	Format/Paragraph/ Paragraph Alignment/ Left
	Center	Centers text in selected paragraphs	Format/Paragraph/ Paragraph Alignment/ Center
	Align Right	Right-aligns text in selected paragraphs	Format/Paragraph/ Paragraph Alignment/ Right
	Numbered List	Creates a numbered list	Format/ Bullets and Numbering/ Numbered
	Bulleted List	Creates a bulleted list	Format/ Bullets and Numbering/ Plain Bullets
	Decrease Indent	Decreases paragraph indentation on nesting level of selected list items	none
	Increase Indent	Increases paragraph indentation on nesting level of selected list items	none
	Highlight Color	Changes the background color of selected text	none
A	Text Color	Changes the color of selected text	Format/Font/Font tab/ Color

For now, we'll only consider one setting in this dialog box:

■ **Paragraph Alignment** specifies that the style will use its default setting for alignment; or you can select left, right, or center.

To fully understand the remaining settings, you need to understand a tiny bit about cascading style sheets. Therefore, we'll defer further discussion until after the section on page 138, titled "A Quick Course in Cascading Style Sheets."

Formatting Lists

In HTML terminology, lists are collections of paragraphs the browser will specially format with leading bullets or numbers. Because lists inherently have a structure to them, creating and updating them is slightly trickier than working with normal paragraphs. Fortunately, FrontPage takes care of this complexity for you.

Creating Bulleted and Numbered Lists

As shown in Figure 5-13, Figure 5-14, and Figure 5-15, FrontPage supports three kinds of bulleted and numbered lists:

- **Picture Bullets.** FrontPage uses a graphic image that you select as the item identifier.

- **Plain Bullets.** FrontPage instructs the browser to display a standard bullet character.

- **Numbered Bullets.** FrontPage instructs the browser to sequentially number the list items.

FIGURE 5-13.
If you choose Bullets And Numbering from the Format menu, you can insert picture bullets from this dialog box.

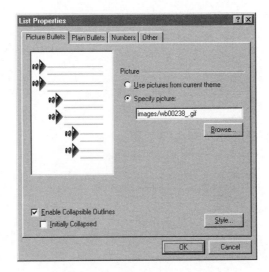

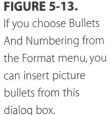
Creating Web Pages

To convert existing paragraphs to a list:

1   Select the desired paragraphs.

2   Do *one* of the following:

- Choose Numbered List or Bulleted List from the Change Style list on the Formatting toolbar.

- Click the Numbered List or Bulleted List icon on the Formatting toolbar.

- Choose Bullets And Numbering from the Format menu.

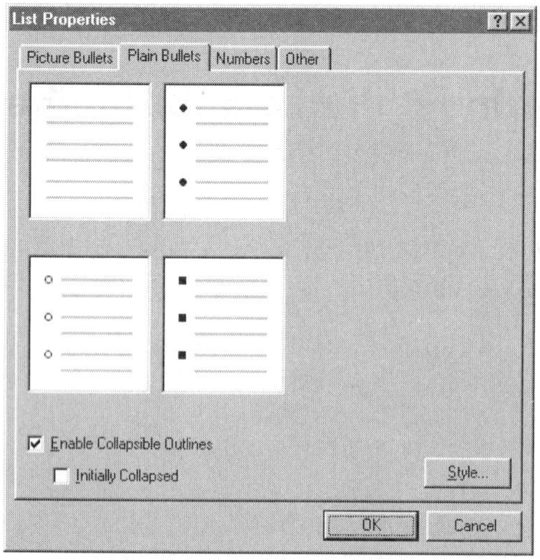

FIGURE 5-14.
FrontPage assigns the properties of normal bulleted lists according to the settings made here.

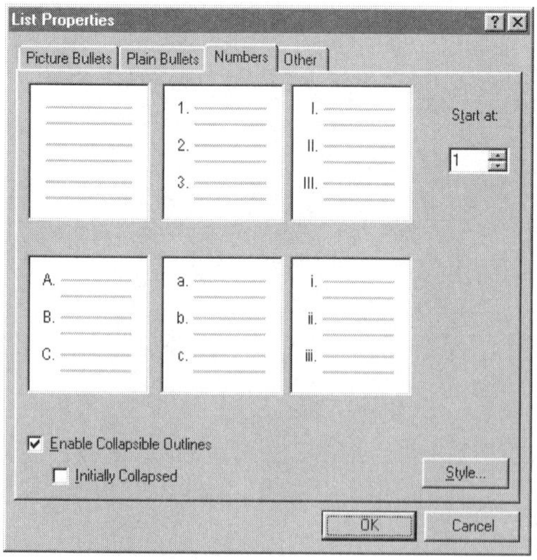

FIGURE 5-15.
The Numbers tab of the Bullets And Numbering dialog box controls the properties of numbered lists.

> **NOTE**
>
> You can't create an Picture Bullet list from the Formatting toolbar. To create an Picture Bullet list, choose the Bullets And Numbering command from the Format menu, and then select the Picture Bullets tab as shown in Figure 5-13. You can also select the Picture Bullets tab by right-clicking an existing plain-bullets list and then choosing List Properties from the pop-up menu.

You can create a new list in two ways. The first is to create normal paragraphs and convert them as just described. The second is this:

1 Place the insertion point where the list should begin.

2 Do *one* of the following:

   - Click either the Bulleted List or the Numbered List button on the Formatting toolbar.

   - Choose Bullets And Numbering from the Format menu, select a style, and then click OK.

3 Enter the text for each item in the list, and press Enter to continue to the next item.

4 To end the list and return to Normal paragraph style, press Enter twice. (If you don't want an extra line of space, press Backspace to delete it.)

> **NOTE**
>
> Remember the convention that two consecutive paragraph endings denote the end of a list. This explains many otherwise curious behaviors that occur around the end of lists.

From the Picture Bullets tab, you can select pictures for your bullets in two ways:

> **SEE ALSO**
>
> For more information about FrontPage Themes, see "Using Existing Themes," page 292.

■ If the current Web or page uses themes, choose the option Use Pictures From Current Theme to use the bullet pictures supplied with the theme.

■ Choose the Specify Picture option if there's no theme in effect or if you don't want the standard theme bullets. Continue by hand-typing the picture's URL or by using the Browse button to locate one. Browsing for an picture is identical to browsing for any other file, except for the addition of the Clip Art button, described in "Adding Pictures to a Page" on page 176.

NOTE

> Picture bullet lists aren't lists in an HTML sense. Rather, they're tables that FrontPage builds and maintains, using the same commands it uses for true HTML lists.

Figure 5-14 shows the Plain Bullets tab of the Bullets And Numbering dialog box, from which you can select any one of several bullet styles that use text symbols rather than pictures. Click the style you want, and then click OK. Click the Style button to set CSS properties.

Figure 5-15 shows the Numbers tab of the Bullets And Numbering dialog box. Click the numbering style you want, verify or change the Start At value for the first paragraph in the list, and then click OK. Click the Style button to set cascading style-sheet properties.

Figure 5-16 shows examples of indented lists using plain bullets, numbered lists, and picture bullets. These are actually lists inside of lists; the entire sublist is part of the text for the item just above it. To begin a sublist:

1 Place the insertion point at the end of the bullet that will precede the first indented bullet.

2 Press Enter to create a new list item.

3 Click the Increase Indent icon on the Formatting toolbar twice. The first click creates a Normal style paragraph, and the second click creates a sublist bullet.

FIGURE 5-16.

Notice that each sublist is included within a parent list.

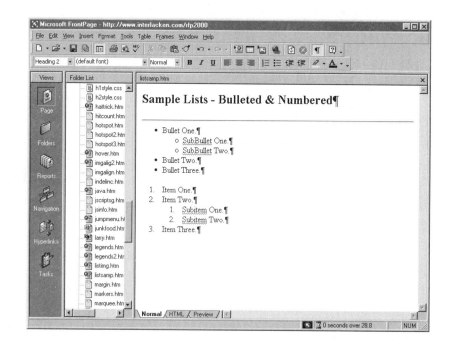

II

Creating Web Pages

⊗ CAUTION

You can't add multiple items to the end of a list without entering text as you go. Placing the insertion point at the end of the list and pressing Enter once will create a new item, but pressing Enter *again* will delete the newly created item and terminate the list.

To convert any item in a list to a normal paragraph, first select it and then click the Decrease Indent icon on the Formatting toolbar. More than one click might be necessary, depending on the original indentation. If you experiment with successive clicks of the Increase Indent and Decrease Indent buttons, you'll see that you can move from level to level, passing through a Normal style level in between list levels.

To continue adding new items at the current list level, simply press Enter at the end of each preceding item.

To change an existing list's overall style, right-click anywhere in the list and choose List Properties from the pop-up menu. Figure 5-17 shows the resulting dialog box.

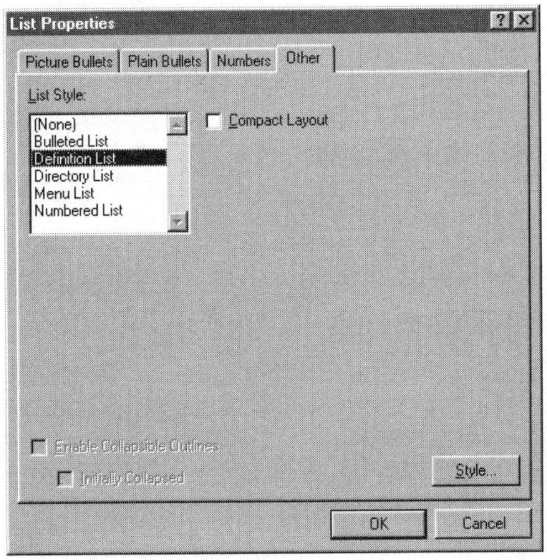

FIGURE 5-17.

The Other tab of the List Properties dialog box contains additional list choices.

- **List Style** changes the list's overall style.

- **Compact Layout** appears only for definition lists. Turning it on displays the definition on the same line as the defined term, provided the defined term is short enough not to overlap.

Creating Collapsible Lists

FrontPage can make multi-level lists *collapsible*. This means that sublists appear and disappear as the visitor clicks the next higher list item that contains them. Figure 5-18 provides an example. FrontPage, running in the back window, displays the collapsible list in its entirety. Internet Explorer, running in the front window, displays details only for entries the visitor has clicked.

FIGURE 5-18.

Collapsible lists expand and contract as the remote user clicks headings.

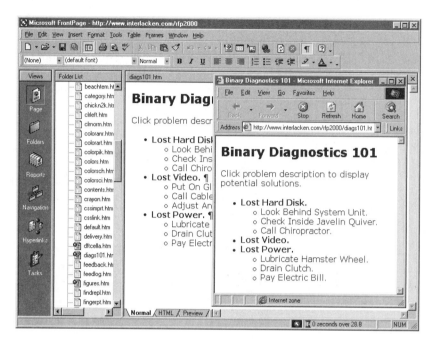

⊗ CAUTION

Collapsible lists don't collapse in Netscape Navigator, at least not through version 4. For Internet Explorer, they require at least version 4. This is because collapsible lists use Dynamic HTML (DHTML) features first introduced in Internet Explorer 4.

Two settings control the behavior of collapsible lists. For convenience, they appear on all four tabs of the List Properties dialog box.

- **Enable Collapsible Outlines,** if turned on, means that sublists should appear and disappear as the visitor clicks the list entry just above them. This check box appears only for lists in a multi-level structure.

- **Initially Collapsed,** if checked, means that the collapsible portion of a list will initially be hidden. Otherwise, it appears. This check box appears only for lists that contain other lists.

Using Other List Types

While the Other tab of the List Properties dialog box lists (among others) directory lists and menu lists, current browsers seem to display these identically to bulleted lists. Nevertheless, you can use this tab to assign the directory or menu list types to be used if the need arises. Bulleted lists are by far the most common of the three and therefore the most universally supported.

The Definition List option on the Other tab combines two HTML styles, Defined Term and Definition, to create a special type of list. The browser displays a Defined Term paragraph flush left followed by an indented Definition paragraph. Glance back at Figure 5-11 to see how the Definition appears in the middle window. To create a defined term and its definition:

1   Type the term you plan to define on its own line.

2   Select Defined Term from the Change Style list on the Formatting toolbar. The paragraph will format as a defined term.

3   Set the insertion point at the end of the Defined Term paragraph, and then press Enter. FrontPage will start a new line and apply the Definition style, indenting the new line.

4   Type the definition of the term.

5   Press Enter. FrontPage will start a new line and begin a new defined term so that you can type a list of terms and definitions without interruption.

6   When you're done with the entire definition list, terminate the list by pressing Enter twice at the end of the final definition line.

Formatting Text Fonts

Controlling fonts on Web pages presents unique difficulties. For one, there's no way of knowing what fonts or font technologies a given remote user will have available. For another, it's unlikely that all the same fonts will be available to any two remote users. Finally, even fonts that appear to be identical, down to their names, may have subtle differences when obtained from different vendors or even from the same vendor when used on different platforms.

The original HTML specification tried to avoid font confusion by avoiding fonts. That is, instead of providing a way to specify fonts by name, it provided ways to flag blocks of text by their structural use in the document. Responsibility for assigning specific fonts then fell to the user's browser.

SEE ALSO

For information on how to format small amounts of text as images, see "Adding Text to Images," page 190.

Some newer versions of HTML *do* support specific font-name assignments, as does FrontPage. However, just because FrontPage lets you specify font names such as DomCasual BT and Elephant doesn't mean those fonts are available to your Web visitors. If the remote system doesn't have a font with the name you specify, it will substitute another font—usually the default browser font, which, if not stylish, will at least be legible.

NOTE

Most browsers correctly substitute a local version of Arial, Helvetica, or Times Roman for any known variation of those names. Font substitution for less common names, however, can be problematic.

FrontPage provides seven font-related icons on the Formatting toolbar. Each icon applies an attribute to the currently selected text, or removes an attribute previously applied. See Table 5-4 (pages 125–126) for help in identifying buttons you're not already familiar with:

- **Font** applies a selected font name.

- **Font Size** increases or decreases font size.

- **Bold** toggles boldfacing on and off.

- **Italic** toggles italicizing on and off.

- **Underline** toggles underlining on and off.

- **Font Color** controls the color in which the browser displays text.

- **Highlight Color** controls a text area's background color.

TIP

You can also toggle boldfacing, italicizing, and underlining of selected words on and off by pressing Ctrl+B, Ctrl+I, and Ctrl+U, respectively.

TIP

Press Ctrl+Shift+> to increase font size of selected words, Ctrl+Shift+< to decrease it. Ctrl+Plus flags text as a superscript and Ctrl+Minus as a subscript.

Five Recommendations for Using Fonts on the Web

Consider these five commonsense suggestions for using font attributes effectively in your Web pages:

1 **Use fonts large enough to read.** Small print is for lawyers. If the verbiage isn't important enough to present legibly, omit it.

2 **Don't waste space with large fonts.** Large amounts of text in a large font slow down the reader and lead to excessive scrolling. In addition, they have far less impact than a pleasing and effective page design.

3 **Stick to mainstream fonts.** If remote users don't have the artistic font you want, their browser will probably substitute an ugly one.

4 **Avoid ransom notes.** Stick to a few well-chosen sizes and styles of type.

5 **Aim for contrast, not clash.** Achieve a pleasing contrast between background and text.

For maximum control of font settings, select the text you want to modify and then choose Font from the Format menu. The resulting dialog box contains the Font tab shown in Figure 5-19 and the Character Spacing tab shown in Figure 5-20.

You can obtain the same dialog box by right-clicking a block of text and choosing Font Properties on the pop-up menu.

FIGURE 5-19.
The Font tab of the Font dialog box provides controls similar to those of any word processor.

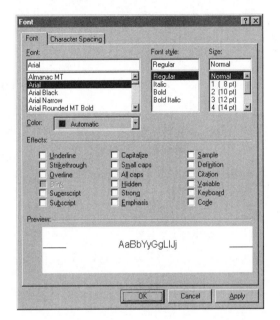

For more information on configuring Front-Page to reflect the capabilities of various browsers, see Chapter 14, "Customizing Your Copy of FrontPage."

SEE ALSO
To learn about applying fonts at the page or site-wide levels, see, "A Quick Course in Cascading Style Sheets," page 138.

The Font tab controls the following settings. Effects flagged (CSS) will appear only in browsers that support cascading style sheets; other browsers will ignore them.

- **Font** selects a specific font name.

- **Font Style** controls the following effects: regular, italic, bold, bold italic.

- **Size** specifies a code from 1 through 7, indicating the relative size of the font. The dialog box lists typical point-size equivalents for convenience, although these can vary by browser and system configuration.

- **Color** provides the usual FrontPage color dialog boxes, beginning with a drop-down list of 16 colors.

- **Underline** underlines text.

NOTE

> The underline setting has no effect on underlining of hyperlinks.

- **Strikethrough** draws a horizontal line through the selected text.

- **Overline** (CSS) draws a horizontal line above text.

- **Blink** flashes text. Web browsers that can't display blinking text will ignore this setting.

- **Superscript** reduces text in size and shifts its baseline upward, like an exponent.

- **Subscript** reduces text in size and shifts its baseline downward, like a footnote marker.

- **Capitalize** (CSS) displays the first letter of each word in upper-case, even if the actual text is lowercase.

- **Small Caps** (CSS) displays reduced-size capital letters in place of any lowercase letters in the actual text.

- **All Caps** (CSS) displays all letters in uppercase, even if the actual text is lowercase.

- **Hidden** (CSS) suppresses display of the selected text.

- **Strong** enhances text to convey a stronger meaning. Most browsers use boldface for this.

- **Emphasis** enhances text to convey extra emphasis. Most browsers use italics for this.

- **Sample** is a sequence of literal characters. This is similar to the typewriter font on the Font tab.

- **Definition.** A definition, typically in italics.

- **Citation** is a style designed to be assigned to a manual, section, or book, typically displayed in italics.

- **Variable.** A variable name, typically in italics.

- **Keyboard** indicates typing by a visitor, as when following a pro-cedure. This is usually similar to the typewriter font.

- **Code.** A code sample. This is usually similar to the typewriter font.

To preview the results of setting the various Font controls, see the Preview box.

The Character Spacing tab controls font settings that require a numeric value. Figure 5-20 shows this tab.

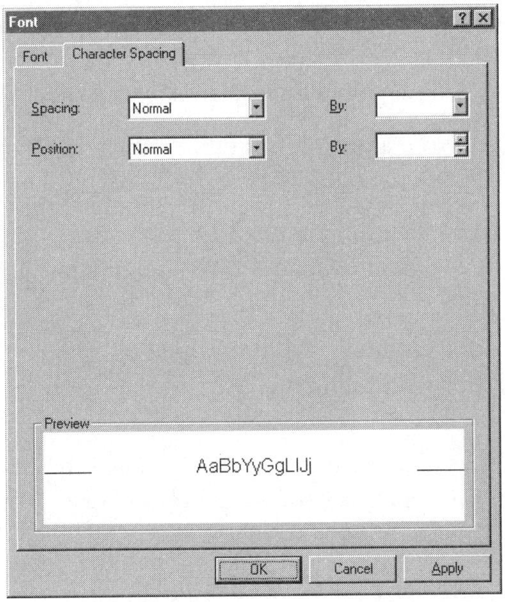

FIGURE 5-20.

The Character Spacing tab controls space between lines and character position relative to baseline.

■ **Spacing.** (CSS) Choose Expanded for extra space between letters, Condensed for less than normal space, or Normal for the default spacing.

■ **By.** Enter a CSS measurement for the amount of extra or lesser spacing you want.

⊘ **SEE ALSO**
To learn about valid CSS measurements, see "Specifying CSS Measurements," page 145.

■ **Position.** A style that sets text to Raised, Lowered, or Normal (the default).

■ **By.** In conjunction with Vertical Position, indicates the number of points by which the text should be raised or lowered from the baseline (the imaginary line on which letters such as *a, e,* and *o* rest).

To preview the results of setting Character Spacing controls, see the Preview box at the bottom of the dialog box.

Creating Web Pages

Aligning Text

HTML provides only four settings for aligning paragraph text: Default, Left, Center, and Right. There are three ways to apply these settings:

- Use the Align Left, Center, and Align Right icons on the Formatting toolbar, as described in Table 5-4 on pages 125–126. Once an alignment is in effect, its button will remain pressed in. To specify default alignment, no alignment button should be pressed in.

- Choose Paragraph from the Format menu, and set the Paragraph Alignment control. See Figure 5-12 on page 125.

- Right-click the paragraph, choose Paragraph Properties from the pop-up menu, and then set the Paragraph Alignment control.

TIP

> The following keystrokes also align text: Ctrl+R toggles right alignment; Ctrl+L toggles left alignment; Ctrl+E toggles centering.

As we'll learn in the next section, cascading style sheets provide the same four options, plus a justified text option that flush-aligns both margins, left and right.

A Quick Course in Cascading Style Sheets

Early versions of HTML had almost no provisions for controlling fonts, colors, indentations, line spacing, and other aspects of typography. Later versions added simple control over fonts and colors, but only for specifically marked blocks of text. Centralized control of typography for an entire page or site remained lacking.

CSS Basics

To provide full typographical control over Web pages, the World Wide Web Consortium adopted a technology called Cascading Style Sheets—CSS for short. Using CSS is generally a two-step process.

1 **Define a style.** A style is a list of typographical properties such as—in English—yellow 16-point Arial bold italic, blue background, and 1-pixel black border. Each different style has a name called a *selector*.

2 **Apply the style to one or more blocks of text.** Sometimes this is automatic and sometimes it requires explicit action on your part, depending on how you go about your work.

The natural language of CSS consists of lines of code—code from which all the WYSIWYG editors and dialog boxes in the world can't shield you completely. Wherever possible, this book will avoid showing code and display the relevant FrontPage dialog boxes instead, but here, while we're talking fundamentals, code it is. Trust me, though; it'll be simple.

First, some definitions:

- A *CSS style* is a collection of properties like font name, font size, font weight, color, background color, border type, border width, and so forth.

- A *CSS rule* is a statement that assigns properties to one or more styles. The following is a CSS rule that assigns two properties (font family and color) to two styles (H1 and H2).

  ```
  H1, H2 { font-family: Arial; color: red; }
  ```

Rules and styles are many-to-many. A single rule can apply to any number of styles, and a single style can be affected by any number of rules.

- A *selector* is the name of a CSS style. For now, we'll consider three types of selectors.

  - *Type selectors* have the same names as HTML tags: P for normal paragraphs, H1 for Heading 1, LI for list item, TD for table detail, and so forth.

    Assigning properties to a type selector modifies all text controlled by the corresponding HTML tag. The first rule below makes all text in table-heading cells italic; the second makes all bold text red.

    ```
    TH { font-style: italic; }
    B { color: red; }
    ```

  - *Class selectors* don't apply automatically to any part of a Web page; instead, you invoke the class selector by name anywhere you want it to apply. The first statement below defines a class called gonzo and the second applies it to one paragraph.

    ```
    .gonzo { color: white; background-color: black; }
    <p class=gonzo>This text will be white on
    black.</p>
    ```

    Note that the class selector begins with a period when you define it, but not when you reference it.

- *ID selectors* work somewhat like class selectors, except that the ID is the name of something in your Web page. Instead of naming a style and then invoking it from page elements, you name the page elements and then define styles for them. The second statement below gives a paragraph the name bruce, and the first statement makes its text bold.

```
#bruce { font-weight: bold; }
<p id=bruce>This text will be bold.</p>
```

You should never give two elements in the same page the same ID. This makes class selectors preferable for most uses. The pound sign prefix on the selector name tells CSS you're defining an ID selector.

ON THE WEB

For more information about the features and use of cascading style sheets, browse these locations.
Microsoft: http://www.microsoft.com/workshop/author/default.asp
World Wide Web Consortium: http://www.w3.org/Style/

CSS Browsers

Because CSS is a relatively new technology, not all browsers support it. CSS support first appeared in version 3 of Internet Explorer and version 4 of Netscape Navigator. Older browsers treat CSS information like they treat HTML tags they don't understand—they ignore them.

Even among browsers that do support CSS, levels of support and details of interpretation tend to differ. As always, the more important your page, the more important your testing, using a variety of browsers.

Lest you discard CSS as too complicated and too poorly supported, consider your only options for controlling typography:

- Make everything an image and suffer the download time.

- Use CSS and deal with browser differences.

- Forget typography and make believe Netscape Navigator 3 is the state of the art.

It's hard to believe CSS can never be the best of these solutions, not even in a percentage of cases.

Where to Put CSS Rules

There's one more point to make, and then we'll look at how to do all this in FrontPage. That point concerns where to put CSS rule statements, and there are three options.

- **Attached to a specific page element.** Recent versions of HTML have a STYLE attribute you use for assigning CSS properties to individual page elements. The HTML code looks like this:

```
<p style="text-transform: upper-case;"> This will
appear in uppercase.</p>
```

FrontPage attaches CSS properties to ordinary page elements in just this way whenever you use the Style button on an element's Properties dialog box.

- **In the <STYLE> section of a Web page.** HTML now includes a pair of special style tags that tell the browser everything between them consists of CSS rules. Most Web pages that use CSS have a single style section, located within the <HEAD> section of the Web page.

```
<HTML>
<HEAD>
<STYLE>
H1 { color: green; }
</STYLE>
</HEAD>
<BODY>
<H1>This heading will be green.</H1>
</BODY>
</HTML>
```

- To enter such rules through FrontPage dialog boxes, choose Style from the Format menu and use the Format button's pop-up menus to set properties.

- Type selectors take effect with no further action on your part.

- To apply class selectors, highlight the desired page element, then choose the selector name from the end of the Format toolbar's Change Style drop-down menu.

- To apply ID selectors, use HTML view to enter an ID= attribute inside the tag you want the rule to affect.

SEE ALSO

For more information on using one style-sheet file in multiple Web pages, see "Shared Cascading Style Sheets," page 160.

■ **In a file you can reference from multiple Web pages.** By putting CSS statements in their own file and then referencing that file in multiple Web pages, you can control the appearance of all those pages from one source. This ensures uniformity and makes it easy to fine-tune or revamp the appearance of an entire site.

CSS Syntax

The syntax—that is, the required format—of CSS statements is different from that of HTML. Note that in the following example:

```
H2, H3 { font-family: Arial, sans-serif; color: blue; }
```

■ The selectors are the first items on the line.

- If a comma is present, it means the properties in this rule apply to both selectors individually: in the example, to H2 and to H3.

- If two selectors are specified with no intervening comma, it means the properties in this rule apply only when *both* selectors are in effect. The following rule, for example, would apply only to H2 text that's also bold:

```
H2 B { color: red; }
```

■ Curly braces enclose the entire list of properties.

■ Each property consists of a property name, a colon, and then one or more values.

■ Commas separate multiple values for the same property.

■ A semicolon indicates the end of a property definition.

Cascading and Inheritance

Any browser that supports CSS starts out with a default set of styles based on built-in logic and whatever preferences the user has in effect. Any CSS rules found in Web pages then override, on a property-by-property basis, the default styles. If multiple rules apply to the same style, the overrides occur in the order they appear. This is part of the *cascading* idea in Cascading Style Sheets.

Another aspect of cascading is that some styles inherit properties from others. This is usually based on the type of HTML tag involved. When you assign a CSS property to a <UL> (Unnumbered List) or <OL> (Ordinal List, a.k.a. numbered list) tag, for example, any subordinate <LI> (List Item) paragraphs will *inherit* the same properties. The rules of inheritance vary somewhat among browsers, but this is still a very useful aspect of cascading.

Integrating CSS and FrontPage

? SEE ALSO

For more information about using HTML view, see Chapter 13, "Working Directly with Code."

Both CSS styles and the rules that define them are rather abstract entities, not particularly amenable to WYSIWYG display. To wrest every drop of function out of Cascading Style Sheets, therefore, you really need to click the HTML tab at the bottom of the Page View window and enter the rules by hand. As seems to be the way of art, the results may be beautiful but the techniques are messy.

FrontPage doesn't completely leave you in the lurch, however. By choosing Style from the Format menu, you'll display the Style dialog box in Figure 5-21, which creates, modifies, and deletes CSS rules at the page level.

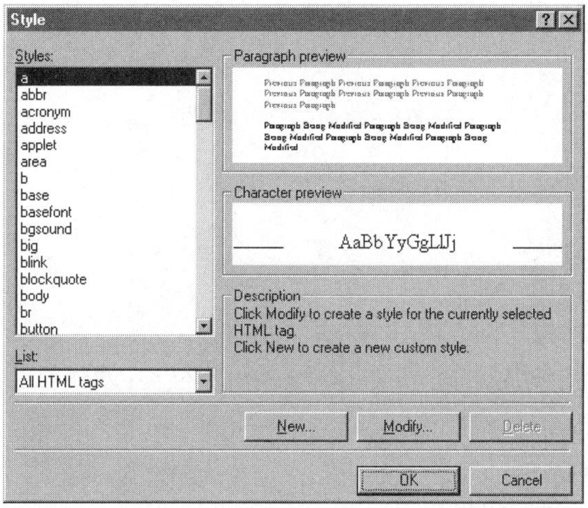

FIGURE 5-21.

From this dialog box, you create, modify, and delete CSS style rules for the current Web page.

When you first bring up the Style dialog box, the Styles list contains the names of all valid HTML tags, whether or not you already have rules defined for them. Note that by definition, this is also a list of valid type selectors.

The Styles list can also display a list of existing rules for the current page. To make this happen, select User-Defined Styles from the list box in the lower-left corner. As you select each rule, the Paragraph Preview box shows the effect of that rule's paragraph properties, the Character Preview box shows the result of its font properties, and the Description box describes its properties in text.

Here's how to create, modify, and delete rules, regardless of whether you've selected All HTML Tags or User-Defined Styles in the List control.

- To create a new CSS rule of any type, click the New button.

- To create or modify an existing rule, highlight its selector name in the Styles list and then click Modify.

- To delete an existing rule, select it in the Styles list then click Delete. However, this is only possible when the List control specifies User-Defined Styles. You can delete any style rules you've created, including those for type selectors, but you can't delete valid HTML tag names.

Clicking either the New button or the Modify button in Figure 5-21 produces the dialog box featured with no unusual fanfare in Figure 5-22. (Oh, OK. Ta-da.)

FIGURE 5-22.
This dialog box is the entry point for setting font, paragraph, border, and numbering properties for a selected CSS rule.

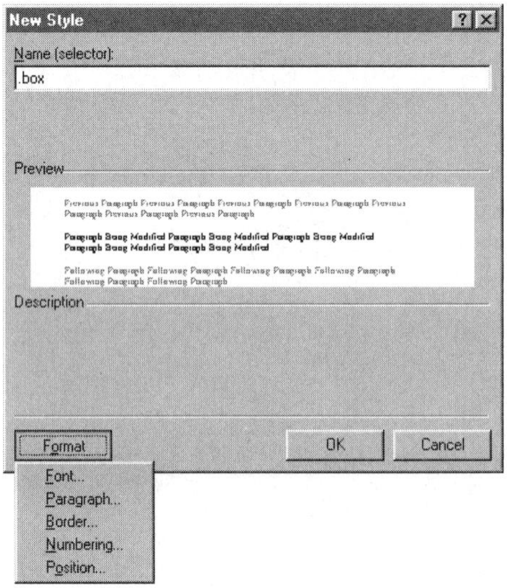

 TIP

FrontPage also displays the dialog box in Figure 5-22 when you click the Style button in various property dialog boxes. However, in such cases, any properties you specify apply only to the current element.

SEE ALSO
For more information about the fifth Modify Style Format choice—Positioning—refer to "Positioning Content with CSS," page 273.

If you selected an existing rule and clicked Modify, the Name (Selector) box will contain the selector name, the Preview area will show a typical paragraph formatted with the rule's current properties, and the Description area will show the same properties as text. To modify the CSS properties for this rule, click the Format button, then choose Font, Paragraph, Bullet, Number, or Position. Each of these five choices displays its own dialog box. We'll consider the last one in Chapter 8 and the first four after this brief announcement.

Specifying CSS Measurements

The values of many CSS properties involve measurements: the height of the characters, the width of a paragraph, the thickness of a border, whatever. The format for specifying these measurements consists of a number followed by a unit of measure, with no intervening spaces. Table 5-5 lists the valid units of measure, and here are some examples.

12pt	12 points
1.5in	$1^1/_2$ inches
7mm	7 millimeters
125%	25% larger than would otherwise be the case.

When possible, it's best to use relative measurements. That way, if the remote user's browser magnifies or shrinks the entire page, your elements retain the correct relative proportions. The same is true when you resize an element's parent and expect subordinate items to scale proportionately.

If you can't use relative measurements, the device-dependent *pixel* measurement should be your second choice. This at least maintains proportion to any images on your page, which the browser always sizes in terms of pixels. In addition, it avoids difficult-to-resolve situations involving odd pixel sizes (for example, trying to display a font 7.5 pixels high).

TABLE 5-5. Cascading Style Sheet Units of Measure

Type	Unit	Name	Description
Absolute	mm	Millimeter	25.4 millimeters equal one inch.
	cm	Centimeter	1 centimeter equals 10 millimeters.
	in	Inch	1 inch equals 25.4 millimeters.
	pt	Point	72 points equals one inch.
	pc	Pica	1 pica equals 12 points. 6 picas equals 1 inch.
Relative	%	Percent	Indicates a degree of magnification compared to the item's normal size. For example, 200% means twice normal size and 50% means half normal size.
	em	Em	1 em equals the point size of the current font.
	ex	Ex	1 ex equals the x-height of the current font. The x-height is the height of the lowercase x character.
Device-Dependent	px	Pixel	1 pixel equals the smallest unit of resolution on the user's display screen.

The main problem with absolute measurements, such as 1in, lies in not knowing what the remote user's computer thinks an inch is. Most video drivers interpret one inch as 72 pixels, so that one point equals one pixel. This convention is far from universal, though, and still subject to the remote user's monitor size and video setting.

The meaning of percentage measurements varies with the type of object. For most types, it's a percentage of the measurement the object would otherwise inherit. For example, a paragraph width of 80% would make the paragraph 80% as wide as it otherwise would be. The following are typical exceptions to this rule:

- For colors, the range 0% to 100% corresponds to the normal RGB values 0 through 255.

- For line height, the percentage value is applied to the surrounding text's point size.

In the context of CSS, an em is a unit of distance equal to the point size of text. Thus, within 12-point text, one em equals 12 points—1/6 inch. The advantage of using ems as a unit of measure is that your other measurements change proportionately when the point size changes.

To specify colors, you can choose from five different measurement schemes:

- **By name.** You can specify colors using the names from Table 4-4, "Web Names for the 16 Original VGA Colors." For example:

  ```
  { color: red ; }
  ```

- **By hexadecimal 12-bit color value.** To specify red, green, and blue colors on a hexadecimal scale from 0 to F, specify three hex digits preceded by a pound sign. For example:

  ```
  { color: #F00 ; }
  ```

- **By hexadecimal 24-bit color value.** Specifying hex digits preceded by a pound sign, six digits control red, green, and blue intensities, each on a scale from 00 to FF. For example:

  ```
  { color: #FF0000 ; }
  ```

- **By decimal 24-bit color value.** To specify red, green, and blue color values on a scale from 0 to 255, use this notation:

  ```
  { color: rgb(255,0,0); }
  ```

- **By percentage color value.** To specify red, green, and blue color values as percentages of maximum intensity, use this notation:

  ```
  { color: rgb(100%,0%,0%); }
  ```

TIP

Remember to specify browser-safe colors wherever possible. The required RGB components for the various notations are:

12-bit: 0, 3, 6, 9, C and F.

24-bit: 00, 33, 66, 99, CC and FF.

Decimal: 0, 51, 102, 153, 204, 255.

Assigning CSS Properties

SEE ALSO
For more information about the fifth Modify Style Format choice—Positioning—refer to "Positioning Content with CSS," page 273.

Recalling Figure 5-22, clicking the Style dialog box's Format button displays a pop-up menu with five categories of CSS properties. The following topics describe the dialog boxes corresponding to the first four.

Assigning CSS Fonts

The dialog box for assigning CSS fonts appears in Figure 5-23. If this looks hauntingly familiar, you're right; it contains everything that Figure 5-19 contained. The difference is that here, you're configuring an abstract style and not a specific Web-page element.

FIGURE 5-23.
This dialog box specifies fonts and related properties for a CSS style.

```
Font                                                        ? X
 Font   Character Spacing

 Font:                          Font style:       Size:
 (Default Font)                 Regular

 (Default Font)                 Regular           10 px
 Abadi MT Condensed Extra Bold  Italic            .5 in
 Abadi MT Condensed Light       Bold              2 mm
 Algerian                       Bold Italic       1 em
 Almanac MT                                       8 pt

 Color:      ■ Automatic

 Effects:
   □ Underline         □ Capitalize
   □ Strikethrough     □ Small caps
   □ Overline          □ All caps
   □ Blink             □ Hidden

 Preview:
                      AaBbYyGgLlJj

                                          OK        Cancel
```

Table 5-6 associates the fields in this dialog box with the CSS properties they control, describes what they do, and itemizes the acceptable values. The same table also lists related CSS properties not accessible through FrontPage dialog boxes, just in case you're bold enough (sorry) to engage HTML view and modify your style rules directly.

TABLE 5-6. CSS Font Properties

Dialog Box Field	CSS Property Name	Description and Values
Font	font-family	A list of font names available on the local system.
Font Style	font-style	Can be *normal*, *italic*, or *oblique*. 　Normal text is upright. 　Italic text is slanted, thinned, and more curved. 　Oblique text is slanted but otherwise resembles normal.
	font-weight	The thickness of the strokes making up a font. Values include: 　A numeric weight from 100 to 900. 　The keywords *normal* (=400) or *bold* (=700). 　The keywords *bolder* or *lighter*, which thicken or weaken strokes compared to the object's parent.
Size	font-size	The height of a font, measured from the top of the tallest character to the bottom of the lowest. Any CSS unit of measure is acceptable.
Small Caps	font-variant	Normal or small-caps. The value *small-caps* replaces lowercase letters with reduced-size capital letters.
(none)	font	This is a shortcut property that accepts any of the values described above. CSS assigns each value to the correct property based on the value's syntax.
Color	color	The color in which text should appear. FrontPage controls this using its standard sequence of color dialog boxes.
Underline Strikethrough Overline Blink	text-decoration	Controls the following modifications to normal text: *underline*, *overline*, *strikethrough*, and *blink*. The default is *none*.
Capitalize All Caps	text-transform	Presents text in a certain case, regardless of how it was entered. The options are: 　*capitalize* (first letter only, all others lowercase). 　*uppercase* (all uppercase). 　*lowercase* (all lowercase). 　*none* (as is, the default).
Hidden	visibility	Values of *hidden* (Internet Explorer) or *hide* (Netscape) make an element invisible. Values of *visible* (Internet Explorer) or *show* (Netscape) make it visible.

Specifying Fonts

No matter what font name you assign to a Cascading Style Sheet property, there's no assurance the remote user has that font available. If the specified font *isn't* available, the Web visitor's browser does its best to pick another font that's similar, but this is far from an exact science. After all, if the visitor's system doesn't have a font like Glouster MT Extra Condensed installed, how's it supposed to know enough about it to pick something similar?

There are three solutions to this problem:

■ **Specify only commonly available fonts.** Fonts that come with Windows, fonts that come with Microsoft Office, and fonts installed with the user's browser are probably available to the vast majority of your Web visitors. Stick to these fonts.

■ **Specify generic fonts.** The following font names have reasonable equivalents on every user's system.

serif	The system-default serif font, such as Times New Roman or Times Roman.
sans-serif	The system-default sans-serif font, such as Arial or Helvetica.
cursive	A font that looks like handwriting.
fantasy	A highly decorative font.
monospace	The system-default monospaced font, such as Courier New or Courier.

It's true that the cursive and fantasy generic fonts still leave you wondering what you're going to get, but the serif, sans-serif, and monospace choices are reasonably specific and highly useful.

■ **Specify multiple fonts.** The font-family property can accept a list of fonts the browser should use, in order of preference. In code, it looks like this:

```
H1 { font-family: Verdana, Arial, Helvetica, sans-serif; }
```

This code makes the browser look first to see if the Verdana font is available, then Arial, then Helvetica, then any sans-serif font. This virtually guarantees that what the remote user sees will conform to your original design.

II

Creating Web Pages

Small Caps

Using normal 12-point characters for capitals and substituting, say, 9-point capitals for lowercase doesn't produce completely satisfactory results because 9-point capitals have thinner strokes than 12-point characters of either case. A true small-caps font has equal-stroke thickness for both the large and small capitals.

Character Spacing

The second tab of the CSS Font dialog box appears in Figure 5-24. Table 5-7 details the corresponding CSS properties.

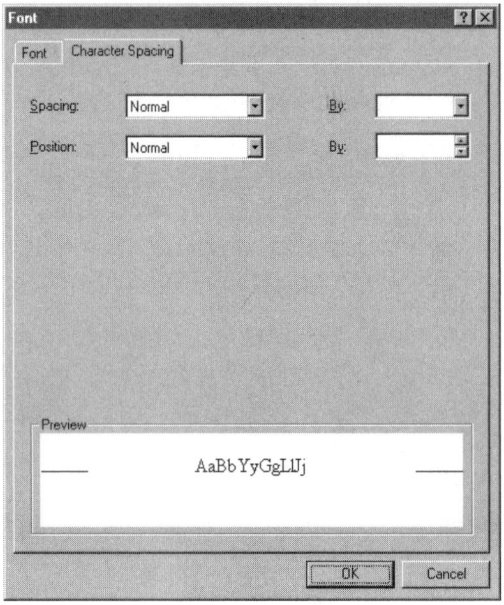

FIGURE 5-24.

This is the second tab of the dialog box from Figure 5-23. It controls letter spacing and vertical positioning.

TABLE 5-7. CSS Letter Spacing and Positioning Properties

Dialog Box Field	CSS Property Name	Description and Values
Spacing	letter-spacing	Expands or tightens the spacing between letters. The default measurement is in pixels.
Position	vertical-align	A positive measurement raises the object that amount above its normal position. A negative measurement lowers it below. See the accompanying text for more options.

Downloadable Fonts—CSS Nirvana

Cascading Style Sheets provide tremendous flexibility for specifying and controlling fonts. Unfortunately, just putting font names in your Web pages doesn't ensure that Web visitors will have those fonts installed on their systems.

The Web desperately needs a way for Web designers to put font files on their Web sites, and for visitors to download them as needed. Designers could stop converting text to graphics, download times would decrease, and Web visitors would see pages as their designers intended. The only losers would be the font companies, who prefer the current system of selling fonts over any new system involving free downloads.

Someday, we hope, we'll have a generally accepted way to download font files just as we do images today. Until then, keep an eye on the following Web locations:

- *http://www.microsoft.com/opentype* is Microsoft's home page for Web typography. OpenType is a joint initiative of Microsoft and Adobe that will produce a single, downloadable font format usable with both Post-Script and TrueType systems.

  From here you can also obtain Microsoft's Web Embedding Fonts Tool (WEFT), which prepares compressed, downloadable font files for an entire Web site.

- *http://www.truedoc.com/* is the home page for TrueDoc, an invention of the digital type house Bitstream Inc. Web designers convert font files on their own systems into TrueDoc files (a process called *burning*) and put the TrueDoc files on their Web sites. Remote browsers download the TrueDoc files and use them to display pages from that site.

  Whenever you create a TrueDoc font file, you have to specify either a site name (like www.whatever.com) or a path (like /~whoever/). This makes the TrueDoc file unusable on any other site or path. Bitstream added this restriction so each Web site has to buy any fonts they use. Unfortunately, if a user visits several sites that deliver the same font via TrueDoc, they'll have to download the font multiple times.

  Bitstream provides a number of free TrueDoc fonts—free, that is, if you don't mind coding Bitstream's site as your font location. Their site also provides an ActiveX control that adds TrueDoc functionality to Internet Explorer.

- *http://www.hexmac.com* is the home location for Typograph, a utility that converts fonts on your system to TrueDoc format. (Be aware, however, that not all fonts have licenses that permit this.)

Position (vertical-align)

This property specifies the alignment of an in-line object relative to the surrounding text. The permissible values are the following:

- *baseline*. The baseline of the child (surrounded) object aligns with the baseline of the parent (surrounding) text.

> **NOTE**
>
> The baseline is the imaginary straight line on which letters in a line of text rest. (The lowercase descenders of letters such as *j* and *g* extend *below* the baseline.)

- *sub*. The baseline of the child object aligns with the parent's preferred baseline for subscripts.

- *super*. The baseline of the child object aligns with the parent's preferred baseline for superscripts.

- *text-top*. The top of the child object aligns with the top of the surrounding text.

- *middle*. The object's vertical midpoint aligns with the parent's baseline raised by one-half the x-height (the height of a lowercase letter with no ascenders or descenders, such as a, e, o, and, well, x). That is, the midpoint of the object would align with the midpoint of such letters as a, e, o, or x in the surrounding text.

- *text-bottom*. The bottom of the child object aligns with the bottom of the parent.

- *percentage*. This value adjusts the child's position by a fraction of the parent's line height. 50% raises the child object half a line.

- *quantity*. This value adjusts the child's position by any CSS measurement. This is the only approach supported through the Position setting in Figure 5-24.

Assigning CSS Paragraph Properties

Cascading style sheets provide amazing control over the layout of paragraphs. The CSS Paragraph dialog box, which appears in Figure 5-25, provides access to some of these, and the Border and Numbering dialog boxes, discussed later in this chapter, provide even more.

Table 5-8 correlates the fields in the FrontPage Paragraph dialog box with the CSS properties they control, and then describes those properties.

The following sections provide additional information about line height and margins.

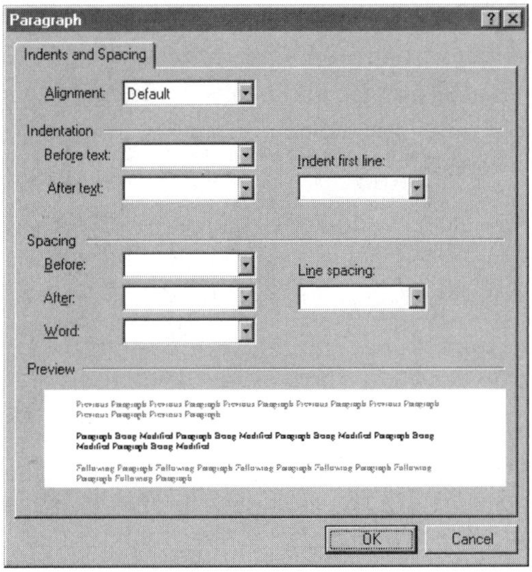

FIGURE 5-25.

The Paragraph dialog box controls paragraph alignment, indentation, and spacing.

TABLE 5-8. CSS Paragraph Properties

Dialog Box Field	CSS Property Name	Description and Values
Alignment	text-align	Controls the horizontal position of text. *left*-aligns text to the left margin (left-aligned, flush-left). *right* aligns text to the right margin (right-aligned, flush-right). *center* aligns the center of each line with the center of the available area. *justify* aligns text to both the left and right margins, spreading the required space as evenly as possible between words in the line.
Indent First Line	text-indent	Specifies first-line paragraph indentation. Negative numbers produce outdents (where the first line extends to the left of second and subsequent lines).
Indent Before Text Indentation After Text Spacing Before Spacing After	margin-left margin-right margin-top margin-bottom	These four properties control the amount of blank space that surrounds a page element's border (or where the border would be, if its thickness weren't zero).
Spacing Word	word-spacing	Adjusts the normal spacing between words. Positive measurements increase spacing and negative values decrease it.
Line Spacing	line-height	Specifies the amount of vertical space reserved for a line. A common value is the font size times 1.2.

II

Creating Web Pages

Line Height

This property controls the height of lines in a paragraph. FrontPage suggests measurements in pixels, but the CSS standard also provides for specifying a percentage or ratio of font size (for example, either 120% or 1.2).

When you specify the line-height property (or most other text measurements) as a percentage, other objects will inherit not the percentage itself, but the result of multiplying. Consider the following example:

```
{ font-size: 12pt ; line-height: 120% ; }
fineprint { font-size: 10pt ; }
```

The default style's line-height property will be 120%x12 points = 14.4 points. Because the default style's line height is a percentage, the fine print class inherits the multiplied result—14.4 points—as its line height.

```
{ font-size: 12pt ; line-height: 1.2 ; }
fineprint { font-size: 10pt ; }
```

In the second example, the default style's line height would again be 14.4 points—1.2x12 points. Because the default style's line height is a ratio, the fineprint class inherits the ratio and recalculates the effective line height as 1.2x10 points = 12 points. This will result in a more attractive display of 10-point text.

Margins

These four settings control the amount of white space reserved around the borders of an element, plus a small buffer zone, called *padding*. Figure 5-26 illustrates the concept not only of margins, but also of padding, a related concept.

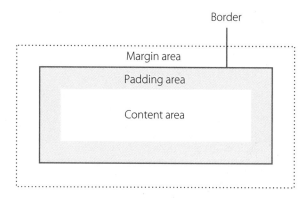

FIGURE 5-26.

Padding surrounds a Web page object and matches its background. Margins surround the padding and match the exterior background. Borders, if specified, appear where the two meet.

■ The *content area* is the space where an image would appear, where text could appear, the space occupied by a table, and so forth, depending on the kind of content.

- *Padding* surrounds the content area, matching its background color and certain other properties.

- If there's a visible *border*, it surrounds the padding area and not just the content area.

- *Margins* surround the padding area and borders, if there are any. Unlike padding—which matches the background of what it contains—margins match the background of whatever surrounds them.

You can specify margin width, border width, and padding width in terms of any CSS measurement. The most common, however, is pixels.

Assigning CSS Borders

Figure 5-27 illustrates the Border tab of the CSS Borders And Shading dialog box. This appears after selecting Border from the Format pop-up menu in Figure 5-22 on page 144.

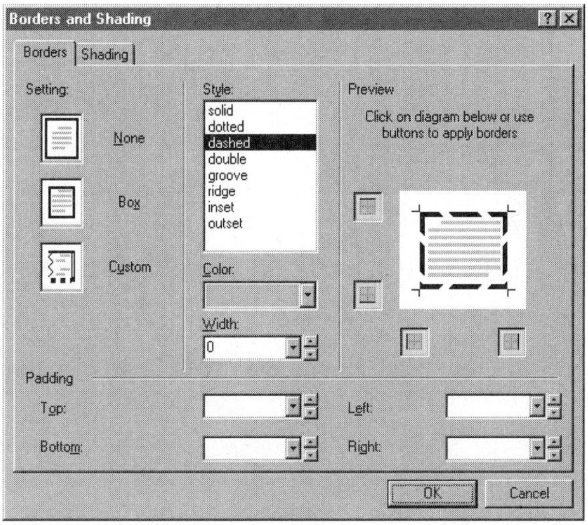

FIGURE 5-27.

The Borders tab controls the visible border around Web page elements, as well as the amount of padding between the border and the page element's contents.

To operate this dialog box:

1 Double-click one of the Setting choices:

- **None** means you don't want any borders. If this is your choice, ignore the remaining steps.

- **Box** means you want borders on all four sides.

- **Custom** means you want borders on one, two, or three sides.

2 Choose the border style you want from the Style list. The Preview area will reflect your choice.

3 Use the Color drop-down menu to specify what color the border should be.

4 Use the Width box to specify how thick the border should be.

5 If you chose Custom (or just changed your mind), click the four icons at the left of and below the preview diagram. Each icon applies or removes borders to a different side—top, bottom, left, or right.

The Padding section is only marginally related to the parts of the dialog box described so far. OK, sorry. Do you recall from the previous section that margin measurements control the amount of space between an element's surrounding and its border? Well, padding controls the amount of space between the border and the element's regular content. Refer again to Figure 5-26 if a picture would clarify this.

Table 5-9 correlates each Border tab setting with the CSS properties it controls.

If you're working with CSS rules by hand, it is often useful to use the *border* and *padding* property names rather than the more detailed properties shown in Table 5-8 and Table 5-9. For example, it's perfectly OK to code:

```
.special { border: 2px solid #900 ; }
```

rather than:

```
.special { border-width: 2px; border-style: solid;
border-color: #900; }
```

The order of any values you specify as border properties isn't important. CSS can figure out that measurements must be border widths, style names must be style values, and color values must be border colors.

In the case of border width and padding width, you can specify anywhere from one to four values. Table 5-10 shows which values control which measurements, depending on the number of values you supply.

The second tab on the Borders And Shading dialog box is—you guessed it and won the bet—Shading. This tab figures prominently in, and in fact virtually dominates, Figure 5-28.

Table 5-11 relates the controls on the Shading tab with their corresponding CSS properties and values.

TABLE 5-9. CSS Border Properties

Dialog Box Field	CSS Property Name	Description and Values
Style	border-style	Specify the type of line used to draw the border—none, solid, dotted, double, and so on.
Color	border-color	Indicate the color you want the border line to be.
Width	border-width	Specify the thickness of the borders. You can specify width using generic values of *thick*, *medium*, or *thin*, or as a specific number of pixels. As before, additional units of measure are supported by the CSS specification.
Preview buttons	border-top border-right border-bottom border-left	These four properties control the type of border drawn on each side of a Web page element. Accepted values are those listed in the Style box in Figure 5-27, plus *none*.
(none)	border-top-width border-right-width border-bottom-width border-left-width	These four properties specify the width of each border side independently. If all four sides should be the same width, it's much easier to use the *border-width* property.
Padding Top Padding Bottom Padding Left Padding Right	padding-top padding-bottom padding-left padding-right	These four settings control the amount of white space reserved between a page element's border and its content.

TABLE 5-10. Use of CSS *border width* and *padding width* Property Values

Number of Values Specified	Top	Source of Value For:		
		Right	Bottom	Left
1	1st	1st	1st	1st
2	1st	2nd	1st	2nd
3	1st	2nd	3rd	2nd
4	1st	2nd	3rd	4th

FIGURE 5-28.
The Shading tab controls the foreground color and background appearance of styled elements on your Web page.

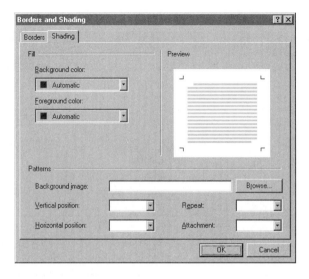

Assigning CSS Numbering

The fourth pop-up menu choice in Figure 5-22 is really a misnomer; the menu says Numbering but the dialog box controls unnumbered bullets as well. Oh well, at least the resulting dialog box is titled Bullets And Numbering, as you can see in Figure 5-29.

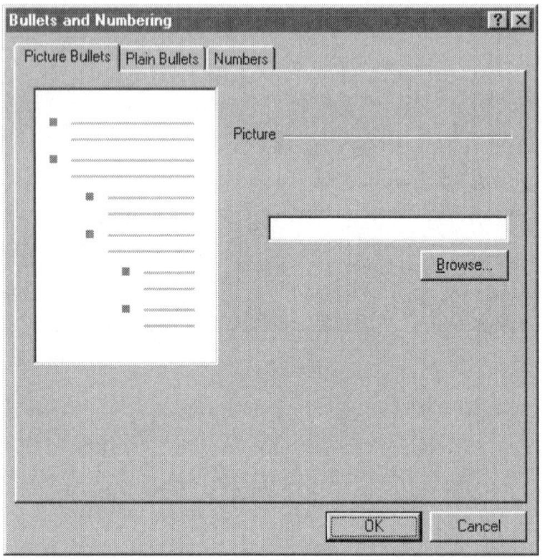

FIGURE 5-29.
Use this dialog box to specify what kind of bullets or numbers should appear for a bulleted or numbered list.

The three tabs are very simple and very much alike:

- The **Picture Bullets** tab provides a text box and accompanying browse button. Together, these specify a picture the browser will use for a bulleted list. This can be any picture the browser can display, though caution suggests a small one.

- The **Plain Bullets** tab displays four ordinary bullet styles: none, solid round, hollow round, and solid square. Click the style you want, and then click OK.

- The **Numbers** tab displays six numbering styles: none, Arabic numerals, upper-case roman numerals, uppercase letters, lower-case letters, and lowercase roman numerals. Click the style you want, change the starting number if needed, and click OK.

The Bullets And Numbering dialog box has the least direct correlation to CSS styles. Nevertheless, Table 5-12 lists the applicable CSS properties.

TABLE 5-11.   CSS Shading Properties

Dialog Box Field	CSS Property Name	Description and Values
Background Color	background-color	Specifies the default color used for filling the background of an element.
Foreground Color	color	Specifies the color used for presenting an object's contents. For many elements, this is the color in which text will appear.
Background Image	background-image	Specifies an image that will fill the background of an element.
Vertical Position Horizontal Position	background-position	Controls positioning of the first (or only) background image. These can be: The keywords *top*, *bottom*, *center*, *left*, and/or *right*, interpreted within the space the page element occupies. Percentages, again interpreted within the page element space. *0% 0%* means *top left*; *100% 100%* means *bottom right*. Any valid CSS measurement, interpreted from the element's top left corner.
Repeat	background-repeat	Controls the repetitive tiling of a background image. *repeat* repeats the background image both vertically and horizontally to fill the entire available area. *repeat-x* repeats the image horizontally only. *repeat-y* repeats the image vertically only. *no-repeat* displays the image only once and doesn't repeat it.
Attachment	background-attachment	Scrolls the background image or keeps it fixed. *scroll* moves the background image along with other content. This is the default. *fixed* keeps the background image stationary, even when other content scrolls.

Assigning Additional CSS Properties

Table 5-13 lists some additional CSS properties that don't appear in any of the FrontPage dialog boxes presented so far. These may be useful if you end up being a CSS fanatic and coding rules by hand in HTML view.

Shared Cascading Style Sheets

CSS provides two ways for groups of Web pages to share one set of styles. The first method requires placing a line such as the following in the Head section of each page that will use the shared styles, where *sharecss.css* is the URL of a master document containing the desired styles.

```
<link rel="StyleSheet" href="sharecss.css"
type="text/css">
```

To insert this statement, select the HTML tab in FrontPage. Place this line on a new line immediately after the *<head>* tag. The file sharecss.css must contain only CSS statements.

This method is subject to two restrictions: you can include only one such statement in a file, and you can't specify any other CSS styles in the same document. If you violate either rule, the browser is supposed to ask which set of styles to use. In fact, there seems to be little uniformity in the way this feature is implemented.

The second method involves adding @import statements to a normal style sheet. For example:

```
<STYLE type="text/css">
 @import "stylecss.css";
 H1 { font-style: Arial, sans-serif; }
</STYLE>
```

This method avoids the restrictions present in the Link statement, but support for it is even less consistent.

FrontPage provides a way to link style sheets to one or more pages in a FrontPage Web, without looking at any lines of code. Here's the procedure.

1 Create a file containing the CSS rules you want, then save it in your FrontPage Web with a ".css" extension.

⭐ **TIP**

> To create a style-sheet file, select Page view, choose New Page from the File menu, then click the Style Sheets tab. FrontPage displays such files as code, but you can still choose Style from the Format menu and make changes using dialog boxes.

TABLE 5-12. CSS Shading Properties

Dialog Box Field	CSS Property Name	Description and Values
Bullet Samples	list-style-type	Specifies the type of list bullet. Permissible values are *disc, circle, square, decimal, lower-roman, upper-roman, lower-alpha, upper-alpha,* and *none.*
Picture	list-style-image	Specifies the URL of an image the browser will display as a list bullet.
(none)	list-style-position	Specifies where the list bullet should appear: *inside* or *outside* the list box. The default is *outside.*
(all)	list-style	A short-cut property that accepts any combination of values described above. CSS assigns the value to the correct property based on syntax.

TABLE 5-13. CSS Properties Not Supported in CSS Dialog Boxes

CSS Property Field	Description and Values
width	The desired width of an element, using any valid CSS measurement.
height	The desired height of an element, using any valid CSS measurement.
float	Specifies an object's alignment: *left, center,* or *right.* Text will flow around left-aligned or right-aligned objects, but not around centered ones. If the property is blank, the object either flows in-line with text or is left-aligned with text not flowing around it, depending on the type of object.
clear	Specifies that an element should be positioned far enough down the page that it clears any left-aligned elements, right-aligned elements, or both. Permissible values are *none* (the default), *left, right,* and *both.*
display	Controls how an element is displayed. *block* means the element starts on a new line, like a paragraph or heading. *inline* means the element flows within a line, as occurs with bold or italic text. *list-item* means the element will appear as an indented box with a preceding label, like a bulleted or numbered list. *none* means the element will not appear.
white-space	Controls the treatment of spaces, tabs, line feeds, and carriage returns. *normal* treats all strings of such characters as if they were a single-space character. *pre* leaves all such characters in place. *nowrap* compresses white space characters like *normal,* but doesn't break lines wider than the browser window.

II

Creating Web Pages

2 If you only want to affect certain files in your Web, select them. This will probably be easiest in Folder view.

3 Choose Style Sheet Links from the Format menu. The foreground dialog box of Figure 5-30 will appear.

FIGURE 5-30.

This dialog box applies a CSS style-sheet file to one or more pages in a FrontPage Web.

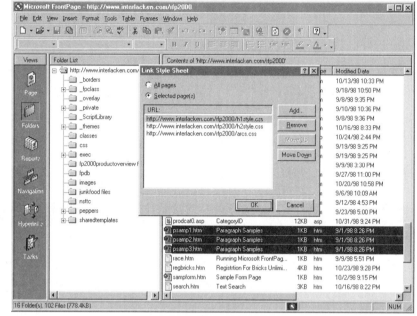

ⓧ CAUTION

If the current FrontPage Web resides on a Web server location (that is, if the top of your Folder List shows an http:// location) the Link Style-sheets dialog box will fail unless that Web server is running the FrontPage 2000 Server Extensions. Earlier versions of the Extensions can't insert style-sheet links based on commands from the FrontPage client.

4 To apply a stylesheet to every page in your Web, select All Pages. To apply it only to the pages you selected in step 2, click Selected Pages.

5 If the style-sheet file you want to apply is already listed, select it. If it isn't, click the Add button to locate the file and add it to the list.

6 Click OK.

Creating Web Documents with Word 2000

Microsoft Word 2000 has several new features that greatly enhance its ability to open and publish files from and to the Web.

■ Like FrontPage, Word's File Open dialog boxes can access not only files on the local hard disk or file server but also, like a browser, files on the World Wide Web.

■ Also like FrontPage, Word 2000 can save files directly to any Web server running the FrontPage Server Extensions (subject, of course, to security restrictions).

■ Word 2000's translation to and from HTML is considerably enhanced, compared to previous versions. Word makes full use of both HTML and CSS to produce the most accurate document rendition possible.

■ Word 2000 uses XML to save any document information not relevant to HTML or CSS. This means Word can save files as HTML and reopen them with all features and codes intact, just as if Word has saved and reopened the document in its native ".doc" file format.

Figure 5-31 shows Word 2000 saving a reasonably complex document directly to a FrontPage Web. The user followed this procedure:

1 Choose Save As Web Page from the Word 2000 File menu.

2 Click the Web Folders icon on the Save As dialog box.

3 Double-click the desired Web server from the list provided

   or

   If the correct server isn't listed, hand-enter the http:// location in the File Name box, then click the Save button.

FIGURE 5-31.
Microsoft Word 2000 can save documents both in native HTML format and directly to a Web server that has the FrontPage Server Extensions installed.

NOTE

Completing a Save or Open operation adds the Web server to the Web Folders list.

4 Unless you want to save the Word document in the Web server's root folder, double-click your way to the FrontPage Web or folder where the document should reside.

5 Click Save.

Although Word 2000 does its best to save every detail of document formatting in the HTML, it may need to make a few compromises. If so, it warns you with a dialog box like the one in Figure 5-32.

FIGURE 5-32.

Word 2000 warns you if any document formatting will be lost in saving documents as HTML.

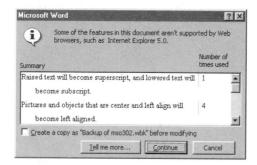

Once the Save operation is complete, you can immediately see the results in FrontPage. Figure 5-33 shows the Word 2000 document saved above open in FrontPage.

There are two things to note about Figure 5-33.

- First, FrontPage isn't Microsoft Word and doesn't achieve the same WYSIWYG display, at least not for Word documents.

- Second, notice the presence of an *fp2000productoverview_files* folder in Page view's folder list. This is where Word 2000 puts all the GIF, JPEG, and other files needed to display the *fp2000productoverview.btm* file correctly.

 If you have Word, save a Web page to your local disk, and later upload the page manually to the Web server; you'll need to upload the *fp2000productoverview_files* folder (and all its contents) as well as the *fp2000productoverview.btm* file. Saving directly to a Web folder accomplishes everything in one step.

Figure 5-34 shows the Product Overview page open in Internet Explorer. As you can see, resemblance to the original document is excellent.

FIGURE 5-33.

FrontPage can open documents saved by Word 2000, just as it can any other HTML file. The *fp2000product-overview files* folder contains images and other files needed to render the *fp2000-productoverview.htm* file correctly.

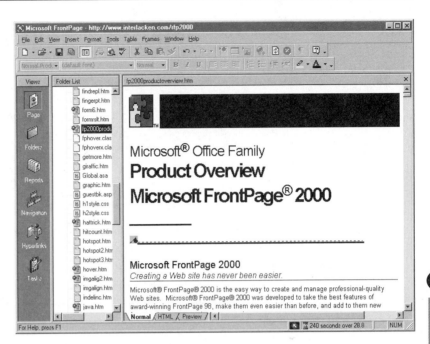

FIGURE 5-34.

Internet Explorer displays Word 2000 documents saved as Web pages with excellent results.

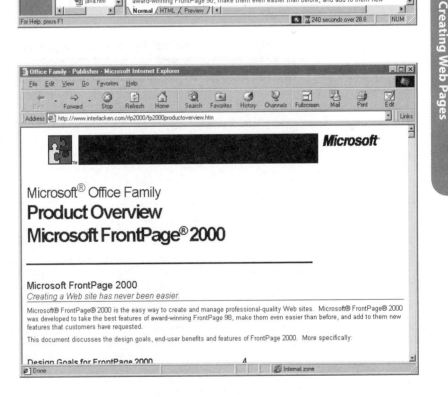

Creating Web Pages

XML—HTML on Steroids?

No, not really. Hype about Extensible Markup Language (XML) has greatly exceeded hard information, leading to widespread misinterpretation and speculation about the nature of XML and what it can do.

In fact, XML consists of tags that can describe the data in any sort of document including, of course, Web pages. For example, here's a piece of XML code that identifies a document as being from Microsoft Office or, more specifically, from Microsoft Word.

```
<xml:namespace ns="urn:schemas-microsoft-
com:office/word" prefix="w"/>
```

To an ordinary browser, XML simply looks like an unknown tag, and the browser ignores it. If the browser—or, for that matter, any other program—understands the XML tags, it can use the XML information for whatever purposes the application requires.

TABLE 5-14.   Print vs. Web Media Comparison

Characteristic	Print	World Wide Web
Delivery	Slow and physical	Immediate and electronic
Organization	Sequential	Hierarchical
Packaging	One cohesive document	Many disjointed pages
Timeliness	Limited by publication and distribution cycle	Up to the second
Response time (next page)	Instantaneous	15-30 seconds, depending on download speed
Typography	High resolution High control Unlimited use of fonts	Low resolution Limited control Limited use of fonts
Images	High resolution Frequently monochrome	Low resolution Usually color
Multimedia	None	Sound, video, animation
User participation	Passive	Interactive

If you're wondering whether to create a new document in Word or in FrontPage, consider Table 5-14. If your document's properties align best with the Print column, choose Microsoft Word. If they align more closely with the World Wide Web column, choose FrontPage. Whichever medium you pick as your primary, consider portability to the other a bonus.

Design Tips—Typography

Typography is the umbrella term for the use of typefaces, a fundamental tool of graphic design, whether on paper or on screen. The shape, color, and style of the letters and symbols that make up text convey meaning as surely as the words and sentences themselves. Effective use of type will enhance and amplify your message, just as ineffective use will weaken it and even confuse viewers or readers.

Originally, fonts used on the Web were totally outside the page creator's control. The page creator specified text styles such as "Heading1," or "Normal," and remote users configured their browsers with desired fonts for each style. In practice, most fonts ended up being a form of Times Roman or Courier.

Choosing fonts for normal text presents a problem because computer monitors typically display only 72 pixels per inch. At such resolutions there are simply not enough pixels to differentiate similar typefaces. Often, there aren't even enough pixels to make fonts legible. For these reasons, overriding the default font for normal text requires great care.

Headings and titles generally use larger type sizes and thus provide more opportunity for artistic type selection. The problem is that there's no good way to ensure that end users have the specified fonts on their systems; nor is there any widely accepted technology for providing temporary, downloadable fonts as Web-page components. As a result, and as a workaround, many Web designers approach typography by rendering text as graphic images.

As always, similar page elements should look alike and dissimilar elements should look different. This means, for example:

- All first-level headings should look alike.

- All normal text should look alike.

- First-level headings and normal text should look different.

Similarly, all hypertext links should look alike, but something other than a link should never look like one. Many other examples are possible.

II

Creating Web Pages

The extent of contrast between different page elements is a matter of judgment, but the result should be a mixture of contrast and unity. If something deserves typographical treatment to make it look different, then make it look *really* different. Insufficient contrast makes the reader stop reading and start analyzing the tiny differences you've created. Insufficient contrast confuses and distracts the reader.

Excessive contrast is similarly distracting. Each Web page should have a unity among all its elements, and all Web pages on the same topic or site warrant a certain unity as well. Choosing different styles and conventions for every page forces your readers to constantly reorient themselves, diverting their attention away from your message.

There are two main uses for bolding and italics on Web pages. In normal text, **bolding** indicates words bearing special emphasis and *italics* denotes special terms—especially the first instance of a special term.

Bolding and italics can also be useful in designing heading fonts. In this context, the entire heading phrase is bolded or italicized to distinguish it from normal text, other headings, or other page elements.

Underlining, by the way, is a crude substitute for italics carried over from the days of typewriters. Now that italics are readily available, there's no longer any need to emphasize text by underlining. Such text can also be confused with a link because browsers are often configured to display hyperlinks with an underline.

The primary dimensions that provide contrast between different kinds of text are:

- **Size.** Font size is normally measured in points, where one point equals 1/72 of an inch. It refers to the vertical range of the entire typeface as measured from the top of the tallest character to the bottom of the lowest "descender," such as the tail of the letter *j*.

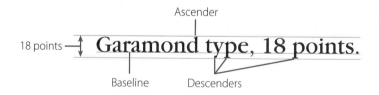

- **Color.** Text, like any other page element, can appear in any selected color. Text color should naturally be integrated with the overall color scheme for the page.

■ **Typeface.** There are thousands of typefaces, and more are being created every day. It's remarkable that there can be so many variations on an alphabet of only 26 letters, and even more remarkable that so many variations of the same letters can be recognizable. Some of the characteristics that differentiate one typeface from another include:

- **Presence or absence of serifs.** Serifs are small, angular extensions added to the ends of character strokes. Fonts such as Times Roman and Garamond have them; Arial and Helvetica don't.

- **Slant of serifs.** Serifs may be angled relative to the baseline or parallel to it, particularly for lowercase letters.

- **Thickness of serifs.** Serifs may be hairline thin or as thick as main character strokes.

- **Stroke transition.** Strokes are the lines and curves that form the body of a character. Stroke transition refers to the difference between the thickest portions of a character and the thinnest.

- **Stress.** This term refers to the angle of an imaginary line drawn through the thinnest portions of a rounded, symmetrical character such as "O."

- **Weight.** The difference between bold and normal text is one of weight, but other degrees of thickness are possible as well. Some typefaces are always thicker than others by design; very thick fonts often have the word black or ultra in their names. In general, the heavier the font, the more attention it attracts. (As we'll see, this is called contrast of extent.) However, a predominance of heavy fonts greatly reduces their effectiveness.

- **Direction.** This property sometimes refers to curvature or rotation of the baseline (effects that, by the way, are more often abused than used properly). Beyond baseline alignment, though, direction can refer to the dimensions of text flow. Sentences or paragraphs fitted into tall, narrow columns have a more vertical direction than text fitted into the full width of a page. The rows and columns of cells in a table have horizontal and vertical dimensions. Items in a list can appear horizontally, in sentence format, or vertically, as bullets in a list (like this one).

- **Proportional vs. monospaced.** Most typefaces are proportional, meaning some characters are wider than others. This is and should be the normal situation; there's no reason for small l and capital W to occupy the same amount of space on a line.

  Monospaced typefaces allocate the same amount of space for every character, much like a typewriter. They are significantly less attractive and less readable than proportional fonts, but may be preferable for program code listings and other applications that need equally spaced characters to align text without using tabs.

- **Form.** This property refers to the overall shape of the letters, numbers, and symbols in the typeface. Uppercase and lowercase letters in the same font obviously have different forms, as do the characters in distinctly different typefaces. In a sense, form is the sum of all the technical properties above.

- **Style.** This is a catchall property that covers everything not covered above. Typefaces are collections of artistic images, after all, and combining a set of technical and artistic properties into a useful and legible font is an artistic endeavor.

Every typeface has a name, but font names may reveal little about their properties. Some, such as Garamond and Baskerville, have a rich history and are named for their designers of a century or more ago, but many are recent creations, driven by market forces, or derivations of the classics. To analyze the contrast or similarity of typefaces, general categories such as the following are more useful.

■ **Oldstyle.** These are some of the oldest, most readable typefaces in common use. They feature slanted, lowercase serifs; moderate transition in strokes; and left-leaning diagonal stress. These characteristics are highlighted in Figure 5-35. Typical oldstyle typefaces include Times Roman and Garamond.

FIGURE 5-35.
Oldstyle fonts have a classic appearance and are among the easiest to read.

Slanted lowercase serifs · Moderate transition in strokes · Diagonal stress

Oldstyle

Times Roman

Many oldstyle fonts are difficult to display on the limited resolution of computer monitors. The limit of 72 pixels per inch simply doesn't provide enough detail to display moderate stroke variations and slanted pixels, especially at small point sizes. Modern fonts are therefore more common in online environments than in print. One aid to viewing fonts is software that smoothes (anti-aliases) the type-faces, such as Microsoft Plus! or Adobe Type Manager. Another is higher-resolution video cards used on larger monitors that can combine to display type up to about 120 pixels per inch, making each character more fully formed.

■ **Modern.** These fonts were invented to have a more mechanical, colder look than oldstyle fonts. Stroke transitions are extreme, stress is vertical, and serifs are horizontal. Bodoni and Elephant are typical modern fonts. See Figure 5-36.

FIGURE 5-36.
Modern fonts eliminate many angular features found in oldstyle type.

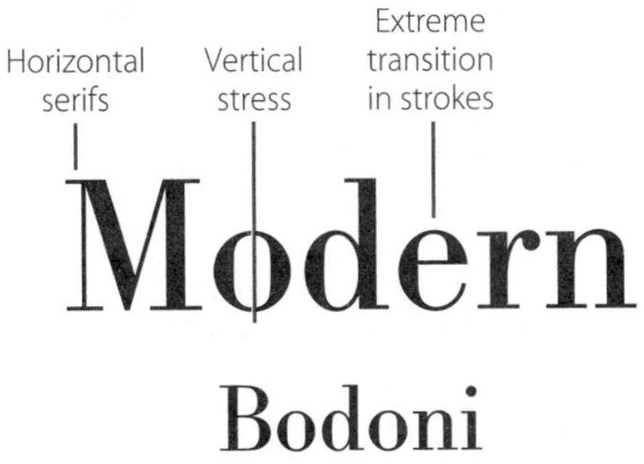

Horizontal serifs   Vertical stress   Extreme transition in strokes

Modern
Bodoni

■ **Slab serif.** Fonts in this category are designed for extra visibility by eliminating fine strokes. They have less stroke transition and thicker serifs than modern fonts, but retain the vertical stress. Century Schoolbook, New Century Schoolbook, and Clarendon are slab serif fonts. See Figure 5-37.

FIGURE 5-37.
Slab serif fonts eliminate the fine details of other serif fonts to enhance casual readability.

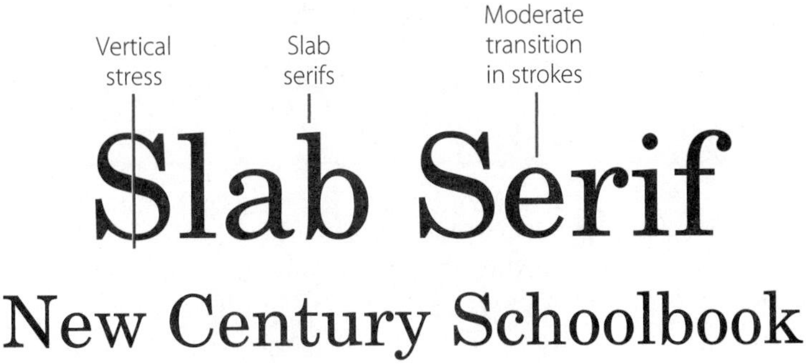

Vertical stress   Slab serifs   Moderate transition in strokes

Slab Serif
New Century Schoolbook

Creating Web Pages

■ **Sans serif.** These fonts have no serifs and display uniform stroke thickness throughout. With no stroke transition there is, of course, no stress. Sans serif fonts have a clean, technical appearance but in general aren't quite as legible as serif fonts. The contrast between serif and sans serif is quite extreme yet attractive, accounting for the common practice of using serifs for body text and sans serifs for headings. Common sans serif fonts include Arial and Helvetica. Figure 5-38 provides an example.

FIGURE 5-38.
A complete lack of serifs gives the sans serif category its name. Sans serif fonts provide an attractive contrast to oldstyle and modern fonts.

No stress   No serifs   No transition in strokes

Sans Serif
Helvetica

■ **Script.** Fonts that resemble handwriting or calligraphy fall into the script category. These are highly stylistic fonts typically used for wedding invitations and advertising. Most are inherently hard to read and even worse at computer monitor resolutions. Exercise great caution when considering a script font for use on a Web page. Figure 5-39 uses Zapf Chancery, a typical example.

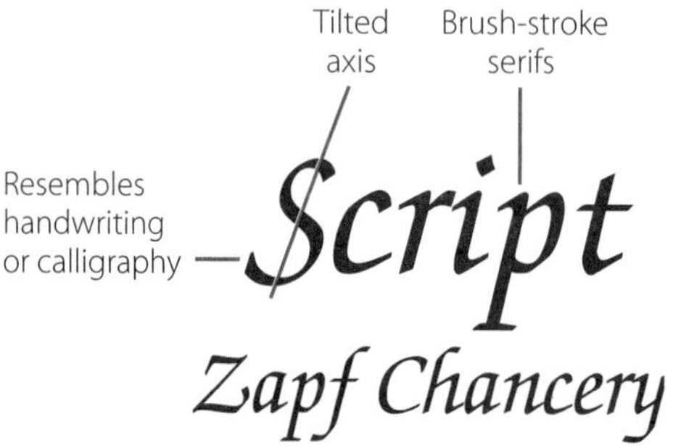

FIGURE 5-39.
Script fonts look like excruciatingly correct handwriting or lettering.

Tilted axis   Brush-stroke serifs

Resembles handwriting or calligraphy —

Script
Zapf Chancery

■ **Decorative.** This category includes a wide variety of highly stylized fonts—you could almost call them fonts with a gimmick. They're eye-catching but hard to read, and overusing them can drive people screaming from the room. Small point sizes look terrible on computer monitors. Used properly, decorative fonts can produce eye-catching logos, headlines, and banners, but overuse is much more common than proper use. Tread carefully. Figure 5-40 illustrates Giddyup, a decorative font with a rough 'n' ready western flair.

FIGURE 5-40.

Decorative fonts are fonts with a gimmick. Use them carefully, if at all.

"Whimsical" — *Decorative*

Giddyup

■ **Symbol.** These fonts range from useful symbols to visual clutter and don't even pretend to contain letters, numbers, and punctuation; they're actually icon collections. Formatting normal characters with a symbol font produces seemingly random sequences of mathematical symbols, foreign language characters, bullets, road signs, or images of almost anything. Figure 5-41 shows the Zapf Dingbats font. (A dingbat is a typographer's term for a symbol or decorative "thingie.")

Symbol fonts are more useful in printed documents than in Web pages. There are far better (and more colorful) icon collections in clip-art libraries and on the Web than any symbol font can provide.

FIGURE 5-41.

Symbol fonts display small icons, bullets, or other non-English characters.

Special characters and icons —

Zapf Dingbats

The primary value in considering these font categories lies in understanding the most common conventions and variations among fonts. The eye is so accustomed to reading different fonts that it takes quite a difference to be obvious.

Figure 5-42 shows an attractive but unusual font—Zapf Humanist. This is a sans serif font with stroke transition, normally an oldstyle or modern

Creating Web Pages

characteristic. Despite its attractiveness, Zapf Humanist's partial similarity to both the sans serif category and to oldstyle and modern makes it—and other fonts like it, such as Optima—difficult to use with either. This highlights the importance of providing sufficient contrast among typefaces used on the same page.

FIGURE 5-42.

Zapf Humanist is a sans serif font with stroke transition. The blend of oldstyle and sans serif characteristics makes Zapf Humanist difficult to use with either.

> **NOTE**
>
> There are dozens of look-alike typefaces that are modeled on (or ripoffs of) the classic designs of Optima, Garamond, Times Roman, Helvetica, and the like.

Contrast in color and size are far more obvious than contrast in the shape of letters. If you decide to use multiple fonts on a page, topic, or site, make sure they're markedly different yet legible and that they work together. When in doubt, use the default font (typically an oldstyle) for body text and a larger sans serif font for headings.

In Summary...

FrontPage 2000 provides powerful commands for entering, importing, and formatting text on Web pages. Similarity to word processing commands and conventions makes these commands easy to use as well.

In the next chapter, we'll complement the formatting of text covered in this chapter with information on how to incorporate graphics and format them for the best possible effect.

CHAPTER 6

Incorporating Graphics

M ost observers credit in-line graphics as the feature that transformed the World Wide Web from a curiosity of academic interest and a means of technical interchange to an amazingly pervasive icon of pop culture. Today, while excessive use of graphics slows download times and keeps visitors away, the lack of graphics drives them away at least as rapidly.

Strictly speaking, HTML is incapable of containing images. Instead, HTML contains the names of image files and some accompanying format codes. On receiving an HTML file, the visitor's browser notes the names and locations of any required image files, retrieves them from the Web server, and displays them as specified in the HTML. Nevertheless, Web pages and the images they contain must work together and, therefore, be designed together too.

Microsoft FrontPage not only supports the full capabilities of HTML for adding graphic images to Web pages, but also permits integrated graphical display and, to a limited extent, graphics editing. This chapter describes these facilities.

Adding Images to a Page

FrontPage can add pictures to your Web page in a variety of ways. One of them is almost sure to meet whatever requirements you encounter.

Inserting Image Files

With FrontPage, adding graphics to a Web page is as easy as drag and drop. Figure 6-1 shows how you can drag images from Page view's Folder List to a page open for editing. As you drag over the open Web page, the insertion point shows where the graphic will appear. You can also:

- Drag images from Windows Explorer into Web pages.

- Drag images from Internet Explorer into Web pages.

- Copy images from other programs to the Clipboard, and then paste them into FrontPage.

- Drag images from one open Web page to another.

- Drag images from one location to another on the same Web page.

FIGURE 6-1.

FrontPage can accept images dropped from the Folder List, from Windows Explorer, or from Internet Explorer.

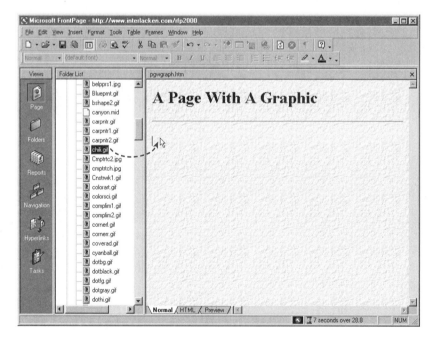

You can also insert images from the FrontPage Insert menu. After opening that menu, first choose Picture, then From File. This produces the Picture dialog box shown in Figure 6-2.

⭐ TIP

When dragging images from the same or another Web page, the default operation is Move. That is, the images disappear from the source location and appear at the drop location. To create a second copy of the source image, either hold down the Ctrl key while dragging or drag with the right mouse button and choose Copy Here from the pop-up menu that appears after releasing it. Copying an image this way doesn't create a new image file; it simply loads the same file into two different locations on the same Web page.

Dragging an image outside FrontPage into FrontPage always performs a copy.

If you have trouble remembering when to use the Ctrl key, try dragging with the right mouse button. Whenever you drop an object after right-dragging it, Windows displays a pop-up menu with Move, Copy, and Cancel options.

FIGURE 6-2.

Use this FrontPage dialog box to locate a desired image.

Shows current folder or location

Displays parent folder
Creates new folder
Lists files and folders

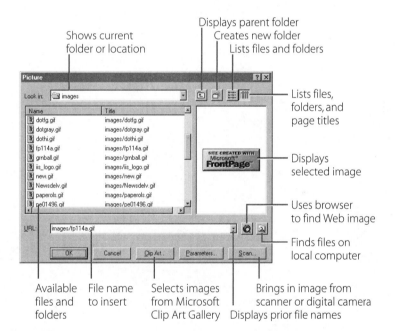

Lists files, folders, and page titles

Displays selected image

Uses browser to find Web image

Finds files on local computer

Available files and folders

File name to insert

Selects images from Microsoft Clip Art Gallery

Brings in image from scanner or digital camera
Displays prior file names

Initially, the Picture dialog box displays files in the starting folder of the current FrontPage Web. To view contents of another folder in the Web, double-click it. To view the parent of the current folder, click the Up One Level button.

The list in the center of the dialog box displays all image files in the current folder. To select one, single-click it. The preview window to the right of the selection list will display the corresponding image.

The Look In and URL fields in combination show the current location. This can be either a Web address or a local file name; thus, you can use this dialog box to retrieve any image on your personal Web server, your intranet, or the World Wide Web. To view your recent selections, click the drop-down arrow at the right of the URL field.

The Browser button uses your Web browser to find an image. See "Locating Images with Your Web Browser," page 179, for more information.

The Files On Local Computer button selects an image from your local disk or network. After you've located the file, FrontPage converts its location to a *file://* URL and enters it in the URL field.

⭐ TIP

> You can also insert image files—or, for that matter, any other type of file—by choosing File from the Insert menu.

Inserting Clip Art

FrontPage uses the same clip-art library as the rest of the Office 2000 suite, enlarged with a handy collection of Web clip art. To select an image from the clip-art library:

■ Click the Clip Art button in the Picture dialog box shown in Figure 6-2.

or

■ Choose Picture from the Insert menu, then Clip Art.

Either way, the Clip Art Gallery window shown in Figure 6-3 will appear.

FIGURE 6-3.

Use this window to select images and pictures from the Office 2000 clip-art library.

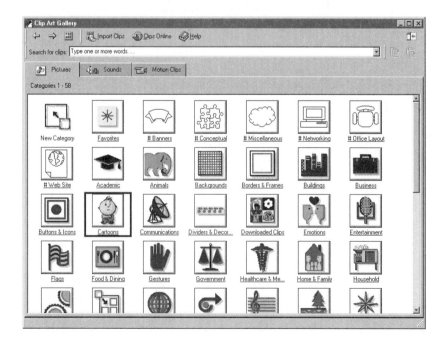

Locating Images with Your Web Browser

The button Use Your Web Browser To Select A Page Or File requires this procedure:

1 Click the button titled Use Your Web Browser To Select A Page Or File, located in the Picture dialog box.

2 Wait for the browser to appear.

3 Display the image in the browser. Note that the browser must display just the image, and not a Web page that contains it. The address displayed in the browser's Location box must end in JPG, JPEG, or GIF.

4 Switch back to FrontPage. The image's Web location will automatically appear in the URL field of the Picture dialog box.

Completing step 3 is easy when the remote Web site provides direct hyperlinks to images, typically through thumbnail previews. Otherwise, it's usually easier to just copy the image's URL out of the Web page and paste it into the Picture dialog box. Here are the procedures.

- In Internet Explorer:

    1 Locate a Web page containing the image you want.

    2 Right-click the image and choose Properties from the pop-up menu.

    3 When the Properties dialog box appears, highlight the contents of the Address (URL) field by double-clicking its value.

    4 Press Ctrl+C to copy the address, or right-click the Address (URL) field and choose Copy from the pop-up menu.

    5 Click OK to close the dialog box.

    6 Return to FrontPage and make sure the Picture dialog box is displayed.

    7 Click the URL box to activate the cursor, then press Ctrl+V or Shift+Insert to enter the URL from step 4.

- In Netscape Navigator:

    1 Right-click the image.

    2 Choose Copy Image Location.

    3 Return to FrontPage and make sure the Picture dialog box is displayed.

    4 Click the URL box to activate the cursor, then press Ctrl+V or Shift+Insert to enter the URL from step 2.

The easiest approach of all, available only in Internet Explorer, is to right-click the Web-page image, choose Copy from the pop-up menu, switch back to FrontPage, and paste the image directly into the Web page.

II

Creating Web Pages

To search the clip-art gallery and find the perfect image:

1 Click the Pictures tab.

2 To search for images by category, click that category.

3 To search for images by keyword, enter the keywords in the Search For Clips box, then press Enter.

4 Either way, review the resulting list of images. If you can't find one you like, scroll to the bottom of the list and look for a Keep Looking icon. If it's there, click it to display more images.

5 To return to a previous list of images or categories, click the Back Arrow button on the Clip Art Gallery's toolbar. To undo a backward jump, click the Forward Arrow button.

A list of Clip Art Gallery toolbar icons is shown in Table 6-1.

TABLE 6-1.   The Clip Art Gallery Toolbar

Icon	Description	Function
	Back	Reverts to the previous page of selections.
	Forward	Advances to the next page of selections (reverses the effect of clicking Back).
	All Categories	Displays the initial category selection list.
Import Clips	Import Clips	Opens a dialog box that adds images to the clip-art library.
Clips Online	Clips Online	Connects via the Internet to a special Web page that can download clip art and add it to your collection.
Help	Help	Obtains help about the clip-art gallery.
	Small Window	Narrows the clip-art gallery window so that only one column of selections appears.
Search for clips: Type	Search for Clips	Searches for clip art based on keywords.
	Copy	Copies the current clip-art picture to the Clipboard.
	Paste	Pastes an image from the Clipboard into the clip-art gallery.

Clicking any picture in the clip-art gallery displays the menu shown below.

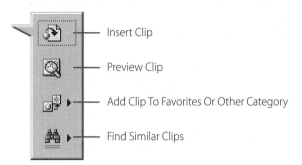

- **Insert Clip** adds the selected picture to your Web page at the current insertion point.

- **Preview Clip** displays the picture at full size.

- **Add Clip To Favorites Or Other Category** displays a drop-down list of clip-art categories. Selecting any category and clicking the Add button adds that picture to that category.

- **Find Similar Clips** searches for pictures that resemble the current one. You can search for the same artistic style, the same color and shape, or the same keywords.

Right-clicking a clip-art picture displays this pop-up menu.

The first five options operate just as you'd probably suspect. Insert adds the image to your Web page; Copy copies it to the Clipboard; Paste adds a Clipboard image to the current collection; and Delete removes the current image from the collection. Select All selects all images currently on display.

The Recover option displays a dialog box with two commands: Compact and Restore. The Compact command compresses and repairs the clip-art database. The Restore command reloads the clip-art library from its installation media.

The Clip Properties choice shows the text description for the current clip, the categories it belongs to, and the current keywords assigned. You can revise any of these properties, or even create new categories of your own.

 SEE ALSO
For information on resizing and resampling images, see "Modifying Image Properties," page 183.

Many clip-art images arrive in FrontPage as Windows Metafile (WMF) files. WMF is a line-drawing format where images consist not of pixels, but of lines, curves, and shapes. WMF is a great clip-art format because you can enlarge, reduce, or reshape such images with no loss of resolution. However, because not all browsers can display it, WMF isn't a good format for Web pages. FrontPage therefore converts WMF files to GIF or JPEG the next time you save the page.

Knowing this, it's best to resize and resample any new clip-art images before saving a Web page. This ensures the image gets saved with the proper size and without loss of resolution.

Inserting Scanned Images

To record an image directly from a scanner or digital camera to a Web page, click the Scan button in the Picture dialog box. This invokes TWAIN-compliant camera, scanner, or other device software and directly passes any image you capture to FrontPage.

Saving Inserted Images

When FrontPage inserts a clip-art image, it holds the image in memory until you save the page. FrontPage then uses the Save Embedded Files dialog box, described in Chapter 4, "Getting Started with Web Pages," to suggest adding the image to your Web. The same thing happens for images from the Clipboard, images retrieved from the World Wide Web, and in fact, any images not already stored in the current FrontPage Web.

Unless you have strong reasons to the contrary, you should accept FrontPage's suggestion and save these files to your Web. Rename them or change the folder where they reside, if you like, but do save them. If you don't, sooner or later they're bound to come up missing from your Web page.

Adding Multimedia Files

To add a video clip to a Web page, choose Picture from the Insert menu and select Video. The Video dialog box appears and is similar to the Picture dialog box shown in Figure 6-2, except that it searches by default for video (AVI) files rather than still images, and it lacks the Scan button.

Page-level settings for a background sound are set in the Page Properties dialog box as described in "General Page Properties" in Chapter 4.

Animated GIF files don't qualify here as multimedia. Insert animated GIFs using the Picture dialog box, as you would for any other GIF or JPG image.

Modifying Picture Properties

Very often, making an image appear on a Web page is only half the job. The remainder involves details of placement and presentation. HTML, and therefore FrontPage, provides a variety of settings for this purpose.

To open the Picture Properties dialog box, do *one* of the following:

- Click the image and choose Properties from the Format menu.
- Right-click the image and choose Picture Properties from the pop-up menu.
- Click the image and press Alt+Enter.

The three tabs of the Picture Properties dialog box are shown in Figure 6-4, Figure 6-5, and Figure 6-7.

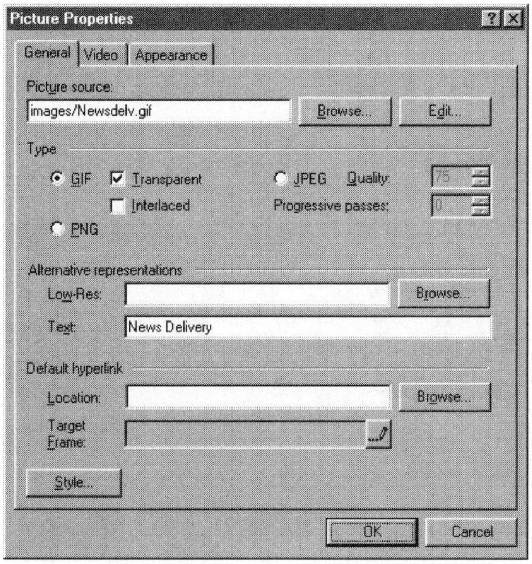

FIGURE 6-4.

This is the first of three tabs in FrontPage's Picture Properties dialog box.

General Picture Properties

You can use the General tab of the Picture Properties dialog box shown in Figure 6-4 to modify the properties of an image. Certain options might be unavailable (dimmed), depending on the context. The full complement of fields includes the following.

- **Picture Source.** This text box specifies the full or relative URL of the image file being modified. It might be read-only, depending on the context.

- **Browse.** If Image Source is modifiable, clicking this button permits browsing the current Web or local file system to locate an image.

SEE ALSO
For information about configuring FrontPage to run the image editor you want, see Chapter 14 "Customizing Your Copy of FrontPage."

- **Edit.** Clicking this button invokes the default editor for the type of image. For example, this might be Microsoft Image Composer or Microsoft PhotoDraw.

- **Type.** This section initially displays the current image type—GIF or JPEG—and permits changing it.

- **GIF.** If turned on, this option button instructs FrontPage to save the image as a GIF file.

- **Transparent.** This box activates or inhibits the GIF transparency feature.

TIP

> Activating transparency accomplishes nothing unless you also designate a transparent color with the Make Transparent tool in the Picture toolbar.

- **Interlaced.** If turned on, this box instructs FrontPage to save a GIF file with interlacing. Interlaced images appear first in coarse resolution, and then with increasing fineness.

CAUTION
Increasing the JPEG compression of a file (by *lowering* the Quality number) discards information that can't be restored later. What's gone is gone. To be safe, save a full-resolution version of any file *before* experimenting with its JPEG quality setting.

- **JPEG.** If turned on, this option button instructs FrontPage to save the image as a JPEG file.

- **Quality.** This is an integer from 1 to 99. Lower numbers increase compression and decrease file size, but permanently decrease image quality. The default is 75.

- **Progressive Passes.** This is similar to the Interlaced feature for GIF images, but with more control. Specify the number of steps in which the JPEG image will appear.

TIP

> Interlaced GIF and progressive JPEG formats provide viewers with coarse images early and full resolution later. This avoids waiting for a complete, full-resolution display.

SEE ALSO

For an explanation of the GIF, JPEG, and PNG file formats, see "Graphic File Formats," page 204.

- **PNG.** If turned on, this option button instructs FrontPage to save the image as a PNG file.

- **Alternative Representation.** The fields in this section control alternate views of an image.

- **Low-Res.** This specifies a low-resolution image the browser will display while downloading the larger image file. You can use the Browse button to find such an image file.

- **Text.** This line of text will appear in browsers that can't display the image. Some browsers that *can* display images will also display this text while the image is downloading, or when the visitor passes the mouse pointer over the image.

SEE ALSO

For information on normal and hotspot hyperlinks, see "Creating and Managing Hypertext Links," page 220.

- **Default Hyperlink.** This section establishes a hyperlink to another location from any part of the current image that has no hotspot defined. The command isn't available for background images.

- **Location.** This field contains the URL the browser should retrieve if the visitor clicks the current image. You can use the Browse button to locate it.

SEE ALSO

For information about assigning CSS properties, see "Assigning CSS Properties," page 147.

- **Target Frame.** This field specifies the frame in which the Location page will appear.

- **Style.** This button accesses the Modify Style dialog box where you can apply cascading style-sheet properties to the current image.

Video Properties

The Video tab of the Picture Properties dialog box, shown in Figure 6-5, controls the display and playback of digitized video such as AVI files.

- **Video Source.** Here you specify the location of the file containing digitized video. It can be in the current Web, on your local hard disk, on a file server, or on the World Wide Web. You can use the Browse button to locate the file.

NOTE

If the Picture Properties dialog box contains both an Image Source and a Video Source entry, the browser will first display the static image and then, when possible, replace it with the first frame of the video.

- **Show Controls In Browser.** If this box is turned on, the browser displays a button for starting and stopping the video and a slide control for positioning replays. Figure 6-6 illustrates this.

Creating Web Pages

- **Repeat.** Settings in this section control the replaying of the video.

  - **Loop** controls the number of times the browser should replay the video.

  - **Forever** overrides the Loop setting and repeats the video continuously.

FIGURE 6-5.

The Video tab of the Picture Properties dialog box controls presentation of full-motion video files.

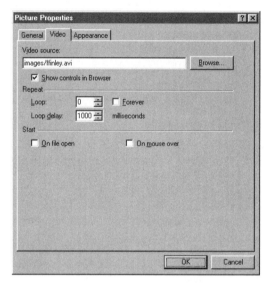

FIGURE 6-6.

FrontPage can configure video clips to appear with playback controls.

(X) CAUTION

Use good judgment when placing video files on Web pages. These files are extremely large by Web standards and might take several minutes to download, possibly frustrating or angering some visitors. Always place warnings on hyperlinks that lead to such downloads so that viewers have a chance to avoid starting a lengthy download.

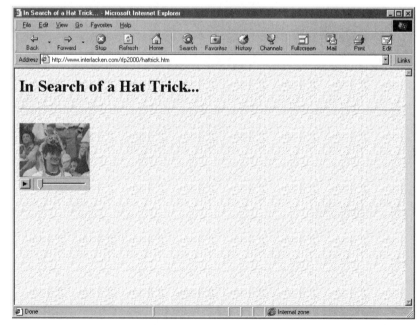

- **Loop Delay** causes a delay between repeat playings. The default is zero; any other value is milliseconds. A five-second delay, for example, would be specified as 5000.

- **Start.** This section controls when the browser plays the video.

  - **On File Open** plays the video as soon as the browser opens the file.

  - **On Mouse Over** plays the video when the mouse pointer passes over the display area.

TIP

You might need to manually increase the Height field on the Appearance tab (discussed next) to accommodate browser video controls.

Size and Placement Properties

The Appearance tab of the Picture Properties dialog box controls image layout and size. Figure 6-7 illustrates this. The dialog box's controls have the following effects:

- **Layout.** This section positions the image on the page.

  - **Alignment** controls vertical positioning of an image and text in the same line. See Table 6-2 for a listing and description of each option. Figure 6-8 presents the same information visually.

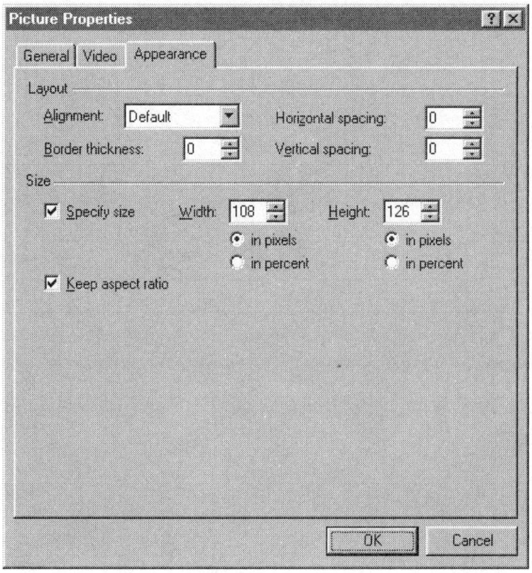

FIGURE 6-7.

The Picture Properties Appearance tab controls page positioning and displayed image size.

- **Border Thickness,** if nonzero, surrounds the image with a border. The specified integer controls the border's thickness in pixels. Hyperlinked images have blue borders; others have black borders.

- **Horizontal Spacing** controls the separation, in pixels, between the image and other elements on the same line.

- **Vertical Spacing** controls separation between the image and any text or images in lines above or below.

■ **Size.** This frame controls the displayed size of an image.

- **Specify Size,** if turned on, indicates you wish to override the natural size of the image.

- **Width** sets the amount of horizontal space the browser should reserve for the image. Click either In Pixels or In Percent to denote the unit of measure.

- **Height** sets the amount of vertical space the browser should reserve for the image. Use the In Pixels or the In Percent buttons to denote the units of height.

- **Keep Aspect Ratio** specifies that changing either the image's height or its width changes the other dimension proportionally.

TABLE 6-2. HTML Image Alignment Settings

Alignment	Description
Left	Floats the image down and left to the next available spot along the left margin; wraps subsequent text around the right side of that image.
Right	Aligns the image with the right margin; wraps subsequent text around the left.
Bottom	Aligns the bottom of the image with the baseline of the current line; see Figure 6-8 for illustrations of this and the following settings.
Baseline	Aligns the bottom of the image with the baseline of the current line.
Absbottom	Aligns the bottom of the image with the bottom of the current line.
Middle	Aligns the baseline of the current line with the middle of the image.
Absmiddle	Aligns the middle of the current line with the middle of the image.
Top	Aligns the image with the top of the tallest item in the line.
Texttop	Aligns the image with the top of the tallest text in the line (this is usually, but not always, the same as Top).

As HTML page design has evolved, most Web designers want more control over image placement than in-line images provide. Of the nine image-alignment settings, Left and Right are probably the most often used. As Figure 6-8 illustrates, in-line images also result in uneven, distracting line spacing. The Left and Right settings provide at least some absolute positioning—the margins—while they also maintain uniform line spacing.

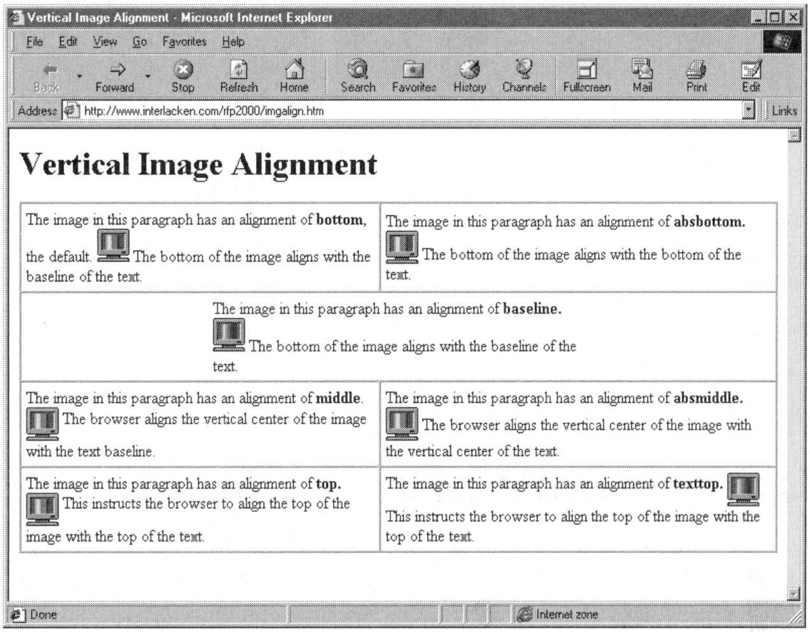

FIGURE 6-8.

This page illustrates various HTML Image Alignment settings.

To center an image by itself, put it in its own paragraph. To center the paragraph, do *either* of the following:

- Select the paragraph and click the Center button on the Text toolbar.

- Right-click the paragraph, choose Paragraph Properties from the pop-up menu, and set the Paragraph Alignment control to Center.

By default, the visitor's browser will inspect all images on a page and allocate window space to display them at their natural size. For at least three reasons, you should consider overriding this behavior and setting an image size at authoring time:

- Using the default behavior, the browser can't allocate window space to an image until it has received enough of the file to determine its dimensions. Not knowing the size of an image might also delay placement—and therefore display—of other page elements. Specifying sizes for all images on a page allows many page elements to appear sooner than otherwise might be possible.

(?) SEE ALSO

For an example of when to expand small images at the browser, see "Using Transparent Images for Page Layout," page 256.

■ Occasionally, you may wish to display an image larger or smaller than its natural size. This used to be rare because downloading a large image and having the browser reduce it takes more time than downloading a smaller one. By contrast, downloading a small image and having the browser expand it results in a loss of resolution. More recently, however, the practice of expanding small images has become surprisingly common.

(?) SEE ALSO

For more information on scripts, see "Working with Script Code," page 418.

■ Older browsers tend to have difficulty with pages containing both scripts embedded in the HTML and images with no preassigned Height and Width. These problems seem to arise when the scripts start to run before all page element locations are determined. Therefore, always specify dimensions—in pixels—for all images on pages that contain scripts.

FrontPage automatically enters heights and widths whenever you specify them in Figure 6-7, and also for all images in the current Web.

Using FrontPage Image Tools

Microsoft provides a useful assortment of image editing functions built directly into FrontPage. These functions certainly don't replace a full-tilt image editor, but they conveniently provide the right tool in the right place, at least a percentage of the time.

Adding Text to Images

Web authors frequently need to add text, such as button titles, to graphics, such as button images. FrontPage supports this operation completely within FrontPage using a feature called Text On GIFs. Figure 6-9 provides some examples.

Applying text to GIF files is quite simple:

1 Add the graphic to the Web page if it isn't there already.

2 Select the graphic by clicking it.

3 Choose the Text tool on the Picture toolbar.

4 A second set of handles will appear within those surrounding the image. Click inside the inner handles to place an insertion marker, and then type your text. If the text doesn't fit, enlarge the text area by dragging its handles.

5 Set font, point size, alignment, color, and other attributes by either selecting the text and then choosing Font from the Format menu or using the buttons on the Format toolbar.

6 When you're done, click outside the graphic to stop text entry and editing.

(?) SEE ALSO

For an explanation of transparency in image files, see "Transparency and Alpha Channels," page 206.

To create headings, titles, and other small amounts of text using special fonts and colors, first use your image editor to create a completely transparent GIF file. Add this file to your Web page, and then use the Text button to add and format the text. The main advantage of this method, compared to just entering the text in your image editor, is having the Text On GIFs feature readily available as you develop other parts of your page.

FIGURE 6-9.

The image at the upper left is the original image; the others make use of the Text On GIFs feature.

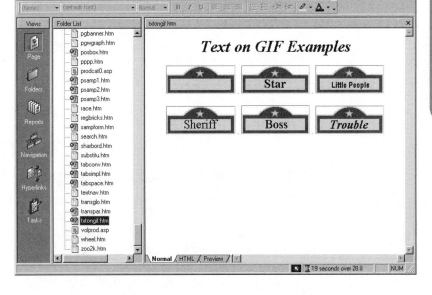

Many Web-page creators keep a collection of transparent GIF files on hand to use for reserving white space or guaranteeing table widths. It's very tempting to stretch a small transparent GIF out to the size of a heading and then use the Text On GIFs feature to display the heading with full control over font and color. There are two precautions to this technique:

- The text must be a different color than the GIF file's transparent color; otherwise, you'll end up with transparent text. Note that a GIF file's transparent color usually isn't readily apparent because, by definition, it's invisible.

You can temporarily disable a file's transparency by right-clicking it, choosing Picture Properties, and turning off the Transparent box.

- FrontPage can't save text on a small image you've merely resized on screen. Such resizing changes only the display size and not the number of pixels stored on disk. And however few those pixels on disk might be, they probably don't provide enough resolution to make your text legible. Resampling (described in "Cropping and Resizing Images," page 197) creates an image permanently sized to the dimensions that appear on your screen.

Follow these steps to ensure the Text On GIFs feature will work correctly:

1 Resize the GIF file by dragging its handles or entering dimensions in the Picture Properties dialog box.

2 Resample the transparent file.

3 Save the Web page.

4 Give the transparent file a descriptive name when prompted.

5 Add the text, using the procedure described earlier in this section.

Creating Thumbnail Images

To minimize download time for large images, it's common practice to display a small preview image (a thumbnail) on the Web page a remote user would first encounter, and display the full-size image only if the visitor clicks the thumbnail. To do this in FrontPage:

1 Insert the full-size image where you want its thumbnail to appear.

2 Select the large image.

3 Select AutoThumbnail from the Tools menu. In one operation, FrontPage will remove the large image, create the thumbnail in its place, and set up a hyperlink from the thumbnail to the large image.

? SEE ALSO

To learn about controlling the size of thumbnail images, see "AutoThumbnail," page 468.

4 Use the thumbnail's handles to resize it if desired.

5 When you save the Web page, FrontPage will display a Save Embedded File dialog box to prompt for the thumbnail's file name. The section just below explains this.

Positioning Images

The Picture button has three buttons that support absolute positioning of images. Absolute positioning means you can specify exact *x-y* coordinates, and that's where the image will appear. The coordinates are measured from the upper-left corner of the browser window to the upper-left corner of the image, but FrontPage shields you from all that.

To absolutely position an image requires a three-step process.

1 Select the image.

2 Click the Positioned Absolutely button on the Picture toolbar.

3 Drag the image into position with the mouse.

Once you flag an image as absolutely positioned, you can drag it whenever it's selected, even during a subsequent editing session.

To arrange positioned images in layers, first select one image then click the Bring Forward or Send Back button. Repeat this for other images as necessary. You can set positioned images in front of or behind regular page content, as well as in front of or behind each other. In Figure 6-10, note that the tree is behind the regular text and the giraffe is in front.

Internet Explorer 4 was the first browser to support CSS2 positioning, which is the technology FrontPage uses for positioning images. Versions of Netscape Navigator up through and including version 4.0 ignore the positioning information, as proven by Figure 6-11.

Rotating and Flipping Images

FrontPage provides four toolbar icons for rotating images (shown in Table 6-3): two to rotate right or left in 90-degree increments, and two more for flipping top-to-bottom and right-to-left. To see their effects, look at the top set of images in Figure 6-13.

FrontPage permits flipping and rotating the same image any number of times. As with other operations that modify the saved file, rotating and flipping open the Save Embedded Images dialog box when you save the Web page, giving you a chance to save the modified image under a new name. This preserves the original file.

II

Creating Web Pages

FIGURE 6-10.

Note how the tree appears behind the text, and how the giraffe appears in front of both the tree and the text. The tree and giraffe are both independent, transparent GIF images, CSS-positioned using the FrontPage graphical interface. The text is ordinary typing, formatted with CSS font attributes.

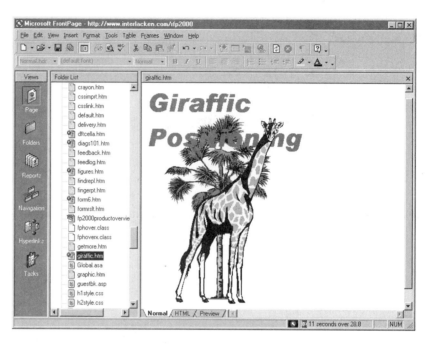

FIGURE 6-11.

Netscape Navigator 4 ignores CSS2 positioning for images.

TABLE 6-3. The FrontPage Picture Toolbar

Icon	Description	Function
	Insert Picture	Adds a picture to the current Web page.
	Text	Superimposes formatted text over an image.
	Auto Thumbnail	Replaces a large image with a smaller one. Also creates a hyperlink so that clicking the small image displays the original one.
	Positioned Absolutely	Marks an image for Pixel Precise Positioning and Layering.
	Bring Forward	Moves an image one position forward from normal browser content.
	Send Backward	Moves an image one position back from normal browser content.
	Rotate Left	Rotates an image 90 degrees counterclockwise.
	Rotate Right	Rotates an image 90 degrees clockwise.
	Flip Horizontal	Reverses an image right to left (mirror image).
	Flip Vertical	Flips an image top to bottom (inverted image).
	More Contrast	Darkens darks, whitens lights, and moves midtones toward dark and light extremes.
	Less Contrast	Darkens lights and whitens darks, moving them closer to the midtone levels.
	More Brightness	Adds white proportionally to every color in the image.
	Less Brightness	Adds black proportionally to every color in the image.
	Crop	Readies the mouse pointer to select a portion of an image and discard the rest.
	Set Transparent Color	Readies the mouse pointer to select a GIF image color and declare it transparent.
	Black and White	Changes an image to monochrome.

II

Creating Web Pages

(continued)

TABLE 6-3. *continued*

Icon	Description	Function
	Wash Out	Lightens an image so that it can be used as a background or so that text can be seen on top of it.
	Bevel	Adds a 3-D border around the edge of an image.
	Resample	Physically converts an image (scaled only in memory) to its new size.
	Select	Readies the mouse pointer for selecting images or hotspots.
	Rectangular Hotspot	Readies the mouse pointer for marking rectangular hotspots.
	Circular Hotspot	Readies the mouse pointer for marking circular hotspots.
	Polygonal Hotspot	Readies the mouse pointer for marking polygonal hotspots.
	Highlight Hotspots	Displays hotspots on selected images against a solid white back ground so that you can review their positions.
	Restore	Restores an image to its last saved contents.

Controlling Contrast and Brightness

The Picture toolbar contains four buttons for modifying brightness and contrast: one each for increasing and decreasing. The results appear in the second set of images in Figure 6-13. Pressing these buttons repeatedly will intensify their effect.

- Increasing contrast makes high intensities higher and low intensities lower. That is, it pushes each color in an image closer to either black or white, whichever is closer.

- Decreasing contrast makes high intensities lower and low intensities higher. In short, it pushes your image in the direction of Seattle weather—all gray.

- Increasing brightness adds white to every color in the image; the darker the color, the more white added. Eventually, the image would become pure white.

- Decreasing brightness adds black to every color in the image; the lighter the color, the more black added. Eventually, the image would become completely black.

Brightness and contrast changes are saved in the image, so for any image you thus modify, FrontPage gives you the opportunity to save the file under a new name.

Cropping and Resizing Images

Cropping is the process of choosing part of an image and discarding the rest. The image becomes smaller in the process. To crop an image in FrontPage:

1 Select the image.

2 Select the Crop tool from FrontPage's Picture toolbar, shown in Table 6-3.

3 Within the selected image, FrontPage will draw a bounding box with handles. Move the handles so that the bounding box encloses the part of the image you want to retain.

Click the Crop tool again or press Enter. FrontPage will discard any pixels outside the bounding box.

When you save the Web page, FrontPage will consider the cropped image a new, unsaved file and present the Save Embedded Files dialog box, shown in Figure 6-5. By default, the dialog box will suggest saving the file in the root directory of your Web with the same file name as the original, uncropped file. Unless you want to overwrite the original file, it's best to rename the cropped file.

⭐ TIP

> It's best to keep all your images in an /images folder rather than the root. FrontPage helpfully provides such a folder when you first create your Web.

To resize an image, simply select it and drag its handles. Dragging the corner handles resizes the image proportionately; the height and width are forced to change by the same percentages. Dragging the top or bottom handle changes only the height, while dragging the left or right handle changes only the width.

Resizing a file with its handles doesn't alter the size of the image file itself; it changes only the amount of screen space the browser must

fill. The actual resizing occurs *after* the file gets delivered to the remote user's browser. Reducing the size of an image this way saves the
remote user nothing in download time. (Unless, of course, you later
resample the downsized image.)

Setting Transparency

All GIF and JPEG images are rectangular. Most real-life objects aren't.
One solution to this dilemma, though a poor one, is to enclose all images in picture frames. This often produces unattractive results. A second and better approach is coloring the unused portions of the image
to match it's surroundings—the Web-page background. However, this
solution also has drawbacks:

- It requires a different image version for each background color.

- Smoothly matching a textured background image generally isn't
  possible.

- Remote users can instruct their browser to ignore background
  images, to ignore background colors, or to ignore both.

The best solution is to make portions of the image transparent, as if
they were printed on a sheet of clear plastic. Figure 6-12 provides an
example of this technique. The image on the left, with a white background, doesn't blend with the textured background. The image on
the right has a transparent background that lets the page's background
image show through.

> Take care that any background you select doesn't obscure fine detail in your
> content. This is particularly troublesome when displaying small fonts over a
> textured background. Consider using a finer background or changing the font
> itself, the font size, or other attributes.

Most GIF file editors have features for handling transparency, but you
can also control transparency from within FrontPage. The FrontPage
procedure is:

1 Add the image to your Web page (if not already present).

2 Make sure the Picture toolbar is displayed. This is the toolbar described in Table 6-3.

> To toggle display of any toolbar, choose its entry from the View menu in FrontPage.

3 Single-click the image to select it.

FIGURE 6-12.

The image on the left has a white background; that on the right is transparent.

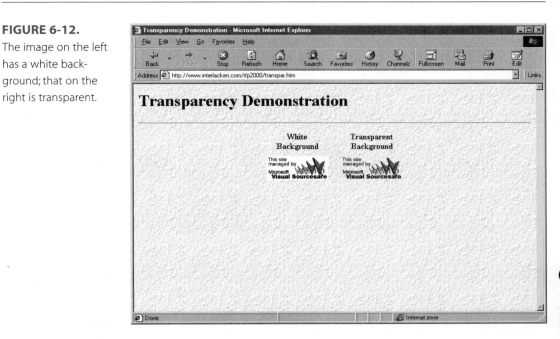

4   Click the Make Transparent button, shown in Table 6-3 on page 195.

5   Move the mouse pointer over the selected image and click any pixel of the color that should become transparent. All pixels matching that color in the image will immediately become transparent.

6   To make a different color transparent, repeat steps 4 and 5. FrontPage can make only one color at a time transparent.

7   To turn off transparency for an image, go to the General tab of the Picture Properties dialog box, shown in Figure 6-4 on page 183, and turn off the Transparent box.

Applying Monochrome and Washouts

The Black And White toolbar button removes all color from an image; that is, it converts it to monochrome. You can undo this operation by clicking the button again, but not after the monochrome image is saved.

To wash out an image, select it and then click the Washout button on the Picture toolbar. You can only wash out an image once per save. To avoid accidentally overwriting the original image file when you save the Web page, FrontPage will prompt you for a new file name and location.

To doubly wash out an image, wash it, save it, and then wash it again.

Figure 6-13 illustrates these and other image effects.

Creating Web Pages

II

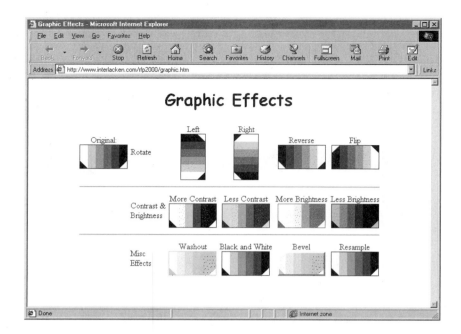

Beveling Edges

This effect lightens the top and left edges of an image while also darkening the bottom and right edges. This creates the effect of a three-dimensional button. After beveling an image and saving the page, you'll once again be prompted for a file name and folder.

Resampling Images

To physically resize an image, you must both resize *and* resample it in FrontPage. First resize the file, and then click the Resample button on the Picture toolbar. Resampling creates a larger or smaller file than the original, rescaled by mathematically averaging pixels.

Unlike resizing, resampling *does* change the file stored on your Web. When you save the Web page, FrontPage presents the Save Embedded Files dialog box, to suggest giving the modified file a new file name and location.

Restoring Images

Until you save an image file, FrontPage can always revert to the version it originally loaded from your Web or other location. To return to this version, click the Restore button on the Picture toolbar. Don't use Restore to reverse only the most recent of several changes; if you wish to do that, instead choose Undo from the Edit menu.

Design Tips

The following sections discuss two important but often overlooked aspects of site design: the color palettes in your images and the total download time for your pages. This advice, however, is far from all-encompassing. When choosing and positioning images for your Web pages, you should also consider color scheme, page layout, and the tendency for images to detract attention from text. In short, you should consider all the design tips sprinkled throughout this book.

Managing Image Palettes

If you have an image that appears properly in an editor or stand-alone viewer but appears grainy in the browser, you should try converting its *palette*. A palette is simply a collection of colors, and most image editors can store, edit, and save palettes—both with individual images and as stand-alone palette files. If you open an image having one palette and then open a palette file describing another palette, most editors provide several options to reconcile the differences. One such option is usually to convert each pixel in the image to the nearest color in the new palette. If the palette consists solely of the 216 browser-safe colors, each pixel in the original image will take on a safe color value, and no dithering or substitution will subsequently occur.

SEE ALSO
For more information about the 216 browser-safe colors, see "Achieving Accurate Rendition—Safe Colors," page 102.

The fixed 216-color palette explains two other problems Web designers often encounter:

- Black-and-white photograph rendition is usually terrible. This is because the browser has only six levels of gray, and four if you exclude black and white. The six available gray levels are:

Color Name	Decimal	Hexadecimal
Black	0-0-0	00-00-00
	51-51-51	33-33-33
	102-102-102	66-66-66
	153-153-153	99-99-99
	204-204-204	CC-CC-CC
White	255-255-255	FF-FF-FF

These six aren't enough shades of gray to display continuous tone grayscale images such as black-and-white photographs.

II

Creating Web Pages

■ Screen shots look terrible because only 8 of the 20 colors reserved by Windows are in the safe palette. Early, 16-color VGA adapters had the following colors indelibly fixed in hardware, and these colors are, by default, now fixed in the Windows mindset as well. They are:

Color Name	Bright	Dark
Black	0-0-0	192-192-192 (light gray)
Red	255-0-0	128-0-0
Green	0-255-0	0-128-0
Blue	0-0-255	0-0-128
Cyan	0-255-255	0-128-128
Magenta	255-0-255	128-0-128
Yellow	255-255-0	128-128-0
White	255-255-255	128-128-128 (dark gray)

All the colors in the Bright column appear in the browser-safe palette, but none of those in the Dark column are in the browser-safe palette. This explains why screen shots converted directly into GIF files don't appear as clearly on Web pages as they did when originally displayed. To obtain a clear display, you'll need to use an image editor to convert the dark VGA colors to their nearest safe-palette equivalents.

Managing Image Download Time

A constant concern for all Web visitors is the time required to download and view a given page. This is less a concern for visitors on local intranets or with high-speed connections than it is for dial-up modem users, but a concern nonetheless. As a Web provider, you should also be concerned with outbound bandwidth. The larger your pages, the fewer pages your server and your Internet connection can deliver per second (or minute).

In general, the time required to download a page is the combined size of all constituent files divided by the bytes per second of available bandwidth. Managing download time thus becomes an issue of managing download bytes. And, because most download bytes occur in image files rather than the HTML, managing download bytes becomes an issue of managing image file size.

FrontPage estimates each page's download time for a typical modem user and displays it in the status bar—for example, the "19 seconds over 28.8" showing in the bottom-right corner of Figure 6-9. This feature permits monitoring the effect of images you add to a page. There are, however, three mitigating factors:

TIP

> To configure the connection speed used for calculating download times, choose Options from the Tools menu, click the Reports View tab, and adjust the control titled "Assume Connection Speed Of."

- Most current browsers cache images and other files. That is, they keep local copies of recently used files. Before downloading any file, the browser checks for a local copy; if one exists, the browser, depending on its configuration, does *either* of the following:

  - Uses it without question, subject to certain timing constraints.

  - Transmits the local copy's date stamp to the server. If the cached copy is outdated, the Web server transmits a new version. If the cached copy is current, the Web server responds with a status code instructing the browser to use the cached version.

  You can maximize the benefits of caching by using stock images and not storing them redundantly on your server. The use of stock images increases caching by reducing the number of different images. Storing all images in, say, an /images folder ensures that the same image has the same URL for all pages on your site. Storing the same image in two different server locations forces the browser to download and cache each copy separately.

- Reducing total image bytes on a Web page suggests using many small image files rather than one large or medium file. This process can go too far, however, because of a factor called *connection overhead*.

  Unless both the browser and the Web server support a feature called *persistent connections,* the HTTP protocol forces the browser to open a new connection for every file it downloads. Thus, a Web page containing 10 images forces the browser to open and close 11 server connections: 1 for the HTML page and 1 for each image. Each of these connections requires processing time on both the browser and server—time that might exceed what's required to download a smaller number of slightly larger files. Stringent balancing of download bytes vs. required connections is seldom warranted, given the number of other variables in effect. Nevertheless, it's good practice to avoid large numbers of very small files.

■ GIF image compression works mainly by consolidating horizontal pixels. That is, rather than sequentially storing 100 white pixels on the same line, the file stores a single instruction to display 100 consecutive pixels, all white.

You can use this information to create images that compress well. Just remember that flat, horizontal areas compress well but complex horizontal areas don't.

JPEG compression is more two-dimensional and thus is less affected by the nature of the image. Flat areas still compress better than highly variegated ones, however. With JPEG files you can also balance quality against image size. To do this, vary the Quality setting in the Picture Properties dialog box. See Figure 6-4 on page 183.

Graphic File Formats

Most current Web browsers can only display two image file formats: Graphic Interchange Format (GIF) and Joint Photographic Expert Group (JPEG). A few browsers also support Portable Network Graphics (PNG), a new high-function alternative. Table 6-4 compares these formats and identifies important differences.

TABLE 6-4. Characteristics of GIF, JPEG, and PNG Formats

	GIF	JPEG	PNG
Colors available	16,777,216	16,777,216	16,777,216
Colors per image	256	16,777,216	16,777,216
Compression	Lossless	Lossy	Lossless
Transparency	One Color	No	Alpha Channel
Translucence	No	No	Alpha Channel
Animation	Yes	No	No
Remembers Gamma	No	No	Yes

NOTE

FrontPage lets you import graphics in any of several other formats—BMP, TIFF, MAC, MSP, PCD, RAS, WPG, EPS, PCX, and WMF—and save them as GIF or JPEG images.

- **Lossy vs. lossless compression.** Storing a bitmapped image may require several bytes of information for each pixel and, if the image is large, may result in very large files. Most bitmapped file formats therefore include provisions for *compression*. Compression uses complex mathematical formulas to identify and abbreviate repeating patterns in the data.

  GIF compression uses a formula that results in zero loss of data from the compression/decompression process—that is, it provides *lossless* compression. The JPEG format supports varying degrees of compression, but most of them fail to guarantee an exact reproduction of the original. Depending on the creator's choice of settings, the resulting image typically loses a measure of color fidelity, sharpness, or contrast. This is called *lossy* compression. The more loss tolerated, the smaller the image file.

SEE ALSO

For information about setting transparency in FrontPage, see "Setting Transparency," page 198.

- **Transparency.** All formats mentioned save rectangular images. The number of horizontal and vertical pixels can be whatever you want, but there's no way to save an image in these formats with circular, ovate, or irregular borders.

  One way to avoid rectangular image shapes is to fill the edge with the same color as the background of your Web page. However, this won't work if the page uses a complex image as a background, or if the remote user has configured the browser to override incoming background colors and images.

  A better solution involves specifying a *transparent* color in the image. Instead of displaying pixels from the image having that color, the browser displays whatever pixels lie behind them—usually the background color or image.

  Even better is an *alpha channel* which, for each pixel, specifies 256 levels of transparency as well as a base color.

- **Animation.** The GIF format includes a provision to accommodate multiple images in the same file and to specify timing sequences among them. This provides a way to present simple animations within the browser without requiring the remote user to install additional animation software.

Creating Web Pages

- **Gamma.** Different computers make different assumptions about the relationship between software color brightness and the resulting monitor brightness (which, by the way, is non-linear). Knowing an image's gamma factor when saved allows another computer, later displaying the image, to achieve better rendition.

Most Web designers prefer the GIF format for text, line art, and icons because of its lossless compression and transparency. JPEG finds use in backgrounds, photographs, and other areas where maximum compression and color fidelity are more important than sharpness.

A new graphic format called Portable Network Graphics (PNG) supports full 32-bit color with an alpha channel, multiple compression methods, gamma information, and additional features that ease cross-platform difficulties. Unfortunately, PNG support in browsers remains far from universal, and PNG images tend to be larger than GIF or JPEG images.

ON THE WEB

For detailed information about PNG, browse http://www.w3.org/TR/REC-png-multi.html.

Images on Web pages remain in separate files and don't become part of the HTML. Instead, the HTML merely includes a reference to the image file's name. As the browser receives the HTML for a page, it identifies any image files needed and downloads them for display.

TIP

Avoid using more than 20 to 30 KB of image files on a Web page. Doing so leads to slow download times for visitors who connect to the Internet by modem.

Advanced Image Properties

The remainder of this chapter discusses several advanced topics related to picture files. You're most likely to encounter these concepts when using an advanced picture editor.

Transparency and Alpha Channels

At times it's quite desirable for parts of a computer graphics image to be transparent:

- When the edges of an object are irregular—that is, anything but rectangular

- When parts of an image must appear translucent

- When parts of an image should blend gradually into the background

Irregular Edges

Figure 6-14 shows a Web page containing two versions of the same image. The version at the left has a solid white background that clashes with the textured background of the Web page. The image at the right has a transparent background that allows the texture to show through clearly.

FIGURE 6-14.

Compare the white background in the image at the left with the transparent background of the image at the right.

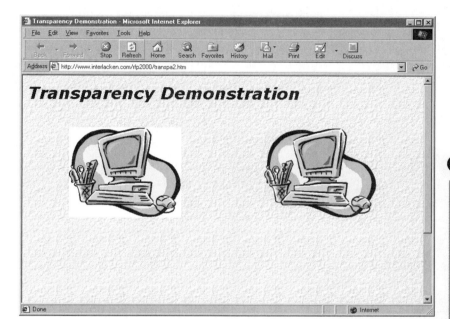

No amount of editing on the left image will make it look as good as the image on the right. No solid color can possibly blend evenly with the surrounding texture, and even adding a textured background to the image will produce slight mismatches as the visitor resizes the browser window.

Using a solid, rather than textured, Web-page background makes it easier to use images with nontransparent backgrounds—though each different background color then requires its own set of images with matching backgrounds. A transparent background allows using the same image file on any Web page.

Anti-Aliasing

Another application that greatly benefits from transparency is *anti-aliasing*. This is a technique that reduces the jagged appearance of curved lines when displayed on a computer monitor. Pixels along a curved edge, rather than being either the object's color or the background color, take on a mixture of the two. Figure 6-15 shows the string "abc" aliased at the left and anti-aliased at the right.

Creating Web Pages

abc abc

Figure 6-16 provides an enlarged view of anti-aliasing. Pixels entirely in the white area are entirely white, and those entirely in the black area are correspondingly black. Pixels along the border, however, are colored gray in proportion to the amount of black or white space that would be occupied at a much higher resolution.

The use of anti-aliasing isn't confined to black-and-white drawings; the concept of proportionately shading edge pixels can apply to any intersection of two colors.

Many graphics programs anti-alias everything by default, but this isn't always desirable. Anti-aliased edges sometimes appear blurry, like a slightly out-of-focus photograph, and sometimes the sharpness of aliased images is more important than the elimination of jagged edges. For this reason, it's important to have both aliasing and anti-aliasing tools at hand.

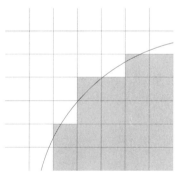 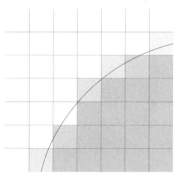

Aliased (jagged) curve   Anti-aliased (smoothed) curve

Translucence

Figure 6-17 shows Microsoft Image Composer editing an image that contains a transparent *sprite*—the magnifying glass. An Image Composer sprite is a sort of image within an image; when you combine several images to form a single composition, Image Composer remembers each subimage as a separate component you can later rearrange or modify. The magnifying glass, the gray background, and the darker gray stripe are each sprites.

FIGURE 6-17.

Note the transparency present in the magnifying glass. The gray background and dark gray stripe show through the glass only partially.

The background and stripe were actually drawn with solid colors; they appear lighter through the magnifying glass because the glass is partially transparent. This is possible because Image Composer uses a 32-bit color model with an 8-bit *alpha channel*.

Implementing Transparency

A problem arises when preparing anti-aliased graphics (or, for that matter, nonrectangular graphics of any kind) for use on various colored or textured backgrounds. One color is known—that of the image—but the second color varies depending on where the graphic is used. The edge pixels need to be shaded not from one color to another, but from a solid color to various degrees of transparency—degrees that allow background colors to partially show through. Complicating the problem, each pixel in the image may require a different amount of transparency.

An *alpha channel* stores a fourth value along with the normal red, green, and blue intensities for each pixel. Each pixel's alpha value indicates the degree of transparency for that pixel, normally with the same precision used for red, green, and blue values. The addition of an alpha channel expands 24-bit color (8 bits each for red, green, and blue) to 32-bit color.

Unfortunately, neither of the two graphics formats commonly used on the Web supports a true alpha channel. Advanced image editors such as Microsoft Image Composer *do* support alpha channels, but saving an image in Web format converts the transparency information to fixed colors based on the editor's current background color. Having alpha-channel support in the image editor and its native file format is less useful than if Web graphics fully supported the feature, but having alpha support in an editor at least provides an easy way to create multiple versions of an image with different background colors.

A common problem involves images anti-aliased for one background but used on another. This results in a sort of halo around the opaque portions of the image. Unfortunately, even editing the image with a program that supports alpha channels won't restore the original transparency information; the alpha channel was lost when the image was saved with a fixed color background. Pixel-by-pixel editing along the edges is often the only remedy to this halo effect.

The JPEG file format doesn't support transparency.

The Graphic Interchange Format—GIF—does support an all-or-nothing sort of transparency. The creator of a GIF file can designate one color in the image as denoting transparency, and a browser will then render pixels that color as transparent. This is better than nothing—but nowhere near as powerful as a full alpha channel.

Of 16,777,216 possible colors, only 256 can exist within any given GIF file. These 256 are the GIF file's palette. Transparency works by designating one palette entry—out of the 256—as transparent. When the browser encounters this palette-entry color, it displays whatever lies behind the GIF image instead of the palette-entry color.

If two palette entries represent the same color, only one of them can indicate transparency. This may explain why you occasionally get incomplete results setting transparency on the basis of color.

Gamma Correction

In a perfect world—or at least a simple one—the brightness of each pixel displayed on a monitor would vary precisely in accordance with the brightness values set by software. For example, a pixel with RGB values of 200-200-200 would appear twice as bright as one with values of 100-100-100. The relationship between software intensity, display-card voltage, and hardware intensity would all be linear. Optimally, the brightness of a monitor pixel would vary directly with the signal from the display adapter, as shown in the first graph of the following figure.

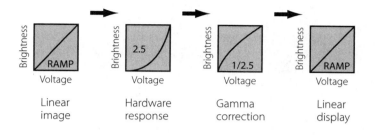

| Linear image | Hardware response | Gamma correction | Linear display |

Of course, real life is nowhere near so simple. Monitors work by blasting electrons at glowing phosphors; the more electrons the brighter the phosphors, but the relationship is hardly linear. For most monitors, brightness equals voltage raised to the 2.5th power:

$$\text{Brightness} = \text{Voltage}^{2.5}$$

In the above formula, voltage is a relative value between 0 and 100 percent, expressed in the range from 0 to 1.

The Hardware response graph shows a typical, real-world graph of monitor brightness vs. display adapter output.

The exponent 2.5 is called a *gamma coefficient*. The exact value varies somewhat, depending on the particular device, but 2.5 is a typical value. The resulting curve relating brightness to voltage is shown Hardware response graph.

Gamma correction is an adjustment that restores linearity between software color values and monitor brightness. It supplies an inverse function, shown in the third graph, and corrects the nonlinearity of the hardware, as shown in the final graph.

Without gamma correction, changes in RGB values close to zero have far less effect than changes closer to 255. Also, a true 50% gray would occur at an RGB value of 193-193-193, not (as you would expect) at 127-127-127:

$$(193/255)^{2.5} = .49836$$

ON THE WEB For more information about gamma and gamma correction, browse the Web site http://www.cgsd.com/papers/gamma_intro.html.

Uncorrected gamma can also have a serious effect on color blending. Doubling each of the intensities in RGB color 50-75-100, for example, would create a nonlinear color shift because doubling 50 would have less effect on the red component than doubling 100 would have on the blue component.

Gamma correction can occur in application software, in the operating system, in the video driver, in the display adapter, or in the monitor. In the PC and Unix environment, however, gamma correction normally appears only in application software. Figure 6-18 shows the Gamma tab of the Microsoft Image Composer Options dialog box.

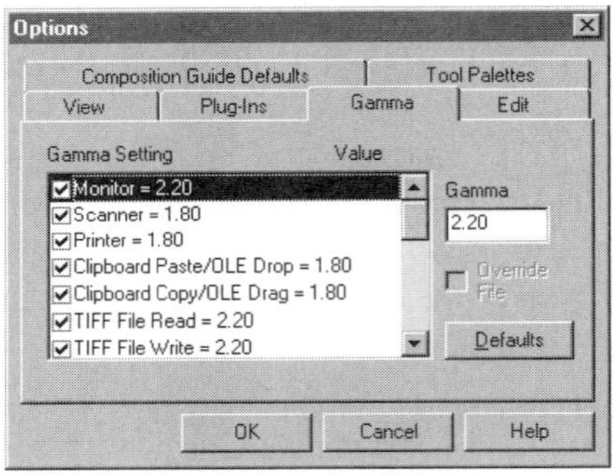

FIGURE 6-18.

Microsoft Image Composer contains this tab to provide control over gamma correction.

PC vs. Macintosh Gamma Correction

Macintosh computers have a gamma correction of 1.4 built into the hardware. Since 2.5 divided by 1.4 is 1.8, 1.8 is the normal gamma correction setting for Macintosh software. This accounts for the muddy appearance of Macintosh-created graphics on a PC, and the bright, washed-out appearance of PC-created images on a Mac. The Mac hardware brightens dark colors in hardware, while the PC hardware does not.

Measuring the gamma of a particular monitor, graphics card, printer, or other device is called *color calibration*. Color calibration requires special color measurement hardware and specially adjustable software, and is generally beyond the scope of this book. However, this may be an area to explore if you plan on doing the most exacting, professional-quality graphics work.

In Summary...

Anything the Web can do with images, so can FrontPage. What's more, FrontPage does it quickly and easily, using Office 2000 conventions familiar to millions of people.

The next chapter deals with how to create and manage hypertext links, including image maps.

Building Hyperlinks

Hyperlinks are the essence of the Web. Without hyperlinks, there would be no point-and-click navigation among Web pages—and without point and click, the Web would be dead. Every time you click some underlined text or an image area and thereby jump to another page, you're using a hyperlink. A Web page lacking hyperlinks is truly a Web page going nowhere.

This chapter describes the most common Web mechanisms for linking Web pages, and discusses how to employ these mechanisms using Microsoft FrontPage:

- Hyperlinks

- Bookmarks

- Hotspots (also called Image Maps)

Without hyperlinks, visitors would have to hand-type the URL of each page they wanted to visit. Given the length and cryptic nature of many URLs, visitors probably wouldn't visit many pages, or would get lost in a thicket of typos along the way.

Bookmarks provide a means for jumping into a Web page not at its top, but at some point further within the page. Essentially, they associate a name with a spot on a Web page and provide a way of jumping to that name.

Hotspots provide a way of jumping to a different Web location depending on which part of an image the visitor clicks. This can be useful when a set of hyperlinks lends itself to visual selection.

How Hyperlinks Work

Despite their impact, hyperlinks are extremely simple mechanisms. Associated with a given string of text or image is the address of another Web page. When the visitor clicks that string of text or that image, the browser retrieves the associated page location.

A uniform resource locator (URL, pronounced "u-r-l") provides, in a single string, all the information required to access a file on the Web. It consists of the following structure:

```
<protocol>://<computername>:<port>/<directory>/<filename>
```

For example:

```
http://www.microsoft.com:80/frontpage/learn.htm
```

The protocol HTTP (often supplied automatically when you hand-type *www* into your browser) tells the browser to use hypertext transfer protocol for formatting and transmitting a request to the named computer. It also sets the default port number to 80. The browser will ask the remote computer to send a file named learn.htm from the /frontpage directory on that site.

The following subsections will examine the remaining URL fields in greater detail.

Internet Computer Names

Computers on the Web actually connect by means of numeric IP addresses and not by name. Site names like *www.microsoft.com, ftp.microsoft.com,* and *www.msn.com* are only for the convenience of visitors. Names like *www.microsoft.com* are simply easier to remember than numeric addresses like 207.68.137.36. With visitors preferring names and computers using numbers, some means are clearly needed to translate from one to the other. The Domain Name System (DNS) provides that service.

DNS names are built in levels. Periods separate the levels, with the highest level at the right end of the name. Names get looked up a level at a time—first com, then microsoft, then www—and possibly on different servers for each level. Table 3-1 lists a few of the most common high-level DNS names. DNS names aren't case sensitive, but they're usually shown in lowercase.

> **> NOTE**
>
> The right-most portion of a DNS name—the suffix—indicates the country that registered the name. The suffixes com, gov, mil, net, and org all indicate the United States. Other suffixes are unique to each country, such as ca for Canada, fr for France, jp for Japan, and uk for United Kingdom.

TABLE 7-1. Common Domain Name Suffixes (Root Domains)

Suffix	Meaning	Example	Site
com	Commercial	www.microsoft.com	Microsoft Corporation
edu	Educational	www.nd.edu	University of Notre Dame
gov	Government	www.odci.gov	Central Intelligence Agency
mil	Military	www.army.mil	United States Army
org	Nonprofit Organization	www.pbs.org	Public Broadcasting Service
ca	Canada	www.canoe.ca	Canadian Online Explorer
uk	United Kingdom	www.ox.ac.uk	Oxford University, England
us	United States	www.state.az.us	State of Arizona

Your Internet service provider or network administrator will either give you the IP address of a local DNS server or arrange to have it configured into your PC automatically. This is an important setting because without, it you can only connect to other machines by numeric IP address.

Web-Site Folders and Files

Any folders and files you create as part of your Web site will become folders and files on your Web server's computer. Factors such as allowable characters, allowable length, and case sensitivity of names depend on the operating system running the Web server. If you develop and test Web sites under an operating system with a different file system than the production Web server, you'll need to understand and account for any file system differences.

Unix file systems are case sensitive, so asking for a file named Index.html will fail if the actual file name is index.html. Windows file systems aren't case sensitive, however, so the same request would work on a Windows-based Web server.

TIP

Case-sensitive names are relatively confusing, even to hard-core Unix visitors, and the normal solution is to use lowercase file names only. This is an excellent habit to acquire.

The FAT file system used for years under MS-DOS and Windows 3.x supported an eight-character file name base plus an optional three-character extension. You should conform to these restrictions if there's any chance of moving your site or any of its files to such a platform, even temporarily. This will involve shortening HTML and JPEG file name extensions to HTM and JPG, respectively. (Note that for clarity, extensions standing alone in this book are printed in capital letters.)

If you link to a page someone else created, you'll have to accept the creator's name for it. When naming Web pages and folders yourself, however, here are some worthwhile tips.

- The maximum length of a file name or folder name under Unix is 32 characters—certainly a practical limit for Web pages as well. Extremely long file names and folder names constitute cruel and unusual punishment when the need to hand-type a Web page address arises; further, they invite error, frustration, and ultimately, perhaps, the visitor moving on to a simpler site.

- It's good practice to use only letters, numbers, hyphens, and underscores in path names and file names used on the Web. Even if allowed by the Web server's file system, characters such as commas, slashes, apostrophes, backslashes, dollar signs, ampersands, and spaces aren't allowable in Web addresses; a percent sign followed by a two-digit hexadecimal code is required in lieu of most special characters. A "simple" folder name like What's New? thus becomes What%27s%20New%3F—decidedly less friendly than whatsnew or whats-new.

Additional URL Features

Three subfields can follow the file name in a URL. Each of them is entirely optional. They are:

- **Bookmarks.** Web designers can give names to certain spots within a page. Hypertext links from within the same page or other pages can then jump directly to those spots. The syntax for a link to a bookmark is a pound sign (#) and the name of the bookmark, appearing immediately after the file name. If the URL consists of the pound sign and bookmark name only, the full path to the current page will be the default. The following are examples of URLs that jump to bookmarks:

```
http://www.foo.com/far/out/place.html#space
#earth
```

- **Query strings.** In some cases, rather than the name of a file to transmit, a URL specifies the name of a program the server should run. Such programs may require command-line arguments, and the query string provides a way to transmit them. As shown in the following example, a question mark indicates the beginning of a query string.

```
http://www.foo.com/scripts/
lookup.exe?cust=123&order=456
```

The query string contains one or more name=value pairs, separated by ampersands (&).

? SEE ALSO

For more information on collecting data at the browser and processing it on the server, see Chapter 10, "Creating and Using Forms," and "Saving Form Results for Later Use," page 700.

- **Path information.** Anything that appears between the name of an executable file and the beginning of a query string is passed to the executing program as path information. The URL below contains the string "zonkers" as path information.

```
http://www.foo.com/scripts/lookup.exe/
zonkers?cust=123&order=456
```

Query strings, path information, and the POST method are three different ways of sending data from a browser to a program on a Web server. The method required by any given program depends on how that program was written.

> NOTE

For a further explanation of the POST method, see "HyperText Transfer Protocol— A Simple Concept" in Chapter 15 on page 483.

Using Relative Locations

In URLs that appear within Web pages, a protocol, a computer name, a port, a path name, and a file name are all optional. In general, it's best to let these values default whenever possible because it minimizes changes when you move pages from one site or folder to another.

- Protocol defaults to that of the page currently on display.

- Computer name also defaults to that of the current page.

- If the URL specifies a computer name, port defaults to the default for the protocol. (For HTTP, the default is 80.) If the URL takes the computer name from the current page, the default port is also taken from the current page.

II

Creating Web Pages

In URLs, file names and folder names are always separated by a slash (/)—even if the Web server is running an operating system (such as MS-DOS or Windows) that normally uses a backslash (\) separator.

- If no path name appears, the path from the current page applies.

- If no file name appears, the browser simply doesn't transmit one. The Web server responds by searching the directory path for one or more preconfigured, default file names. If the path contains no default file, the server transmits either a list of files or a Not Found message, depending on its security configuration.

- Although a path name and a file name are both optional, at least one is required.

Note that except for the file name, these defaults work from within Web pages and not from the Address or Location field of your browser window. Suppose, for example, the browser window displays the following URL:

```
http://www.microsoft.com/frontpage/learn.htm
```

To jump to the What's New page, you'd have to change the browser's Address or Location box to:

```
http://www.microsoft.com/frontpage/brochure/whatsnew.htm
```

This entire string isn't required within the definition of the learn.htm file, however. Within learn.htm, you could specify simply:

```
brochure/whatsnew.htm
```

and allow the rest of the URL to default. The browser will add: *http://www.microsoft.com/frontpage/* in front of *brochure/whatsnew.htm* for you.

Creating and Managing Hypertext Links

The most common form of Hypertext link is the anchor. With this type of link, clicking underlined text or an outlined picture takes you to another page. A simple anchor has the following HTML syntax:

```
<A HREF=/contact.html>Click here for contact
information.</A>
```

The browser would display this code as:

<u>Click here for contact information.</u>

and clicking it would jump to the contact.html page in the current server's home folder. The A in <A HREF= stands for anchor, and HREF means

Hypertext Reference. Content between the <A...> and </A> appears as a link, and clicking it jumps to the HREF location.

TIP

> Hyperlinked images work virtually the same as hyperlinked text. Format the anchor tags just as you would for text, but put the HTML to display the image between them.

Of course, a major reason FrontPage exists is to isolate you from HTML tags such as <A HREF=>. The procedure for creating a Hypertext link in FrontPage Editor is as follows:

SEE ALSO

If windows like Figure 7-1 are starting to look familiar, you're paying attention. The dialog boxes shown in Figure 1-13 and Figure 6-2 are quite similar.

1 Select the text or image you wish to create a hyperlink for.

2 Choose Hyperlink from the Insert menu or click the Hyperlink button on the Standard toolbar. The Create Hyperlink dialog box in Figure 7-1 will appear.

3 Specify the hyperlink's target location in the URL field.

4 Click OK.

FIGURE 7-1.
FrontPage uses this dialog box to create a hyperlink for a selected text string or image to another page in the current Web.

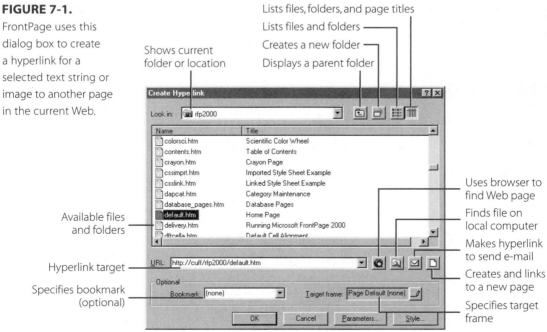

Lists files, folders, and page titles
Lists files and folders
Creates a new folder
Shows current folder or location
Displays a parent folder

Uses browser to find Web page
Finds file on local computer
Available files and folders
Makes hyperlink to send e-mail
Hyperlink target
Creates and links to a new page
Specifies bookmark (optional)
Specifies target frame

Drag and Drop Hyperlinking

If you're working with a FrontPage Web—either disk-based or server-based—creating hyperlinks within your Web is even easier than described in the rest of this section. Just:

1 Open the page that should contain the hyperlink.

2 Locate the hyperlink target in the Folder list.

3 Drag the target onto the open page.

FrontPage will create a hyperlink to the page you dragged, using that page's title as the hyperlink text.

All other options in the Create Hyperlink dialog box are variations on this pattern. For example, there are six ways to accomplish step 3 on the previous page:

- Click any entry in the large list box in the center of the dialog box. FrontPage will enter its location in the URL box.

- Click the browser button (the globe with the spyglass) and locate the target page with your browser. When you switch back to FrontPage, FrontPage will get the current page from the browser and enter it in the URL box.

> **⊗ CAUTION**
>
> Linking directly to a file on your computer is usually a bad idea, because remote users don't have access to the files on your computer. It's better to first import the file to the current FrontPage Web, and then create a hyperlink to that location.

- Click the local file button (the folder with the spyglass) and locate a file on your computer. FrontPage will enter this file name in the URL box for you.

- Click the mail icon (the envelope) and type an Internet e-mail address. FrontPage will enter a URL that launches the remote user's e-mail program and creates a message addressed to the specified recipient.

- Click the new-page button (the blank document) to create a new page and link to it. FrontPage will enter the newly created file's name in the new hyperlink. The resulting New dialog box is the one that appeared previously in Figure 1-6 and Figure 4-2.

- Enter the target location by hand, either by typing or by pasting with the Ctrl+V or Shift+Ins keystrokes.

The large selection list in the center of Figure 7-1 pertains to the current Web. As usual, you can open a folder by double-clicking it. To revert to a parent folder, click the Up One Level button. Clicking the

List and Details buttons toggles the list between displaying files and displaying detailed file information.

The Bookmark control at the bottom of Figure 7-1 permits jumping not only to a particular page, but even to a particular location within that page. The next section in this chapter discusses bookmarks.

? SEE ALSO

For more information on using frames, see "Creating and Editing Frames," page 261.

The Target Frame control specifies which frame should display the hyper-linked page. This presumes that the current Web page will appear within a frameset. You may also select New Window. This instructs the browser to open a new browser window and display the linked page there.

Clicking the Parameters button in the Hyperlink dialog box displays the dialog box shown in Figure 7-2. Here, by clicking the Add button, you can add parameter names and values that FrontPage will append to the URL. This can be useful for sending data from the Web page to a program or script that runs on the Web server, and without using an HTML form. To modify or delete an existing parameter, select it, then click Modify or Remove. To clear all the parameters, click Clear.

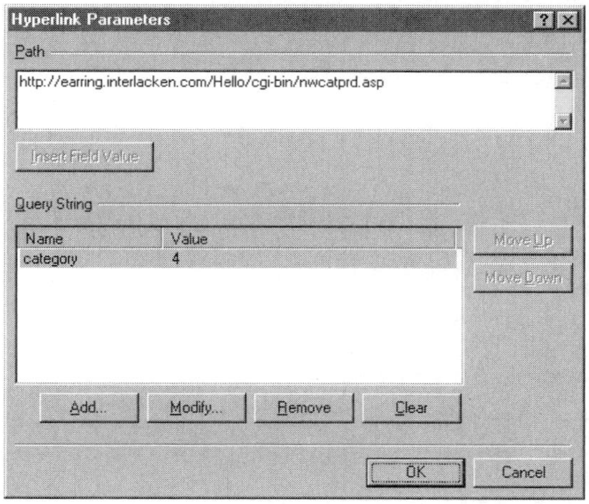

FIGURE 7-2.

Clicking the Param-eters button in Figure 7-1 displays this dialog box, which specifies parameter names and values passed to server-side programs as a query string.

? SEE ALSO

For more information about the structure of URLs see, "How Hyper-links Work," page 216.

Clicking the OK button in Figure 7-1 will establish a link from the text or image you selected in FrontPage to the location specified in the URL box.

To remove hyperlinking from a given text string or image, right-click the hyperlink and select Hyperlink Properties from the pop-up menu. The hyperlink's URL will be highlighted. Press the Backspace key to erase it, and then click OK.

Setting and Using Bookmarks

Sometimes, especially when a Web page is long, it's desirable for hyperlinks to point somewhere other than the top of a page. Bookmarks provide this handy function. They allow hyperlinks to jump from one location to another within the same page, or even from one page to any location in another page. To define a bookmark:

1 Open the target page in FrontPage.

2 Select the page element you want the hyperlink to jump to. This is where you'll insert the bookmark.

3 Choose Bookmark from the Insert menu. The Bookmark dialog box shown in Figure 7-3 will appear.

FIGURE 7-3.

Bookmarks move viewers to specific page locations.

4 Type the name of the bookmark in the field titled Bookmark Name. Use a unique name for each bookmark on a page.

5 Click the OK button. Dotted underlining, as pictured in Figure 7-3, will denote the bookmark's location.

The other buttons in Figure 7-3, perform the following functions.

- **Clear.** To delete a bookmark, double-click its name in the list titled Other Bookmarks On This Page, and then click the Clear button after it appears in the Bookmark Name field.

- **Goto.** To move the insertion point to an existing bookmark, select its name in the list titled Other Bookmarks On This Page, and then click the Goto button.

To set up a hyperlink that jumps to the bookmark:

1 Open the page that will contain the hyperlink.

2 Specify the hyperlink's target URL in the normal way.

3 If the FrontPage dialog box has a Bookmark field, enter or select the bookmark's name there. Otherwise, append a pound sign (#) and the bookmark's name to the URL.

Figure 7-4 shows adding a hyperlink from one spot in a page to another. The dotted underlining below the heading Backup indicates the presence of a bookmark. The bookmark's name is backup, a fact you could confirm by right-clicking the underlined text and selecting Bookmark properties.

FIGURE 7-4.

A hyperlink is being added from the Backup menu bar text to the Backup heading on the same page.

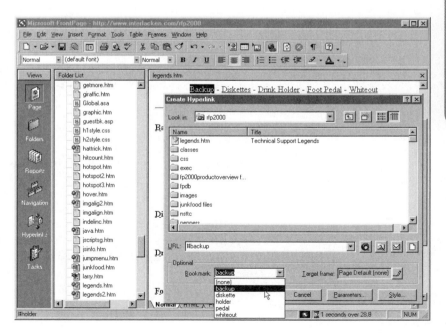

To establish the hyperlink, the page creator took these steps:

1 Highlighted the word "Backup" in the menu bar at the top of the page.

2 Clicked the Hyperlink button on the Standard toolbar.

3 Selected the page containing the bookmark.

4 Dropped down the Bookmark list.

5 Selected backup.

The page creator will finish by clicking the OK button.

If the page containing the bookmark isn't in the current Web, the drop-down list of bookmarks might not be available. In this case, simply type the bookmark name.

Creating and Using Hotspots

Hotspots provide another form of hyperlinking—one that permits assigning different URLs to different parts of an image. Another name for hotspots is *image maps*.

Hotspots are portions of an image that function as hyperlinks. The most common uses for hotspots are in menu bars and maps, though you can use hotspots for any application that requires jumping to different locations in response to clicking different areas of an image.

To add hotspots to an image in FrontPage:

1 Single-click the image to select it.

2 Select the Rectangular Hotspot, Circular Hotspot, or Polygonal Hotspot tool from the Picture toolbar described in Table 6-3 on page 195.

3 When using the Rectangular or Circular Hotspot tools, drag the mouse pointer over the portion of the image that should define the hotspot. When using the Polygon tool, click the mouse pointer at each corner. To close the polygon, double-click the next-to-last point, and the final line will be drawn to the starting point.

4 When dragging is complete, FrontPage will open the Create Hyperlink dialog box. This is the same dialog box used for setting up hyperlinks both from text and from entire images. Define the hyperlink as described in the next section, and then click OK.

5 Repeat steps 2, 3, and 4 to define additional hotspots for the same image.

6 To define a hotspot for the image as a whole, click any portion that's not already a hotspot and specify its URL in the usual way.

When you select an image that has hotspots, FrontPage displays the clickable areas as shown in Figure 7-5. The figure shows a single image with eight hotspots.

FIGURE 7-5.

If an image's hotspots are difficult to see, the Highlight Hotspots button will toggle the Images to a solid white background.

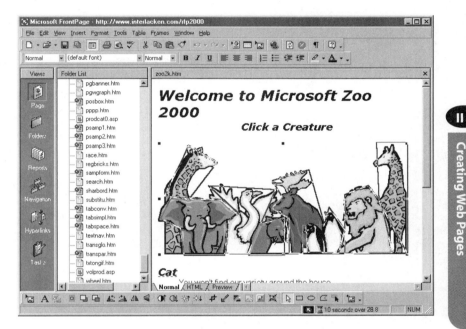

- To modify a hotspot area, select it once by single-clicking, and then drag the edges or corner handles.

- To modify a hotspot hyperlink, double-click the hotspot area, or right-click it and choose Picture Hotspot Properties from the pop-up menu.

⭐ TIP

A frequent criticism of hotspots—and of image hyperlinks in general—is the lack of visual clues they provide. Visitors are reduced to moving the mouse pointer over an image and watching for the pointer to indicate a hyperlink, or to clicking images at random to discover what they do. If the image you're creating a hyperlink for lacks obvious visual clues, be sure to provide instructions in the surrounding text.

Creating Web Pages

In Summary...

FrontPage provides easy-to-use dialog boxes for constructing all types of hypertext links. Chapters later in the book will discuss ways that even generate hyperlinks automatically, particularly the section in Chapter 21 titled "Using Web-Level FrontPage Components." For now, though, the next topic is Page Layout. I'll meet you in Chapter 8.

Page Layout

This chapter describes the three most common appoaches to formatting Web pages, and how Microsoft Front-Page supports each one. The approaches are:

- Tables
- Frames
- CSS positioning

HTML tables, originally designed for displaying simple text in rows and columns, have become an important layout technique for Web pages as well. Tables are among the most flexible means for arranging page elements spatially and maintaining their proper appearance as the remote user resizes the page. Because so many people use Excel to create and process tabular data, we'll also look at Excel 2000's capability to save tabular data, including formats and formulas, as a Web page.

Frames are another popular way to subdivide the browser window into functionally distinct areas. A *frameset* defines the size, location, and name of each frame, and ordinary Web pages provide content for each frame. A hyperlink in one frame can change the Web page displayed in another.

CSS positioning—sometimes called CSS2—extends the original Cascading Style Sheet specification with new commands that precisely control the size and placement of elements on a Web page. If this sounds too good to be true, you're right. Once a new technology like CSS comes out, it's usually a long time until all your Web visitors have a browser that supports it.

Internet Explorer 4 and Netscape Navigator 4 were the first browsers to support CSS positioning, and they both support it differently. FrontPage currently limits its support of CSS positioning to that supported by version 4 of both browsers, and fear not, this chapter certainly discusses that capability. It also provides a brief introduction to the rest of CSS2, just in case you're ready (or desperate enough) to work with the code by hand.

The chapter concludes with a look at PowerPoint 2000's HTML facilities and with some tips on designing pages your visitors will find both attractive and intuitive.

Creating and Editing Tables

Tables are an incredibly useful addition to HTML. Before tables were available, HTML offered no practical means to organize content horizontally or in grids. The entire World Wide Web was left-justified.

For ease of learning, the following discussion will use very simple grids as examples. A later section titled "Using Tables for Page Layout," on page 248, will describe how to use tables for laying out more complex content. As each feature is introduced, refer to Table 8-1 to identify the relevant toolbar buttons.

Creating a New Table

FrontPage provides five distinct ways to create HTML tables. The method you choose depends on your preferences and the type of content you want to display. The five methods are:

- Drawing with the mouse
- Using the Insert Table button
- Inserting a table using menus
- Converting text to a table
- Pasting tabular data

TABLE 8-1.   The FrontPage Table Toolbar

Icon	Description	Function	Menu Command
	Draw Table	Creates a new table sized in accordance with mouse dragging.	Table/Draw Table
	Eraser	Erases any cell walls you drag the mouse across; merges affected cells.	Table/Merge Cells
	Insert Rows	Inserts rows above the current selection.	Table/Insert Rows Or Columns
	Insert Columns	Inserts columns left of the current selection.	Table/Insert Rows Or Columns
	Delete Cells	Deletes currently selected cells.	Table/Delete Cells
	Merge Cells	Combines two or more cells into one cell that spans multiple rows or columns.	Table/Merge Cells
	Split Cells	Divides one cell into several (opposite of Merge Cells).	Table/Split Cells
	Align Top	Aligns contents to the top of a cell.	Table/Properties /Cell/ Vertical Alignment/Top
	Center Vertically	Aligns contents to the middle of a cell.	Table/Properties /Cell/ Vertical Alignment/Middle
	Align Bottom	Aligns contents to the bottom of a cell.	Table/Properties/Cell/ Vertical Alignment/Bottom
	Distribute Rows Evenly	Fixes table height to its current value in pixels and row height to uniform values.	Table/Distribute Rows Evenly
	Distribute Columns Evenly	Fixes table width to its current value in pixels and column width to uniform values.	Table/Distribute Columns Evenly
	Fill Color	Sets background color for the entire table, if selected, or for selected cells.	Table/Properties/Cell or Table/ Background Color
	AutoFit	Removes all overrides to the natural height and width of a table and its cells.	Table/AutoFit

The remainder of this section will provide step-by-step instructions for each of these methods.

Drawing a Table with the Mouse

To create a table by drawing:

1 Choose Draw from the Table menu or click the Draw Table button on the Table toolbar. The mouse pointer will take on the shape of a pencil.

2 Point to where you want one corner of the table to appear, hold down the mouse button, and then drag to the table's opposite corner.

3 Release the mouse button to create the table. Note the following:

   • All such tables are sized in pixels.

   • All such tables initially consist of one cell. You can create rows and columns within the table by drawing lines with the Draw Table button.

   • FrontPage will do its best to position the table where you drew it, though the limitations of HTML still apply.

   • If you draw two tables that overlap horizontally, FrontPage will locate the second inside the first. HTML doesn't allow horizontally overlapping tables.

4 Right-click the new table, and then choose Table Properties from the pop-up menu.

5 In the Table Properties dialog box, shown later as Figure 8-5, specify additional properties as required, and then click OK.

Using the Insert Table Button

This method also creates a table at the insertion point but, unlike the draw method, it lets you choose the number of cells in the table. There are two ways to use the Insert Table button: clicking and dragging.

To use the Insert Table button in clicking mode:

1 Place the insertion point where the table should appear.

2 Click the Insert Table button on the Standard toolbar. A small grid of table cells will appear.

3 Move the mouse pointer over the grid until it shades the number of cells you want.

4 Click the mouse again to insert the table.

5 To cancel table creation, click the Cancel area at the bottom of the grid. (It won't say Cancel unless the mouse is over it.)

To use the Insert Table button in dragging mode:

1 Place the insertion point where the table should appear.

2 Click the Insert Table button on the Standard toolbar and hold down the mouse button. A small grid of table cells will appear.

3 Drag the mouse pointer across the grid, selecting the number of rows and columns you want. To enlarge the grid, drag beyond its right or lower edge.

4 Release the mouse button to insert the table.

5 To cancel table creation, drag the mouse pointer beyond the grid's upper or left edge, then release the mouse button.

In general, the dragging method is superior because it can enlarge the supplied grid.

Inserting a Table Using Menus

Choosing a menu option and filling out a dialog box provides more control over a new table's attributes than either method above. To take this approach:

1 Place the insertion point where the table should appear.

2 Choose Insert from the Table menu, and then choose Table. The Insert Table dialog box shown in Figure 8-1 will appear.

3 Specify characteristics for the table.

4 Click OK.

FIGURE 8-1.

This dialog box adds a table to a Web page.

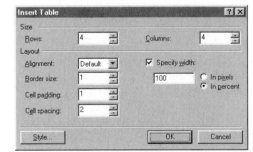

The available properties are described below. You can modify any of these properties later without re-creating the table.

■ **Size** controls the dimensions of the table in terms of rows and columns.

- **Rows** specifies the number of horizontal rows the table should have.

- **Columns** specifies the desired number of vertical columns.

- **Layout** controls page positioning and appearance.

  - **Alignment** specifies where you want the table positioned on the page. Choices are Default, Left, Center, and Right. Default lets the browser do what it wants, which is normally to left-align tables. Left and Right align a table to the corresponding margins, while Center positions it in the center of the page.

  - **Border Size** specifies the thickness in pixels of a border that will surround the table. A border size of zero specifies no such border and no interior gridlines.

  - **Cell Padding** indicates the number of pixels to insert between a cell's margin and its contents.

  - **Cell Spacing** indicates the number of pixels that should appear between the margins of adjacent cells.

Figure 8-2 illustrates the difference between cell padding and cell spacing. Distinguishing cell padding from cell spacing is easier when cell borders are turned on. Figure 8-2 also illustrates tables within tables.

FIGURE 8-2.

This Web page illustrates the difference between cell spacing and cell padding. Spacing occurs outside the margin, and padding occurs within. Note also that the four 3x3 tables are located within the cells of a 7x2 table.

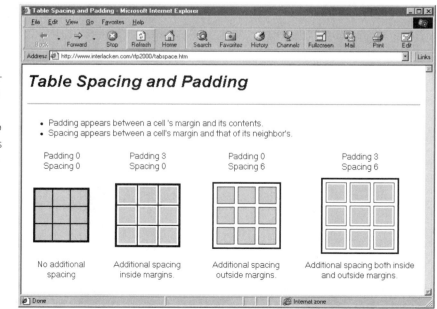

CAUTION

Most Web browsers treat design-time table measurements as approximations and not as concrete specifications.

- **Specify Width** specifies the width of the table, provided the check box is turned on. The next two settings control the units of measure. If the box is turned off, the browser sizes the table.

  - **In Pixels** specifies the width of the table in pixels.

  - **In Percent** sizes the table as a percentage of available space at browse time. A table width of 100% stretches the table across all available space.

- **Style** applies cascading style-sheet properties to the table.

Figure 8-3 shows the result of inserting a table with the properties given in Figure 8-1.

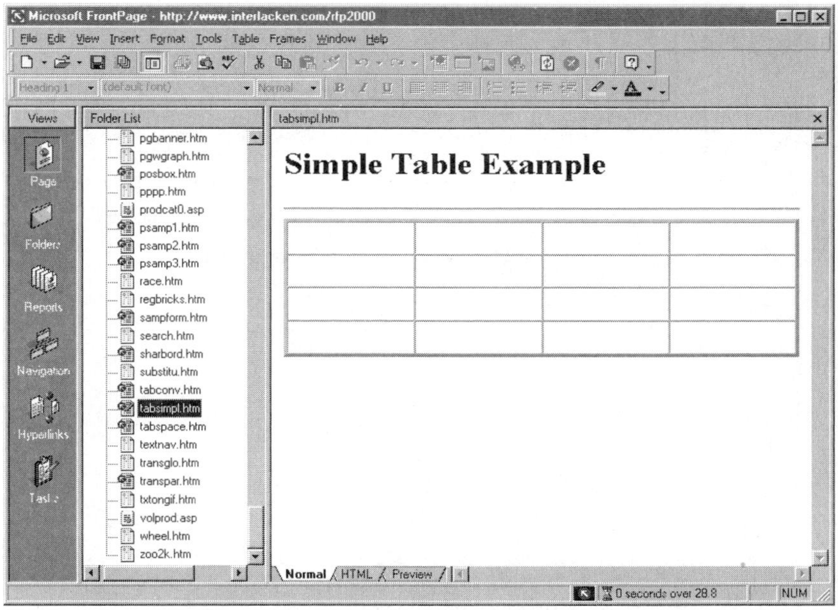

FIGURE 8-3.

This table was created from the Insert Table dialog box of Figure 8-1 on page 233.

Converting Text to a Table

To create a table from existing text:

1 Select the text you want converted to a table by dragging the mouse pointer across it.

2 Choose Convert from the Table menu, then choose Text To Table.

3 When the dialog box titled Convert Text To Table appears (shown in Figure 8-4), choose one of the following:

  - To convert each paragraph in the text to a full row in the table, click Separate Text At Paragraphs.

- To divide each row's text into columns based on the presence of tab characters or commas, click Tabs or Commas, respectively.

- To divide each row's text into columns based on some other character, click Other and enter the character you want in the space provided.

- To draw a one-celled table around the selected text, choose None.

4 Click OK.

Figure 8-4 shows actual results. After you click OK, the selected text will become another table like the one shown.

FIGURE 8-4.

The Convert Text To Table command builds a table from existing plain text.

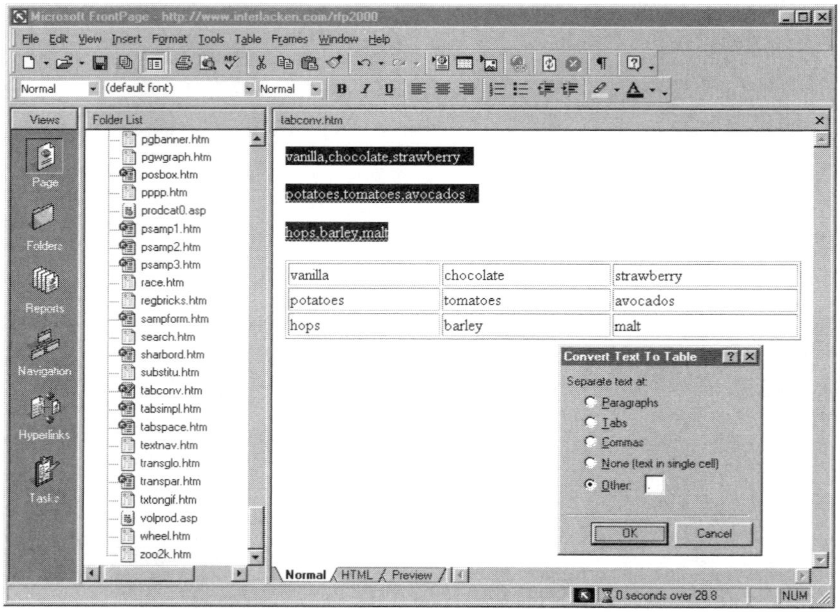

TIP

To convert an existing table to text, first select the table, then choose Convert from the Table menu, and finally choose Table To Text. Each cell in the table will become an ordinary paragraph.

Pasting Tabular Data

Another way to create a table in FrontPage is to paste tabular content from other programs, such as a table from a word processor or database, or cells from a spreadsheet. If FrontPage doesn't automatically create a table, use the Paste Special command from the Edit menu to format the text as you paste it. If necessary, then use the Convert Text To Table command (just discussed) to complete the table.

Modifying an Existing Table

Regardless of how you create a table, you probably won't get it exactly right on the first try. Most people spend considerably more time modifying and refining existing tables than creating new ones.

The Table Properties dialog box contains settings that affect an entire table. There are two ways to open this dialog box:

■ Set the insertion point or selection anywhere in the table, choose Properties from the Table menu, and then choose Table.

■ Right-click anywhere in the table, and then choose Table Properties from the pop-up menu.

Either action displays the Table Properties dialog box shown in Figure 8-5. The following settings are available.

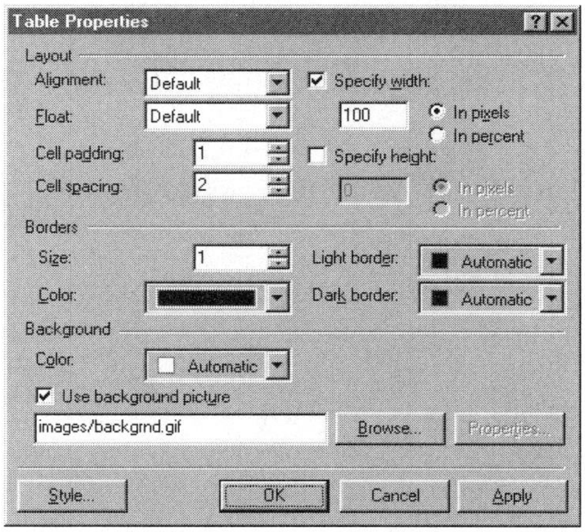

FIGURE 8-5.

This dialog box provides access to settings that affect an entire HTML table.

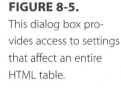

Layout

This section controls page positioning and appearance.

■ **Alignment** specifies the table's horizontal page positioning.

   • **Default** specifies no special alignment for the table. At display time, browser defaults will apply; this usually results in a left-aligned table with no text wrapping.

- **Left** and **Right** place the table in an HTML division that aligns its content to the specified margin. No text will wrap around the table.

- **Center** places the table in an HTML division that centers its content. No text will wrap around the table.

■ **Float** controls left and right positioning of the table.

- **Default** specifies no special alignment for the table. At display time, browser defaults will apply, usually producing a left-aligned table with no text wrapping.

- **Left** and **Right** align the table to the left or right margin, respectively; both allow text to flow around it.

■ **Cell Padding** indicates the number of pixels between the edges of each cell and its contents.

■ **Cell Spacing** indicates the number of pixels between adjacent cells.

■ **Specify Width** controls the amount of horizontal space the table occupies. To apply this setting, you must turn on the check box, specify a value, and indicate a unit of measure.

- **In Pixels** indicates the width value is specified in pixels.

- **In Percent** indicates the width value is a percentage of available space at browse time.

TIP

When you specify the dimensions of any Web-page object as a percentage, that percentage is relative to the object's immediate container. Thus, depending on where it appears, an object sized at 50 percent might occupy 50 percent of the browser window, 50 percent of a frame, or 50 percent of a table cell, whichever is most specific.

■ **Specify Height** controls the amount of vertical space the table occupies. To apply this setting, you must turn on the check box, specify a value, and indicate a unit of measure.

- **In Pixels** indicates the height value is specified in pixels.

- **In Percent** indicates the height value is a percentage of available space at browse time.

? SEE ALSO
Refer to "Choosing Page Colors," page 107, for advice on selecting colors.

Border

This section provides control over the table's border colors.

- **Size** specifies the thickness of a border that surrounds the table. A size of zero suppresses both the border and interior grid.

- **Border** specifies a solid color for drawing the border that surrounds the table.

- **Light Border** overrides the color of the top and left table borders.

- **Dark Border** overrides the color of the right and bottom table borders.

> NOTE

According to common GUI guidelines, the light source for three-dimensional images is above and to the left. Thus, to make a raised object look three-dimensional:
- Make the top and left edges light, as if catching light directly.
- Make the bottom and right edges dark, as if in shadow.

Pages take on a very confusing perspective if different objects appear lighted from different directions.

Background

These options control the table's background picture or color.

- **Use Background Picture** gives the table a background picture. To use this feature, turn on the check box and specify the background picture's file name and location in the current Web.

- **Browse** displays the Select Background Picture dialog box for finding a background picture. It looks through the current Web, the local file system, or the FrontPage clip-art library.

- **Properties** displays the Picture Properties dialog box shown in Figure 8-6 (page 242), which alters the properties of the specified background picture.

- **Background Color** controls the table's background color.

Adding Rows and Columns to a Table

Two methods are available for adding rows or columns to a table: menus and the toolbar. To add rows or columns using menus:

1 Click any cell that will adjoin the new row or column.

2 Choose Insert from the Table menu, and then choose Rows Or Columns.

3 In the resulting dialog box, click either the Columns or Rows option button, indicating what to insert.

4 Indicate the number of rows or columns to insert. If you choose to insert columns, the text label changes from Number Of Rows to Number Of Columns.

5 For rows, indicate whether to insert above or below the current selection. For columns, specify right or left.

6 Click OK.

Here's the toolbar procedure for adding rows to a table.

1 Select one or more existing rows that will appear under the new row. (See the sidebar opposite, "Selecting Table Cells.")

2 Click the Insert Rows button on the Table toolbar.

3 Above your selection, FrontPage will insert as many rows as you selected.

★ TIP

When you insert rows using the toolbar, FrontPage inserts them above the selected rows. When you insert columns, they appear to the left of whatever columns you selected.

To add columns to a table via the toolbar:

1 Select one or more existing columns that will appear to the right of the new column or columns.

2 Click the Insert Columns button on the Table toolbar.

3 FrontPage will insert an equal number of columns just left of your selection.

HTML tables are quite flexible and don't require all rows to have the same number of cells. To add cells to a single row:

1 Click inside the cell just left of where you want the new cell inserted.

2 Choose Insert Cell from the Table menu.

In Figure 8-6, the insertion point was in the cell numbered 3 when the FrontPage user inserted a cell. The new cell appeared between existing cells 3 and 4.

FrontPage can also merge adjacent cells to span several rows or columns. Figure 8-7 illustrates this concept; note the large cells in each corner that occupy the space normally occupied by two. The procedure for merging cells is described on page 242.

Selecting Table Cells

There are three approaches to selecting cells, rows, columns, or an entire table.

Using Menus

Click any cell in the desired range, choose Select from the Table menu, and then choose one of the following commands:

- Table
- Column
- Row
- Cell

Using Mouse Movements at the Table Margins

- To select columns or rows, move the mouse pointer over the top margin (to select columns) or over the left margin (to select rows). Click when the mouse pointer changes to a thick arrow.
- To select multiple columns or rows, proceed as above but drag.

Clicking Cells

- To select a single cell, press Alt and click the cell.
- To select a range of cells one cell at a time, hold down Ctrl+Alt and drag the mouse pointer across each one. As an alternative to dragging, click each cell you want to select while pressing Ctrl+Alt.
- To select a contiguous range of cells, drag from one corner of the selection to the opposite corner. You can also click one corner cell and then click the opposite corner while pressing the Shift key.
- To add cells to a selection, hold down Shift while clicking the additional cells.
- To deselect cells from a group of selected cells, click the cells while pressing the Ctrl+Alt key combination.
- To select the entire table, click the top or left table margin while pressing the Alt key.

1 Select the cells you want to merge. They must be contiguous and form a rectangular block—no L-shapes or other irregular shapes.

2 Choose Merge Cells from either the Table menu or the Table toolbar.

FIGURE 8-6.

A user added one cell to this table between cells 3 and 4 of the second row.

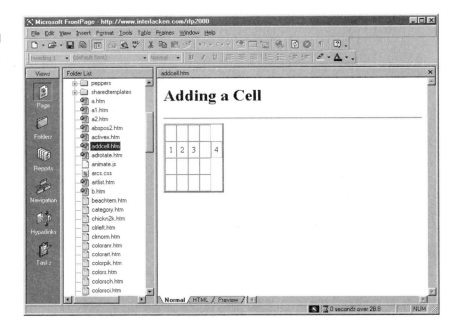

FIGURE 8-7.

The oversized cells in the corner of this table resulted from merging cells in a 4x4 table.

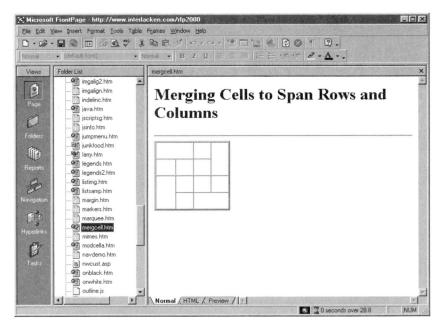

II

Creating Web Pages

(X) CAUTION

Merging two cells into one produces quite a different result than deleting one of them. *Merged* cells span multiple rows or columns— whatever space the individual cells occupied before the merge. *Deleting* a cell forces adjacent cells to move in from below or from the right.

The only tricky part of this procedure is selecting the cells. Refer to the sidebar "Selecting Table Cells" (page 241) for details.

To split cells already merged, select them, and then either click the Split Cells toolbar button or choose the Split Cells command from the Table menu.

Adding a Table Caption

To give the table a caption, click anywhere in the table, choose Insert from the Table menu, and then choose Caption. FrontPage will create a blank caption above the table and set the insertion point there. Type the caption wording you want. To move the caption below the table:

1 Click the caption, choose Properties from the Table menu, and then choose Caption. (Alternatively, right-click and choose Caption Properties from the pop-up menu.)

2 Choose the caption position you prefer: Top Of Table or Bottom Of Table.

3 Click OK.

Figure 8-8 shows a simple 4x4 table containing some data. Inserting the text was a simple matter of placing the insertion point inside each cell, and then typing. The same approach works for inserting images and other objects—even additional tables—into a cell. You can set the same properties for items within a cell that you can set for them elsewhere on the page.

FIGURE 8-8.

Like a browser, FrontPage adjusts default column height and row width, based on cell contents and window size.

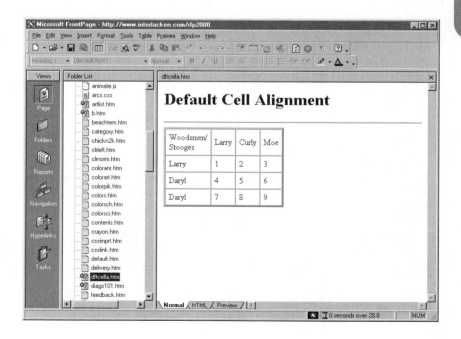

By default, the rows and columns in a table grow in height and width to accommodate cell content. Browsers—and FrontPage as well—normally try to minimize white space by widening columns whose cells contain a lot of text. At the same time, they try to keep columns wide enough not to truncate any images or other fixed-width objects. If possible, the browser sizes the table horizontally to fit within the available display area.

Adjusting Cell Properties

Although the table layout in Figure 8-8 looks generally pleasing, several aspects beg improvement. The numeric entries should allow for two-digit numbers and therefore should be right-justified, for example, and the column headings might look better bottom-aligned. You can make these kinds of adjustments in the Cell Properties dialog box. To specify cell properties:

1   Select one or more cells using *one* of these methods:

  - Set the insertion point in a cell.

  - Select content in one or more cells.

  - Use any of the methods cited in the sidebar "Selecting Table Cells."

2   Choose Properties from the Table menu, and then choose Cell.

  or

  Right-click the cell and choose Cell Properties from the pop-up menu.

Step 2 will display the Cell Properties dialog box shown in Figure 8-9.

This controls the following properties for the selected cells.

Layout

These four controls determine how objects in the selected table cell are displayed. Note that all the following properties can be applied to a single cell or a block of cells.

- ■ **Horizontal Alignment** controls lateral positioning of the cell's contents. There are three possibilities:

  - **Left** aligns the cell's contents to the left border. This is the default.

  - **Center** positions the cell contents an equal distance from the left and right borders.

  - **Right** aligns the cell's contents to the right border.

FIGURE 8-9.

The Cell Properties dialog box exposes settings for any number of selected table cells.

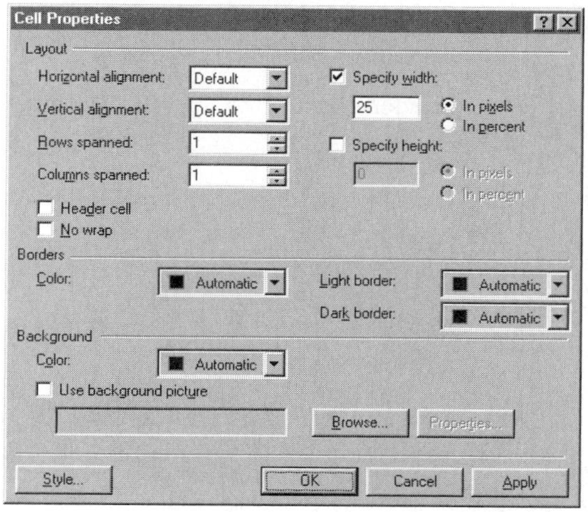

- **Vertical Alignment** controls vertical positioning of the cell's contents. Again, there are three possibilities:

  - **Top** aligns the cell's contents to the top of the cell. Any white space appears at the bottom.

  - **Middle** distributes any vertical white space half above and half below the cell's contents. This is the default.

  - **Bottom** aligns the cell's contents to the bottom of the cell. Any white space appears at the top.

- **Rows Spanned** indicates the height of the cell in terms of normal table rows.

- **Columns Spanned** indicates the width of a cell in terms of normal table columns.

> **NOTE**
>
> HTML provides no definitive way to size either cells or entire tables. Any dimensions you specify are merely suggestions that the browser might override. Inserting a transparent image often provides better control of minimum cell dimensions than do the settings in the Cell Properties dialog box. For more information about this technique, refer to "Using Transparent Images for Page Layout" on page 256.

- **Specify Width** signifies that a minimum width is in effect. To use this setting, you must turn on the check box, specify a value, and indicate a unit of measure.

- **In Pixels** indicates that the Specify Width text box contains a value in pixels.

- **In Percent** indicates that the Specify Width text box specifies a percentage of table size.

■ **Specify Height** signifies that a minimum height is in effect. To use this setting, you must turn on the check box, specify a value, and indicate a unit of measure.

- **In Pixels** indicates that the Specify Height text box contains a value in pixels.

- **In Percent** indicates that the Specify Height text box specifies a percentage of table size.

■ **Header Cell** indicates, if turned on, that the selected cell contains headings. This normally causes any text to appear in bold.

■ **No Wrap** indicates, if turned on, that the browser mustn't wrap text in the selected cell.

Merging cells and setting a span accomplish similar end results, but they aren't the same. *Merging* combines two or more cells into one wider cell that spans multiple rows or columns; cells not involved in the merge retain their former positions. *Setting a span* widens one cell to cover multiple rows or columns, pushing any following cells down or to the right.

Borders

This feature controls the border colors of the selected cell.

■ **Color** specifies a solid color for drawing the cell border.

■ **Light Border** specifies a color for drawing the top and left cell borders.

■ **Dark Border** specifies a color for drawing the right and bottom cell borders.

Background

This feature controls the background picture or color for the selected cell.

■ **Color** controls the color of the cell's background.

■ **Use Background Picture** indicates, if turned on, that the cell will have a background picture. The associated text box specifies a location and file name in the current Web.

- **Browse** presents a dialog box that browses the current Web, the local file system, or the FrontPage clip-art library for a background picture.

- **Properties** displays the Picture Properties dialog box, shown in Figure 6-4, on page 183, which alters the properties of the specified background picture.

Cell Formatting—An Example

Compare Figure 8-8 and Figure 8-10. The latter figure reflects the following edits.

- The cells in the top row have a background color of 204-204-204.

- The text in the top row of cells is bold.

- The cells in the top row have a vertical alignment of Bottom.

- The cells containing numbers have a horizontal alignment of Right.

FIGURE 8-10.

Although still simple, this table is considerably enhanced from that in Figure 8-8.

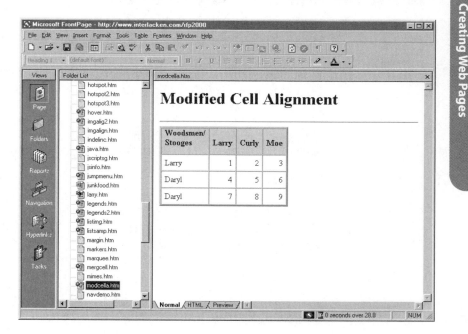

FrontPage provides two commands that attempt to produce uniform row and column sizes. Each appears in FrontPage on the Table menu as well as on the Table toolbar.

■ **Distribute Rows Evenly** sets the height of the currently selected table to its present value in pixels, divides this value by the current number of rows, and sets the height of each cell to the resulting value.

■ **Distribute Columns Evenly** sets the width of the currently selected table to its present value in pixels, divides this value by the current number of columns, and sets the width of each cell to the resulting value.

Unfortunately, the power of these commands is greatly diminished by HTML's weak control over the dimensions of table cells. Browsers consider cell dimensions specified in the HTML as initial suggestions only. You can specify all the cell dimensions you want, but the browser, reacting to the user's current display window, will *still* apply its cell-sizing logic.

Using Tables for Page Layout

It bears repeating that, despite its popularity, HTML is one of the *worst* page description languages in use. Its inventors, in the interest of device independence, stripped HTML of virtually all capabilities to control page appearance. And page authors, in the interest of visual communication, have tried to regain page control ever since.

HTML provides only a basic assortment of paragraph styles. Normal text, headings, code listings, and so forth are all *flush left*—that is, aligned to the left margin, with no provision for indentation. Only a few styles, such as bulleted lists, numbered lists, and definition lists, provide built-in horizontal alignment.

More advanced objects, such as images, tables, Java applets, and ActiveX controls, are flush left by default but can also be centered or *flush right* (aligned to the right margin). When aligned to the left margin, text can optionally flow around nontext objects. Text always flows around right-aligned objects.

From a page-layout standpoint, grids are among the most time-honored techniques. Newspapers have the most obvious layout grids, usually followed by magazines and brochures in that order. From billboards to business cards, the elements of graphic design tend to be first, rectangular and second, lined up in rows and columns.

Tables and frames are the most common tools used for HTML page layout, and both of them arrange content in rectangular grids. Of the two, tables offer the most flexibility, but frames offer less repetition of content.

Grid Layout Principles

Robin Williams, in *The Non-Designers Design Book*, identifies four key elements of effective graphic-arts page design. The first two concepts should be quite familiar from earlier discussions regarding color and typography. The third and fourth concepts, however, are new to this chapter.

- **Contrast.** This is the idea that different kinds of page objects should each be identified by a different look. Titles, headings, body text, hyperlinks, and legal disclaimers, for example, should each be differentiated by a unique appearance.

- **Repetition.** This concept directs that similar page objects should look alike. All body text should look the same, as should all level-1 headings, all level-2 headings, and so forth. Giving like objects different appearances can be extremely confusing to the reader.

- **Alignment.** This concept addresses the positioning of each element in a composition. Elements should appear to be organized according to some plan, not haphazardly.

  Proper alignment generally involves drawing imaginary horizontal and vertical lines through the composition, and then aligning related objects along those lines. Similar objects should generally be aligned similarly to each other. Unlike objects may likewise have unlike alignment, but they can also be differentiated in some other way.

- **Proximity.** This principle holds that related objects should be closer together than unrelated objects. This leads to techniques such as ordering similar items together, decreasing blank space between related items, and increasing blank space between unrelated items.

HTML Tables as Layout Grids

HTML is a relatively poor page-layout environment. HTML, after all, was designed for simple documents and simple authoring. No one at the time thought of assembling graphic compositions rivaling brochures and magazine ads. Basic HTML had almost no typographical or page-layout controls, thus stripping page designers of their most important tools. HTML page layout is further complicated by its variable page dimensions (according to the viewer's browser dimensions), which in turn complicate spatial positioning.

Tables constitute a major weapon in the battle to control page layout. They provide a way to split the page into horizontal and vertical sections, and thus to lay out page elements spatially. Whoever invented HTML tables may have imagined simple grids like that shown in Figure 8-8, but what has evolved are some of the most attractive and complex pages seen today on the World Wide Web.

The cells in an HTML table can have visible or invisible borders. Tables are required for most page layouts, and invisible borders are usually preferable. Creating a page layout with tables first involves deciding how many horizontal and vertical cells the composition requires, and then merging cells for objects that need to span more than one row or column.

> **NOTE**

In graphic design, even text is rectangular. Designers often think of headlines, titles, body text, and other elements as if they were colored rectangles rather than words, letters, and punctuation. It's quite common to call body text *gray space*, for example.

SEE ALSO
For more information about frames, see "Creating and Editing Frames," page 261.

HTML Frames as Layout Grids

Using HTML frames begins with defining a *frameset* that divides the browser window into zones called *frames*. Each frame displays a different Web page, and clicking hypertext in one frame can change the page displayed in another. A typical use of frames involves a menu list in one frame and an information display in another. As the remote user clicks different menu items, the information frame displays corresponding Web pages.

SEE ALSO
For the technical details of HTML page layout, refer to Chapter 5, "Adding and Formatting Text." See also "Assigning CSS Properties," page 147; "Creating and Editing Tables," page 230; and "Creating and Editing Frames," page 261.

Tables and frames both divide the browser window into horizontal and vertical areas, but they solve two quite different problems. Tables are relatively static *x-y* grids, but you can define as many rows and columns as you need. Frames provide a means to replace parts of the browser display while preserving others, but their size and positioning is much less precise. A 5-row by 5-column table is relatively easy to work with, but a 25-frame frameset would be a nightmare.

Table Layout Mechanics

Figure 8-11 illustrates a simple Web page laid out with HTML tables. You may recognize this as the same Web page shown in Figure 2-2 on page 41, except that back then we were talking about the wonders of WYSIWYG editing. This time we're discussing the wonders of tables.

The heading and the horizontal line in Figure 8-11 are just ordinary, centered HTML elements. The four icons, the four category titles, and the kicker occupy a table three columns wide and four rows tall—the table FrontPage makes visible in Figure 8-12. The four cells in column 3 are merged.

FIGURE 8-11.
HTML tables make possible the two-dimensional layout of this Web page.

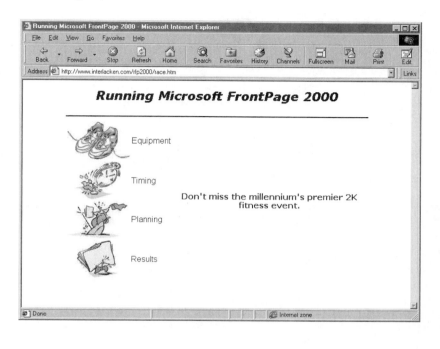

FIGURE 8-12.
Here is the Web page of Figure 8-11, displayed in FrontPage.

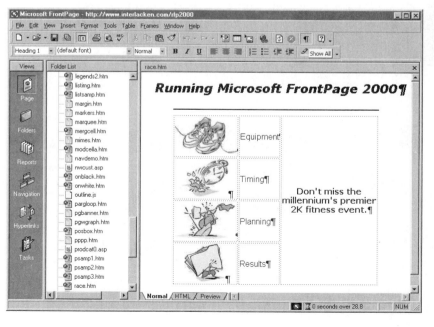

Notice how using a table aligns the category titles along a vertical grid line even though the four icons are different widths. The titles are like items and therefore should have a like appearance and like alignment. Because each icon and its category title are related, they too should have like alignment. The two-dimensional table lets us use one type of alignment—vertical—to indicate like elements and another type of alignment—horizontal—to indicate associated content.

The kicker isn't associated with any one category, and therefore shouldn't be lined up with any of them. Centering it vertically ensures it won't line up with any of the categories, and using a different font further signals the reader that this is something other than a category title. Centering the kicker horizontally further differentiates it from the other, left-justified text. In addition, the centered text fills in the large empty space a bit.

The layout table and the horizontal bar are set to 80% of the page width. This compacts the main content a bit, which is important because there just isn't much *of* it. Too much white space (that's what designers call any kind of empty space) in the middle of the page makes the intended message seem unimportant. White space around the edges focuses attention inward. Making the horizontal line and the table the same width gives the table a sort of false right edge, symmetrical with the more obvious left edge.

Figure 8-13 shows another, somewhat similar, layout done with an HTML table. There are three columns and four rows, which FrontPage makes visible in Figure 8-14. Cells 2 and 3 in row 1 are merged to provide a large, somewhat encompassing, space for the heading. Rows 3 and 4 in column 1 are not only merged but also given a gray background; this creates an area that's visually distinct from the rest of the page, particularly the elements to its right.

The gray area on the left will probably become a menu of hyperlinks, although no links currently exist. (After all, this is only an exercise done for the sake of example.) Each pair of bullets is clearly associated with the icon to their left. The title area, the news delivery icon, and the menu bar frame the rest of the content and add a sense of unity to the page.

Figure 8-15 shows a considerably more complicated use of tables for page layout. This page uses a 4-column, 5-row table for its main grid, but four of the resulting cells themselves contain tables. Can you spot them?

FIGURE 8-13.

Here's another Web page that uses tables for page layout.

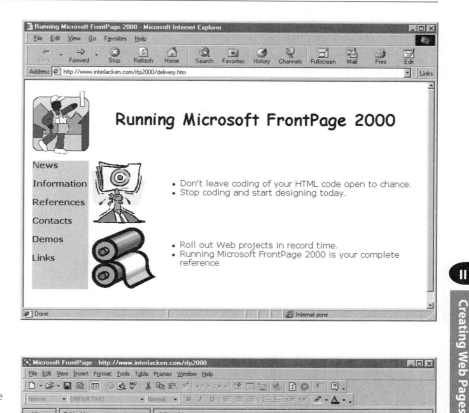

FIGURE 8-14.

FrontPage shows the page layout table. Note the two large cells, which are merged, and the background color that visually bounds the menu area.

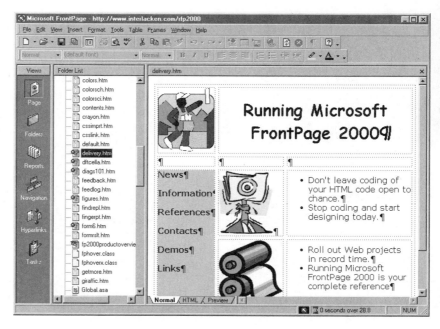

I'll tell you where the four tables are in a moment, but first you need to understand the merged cells in the main table. The following cells are merged:

- In row 1, cells 2 and 3.

- In row 2, cells 2 and 3.

- In row 4, all four cells. They contain a horizontal line.

- In row 5, cells 2 and 3.

OK, now here are the "inside" tables. They're more visible in Figure 8-16.

- A one-celled table occupies columns 2 and 3 (merged) of row 2. Its width is 100% so it completely fills the cell that contains it, and it supplies the border and background color for the text.

- Two more one-celled tables occupy cells 1 and 4 of row 2. They supply a wide margin and a background color for the side text.

- A 3x3 table occurs within columns 2 and 3 (merged) of row 5. This supplies formatting, a border, and a background color for the list of sites.

This page could use a bit more work managing white space; there's probably too much of it above and below the heading, and too little above and below the bullet lists. The content is a bit weak as well, as there are no obvious hyperlinks other than the listed events and the external links. What about dates, tickets, and location, for example? But the purpose of this example is to illustrate tables within tables, and I think it's well-enough developed for that. Adding more content would push the bottom of the page below the end of the screen shot, and you couldn't see it anyway.

★ TIP

> A high percentage of Web visitors will never scroll down your page. If you don't get their attention in the first 800x600 browser window, you probably won't get their attention at all.

If you think the use of tables, as described above in some detail, seems convoluted compared to other page-layout techniques, you're right! HTML itself was never designed for this kind of work—nor, most likely, were tables. Nevertheless, advanced use of tables permits a degree of layout control that would be impossible using any other technique. Fortunately, FrontPage can make creating and formatting complex tables easier by reducing the need for arcane syntax and HTML tags.

FIGURE 8-15.
This Web page uses tables within tables for its page layout.

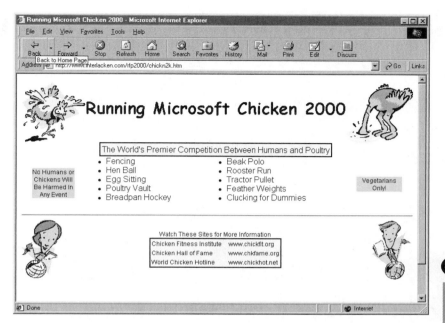

FIGURE 8-16.
FrontPage makes the invisible layout tables in this Web page visible.

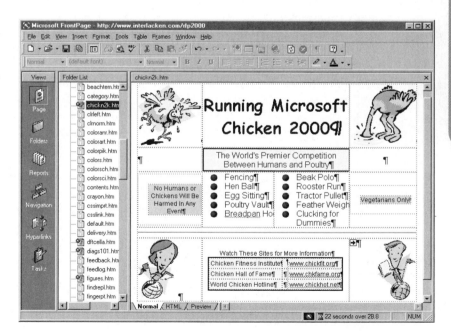

Creating Web Pages

Using Transparent Images for Page Layout

In an effort to keep Web pages device-independent, HTML provides very little support for absolute positioning. HTML "thinks" in terms of flowing text, not in terms of objects placed on an x-y grid. This is greatly frustrating when presenting commercial art rather than, say, a research paper. Tables and frames (described shortly) provide page designers with a coarse measure of x-y positioning, but for fine control, many designers have adopted the use of transparent GIF images. Anywhere they want some blank space on the page, they simply locate a completely transparent GIF image. Some cases where this works extremely well include:

- Indenting the first line of a paragraph

- Spacing fractional lines between paragraphs

- Indenting objects from a window, frame, or table margin

- Guaranteeing a minimum width for a table column

Note that in a completely transparent GIF image, every pixel is the same color—the transparent color. Clever designers therefore keep a one-pixel by one-pixel transparent GIF file in their bag of tricks. This is the smallest possible file to download, and specifying an appropriate height and width for it (in the Appearance tab of the Image Properties dialog box shown in Figure 6-7) will stretch the file to any required size. Remember to turn off the Keep Aspect Ratio feature so that you can independently set the width and height. The same file can be used over and over again in different locations, simply by specifying different sizes of it each time.

Working with one-pixel transparent GIF images presents a unique problem with WYSIWYG editors such as FrontPage; such images are quite difficult to locate, select, and modify. For this reason you may find it easier to work with slightly larger files. As shown below, GIF file compression reduces the overhead to almost nothing. The File Size column shows the size of the transparent GIF file saved with 1-bit color.

Pixels	File Size (Bytes)
1x1	42
5x5	45
9x9	49

Creating Web Documents with Excel 2000

Faced with a need to display any sort of data in tabular format, most Microsoft Office users turn to Excel. Of course, Excel's capabilities go far beyond tabular presentation; for many users and applications, Excel is the tool of choice for numerical and financial analysis.

Regardless of your reasons for using Excel, sooner or later you'll probably develop results in Excel that you want to distribute via the Web. Excel 2000 provides excellent facilities for this, facilities that greatly resemble those we saw in Chapter 5, "Adding and Formatting Text," regarding Microsoft Word.

Figure 8-17 shows the first step in making Excel 2000 save a simple spreadsheet to the Web. The process begins with making the desired sheet current and then choosing Save As Web Page from the File menu.

FIGURE 8-17.

Excel 2000's Save As Web Page command begins the process of publishing spreadsheet data on the Web.

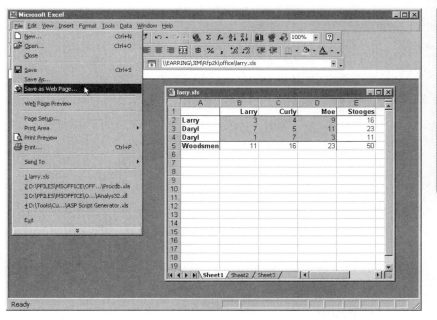

Excel next displays the dialog box shown in Figure 8-18. This dialog box bears the expected Office family resemblance to File dialog boxes we've seen before. Table 4-1, on page 86, describes the toolbar icons. The History, My Documents, Desktop, and Favorites icons save to various locations on the local disk or file server, but from a FrontPage point of view, Web Folders is the most interesting option. This option not only creates an HTML version of the spreadsheet, but adds it directly to a FrontPage Web.

Clicking Web Folders displays a list of recently used FrontPage Web locations: that is, a list of server names for server-based Webs and a list of file locations for disk-based Webs. To produce the display in Figure 8-18, I double-clicked the entry for the www.interlacken.com Web server, and then double-clicked the entry for the rfp2000 Web.

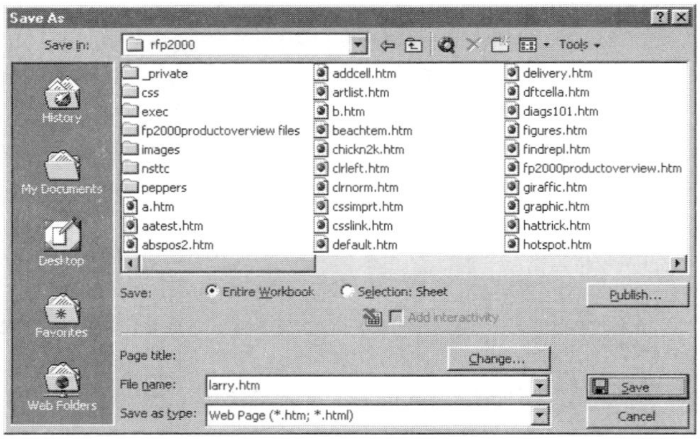

FIGURE 8-18.

This is Excel 2000's Save As Web Page dialog box. Note the specialized options just below the files list.

If the Web server or disk-based Web location you need doesn't appear automatically, you'll have to enter it the first time by hand. For server-based Webs, use URL notation like http://www.interlacken.com. For disk-based Webs, enter a full path such as C:\My Webs\rfp2000.

Just below the large file and folder listing are several controls unique to Excel.

- **Save Entire Workbook** saves everything in the current Excel workbook as HTML.

- **Save Selection: Sheet** saves only the currently selected portion of the current sheet.

- **Add Interactivity** adds some ActiveX controls to the Web page so Web users can work with data interactively. For example, they can sort displayed data, play what-if games, operate PivotTables, and see results on linked graphs.

- **Publish** displays the dialog box of Figure 8-19, which contains additional options.

⊗ CAUTION

Pages saved with Add Interactivity in effect will display correctly only if the browser can display ActiveX controls. This includes Internet Explorer 3 and above.

The Publish As Web Page dialog box shown in Figure 8-19 provides additional flexibility regarding the HTML version of the spreadsheet.

- **Choose** provides a selection list of currently open spreadsheet objects you can publish.

- **Add Interactivity With** controls what Web visitors can do with the displayed data. For this to work, the visitors must be using Internet Explorer and have access to some ActiveX controls packaged with Excel 2000.

- **Publish As** controls where the output HTML file (or files) will reside.

FIGURE 8-19.

This dialog box provides additional control over the conversion of Excel spreadsheets to Web-page format.

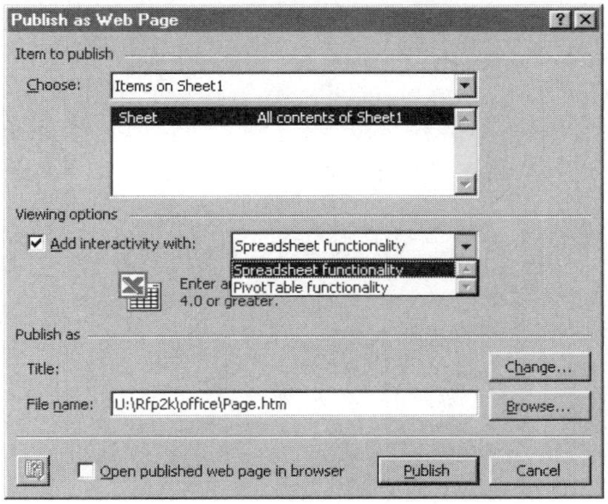

Clicking the Save button converts the spreadsheet to an HTML file and adds it to the specified Web. Internet Explorer shows the results in Figure 8-20. Note the excellent preservation of borders, shading, and fonts.

FIGURE 8-20.

When displayed by Internet Explorer, the spreadsheet saved as HTML in Figure 8-18 retains its original appearance.

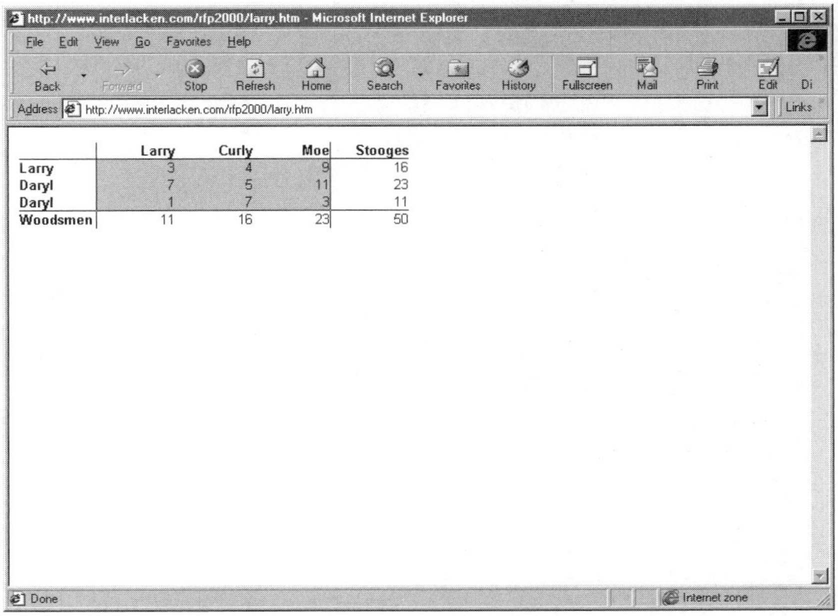

Since Excel saved it in a FrontPage Web, you may wonder if FrontPage can open the HTML version of the spreadsheet. It can. What's more, you can visually enhance the HTML version, save it, reopen it in Excel, and still have all the formulas and other features work. This is possible because Excel saves all the spreadsheet-related information inside the HTML file as XML statements. FrontPage takes care not to modify the XML statements, so the spreadsheet information passes through unchanged.

Figure 8-21 shows FrontPage editing the larry.htm file saved from Excel. I've inserted some clip art and a title. If you're curious what XML looks like, open the larry.htm file on the CD accompanying this book and switch into HTML view.

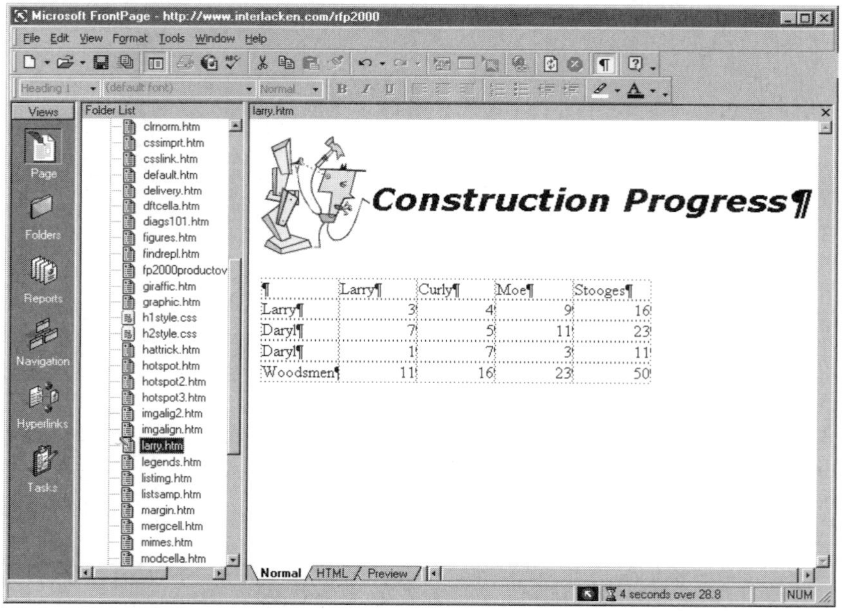

FIGURE 8-21.

FrontPage can edit and enhance Web pages saved by Excel. The Excel-related information, saved as XML statements, passes through unchanged.

Saving the modified file in FrontPage and opening it in Excel produces the spreadsheet shown in Figure 8-22. All the formulas still work and yes, Excel can directly open files residing in FrontPage Webs, even server-based Webs. Just click the Web Folders icon in Excel's File Open dialog box.

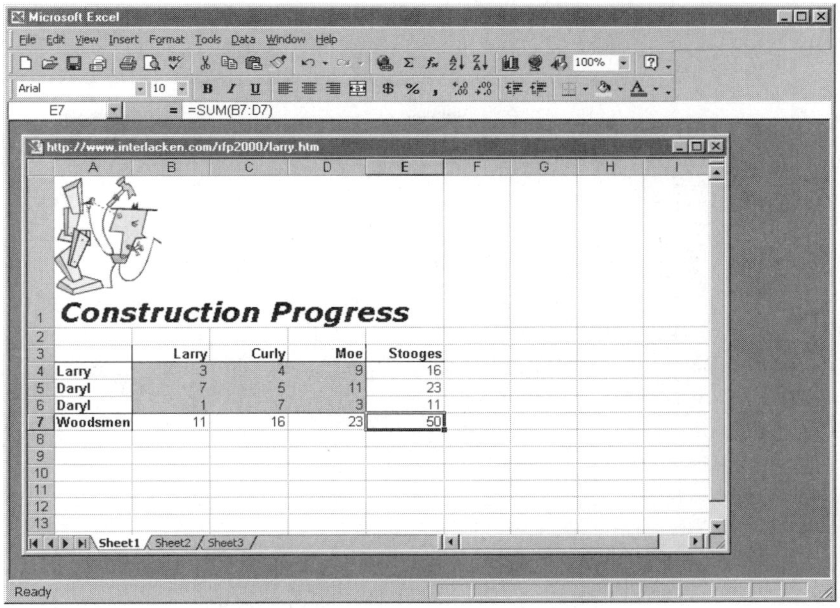

FIGURE 8-22.

Despite being saved as HTML, then modified and saved in FrontPage, the spreadsheet is still fully functional in Excel. Note the Excel file name, an HTML file opened from a Web location.

Creating and Editing Frames

Whether arranging simple columns of data or complex page layouts, tables are among the most powerful page-composition tools on the Web. A major shortcoming, however, is that tables aren't dynamic. The browser can't replace the contents of a table or cell without redisplaying the entire Web page.

Another approach divides the browser window into zones called *frames*. As introduced earlier in this chapter, a special Web page called a *frameset* defines the overall frame layout but provides no actual content. Instead, each frame displays a self-sufficient Web page. The frameset tells the browser what pages to load initially; later, hyperlinks reload individual frames in response to user selections.

Understanding Frame Fundamentals

Figure 8-23 shows a Web display that uses frames. Creating this display requires four HTML files:

- One HTML file to define the frame areas, giving each frame a position, name, and frame source. This file is called a frameset, and it contains no visible content of its own.

■ Each frame has a property, called its *frame source,* that specifies the URL of the Web page that provides its content. The frameset specifies an initial frame source for each frame.

The labels in Figure 8-23 show the frame names and sources for each of the three frames that make up the frameset. The fact that Figure 8-23 displays four HTML files *at once* is a key concept. The browser's Location line shows only one URL, but three more are hidden. To see the other URLs, right-click the content area of a frame and choose Properties from the pop-up menu. Figure 8-24 illustrates this.

FIGURE 8-23.

This display involves use of four HTML files: one to define the three frame areas, and one per frame to provide content.

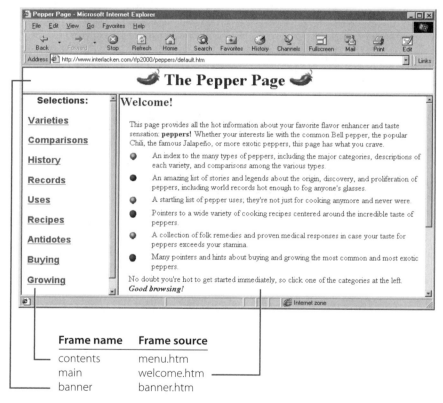

A frameset can also be the source of another frame; that is, you can have framesets within frames. This can become extremely confusing, but it works.

Once a frameset and its frame sources are on display, hyperlinks in any frame can display new content in the same frame, a different frame, or a different window. A link attribute called the *target frame* specifies—by name—which frame a given hyperlink should affect. The browser looks for the target frame in three locations. In order, these are:

1 **The hyperlink itself.** Dialog boxes like that in Figure 7-1 on page 221 specify the target frame for an individual hyperlink.

2 **A default target frame.** The Web page containing the hyperlink can specify a default target frame. This applies to all hyperlinks on that page that don't specify an explicit target frame. Figure 4-6 on page 93 shows the Page Properties dialog box, where a default frame can be specified.

3 **The current frame.** If the hyperlink target frame and the default target frame are both absent, hyperlinks display their contents in the frame in which they occur, just as you'd expect on a page with no frames.

If you specify a target frame that doesn't exist, the browser will usually display the named HTML file in a new window. This could happen to you! Always double-check frame-name spellings, especially if a frameset isn't working properly.

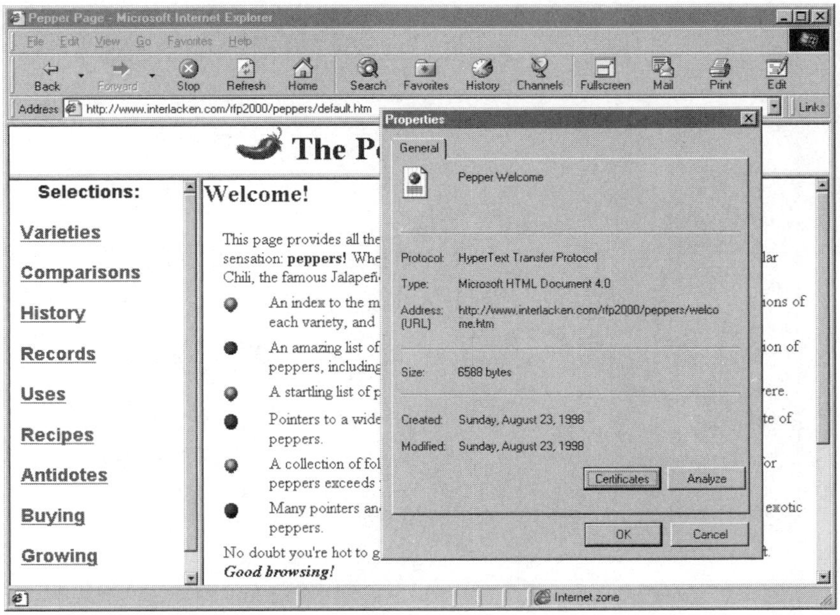

FIGURE 8-24.

The Page Properties dialog box for the main "Welcome!" frame shows a URL different from that of the frameset.

The most frequent use of the target frame on today's Web pages can be seen in Figure 8-23. Note the menu of hyperlinks in the left frame. When the viewer clicks one of these hyperlinks, the page appears in the main frame to the right—you wouldn't want the content to appear in the menu frame, making further menu choices unavailable. By setting each hyperlink's target frame (or the menu page's default target frame) to Main, you ensure that the menu remains visible in the left frame (as does the banner in the top frame) even as the content displayed in the right frame changes.

In addition to the frame names you create as part of a frameset, the four built-in target frame names listed in Table 8-2 may be useful. FrontPage sometimes identifies these by the Common Target names listed in column 2.

Frames provide a certain (and welcome) continuity as visitors traverse your site. An arrangement such as that shown in Figure 8-23 constantly displays your site's banner in the top frame and a menu of common hyperlinks in the left frame, no matter which page visitors browse in the main window. However, this structure has disadvantages as well.

TABLE 8-2. Built-in Frame Names (No User Definition Required)

HTML Code	Common Target Name	Browser Action
_new	New Window	Loads the hyperlink target into a new window.
_self	Same Frame	Loads the hyperlink target into the frame that contains the hyperlink. This is useful for overriding a page's default target frame on selected hyperlinks.
_parent	Parent	Loads the hyperlink target into the parent of the frame that contains the hyperlink. That is, the hyperlink target will replace the entire frameset that defines the frame containing the hyperlink.
_top	Whole Page	Loads the hyperlink target into the full window of the Web browser, replacing all prior framesets. This is commonly used as the exit door from a framed page back to a single-HTML, full-page display.

- Managing frame names is a manual process, by nature tedious.

- Hyperlinking to specific frameset combinations can be difficult. When another hyperlink loads the entire frameset, the default frame sources will always load. To load the frameset with a different combination of sources, you'll have to create (and perpetually maintain) a second version of the frameset.

Creating and Modifying Framesets with FrontPage

Creating a new frameset in FrontPage 2000 is fairly simple. As with tables, you'll spend far more time modifying than creating.

1 In Page view, choose New from the File menu, and then choose Page. Then, when the New Page dialog box appears, click the Frames tab. The New dialog box shown in Figure 8-25 will result.

2 Single-click the listed framesets until you find the one closest to your needs. The description and preview boxes display information about each selection and an image of it.

3 Click OK. FrontPage will display the new frameset as shown in Figure 8-26.

FIGURE 8-25.

FrontPage offers a variety of prebuilt framesets that are useful as starting points for your own work.

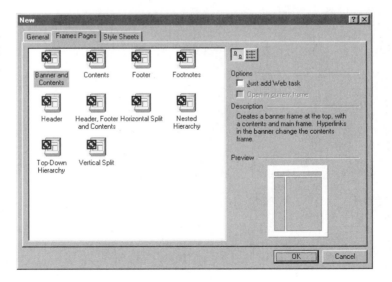

This is a new frameset, ready for content in each frame. In and of itself, a frameset contains no content. A new frameset is much like a picture frame with no picture. In place of content, FrontPage therefore displays three buttons in each new frame.

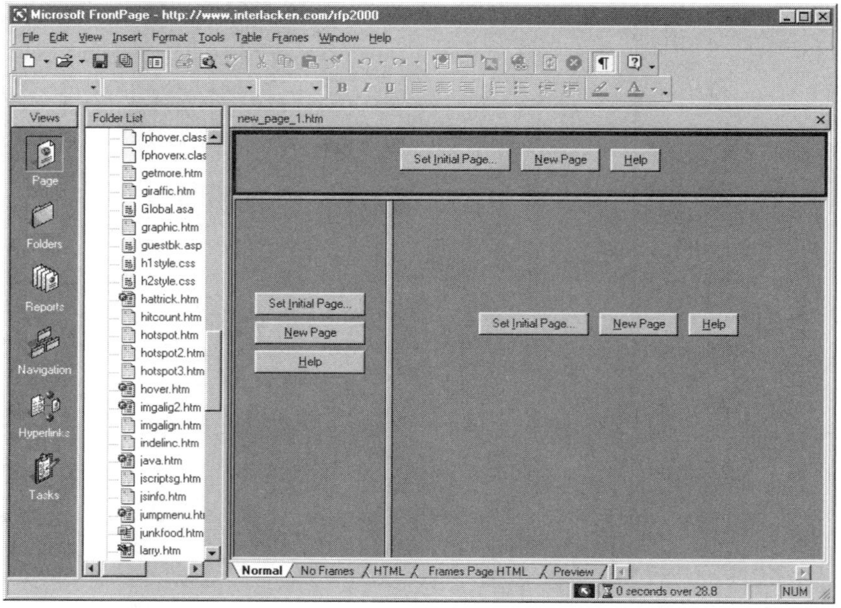

FIGURE 8-26.

Creating a new frameset doesn't automatically create target pages for each frame.

- **Set Initial Page.** This button displays the Create Hyperlink dialog box from Figure 7-1. To initialize the frame with an existing Web page, use this dialog box to find it, and then click OK.

- **New Page.** Click this button to create a new Web page whose content will fill the frame when the frameset opens. No templates are offered for new pages used as frame targets; instead, FrontPage fills the frame with a blank page and prompts you for a name and title when you first save the frameset.

- **Help.** Click this button for more information.

When displaying a frameset, FrontPage displays not only the frame positions but also their default targets in fully editable, WYSIWYG mode. Clicking each of the New Page buttons in the frameset of Figure 8-26 and supplying preliminary content thus produces the results shown in Figure 8-27.

FIGURE 8-27.

Now the frameset of Figure 8-26 is populated with new target pages and some initial content. Saving this view saves four files: the frameset itself, and each of three target Web pages. The dark line around the top frame indicates the active frame.

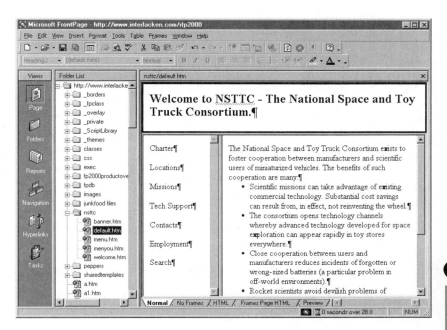

When you first save the frameset, FrontPage will prompt not only for the frameset file name but also, in turn, for the file name of each new target. Subsequently, when you save the frameset, FrontPage also saves any open target pages you've modified.

- To save a specific target page, select its frame, and then choose Save Page from the Frames menu.

- To save the page under another name, select its frame, and then choose Save Page As from the Frames menu.

To change the default target for a frame, click anywhere within it and then choose Properties from the Frames menu. (Alternatively, right-click the frame and then choose Frame Properties from the pop-up menu.) Update the Initial Page field, possibly by using the Browse button, and then click OK.

Frames are always tiled in a window. This means frames never overlap each other and the complete frameset always fills the entire browser window. The only way to add a frame, therefore, is to split an existing one. To do so:

1   Select the frame you want to split.

2   Choose Split Frame from the Frames menu. The following dialog box will result.

- Select Split Into Columns to divide the frame vertically.

- Select Split Into Rows to divide the frame horizontally.

3 Click OK.

4 FrontPage will display a new frame containing the same three buttons it displays in new framesets. Click one.

- **Set Initial Page** specifies an existing page.

- **New Page** creates a new blank page.

- **Help** displays additional information.

To delete a frame, first select it, and then choose Delete Frame from the Frames menu. This deletes only the frame and *not* the Web page configured as its default target.

You can specify the dimensions of a frame in three ways: by percentage, by relative sizing, or by pixels.

- Percentage states what fraction of the frameset's available height or width a given frame will occupy. This has the advantage of changing proportionately, depending on the size of the remote user's browser window.

- Relative sizing assigns a sizing factor to each frame, and then divides the available space proportionately. For example, if the frameset consists of three horizontal frames with relative heights of 10, 20, and 30, the three frames receive 10/60, 20/60, and 30/60 of the browser window, respectively. (To calculate the denominator, just add the values.)

- Specifying frame sizes in pixels seems at first to offer more absolute control, but only if you know in advance the size of all objects in the frame. Remember, for example, that in most cases you won't know the actual font sizes the remote user has chosen for various kinds of text.

To resize a frame, you can use two methods. First, to resize a frame visually in FrontPage, move the mouse pointer over the frame border until it becomes a double-headed arrow, and then hold down the mouse button and drag the border to the desired position.

Second, using menus, you can resize frames relative to each other, as a percentage of available space, or as a specific number of pixels. These settings are part of the Frame menu, which you can display *either* of two ways:

- Left-click the frame, and then choose Frames Properties from the Frame menu.

- Right-click the frame, and then choose Frame Properties from the pop-up menu.

Saving Individual Frames

The Save Page As command on the Frames menu saves the contents of the current frame, using a new file name. However, it *doesn't* automatically update the frame's Initial Page setting. This means FrontPage temporarily displays the *wrong* Web page in the saved frame. FrontPage recovers by reloading the last-saved version of the frame's Initial Page when you switch to another frame or, if you immediately close the frameset, the next time you open it.

Suppose, for example, that a frame's Initial Page is apples.htm. You modify the frame's content and save the results as oranges.htm. FrontPage will temporarily display the contents of oranges.htm even though the frame's Initial Page remains apples.htm. FrontPage loads the last-saved version of apples.htm when you switch to another frame.

The behavior just described is perfect if you want to open the frameset, save a modified version of one source page, and leave the original frameset and source page unchanged. Obviously, your assessment of perfection will differ if you intend something else.

To save a frame's content as a new Web page *and* point the frame's Initial Page setting to it, first use the Frame menu's Save Page As command; then, with the same frame displayed, use the Frame Properties dialog box to update the Initial Page field.

To change a frame's content and save it under *both* the existing name *and* a new one, you'll have to save the target twice—first using the Frame menu's Save Page command, and then using its Save Page As command.

Either method displays the Frame Properties dialog box shown in Figure 8-28. It controls the following settings for the current frame:

- **Name.** Enter the name that hyperlinks will specify to load their contents into the selected frame.

- **Initial Page.** Specify the URL of the Web page that will initially appear in the frame (that is, when the browser first loads the frameset). The Browse button can be used to locate the page.

- **Frame Size.** The fields here control the frame's display size. As you might expect, frames have two dimensions.

  - **Width/Column Width.** This setting normally controls the width of a frame. However, if the frame resides in a column with other frames of uniform width, the caption will be Column Width (as it is in Figure 8-28) and the setting will control all frames in the column. In either case, specify both a width and the corresponding unit of measure.

  - **Height/Row Height.** This setting normally controls the height of a frame. However, if the frame resides in a row with other frames of uniform height, the caption will be Row Height and the setting will control all frames in the row. In either case, specify both a height and the corresponding unit of measure.

- The preceding measurements have three possible units of measure: Relative, Percent, and Pixel.

  - **Relative** units specify frame sizes relative to each other. If the frameset is divided horizontally into two frames with relative sizes of 1 and 4, the frame will occupy 1/5 and 4/5 of the available window space, respectively. Relative sizes of 2 and 8 would produce identical results, as would 5 and 20.

  - **Percent** units allocate portions of the frameset. A frame sized at 33 percent would occupy 1/3 of the horizontal or vertical space available to the frameset.

  - **Pixel** dimensions are straightforward. The frame will occupy the specified number of pixels or dots on the remote user's monitor.

- **Margins.** These options control the size of margins within the selected frame.

- **Width.** Specify the number of pixels you want between the frame contents and the left and right borders. The number applies to both the left border and the right border.

- **Height.** Specify the number of pixels you want between the frame contents and the top and bottom borders. This value applies to both the top and bottom borders.

? SEE ALSO
For descriptions of the first five tabs in the Frame Page dialog box, refer to "Specifying Page-Level Attributes," page 92.

■ **Options.** Two frame properties are controlled by these settings.

- **Resizable In Browser.** If this box is turned on, the browser can resize the frame based on the size of the window.

- **Show Scrollbars.** The choices in this list box control when the browser will display scroll bars for the frame.

  If Needed. The browser will display scroll bars whenever the frame's contents are larger than the current window.

  Never. The browser never displays scroll bars for the frame.

  Always. The browser always displays scroll bars for the frame, even if the entire contents of the page fit within it.

■ **Frames Page.** Clicking this button displays the Page Properties dialog box for the frameset that contains the current frame.

■ **Style.** Clicking this button displays the standard FrontPage CSS Style dialog box. Any cascading style sheet properties you specify will become defaults for the current frame.

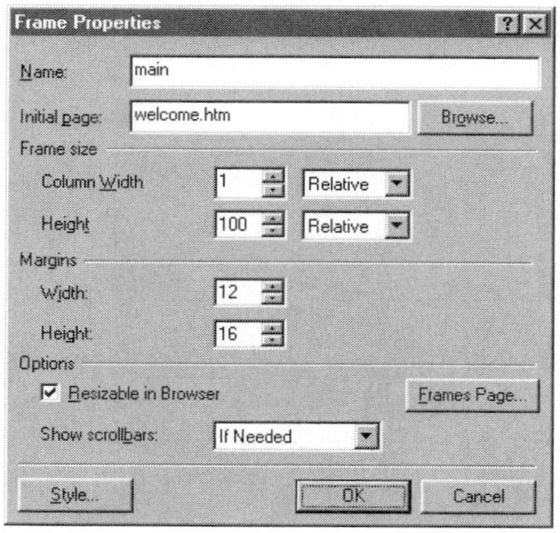

FIGURE 8-28.
The Frame Properties dialog box controls the name, size, and other settings pertinent to a frame.

II

Creating Web Pages

The Page Properties dialog box for a frameset is quite similar to that of a normal page; it consists of the five tabs shown in Figures 4-6, 4-7, 4-8, 4-10, and 4-12, plus the Frames tab shown here in Figure 8-29.

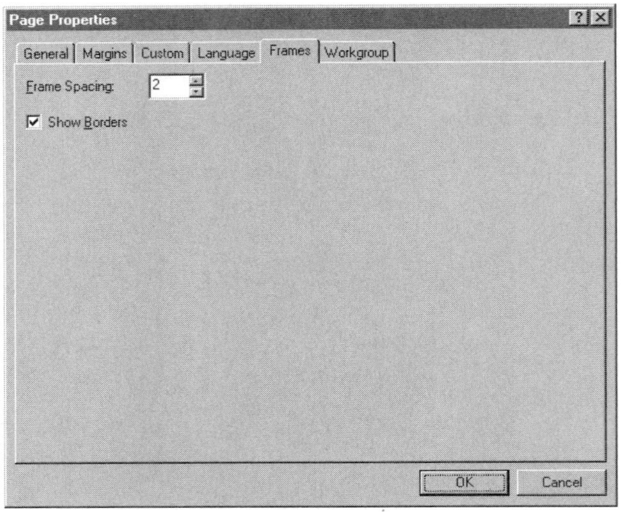

FIGURE 8-29.

The Frames Page button on the Frame Properties dialog box opens this version of the Page Properties dialog box, which contains an additional tab: Frames.

The Frames tab contains two settings:

- **Frame Spacing** specifies the number of pixels the browser will insert between frames. If Show Borders is also turned on, the space will display as a border; otherwise, the frame contents will appear to be separated by this amount of neutral space.

- **Show Borders** specifies, if turned on, that the browser should display visible borders between frames of the thickness specified in Frame Spacing.

> **NOTE**
>
> FrontPage will display borders even if Show Borders is turned off. To view the page without frame borders, click the Preview tab at the bottom of the Front-Page window, or preview the page in your browser.

To open a normal editing window for a page already open in a frame, click anywhere in that frame, and then choose Open Page In New Window from the Frame menu. You can edit in the larger window and switch back to the framed page (use the Ctrl+Tab shortcut) to check its appearance there.

Today most browsers support frames, but this obviously wasn't true when frames were first introduced. The frames specification therefore provides a way to embed an ordinary Web page in a frameset. A frames-capable browser will ignore the ordinary Web page, while a frames-deficient browser will ignore the frameset information.

NOTE

> A major tenet of HTML is that browsers should silently ignore anything they don't understand. This smoothes adoption of new HTML features by allowing older browsers to run as they always have—though the lack of error messages can make debugging maddeningly difficult.

To display the page that a frames-deficient browser will display, open the frameset and then click the No Frames tab at the bottom of the window. This tab is visible in Figure 8-27. FrontPage initializes the No Frames page with a message stating *This page uses frames, but your browser doesn't support them,* but you can replace this with a complete Web page if you want.

When designing a frame-based site, keep in mind that not all visitors have frames-capable browsers, and that other visitors simply don't like frames. This means you should either provide a parallel set of nonframes pages or include adequate hyperlinks on a single set of pages so that non-frame users can also navigate your site.

Framesets appear in Navigation view as ordinary Web pages. A frameset's default target pages aren't automatically made children in Navigation view, nor are Navigation-view children automatically designated default target pages.

Take great care when using themes and frames in the same Web. Backgrounds, color schemes, and graphic elements that look good on single Web pages are often distracting when displayed multiple times, once in each frame.

Combining shared borders and frames is almost never a good idea because the shared border content will appear redundantly in every frame of a frameset.

Positioning Content with CSS

Pixel-precise positioning and layering of page elements has long been a dream of Web designers. They yearn for the relative simplicity of print design, where they can put things at specific page locations and not worry about readers changing the page dimensions after the fact. Well,

CSS positioning provides just that capability (although, as we'll see, it can't stop Web visitors from having different sized monitors or from resizing the browser window).

Introducing CSS Positioning

Release two of the Cascading Style Sheet specification provides three kinds of positioning:

- **Static** positioning is the kind browsers have supported since the beginning. This remains the default.

- **Relative** positioning lays out the Web page normally, but then, just before displaying any positioned elements, shifts them up, down, right, or left of their normal locations. The browser flows other content around the space where the relative position element *would have been* had it not been positioned.

- **Absolute** positioning makes an element appear at specific *x-y* coordinates, measured from the top-left corner of some *container* to the top-left corner of the element. The browser reserves *no space* for the absolutely positioned element; the element just appears at the specified location. Other content doesn't flow around it.

The default container is the current Web page. You specify measurements in terms of top-left corners, so the CSS statement to display something 20 pixels below the top of the browser window is:

```
top: 20px;
```

The command to place something 30 pixels from the left edge of the browser window is:

```
left: 30px;
```

Combining this with the command that invokes absolute positioning produces this HTML:

```
style="position: absolute; top: 20px; left: 30px;"
```

CSS positioning supports more properties than just position, top, and left, but those three will do for now. If you're curious about the rest, browse through Table 8-3. If you're curious about whether FrontPage makes you type code like the above, you can be sure it doesn't. We'll get to that shortly.

So, what can you position? Well, all browsers can do static positioning because that's what they've been doing all along. In addition:

- Netscape Navigator 4 can apply:

  - *relative* or *absolute* positioning to *spans*, *divisions*, and *block elements*.

- Internet Explorer 4 can apply:

  - *relative* positioning to any page element.

  - *absolute* positioning to the element types listed in Table 8-4.

TABLE 8-3. CSS Positioning Properties

Property	Values	Interpretation
position	static	Tells the browser to position content normally. No special positioning is in effect.
	relative	Positions content relative to its normal page location.
	absolute	Positions content relative to the top-left corner of its container.
top, left	auto, \<length\>, \<percent\>	Controls the placement of elements assigned relative or absolute positioning.
width, height	auto, \<length\>, \<percent\>	Controls the size of positioned elements.
z-index	auto \<number\>	Controls the visual precedence of positioned elements that overlap. Static elements have a z-index of zero.
visibility	inherit visible hidden	Controls whether an element is visible. The inherit value adopts the visibility of the parent container.
clip	auto, rect (\<top\> \<right\>, \<bottom\>, \<left\>)	Defines what portion of an absolutely positioned element is visible.
overflow		Controls what happens if an element's content exceeds its height or width:
	visible	Enlarges the container to display all the content.
	hidden	Hides the additional content.
	auto	Displays scroll bars as necessary.
	scroll	Displays scroll bars at all times.

TABLE 8-4. Valid Absolute Positioning Elements in Internet Explorer 4

Navigator Positionable	Internet Explorer Positionable	Internet Explorer Unique Elements	Form Elements
Divisions	Images	Fieldsets	Buttons
Spans	Applets	Iframes	Input Elements
Block Elements	Objects		Select Lists
Tables			Text Areas

A *block element* is anything that causes line breaks before and after itself. Normal paragraphs are the most common block elements, followed by the various heading types.

Divisions and spans are two HTML tags that mark sections of a Web page. A division starts where you put a <DIV> tag, ends where you put a </DIV> tag, and creates line breaks before and after itself. A span starts with <SPAN>, ends with </SPAN>, and flows continuously with surrounding elements.

Divisions and spans are normally invisible. (Their content, of course, is normally visible.) This presents a problem for WYSIWYG editors like FrontPage, because what you see is nothing. FrontPage has a way of handling this, but once again, this is something we'll get to shortly.

A *container* is any page element that establishes a coordinate system for positioned elements within it. The default container, and the only one Netscape Navigator 4 recognizes, is the body of the Web page. Internet Explorer 4 also supports divisions inside one another, positioning the inner division relative to the top-left corner of the outer division. In the same situation, Netscape 4 ignores the inner division.

Why am I telling you all this? Well, the FrontPage editor supports only a portion of the total CSS positioning specification. For example, FrontPage sometimes has trouble dealing with relative positioning, and it won't put one DIV inside another. Furthermore, it can't apply background colors, background images, borders, margins, and padding to any DIVs or SPANS you create. If you want to use these sorts of features, you either need to take a reality pill or go into HTML view and deal with the code. (The CSS coding examples in Chapter 5 may be helpful in this regard.)

Positioning in FrontPage

There are three ways to control positioning in FrontPage:

■ An Insert Positioning Box command that creates an empty, relatively positioned division.

■ A Positioning toolbar that applies absolute positioning to existing content and modifies positioning properties.

■ A Positioning dialog box that adds or modifies positioning properties for existing content.

When working with positioned content, it's best to have the Standard toolbar's Show All option enabled. This is the button with the ¶ paragraph symbol on it. With Show All in effect, FrontPage displays a hairline box around any positioned element. Figure 8-30 shows this option in effect.

FIGURE 8-30.

With the Show All toolbar option in effect, FrontPage displays hairline borders around positioned divisions. This greatly facilitates editing.

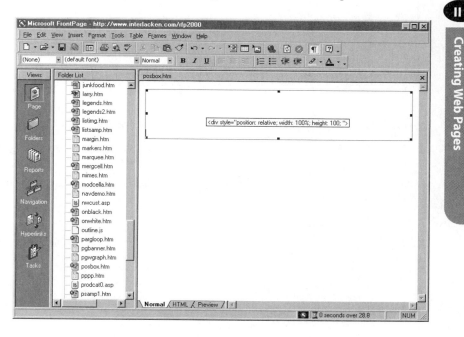

In addition, whether or not Show All is in effect, FrontPage displays sizing handles around any positioned content you select. You can resize the positioned area by dragging its handles. To reposition it, move the mouse pointer over the area's outer edge and watch for the pointer to take on this shape:

Whenever the pointer has this shape, you can hold down the mouse button and drag the positioned content around the page.

Using the Positioning Toolbar

FrontPage provides a special toolbar for controlling position properties, namely the Positioning toolbar described in Table 8-5. All the controls on this toolbar have equivalents on the Positioning dialog box described in the next section.

The Positioning toolbar doesn't support relative positioning, but it can switch areas between static and absolute. To absolutely position one or more existing Web page elements:

1 Display the Positioning toolbar. That is, choose Toolbars from the View menu, and then choose Positioning.

2 Select the Web-page elements you want to position. This can be a single element or a contiguous set.

3 Click the Absolutely Positioned button on the Position toolbar. At this point:

- If you selected a single element (other than a block element) that appears in Table 8-4, FrontPage will add absolute positioning to that element's properties.

- If you selected a block element, multiple elements, or an element not included in Table 8-4, FrontPage draws a division around the selected content and adds absolute positioning to that division's properties.

- If the selection includes only part of a block element, FrontPage extends the selection to include the entire block element.

As usual, handles and possibly hairline borders will appear around the positioned area.

Absolutely positioning an element or area generally won't cause it to move. The absolutely positioned area, however, will no longer reserve any space on the ordinary page area. This means any elements that previously followed the now-positioned content may now flow under it, resulting in a sort of double exposure.

Once positioning is in effect for an element, clicking it always redisplays the handles. There are two ways to resize an absolutely positioned element:

- By dragging the handles with the mouse.

- By typing a height or width into the Positioning toolbar.

TABLE 8-5.   The FrontPage Positioning Toolbar

Icon	Description	Function
	Absolutely Positioned	Toggles the currently selected page element between absolute and static positioning.
Left: 268	Left	Controls the distance between the left edge of a positioned element's container and the left edge of the positioned element.
Top: 22	Top	Controls the distance between the top of a positioned element's container and the top of the positioned element.
Width: 177	Width	Controls the width of a positioned element.
Height: 19	Height	Controls the height of a positioned element.
Z-Index: -1	Z-index	Controls the precedence of overlapping positioned elements.
	Bring Forward	Increases the z-index of a positioned element by one.
	Send Backward	Decreases the z-index of a positioned element by one.

To relocate an absolutely positioned element or division, first click it to make handles appear, then:

- Click the numeric values in the Positioning toolbar's Left or Top fields, then type in the coordinate you want.

- Drag the element of position by its edges. The "move" mouse pointer will appear when the mouse is in the required position.

Figure 8-31 shows a Web page with absolute positioning in effect for five elements: the four mime images and the heading paragraph, "Great Leaping Mimes." Making such an arrangement work in Netscape Navigator 4 is a nuisance because FrontPage positions single images by adding in-line style properties—attached directly to the images—and not by putting them inside positioned divisions.

To avoid this problem and force FrontPage to surround the image with a new division:

1 Enter a character or word next to the image.

2 Select that character or word *and* the image.

3 Click the Absolutely Positioned button on the Positioning toolbar.

4 Delete the character or word you entered in step 1.

Here's the reason this works. Recall, if you will, from the previous section, that Internet Explorer can position individual images but Netscape Navigator cannot. When you select an image and then apply Absolute Positioning, FrontPage acts in accordance with Internet Explorer's behavior and just positions the image. The HTML looks like this:

```
<img border="0" src="images/mimerest.gif"
style="position: absolute;
width: 131; height: 107; top: 44; left: 286; ">
```

FIGURE 8-31.

The four images and the title string are each absolutely positioned elements. Z-indexing governs display of overlapping elements.

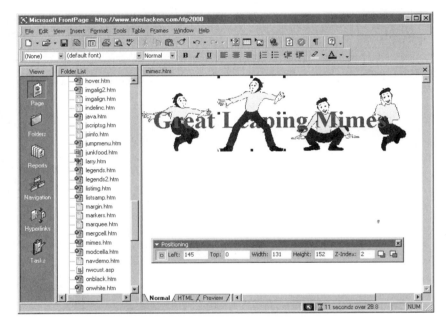

Unfortunately, Netscape Navigator, at least through version 4.0, ignores this positioning information. Netscape needs the image positioned within a division, like this:

```
<div style="position: absolute;
width: 131; height: 107; top: 44; left: 286;">
<img border="0" src="images/mimerest.gif"
width="131" height="107">
</div>
```

Including some text along with the image makes FrontPage create a DIV instead of just positioning the image directly, and the DIV remains in place even after the text is deleted.

The results appear in Figure 8-32.

Note in Figure 8-31 how three mimes appear behind the title and one in front. This is an example of z-indexing. Positioned content with larger z-index values appears in front of any content with lesser z-index values. Both positive and negative numbers are acceptable as z-index values; ordinary page content has an implied z-index of zero. If two overlapping elements have the same z-index, the one defined first in the HTML appears behind the one defined later.

FIGURE 8-32.

With care taken during page creation, Netscape Navigator 4 can also display positioned content.

To assign a z-index value via the Positioning toolbar, first select it, then either:

■ Click the Bring Forward or Send Backward button on the Formatting Toolbar

or

■ Enter a new value in the Z-Index text box and press Enter.

Using the Positioning Dialog Box

To position elements by menu, first select the content you want to position, then select Positioning from the Format menu. The dialog box in Figure 8-33 will appear.

- **Wrapping Style** controls the alignment of elements within a division or span. The choices are None (default alignment), Left, and Right.

- **Positioning Style** controls the type of positioning: None (the default, which CSS2 calls static), Absolute, or Relative.

- **Left** and **Top** control the positioned element's actual position, measured from the top-left corner of the element's container to the top-left corner of the element itself.

- **Width** and **Height** control the positioned element's size.

- **Z-Order** controls the element's display precedence compared to that of overlapping elements; that is, it controls the element's z-index.

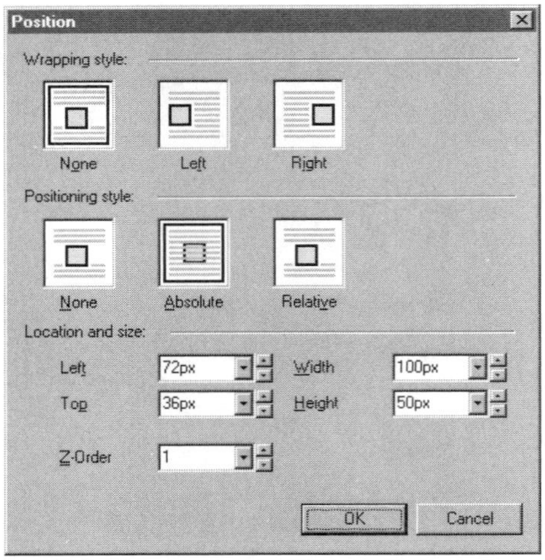

FIGURE 8-33.

The Positioning dialog box controls the same properties as the Positioning toolbar, plus Wrapping Style and Relative Positioning.

Using the Positioning dialog box to modify existing properties is trickier than it might first appear. A problem occurs when:

- The positioned element is a division.

- You select an element inside that division.

- You then display the Positioning dialog box.

When the Positioning dialog box appears, it won't show the existing positioning properties. Furthermore, after you enter some properties and click OK, FrontPage will create a *new* division inside the existing one. This is almost certainly not what you want. If you're trying to modify existing positioning and the existing properties don't appear, try clicking Cancel and selecting the division rather than its contents. If that doesn't work, try making your change through the Positioning toolbar.

Positioning Tips

When working with overlapping positioned content, selecting a particular division can be maddening. Selecting some other division that overlaps the same space is way too easy. For this reason, it's very good practice to keep divisions as short and narrow as possible, minimizing the overlap and hence the problems.

Mixing positioned and unpositioned content is tricky as well. With part of a Web page changing with the remote user's browser environment and part being, "nailed in place," it's very easy to produce a page that looks right only under the most perfect conditions. Here are a few suggestions to minimize this problem.

- Reserve white space on your page with a 1-pixel-wide transparent GIF file. Make this file as tall as your positioned content (assuming, of course, the white space won't move and the positioned content is fixed in height), and then locate the positioned content over the white space.

- Use a relatively positioned division as a container for your absolutely positioned content, because normal page content flows *around* a relatively positioned division. Unfortunately, Netscape Navigator 4 doesn't deal well with positioned content inside other positioned content.

- Absolutely position everything on your page. This avoids mixing free-flowing and absolutely positioned content, but it may require your visitors to adjust their browser window.

Creating Web Documents with PowerPoint 2000

A high percentage of PowerPoint documents are presentations designed for widespread public distribution—at least public within some bound. The Web is an excellent vehicle for such distribution, given of course a means of converting PowerPoint presentations to HTML. The Save As Web Page feature in PowerPoint 2000 provides that means.

Figure 8-34 shows a hypothetical PowerPoint presentation created for the sake of example.

FIGURE 8-34.

This is page 3 of 7 in a PowerPoint presentation created from the Bad News template.

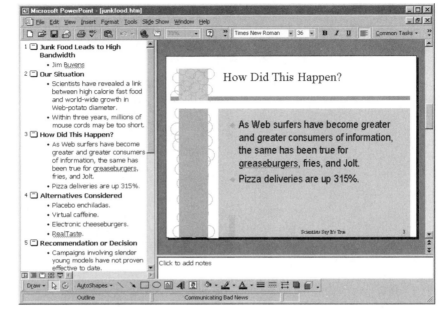

The procedure for converting PowerPoint 2000 presentations to HTML is the same as in Word and Excel 2000: choose Save As Web Page from the File menu. (This saves the entire presentation, by the way, and not just the current presentation page.) Choosing Save As Web Page results in the dialog box of Figure 8-35.

FIGURE 8-35.

PowerPoint 2000 follows Office conventions in its Save As dialog box.

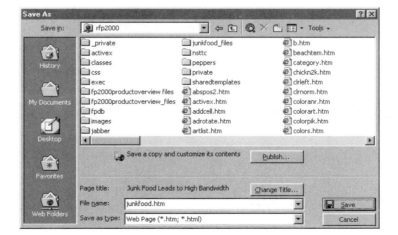

As usual, the procedure for saving to a FrontPage Web is to click Web Folders, double-click the correct server-based or disk-based Web location, then double-click through any necessary folders or subwebs. To save the presentation with standard options, click the Save button. To modify the Save options, click the Publish button and negotiate the dialog box of Figure 8-36.

■ **Publish What?** controls which presentation pages the Web version will contain. This can be the complete presentation, a selected range of slide numbers, or a list of slide numbers separated by commas.

■ **Display Speaker Notes** controls whether or not PowerPoint speaker notes will be visible to Web visitors.

■ **Web Options** provides the additional options on the four-tabbed dialog box shown in Figure 8-37.

■ **Browser support** controls the type of HTML PowerPoint will create.

   • **Microsoft Internet Explorer 4.0 Or Later (High Fidelity)** creates Web pages that look very much like the native PowerPoint versions, but which display only on Internet Explorer 4.0 or above.

   • **Microsoft Internet Explorer Or Netscape Navigator 3.0 Or Later** creates simpler Web pages that display on more browsers.

   • **All Browsers Listed Above (Creates Larger Files)** creates files that test the browser type and display slides the best way possible. However, this creates larger Web pages than either of the first two methods used alone.

■ **Publish A Copy As** creates a local copy of the Web presentation.

■ **Open Published Web Page In Browser** starts Internet Explorer and displays the presentation once it's saved.

Clicking the Web Options button in Figure 8-36 displays the four-tabbed dialog box that appears in Figure 8-37.

■ The **General** tab controls the presence and appearance of navigation buttons, animation, and graphics sizing.

■ The **Files** tab controls placement and naming of support files, updating of associated hyperlinks, and how opening of HTM files should be handled.

■ The **Pictures** tab controls the use of advanced image formats.

■ The **Encoding** tab controls the Web page's character set.

FIGURE 8-36.

This dialog box controls PowerPoint Web publishing settings.

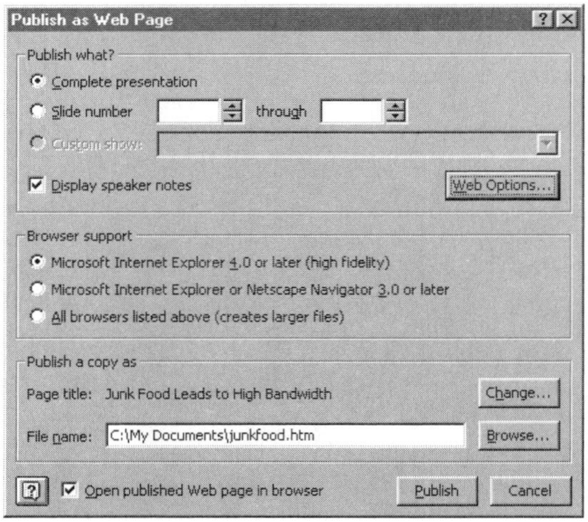

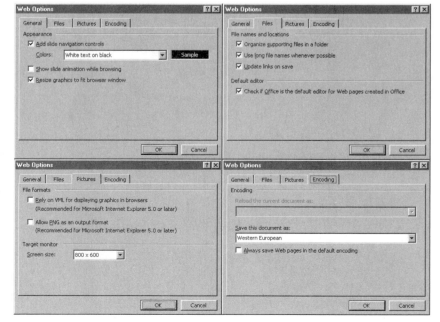

NOTE

Since every file you create using Office 2000 can be saved as a Web page, a problem arises: which application should Windows start when you double-click an HTM file? By default, Office 2000 starts a helper application that determines which program saved the selected HTM file, and then starts that application.

FIGURE 8-37.

These four tabs control how PowerPoint saves presentations for use on the Web.

As shown in Figure 8-38, the Web page that PowerPoint actually creates is a frameset with a menu of slide titles at the upper left, the slides themselves at the upper right, an Outline button at the lower left, and Forward and Back button at the lower right.

FIGURE 8-38.

PowerPoint 2000 publishes presentations as framesets, with a menu at the left and navigation buttons at the bottom.

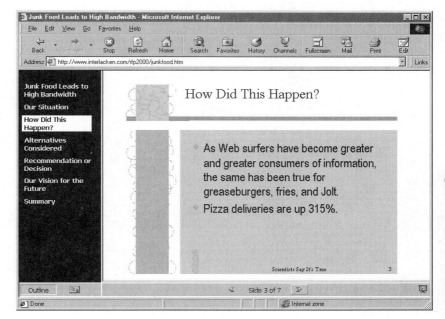

The file you specify in Figure 8-34 on page 284 becomes the frameset, and all the files required for the actual presentation pages go in a folder named with the frameset's base name, a space, and the word "files." Saving the file *junkfood.ppt* as HTML, for example, creates a frameset named *junkfood.htm* and a folder called *junkfood files*. As illustrated in Figure 8-39, this folder can contain quite a few files—probably more than you'd care to update by hand. Nevertheless, if you ask PowerPoint to open the frameset file, it's perfectly capable of retrieving all the original presentation text, graphics, and settings from the associated folder with full functionality, just as if you'd saved and reopened the same presentation in native PowerPoint format. Again, XML information saved within the HTML files makes this possible.

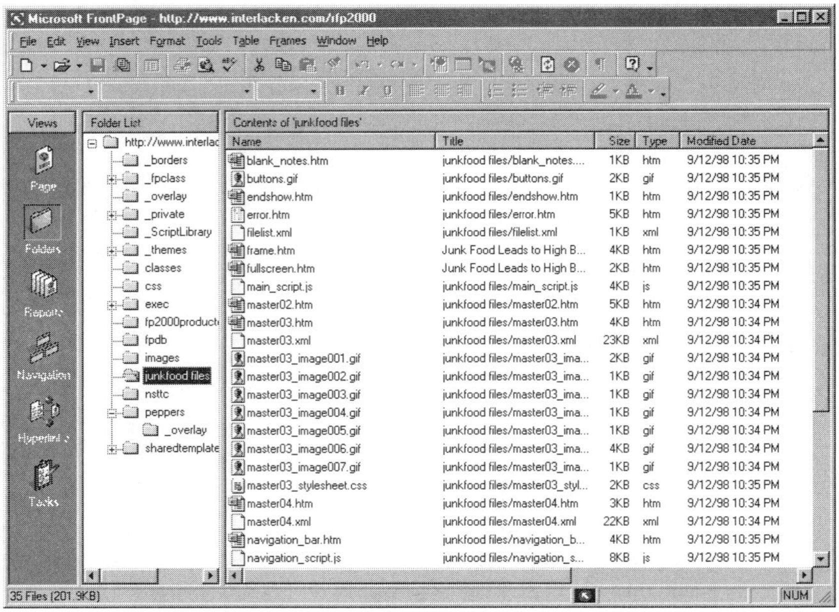

FIGURE 8-39.

A folder such as this, associated with each presentation frameset PowerPoint creates, contains all the detail files needed to display the presentation.

Additional Topics in Page Layout

As you're designing Web pages, don't overlook the use of shared Cascading Style Sheets, described in Chapter 5 under the heading of (what else?), "Shared Cascading Style Sheets." Using the same CSS specifications on all pages in your site—or at least all pages of the same type—is a powerful tool for maintaining an attractive and consistent appearance.

Color Masters provide another way to standardize colors and background images across groups of pages. This simple but limited facility has been part of FrontPage since the early versions, and is still adequate for many tasks. For more information, consult the sections titled, "Color Masters," in Chapters 1 and 20.

Themes provide an easy way to assign rich, uniform formatting to single pages, groups of pages, or an entire Web site. FrontPage includes dozens of professionally designed themes you can use right out of the box. You can also modify the supplied themes or design new ones. For more information about themes, consult the next chapter.

In Summary...

FrontPage 2000 supports every page-layout technique currently available: tables, frames, and CSS positioning. In addition, it cooperates with other Office 2000 applications to support seamless publishing of many kinds of documents.

The next chapter will describe themes, a means to uniformly impart an attractive appearance to selected Web pages or an entire site.

II

Creating Web Pages

CHAPTER 9

Using FrontPage Themes

Despite the fact than many beginning Web designers ignore it, communicating with color is something all successful Web pages must do. Human perception of color is, after all, an artistic study, and many Web beginners, feeling they lack artistic talent, find this intimidating.

Microsoft FrontPage themes provide an answer for people who don't know color but can recognize something they like. Themes are professionally designed style packages that include a color scheme, font scheme, and graphic page elements you can apply to single pages or an entire Web with one command.

Time and talent permitting, you can modify the supplied themes to your heart's desire, even creating new themes if you want. To multiply the value of your efforts, any themes you create in FrontPage are available to other Office 2000 applications as well.

This chapter first walks you through the process of assigning themes to existing pages or Webs, then covers the mechanics of modifying themes to create new ones. Finally, it presents an introduction to color theory, just in case you'd like some help understanding why some colors look so good together and others obviously don't.

Using Existing Themes

Figure 9-1 shows the FrontPage Themes window, the focal point for applying, modifying, and removing themes. To display it, choose Theme from the Format menu.

FIGURE 9-1.

FrontPage themes impart a consistent, predesigned appearance to individual pages or all pages in a Web.

The large list box at the left of the window shows the available themes. Selecting a theme previews its appearance in the large area titled Sample Of Theme. After finding a theme you like, click OK to apply it to one or more Web pages. The following controls manage the details:

■ **Apply Theme To** controls which pages clicking OK will affect.

- **All Pages** will be dimmed unless a FrontPage Web is open. If available, it means the theme you specify will become the default theme for all pages in that Web.

- **Selected Page(s)** means the theme will apply to the current page in Page view or, if another view was on display, to whatever pages were selected. Themes assigned with this option override themes assigned with All Pages.

■ **Vivid Colors.** Some themes provide two sets of colors: one muted and one vivid. Turning on this box selects and previews the vivid set.

CAUTION

Once you apply a theme, there's no Undo command that restores your Web to its prior appearance. Removing a theme returns pages to their default. Always back up your Web first or work from a copy.

- **Active Graphics.** If a theme contains animated graphics, turning on this box will activate them. Tread carefully here; the novelty of flashing lights can wear off quickly.

- **Background Image.** This option determines whether a background image will be used. Most themes substitute a solid background color if this option is turned off.

- **Apply Theme Using CSS.** If this box is turned on, FrontPage will apply theme attributes by using CSS commands. If it's off, FrontPage will use standard HTML commands.

? SEE ALSO

For information about the Delete and Modify buttons, see below, "Creating and Modifying Themes."

The Apply Theme To All Pages option adds another choice to the top of the themes list, namely (Default) <theme> (where <theme> is the name of the theme you selected).

- If you assign (Default) <theme> to one or more selected pages, subsequently changing the default will affect those pages.

- If you assign a specific theme to the same pages, subsequently changing the default won't affect them. This holds true even if the theme you assign is currently the default.

After applying a theme and opening a Web page, you may be surprised to find it less elaborate than the preview. This happens because the preview includes page banners, navigation bars, hover buttons, dividers, and other FrontPage components your pages don't contain. Alas, there's no solution but to edit each page and insert the desired elements. FrontPage can't guess which text you intended to be the heading, for example, when you originally created each page.

You may also be surprised, after applying a theme, that FrontPage suppresses many of its normal formatting commands for the affected pages. You can't override themes on an element-by-element, attribute-by-attribute basis.

Creating and Modifying Themes

FrontPage themes are one area where you truly can't make something out of nothing. The only way to create a new theme is to modify an old one and save it under a new name.

To modify a theme, first display the Themes window by choosing Theme from the Format menu. As before, this displays the window shown in Figure 9-1. To create or modify a theme, select any theme listed and then click the Modify button (which appears beneath the theme preview). As shown in Figure 9-2, this displays five additional buttons between the theme preview and the Modify button.

FIGURE 9-2.

Clicking the Modify button in Figure 9-1 displays an additional row of buttons under the preview area.

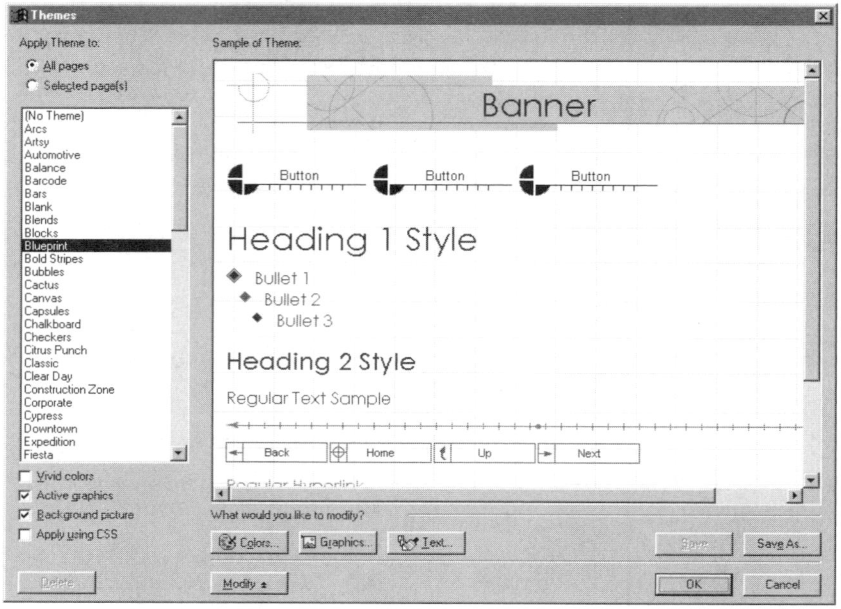

Use the Colors, Graphics, and Text buttons to modify the existing theme, and then use the Save or Save As button to save it under the same or a different name. No changes will take effect until you click Save or Save As.

Modifying Theme Colors

Clicking the Colors button in Figure 9-2 displays the Modify Theme window shown in Figure 9-3. The three tabs at the upper left offer three ways to choose a color scheme. The option buttons at the bottom control which set of colors you're configuring: normal or vivid.

? SEE ALSO
For an explanation of color terms like vivid, bright, and saturated, see "Design Tips—Color," page 301.

By default, a theme's normal and vivid colors are the same. The vivid color set, should you care to define it, is usually similar to the normal set but brighter or more saturated. You can switch between color sets by clicking any Normal Colors or Vivid Colors option button.

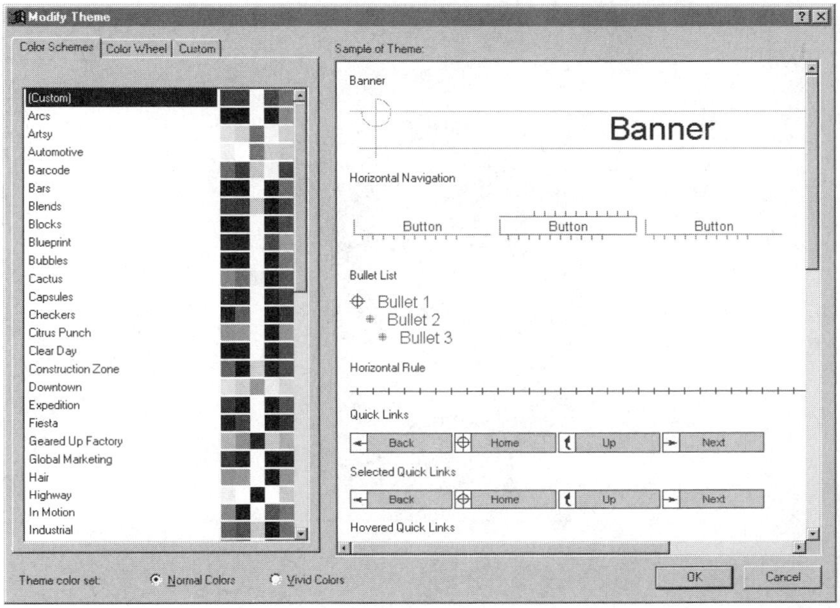

FIGURE 9-3.

Clicking a named color scheme at the left applies a set of colors to the Sample Of Theme area.

Using the Color Schemes Tab

Figure 9-3 also shows the first means of picking colors: the Color Schemes tab. Color schemes are preselected sets of colors that usually look good together. To try out a given color scheme, just select its entry in the list and view the results in the Sample Of Theme pane.

Note that the list of color schemes is different than the list of themes. Figure 9-1 shows a Bold Stripes *theme,* for example, but Figure 9-3 has no Bold Stripes *color scheme.* Similarly, there's an Arcs *color scheme* but no Arcs *theme.* This proves there's no link between theme names and color-scheme names other than the choices you make.

Using the Color Wheel Tab

Figure 9-4 shows the two remaining color-choice tabs: Color Wheel and Custom. The Color Wheel tab makes use of the Hue, Saturation, Brightness (HSB) color model described in detail later in this chapter. The Custom tab is covered in the section immediately following this one.

■ **Hue** refers to a true, pure color value. The Color Wheel tab represents hue as degrees of rotation around the wheel inside the black rectangle. Red, blue, and green, for example, are at 9 o'clock, 1 o'clock, and 5 o'clock.

II

Creating Web Pages

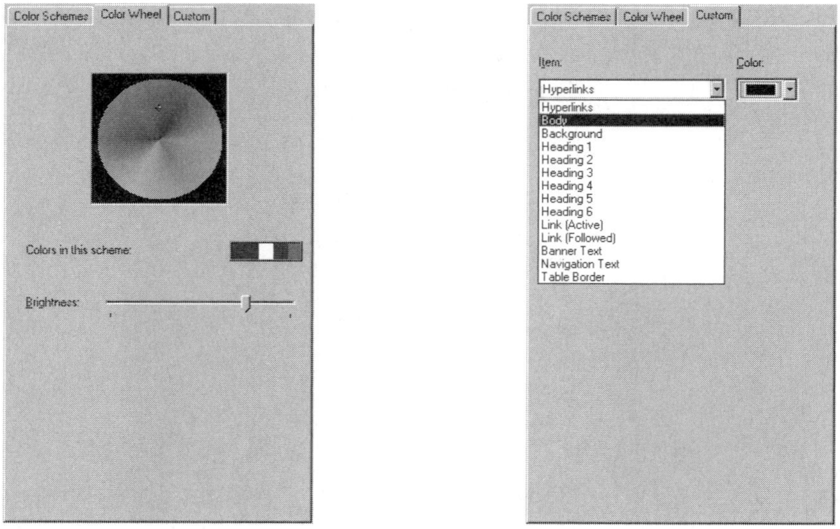

FIGURE 9-4.
These tabs provide additional ways to specify theme colors.

Note the white dot superimposed on the color wheel inside the black rectangle. Dragging this dot around the circle changes the selected hue.

■ **Saturation** measures the purity of a color: that is the lack of neutral colors diluting it. To increase saturation, drag the white dot closer to the center of the circle. To decrease saturation, drag it closer to the edge.

■ **Brightness** measures the intensity of a color. If brightness is zero, for example, the result is black. The Color Wheel tab's brightness slider controls brightness.

> NOTE

> Because the eye perceives color in three dimensions—red, green, and blue—no two-dimensional arrangement can ever display a complete set of colors.

The bar titled Colors In This Scheme shows the colors FrontPage will use in building the theme. These change as you drag the white dot around the wheel. The Sample Of Theme preview changes only when you *stop* dragging: that is, when you release the mouse button.

A reasonable person might ask how, after they choose one color with the wheel and slider, FrontPage loads five colors into the Colors In This Scheme bar. Well:

■ The color you select is the normal text color; and it appears fourth in the color bar.

- The color that appears third is the background color, which can't be changed from the Color Wheel tab. To change the background color, use the Color Schemes tab or the Custom tab.

- FrontPage calculates the remaining three colors.

The Color Bar method of choosing colors may seem confusing at first, but it's actually quite advanced. The "Design Tips—Color" section later in this chapter provides more background for understanding this approach.

Using the Custom Tab

The Custom color-scheme tab, shown at the right of Figure 9-4, provides direct control over 14 element types controlled by a theme. To change the color of any type, first select it from the drop-down list. Then, drop down the color control and choose the exact color you want. This uses the same series of dialog boxes shown previously in Figure 4-14, Figure 4-15, and Figure 4-16.

Modifying Theme Graphics

Clicking the Graphics button in Figure 9-2 produces the display of Figure 9-5. This window specifies the images FrontPage will use in each of 11 situations.

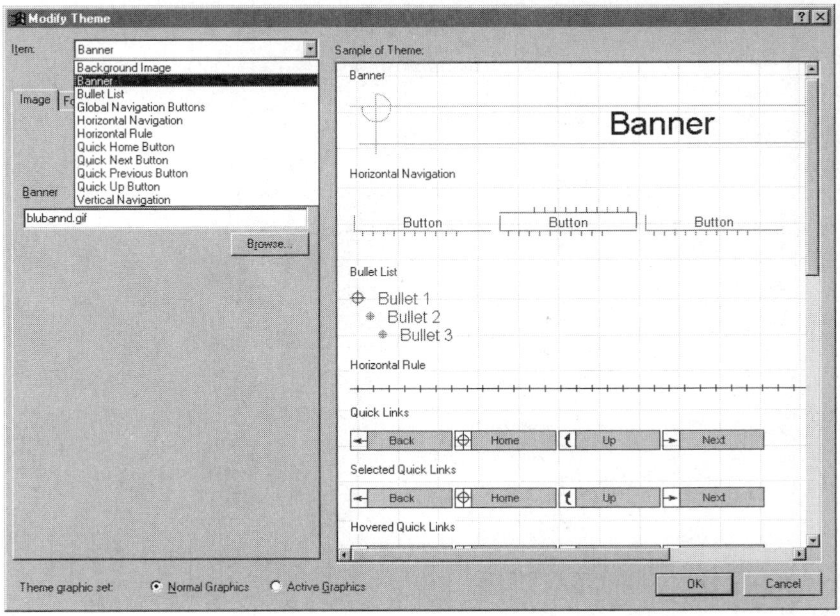

FIGURE 9-5.

The Image tab of this window specifies the picture files Front-Page will use on pages controlled by a specific theme. (Note: This screen shot is slightly modified so both the drop-down list and the Banner box are visible.)

II

Creating Web Pages

? SEE ALSO

For a brief introduction to Navigation Bars and to Navigation view, which provides the data for them to work, see "Navigation View," page 55.

? SEE ALSO

To learn how FrontPage superimposes text over images, see "Adding Text to Images," page 190.

? SEE ALSO

For more information about the Page Banner component, see "Banner Ad Manager," page 358.

- **Background Image** controls the image that fills the background of the Web page.

- **Banner** controls the image that will appear behind the page title.

- **Bullet List** controls the image that marks each item in a bullet list.

- **Horizontal Rule** specifies an image used in place of HTML's normal horizontal-rule element.

The remaining seven image types are all used by the Navigation Bar component described in Chapter 20 under the heading, "Navigation Bars."

After selecting an item from the Item list, hand-type the name of the image you want FrontPage to use or use the Browse button to find it. The Sample Of Theme area will preview your choices.

The Font tab is mostly hidden in Figure 9-5 but appears clearly in Figure 9-6. This tab specifies the font the Page Banner component will superimpose over the banner image as well as the fonts the Navigation Bar component will superimpose over the various navigation images.

A common question is whether you can specify page-banner text without entering it in Navigation view. Sorry, you can't. Another question concerns creating Navigation-bar options without arranging pages in Navigation view, and again, you can't.

FIGURE 9-6.

The Font tab of the Modify Theme Graphics window controls the appearance of text that appears in page banners and navigation bars.

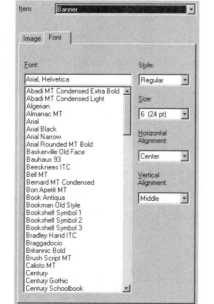

Modifying Theme Text

Clicking the Text button in Figure 9-2 on page 294 displays the window shown in Figure 9-7. This specifies the font and other characteristics of body and heading text that appears on pages controlled by the theme.

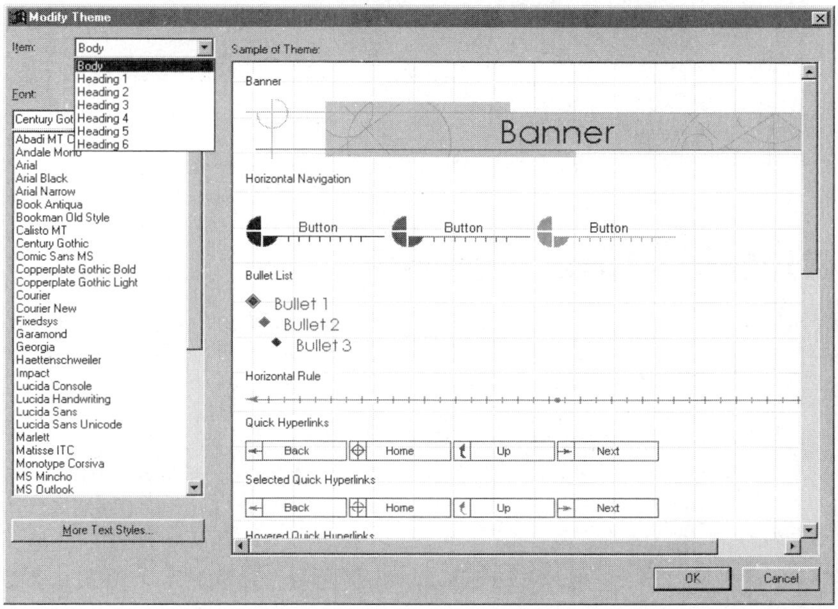

FIGURE 9-7.

The Modify Theme window controls the appearance of body and heading text. The More Styles button provides access to the usual CSS properties.

To specify a font, select the element you want to control and then click the desired font in the list provided. To specify multiple fonts in order of preference, separate the font names with commas.

The More Text Styles button provides access to CSS properties, using the dialog box first seen in Figure 5-23. This provides control not only over font family, but also over font size, weight, style, color, and all the usual CSS selectors and properties.

Saving Modified Themes

Once you've created a modified theme that satisfies you, click the Save button in Figure 9-2 to save it under the same name, or click Save As to save it under a new name. If you click Save As, FrontPage will show the following dialog box to prompt for a theme name.

Creating Web Pages

Some themes, such as those supplied with FrontPage, are flagged read only. In this case, the Save button will be dimmed and you'll have to use Save As.

Once you've saved a theme, you can use it in any Web pages you create.

Distributing Themes

Themes you save in FrontPage reside in a folder accessible to other Office 2000 applications as well. Not all Office 2000 applications use such themes, but those that do—including Word 2000—have access to them immediately.

There are two ways to distribute themes from one computer to another: by direct file copy or by Web.

Distributing by Direct File Copy

To distribute a theme to computers other than your own requires copying one folder that contains two files. By default, this folder resides at the path:

> C:\Program Files\Common Files\Microsoft Shared\Themes

The folder, the two files, and the theme will generally have similar names; for example, the Blueprint theme resides in the Blueprnt folder, and the two files are named Blueprnt.elm and Blueprnt.inf.

To copy a theme from one computer to another, copy its folder to an intermediate location—such as a diskette, file server, or FTP location—and then copy it from there into the Themes folder on the other computer.

Figure 9-8 shows the Themes folder, the Blueprnt folder, and the two files on a typical Windows 98 installation.

Distributing by Web

When you apply a theme to a page in a FrontPage Web, FrontPage copies the theme files into that Web. Then, when another FrontPage user opens the same Web, their Themes list contains two kinds of entries:

- Themes residing on their local system.

- Themes residing in the current FrontPage Web.

If the second FrontPage user applies a theme that resides only on the FrontPage Web, FrontPage will offer to download the theme and install it locally. This provides an efficient means to propagate themes as required to those who need them.

FIGURE 9-8.

Themes reside in a common files area accessible to other Office 2000 applications. To install a theme on another computer, copy it to that computer's Themes folder.

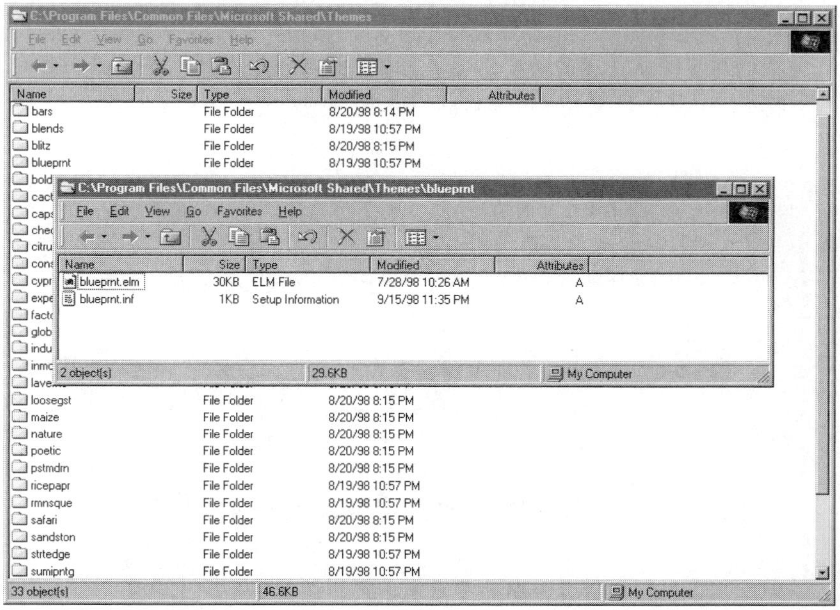

Design Tips—Color

Creating attractive and effective Web pages is a surprisingly difficult proposition. First, Web pages require a different organization and layout than letters, memos, presentations, books, reports, or other documents that beginning Web authors may be more familiar with. The aesthetics and metaphors of Web pages are more like graphic-arts compositions: brochures, magazine pages, posters, handbills, and the like. Second, limitations inherent in HTML severely constrain use of the most common graphic composition techniques: images, typography, color, and page placement and orientation.

Reading this section won't magically transform you into a graphic artist, but it does provide a brief introduction to the graphic and artistic design of Web pages. If you find the material intriguing, try browsing the graphic-arts section of your local bookstore or library, or visit a large art supply store. As long as you keep your handheld computer out of sight, no one will point or laugh.

You'll find color and the study of color to be remarkably multifaceted. Perception of color is a biological and emotional process, not a technical one, and it defies precise scientific analysis. Computer graphics deal with color literally by the numbers, while the artist's view of color—arguably the far better developed—is totally subjective. No graphics card or monitor deals with colors as cool, warm, happy, sad, playful, or serious. Nevertheless, these are the moods we as Web designers seek to convey through our use of technology.

This section briefly introduces the physical nature of color and describes how the human eye perceives it. It then explains how computers (and thus Web browsers) create color images, and then integrates into these discussions several artistic views of color. Finally, it returns to the technical details of implementing the aesthetic colors you choose.

Grasping this material will give you at least a jump-start at understanding how Web visitors will respond to the colors in your site and how to choose colors that invoke the emotional responses you wish to convey to get the maximum impact you want.

Technical Models of Color

In a physical sense, colors correspond to different wavelengths of light. Focusing a beam of white light through a prism—as shown in Figure 9-9—divides it into many beams, each with a single unique hue. The prism works by deflecting each wavelength by a different amount.

FIGURE 9-9.

A glass prism divides white light into its constituent wavelengths.

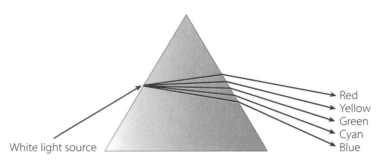

White light source
Red
Yellow
Green
Cyan
Blue

Objects in nature emit or reflect various amounts of light at various wavelengths, and the human eye interprets these combinations as colors. Astonishingly, experts estimate the eye can discriminate about two million different colors.

Fortunately, producing life-like color images doesn't require monitors and video cards capable of generating all the wavelengths found in nature. The eye interprets the infinite range of natural colors in terms of just three: red, green, and blue. Rather than emitting true yellow light, for example, a video system can emit equal amounts of red and green light instead.

If you shone a beam of true yellow light through a prism, a single yellow beam would emerge. The same prism would separate a mixture of red and green light into red and green beams. Nevertheless, both beams, the true yellow and the red-green mix, would look the same to us humans.

RGB—The Red, Green, and Blue Primary Colors

Computer monitors emit only three colors of light: red, green, and blue. Mixing and blending these three colors in various intensities allows the monitor to mimic any color our eyes can perceive. The face of the monitor is divided into a series of dots called *pixels* (picture elements), while a graphics card inside the PC controls the red, green, and blue intensities of each pixel.

NOTE

> An image 200 dots wide and 75 dots tall contains 15,000 pixels.

All current graphics cards trace their ancestry to the original Video Graphics Adapter (VGA) developed by IBM. This device produced a display 640 pixels wide, 480 pixels high, and 16 fixed colors in depth. Since then, capabilities have grown to typical resolutions of 800x600, 1024x768, 1152x864, 1280x1024, 1600x1200, and other variations, and color depth has increased from 16 fixed colors to 256, 65,536, and 16,777,216 programmable colors.

Video cards supporting 256, 65,536, and 16,777,216 colors devote 8, 16, or 24 bits of video memory per pixel. The 24-bit color system is the easiest to understand and program. For each pixel on the display, the graphics card provides 8 bits of memory that specify 256 intensities of red. An additional 8 bits specify 256 intensities of green, and 8 more control 256 intensities of blue. A value of zero indicates no color; 255 indicates maximum color. Each color value of 0 through 255 occupies 8 binary digits, so the entire scheme is called 24-Bit Red, Green, Blue (RGB) Color. Multiplying 256 reds times 256 greens times 256 blues equals 16,777,216 combinations. Therefore, 24-Bit RGB Color is synonymous with 16 Million Color Mode.

Creating Web Pages

FrontPage and many other Windows applications prompt for colors using the Windows dialog box shown in Figure 9-10. You can choose from the basic or custom colors at the upper left by clicking them. The large rectangle at the right shows a pixel-by-pixel array of colors you can choose by clicking, and the vertical bar at the far right controls darkness or lightness.

FIGURE 9-10.

This standard color-choice dialog box is provided by Windows and used by FrontPage and many other applications.

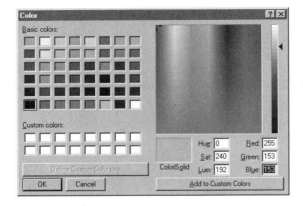

? SEE ALSO

For an explanation of the color array and the Hue, Sat, and Lum settings shown in Figure 9-10, see "HSL—The Hue, Saturation, Luminance Color Model," page 320.

The Red, Green, and Blue values at the lower right of Figure 9-10 specify color intensities in the range 0 through 255, the range discussed earlier in this section. For the most part, this book refers to colors by RGB value. The currently selected color in Figure 9-10, for example, would be 255–153–153.

Some applications require hexadecimal, rather than decimal, RGB values. In hexadecimal (sometimes called simply "hex") the first digit is the 16s place, so hex 23 is (2x16) + 3, or decimal 35. Hex 80 is (8x16) + 0, or decimal 128. The letters *A* through *F* are the hex digits that represent decimal values 10 through 15. In Web pages you'll often see color codes like #9900CC. This represents hex RGB colors 99, 00, and CC, which are 153, 0, and 204 in decimal. A few really detestable programs require entering the true decimal equivalent of hex 9900CC, which is 10,027,212.

★ TIP

You can use the Microsoft Windows Calculator (in Scientific View) to convert decimal values to hexadecimal and vice versa. To convert hexadecimal to decimal, click Calculator's Hex button, enter the number, and then click Calculator's Dec button. To convert decimal to hex, reverse these steps.

Color Notation by the Numbers

With 16,777,216 colors available, referring to them all with vague names like Blanched Almond, Honey Dew, and Moccasin quickly becomes tiresome. Instead, most Web applications denote colors in terms of their red, green, and blue (RGB) intensities. Here are some typical colors specified as RGB combinations.

Color	Decimal			Hexadecimal		
	Red	Green	Blue	Red	Green	Blue
Black	0	0	0	00	00	00
White	255	255	255	FF	FF	FF
Gray	128	128	128	80	80	80
Bright Red	255	0	0	FF	00	00
Bright Green	0	255	0	00	FF	00
Bright Blue	0	0	255	00	00	FF
Dark Red	128	0	0	80	00	00
Dark Cyan	0	128	128	00	80	80

A 256-color graphics adapter also uses a 24-bit color notation. Despite dedicating only 8 bits per pixel, these adapters can display any 24-bit color a programmer desires; the trick is that 8-bit video cards can display only 256 different 24-bit colors at any given time. The video driver supplies the card with a table of 256 colors, and then tells the video card which of these 256 colors to display in each pixel. The phrase that describes this is "256 colors from a palette of 16,777,216."

Some 16-bit graphics adapters display 65,536 colors from a palette of 16,777,216; some display 65,536 fixed colors. An adapter that provides 65,536 fixed colors in "64K mode" usually produces better results if configured to use 256 programmable colors instead. Note that a graphics adapter operating in 64K mode can display 65,536 colors because 64KB = 64x1,024, or 65,536.

SEE ALSO

For information on choosing colors that Web browsers will display smoothly with 256-color display adapters, see "Achieving Accurate Rendition—Safe Colors," page 102.

CMY—The Cyan, Magenta, and Yellow Subtractive Colors

The Red, Green, Blue (RGB) color system described above is an *additive* system; it describes how to form colors by combining beams of light from luminous sources. The colors red, green, and blue are called *primary colors* because the eye responds to them directly.

II

Creating Web Pages

Paints and pigments absorb light rather than generate it, and thus require a completely different model of color. If you mix red and green light, the result is yellow. If you mix perfectly red and perfectly green paint, the result is black. This is the *subtractive* color system.

Subtractive colors are passive. The ink or paint isn't luminous of itself; it only reflects light shone upon it. Red paint reflects red light but absorbs green and blue. Green paint reflects green light but absorbs red and blue. Combining two such paints produces a surface that absorbs all three colors—that is, a surface that appears black.

⊗ NOTE

> In practice, pigments don't reflect or absorb all colors of light perfectly. This is why mixing red and green paint usually produces a brown or gray color.

The simplest and most elementary subtractive colors are those that absorb only one primary color. As shown in Table 9-1, these colors are Cyan, Magenta, and Yellow. Most color reproduction processes, such as color printing and color photography, work by blending these three colors. The CMY color scheme is as common in the printing industry as RGB is for computers. Because of its use in printing, the subtractive color scheme is sometimes called *process color*.

TABLE 9-1.   Additive and Subtractive Colors

Subtractive Color	Absorbs Primary	Reflects Primaries
Cyan	Red	Green, Blue
Magenta	Green	Red, Blue
Yellow	Blue	Red, Green

To produce red, the subtractive process uses a combination of magenta and yellow pigments. The magenta pigment absorbs green and the yellow pigment absorbs blue, so the combination reflects only red to the viewer.

In practice, producing black through a mixture of cyan, magenta, and yellow pigments is quite difficult; natural pigments are seldom so perfect that light of all wavelengths is absorbed completely. Most printing equipment therefore provides black ink as well as cyan, magenta, and yellow. You might think that a cyan, magenta, yellow, and black system would be called CMYB but it's not; the actual term is CMYK.

Both the CMY and CMYK systems use percentages between 0 and 100 for measuring intensity. Zero means no absorption and 100 means complete absorption. A typical CMYK color specification appears below.

C   40

M   100

Y   0

K   45

It's extremely unusual to specify computer display colors in terms of the CMY or CMYK systems; the RGB system is much more appropriate. Occasionally, though, the need may arise to convert CMY color values to RGB. In such cases, the following approximate formulas will help.

Converting CMYK to CMY

Cyan   = Min (1, (Cyan * (1 − Black)) + Black)

Magenta = Min (1, (Magenta * (1 − Black)) + Black)

Yellow   = Min (1, (Yellow * (1 − Black)) + Black)

To convert the CMYK color 40-100-0-45 to CMY, compute as follows:

Cyan   = Min (1, (0.40 * (1 − 0.45)) + 0.45) = Min (1, 0.22 + 0.45) = 0.67

Magenta = Min (1, (1.00 * (1 − 0.45)) + 0.45) = Min (1, 0.55 + 0.45) = 1.00

Yellow   = Min (1, (0.00 * (1 − 0.45)) + 0.45) = Min (1, 0.00 + 0.45) = 0.45

Converting CMY to RGB

Red   = 255 * (1 − Cyan)

Green   = 255 * (1 − Magenta)

Blue   = 255 * (1 − Yellow)

To convert the CMY color 67-100-45 to RGB, compute as follows:

Red   = 255 * (1 − 0.67)   = 255 * (0.33)   = 84

Green   = 255 * (1 − 1.00)   = 255 * (0.00)   = 0

Blue   = 255 * (1 − 0.45)   = 255 * (0.55)   = 140

Converting RGB to CMY

Cyan   = 1 − (Red / 255)

Magenta = 1 − (Green / 255)

Yellow   = 1 − (Blue / 255)

(X) CAUTION

The formulas at the right are adequate for general work but nevertheless are imperfect. Achieving a perfect match between primary and subtractive colors requires adjustments for viewing conditions, lighting, monitor phosphors, monitor brightness, monitor contrast, printing inks, paper, type of printing process, and additional factors.

II

Creating Web Pages

Converting the RGB color 84-0-140 to CMY produces the expected result:

Cyan	= 1 – (84 / 255)	= 1 – 0.33	= 0.67
Magenta	= 1 – (0 / 255)	= 1 – 0.00	= 1.00
Yellow	= 1 – (140 / 255)	= 1 – 0.55	= 0.45

Converting CMY to CMYK

Black	= Min (Cyan, Magenta, Yellow)
Cyan	= (Cyan – Black) / (1 – Black)
Magenta	= (Magenta – Black) / (1 – Black)
Yellow	= (Yellow – Black) / (1 – Black)

Converting the CMY color 67-100-45 to CMYK works as below (find the black value *first* so that you can use it in the C, M, and Y formulas).

Black	= Min (0.67, 1.00, 0.45)		= 0.45
Cyan	= (0.67 – 0.45) / (1 – 0.45)	= 0.22 / 0.55	= 0.40
Magenta	= (1.00 – 0.45) / (1 – 0.45)	= 0.55 / 0.55	= 1.00
Yellow	= (0.45 – 0.45) / (1 – 0.45)	= 0 / 0.55	= 0.00

Artistic Color Models

The RGB and CMY color models provide a way to numerically classify and then mechanically reproduce colors. This is valuable information for Web-page creators, who almost universally need a way to specify colors and be relatively confident that Web browsers can reproduce them on the remote user's computer. However, neither the RGB nor CMY color models provide any guidance on choosing colors that look good together, display well, and convey a desired image or mood. Providing this kind of advice is the province of art, artists, and artistic expression.

Artists seldom deal with colors numerically; to them, colors are tubes of pigment having traditional names and obtained from art-supply stores. The artist is far more concerned with human perception of color than the technology of color reproduction; mixing pigments to produce desired colors is a means to an end and not an end in itself.

Think about the front outside wall of your house or building. Most scientific or technically oriented folks would say that the wall is always the same color; very few would say its color constantly changes. In an artistic sense, however, the wall is many colors at once, and those colors change all the time! It's completely obvious, in an artistic sense, that the wall appears to be a different color in the morning and in the afternoon, a third color in the evening, and another at night. A painting would have to use different colors to show the wall in sunlight or in shade, on sunny days or overcast, in winter or summer. (Think of Monet's series of paintings of water lilies.) The paint on the building wall doesn't change, but the human perception of it does. The artist is concerned with reproducing the human perception of the wall rather than the original color of the house paint.

Fortunately, Web authors seeking to produce attractive pages needn't become proficient oil painters or artists. There are no absolutes in the field of art, but there *are* relatively simple guidelines you can use to choose colors intelligently—colors that work well together and transmit the message you desire.

Color Wheels

A common artistic approach to color involves arranging hues around the edges of a wheel, as shown in Figure 9-11. Colors appear around the wheel's edge in spectral order: the order produced by splitting white light with a prism.

TIP

> To view Figure 9-11 and others in color, use your browser to open them from the Internet or from the CD in the back of this book. The Internet URLs are those that appear in the figures, such as http://www.interlacken.com/rfp2000/colorsci.htm. The corresponding CD file name would be D:\rfp2000\colorsci.htm (assuming D: is the letter of your CD-ROM drive).

The arrangement of colors in Figure 9-11 seems technically correct— the primary colors red, green, and blue are spaced evenly, in spectral order, and diametrically opposed to their subtractive opposites. Note that 180° across from red is cyan, which absorbs red and reflects only green and blue.

There's nothing hard and fast about a color wheel; you can arrange any number of colors in any order you want. The Corel Draw dialog box shown in Figure 9-12, for example, includes a color wheel with six labeled color positions, red at 3 o'clock rather than 12, and the colors red, green, and blue arranged counterclockwise.

Creating Web Pages

FIGURE 9-11.

This color wheel arranges the standard RGB and CMY colors uniformly. This is correct in a technical sense—but seldom produces artistic results.

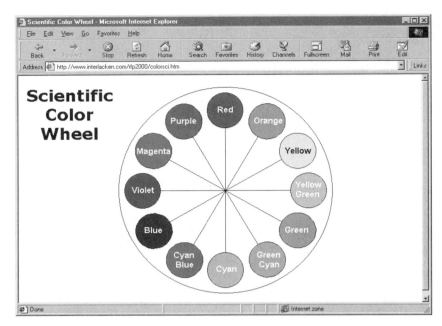

FIGURE 9-12.

This color dialog box from CorelDraw features a technically oriented color wheel. Moving the highlight around the triangular area controls saturation and brightness.

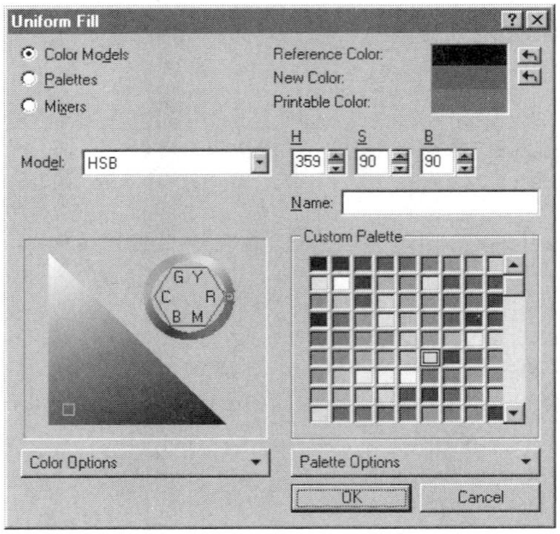

Color Harmony

Properly constructed color wheels serve a very important purpose for beginning designers and artists: they provide guidance in selecting colors that work well together. This technique is called *color harmony*.

The theory of color harmony maintains that drawing a regular polygon inside a color wheel automatically selects colors that are harmonious—that is, pleasing together, like the musical notes that constitute a chord.

> **Purple, the Unnatural Color**
>
> The visible spectrum of color extends continuously from red to blue, with stops along the way as shown below.
>
> Red—Yellow—Green—Cyan—Blue
>
> The eye sees yellow in either of two ways:
>
> ■ When it sees true yellow light.
>
> ■ When it sees a mixture of red and green light.
>
> A similar effect occurs with cyan. We see this color either because we see real cyan light or because we see a mixture of green and blue light.
>
> Something interesting happens when the eye sees a mixture of red and blue light—it sees purple, a color that doesn't exist as a single wavelength of light. Purple, in this sense, is an artificial color.
>
> Purple pigment has rather exacting requirements: it must absorb the broad middle of the visible spectrum and reflect only the high and low extremes. This explains somewhat why purple is a color seldom found in nature.

Colors opposite each other on the wheel are complementary—that is, opposites in a pleasing way. Adjacent colors are similar—that is, they transition smoothly. Stating this another way, opposite colors have maximum contrast of hue, whereas adjacent colors have minimal contrast of hue.

Color harmony provides an appealingly simple approach to choosing attractive color schemes for Web pages or any other purpose. Here's how to achieve color harmony:

1 Select a key color—a color that must appear in the color scheme because of requirement or preference.

2 Locate that color on the color wheel.

3 Select two, three, or four harmonious colors by imagining a line, triangle, or square inside the wheel and noting the colors at the ends or corners. (See the upper-left, lower-left, and lower-right examples in Figure 9-13.)

4 Alternatively, choose the complementary (opposite) color plus one or two similar colors—similar either to the key color or to the complement. (See the upper-right example in Figure 9-13.)

If this seems too simple, you're right; there are several details we haven't discussed yet. Nevertheless, the simple techniques of color wheels and color harmony prove you needn't be Vincent van Gogh or Andy Warhol to design an attractive color scheme.

FIGURE 9-13.

Colors spaced evenly around the wheel are harmonious—that is, they're usually pleasing to the eye when used together. Opposite colors are complementary, and adjacent colors are similar.

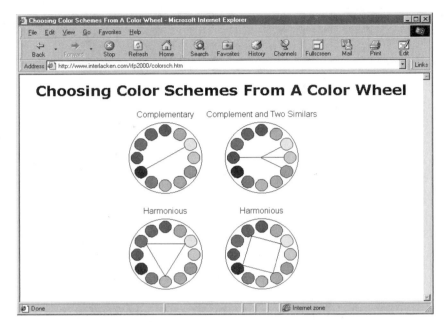

The Artistic Color Wheel

The first step to achieving true color harmony is adjusting the colors in the wheel. A color wheel with red, green, and blue evenly spaced—and with cyan, magenta, and yellow in direct opposition—doesn't take the flesh-and-blood characteristics of the eye and mind into account.

Artists, with hundreds of years of art history to guide them, consider the primary colors to be red, yellow, and blue. You can show artists all the prisms, computer monitors, and printer's inks you want, but they'll swear that red, yellow, and blue are the colors with the most visual contrast and the highest recognition. Conversely, blue and green have too little visual contrast for both to be artistic primaries.

A color wheel with red, yellow, and blue as the primaries appears in Figure 9-14, on the next page. Green, cyan, and magenta appear interspersed among the primaries in their usual order; in fact, the overall order of the wheel is unchanged. The colors from red to green have simply been stretched to occupy the entire right side of the wheel, and the colors from green through blue and back to red have been compressed into the left semicircle. This arrangement fulfills two objectives:

- It takes into account the color perception of the human eye and mind.

- It produces better—more harmonious—results.

Figure 9-15, on the next page, shows the same color wheel as Figure 9-14, except that color names are replaced by RGB values. Note that the additive and subtractive primaries have color values of 0 or 255 only; these are extremely vivid—some would say fully saturated—colors. The remaining colors are quite vivid as well; the extreme intensities of 0 and 255 predominate except where it's necessary to generate hues between two adjacent colors.

FIGURE 9-14.

Here is the sort of color wheel most artists use. The primary colors are red, yellow, and blue.

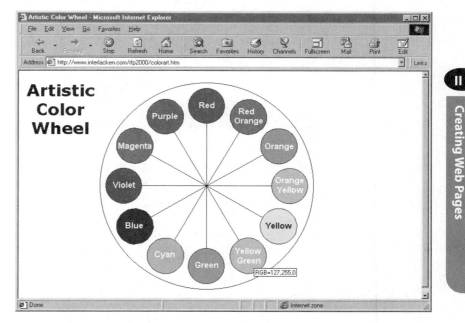

The terms hue, shade, tint, and color deserve some explanation. Many people use these terms somewhat randomly or interchangeably, but in color theory they have very specific meanings.

- A color's hue is its true, pure color. A hue relates to a single wavelength of light.

- Tints are a mixture of the pure hue with white.

- Shades are a mixture of the pure hue with black.

- The same hue can have thousands of tints and shades.

FIGURE 9-15.

This artistic color wheel shows RGB color values that correspond to the color names in Figure 9-14.

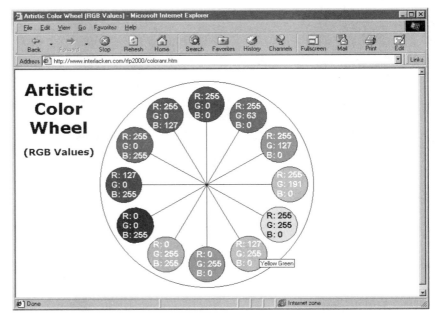

Elementary Color Schemes

Because human judgment and interpretation are involved, choosing effective color combinations can never be a completely scientific process. Nevertheless, some approaches are more consistently successful than others. The 10 schemes listed below have been used repeatedly and have stood the test of time.

- **Achromatic.** Use no color at all; the composition consists entirely of grays. A black-and-white photograph is achromatic.

- **Monochromatic.** Use various tints and shades, but only one hue. This lends a soft appearance and sense of unity.

- **Neutral.** Use a single hue, but neutralize it by adding its complement or black. The result is more muted than a monochromatic scheme might be.

- **Analogous.** Use tints or shades of three consecutive color-wheel colors.

- **Complementary.** Use two colors 180° apart on the wheel. Beware of excessive contrast, especially when choosing vivid colors.

- **Clash.** Choose a starting color for this extremely harsh yet eye-catching scheme, and then choose the hue to the left or right of its complement. That is, choose two colors 150° or 210° apart.

- **Split Complementary.** Use a starting color and the two colors adjacent to its complement—that is, 150° or 210° degrees around the wheel. Two similar colors clashing with another often produces a certain balance, especially if you avoid vivid colors.

- **Primary.** Use red, yellow, and blue.

- **Secondary.** Use green, violet, and orange.

- **Tertiary.** Use any colors other than red, yellow, blue, green, violet, and orange, but that are equally spaced around a color wheel.

Perhaps by now you've realized there are many ways to choose contrasting colors that are pleasing and compatible. In fact, there are seven. These are the topic of the next section.

Seven Kinds of Color Contrast

Johannes Itten, a pioneer in the study of color, identified seven kinds of contrast that occur between colors. The first three pertain to physical properties of light:

- **Contrast of hue.** Choosing colors from different positions on the color wheel (or spectrum) is the simplest and most obvious way to achieve color contrast. Contrast of hue is greatest among primary colors, less among their complements, and least among tertiary and other mixed hues. Stained glass windows have very high contrast of hue.

- **Contrast of saturation.** The purity of a color is expressed as its degree of saturation. Painters and artists control saturation by starting with an extremely vivid pigment and then diluting it with white, black, gray, or the original color's complement.

- **Contrast of light-dark (brightness).** Two colors of the same hue can differ greatly; a dark, near-black shade and a light, near-white tint of the same color exhibit this kind of contrast. A black-and-white photo consists entirely of light-dark contrasts, though this kind of contrast can occur with any hue. The human eye responds more precisely and reliably to contrast of light-dark than to contrast of hue. Extreme light-dark contrast is usually more legible and less jarring than extreme contrast of hue. In the absence of light-dark contrast, fine text is usually illegible.

The remaining four color contrasts pertain to human perception and interpretation of light.

- **Contrast of cold-warm.** Colors on the green-blue side of the color wheel are classified as cool, while those on the red-yellow side are warm. Compositions involving all warm or all cool colors are usually more pleasing than those in which colors of both types appear. Cool colors are usually deemed sedate and warm colors stimulating. Wall and fixture colors in psychiatric wards and fast-food restaurants are designed accordingly.

- **Contrast of complements.** This is the contrast that occurs between any two colors that are directly opposite on a continuous color wheel. Combined, they will always produce black, white, or gray; adding their respective RGB components will produce three equal numbers. Using complementary colors, especially in combination with intermediate colors, can produce a strong yet pleasing sort of contrast. Vivid complements, however, can clash violently.

Controlling Color Saturation

In computer graphics, saturated colors have RGB components as extreme as possible; the three primaries, red, green, and blue, for example, are fully saturated at RGB values of 255-0-0, 0-255-0, and 0-0-255. Cyan, magenta, and yellow are fully saturated at 0-255-255, 255-0-255, and 255-255-0. Intermediate hues are fully saturated when one RGB component is 0 and another is 255.

Here's how you can control the saturation of a color:

- To add white to a color, increase its low RGB values uniformly. Adding some white to vivid blue (0-0-255), for example, could produce 102-102-255. Adding even more white would produce colors like 151-151-255 and 204-204-255.

- To add black to a color, uniformly decrease its high RGB values. Adding some black to vivid blue (0-0-255) might produce a color like 0-0-153. Adding more black would produce 0-0-102 or 0-0-51.

- To add gray, increase the color's low RGB values and decrease its high RGB values simultaneously. Adding gray to vivid blue (0-0-255) produces colors like 102-102-153.

- To create the complement of a color, invert its RGB values. The complement of vivid blue (0-0-255) would be 255-255-0 (yellow).

- **Simultaneous contrast.** When two colors are adjacent, the eye sees the duller color as tinged by the complement of the brighter color. When the eye shifts away from a bright color, such as yellow, to a dull color, such as gray, it experiences a sort of boomerang or overshoot effect and mistakenly senses the opposite of the "missing" color. This explains why a gray spot in a yellow background appears blue, or a black thread in a red fabric looks green. Color experts can use this effect constructively, but for beginners it's more often an explanation of why their work doesn't look as expected.

- **Contrast of extent.** The degree to which a color predominates a composition depends not only on its intensity—its brightness—but also on its *extent*—the amount of space it occupies. If all the major colors in a composition have equal impact on the viewer, based on their intensities and extents, the result is harmonious. If not, the result is expressive. Expressive results have greater visual contrast.

Evaluating Contrast of Extent

A complicating factor in judging contrast of extent is that the eye reacts more strongly to some colors than to others. Comparing yellow and violet colors of equal intensity, for example, the eye will perceive yellow as about three times as bright. The following relative intensities are generally accepted.

Yellow	Orange	Red	Violet	Blue	Green
9	8	6	3	4	6

Because orange appears twice as bright as blue, blue must have twice the area of the orange for the two colors to have equal impact. Intermediate combinations are also possible. Here are three possible brightness effects controlled by the extent of the two colors:

Extent of Color	Perceived Brightness
Blue area is twice orange area.	Blue appears as bright as orange.
Blue area equals orange area.	Orange appears twice as bright as blue.
Orange area is twice blue area.	Orange appears four times as bright as blue.

Contrast of extent is a tool, not a rule. To reduce the impact of a color, use less of it in terms of area, brightness, or both. To increase a color's impact, increase its brightness or surface area.

Of these seven contrasts, three are physical properties of light, and four are properties of human perception. Cold-warm, complements, simultaneous, and extension contrasts are perceptual and serve primarily to explain human perception of color in compositions—Web pages or any other. These contrasts are important, but the page creator achieves them indirectly by manipulating the physical color properties.

The physical properties of perceived color are hue, saturation, and brightness. Choosing and blending computer graphics colors using these dimensions is clearly more natural than specifying direct RGB value, and this is the objective of the HSB color model described in the next section.

? SEE ALSO

For an example of FrontPage using the HSB system for color control, see Figure 9-4 on page 296.

HSB—The Hue, Saturation, Brightness Color Model

Figure 9-16 shows a typical color dialog box that selects colors based on hue, saturation, and brightness.

- Hue is specified as degrees of counterclockwise rotation around the color wheel, starting from red at 3 o'clock.

- Saturation varies along the vertical axis of the triangle from 100 at the bottom to 0 at the top; 0% saturation (at the upper corner) results in white.

- Brightness varies along the horizontal axis of the triangle from 100 at the left to 0 at the right; 0% brightness (at the right corner) is black.

- The selected hue is most vivid at the lower-left corner of the triangle, where saturation and brightness are both 100%.

- For any given hue, the triangle displays every possible tint and shade.

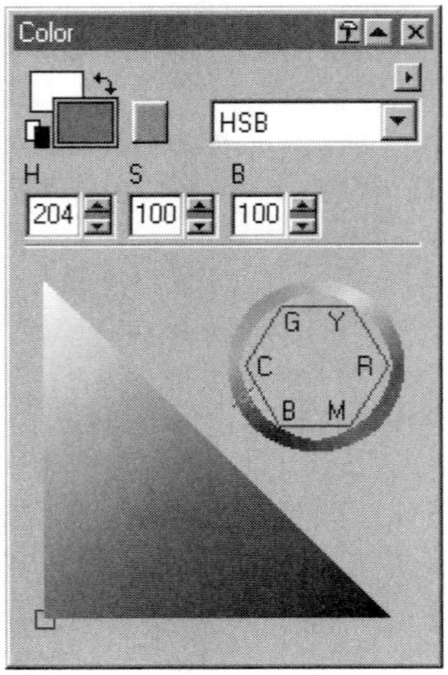

FIGURE 9-16.

This color dialog box from Corel Photo-Paint selects hue as degrees of rotation around the color wheel, saturation along the vertical edge of the triangle, and brightness along the horizontal edge.

Figure 9-17 shows how Microsoft Image Composer supports the HSB model, but Image Composer uses the alternate term HSV, which stands for Hue, Saturation, Value. The top edge of the banded rectangle is essentially a color wheel rolled out flat.

- The slider marked with a triangle along the top edge (or the Hue slider to the right) selects hue.

- The slider next to the tall narrow rectangle (or the Sat slider to the right) controls saturation.

- The slider marked with a triangle along the left edge of the banded rectangle (or the Value slider to the right) controls brightness.

HSB color dialog boxes provide a natural way to make and refine color choices. Finding a pleasing hue with an RGB dialog box requires varying three independent color components in search of a satisfactory combination; the same operation in HSB requires varying only one dimension.

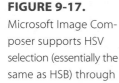

FIGURE 9-17.
Microsoft Image Composer supports HSV selection (essentially the same as HSB) through this color dialog box.

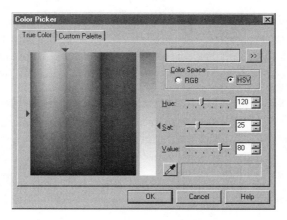

Choosing tints and shades is also quite intuitive under the HSB system. Artists lighten vivid colors by adding white pigment; to accomplish the same result with computer graphics, you can either calculate proportional increases in all three RGB components (using the RGB system) or simply vary the saturation setting (using HSB).

Similarly, artists darken vivid colors by adding black. In computer graphics, you can either calculate proportional decreases in all three RGB components or simply decrease the brightness setting.

Table 9-2 and Table 9-3 compare the RGB and HSB settings for various shades and tints of blue and orange. Blue, being a primary color, has a relatively simple progression of RGB values; to decrease brightness, decrease the blue value. To decrease saturation, increase red and green. Increasing brightness and saturation work the same, in reverse.

> Ignore the HSL column for now. The next section will discuss this additional color model.

Varying orange—a more complex, tertiary color—is more difficult. Decreasing brightness requires proportional decreases in both the original red and green values, and decreasing saturation requires proportionally increasing green and blue. Varying the appearance of a color while maintaining the same hue is considerably easier using the HSB model than the RGB model.

In summary:

- To obtain progressively lighter tints using the RGB model, proportionally increase any components not already at maximum. To obtain lighter tints using the HSB model, decrease saturation.

- To obtain progressively darker shades using the RGB model, proportionally decrease any nonzero components. To obtain darker shades using the HSB model, decrease brightness.

HSL—The Hue, Saturation, Luminance Color Model

For reasons no doubt lost in antiquity, the standard color selection dialog box provided with Windows and used by most applications doesn't support the HSB color model. Instead, it supports RGB and another model called HSL—hue, saturation, luminance.

- Hue is the same measurement used in the HSB system, except that the color wheel is divided into 240 (rather than 360) increments.

- Saturation ranges in value from 0 to 240, and has a different meaning than saturation in the HSB model. In HSL, a saturation of 0 means the color is gray and 240 means the color contains no gray.

- Luminance denotes the brightness of gray referred to by saturation. A luminance of 240 means white, 120 means 50% gray, and 0 means black.

HSL's fascination with gray stems from its origins in the television industry. Luminance is the black-and-white portion of a television signal. The inventors of color television modified the black-and-white television signal, adding hue and saturation data in such a way that monochrome sets would ignore them.

TABLE 9-2.   Saturation and Brightness Settings for the Color Blue

Color	RGB Model			HSB Model			HSL Model		
	Red	Green	Blue	Hue	Satu-ration	Bright-ness	Hue	Satu-ration	Lumi-nance
Black	0	0	0	240	100	0	160	240	0
Shade of blue	0	0	51	240	100	20	160	240	24
Shade of blue	0	0	102	240	100	40	160	240	48
Shade of blue	0	0	153	240	100	60	160	240	72
Shade of blue	0	0	204	240	100	80	160	240	96
Vivid blue	0	0	255	240	100	100	160	240	120
Tint of blue	51	51	255	240	80	100	160	240	144
Tint of blue	102	102	255	240	60	100	160	240	168
Tint of blue	153	153	255	240	40	100	160	240	192
Tint of blue	204	204	255	240	20	100	160	240	216
White	255	255	255	240	0	100	160	240	240

TABLE 9-3.   Saturation and Brightness Settings for the Color Orange

Color	RGB Model			HSB Model			HSL Model		
	Red	Green	Blue	Hue	Satu-ration	Bright-ness	Hue	Satu-ration	Lumi-nance
Black	0	0	0	48	100	0	32	240	0
Shade of orange	51	0	0	48	100	20	32	240	24
Shade of orange	102	0	0	48	100	40	32	240	48
Shade of orange	153	0	0	48	100	60	32	240	72
Shade of orange	204	0	0	48	100	80	32	240	96
Vivid orange	255	204	0	48	100	100	32	240	120
Tint of orange	255	214	51	48	80	100	32	240	144
Tint of orange	255	224	102	48	60	100	32	240	168
Tint of orange	255	235	153	48	40	100	32	240	192
Tint of orange	255	245	204	48	20	100	32	240	216
White	255	255	255	48	0	100	32	240	240

II

Creating Web Pages

Any Color Black You Want

According to legend, someone once asked Henry Ford to start manufacturing cars in more than one color. Ford reportedly answered, "Fine. We'll build cars in any color black you want."

Sharp-eyed readers may notice that while the RGB columns in Tables 9-2 and 9-3 (on the previous two pages) both show black as 0-0-0 and white as 255-255-255, the HSB values for black and white differ:

Color	Table	Hue	Saturation	Brightness
Black	9-2	240	100	0
	9-3	48	100	0
White	9-2	240	0	100
	9-3	48	0	100

In the HSB model, a brightness of zero indicates zero light—the color black. Hue and saturation are irrelevant under these conditions. Think of it this way: if you were sitting in a dark room, leaving a red light turned off would produce the same effect as leaving a green light turned off.

Similarly, there are no hues of white. Zero percent of any hue is still zero. When saturation is zero:

■ Hue is irrelevant.

■ Varying brightness from 0% to 100% produces a grayscale extending from black to white.

Although irrelevant, the hue values for both black and white in Table 9-2 and Table 9-3 were repeated, for the sake of uniformity, as they appeared elsewhere in the same table. The black saturation values were treated similarly.

Figure 9-18 shows a typical Windows color dialog box with HSL support.

■ The top edge of the banded rectangle corresponds to the hues in a standard, continuous color wheel. You can select hues by dragging the crosshairs within the banded rectangle left and right, or by typing a number between 0 and 239 into the Hue text box.

■ The banded rectangle's vertical dimension represents saturation. Note that the lower edge is 50% gray, not black or white. To vary the saturation setting, either move the crosshairs up or down, or type a number between 0 and 240 into the Sat text box.

■ The tall narrow rectangle at the right of the dialog box controls luminance. To vary luminance, drag the slider up and down, or type a number between 0 and 240 into the Lum text box. Remember, 240 means white, 0 means black, and the value 120 produces the most vivid hue.

FIGURE 9-18.

This standard Windows color dialog box simultaneously supports the HSL and RGB color models.

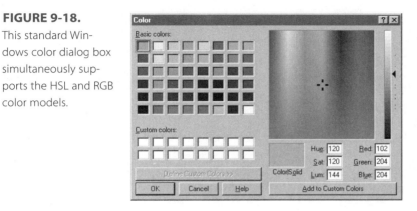

As illustrated in Table 9-4, varying HSL saturation is equivalent to varying *both* HSB saturation *and* HSB brightness. This makes sense when you consider that varying gray (which HSL defines as saturation) is equivalent to simultaneously varying a mixture of white (HSB saturation) and black (HSB brightness).

TABLE 9-4.   Corresponding Effects of HSL Saturation

Color	RGB Model			HSB Model			HSL Model		
	Red	Green	Blue	Hue	Satu-ration	Bright-ness	Hue	Satu-ration	Lumi-nance
Gray	127	127	127	240	0	50	160	0	120
Dull blue	102	102	153	240	33	60	160	48	120
Dull blue	51	51	204	240	74	80	160	144	120
Vivid blue	0	0	255	240	100	100	160	240	120

Most Web-page creators find the HSL model more difficult to understand than either RGB or HSB. However, it does provide a way to vary colors without affecting hue, and its frequent appearance in Windows color-dialog boxes makes learning it worthwhile.

Other Dimensions of Color

Most of us have developed rich associations between colors, other sensory perceptions, and the moods they invoke. Some of these associations are physical, such as red, the color of fire, denoting warmth. Some are societal, such as purple being associated with royalty, and others seem quite arbitrary. Whatever the origins, these associations identify color as a communications channel—a channel by which your Web pages will, by design or by default, communicate with your visitors. Some of these associations are as follows:

- **Hot.** A combination of highly saturated red hues produces red at its strongest and conveys an image of heat. Hot colors are strong and bold; they demand attention. They stimulate the nervous system, sometimes to the point of raising blood pressure.

- **Cold.** Consisting of highly saturated blues, cold colors are directly opposite hot. They invoke sensations of snow and ice; they slow bodily functions and induce a sense of calm. Saturated greens and blue-greens are cold colors.

- **Warm.** Any hue containing red is warm, but mixtures of red and yellow are particularly so. Warm colors are spontaneous, soothing, and enticing.

- **Cool.** These colors differ from cold by containing yellow; this produces yellow-green, green, and blue-green hues such as turquoise. Cool colors are lush, deep, spring-like, and soothing.

- **Light.** Light colors are mostly white, with just a tint of hue; hues appear in such small proportion that contrast among them is minimal. They convey airiness, free flow, rest, and relaxation. Light colors have all three RGB components at or near maximum, or an HSB brightness near maximum.

- **Dark.** Vivid hues mixed with black produce dark colors. Electronically, none of the RGB components is likely to exceed 127. In HSB terms, brightness will be less than 50. Dark colors are dense, somber, and masculine in effect, and they suggest autumn or winter. Compositions composed entirely of dark colors are seldom effective, but dark colors provide excellent contrast against light.

- **Pale.** These are soft pastel colors formed with diminished hues and at least two-thirds white—that is, with all three RGB components at 170 or more. Pink, light blue, and ivory are typical results. Soft and calming, pale colors are frequently used for interiors of homes and offices.

- **Bright.** Colors lacking black or white dilution are vivid, saturated, and therefore bright. Bright colors attract attention from a distance, but if overused at close quarters they can be overpowering and harsh.

Color Contrast on Web Pages

A rule of thumb states that attractive color schemes consist of three (or at most four) predominant colors. On Web pages, these are usually the background color, the normal text color, and a highlight color.

- For easy reading, the most contrast is between normal text and the background. The background is usually light and the text dark.

- The highlight color is used for elements like edge trim, icons, and headings. Consider using a complement of the background hue, but with similar saturation and brightness. Contrast between the highlight and background should generally be less than the contrast between normal text and the background. More contrast against the background may be required for heading text, though, if heading text and normal text will be different colors.

- Use icons and graphics related to the background color. Against a light blue background, for example, use icons featuring either dark, cool colors or complementary earth tones. Avoid icons with poor edge contrast against the selected background color; these confuse the eye.

- Choose similar colors for hyperlink text and visited hyperlink text. These should probably be similar hues with equal saturation and brightness rather than equal hues of different saturation. Make sure that both hyperlink colors have enough contrast against the background to be legible, but near enough to each other to suggest a like function. Hyperlink text and visited hyperlink text are usually brighter than normal text.

- Avoid not only more than three major colors per page, but also more than two or three contrast types. Using too many kinds of contrast on the same page is visually disorienting.

Choosing Harmonic Color Schemes

Figure 9-19 shows the Color Harmony Chooser, a Dynamic HTML (DHTML) page that illustrates several points of color selection and color harmony. The page is highly interactive, and manipulating a color scheme by its attributes is simply a great way to learn by doing. To use this Web page:

1 Load the colorpik.htm file from the CD accompanying this book, from a copy of the rfp2000 Web installed on your PC, or from the Internet. The Internet URL is:

   http://www.interlacken.com/rfp2000/colorpik.htm

2 Choose the following settings in the Options area:

- **Wheel.** Specify the color wheel you wish to use (Scientific or Artistic).

- **Click Chooses.** Specify which color clicking the color wheel will select (the background color, the foreground color, or the highlight color).

- **Auto-Choose.** Specify the direction to use when picking colors other than the one chosen by clicking. For example, if clicking chooses the background color and Auto-Choose is clockwise, the chooser will advance 120° clockwise to choose the foreground color, and another 120° clockwise to choose the highlight color.

- **Browser Safe Colors.** Turn this box on to correct all calculated colors to browser-safe values. Turn it off to display calculated colors without adjustment.

3 Click any color on the color wheel.

- The B, F, and H dots will indicate the base colors chosen for the background, foreground, and highlight of a color scheme.

- The same three colors—and their color values—will appear in the left rectangle under the Background, Foreground, and Highlight color headings.

4 The Shade and Tint drop-down lists modify the base colors, which are quite vivid, by adding percentages of black or white. Increasing the Shade value decreases brightness, while increasing the Tint value decreases saturation. Under each color heading, the rectangle at the right shows the result of applying the chosen tint and shades to the color at the left.

5 Review the color scheme displayed beneath the color wheel, and then repeat steps 1 through 3 until the results are pleasing.

6 Use the right-most color values under each color heading for your Web page or theme.

ON THE WEB

Internet Explorer 4 was the first browser to support the full DHTML specification, and is the only known browser that displays the Color Harmony Chooser correctly. To check for a newer version of the chooser, browse: http://www.interlacken.com/rfp2000/colorpik.htm

Dynamic HTML

Browsers with Dynamic HTML (DHTML) capability can change the content of Web pages after they've been initially displayed.

- Web page elements detect events like the page being loaded, images being clicked, and list items being selected.

- These events cause specified blocks of program code (usually JavaScript) to execute.

- This program code changes the attributes of existing Web page elements, removes existing elements, or adds new ones.

DHTML presents a problem for WYSIWYG editors like FrontPage, because documents need to remain static for editing. This means that for complex pages like the Color Harmony Chooser in Figure 9-19, a considerable part of the work needs to be done with lines of code in HTML view.

FIGURE 9-19.

This Web page computes and displays harmonic color schemes based on a key color you select.

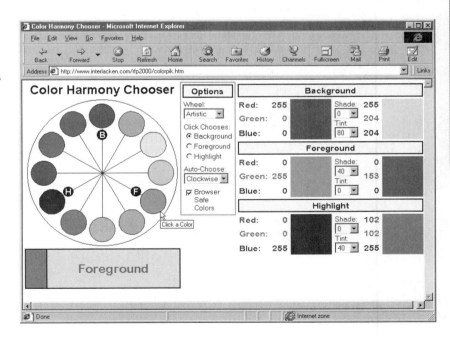

To try color schemes other than three colors 120° apart:

1 Set Auto-Choose to None.

2 Set Click Chooses to Background, then click the desired background color.

3 Set Click Chooses to Foreground, then click the desired fore-ground color.

4 Set Click Chooses to Highlight, then click the desired highlight color.

5 Fine-tune colors with the Tint and Shade controls.

In Summary...

FrontPage themes provide a great way to uniformly apply profession-ally designed color schemes to your Web page. If none of the supplied themes meets your needs, you can modify the existing themes and cre-ate new ones.

Color theory, color harmony, and rules of color contrast provide a struc-tured way of looking at colors that even the most technically inclined, artistically challenged Web designer can appreciate. The brief introduc-tion presented here may not qualify you as a master artist, but it's prob-ably enough to boost your Web pages above average.

The next chapter introduces the topics of HTML forms which, through familiar user interface elements, gather information from your Web visitors.

CHAPTER 10

Creating and Using Forms

The vast majority of current Web pages consists of text, images, and hyperlinks. Such pages are relatively easy to create and deliver, and they provide a valuable electronic publication service. Still, regardless of visual appearance, there's only so much a designer can to with so-called *flat* Web pages. Simple hyperlinks can't provide the full-function interface required for data entry, data retrieval, and a rich user experience. This chapter is the first of several that explain how to bring such interactivity to your site.

HTML forms add text boxes, radio buttons, check boxes, push buttons, and other user interface controls to your Web pages. Designing an HTML form, however, is only half the battle. Once your Web visitors enter data, click the Submit button, and the browser transmits the data to the server, the Web server needs some kind of program to collect the Web visitor's data and to do something with it. Such a program might save the data in a file, save it in a database, send it as e-mail, make Web pages out of it, or whatever. Chapters 21 and 22 will discuss how Microsoft FrontPage software installed on the Web server provides those functions.

HTML Forms

Pages that collect input data are a familiar feature of the Web. Figure 10-1 provides an example. Such pages contain one or more *HTML forms* that operate in a relatively simple way.

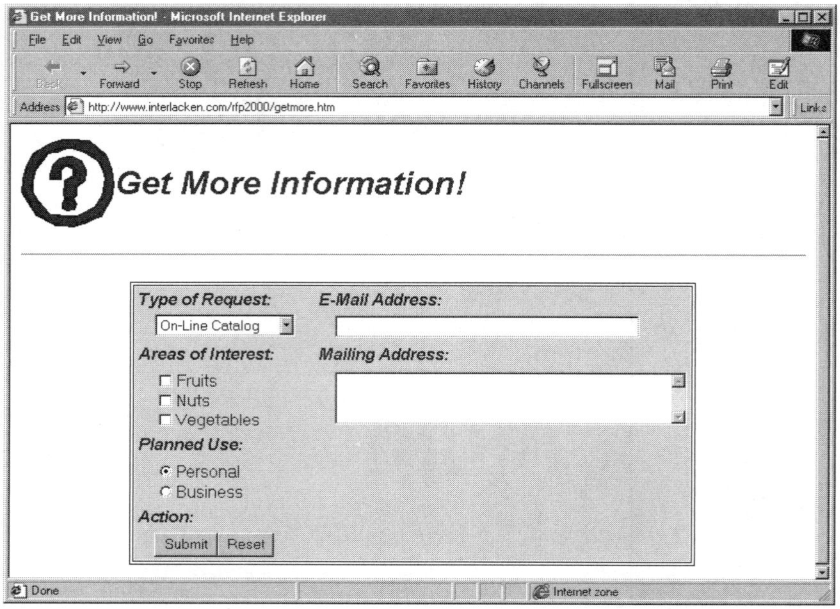

FIGURE 10-1.

This page shows a typical HTML form. It collects data from the Web visitor and submits it to some process.

- Each form occupies a specific area on a Web page. A single Web page can contain one or more forms.

- Within each form are one or more form elements. Table 10-1 lists the available types.

- Each element on the form has a name and a value. The name internally identifies the input field, while the value reflects its current value.

- One element in the form—either a push-button or picture-form field—must act as the Submit button. When the Web visitor clicks this element, the browser:

  - Encodes all the element names and values in the form.

  - Transmits the data to a Web server for processing. The form's Action property contains a URL (referred to as the Action URL) that starts the necessary program on the server.

TABLE 10-1.   Form Element Types

Appearance	Description	Typical Uses
(One-Line Text Box image)	One-Line Text Box	Short, one-line text strings.
Scrolling Text Box	Scrolling Text Box	Multiple-line text such as suggestions or comments.
☐ Check Box	Check Box	Independent fields having only two values, such as yes/no or true/false.
◉ Radio Button	Radio Button	A list of choices where only one at a time can be selected.
Drop-Down Menu ▼	Drop-Down Menu	A list of choices. A Web visitor can select one listed item or several, depending on restrictions set by the page creator. If the menu is sized so that only one choice is visible, a button at the right drops it down to permit selection. If the menu is sized so that two or more choices are visible, a scroll bar replaces the drop-down button.
Push Button	Push Button	A button that transmits the form contents to the server, clears the form, or invokes a script.
(Any chosen picture)	Picture Form Field	A picture that, when clicked, transmits the form contents to the server.
(Invisible)	Hidden	An invisible element the browser transmits with the server.

? SEE ALSO

For more information about using browser scripts, see "Working with Script Code," page 418.

Using a Submit button and transmitting form data to a Web server is the original—and still most common—way of processing HTML forms. More recently, script languages like VBScript and JavaScript have also gained access to form elements. Script code can respond to form-element events such as gaining focus, losing focus, mouse movements, and clicking.

Browser scripts are small blocks of program code that appear within HTML and execute on the Web visitor's computer. The capabilities of browser scripts are intentionally limited for security reasons, but two capabilities they retain are setting form-element properties and responding to form-element events.

Drawing Forms in FrontPage

FrontPage can easily add forms and form elements to your Web pages. To add an HTML form to any Web page:

1 Set the insertion point where you want the first form element to appear.

2 Choose Form from the Insert menu, and then choose Form from the resulting menu. This creates a form, indicated in FrontPage by dashed lines, containing only a Submit and a Reset button.

3 For each element you want in the form, set the insertion point inside the form, choose Form from the Insert menu, and select the type of form element you want. The graphic below illustrates the Insert Form menu choices.

TIP

If you add a form element outside any existing HTML form, FrontPage will automatically create a new form that surrounds the new form element.

To expand the form, simply add more content—whether it's text, images, tables, more form elements, or any other valid objects. You can add content by direct insertion, by dragging, or by cutting and pasting.

Form elements appear in-line with text. Thus, to put two form elements on different lines, you'd have to insert a paragraph ending or line break between them. To line up form elements horizontally or vertically with others—or with surrounding HTML objects—organize them into a table. One common approach is to place field captions and corresponding form elements in consecutive columns. Another is to place each caption and field element pair within a single cell.

To create a second, separate form, insert a form element *outside* the boundaries of the existing form.

Figure 10-2 shows the form of Figure 10-1 open in FrontPage. The heavy dashed lines show the form's boundaries. An HTML table keeps the various form elements aligned horizontally and vertically.

FIGURE 10-2.

FrontPage created the form pictured in Figure 10-1.

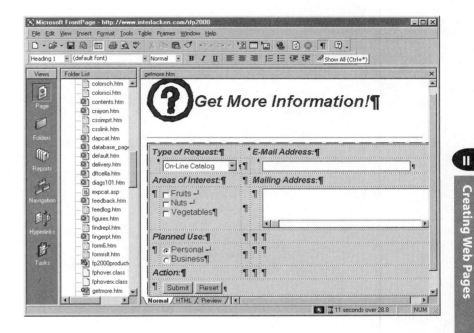

Creating an HTML form visually is only part of the job. You must also configure the properties of both the form itself and each form element. The next section in this chapter describes how. Even so, collecting data from the Web visitor is only half the battle. You also need to provide a way to *process* the data once it reaches the Web server, and Chapters 21, "Using Server-Side FrontPage Components," and 22, "Accessing Databases with FrontPage," will provide the details.

SEE ALSO

For more information about using browser scripts, see "Working with Script Code," page 418.

Setting HTML Form Properties

An HTML form is only a data-entry template and does no processing on its own. To process or save data entered on HTML forms, you'll need to follow *one* of these approaches:

- Correctly invoke features of the FrontPage Server Extensions.

- Obtain server-side programs or scripts from another vendor and correctly invoke them.

■ Arrange for custom script or custom server-side programming.

In any event, your form will need to use the element names and values these methods expect.

To view or modify the form's properties, right-click anywhere in the form and choose Form Properties from the pop-up menu. (Alternatively, set the insertion point anywhere within the form, choose Form from the Insert menu, and then choose Form Properties.) This displays the Form Properties dialog box shown in Figure 10-3, which controls the following properties.

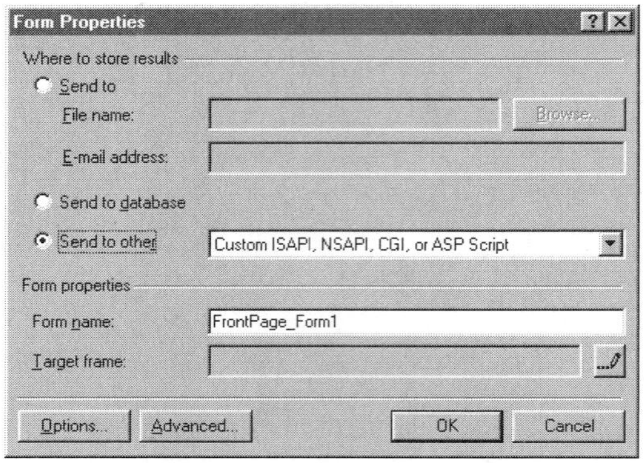

FIGURE 10-3.

This is FrontPage's Form Properties dialog box.

■ **Where To Store Results** indicates the type of action that will process data entered in the form.

SEE ALSO

For detailed information about the Send To File Name and Send To E-Mail Address options, see "Saving Form Results for Later Use," page 700.

• **Send To File Name** adds data in the form to a file on the Web server. This file can be either a Web page that gets longer and longer with each submission, or a data file suitable for later processing in Excel, Access, or some other offline program. The associated text box specifies the name of the file—on the Web server—that will receive the data.

• **Send To E-Mail Address** sends an electronic mail message containing the data in the form. Each time a Web visitor clicks the form's Submit button, it generates one message. Enter the receiving e-mail address in the associated text box.

• **Send to Database** sends the form data to a database on (or accessible to) the Web server. This requires that the database has an ODBC database connection on the server, that you specify the name of that connection, and that you specify

 **SEE ALSO**

For more information about the Send To Database option, see Chapter 22, "Accessing Databases with FrontPage."

the name of the table where the new records will reside. In addition, you must give each form element the same name as the column (within the database table) where it should appear.

- **Send to Other: Custom ISAPI, NSAPI, CGI, Or ASP Script** sends the form data to a server-based program that's not part of FrontPage. You must consult the program's documentation or designer to determine what input it requires for proper operation.

- **Send To Other: Discussion Form Handler** places the information entered into the form onto a discussion-type site. It's discussed later, in "Creating and Managing Discussion Sites," page 712.

- **Send To Other: Registration Form Handler** is used to collect registration data from visitors to a site. See "Enabling User Self-Registration," page 708.

■ **Form Properties** controls the form's name and, if it appears with a frameset, the frame where results of its processing should appear.

- **Form Name** gives the form a name. This field is optional unless needed by a script or custom form handler.

SEE ALSO

For more information about framesets, see "Creating and Editing Frames," page 261.

- **Target Frame** specifies the name of a frame in which output from the server-based program should appear. This field is optional.

■ **Options** displays different dialog boxes, depending on what you chose to do with the form results. Three are discussed here.

- If you chose either Send To File Name or Send To E-Mail Address, the Options button invokes the form handler dialog box titled Options For Saving Results Of Form.

- If you choose Send To Database, the Options button displays a dialog box for specifying the name of the database connection and the name of the data accumulation table within that database.

- If you chose Custom ISAPI, NSAPI, CGI, Or ASP Script, the Options button displays the Options For Custom Form Handler dialog box of Figure 10-4 with these settings:

  Action must contain the URL of the server-side program. It's your responsibility to provide this program or ensure that it exists.

FIGURE 10-4.

Use this dialog box to specify a custom program for processing form data.

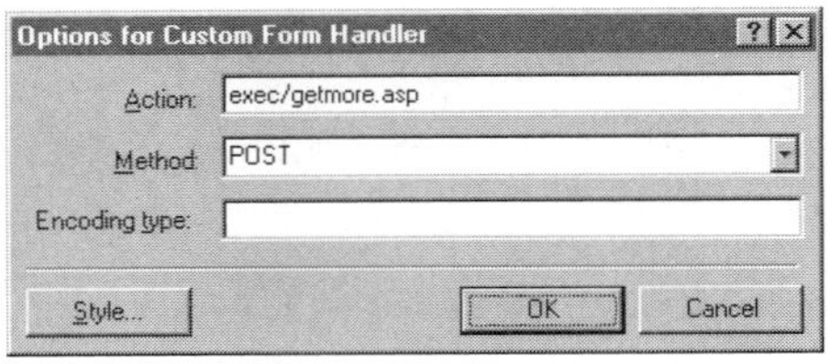

Method specifies POST or GET, whichever the server-side program requires. These are two different ways of transmitting form data to a Web-server program. POST, which transmits data in the HTTP headers, is newer, less restrictive, and generally preferred. GET is subject to length and other restrictions because it transmits form data as part of the URL.

Encoding Type indicates the encoding method used for passing form data to a server-side program. This method permits transmission of reserved characters such as carriage returns and slashes. The only valid entries are blank and *application/x-www-form-urlencoded,* which mean the same thing.

■ **Advanced** displays the Advanced Form Properties dialog box of Figure 10-5, which controls hidden form fields.

The Advanced Form Properties dialog box controls *hidden* fields—fields whose names and values are both coded into the HTML. The Web visitor can neither see nor alter these fields; they're totally under control of the page creator. Hidden fields usually contain application data that's constant or parameters that control the actions of a server-side program. This permits changing the behavior of the server-side program through changes to the HTML—a much easier process than changing the program itself.

FIGURE 10-5.

This dialog box maintains hidden fields on an HTML form.

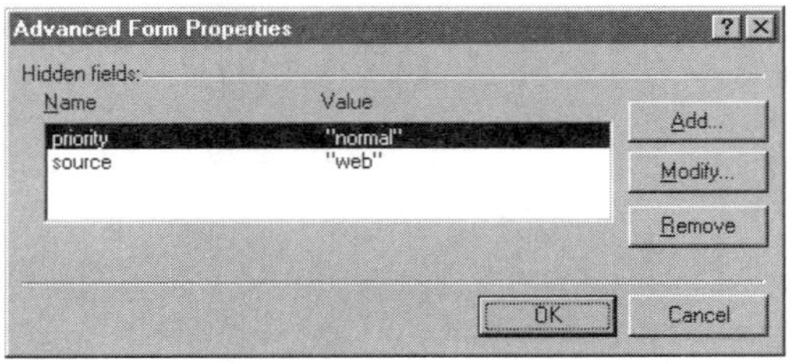

To add a hidden field:

1 Click the Add button in the Hidden Fields section.

2 In the resulting dialog box, enter the hidden field's name and value in the respective text boxes.

3 Click OK.

Arranging Form Elements

Some general guidelines will help you choose form element types and arrange them effectively.

- Place required fields, key fields, and other important fields near the upper-left area of the form to give them top prominence.

- Group fields in naturally expected sequences such as Name, Address, City, State/Province, ZIP Code/Postal Code.

- Group related fields by placing them close together. Make the groups distinct by using white space, indentation, or graphic elements.

- Put lengthy fields—such as comments or special instructions—at the bottom of the form.

- Use ordinary HTML text for field captions.

- Use one-line text boxes for single fields consisting of plain text.

- Use scrolling text boxes for multiple lines of free-form text, such as comments.

- Use check boxes for yes/no or true/false choices. Checked means Yes or True. For a list of yes/no items, use a series of check boxes.

- Use radio buttons for lists where only one item at a time can be selected.

- Use drop-down menus that allow multiple selections as a substitute for check boxes.

- Use drop-down menus that permit only single selections as a substitute for radio buttons.

- Use HTML tables to align captions and form elements horizontally and vertically.

- If groupings appear repeatedly—such as an order requiring multiple lines for each item ordered—create an HTML table with a row for each grouping and a column for each field.

- Put the Submit and Reset buttons at the bottom of the form. This provides some assurance that the visitor has reviewed the entire form before submitting it.

Part II

Creating Web Pages

To change a hidden field:

1 Select the field to change.

2 Click the Modify button.

3 Correct the field value.

4 Click OK.

To delete a hidden field, select it and click the Remove button.

Setting Form Element Properties

There are three ways to modify the basic properties of a form element:

- **Double-clicking** the element you want to modify.

- **Right-clicking** the element you want to modify, and then choosing Form Field Properties from the pop-up menu.

- **Using keystrokes** to select the form element you want to modify, and then holding down the Alt key while pressing Enter.

The dialog box you see will depend on the type of form element. A section later in this chapter titled "Form Element Properties" will discuss the dialog boxes for each type of form element.

Validating Form Input

Most applications involving HTML forms require constraints on form input. Certain fields are generally required, for example—meaning it's an error to leave them blank. Other fields must conform to certain patterns; such as U.S. Postal ZIP consisting of five numeric digits.

FrontPage supports these requirements with a feature called *validation*. Working in Page view, the designer specifies value constraints using convenient dialog boxes. FrontPage then enforces these constraints by adding JavaScript or VBScript code to the Web page. If the visitor violates the constraints, the browser transmits no data to the server but instead displays an error message. Figure 10-6 provides an example of this.

Validation is available for text boxes, drop-down menus, and radio buttons. Check boxes have only two values, both presumably valid, and therefore need no validation. Similarly, there's no validation for either push buttons or submit pictures because there's no wrong way to click them.

The Web Settings Advanced dialog box, discussed in Chapter 14, "Customizing Your Copy of FrontPage," controls the language FrontPage will use when creating script code. The setting that governs validation script code is Default Scripting Language, Client. Choosing JavaScript or VBScript instructs FrontPage to create validation scripts in those languages.

CAUTION
VBScript validation scripts won't work in Netscape Navigator versions 4.0 and earlier. Check later versions for compatibility.

There are two ways to specify validation rules for form elements that support them:

- Open the element's Properties dialog box and click the Validate button.
- Right-click the element you wish to modify and choose Form Field Validation from the pop-up menu.

The following sections on each form element will discuss the applicable validation rule settings.

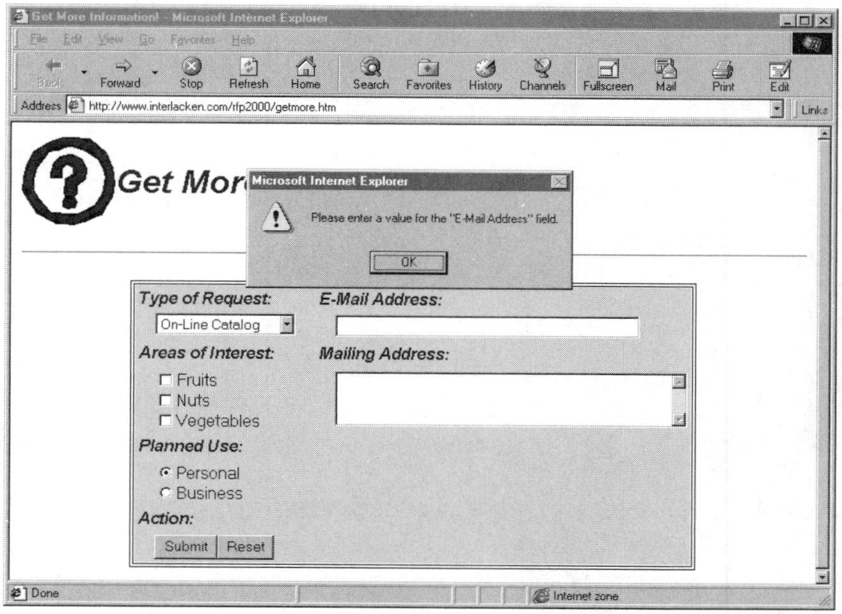

FIGURE 10-6.
Validation code in this page's HTML displayed an error message when the visitor clicked the Submit button.

Form Element Properties

The following sections describe the available settings and validation rules for each type of HTML form element.

One-Line Text-Box Properties

You can change the position of an existing one-line text box by dragging or by cutting and pasting. In addition, you can change its width by selecting the element and then dragging its left or right handles. For other kinds of changes, however, you'll need to display the element's property sheet. Figure 10-7 displays the property sheet for a one-line text box. It provides the following entries:

- **Name** designates an internal name for the field. For a given field to be processed, you must give it the name expected by the script or server-side form handler. If you—rather than the form handling programmer—get to name the field, use short, lowercase names with no special characters or hyphens.

- **Initial Value** optionally supplies a data value that appears when the browser first displays the form or when the Web visitor clicks the Reset button.

- **Width In Characters** specifies the width of the field in typical display characters.

- **Tab Order** controls the order in which fields receive the focus when the visitor presses the Tab key. The current field receives the focus after any fields with lower tab-order values, but before any fields with higher values.

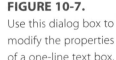 **NOTE**

> *Receiving the focus* means that a text box or other control is highlighted and will receive any keystrokes the Web visitor generates. Fields gain focus and lose focus as the visitor presses the Tab key or clicks different fields with the mouse.

- **Password Field,** if turned on, instructs the browser to display asterisks in place of whatever characters the visitor actually types.

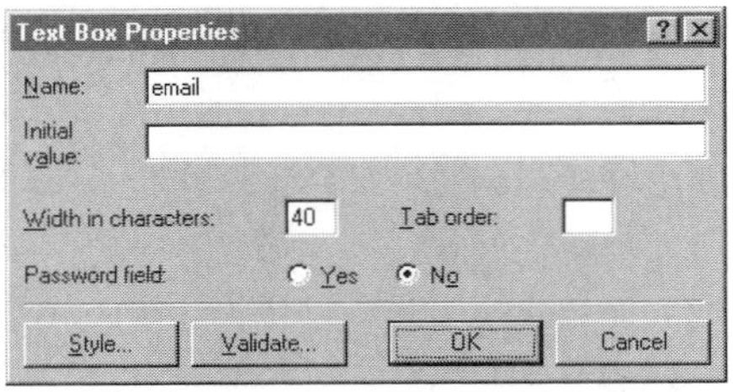

FIGURE 10-7.

Use this dialog box to modify the properties of a one-line text box.

Text Box Properties	? ✕
Name:	email
Initial **v**alue:	
Width in characters: 40	**T**ab order:
Password field: ○ **Y**es ● **N**o	
Style... **V**alidate...	OK Cancel

Clicking the Validate button in Figure 10-7 displays the Text Box Validation menu shown in Figure 10-8. The latter figure is actually a *composite* shown with all fields active, for clarity; in practice, one or more fields will be disabled, depending on the Data Type selected.

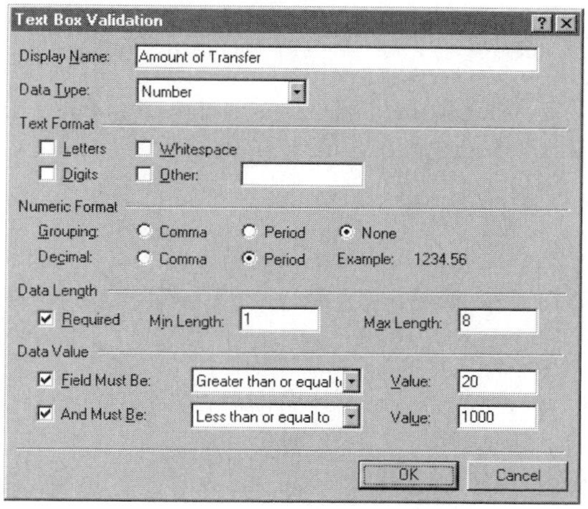

FIGURE 10-8.

This dialog box sets constraints on values entered in a one-line text box.

These are the available properties:

- **Display Name** gives the field a name that will appear in error messages. Normally, this should agree with the field's caption on the Web page. If you don't specify a display name, error messages will use the internal name from the element's property sheet.

- **Data Type** specifies the type of data the field can contain.

  - **No Constraints** indicates that the field can contain any type of data.

  - **Text** indicates that the field can contain alphanumeric or linguistic expressions.

  - **Integer** means that the field can contain only whole numbers.

  - **Number** means that the field can contain only whole or decimal numbers.

- **Text Format** indicates what kinds of text characters are valid. FrontPage enables this section only if Data Type is Text.

  - **Letters** indicates that alphabetic characters are valid.

  - **Digits** indicates that numeric characters are valid.

  - **Whitespace** means that spaces, tabs, carriage returns, and line feeds are acceptable.

  - **Other** indicates that additional characters are acceptable. Enter the acceptable characters in the text box provided.

- **Numeric Format** sets the format of numbers. FrontPage enables this section only if Data Type is Integer or Number.

  - **Grouping** indicates which characters, in addition to numeric digits, are valid in a numeric field.

    Comma means the comma character is permissible, as in 12,345,678.

    None means that no punctuation is permissible, as in 12345678.

    Period means the period character is permissible, as in 12.345.678.

  - **Decimal** indicates which character is acceptable as a decimal point. This field is disabled if Data Type is Integer. Note that the grouping character and the decimal character can't be the same.

    Comma means the comma is acceptable as a decimal point.

    Period means the period is acceptable as a decimal point.

- **Data Length** sets the length restrictions on data entered in the field.

  - **Required,** if turned on, indicates that the field can't be left blank.

  - **Min Length** indicates the fewest characters the field can contain.

  - **Max Length** indicates the most characters the field can contain.

- **Data Value** properties set range constraints on values entered in the text box. If the data type is Number or Integer, FrontPage will use numeric comparisons. If the data type is Text or No Constraints, FrontPage will use alphabetic comparisons.

  - **Field Must Be** sets a range limit on the value Web visitors enter. To use this feature, check this box and then specify a comparison and a boundary value. The available comparisons are Less Than, Greater Than, Less Than Or Equal To, Greater Than Or Equal To, Equal To, and Not Equal To.

  - **Value** specifies the boundary value. Comparison against this value must be true or an error will occur. If, for example, Field Must Be reads *Greater Than 10* and the visitor enters *9*, the visitor will get an error message.

- **And Must Be** specifies a comparison to enforce a second range limit on the value in the one-line text box. The Value property on this line works as above.

Scrolling Text-Box Properties

The dialog box for changing the properties of a scrolling text box appears in Figure 10-9. The available properties are the following:

- **Name** designates an internal name for the field. This name must be known to the script or server-side form handler.

- **Initial Value** optionally supplies a data value that appears when the browser first displays the form or when the visitor clicks the Reset button.

- **Width In Characters** sets the width of the box in units of typical display characters.

- **Tab Order** controls the order in which fields receive the focus when the Web visitor presses the Tab key.

SEE ALSO
For information on CSS, see "A Quick Course in Cascading Style Sheets," page 138.

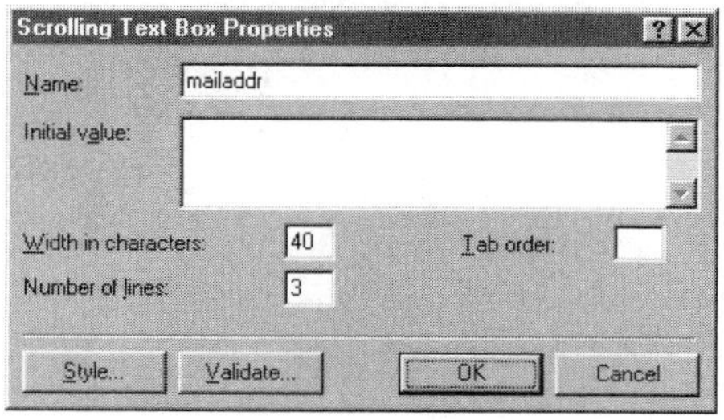

- **Number Of Lines** sets the height of the box in lines.

- **Style** sets cascading style-sheet properties for the text box.

- **Validate** displays the same validation dialog box as for one-line text boxes. Refer to the previous section for details.

FIGURE 10-9.

This dialog box sets constraints on values entered in a one-line text box.

Check Box Properties

The dialog box shown in Figure 10-10 controls the properties of a check box. The following properties are available:

- **Name** gives the field an internal name. This must be the name the script or server-side form handler expects.

- **Value** specifies a string the browser will transmit to the server or script if the box is checked. If the box configured in Figure 10-10 is turned on when the visitor clicks Submit, the browser will transmit fruits=on. If the box isn't checked when the visitor clicks Submit, the browser sends neither the name nor the value.

- **Initial State** specifies how the browser initializes the check box—on or off—when it first displays the form or later responds to the press of a Reset button.

- **Tab Order** controls the sequence, as the Web visitor presses the Tab key, in which this control receives the focus, compared to other controls.

- **Style** specifies cascading style-sheet properties for this element.

There's no Validation property for check boxes—it's hard to imagine what an invalid check-box entry would be.

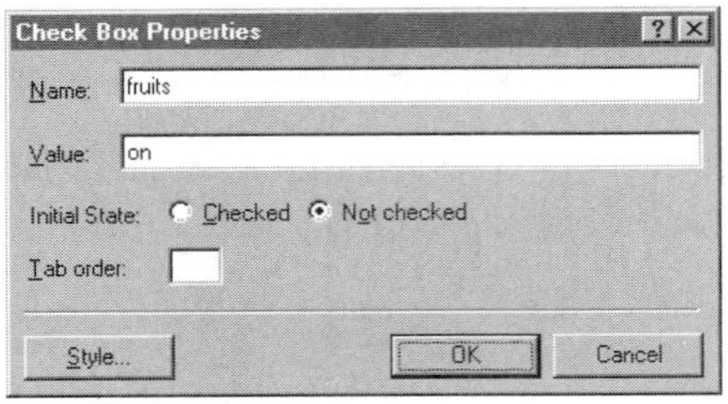

FIGURE 10-10.

This dialog box controls the properties of a check box.

Radio Button Properties

Like lobbyists, heartaches, and rock band aficionados, radio buttons appear in groups. Of all radio buttons in a group, only one at a time can be turned on. No other HTML form elements interact this way.

The grouping mechanism for radio buttons within a form is quite simple: all buttons with the same name are in the same group. Conversely, to group a set of radio buttons, give them all the same name.

Assigning duplicate names to form elements is usually an error, but in the case of radio buttons it's a necessity. Each like-named radio button, however, must have a different value so the server can determine which button was selected when the Web visitor clicked Submit. The browser transmits the clicked radio button's value and no others.

Figure 10-11 shows the properties dialog box for radio buttons. It provides access to the following settings.

- **Group Name** supplies the internal name of all radio buttons in the same group as this button. This name must be known to the script or server-side form handler.

- **Value** designates a string the browser will transmit if this radio button is selected when the visitor clicks Submit. Be sure to give each radio button in the same group a different value.

- **Initial State** initializes the radio button—on or off—when first displayed or when the visitor clicks the Reset button.

NOTE

Setting the initial state of one radio button to Selected sets the initial state of all other buttons in the same group to Not Selected.

- **Tab Order** controls the order in which this element receives the focus when the visitor presses the Tab key. Radio buttons in the same group should almost always have consecutive Tab Order values.

- **Style** assigns cascading style-sheet properties.

- **Validate** displays the Radio Button Validation dialog box that appears in Figure 10-12.

  - **Display Name** gives the button group a name that will appear in error messages. This field is disabled unless the following field is checked.

  - **Data Required,** if checked, displays an error if the visitor clicks Submit and no radio buttons in the group are selected.

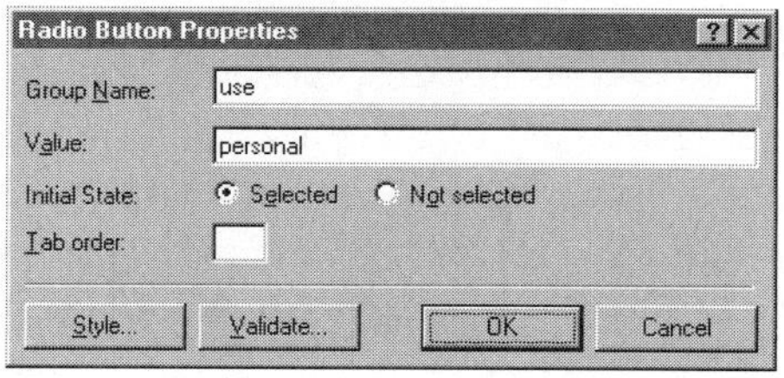

FIGURE 10-11.

This is the Radio Button Properties dialog box.

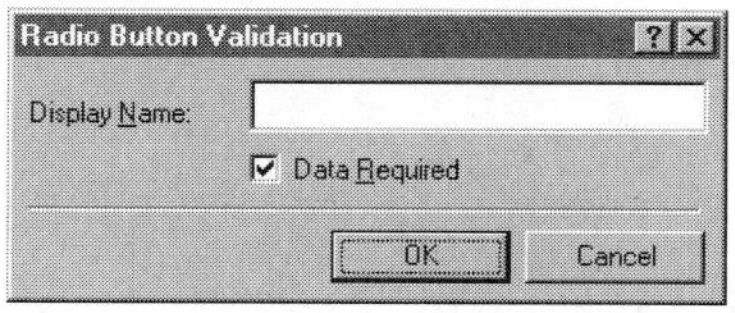

FIGURE 10-12.

This is the validation dialog box for radio buttons.

Normally, a visitor can't turn off all the radio buttons in a group. The only way to turn off a button is to turn on another button in the same group. It's possible, however, to have all radio buttons in a group turned off when first displayed. This, together with the Data Required valida-tion rule, assures that the visitor made a conscious choice and didn't simply take the default.

Changing the validation rules for one radio button automatically changes them for all buttons in the same group.

Drop-Down Menu Properties

The property sheet for drop-down menus appears in Figure 10-13. It offers access to the following settings.

- **Name** assigns an internal name to the menu. This name must be known to the script or server-side form handler.

- **Choice - Selected - Value** contains a row for each entry in the drop-down list. Use the five buttons at the right to maintain this table.

  - **Add** displays the Add Choice dialog box, with the same choices as the one in Figure 10-14. Enter the following fields:

    Choice specifies the text the browser will display to the Web visitor.

    Specify Value controls the value transmitted if this choice is selected when the visitor clicks the Submit button. If this set-ting is on, the browser transmits the value in the associated text box. Otherwise, it transmits the value in the Choice box.

    Initial State determines whether the current choice is se-lected when first displayed and when the visitor clicks Re-set. There are two settings: Selected and Not Selected. If the Allow Multiple Selections option described below and shown in Figure 10-13 is No, setting the initial state of one choice to Selected also sets the initial state of all other choices to Not Selected.

  - **Modify** displays the dialog box shown in Figure 10-14 for the currently selected choice. Make any changes and then click OK.

  - **Remove** deletes the currently selected choice.

  - **Move Up** moves the currently selected choice one position higher in the list.

  - **Move Down** moves the currently selected choice one po-sition lower in the list.

FIGURE 10-13.
Use this dialog box
to control property
settings of drop-down
menus.

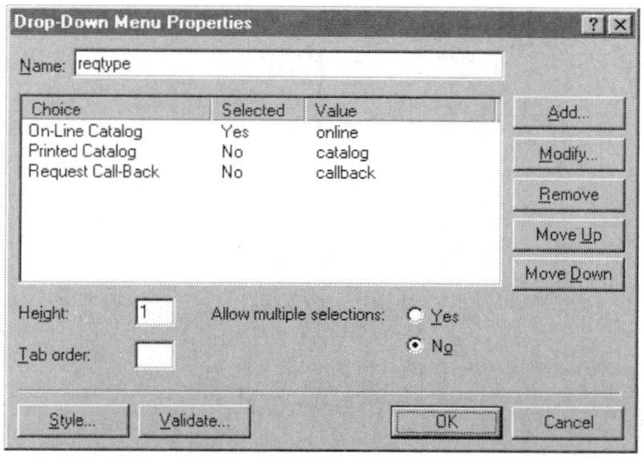

FIGURE 10-14.
The Add Choice and
Modify Choice dialog
boxes contain identi-
cal fields for adding or
modifying entries in a
drop-down menu.

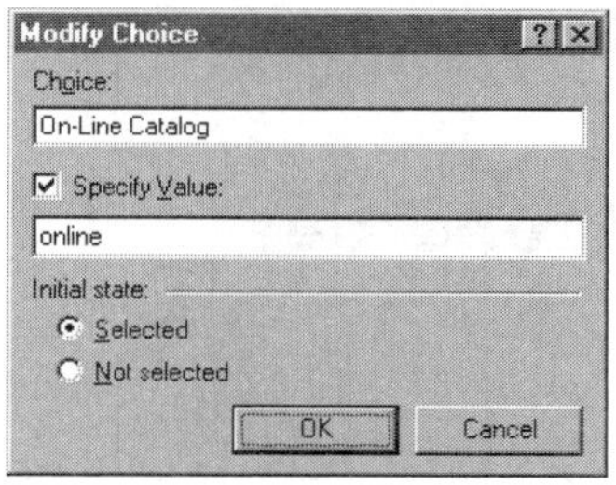

- **Height** specifies the height of the displayed list in lines. A one-line list has a drop-down button at the right. Lists two or more lines high have scroll bars at the right.

NOTE

A drop-down menu with a height of one displays in Windows as a drop-down list. Drop-down menus with heights greater than one display as scrollable list boxes.

- **Allow Multiple Selections** should be set to No if only one selection at a time can be selected. Specify Yes if two or more items can be selected simultaneously.

- **Tab Order** controls the order in which fields on the same form receive the focus as the Web visitor presses the Tab key.

- **Style** controls cascading style-sheet properties.

- **Validate** displays the Drop-Down Menu Validation dialog box shown in Figure 10-15. The available entries are the following.

  - **Display Name** gives the drop-down menu a name that will appear in error messages.

- **Data Required,** if turned on, displays an error if the visitor clicks Submit and no choices in the menu are selected.

- **Disallow First Item** prevents submitting the form with the first choice of this menu still selected. In such cases, the first menu choice is typically a prompt to select a subsequent choice. This assures that the visitor makes a conscious choice and doesn't simply accept the default.

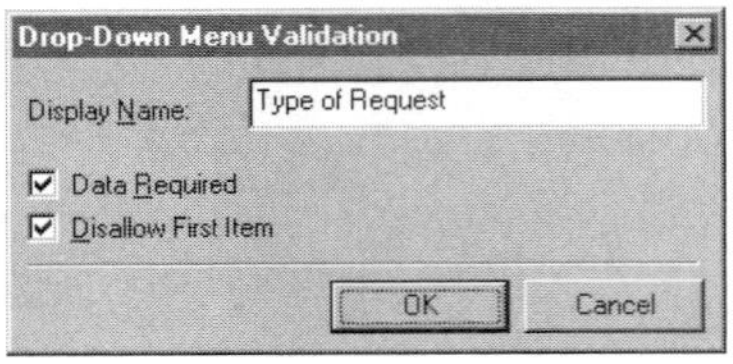

FIGURE 10-15.

This is the validation dialog box for drop-down menus.

Push Button Properties

Figure 10-16 shows the dialog box for push buttons. The available fields are these:

- **Name** denotes the internal name of the field. This is optional for push buttons.

- **Value/Label,** if specified, serves two purposes:

  - It becomes the button's visible caption.

  - If the push button has both a Name and a Value/Label, the browser will transmit the name=value pair when the Web visitor clicks the button. This tells the server which of several buttons the visitor clicked.

- **Button Type** determines the type of push button.

  - **Submit** specifies that clicking this button submits the form. It also sets the default label to Submit.

  - **Reset** indicates that clicking this button resets a form to its initial state. It also sets the default label to Reset.

  - **Normal** assigns no predetermined action for the button. However, a script can respond to button clicks and perform any programmed action. Choosing button type Normal sets the default label to Button.

- **Tab Order** determines the sequence in which the button receives the focus when the visitor presses the Tab key.

- **Style** sets cascading style-sheet properties for the button.

- **Form** opens the Form Properties dialog box for specifying what to do with the form results once the push button submits them.

There are no validation features for push buttons—either you click a push button or you don't.

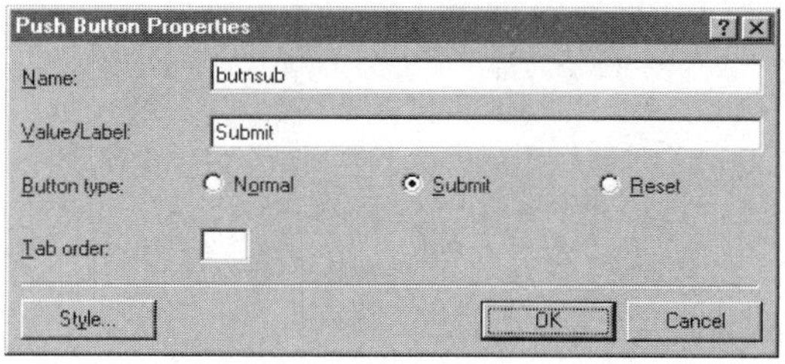

FIGURE 10-16.

This dialog box controls push button properties.

Picture Form-Field Properties

A picture form field works much like a submit push button. Clicking a picture form field submits the form's data using the form's Action URL.

To insert a picture form field, choose Form Field from the Insert menu in FrontPage, and then select Picture. Choosing Picture from the Insert menu inserts only an ordinary image, even when inserting into a form area.

Figure 10-17 shows the dialog box for setting the properties of a picture form field. The single property—Name—on the Form Field tab identifies the picture form field and gets transmitted to the server when the Web visitor clicks the picture. No validation is available. The remaining tabs are the same as those shown in the Picture Properties dialog box of Figure 6-4, Figure 6-5, and Figure 6-7.

The Style button can be used to assign cascading style-sheet properties to the picture. The Form button displays the Form Properties dialog box, already shown in Figure 10-3.

FIGURE 10-17.
This is the property
sheet for picture
form fields.

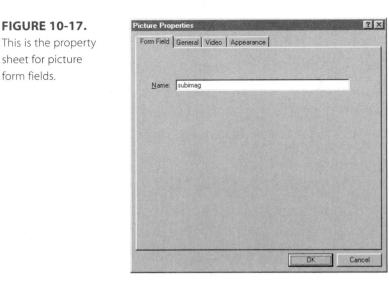

Label Properties

Normally, the text that visually identifies form elements to the Web visitor is just that: ordinary text. Only visual proximity associates the label with its control.

HTML labels associate a form field's descriptive text with the form field itself. Clicking the descriptive text then has the same effect as clicking the form field.

To "officially" designate text as the label of an HTML form element:

1 Enter the label text inside the HTML form and directly adjacent to the form element.

2 Select both the text and the form element.

3 Choose Form Field from the Insert menu, and then select Label.

This will designate the selected text as the selected control's label. A thin dotted box will surround the text in FrontPage, and HTML view will display a label tag preceding the text you selected and referencing the internal name of the form element.

To remove the label designation, select the label, choose Form Field from the Insert menu, and then select Remove Label.

Using the Form Page Wizard

FrontPage provides a wizard to help you get started creating HTML forms. This wizard has so many options that only a representative sample appears here.

The Form Page Wizard is unlikely to produce a finished page tailored to your complete satisfaction, but it can give you a good starting point or at least some quick ideas. If you don't like the results you first achieve, keep rerunning the wizard with different options until results improve.

To run the wizard:

1 Start FrontPage.

2 If you want the new Web page to reside in a FrontPage Web, open that Web.

3 Choose New from the File menu.

4 From the Page tab, choose Form Page Wizard and then click OK.

5 When the banner pictured in Figure 10-18 appears, click Next to continue.

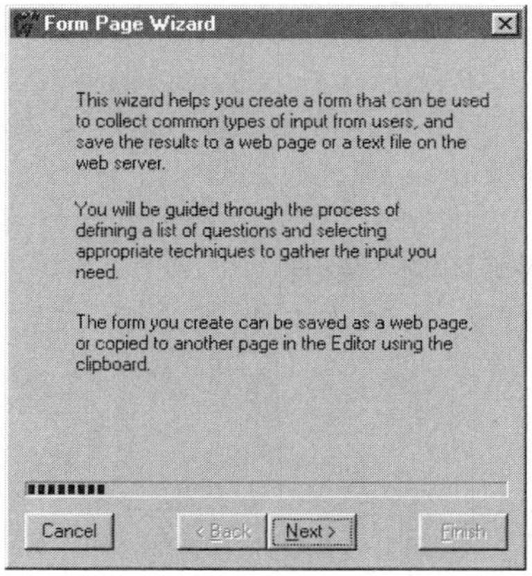

FIGURE 10-18.

Click Next to proceed past the Form Page Wizard banner.

6 When the wizard displays the dialog box shown in Figure 10-19, on the following page, enter a title for the page and a file name in the current Web, and then click Next.

7 The wizard will next display the dialog box shown in Figure 10-20, which contains a list of the major questions the form will ask. To add questions, click the Add button to display the dialog box shown in Figure 10-21.

8 From the list at the top of Figure 10-21, select the type of input to collect for the current question. In the text box at the bottom, review the suggested prompt and make any necessary changes. Click Next.

9 Figure 10-22 displays a typical dialog box the wizard might display next. Each type of input in the previous step results in a different dialog box with different fields, in this step. Select the fields you want to collect, revise the base name for those fields if necessary, and then click Next.

10 Repeat steps 6, 7, and 8 as often as necessary to collect all the input you need. To start over, click the Clear List button in Figure 10-20. When finished, click Next.

11 When the dialog box shown in Figure 10-23 appears, indicate how you want the list of questions presented, whether you want a table of contents, and whether to use tables for form-field alignment. Click Next when finished.

12 The next dialog box, pictured in Figure 10-24, controls how you want to capture the input fields you've specified. The options are described below the figure.

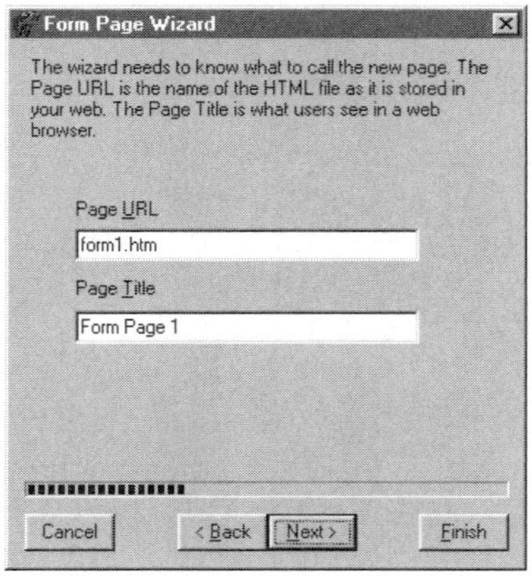

FIGURE 10-19.

Give the new form page a location in the current Web and a title.

FIGURE 10-20.
This dialog box builds a list of major questions for the Web visitor.

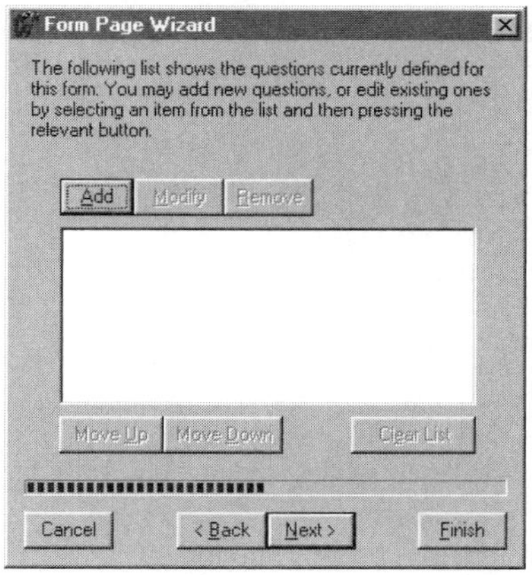

FIGURE 10-21.
This Form Page Wizard dialog box prompts for the type of input to collect for a question.

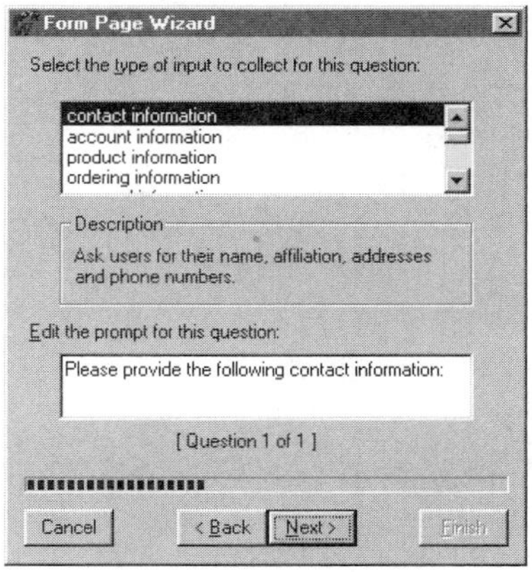

FIGURE 10-22.
Choose the data elements you wish to collect from the visitor.

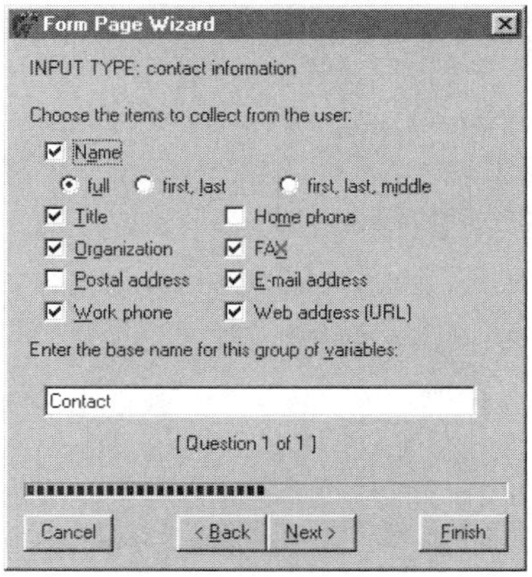

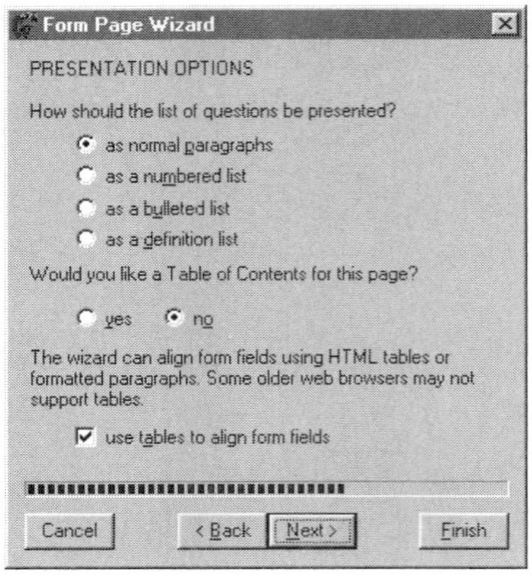

FIGURE 10-23.

This dialog box from the Form Page Wizard controls high-level aspects of form page layout.

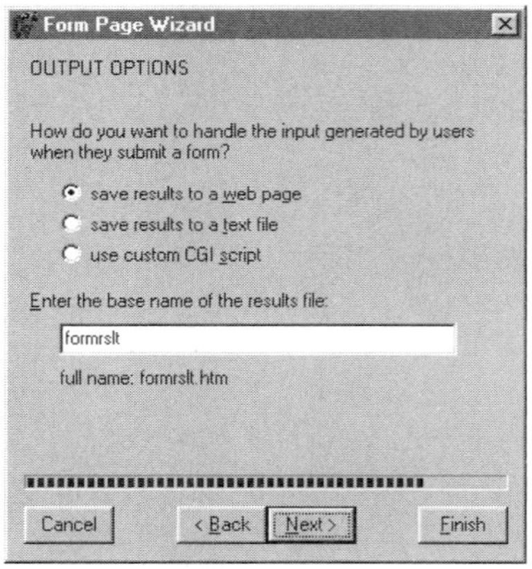

FIGURE 10-24.

This dialog box controls how form data is saved.

? SEE ALSO

For details on saving form results, refer to Saving Form Results for Later Use," page 700.

X CAUTION

The options Save Results To A Web Page and Save Results To A Text File use facilities in the FrontPage Server Extensions. Make sure the extensions are installed on any Web servers you plan to use, and check that your application is properly configured.

- **Save Results To A Web Page** creates a new Web page whenever a Web visitor submits the form.

- **Save Results To A Text File** saves submitted data in a text file on the server. Various programs can import data from such files at a later time.

- **Use Custom CGI Script** assumes a Web programmer will write a custom process to store the data.

- **Enter The Base Name Of The Results File** designates the name of the Web page or text file (minus the HTM or TXT extension) where the form results will be saved. This page or file will be located in your Web, on the server from which the Web visitors access the HTML forms page.

If you choose Use Custom CGI Script, this field is disabled.

13 Figure 10-25 shows the final dialog box in the Form Page Wizard. You can use the Back and Next buttons to review and correct your work. When done, click Finish to create the page as specified.

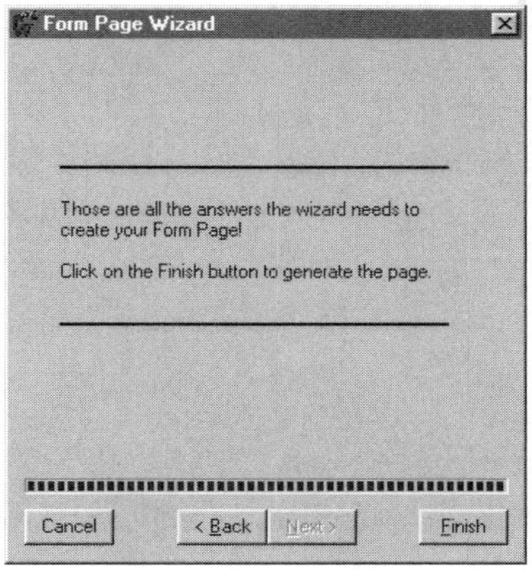

FIGURE 10-25.

This is the final confirmation dialog box in the Form Page Wizard. Click Finish to build the page.

Figure 10-26 and Figure 10-27 show typical results from running the Form Page Wizard. Rerun the wizard as often as necessary to optimize results, and then finalize layout and appearance by editing the page directly. It's a good idea to test data collection features often, to ensure any problems from changing the form manually show up right away and can be dealt with.

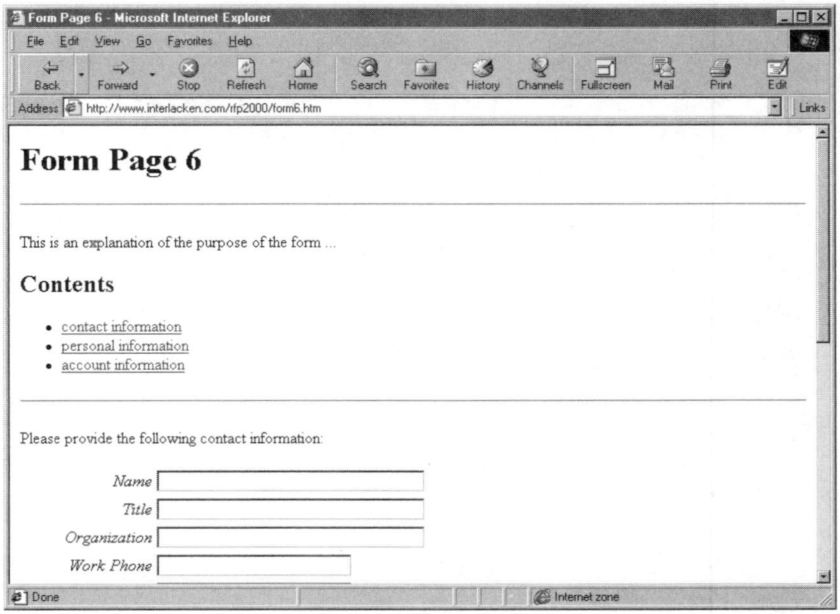

FIGURE 10-26.

This is the top half of a page generated by the Form Page Wizard.

In Summary...

HTML forms are a proven and popular way for your Web visitors to interact with your site. Form design is only half the battle—the other half being the processing of forms on the Web server—but it's a highly necessary part of the process.

The next chapter introduces FrontPage components, which can add interactivity to your pages with no programming and no Web server involvement.

CHAPTER 11

Using Page-Level FrontPage Components

Microsoft FrontPage provides a number of intelligent objects called FrontPage components that add function to your site and ease maintenance by performing tasks automatically. Once configured, these components run whenever an author saves a page or, in some cases, whenever a Web visitor browses it.

When you add a FrontPage component to a page, FrontPage inserts a number of hidden commands and settings. When FrontPage saves the page, the commands generate HTML based on these hidden settings. The HTML content is visible to Web visitors but the commands and settings are not.

Some FrontPage components work only if you store your pages in a FrontPage Web. Others require special software on the Web server, namely the FrontPage Server Extensions. For discussion of such components, refer to Chapters 20, "Using Web-Based FrontPage Components," and 21, "Using Server-Side FrontPage Components."

? SEE ALSO

For introductory material on FrontPage components, refer to "Automatic Content with FrontPage Components," page 23.

The FrontPage components described in this chapter require neither FrontPage Webs nor the FrontPage Server Extensions. There are eight such components.

- **Banner Ad Manager** continuously displays a series of pictures, based on a time interval you specify. The pictures continue to change as long as the remote user keeps your Web page on display.

- **Comment** inserts text visible in FrontPage but not in a browser.

- **Date and Time** displays the date a page was last edited or updated.

- **Hover Button** displays a graphic button that changes appearance when a Web visitor's mouse pointer passes over it. Clicking the button activates a hyperlink.

- **Include Page** displays the contents of one Web page within another. Included pages typically contain blocks of content that appear repetitively throughout a site. Including this content many times from one master copy ensures uniformity and eliminates the need for redundant maintenance.

- **Marquee** scrolls one line of text across an area of the screen.

- **Scheduled Include Page** works like the Include Page component, but only between two given dates. Outside those dates, the Include Page component will display a different page or nothing.

- **Scheduled Picture** works like Scheduled Include Page but displays a picture rather than another Web page. Turning icons on and off automatically is a common use.

Banner Ad Manager

This FrontPage component displays a series of pictures, one at a time, at a particular location on your Web page. Clicking any picture in the series can jump the user to another Web location. The list of pictures, the time interval and transition among them, and the hyperlink location are all under your control.

Many ad rotators on the World Wide Web rotate pictures only once, when a user requests a certain Web page. The Banner Ad Manager, by contrast, continuously rotates pictures even if the user doesn't reload the Web page. Many ad rotators also jump to a different Web page depending on the picture currently displayed, but the Banner Ad Manager always jumps to the same location. Figure 11-1 illustrates a page containing a Banner Ad Manager.

FIGURE 11-1.

The Banner Ad Manager component replaces a picture at timed intervals. The picture on this page changes every five seconds.

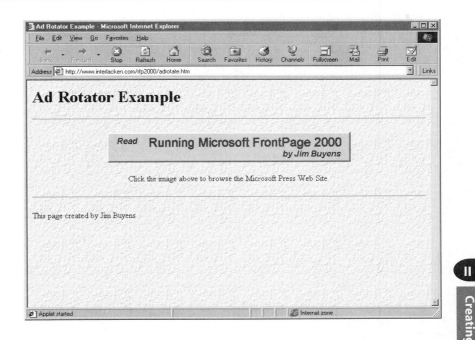

Three pictures are involved in the rotation of Figure 11-1: the one in the figure plus the two shown below.

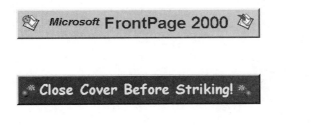

To insert a Banner Ad Manager you must first, of course, obtain or prepare the pictures. It's best but not required that all the pictures be the same size. When you specify a list of pictures that vary in size, the browser pads or crops them. This might not give the effect you want.

> The most common size for advertising banner pictures on the World Wide Web is 468 pixels wide by 60 pixels high.

To insert a Banner Ad Manager, first create or open the Web page in FrontPage. Choose Components from the Insert menu, and then select Banner Ad Manager. The Banner Ad Manager dialog box shown in Figure 11-2 will appear.

- **Width** and **Height** control the amount of space available for displaying the pictures. If a picture is smaller than specified here, FrontPage will surround it with neutral space (gray). If a picture is larger, FrontPage crops the excess height or width.

- **Transition Effect** controls the way each picture transitions into the next.

  - **None** switches directly from one picture to another with no special effect.

  - **Blinds Horizontal** replaces each existing picture with successively wider horizontal strips of its replacement.

  - **Blinds Vertical** replaces each existing picture with successively wider vertical strips of its replacement.

  - **Dissolve** fades out existing pictures until only a new picture remains.

  - **Box In** displays new pictures in a rectangle that grows inward from the edges of the existing picture.

  - **Box Out** displays new pictures in a rectangle that grows outward from the center of the existing picture.

- **Show Each Image For (Seconds)** specifies the number of seconds each picture will remain on display before transitioning to the next picture.

- **Link To** specifies where the browser will jump if the user clicks any picture in the rotation. A single Banner Ad Manager jumps to a single location, no matter which banner picture the user clicks.

TIP

You might expect that the Banner Ad Manager would jump to a different location for each picture it displays. Well, it doesn't. You can configure only one hyperlink location, and all the pictures jump there.

CAUTION

FrontPage uses a Java applet to display your rotating pictures, and Java applets can't be transparent. If you include any transparent GIF pictures in the rotation, they display with the applet's background (a plain gray) and not that of your Web pages. For this reason, it's usually best to avoid using transparent pictures with the Banner Ad Manager component.

SEE ALSO

For more information about FrontPage Webs, refer to Chapter 18, "Creating and Managing FrontPage Webs."

- **Browse** displays the Select Banner Ad Hyperlink dialog box. You can browse the current Web, your local file system, or the World Wide Web to select the Link To location.

- **Pictures To Display** lists the pictures the Banner Ad Manager will rotate. FrontPage displays the listed pictures in order, from top to bottom, and then restarts at the top.

- **Add** inserts a picture at the bottom of the list. FrontPage displays its normal picture-browsing dialog box so that you can search the FrontPage Web, the World Wide Web, your local disk, or the clip-art library.

- **Remove** deletes the currently selected item from the Pictures To Display list.

- **Move Up** moves the currently selected picture one position higher in the Pictures To Display list.

- **Move Down** moves the currently selected picture one position lower in the Pictures To Display list.

Whenever you insert a Banner Ad Manager, FrontPage actually creates the HTML to invoke a Java applet that's named *fprotate.class*. The rotator won't work unless this applet, plus another one called *fprotatx.class*, is available from any Web server that displays your page.

Whenever you save a Web page that contains a Banner Ad Manager component, FrontPage first determines whether you're saving it to a FrontPage Web. If not, FrontPage offers to make the Web page's folder into a disk-based, FrontPage Web. The dialog box containing this prompt appears in Figure 11-3.

Once you're saving to a FrontPage Web—either an existing Web or one you just created—FrontPage checks a hidden folder called *_fpclass* to see if the required Java applets are present. If not, it adds them. Thereafter, whenever you use the FrontPage Publish feature for uploading to another Web server, FrontPage will create the *_fpclass* folder on the remote server and upload the Java applets automatically.

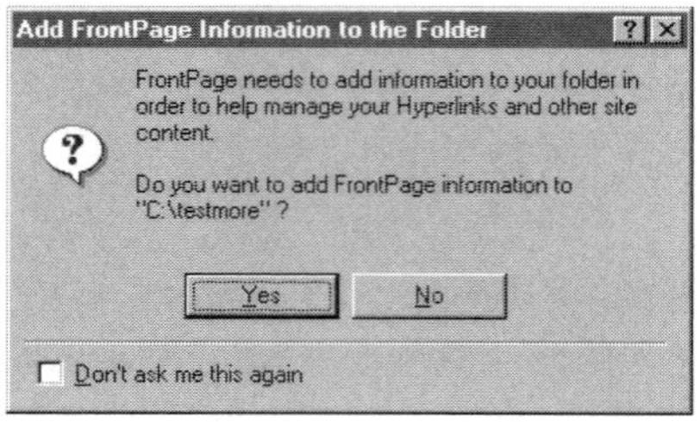

FIGURE 11-3.

This dialog box prompts before adding FrontPage Web information to an ordinary disk folder.

If you choose not to convert your folder to a FrontPage Web, you'll need to copy, rename, position, and upload the Java applets manually. By default, they're located in the folder:

C:\Program Files\Microsoft Office\Office\fpclass

and they have the file name extension CLS.

TIP

To make the _fpclass folder visible in FrontPage, choose Web Settings from the Tools menu, select the Advanced tab, and turn on the option titled Show Documents In Hidden Directories.

Whatever Happened to WebBots?

As you may have noticed, FrontPage 2000 has no components called WebBots and no menus or dialog boxes that refer to that term. This may cause a shock, given that WebBots were at one time a heavily promoted feature of FrontPage.

WebBots still exist; they're just called FrontPage components now. If you look at the raw HTML for a Web page featuring a FrontPage component, you'll still see information coded with "webbot" comments. The WebBot mechanism is a way to collect properties using dialog boxes in FrontPage and then save the information in two forms for the Web page—as properties and as the HTML necessary to implement them.

FrontPage stores WebBot properties as special HTML comments. This ensures that browsers will ignore the original property information, which they may not understand. The generated HTML, which the browser *does* understand, can consist of any valid statements. It can, for example, be ordinary content, JavaScript code, VBScript programming, code that invokes Java applets or ActiveX controls, or HTML that sends transactions back to the Web server.

As the range of technologies used by FrontPage components has grown, the original term *WebBot* has become too narrow. Thus, the more general term *FrontPage component* is now more appropriate, even though FrontPage still uses the WebBot approach internally.

TIP

Few Web pages consist of a single file. Most of them require not only a main HTML file, but also a collection of pictures, and some require additional files such as Java applets, ActiveX controls, CSS style sheets, and more. When you upload a FrontPage Web to a Web server, the FrontPage Publish feature identifies all required files and copies them automatically. If you upload your own files, however, be sure you understand all the files your page requires.

Comment

The Comment component adds hidden text to a Web page. You can use Comment components to makes notes to yourself, to plant short explanations for other page authors using your Web, or to associate any other textual information with a Web page. Be aware, however, that comments consume download time and that remote users can see them by using the View Source command in their browser.

"Inserting Comments," on page 118, describes the procedure for entering comments in FrontPage.

Date and Time

The Date and Time component displays the date a page was saved manually or updated by any means. Such dates are maintained by FrontPage, and don't necessarily correspond to the page's file system date.

To insert a Date and Time component, set the insertion point and then choose Date And Time from the Insert menu. Figure 11-4 shows the Date And Time Properties dialog box that appears.

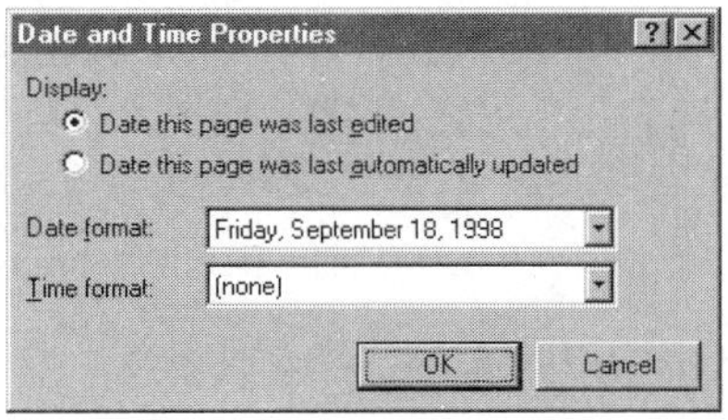

FIGURE 11-4.
This dialog box configures the Date and Time component.

- **Display** controls the significance of the displayed date.
  - **Date This Page Was Last Edited** displays the date someone last saved the page with FrontPage.

- **Date This Page Was Last Automatically Updated** displays the date a page last changed because of manual editing or automatic updating caused by a change elsewhere in the FrontPage Web.

  ■ **Date Format** selects a date format or (None) from the list provided.

  ■ **Time Format** selects a time format or (None) from the list provided.

A common use for the Date and Time FrontPage component is indicating a version date at the bottom of a Web page.

Hover Button

Hyperlinked text, pictures, and push buttons are well-established fixtures on the Web, though they're hardly original. Some links undoubtedly deserve something that gains more attention, and this is what the hover button component can provide.

A *hover button* is another small Java applet supplied with FrontPage. The applet displays a button—actually just a mouse-sensitive rectangle— with a solid-color background and a text caption. The applet changes appearance when the mouse moves over it, and jumps to a hyperlink location when the remote user clicks it.

Figure 11-5 shows a Web page with seven hover buttons, one for each background effect. Because the mouse pointer is positioned on the button with the Glow effect, it displays a gradient background while all the others are solid. The gradient remains in effect only while the mouse pointer is over the button; otherwise, the button's background is solid like all the others.

To create a hover button, open the Web page in FrontPage, choose Component from the Insert menu, and then select Hover Button. The Hover Button dialog box shown in Figure 11-6 will appear, prompting for the following settings:

- **Button Text** specifies the text the button will display.

- **Link To** controls the jump taken when the button is clicked. Clicking the Browse button displays the standard Browse Hyperlink dialog box.

- **Button Color** specifies the button's normal background color—that is, its color when the mouse isn't over it. This displays the usual 16 boring and somewhat inappropriate color choices from the original

VGA card. As usual, it's best to choose Custom and specify RGB values having some combination of 0, 51, 102, 153, 204, and 255.

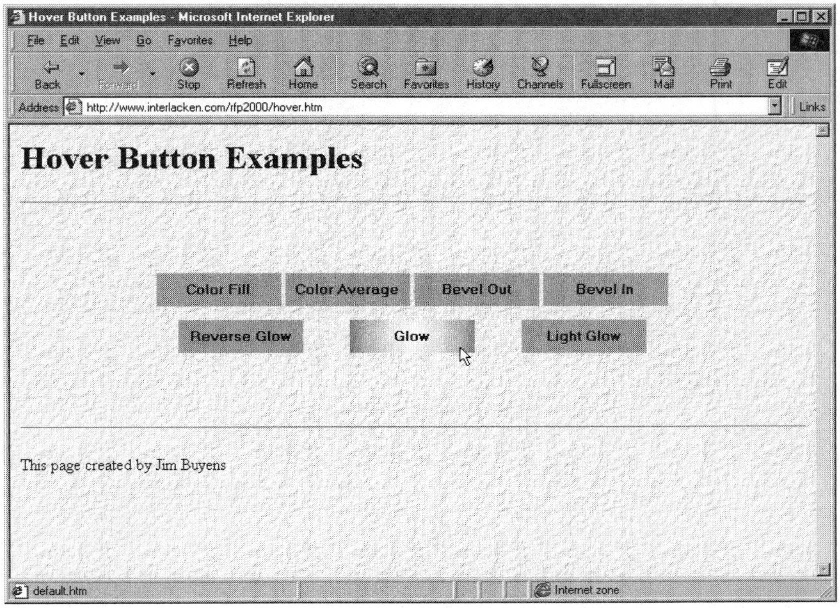

FIGURE 11-5.

These buttons demonstrate all seven background effects available to hover buttons. Only the Glow effect is visible here, because that's where the mouse is positioned.

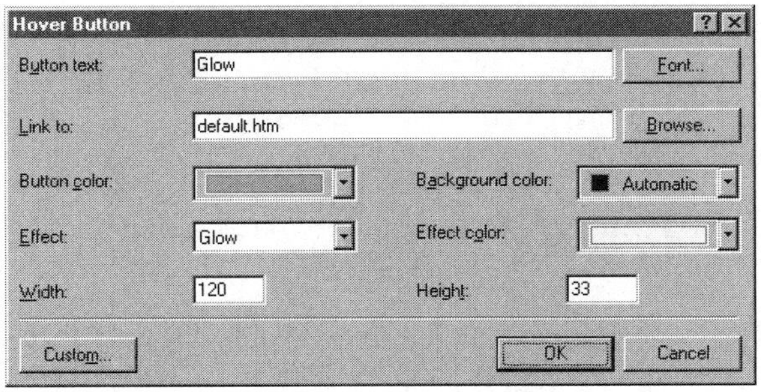

FIGURE 11-6.

This is the dialog box for configuring hover buttons.

- **Background Color** specifies the button's background color when the mouse is over the button.

- **Effect Color** specifies an accent color to display when the mouse is over the button.

- **Effect** determines how the button will appear when the mouse passes over it. The available choices and their effects are listed here:

  - **Color Fill** means the effect color will replace the background color.

Creating Web Pages

- **Color Average** means the background color will change to the average of its red, green, and blue components combined with those of the effect color.

- **Glow** means the button's center will take on the effect color, its left and right edges will retain the background color, and areas in between will display a gradient. This is the effect shown in Figure 11-5.

- **Reverse Glow** means the button's center will retain the background color, the edges will take on the effect color, and areas in between will display a gradient.

- **Light Glow** means the button's left and right edges will retain the background color, its center will display a lighter tint of the same hue, and areas in between will display a gradient. The effect color is ignored with this setting.

- **Bevel Out** gives the effect of popping up the button by lightening the top and left edges, darkening the bottom and right, and lifting the text slightly up and to the left.

- **Bevel In** gives the effect of pressing the button by darkening the top and left edges, lightening the bottom and right, and moving the text slightly down and to the right.

■ **Width** and **Height** determine the button's size in pixels. After selecting a hover button, you can also resize it by dragging its handles. (These are the eight small squares that appear around the edges.)

■ **Font** and **Custom** open additional dialog boxes for setting more hover-button options.

The Font button displays the Font dialog box shown in Figure 11-7. This dialog box controls the appearance of the button's label.

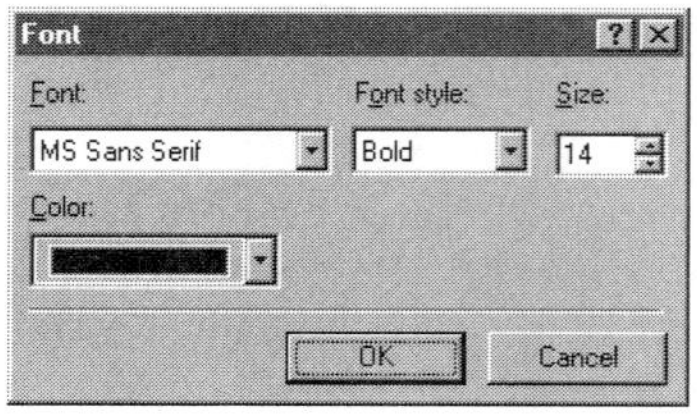

FIGURE 11-7.

The Font dialog box appears when you click the Font button shown in Figure 11-6 and controls the font, style, color, and size of a hover button's label.

■ **Font** sets the label's typeface. For maximum portability across systems, the list of typeface choices is limited.

■ **Font Style** selects normal, bold, italic, or bold italic type.

■ **Size** controls the font size in points.

■ **Color** determines the color of the text. Choices, as usual, include the boring and inappropriate 16 VGA colors, plus default and custom.

The Custom button in Figure 11-6 opens the Custom dialog box shown in Figure 11-8. Four settings are available for creating additional special button effects.

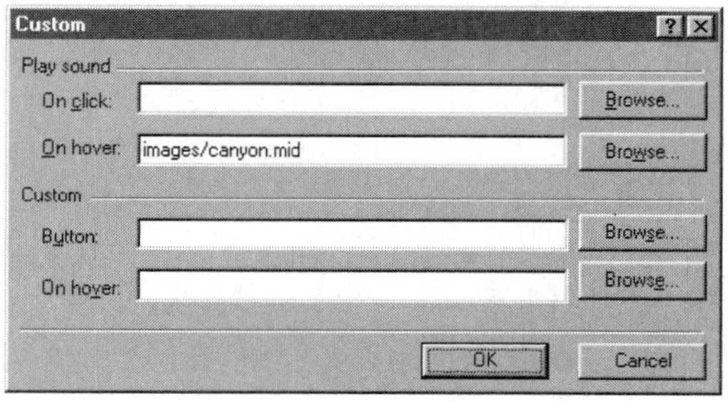

FIGURE 11-8.

This Custom dialog box controls additional hover-button effects.

■ **Play Sound** specifies sound files the browser will play under certain conditions. It's best to use small, brief sound files. Both settings are optional.

• **On Click** specifies a sound that will play when the Web visitor clicks the button.

• **On Hover** specifies a sound that will play when the Web visitor moves the mouse pointer over the button.

■ **Custom Picture** identifies picture files that display within the hover button. Both settings are optional. If you specify both a picture in this dialog box and a text caption in the main Hover Button dialog box, the caption will appear superimposed over the picture.

• **Button** names a picture that will appear inside the hover button when the mouse pointer isn't over it.

• **On Hover** names a picture that will appear when the mouse pointer passes over the hover button.

⭐ TIP

To avoid alignment problems, it's best if the hover button and any custom pictures are the same size.

II

Creating Web Pages

You can use the Browse buttons near each choice to locate files in the current Web, on the World Wide Web, or on the local file system.

Like the Banner Ad Manager component, hover buttons depend on two Java applets being available when the remote user browses the Web page, applets named *fphover.class* and *fphoverx.class*. Be sure to upload these applets along with your Web pages, using the same procedures and precautions described for Ad Banners.

Include Page

FrontPage's Include Page component merges the content of one Web page into another. Included pages usually contain page segments rather than full-blown page layouts—segments that appear on several or all pages in a site. Including the same segment on several pages guarantees that it will look the same everywhere. Later, if a change to the segment is required, only one location needs to be updated.

Figure 11-9 shows two typical candidates for the Include Page component. The upper segment is a picture with hotspots, and the lower one is a plain-text copyright notice. Each segment is an ordinary, freestanding Web page but consists entirely of content to be included as part of other pages. The file names are jumpbar.htm and signatur.htm, respectively. To include these segments in another Web page:

1 Construct the segment to be included on its own page just as you would any other Web page.

NOTE
The _private folder in a FrontPage Web is an excellent place to keep Web-page segments used by the Include Page component. This folder (thanks to the leading underscore in its name) is accessible to you while editing but not to remote users when browsing.

2 Use FrontPage to open the page that will include the segment.

3 Set the insertion point where the included content should appear (that is, click that spot).

4 Choose Component from the Insert menu, then choose Include Page from the menu shown below.

5 The Include Page Component Properties dialog box shown in Figure 11-10 appears next. Click the Browse button, locate the page you wish to include, and then click OK. You can also type the path and file name directly in the text box.

TIP

To simultaneously view pages from the same Web in two or more open windows, first open the Web normally. Then, to create additional windows, choose New Window from the Window menu.

FIGURE 11-9.

FrontPage displays two pages suitable for inclusion in other pages.

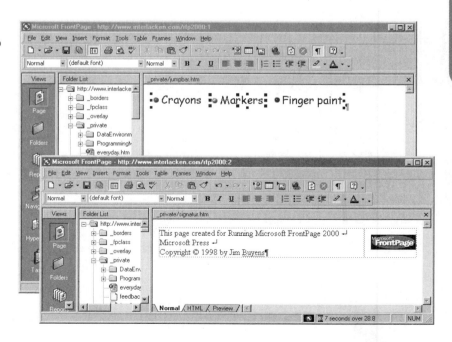

FIGURE 11-10.
Specify the page
segment to be dis-
played at the inser-
tion point in your
currently open page.

Figure 11-11 shows a Web page that includes both files shown in Figure 11-9.
Note that included content takes on the properties of the page that includes
them—background, color scheme, and so forth. The included portions look
no different than if they'd been cut and pasted into the parent page.

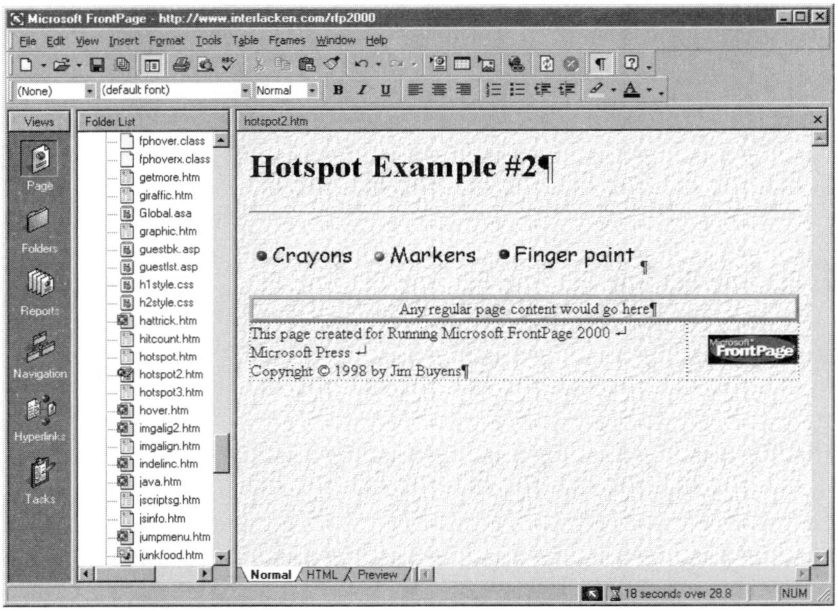

FIGURE 11-11.
Included portions of a
Web page take on the
appearance of the
parent page.

There's an implied line break before and after every Include Page component. That is, the included content occupies the entire display width
and doesn't flow continuously with surrounding content. If this presents
a problem, expand the amount of included content. Include entire paragraphs, for example, and not single words. Alternatively, use the Substitution component for words or phrases.

To change the included content, edit the source page. There are two ways
to change the properties of this or any other FrontPage component:

- Double-click any area it occupies.

- Right-click the area and choose the component's Properties option
  from the pop-up menu.

The Include Page component places a full copy of the included content in each Web page that uses it, for two reasons. First, merging content at browse time would consume more resources on the Web server. Second, merging content at authoring time produces pages that display correctly even on Web servers that don't have the FrontPage Server Extensions installed.

Of course, when you update a page that's included in other pages, you expect all the pages to reflect the new content. To do this, FrontPage maintains an index of pages in which each included page appears. Then, when you save the included page, FrontPage updates all the pages in which the saved page appears.

This indexing information is just the sort of thing you might expect to find in a FrontPage Web. If so, you'd be right. You can use the Include Page component for pages that don't reside in a FrontPage Web, but it becomes a one-way deal. You can open a Web page and refresh its included content, but updating an included file won't update all the other files that include it.

Whenever you save a page that contains a Scheduled Include Page component (or a Scheduled Image component as described in the next section), FrontPage checks to see if you're saving it to a FrontPage Web. If not, it uses the dialog box seen before as Figure 11-3 to suggest converting the page's folder into a FrontPage Web.

- If you answer Yes, FrontPage creates the folders and files that make the difference between an ordinary folder and a FrontPage Web. Thereafter, whenever you use FrontPage to update an included page, FrontPage will update all pages in the same Web that include it.

- If you answer No, FrontPage will not have an index of which pages include other pages. Therefore, updating an included page *won't* update included copies.

Whether or not your page resides in a FrontPage Web, updating it with ordinary programs like Notepad won't update FrontPage's various indexes, and won't propagate changed pages to others that include them. These are functions of the FrontPage software only. If you don't use FrontPage for all changes to your Web, run the Recalculate Hyperlinks command (on the Tools menu) in FrontPage after using other editors.

II

Creating Web Pages

Marquee

The Marquee component displays a line of text that scrolls automatically across the browser window. It uses a facility introduced in Internet Explorer 3, but not available in Netscape Navigator, at least through version 4.0. Browsers lacking built-in marquee support display the marquee text statically.

To add a marquee to your Web page:

1 Open the page in FrontPage.

2 To convert existing text to a marquee, select it. To create a marquee that uses new text, just set the insertion point where you want the marquee to appear.

3 Choose Components from the Insert menu, and then choose Marquee. The Marquee Properties dialog box shown in Figure 11-12 will appear.

4 Configure the marquee by setting the dialog box options as described below, and then click OK.

FIGURE 11-12.

This dialog box configures a FrontPage marquee.

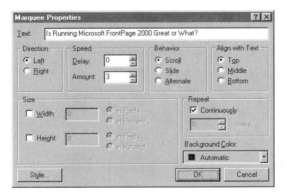

The Marquee Properties dialog box provides the following options:

■ **Text** specifies the verbiage the marquee will animate. Any text you selected before starting the marquee command will appear here.

■ **Direction** controls how the marquee text will move—toward the left (the usual choice) or toward the right.

■ **Speed** controls how quickly the marquee will move.

- **Delay** specifies the number of milliseconds between each motion of the marquee.

- **Amount** specifies how many pixels the marquee will shift in each step.

■ **Behavior** determines the type of motion.

- **Scroll** advances the marquee continuously across the screen in accordance with the Direction setting. Motion continues until the trailing edge of text reaches the end of the marquee area.

- **Slide,** like scroll, advances the marquee continuously across the screen. Motion continues until the leading edge of text reaches the end of the marquee area, where it stops.

- **Alternate** moves the marquee text back and forth within the available area. In this method the marquee text is always completely visible, for maximum impact.

■ **Align With Text** specifies how the marquee should align with surrounding text.

- **Top** aligns the marquee with the top of normal text.

- **Middle** aligns the marquee with the middle of normal text.

- **Bottom** aligns the marquee with the bottom of normal text.

■ **Size** determines the screen area occupied by the marquee.

- **Width** controls the marquee's horizontal dimension. The default is to occupy all available width: the entire browser window, table cell, frame, or other container.

  To choose a specific width, turn on the check box, enter a value, and then indicate unit of measure as either pixels or percent.

- **Height** controls the marquee's vertical dimension. The default is to accommodate only the marquee text, including its formatting.

  To choose a specific height, turn on the check box, enter a value, and then indicate unit of measure as either pixels or percent.

■ **Repeat** controls how often the marquee will redisplay the moving text.

CAUTION

If you specify Movement as Scroll and then set Repeat to a specific number of times, movement will stop with little or nothing visible in the marquee area.

Creating Web Pages

- **Continuously** means the marquee will continue moving text as long as the remote user's browser displays the Web page.

- **Times** specifies how many times the marquee effect will repeat.

- **Background Color** gives the marquee its own background color. The default is the Web page's background color.

- **Style** lets you assign cascading style-sheet attributes to the marquee.

To modify an existing marquee, either select it and choose Marquee Properties from the Edit menu, or right-click and choose Marquee Properties from the pop-up menu.

To change a marquee's font, font size, text color, or other text properties, either select the marquee and use the normal format menus, or open the Marquee Properties dialog box and click Style to apply cascading style-sheet attributes.

Figure 11-13 shows a marquee in FrontPage's Preview mode. Assigning a behavior of Alternate makes the text bounce back and forth between the two icons. This effect is achieved by placing the two icons and the marquee in the left, right, and center cells of a one-row, three-column table.

FIGURE 11-13.

The marquee in this Web page continuously bounces the text left and right between the two icons.

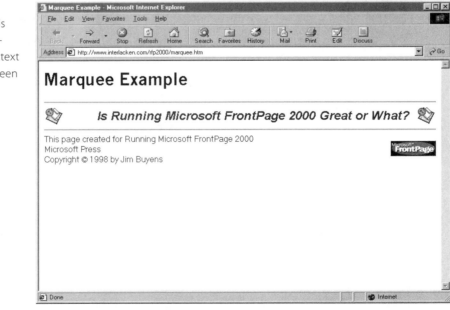

Scheduled Include Page

As often as content on the Web changes, it's not surprising that the need to make scheduled changes is a common requirement. Figure 11-14, for example, shows two Web-page segments that might appear on the same page at different times—the upper during January and the lower during other months.

FIGURE 11-14.

Here are two segments that might appear on the same Web page at different times.

FrontPage supports scheduled changes with the Scheduled Include Page component. This component works much like the Include Page component described earlier, but adds three features:

- A start date.

- A stop date.

- An optional URL.

Inserting a Scheduled Include Page is much like inserting an Include Page component: set the insertion point, choose Component from the Insert menu, select Scheduled Include Page, and click OK. The dialog box for the Scheduled Include Page component appears in Figure 11-15. The available settings are:

- **Page Link To Include.** Identify the pages you want the Scheduled Include Page component to display.

- **During The Scheduled Time.** Enter the Web location of the content you want Web visitors to see during the scheduled period.

- **Before And After The Scheduled Time (Optional).** Enter the Web location of the content you want Web visitors to see before and after the scheduled period. If you leave this field blank, nothing will appear. Click Browse to locate the page in the current Web.

■ **Starting.** Specify the year, month, day, and time Web visitors should begin seeing the scheduled content. To begin showing the new content immediately, enter a past date.

■ **Ending.** Specify the year, month, day, and time Web visitors should stop seeing the scheduled content. To keep showing the new content indefinitely, enter a date far in the future.

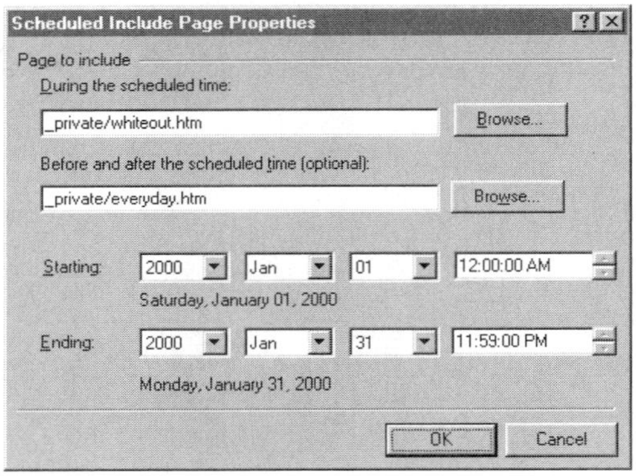

FIGURE 11-15.

This dialog box controls the properties of a Scheduled Include Page component.

Figure 11-16 shows Internet Explorer displaying the Scheduled Include Page component configured in Figure 11-15. The current month isn't January 2000.

SEE ALSO
The fpsrvadm.exe program described in "Administering the FrontPage Extensions from the Command Line," page 566, can be run from a scheduled batch file to recalculate hyperlinks.

The Scheduled Include Page component, like the Scheduled Image FrontPage component described next, suffers one nagging flaw: the scheduled change isn't completely automatic. Even on a Web server running the FrontPage extensions, there's no automatic process for the scheduled content to be inserted, replaced, or removed at the specified time. To ensure proper timing of Scheduled Include Page components, you must do *either* of the following:

■ Make some change to your FrontPage Web every day. (For example, change the value of some configuration variable.)

■ Arrange with your server administrator to recalculate hyperlinks in batch mode on a nightly basis.

If your page resides in an ordinary disk folder rather than a FrontPage Web, saving it will result in the prompt of Figure 11-3 on page 362. If you answer No, the schedule will take effect only if you open and save the Web page.

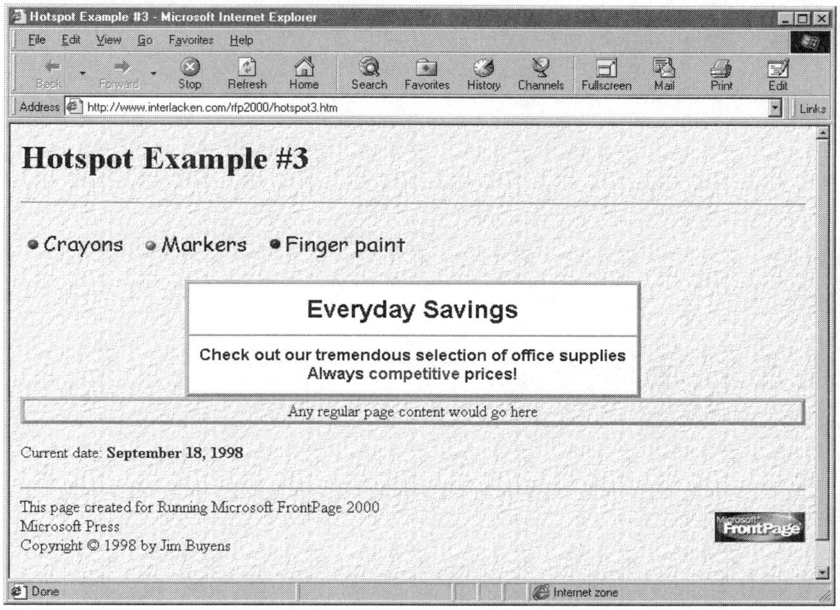

FIGURE 11-16.
This is the Web page configured in Figure 11-15. The everyday.htm segment appears because the current date isn't January 2000.

Scheduled Picture

The Scheduled Picture component works almost exactly like the Scheduled Include Page component. The differences are:

■ The Scheduled Picture component conditionally displays a single picture rather than an arbitrary block of content.

■ Conditionally displayed pictures flow in-line with text. There are no automatic paragraph breaks before and after a scheduled picture.

Figure 11-17 shows the Scheduled Picture Properties dialog box. This dialog box and the procedure for invoking it parallel those for the Scheduled Include Page component exactly; refer to the previous section for details.

Scheduled pictures suffer the same timing nuisance as scheduled include pages; for date changes to take effect, you must somehow initiate a hyperlink recalculation.

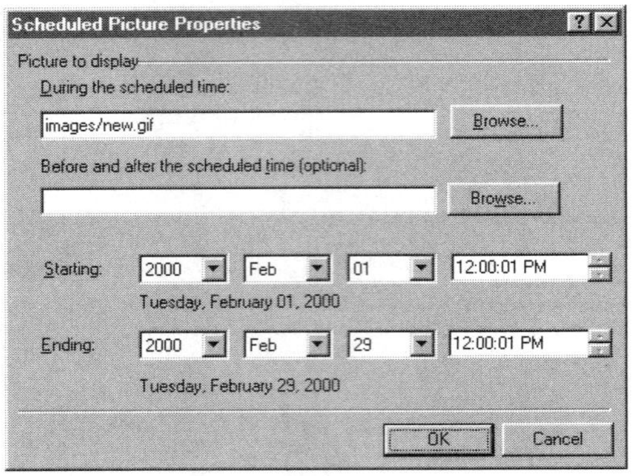

FIGURE 11-17.

This dialog box sets the properties of a Scheduled Picture component.

In Summary...

This chapter introduced the FrontPage components you can use, albeit with occasional difficulty, even if you don't keep your Web pages in a FrontPage Web. These components are useful features by themselves, but at least some of them begin to illustrate the advantages of FrontPage maintaining and acting upon accurate cross-reference information—information available only in a FrontPage Web. If this is starting to make sense, consider a temporary detour through Chapter, 18, "Creating and Managing FrontPage Webs."

The next chapter discusses a variety of techniques for further activating your site.

CHAPTER 12

More Ways to Activate Your Site

This chapter describes seven ways to enhance your Web pages beyond the mundane dimensions of height and width, and into the active dimension of time. These techniques range from the simple to the complex, but they all involve motion or interactivity.

- **Page transitions** make Web pages appear or disappear with a series of fades, wipes, and other effects.

- **Animation** applies special effects to text, graphics, and other elements on a Web page. For example, you can make the page heading drop in from above and have section headings fly in from the left or right.

- **Video images** provide a way to play movies and other animations inside the browser window.

- **Plug-ins** are software modules that add capabilities to applications. As used with browsers, plug-ins usually occupy a space within the visible window and display file types the browser alone cannot. Microsoft Front-Page creates the HTML that flags a file for plug-in processing, and then the browser selects plug-in software based on the type of file.

- **ActiveX controls** are program modules that provide any function a Windows program can implement. On a Web page, they most commonly acquire screen space and display specialized content. However, their use of Windows-specific technology limits their use on other platforms, and many people consider their free access to all system resources a security risk.

- **Java applets** are programmed objects that, like ActiveX controls, can occupy space on a Web page and respond to user input. Java applets can run on any computer that has a Java interpreter but, for security reasons, their capabilities on the local computer are severely limited.

- **Design-Time Controls** are similar to ActiveX controls, except that they're designed to support the Web authoring environment rather than run inside a browser. A Design-Time Control loaded into FrontPage works very much like a FrontPage component.

This chapter will concentrate not on programming these last four objects, but on using FrontPage to enter, manage, and integrate them. Complete treatments of browser objects, server objects, and programming techniques require full-length books in themselves.

Animating Page Content

At two different levels, FrontPage can animate the way your Web pages come into view. At the page level, you can have FrontPage animate the way one Web page replaces another. Or, at the level of individual objects, FrontPage can animate the way objects appear on the page.

Both these capabilities require the Dynamic HTML features of Internet Explorer 4. For browsers that lack these features, the Web pages simply appear without animation.

Animating Page Transitions

Figure 12-1 shows, in frozen form, an animation effect in progress as one Web page replaces another. Instead of just erasing the screen and painting the new page normally—from top to bottom—the browser displays it in an ever-widening circle. In this way the Black On White page gradually replaces the White On Black page.

To set page transitions, open the dialog box shown in Figure 12-2 by choosing Page Transition from the Format menu.

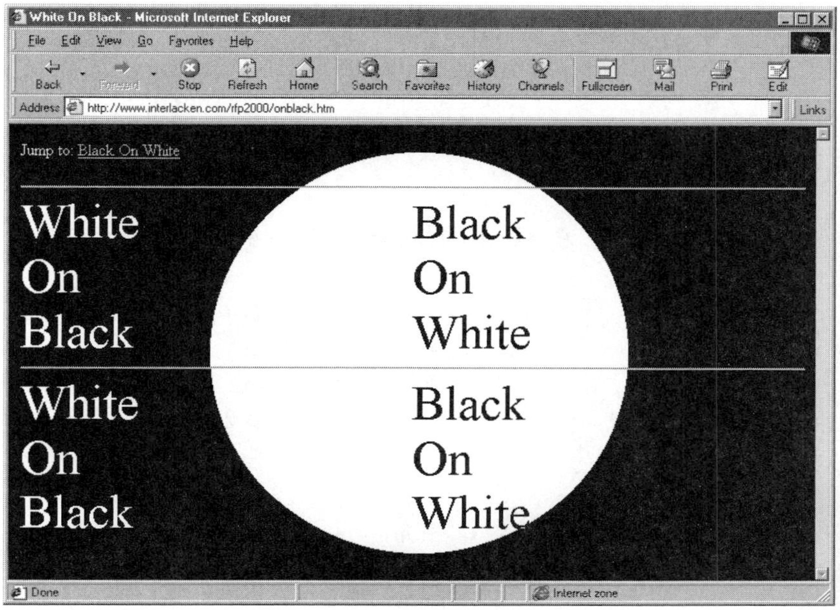

FIGURE 12-1.

The page with the white background is gradually replacing the page with the black background. You control such effects using the Page Transition command on the Format menu.

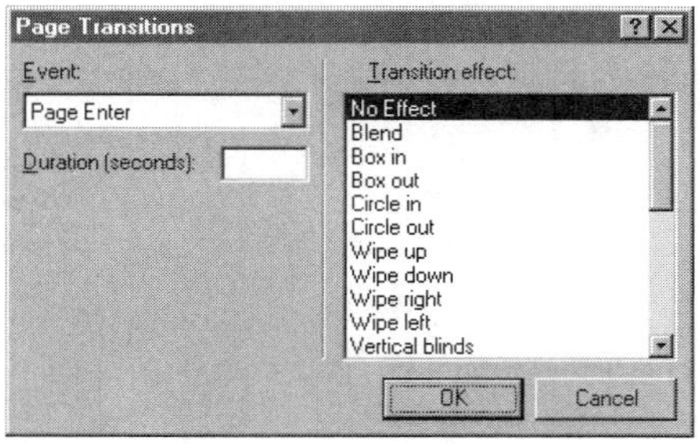

FIGURE 12-2.

This FrontPage window defines page transitions for Web pages.

II

Creating Web Pages

■ **Event** specifies when the page transition will occur.

- **Page Enter** displays a transition effect as the currently edited page appears on the Web visitor's browser.

- **Page Exit** displays a transition effect as the currently edited page disappears from the visitor's browser.

- **Site Enter** displays a transition effect as the currently edited page appears on the visitor's browser, provided the previous page was from a different Web site.

- **Site Exit** displays a transition effect as the currently edited page disappears from the visitor's browser, provided the next page is from a different Web site.

- **Duration (Seconds)** specifies how long the transition effect will last.

- **Transition Effect** controls the animation pattern with over 20 effects. You can guess from each transition's name the type of effect it will produce. But the best way to become familiar with these effects is to simply try them on your own system.

Animating Page Objects

In addition to animating the appearance and disappearance of entire Web pages, FrontPage can animate the way individual elements arrive on-screen, react to mouse activity, or both. Headings, images, and other objects can fly in from various borders, drop in one word at a time, spiral in, zoom in, and so forth. In addition, the appearance of objects can change as the mouse pointer passes over them.

Figure 12-3 shows such a page-load animation in progress. The heading line, including the graphic, has already flown in from the right. Now, the items on the menu bar in the Web page are flying in one word at a time from the top of the window. *Backup, Diskettes, Drink Holder*, and *Foot Pedal* have already arrived and *Whiteout* is en route.

FIGURE 12-3.

The menu bar on this Web page is flying in word by word from the top.

FrontPage creates these effects by adding browser scripts to your Web page. These scripts are written in JavaScript and use the positioning and overlap features provided by Dynamic HTML (DHTML). Internet

Explorer 4 was the first browser to support these features; others may follow. Applying animation effects in FrontPage 2000 is quite simple.

1 Set the insertion point anywhere within the element you wish to animate. This will usually be a paragraph.

2 Locate the DHTML Effects toolbar described in Table 12-1. If it isn't visible, choose Toolbars from the View menu, then choose DHTML Effects.

3 Use the Event drop-down list (labeled On) to specify the event that triggers the effect. There are four possibilities.

- **Click** means the effect occurs whenever the Web visitor clicks the element.

- **Double-Click** means the effect occurs whenever the Web visitor double-clicks the element.

- **Mouse Over** means the effect occurs whenever the Web visitor moves the mouse pointer over the element.

- **Page Load** means the effect occurs whenever the Web visitor loads or reloads the page.

4 Use the Effect drop-down list (labeled Apply) to choose the effect you want. As illustrated in Table 12-2, the choice of effects varies depending on the trigger event.

5 If the Effect Settings list is enabled, click the drop-down button and choose one of the listed options.

TABLE 12-1.   The FrontPage DHTML Effects Toolbar

Icon	Description	Function
On < Choose an event >	Choose An Event	Specifies what condition triggers the effect.
Apply < Choose an effect >	Choose An Effect	Specifies what effect will occur, such as a change of font or position.
< Choose Settings >	Effect Settings	Specifies details of the effect, such as color, font, or direction of movement.
Remove Effect	Remove Effect	Cancels DHTML effects.
	Highlight Dynamic HTML Effects	Controls whether FrontPage will indicate, by means of a light blue background, which elements have DHTML effects.

TABLE 12-2. Effects Available for DHTML Events

Event (On)	Effect (Apply)	Description	Settings
Click, Double-Click	Fly Out	Moves the animated element off-screen.	Direction of movement
Mouse Over	Formatting	Changes the appearance of text.	Fonts (including font colors) and borders
Page Load	Drop In By Word	Moves text on screen from the top, a word at a time.	(none)
	Elastic	Moves the entire element on screen from the right or bottom, overshoots, then corrects.	From right or from bottom
	Fly In	Moves the element on screen from any side or corner.	Side or corner, entire element or a word at a time
	Hop	Moves the element slightly up, right, down, and then left.	(none)
	Spiral	Moves the element from the upper-right corner to its proper place, using a spiral motion.	(none)
	Wave	Moves the element slightly down, right, up, and then left.	(none)
	Wipe	Gradually reveals the element.	Left to right, top to bottom, or from middle
	Zoom	Text starts out either very large or very small, then zooms to normal size.	In (reduced text becomes normal) or out (enlarged text becomes normal)

When you select a picture and then use the DHTML Effects toolbar, the toolbar will offer different effects than shown in Table 12-2. The effects offered are shown in Table 12-3.

TABLE 12-3.   Additional Effects offered on the DHTML Toolbar

Event (On)	Effect (Apply)	Description	Settings
Click	Fly Out	Moves the picture off-screen	Direction of movement
	Swap Picture	Replaces the picture with another picture	Location of the replacement picture
Double-Click	Fly Out	Moves the picture off-screen	Direction of movement
Mouse Over	Swap Picture	Replaces the picture with another picture	Location of the replacement picture
Page Load		Same as Page Load in Table12-2	

The Swap Picture Effect

The Swap Picture effect offers a flexible alternative to Hover Buttons if you proceed as follows.

1 Create two versions of a picture you want to use as a button.

- One will be the picture as it normally appears.

- The other will be an alternate version that appears when the Web visitor passes the mouse over the picture area. (Note that both images should be the same size.)

2 Add the "normal" picture to your Web page and build the desired hyperlink.

3 Select the "normal" picture, and then display the DHTML Effects toolbar.

4 In the DHTML Effects toolbar:

- Set On to Mouse Over.

- Set Apply to Swap Picture.

- Set the third drop-down list to Select Picture.

5 Use the resulting Picture dialog box to specify the "alternate" picture.

It is important that you perform these steps in the order given. If you specify the DHTML effects first and then the hyperlink, FrontPage might discard the DHTML effects.

To remove an effect, first select the element, making sure the DHTML Effects toolbar displays the effect you want to remove. Then, click the toolbar's Remove Effect button.

FrontPage can visually indicate elements with DHTML effects by showing them with a light blue background. This occurs only in Page view, and not in the Web visitor's browser. However, if you find the blue background in Page view distracting, you can toggle it on and off by clicking the Highlight Dynamic HTML Effects button on the DHTML Effects toolbar.

The various DHTML Effects animations run only once. There's no way to make them run continuously, and that's probably a good thing. Once your page is on display, you want Web visitors to read your content and not to sit there watching cartoons.

Highlighting hyperlinks is a common use for Mouse Over effects. When the mouse pointer passes over hyperlinked text, the text can change color, get larger, change font, and so forth.

Presenting Video

FrontPage can insert video clips into your Web pages as easily as it inserts still images. Delivering video requires no special software in Front-Page or on your Web server, but displaying it requires a player on the remote user's browser. The most common video formats on the Web are Audio Visual Interleaved (AVI) from Microsoft and QuickTime (formerly called Active Movie (MOV)) from Apple. Web visitors can obtain player software from these companies' Web sites, or through their browser suppliers.

It's good practice and common courtesy to provide hyperlinks that download players for video clips or other multimedia elements used on your Web pages.

- For information about downloadable Microsoft browser features, browse:
  http://www.microsoft.com/windows/ie/download/default.asp

- For information about downloadable Netscape browser features, browse:
  http://www.netscape.com/plugins/index.html

- For more information about QuickTime, including download locations, browse:
  http://www.apple.com/quicktime/

The section "Adding Multimedia Files" on page 182 describes the mechanics of adding video files to pages in your Web.

Incorporating Plug-Ins

A plug-in is a piece of software that takes over a section of the browser window and displays something in it. Usually the display is from a file obtained from the Web server, and most often is some kind of multi-media file. Netscape Communications originally devised plug-ins, and Internet Explorer now supports them. Plug-ins generally aren't as con-figurable (via HTML) as other approaches to multimedia, but support by both browsers is a strong point.

Displaying a given file with a plug-in requires two things. First, the file has to be specially marked in the HTML. Second, the Web visitor's browser must have a plug-in available for the given type of file. Some plug-ins come with the browser itself, and Web surfers can install more from various Internet sites. In general, the Web author doesn't know which, if any, plug-in software will process a given file type. This can vary considerably depending on the type of computer, the type of browser, and the browser's configuration.

FrontPage can't install plug-ins on the remote user's browser, or per-form browser configurations. It can, however, flag files on a Web page for plug-in processing. To begin, choose Advanced from the Insert menu, then choose Plug-In. Figure 12-4 shows the dialog box that results.

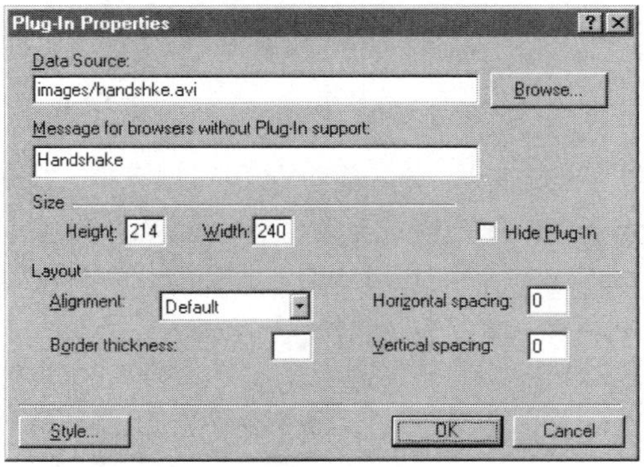

FIGURE 12-4.
This dialog box creates instructions for the browser, telling it to display the named file using a plug-in.

Here are the fields included in this dialog box.

- **Data Source** specifies the name of the file the plug-in should process. This can be a relative or fully qualified URL.

- **Message For Browsers Without Plug-In Support** provides text that will appear if the browser doesn't support plug-ins.

- ■ **Size** specifies how much window space the plug-in will consume.

  - • **Height** specifies a height in pixels.

  - • **Width** specifies a width in pixels.

  - • **Hide Plug-In,** if turned on, specifies that the plug-in will occupy no window space. This can be appropriate for non-visual files, such as sound clips.

- ■ **Layout** controls how the plug-in appears on the Web page.

  - • **Alignment** controls the plug-in's positioning relative to surrounding text. Refer to Table 6-2 on page 188 for the list of choices.

  - • **Border Thickness** controls the thickness, in pixels, of a black border surrounding the plug-in.

  - • **Horizontal Spacing** sets the horizontal spacing, in pixels, between the plug-in and the nearest element on the same line.

  - • **Vertical Spacing** sets the vertical spacing, in pixels, between the plug-in and the lines above and below it.

- ■ **Style** applies cascading style-sheet properties to the plug-in display.

Figure 12-5 shows Netscape Navigator using a plug-in to display the AVI file configured in Figure 12-4.

FIGURE 12-5.

Netscape Navigator uses a plug-in to display the AVI file configured in Figure 12-4.

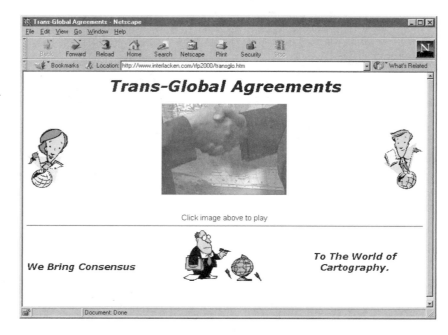

 **SEE ALSO**

For more information about MIME types, see "MIME Types and Other Curiosities," page 490.

 **SEE ALSO**

For information about configuring MIME tables in Microsoft Web servers, see Chapter 16, "Installing and Configuring Your Web Server."

A common plug-in problem involves Multipurpose Internet Mail Extension (MIME) types. The file type a browser uses for selecting a plug-in usually isn't a file name extension, it's a MIME type that the Web server assigns. The MIME type for an AVI file, for example, is usually video/x-msvideo. Correctly displaying the file thus requires a two-step translation.

- First, the Web server translates the file name extension to a MIME type.

- Second, the browser uses the server-supplied MIME type to select a plug-in.

Incorrect Web server configuration is a common cause of plug-in files that fail to appear properly. After eliminating browser configuration as the source of a problem, ask the Web server's system administrator to check the server's MIME type table. Be sure to provide the file name extensions you're using and the MIME type you'd like assigned.

Incorporating ActiveX Controls

Microsoft's vision of uniting Windows and the World Wide Web naturally involves a merger of Windows programming objects and active Web pages. This section explains how to incorporate such objects, called ActiveX controls, into your Web page.

ActiveX—A Brief Introduction

ActiveX controls are reusable software modules you can place on a Web page to extend the capabilities of HTML. The modules are actually Windows DLLs—dynamic link libraries—but usually have an OCX file name extension. They're closely related to OLE objects, widely used in Windows programming. ActiveX controls were initially available only for Windows platforms but their applicability is growing over time.

ActiveX controls run like any other OLE object on your computer. Not only can they manipulate the browser display and interact with scripts, they also can make any changes to the local system that the current local user could make. A Digital Signature scheme ensures that whoever downloads an ActiveX control knows who created it and thus whom to prosecute if the control is mischievous or destructive!

ActiveX controls have properties, methods, and events.

- **Properties** are data values accessible by the control and externally accessible. Depending on how a control is written, a given property might be updateable or made read-only to external processes.

■ **Methods** are software routines, programmed into the control, that external processes can trigger.

■ **Events** are external incidents that trigger code to execute. Event routines run in response to external stimuli, such as mouse clicks, keystrokes, and incoming data.

On Web pages, scripts modify ActiveX properties, invoke their methods, and respond to their events. In most cases, therefore, using ActiveX controls requires the ability to create scripts with JavaScript or VBScript. You don't need to write scripts, however, if your sole objective is to display preset data.

ActiveX controls come from a variety of sources. Sometimes they get installed as parts of other software on your computer, and sometimes they get installed because of a Web page that uses them and provides a download location.

Inserting ActiveX Controls

To begin adding an ActiveX control to a Web page, choose Advanced from the Insert menu, and then select ActiveX Control. The Advanced submenu shown in Figure 12-6 appears.

FIGURE 12-6.
This submenu provides options to insert advanced elements into a Web page.

Choosing ActiveX Control from the Advanced submenu displays the dialog box shown in Figure 12-7. Select the control you want, then click OK.

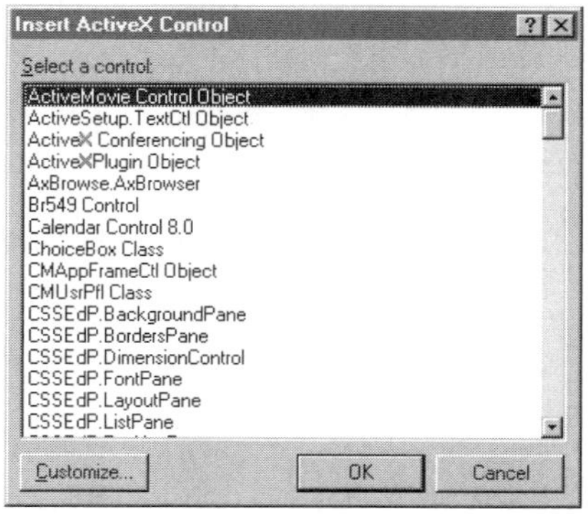

FIGURE 12-7.
To add an ActiveX control to your Web page, select it from this list, and then click OK.

Immediately after you click OK, FrontPage adds the selected control to your Web page at the current insertion point. If the control generates a display, it will appear in Page view. If it doesn't, the control will just occupy a blank space. Either way, FrontPage surrounds the area with sizing handles. You can drag, cut, copy, paste, and resize in all the usual ways.

The Customize button displays a complete list of ActiveX controls installed on your system, along with check boxes that include or exclude specific controls from the first list. Figure 12-8 illustrates this. You'll probably discover many more controls than you expect; the list includes all controls installed on your system by any software, plus any controls you've downloaded from Web pages. Importantly, in the Location box, it also displays the control's file name.

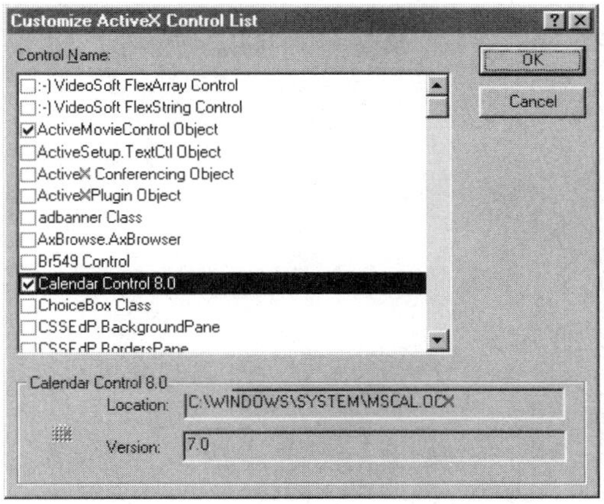

FIGURE 12-8.

Clicking Customize in Figure 12-7 displays this dialog box, where you can include or exclude controls from the Insert ActiveX Control list.

Once you've inserted an ActiveX control, you can set its properties by double-clicking it. If you prefer, you can also right-click it and choose ActiveX Control Properties, single-click it and press Alt+Enter, or single-click it and choose Properties from the Format menu. Any of these techniques will produce a dialog box resembling Figure 12-9.

The last two tabs in Figure 12-9, Object Tag and Parameters, are generic and appear for all ActiveX controls. The rest are specific to the particular control. The Object Tag tab appears in Figure 12-10 and contains the following fields.

- **Name** gives the control a name. Scripts on the same Web page can use this name to reference the control.

■ **Layout** specifies the control's page placement and appearance.

- **Alignment** specifies the control's position relative to surrounding text. Table 6-2, "HTML Image Alignment Settings," on page 198, describes the possible values.

- **Border Thickness,** if nonzero, surrounds the control with a border. The specified integer controls the border's thickness in pixels.

- **Horizontal Spacing** controls the separation, in pixels, between the control and neighboring elements on the same line.

- **Vertical Spacing** controls the separation between the control and any text or images present in lines above or below it.

FIGURE 12-9.

The Active Movie control displays this property sheet. Other controls may display more or fewer tabs, but all controls display the Object Tag and Parameters tabs.

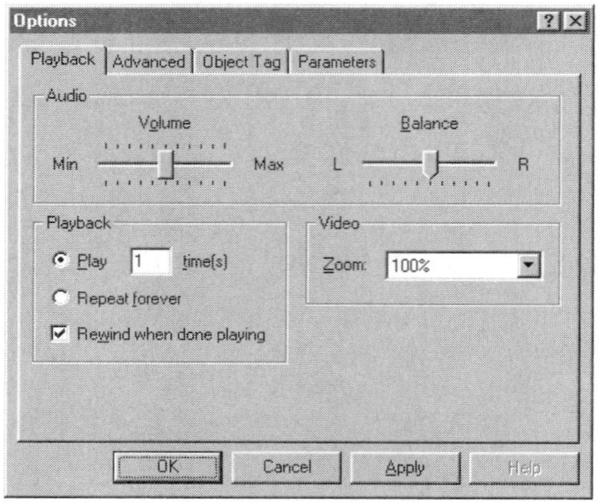

FIGURE 12-10.

The Object Tag properties for an ActiveX control pertain to size and placement on the Web page, and to download location. The browser, and not the ActiveX control, uses this information.

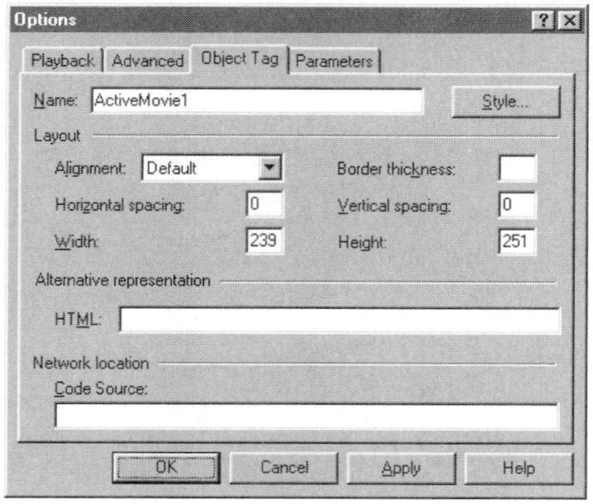

- **Width** specifies, in pixels, the horizontal space available to the control.

- **Height** specifies, in pixels, the vertical space available to the control.

You can also resize the area available to an ActiveX control by selecting the control in FrontPage and then dragging its handles.

■ **Alternative Representation** specifies what a browser should display if it doesn't support ActiveX controls.

- **HTML** supplies HTML to display if a browser doesn't support ActiveX controls. This can be plain text, HTML tags, or both.

■ **Network Location** optionally specifies a network location for the control and its data. This feature allows capable browsers such as Internet Explorer to fetch and install the control on demand.

- **Code Source** provides the URL of the file containing the ActiveX control. If a control isn't installed on a Web visitor's computer, browsers such as Internet Explorer can download and install it using this URL.

If you want Web visitors to download an ActiveX control from your site, copy it into your Web from the location shown in Figure 12-8, then specify its URL in the Code Source field. Alternatively, you may wish to specify a Code Source location at a provider's Web site rather than your own, to ensure that Web visitors will get the most current version.

The Parameters tab, shown in Figure 12-11, provides a general-purpose way to establish settings for the control. Whether or not default entries appear depends on the control, and entries that do appear may be redundant with settings on tabs other than Object Tag and Parameters. With luck, any parameters you need to work with will appear on control-specific tabs or with recognizable names on the Parameters tabs. If good luck eludes you, you'll have to locate and consult documentation from the control's supplier. The next two sections in this chapter address these issues in greater detail.

Be sure to observe copyright restrictions when distributing ActiveX controls.

II

Creating Web Pages

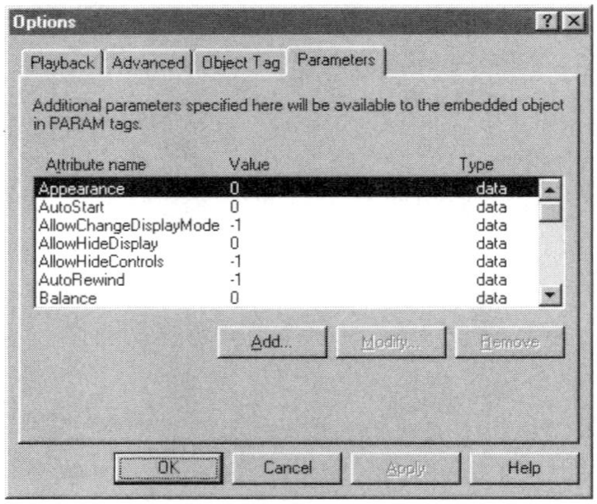

FIGURE 12-11.

The Parameters tab supplies values that the ActiveX control expects and uses.

You can revisit the ActiveX Control Properties dialog box in four ways:

- Double-click the control in FrontPage.

- Right-click the control, and then choose ActiveX Control Properties from the pop-up menu.

- Select the control and press Alt+Enter.

- Select the control, and then choose ActiveX Control Properties from the Edit menu.

Figure 12-12 shows FrontPage displaying two ActiveX controls, while Figure 12-13 shows Internet Explorer displaying the same page. Neither control executes in the FrontPage environment—objects in FrontPage need to "hold still" for editing. This means ActiveX controls don't respond interactively, as they would in a browser situation. Some controls don't even display in WYSIWYG mode.

Using Local-Property Editing

If an ActiveX control is installed on your computer and supports local-property editing, its property sheet will display three or more tabs. Figure 12-14, for example, shows a tab titled General displayed for the Microsoft Calendar control. The Object Tag and Parameters tabs follow as usual.

The General tab lists the available properties for the control and their current values. To change a parameter, select it, modify the existing value in the text box at the top of the dialog box, and then click the Apply button. When finished, click the OK button in the preview window.

Each control that supports local-property editing will display its own set of tabs and properties. Recall for example the total of four tabs displayed by the Active Movie control, shown in Figure 12-9.

FIGURE 12-12.

Here FrontPage displays two ActiveX controls on a page—a Label Object displaying slanted text and a Calendar Control displaying a calendar. Neither object executes in FrontPage.

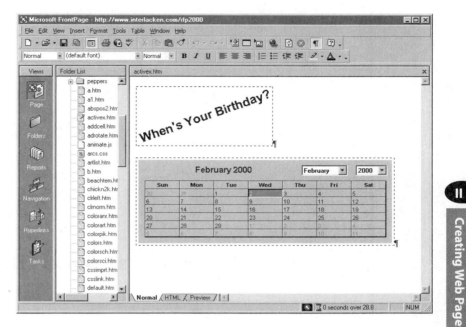

FIGURE 12-13.

The page edited in Figure 12-12 displays correctly in Internet Explorer.

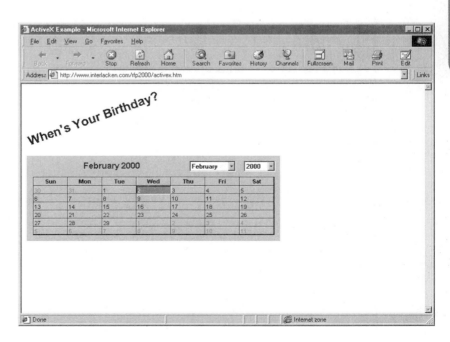

Creating Web Pages

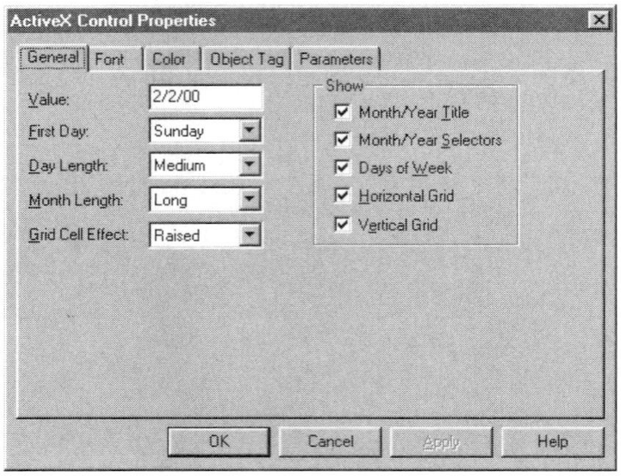

FIGURE 12-14.

This is the local-property editing dialog box for the Microsoft ActiveX Calendar control.

As you can imagine, local-property editing is a much-appreciated feature among Web-page developers who use ActiveX controls, and most new controls include it. Local-property editing does increase the size of the control, however, making it bulkier and thus slower for the remote user.

Using the Object Parameters Dialog Box

Most ActiveX controls now support local property editing. However, for those that don't (or aren't locally installed), FrontPage displays only the Object Tag and Parameters tabs. This is the case in Figure 12-15, which shows the property sheet for a Label control. Initially, the parameter table will be blank, and you'll have to add all required parameters manually, one by one. The procedure for adding a parameter is:

1 Obtain a list of the control's required and optional parameters. This information usually comes as documentation from the control's provider.

2 Click the Add button in Figure 12-15. The dialog box shown in Figure 12-16 will appear.

3 Specify parameters using the following fields.

- **Name** identifies the parameter. This name must be spelled exactly as shown in the control's documentation.

- **Media Type** specifies the Multipurpose Internet Mail Extension (MIME) type of the specified value. Media type can only be specified for the Page parameter type.

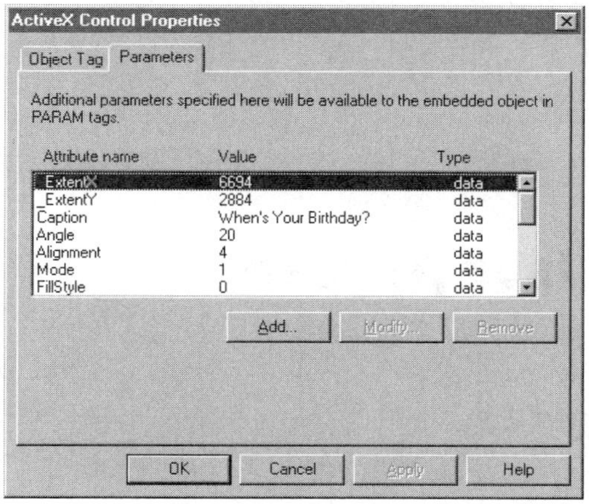

FIGURE 12-15.

The Parameters tab manages parameters for ActiveX controls that don't support local property editing.

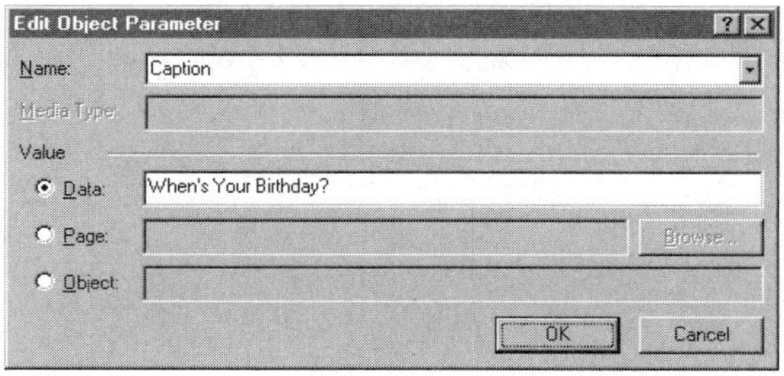

FIGURE 12-16.

The Edit Object Parameter dialog box specifies parameters of ActiveX controls that don't support local editing.

- **Data** is one of three ways to specify the chosen parameter's type and value. Select the type setting specified in the control's documentation. Choosing Data indicates that the parameter's value consists of data. Type the data into the associated text box.

- **Page** indicates that the parameter's value is the URL of a file. Enter the URL in the associated text box or use the Browse button to locate the URL.

- **Object** indicates that the parameter's value is the name of another ActiveX control on the same page. Type the name of the control in the associated text box.

4 Click OK to close each dialog box.

To modify an existing parameter:

1 Select it from the list shown in Figure 12-15, and then click the Modify button. (Alternatively, double-click the parameter's line in the list.)

2   Change whatever settings require correction.

3   Click OK to close each dialog box.

To remove a parameter setting, select it and click the Remove button.

Incorporating Java Applets

Java is a popular programming language closely resembling C++ but with restrictions that help the innocent avoid hanging themselves. A team at Sun Microsystems invented Java, and Sun remains its guiding authority.

Java programs don't compile to a processor's native instruction set; instead, they compile to the instruction set of an imaginary computer called the *Java virtual machine*. Java programs are portable to any type of computer and any operating system that has a virtual machine emulator. The emulator is a piece of software that carries out Java virtual machine instructions using local native instructions so that the compiled Java program can run.

Java applets are small Java programs that run as part of a Web page. Applets are considerably less capable than ordinary programs—even ordinary Java programs. Applets can take up space on the screen, play sounds, modify the browser window, interact with scripts, and open various connections to the machine that delivered the applet to the visitor's browser. Applets can't, however, make changes to the local machine's files or hardware settings. The collective name for these restrictions is *the Java sandbox*. The idea is that an applet, playing within its sandbox, can't do anything at all to your computer, therefore it can't do anything bad.

About GraphicsButton

The examples in this section use a freeware Java applet called GraphicsButton. It displays a button with a specified picture on its face and jumps to a specified Web location when a user clicks it. In addition, the edges of the button depress when the user clicks the button.

To obtain GraphicsButton, its documentation, and other information about Java, visit PineappleSoft at *http://www.pineapplesoft.com/goodies/index.html*.

Applets reside on a Web server. You can locate many freeware or shareware applets on the Web, download them to your own site, and use them in your pages. Browsers download applets just as they do images or other files used on a Web page, but of course the browser runs the applet rather than displaying it as an image.

Applets, like ActiveX controls, have properties and methods. The ActiveX distinction between methods and events is discarded in Java; both are simply considered methods.

To add a Java applet to one of your Web pages:

1 Obtain a copy of the applet and its documentation.

2 Import the applet file, which normally has a file name extension of CLASS, into your Web. You'll probably find it convenient, as many Web developers do, to place all Java applets in a folder called *classes*.

3 Use FrontPage to open the Web page that will contain the applet.

4 Choose Advanced from the Insert menu, and then choose Java Applet. This will produce the dialog box shown in Figure 12-17.

5 Fill out the fields in the dialog box as follows:

- **Applet Source** specifies the name of the Java applet file. Don't specify a complete URL or a path of any kind.

- **Applet Base URL** specifies the URL path to the applet file. Don't include http://, the computer name, the port number, or the name of the applet file itself.

- **Message For Browsers Without Java Support** controls what a browser should display if it doesn't support Java applets.

- **Applet Parameters** lists settings used by the applet. Use the Add button in this group box to specify a name and value for each required applet parameter. The next step describes this process in detail. Consult the applet's documentation for a list of mandatory and optional parameter names and data values.

- **Size** allocates screen space for the applet.

  Width specifies, in pixels, the horizontal space available to the applet.

  Height specifies, in pixels, the vertical space available to the applet.

- **Layout** controls the applet's positioning.

  Horizontal Spacing controls the separation, in pixels, between the applet and neighboring elements on the same line.

Vertical Spacing controls separation between the applet and any text or images present in lines above or below it.

Alignment specifies the control's position relative to surrounding text. Table 8-1, page 231, describes the possible values.

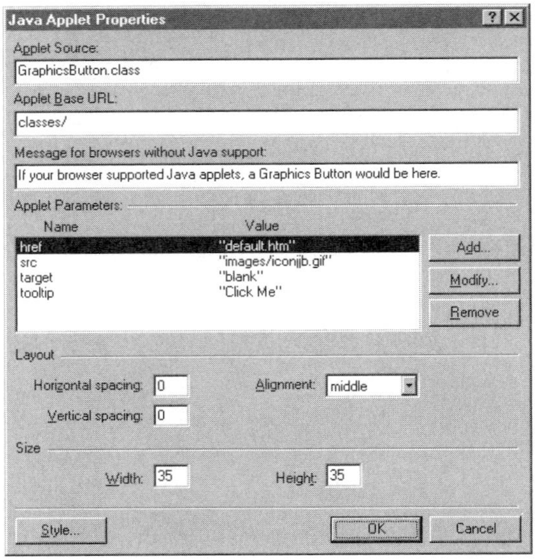

FIGURE 12-17.

This dialog box adds a Java applet to a Web page.

6 Clicking the Add button in the Applet Parameters dialog box shown in Figure 12-17 produces the Set Attribute Value dialog box of Figure 12-18. Enter data using the following fields.

- **Name** specifies the name of the parameter, spelled exactly as described in the applet's documentation.

- **Specify Value** indicates whether the parameter takes a value. Turn the box on for a parameter that takes a value, and turn it off for keyword parameters.

- **Value** supplies the parameter's desired value.

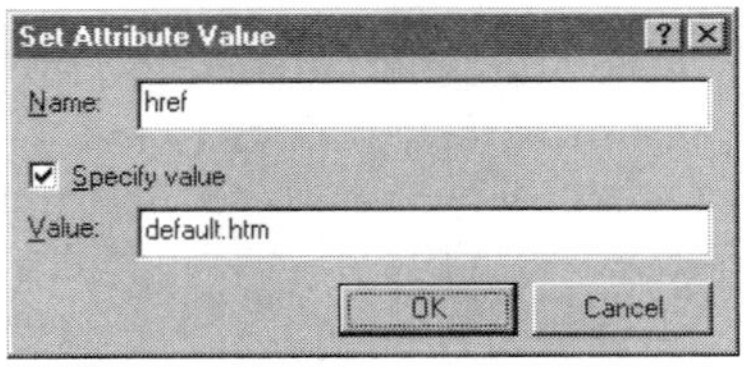

FIGURE 12-18.

This dialog box sets parameter values for Java applets.

To modify a parameter setting:

1 Select its entry in the Applet Parameters table (Figure 12-17) and click the Modify button. (Alternatively, double-click the table line for the desired parameter.)

2 Change whatever settings require correction.

3 Click OK.

To remove a parameter, select it and click the Remove button.

Figure 12-19 shows the GraphicsButton applet open in both FrontPage and Internet Explorer. Like ActiveX controls, Java applets don't execute within FrontPage; this accounts for the difference in their appearance.

FIGURE 12-19.
Because Java applets don't execute in FrontPage, only by browsing them can you display their true appearance.

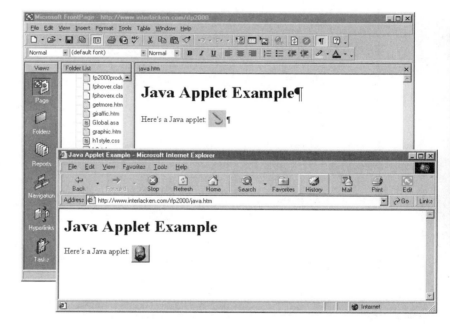

Incorporating Design-Time Controls

The use of ActiveX controls isn't limited to enhancing and extending Web pages. Most computers running Windows operating systems have hundreds, if not thousands, of ActiveX controls having little or nothing to do with Web browsing; they're used with Microsoft Office applications, other programs from Microsoft and third-party vendors, and by Windows itself. Given all this, you might wonder if adding ActiveX controls to FrontPage might add new editing features, just as adding controls to Web pages adds new browsing features. Design-Time Controls (DTCs) provide a glimpse of the answer.

The idea of a DTC is relatively simple. You add the control to an editing window—an open window in Page view, for example—and the control displays whatever is useful to the Web designer. Opening the control displays a property sheet, hopefully of the intuitive and usual sort. Whenever the Web designer saves the page, the editing application notifies the control and the control emits HTML that does whatever the designer specified.

Currently, most DTCs are designed for use with Microsoft Visual InterDev, a high-end Web development application geared more for programmers and hard-core HTML types than the general population. Nevertheless, FrontPage provides some support for DTCs.

The FrontPage procedure for adding a DTC to a Web page is relatively simple:

1 Set the insertion point where you want the control to appear.

2 Choose Advanced from the Insert menu, then choose Design Time Control. Figure 12-20 shows the dialog box that results.

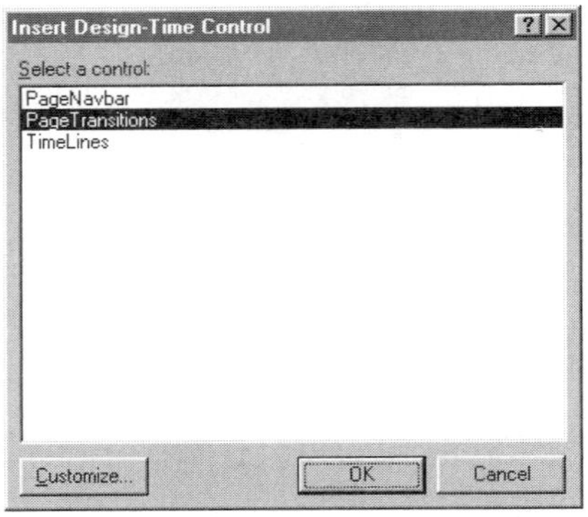

FIGURE 12-20.

The Insert Design-Time Control dialog box adds a DTC to your Web page.

3 Choose the desired control.

4 Click OK.

If no DTCs are installed on your computer, the Insert Design-Time Control menu option will be dimmed. In addition, it's possible that some DTCs installed on your computer may not be listed. To search for additional DTCs, click the Customize button in Figure 12-20. The dialog box shown in Figure 12-21 will result. To make any listed DTC appear in the insert list, turn on its option box, then click OK.

FIGURE 12-21.

This dialog box results from clicking the Customize button in Figure 12-20. It controls which DTCs appear in the Insert Design-Time Control list.

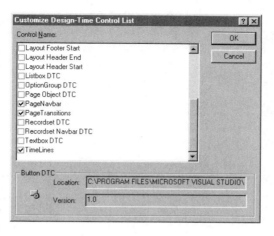

Once inserted, a DTC may or may not present a WYSIWYG appearance. There are three possible reasons for this.

- WYSIWYG display may be turned off. To toggle WYSIWYG display of DTCs, choose Advanced from the Insert menu, then choose Show Design-Time Controls.

- The control may not be written to provide WYSIWYG display. Remember, the two main functions of a DTC are first, collecting settings during Web-page editing and second, writing HTML as the Web page is saved. There's no specific requirement to collect settings in WYSIWYG fashion.

- The control's output might not consist of visible page elements. For example, the DTC might create a timer that controls other elements on the page, or that opens database connections.

Figure 12-22 shows FrontPage editing a page that uses the Page Transitions control supplied with Microsoft Visual InterDev. This is a non-WYSIWYG DTC.

CAUTION

The ability to display page transitions depends on the browser version. Netscape browsers up to and including version 4 lack this capability and ignore transition effects.

To configure a DTC, right-click it and then choose Design-Time Control Properties from the pop-up menu. Figure 12-23 shows a typical result, namely the property sheet for the Page Transitions DTC.

The Page Transition tab presents the following options.

- **Page Enter** specifies effects the browser should use when switching to the current page from somewhere else.

- **Transition** specifies the desired effect. The choices are a variety of fades and wipes.

II

Creating Web Pages

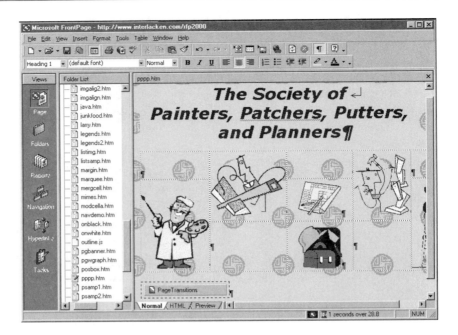

■ **Duration** specifies how long the effect should last (in seconds).

■ **Preview** displays the effect in the Preview box at the right. Figure 12-23 shows a preview in progress.

■ **Page Exit** specifies effects the browser should use when switching from the current page to another. The options are the same as those for Page Enter.

The Site Transition tab is very similar to the Page Transition tab, but specifies effects that occur when Web visitors enter and leave your site. The browser detects a change of site by comparing the computer names in successive URLs.

Figure 12-24 shows Internet Explorer starting to display the Web page from Figure 12-23. The new page appears from the center of the window and grows outward.

The major strength of Design-Time Controls is their potential to work in several different Web page editors. In theory, software developers can write modules once and sell them in a variety of environments. In practice, DTCs require very specific features from the Web-page editor, and most of them work only with Visual InterDev. FrontPage, for example, has tended to stay with its original WebBot approach (now called FrontPage components). Nevertheless, if a Design-Time control works with FrontPage, you might as well take advantage of it.

FIGURE 12-23.

This dialog box specifies properties for the Page Transition DTC.

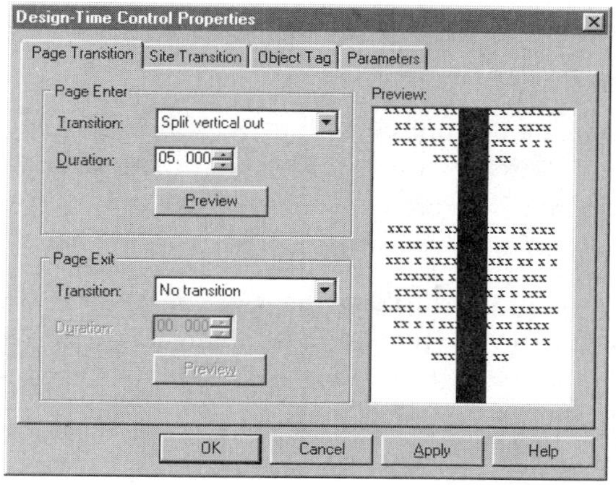

FIGURE 12-24.

Here's Internet Explorer starting to display the Web page in Figure 12-23. The new page is growing from the center line outward.

> **NOTE**
>
> Many of the DTCs that come with Visual InterDev integrate closely with that product's database features, and not with the database features in FrontPage.

In Summary...

The techniques presented in this chapter may seem far afield of what people do with ordinary HTML, but that's the point. FrontPage supports virtually every hot technology on the Web, and does so in a very friendly, easy-to-use way.

Speaking of HTML, that's the topic of the next chapter. If you know HTML, could stand to learn it, or have a friend who could, you'll be glad to know that FrontPage provides full access to the code behind your Web pages.

Working Directly with Code

One of the principal reasons Microsoft FrontPage exists is to free page creators from ever having to look at inscrutable HTML code. Occasionally, however, people who know HTML decide they're doing a certain task the hard way and scream, "Just let me see the blasted code and I'll fix it!" FrontPage *can* look under the hood, and does so skillfully. This chapter will show you how.

Scripts are segments of program code—usually small ones—that add automation and interactivity to Web pages. In many cases, FrontPage can write such scripts for you, but to go beyond what's offered you'll need to lay your own code. Here too, FrontPage provides outstanding features.

Finally, FrontPage 2000 now includes Visual Basic for Applications. This means you can develop scripts and macros that customize FrontPage and automate commonly used procedures.

The common element in these topics is, of course, dealing with lines of code. Your interest in dealing with code will probably vary depending on what you're trying to do and how desperate you are to do it. Regardless, FrontPage is ready when you are.

Working with HTML Code

Despite having FrontPage's powerful WYSIWYG editor, some page creators simply can't be happy without looking at and dealing with HTML code. This section describes how FrontPage does just that.

HTML Basics

Tags define the basic structure of HyperText Markup Language—HTML. Tags begin and end with <angle brackets>. Anything inside the brackets is formatting and control information; everything else is page content.

The first word inside the <angle brackets> determines the type of tag: <P> is a paragraph tag, <IMG> is an image tag, and <TABLE> is the tag that defines a table, for example. Additional expressions within the angle brackets specify *attributes*—characteristics of the page element the tag defines. The following tag, for example, defines a horizontal rule. The attribute WIDTH="80%" tells the browser to make the rule 80% as wide as its container.

```
<HR WIDTH="80%">
```

 TIP

> An element's *container* is an element that surrounds it and limits its size. The browser window is the most common container, but frame windows, table cells, and other elements are also containers for the elements within them.

Spaces, tab characters, and line endings separate attributes within the same tag. The number of such characters is irrelevant; one space is as good as 100 as far as HTML is concerned. Most attributes consist of a keyword and a value separated by an equal sign, although some consist of a keyword alone. The value needs to be enclosed in quotes if it contains any characters other than letters, numbers, percent signs, and hyphens.

Some tags, like <HR> (horizontal rule) and
 (line break), stand alone but many others occur in pairs: one like <B> (bold) to start an effect, and another like </B> (cancel bold) to end it. The ending tag always has the same identifier as the opening tag, preceded by a slash. Ending tags have no attributes.

Text in HTML tags is non-case-sensitive. The tags <p align=center> and <P ALIGN=CENTER> are perfectly equivalent.

The following six lines of HTML appear in nearly all Web pages.

```
<HTML>
  <HEAD>
  </HEAD>
  <BODY>
  </BODY>
</HTML>
```

■ <HTML> and </HTML> mark the beginning and end of a Web page.

■ <HEAD> and </HEAD> mark the beginning and end of the head section, a block of code guaranteed never to appear to Web visitors. The head section typically contains entries such as:

  • The page's title (enclosed by <TITLE> and </TITLE> tags).

  • Style sheets (enclosed by <STYLE> and </STYLE> tags).

  • Scripts (enclosed by <SCRIPT> and </SCRIPT> tags).

  • <META> tags, which generally describe the page and provide keywords for Internet search engines.

■ <BODY> and </BODY>, which mark the Web page's displayable area.

A complete course in HTML, complete with listings, descriptions, and examples of every defined tag, is clearly beyond the scope of this book. Fortunately, though, hundreds of others are available to fill the vacuum. Visit your local bookstore and browse a number of them, searching for one or two that start from your level of expertise and explain whatever you're ready to learn next. Hopefully, of course, FrontPage will create all the HTML you ever need, and you'll never have to deal with the code directly. The rest of this section is for those who wish to fine-tune their Web pages, for the curious, and for those who already know how to do something in HTML and prefer not to learn another approach (even if it *is* easier, dig, dig).

Revealing Tags in Page View

Figure 13-1 shows FrontPage displaying the Web page previously seen as Figure 4-4, this time with the Reveal Tags option in effect. There are two ways of turning Reveal Tags on and off:

■ Choose Reveal Tags from the View menu.

■ Press Ctrl+/.

FIGURE 13-1.
The Reveal Tags feature shows the location and type of HTML tags in the body of a Web page. For details about a specific tag, rest the mouse pointer over it and wait for a ScreenTip to appear.

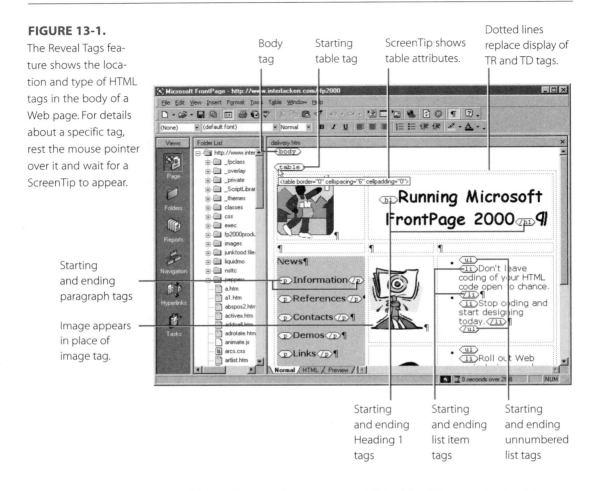

FIGURE 13-1.
The Reveal Tags feature shows the location and type of HTML tags in the body of a Web page. For details about a specific tag, rest the mouse pointer over it and wait for a ScreenTip to appear.

Body tag

Starting table tag

ScreenTip shows table attributes.

Dotted lines replace display of TR and TD tags.

Starting and ending paragraph tags

Image appears in place of image tag.

Starting and ending Heading 1 tags

Starting and ending list item tags

Starting and ending unnumbered list tags

Reveal Tags doesn't give you any additional editing capability; it just keeps you informed about the HTML FrontPage creates. It's also useful for locating HTML with no visible appearance, such as paragraphs with nothing in them.

There's something else Reveal Tags doesn't do: it doesn't reveal tags FrontPage indicates another way. Note the table in Figure 13-1, for example. The opening <TABLE> tag is visible, but not the <TR> and </TR> tags that delimit each row, and not the <TD> and </TD> tags that bound each cell. The dotted lines around each table cell, however, provide the same information. The closing </TABLE> tag is below the displayable portion of the window.

Don't overlook the following commands, which control the visibility of elements Reveal Tags doesn't display.

- The Show All button on the Standard toolbar, described in Chapter 4, "Getting Started with Web Pages." This controls the visibility of block endings, line endings, and table cells, and anchor icons that show the physical position of repositioned content.

- The Highlight Dynamic HTML effects button on the DHTML Effects toolbar, described in Chapter 12, "More Ways to Activate Your site." This controls the visibility of spans and divisions involved in such effects.

- Sizing handles, which appear around images, hotspots, Text on GIF elements, and so forth.

Using the Insert HTML Component

FrontPage makes every effort to support every feature of HTML, and to save Web pages with all the formatting and features they had when opened. Occasionally, however, it might be necessary to insert pieces of HTML that FrontPage absolutely won't touch. This isn't as crazy as it sounds, for the following reasons:

- Keeping up-to-date with every new HTML feature is an extremely difficult task, especially given the constant succession of browser upgrades.

- Accommodating obsolete features is difficult as well.

- Pages newly imported into FrontPage might contain syntax errors or incorrect codes, particularly if previously maintained by hand.

- Something about the HTML is trickier than FrontPage expects. For example, the page may contain incomplete HTML fragments joined together later by scripts (a technique described later in this section).

The Insert HTML component inserts a block of HTML directly into your Web page. FrontPage doesn't check this HTML at all, doesn't display it, and doesn't integrate the HTML with neighboring objects. To use this feature:

1 Open the Web page in FrontPage.

2 Set the insertion point where you want the new HTML to be placed.

3 Choose Advanced from the Insert menu, and then choose HTML.

4 When the HTML Markup window shown in Figure 13-2 appears, enter the HTML and then click OK.

Insert HTML components appear as question-mark icons in FrontPage; one of them appears just left of the Insert HTML dialog box in Figure 13-2.

- To modify an Insert HTML component, double-click the question-mark icon. Alternatively, select it and then choose Properties from the Format menu.

- To delete an Insert HTML component, select it and then either press the Delete key or choose Delete from the Edit menu.

Why use the Insert HTML component in Figure 13-2? Well, it wouldn't be a very useful example otherwise, but there's still another reason. The inserted HTML is an ordinary IMG tag but the file name ../images/ <% =strPict %>.gif is rather peculiar. As explained later in this chapter, <% =strPict %> is a special expression that the Web server will replace with the name of an image file, selecting a different file for each time of day. To FrontPage, though, angle brackets within angle brackets are a no-no that requires correction—correction that would ruin the effect we're trying to achieve. The Insert HTML component provides a solution.

FIGURE 13-2.

The Insert HTML component inserts and modifies HTML outside the control of FrontPage.

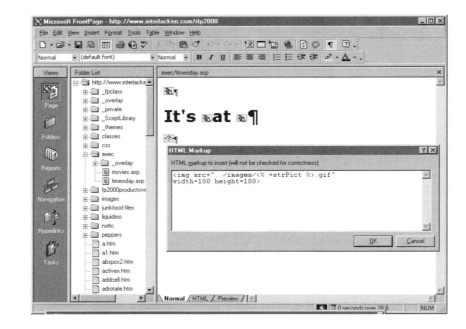

It's not unusual to find Insert HTML components in newly imported HTML code. These often reflect marginal or incorrect syntax in HTML that was previously maintained by hand. You can view the incorrect code by double-clicking the icon. You can either delete the bad HTML and re-create it using FrontPage tools or correct the bad HTML in place.

If there's no need to isolate the code in an HTML Markup component, you can convert it to regular HTML through the following procedure:

1   Open the HTML Markup component (by double-clicking, for example).

2   Select the HTML code you want to remove.

3   Cut the HTML into the Clipboard by using the keystrokes Shift+Delete or Ctrl+X, or by right-clicking the selection and choosing Cut from the pop-up menu.

4   Click OK to close the HTML Markup dialog box.

5   Set the insertion point where you want the HTML code to appear. This will probably be just right or just left of the HTML Markup component.

6   Choose Paste Special from the Edit menu, click Treat As HTML, and then click OK.

7   If the Insert HTML component is now empty, select it and press the Delete key to delete it.

If someone gives you a piece of HTML code, such as the code to use a non-FrontPage hit counter or mailer, first try pasting it directly into your Web page with Edit, Paste Special, Treat As HTML. If this works, it permits a much better WYSIWYG display than using the Insert HTML component. It also facilitates editing and provides much better integration with your other content. If it doesn't, there's always the Insert HTML component to fall back on.

Overuse of the Insert HTML component generally indicates a problem. Except in rare cases, FrontPage should handle your HTML well enough that the "hands-off" aspect of Insert HTML isn't necessary.

Editing Code in HTML View

> **⊗ CAUTION**
>
> In Normal view, where FrontPage creates all the HTML for you, HTML errors are extremely rare. In HTML view, you create the HTML, and errors are quite possible. FrontPage doesn't check your HTML for accuracy as you work.

The topics presented so far have skirted the issue of viewing and editing a Web page in its entirety as HTML code. Well, the buck stops here. To view all the HTML for a Web page in one editable window, select the HTML tab at the bottom of the FrontPage window. A display like that in Figure 13-3 will result.

Of course the display in Figure 13-3 is fully editable as text; you can cut, copy, paste, delete, find, replace, undo, open, and save using the normal FrontPage commands and keystrokes. But as a bonus, almost all of FrontPage's menu commands are available as well! You can insert tables, hyperlinks, pictures, FrontPage components, and other elements using the same commands you learned in Normal (that is, WYSIWYG) view. Simply set the insertion point within the HTML, then use the menu bar as usual.

FIGURE 13-3.

FrontPage readily displays an HTML version of the current Web page. Changes take effect on closing the window.

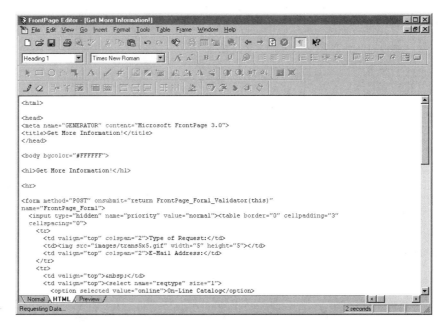

 In some cases you can modify the properties of existing Web-page elements with FrontPage menus, even though you're working in HTML view. There are three ways to use this feature:

> **X CAUTION**
>
> Be sure to set the insertion point correctly before inserting a new element. For example, don't try to insert a new picture inside the HTML for an existing one.

■ Right-click the element, and then choose Tag Properties from the pop-up menu.

■ Set the insertion point within the element, and then choose Properties from the Format menu.

■ Set the insertion point within the element, and then press Alt+Enter.

If you choose HTML view while editing a frameset, FrontPage will display the HTML for all open-target pages, using the same frame arrangement as Normal view in FrontPage. To view the frameset HTML, choose the Frames Page HTML tab shown at the bottom of Figure 8-27.

> **★ TIP**

> Finding the correct location to insert HTML can be difficult in FrontPage's HTML mode, especially if you're not a whiz at HTML. To make this job easier, set the insertion point in FrontPage's Normal view before switching to HTML view. FrontPage will usually highlight the same general area in HTML view.

If you're accustomed to maintaining HTML by hand, you've probably developed indentation styles and other conventions to make the HTML more readable. FrontPage can either preserve the format of your existing code, or adopt whatever conventions you prefer. The next section describes this feature.

Personalizing HTML Format

When FrontPage opens a Web page, it reads the HTML into a set of internal tables best suited for WYSIWYG display and editing. Then, when it saves the Web page, FrontPage writes completely new HTML.

Previous versions of FrontPage saved HTML with some accommodations to human readability, but not many. The resulting HTML frequently bore little resemblance to the original, even if the changes made in FrontPage were quite minor.

If FrontPage is your only Web-page editor, you may not care what your HTML looks like. As long as the browser can understand the HTML code, who cares whether human beings can? Nevertheless, for many page authors—old-timers, pioneers, programmers, and the terminally fastidious—readability of HTML remains a concern. FrontPage 2000 helps in two new ways:

■ **100% HTML Source Code Preservation** means FrontPage remembers the order, capitalization, and surrounding white space for each tag in the page. 100% Preservation means that opening and saving any Web page produces no change in formatting. If you have lots of HTML code formatted just the way you like it, this is the option for you.

As you edit pages with Source Code Preservation in effect, FrontPage does its best to maintain formatting of modified code, and it tries to use comparable styles for inserted code.

■ **Personalized HTML** lets FrontPage reformat your code as before, but provides detailed control over the formatting. If you maintain HTML code that's inconsistently or badly formatted, this option should probably be your choice. It's also a good choice if you prefer entering HTML without regard to format and then letting the computer line up the results.

The HTML Source tab shown in Figure 13-4 provides the means for selecting these options. To display this tab, choose Page Options from the Tools menu, then click the HTML Source tab.

FIGURE 13-4.

The HTML Source tab provides control over the formatting of HTML code edited by FrontPage.

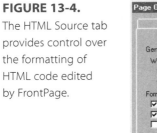

The HTML source tab provides these options:

- **When Saving Files** provides the choice between 100% HTML Source Code Preservation and Personalized HTML.

    - **Preserve Existing HTML** is the option that provides 100% HTML Source Code Preservation.

    - **Reformat Using The Rules Below** provides Personalized HTML.

- **Tag Names Are Lowercase,** if turned on, tells FrontPage to use lowercase letters for the names of HTML tags. Example: <p> and </p> rather than <P> and </P>.

- **Attribute Names Are Lowercase,** if turned on, tells FrontPage to use lowercase letters for HTML attributes. Example: src="trans5x5.gif" rather than SRC="trans5x5.gif"

- **Allow Line Breaks Within Tags,** if turned on, means FrontPage can start writing HTML on a new line even though it's in the middle of a tag. If turned off, FrontPage won't split tags onto multiple lines, regardless of how long the tag becomes.

FrontPage will insert line breaks only where white space is valid.

■ **Indent** specifies to what extent FrontPage will indent tags flagged (as described shortly) Indent Contents. The measurement consists of an amount and a unit of measure (spaces or tabs).

> **NOTE**
>
> For readability, experienced HTML coders usually indent complex, multi-line structures such as tables and lists. All <TR> (table row) tags, for example, might begin on a new line, indented two more spaces than their parent <TABLE> tag. <TD> (table detail) tags might also start on a new line, indented two spaces more than their preceding <TR> tags. This produces an indented code listing that's easy to read.

■ **Right Margin** specifies the maximum number of characters on a line of HTML. FrontPage will insert a line break rather than create lines longer than this setting.

■ **Tags** is a list box with an entry for each valid HTML tag. FrontPage remembers the following settings on a tag-by-tag basis.

  • **Line Breaks** specifies when FrontPage should insert line breaks before and after the start and end of a tag. Table 13-1 lists and describes these settings.

  • **Omit Start Tag,** if turned on, tells FrontPage to suppress an element's starting tag. This is valid for only a few tags, such as <HTML>.

  • **Omit End Tag,** if turned on, tells FrontPage to suppress an element's ending tag. This pertains to certain tags, like <P> (paragraph), whose ending tags are optional.

  • **Indent Contents,** if turned on, tells FrontPage to indent each occurrence of this tag relative to its parent. The Indent properties described above specify the amount of indentation.

■ **Base On Current Page** instructs FrontPage to analyze the current page, determine its formatting styles, and set all the Formatting fields on the HTML Source tab accordingly.

■ **Reset** restores all Formatting settings to their original values.

TABLE 13-1. Automatic Line-Break Settings

Setting	Description	Example
Before Start	The number of line breaks to insert before an element's starting tag.	Before <TABLE>
After Start	The number of line breaks to insert after an element's starting tag.	After <TABLE>
Before End	The number of line breaks to insert before an element's ending tag.	Before </TABLE>
After End	The number of line breaks to insert after an element's ending tag.	After </TABLE>

Working with Script Code

In the most general sense, a script is a set of instructions that describes how certain entities are to interact. The script for a stage play, for example, describes in some detail what the actors say, how they should interact, and when they enter and exit the scenes. In a computer sense, scripts are lines of high-level programming code that control the communication, interaction, loading, and termination of software components.

Scripts in Web pages are an extremely useful addition to the Web. Special HTML tags mark blocks of text as script code, specify the script language used in that block, and control whether the script runs on the server or within the browser. The server looks for server-side script code while transmitting Web pages; correspondingly, the browser watches for browser-side scripts as it receives pages. In either case, the server or browser examines and compiles the code immediately.

Various computer languages have come into use for scripting: awk, sed, Perl, REXX, VBScript, and JavaScript are a few examples. These languages are more general than macro languages tied to a specific program, yet less formal than large-scale development languages such as C and Pascal. Because most scripts are short bits of code connecting other objects and methods, programmers generally view great rigor in a script language as excess baggage. Instead, "quick" and "dirty" are the watchwords.

Code that runs during Web-page transmission can insert HTML at the location that triggers the script. This makes any aspect of the page programmable; indeed, you could create a Web page that consisted of a script only. Such a script would need to write all the HTML required to display what you wanted the Web visitor to see. More common, however, is to author the static (unchanging) parts of the page in an HTML editor such as FrontPage and to code only the variable portions as scripts.

Like programs in most computer languages, scripts can define subroutines. When a browser receives code not within the bounds of a subroutine, it compiles and executes the code immediately. Code declared as a subroutine is compiled immediately but stored for later execution. There are three ways to invoke stored script routines:

- A block of immediate code residing elsewhere in the Web page can call the routine.

- Code in one stored routine can call another.

- Stored routines can respond to events such as the window loading, a particular form element gaining or losing the input focus, or the Web visitor clicking a push button.

Scripts have access to a variety of built-in objects belonging to the browser: the current window, the current URL, and HTML objects such as form elements, hyperlinks, and images. Each of these objects has an assortment of properties, some of which the script can modify.

Scripts, Scripts, and CGI Scripts...

Script languages have been used for server-side programming since the earliest days of the Web. A URL specified the name of the script and the server launched it. The script retrieved any HTML form values from the tail of the URL or from form elements, performed any required processing, and wrote a complete HTML stream for transmission to the remote user. This is how common gateway interface (CGI) and Internet Server Application Programming Interface (ISAPI) work. CGI programs in particular are so often written in script languages such as Perl that many programmers and administrators use the term scripts for all CGI and ISAPI programs, even if they're written in C, C++, or some other formal programming language.

CGI and ISAPI scripts aren't the subject of this section. The scripts discussed here are HTML scripts—scripts whose source code is stored line-by-line within a Web page's HTML and executed directly from that location.

Developers place script statements within <SCRIPT> and </SCRIPT> tags in the HTML. Script statements are executed as the browser loads the page, and they may write data into the browser's input stream. The following statement, for example, writes the page's Last-Modified value into the browser window as if the data had come directly from the HTTP server:

```
document.write(document.lastModified)
```

If the browser finds a subroutine defined within <SCRIPT> and </SCRIPT> tags, the browser stores it for future use. Code found later in the page can then execute the routine.

Events on the page can also trigger script code. There's an *onClick* event, for example, that occurs when the Web visitor clicks a button. If the Web page creator supplied code for that event, the code executes whenever the visitor clicks that button.

The use of "under construction" phrases and icons on the World Wide Web has become an almost comical cliché; in reality, everything on the Web changes *constantly* or quickly becomes obsolete. Inevitably, making all these changes becomes tiresome, so savvy page creators, wearing their construction hard hats, search for ways to automate the work. Script languages meet this need.

Script languages can also provide a customized display for each visitor. Scripts can respond to database results or to a variety of environmental factors, effectively working as self-modifying HTML. They can also provide a measure of interactivity for the remote user without the delay of sending data back to the server and waiting for a response.

Interesting (or not) as the above introduction may be, this book is about creating Web pages with FrontPage and not about the details and nuances of writing scripts. To gain true proficiency in writing scripts, you should obtain one or more books dedicated to that subject alone. FrontPage does have the capability to create certain kinds of scripts without programming, however, and to store script code within Script components in FrontPage. The remainder of this section will discuss these facilities.

Script Languages

A full explanation of script language programming is beyond the scope of this book. Still, the increasing use of such languages makes FrontPage's support of them a critical feature.

Hiding Scripts from Older Browsers

Browsers that don't support scripting easily ignore <SCRIPT> and </SCRIPT> tags, but what of the code between them? An older browser can easily ignore unknown tags, but has no reason to ignore content between unknown opening and closing tags. In the case of <SCRIPT> tags, the old browser will generally try to interpret the script code as HTML, and this can get ugly fast.

To prevent this, experienced coders often enclose script code in HTML comments as shown below.

```
<SCRIPT>

<!--

alert("Your message could appear here.");

//-->

</SCRIPT>
```

The <!-- and --> tags mark the beginning and end of an HTML comment. Script languages successfully ignore the opening <!-- tag, but the closing --> tag presents a problem: a double minus sign is a valid JavaScript operator. Prefixing the closing tag with // marks it as a JavaScript comment as well as an HTML comment.

FrontPage can process JavaScript and VBScript code from three sources.

- User-written code
- Code written by a FrontPage Wizard
- Code written by FrontPage to validate form fields

There are two script languages commonly used on Web pages.

- **JavaScript** is the invention of Netscape Communications and first appeared in Netscape Navigator. Originally called LiveScript, this language has little in common with the Java programming language except that both bear a general resemblance to C++.

  JavaScript runs under both Netscape Navigator and Microsoft Internet Explorer, subject to slight implementation differences.

- **VBScript** is the invention of Microsoft and first appeared in Internet Explorer. VBScript is a subset of Microsoft Visual Basic for Applications, which is a subset of the Visual Basic retail product. Curiously, VBScript has no visual aspect of its own; instead, it runs within the visual interface of the application that invokes it.

VBScript runs under the Internet Explorer browser and, on the server side, under Microsoft Internet Information Server or Microsoft Personal Web Server. Because of differences in their environments, objects, methods, and events on the server differ from those on the browser.

JavaScript

Netscape Communications invented JavaScript to provide browser-side scripting for its popular Navigator browser. The language was originally named LiveScript, but Netscape renamed it when the company adopted Sun Microsystem's Java language for use in components. JavaScript and Java both resemble C++ but otherwise have little in common.

> **NOTE**
>
> Other names for JavaScript include ECMAscript and JScript. ECMA is the European Computer Manufacturer's Association, the standards body that holds the official language specification. JScript is Microsoft's official name for its implementation of JavaScript.

Browser Support for Scripts—or Not

Support for browser scripts varies widely. Some browsers support no scripting at all, some support only JavaScript, and some support both JavaScript and VBScript. In addition, the level of support varies with the browser version. Even among browsers that do support scripting, most provide a way for Web visitors to turn it off.

If you decide to use scripting on a Web page, be sure to:

- Test the script with all common browsers.

- Note (perhaps at the bottom of the page) the minimum browser version the visitor should have.

- Provide a way for visitors to navigate your site even if they lack script support.

Figure 13-5 shows FrontPage editing some JavaScript in a Web page. The script appears between the <SCRIPT> and </SCRIPT> tags. The *document.write* method writes data into the Web page as if it had come from the server. The expression document.lastModified supplies the Web page's date and time stamp—the date recorded in the Web server's file system.

FIGURE 13-5.

FrontPage can insert JavaScript or VBScript into Web pages. This script displays the date the page was last updated.

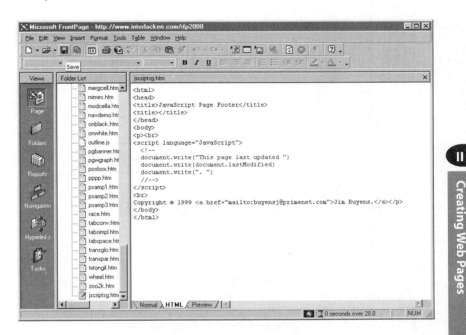

FrontPage does nothing with such code after inserting it; if you switch back to WYSIWYG view, FrontPage merely displays a J icon where the code resides. FrontPage doesn't verify the code for correctness or try to execute it. To see the code run, switch to Preview mode or open the page with a browser.

The JavaScript language tends to be a work in progress; various bugs and limitations appear and disappear with every browser version. Be sure to test your scripts under all recent versions of each browser you care about. As long as JavaScript remains the only script language available on both Netscape Navigator and Internet Explorer, it will probably remain the preferred language for populations of mixed browsers.

VBScript

The VBScript language serves all the same purposes and objects as JavaScript, but is based on Microsoft Visual Basic Scripting Edition. VBScript lacks many familiar Visual Basic features such as a GUI development environment, GUI run-time displays, file input and output, and the ability to call system services. However, its syntax is very familiar to thousands of Visual Basic developers, and it interfaces very well with ActiveX controls.

On the browser, VBScript provides roughly the same capabilities as JavaScript. However, as of version 4, Internet Explorer is the only browser to support it. This severely limits the usefulness of browser-side VBScript in environments where Netscape Navigator is common. Internet Information Server, however, provides server-side support for VBScript. Although scripts running on the server can't interact directly with the remote user, they produce "plain vanilla" HTML as output and thus operate the same with any browser. They can also interact with server-side components and with such services as database systems.

Browser-Side Scripting

All modern browsers have features for running program code that arrives nestled inside Web pages. Such code may customize the page based on the date, the type of browser, or other factors. In addition, it can respond to events—like button clicks—that occur after the page is loaded. These features can significantly enhance your Web pages.

Generating Browser Scripts

The section "Validating Form Input" in Chapter 10, has already described one method of generating browser scripts. Establishing validation rules for form elements generates script routines the browser runs when the Web visitor clicks the form's Submit button. If the script detects no form element fields having values outside the prescribed range, it submits the form normally. If the script detects an incorrect value, it displays an error message to the visitor and submits nothing.

Coding Example 1: Displaying Current Information

Figure 13-5 showed a script that obtains and displays real-time information each time a Web visitor loads a page. Figure 13-6 shows the same page in Preview mode.

> **NOTE**
>
> Preview mode displays the current Web page using whatever version of Internet Explorer is installed on your system.

FIGURE 13-6.

Here, in Preview mode, FrontPage runs the script shown in Figure 13-5.

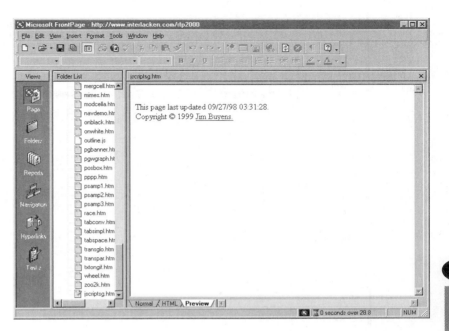

The Web page fragment in Figure 13-6 is suitable for inclusion at the bottom of many different pages, a job made easy by the Include Page component. Of course, the information available to a script isn't limited to Date Last Modified; Figure 13-7 shows a Web page displaying a selection of more useful information.

Each property value displayed in Figure 13-7 comes from a one-line script such as the following:

```
<script>document.write(document.title)</script>
```

As proven by Figure 13-8, there are eight scripts in all: one to display each property. Each J icon represents a <script></script> tag pair.

Of course, scripts aren't limited to just writing static values into the HTML stream. They can define variables, make comparisons, branch, manipulate text, perform arithmetic, run subroutines, and all the other things that programming languages do. They aren't limited to writing simple values into table cells, either; they can write any sort of HTML they wish, and the browser will interpret it just as if the HTML had arrived from the server. You could even check the date, the browser version, or any other value and create different HTML accordingly. It boggles the mind.

FIGURE 13-7.

Scripts written in Java-Script obtain and display all the information in the center row of this HTML table.

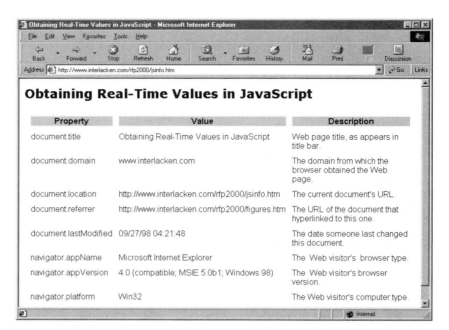

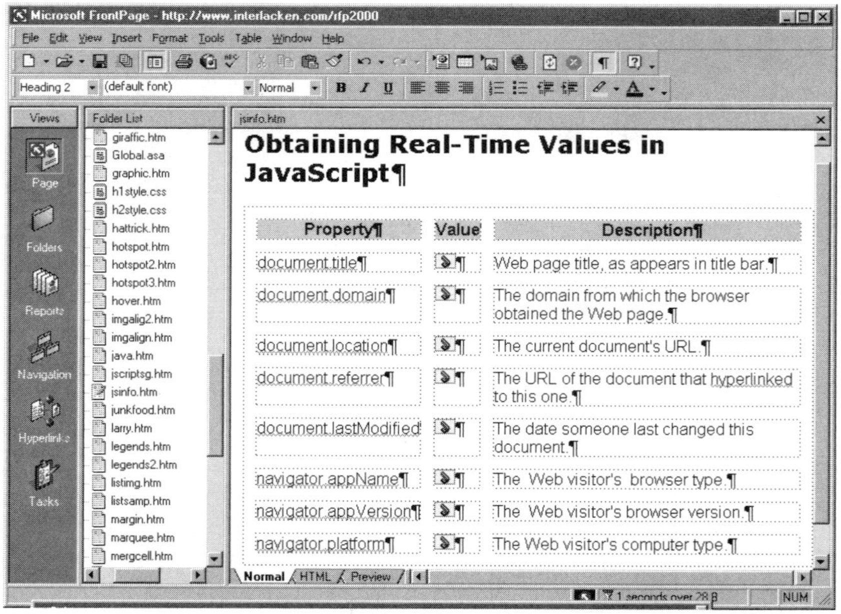

FIGURE 13-8.

Each property value displayed in Figure 13-7 comes from its own script, and each script shows up in WYSIWYG view as a J icon in the Value column.

If a script can create customized HTML as the Web page loads, you may wonder if a script can change a Web page already on display: add, modify, or remove things like text, images, hyperlinks, and table cells, for example. The answer is yes, and this is what Dynamic HTML is all about. The catch is that Dynamic HTML first showed up in Netscape Navigator 4 and Internet Explorer 4, and the two implementations are quite different. This, plus the inherent complexity of the task, can make DHTML programming a daunting task.

Double-clicking J icons like those in Figure 13-8 displays the prompt shown in Figure 13-9. If you click Yes, FrontPage will start another program called Microsoft Script Editor and load your Web page into it. If you click No, FrontPage displays your page in HTML view.

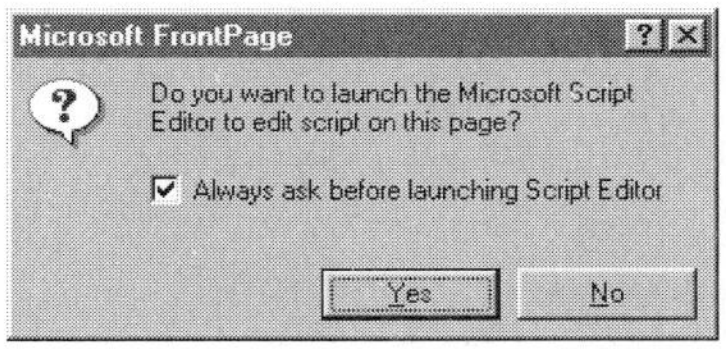

FIGURE 13-9.

This prompt offers to start Microsoft Script Editor, a specialized editor for working with program code.

A section later in this chapter discusses Microsoft Script Editor in some detail. Hold on to your seat, because this is basically the same editor professional programmers use to develop applications in C++ or Java. For now, however, we'll edit script code by switching to HTML view or by answering No to the prompt just above.

Coding Example 2: Changing Content

This example performs some simple comparisons and produces different HTML as a result. It flags items with:

- A New! or Upd! (updated) icon if they're less than 14 days old.

- A graphic bullet if they're more than 14 days old.

Figure 13-10 shows the Web page displayed by a browser, while Figure 13-11 shows it open in FrontPage.

The Script component at the top of Figure 13-11 defines a function named newicon(). This function accepts two arguments named *effDate* and *act*. The *effDate* argument accepts the effective date of the listed item.

The *act* argument accepts an action code—"a" for added items and "u" for updated ones. The function then creates two date objects and computes their difference. The date object named *today* contains the current date and the one named *added* contains the date received in *effDate*.

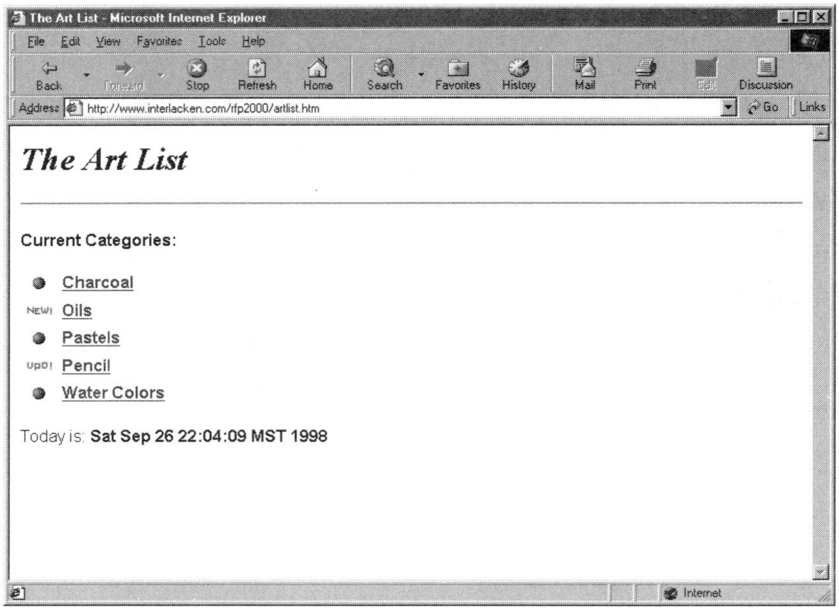

FIGURE 13-10.
JavaScript programming in this page's HTML displays a New! or Upd! (updated) icon for items less than 14 days old, but displays a graphical bullet for items that are older.

JavaScript dates are actually very large integers that count time in milliseconds. Subtracting two dates therefore produces a difference in milliseconds. To convert milliseconds to days, the script divides the number by 24 * 60 * 60 * 1000 (24 hours times 60 minutes per hour times 60 seconds per minute times 1,000 milliseconds per second). The script saves the result in days to the variable named *days*.

- If the variable *days* is less than 14 and *act* is "u," the script writes the characters <IMG SRC=images/upd.gif HEIGHT=11 WIDTH=28 BORDER=0> into the HTML stream as if they had come from the server. This is the function of the document.write statement. The characters shown constitute an HTML image tag.

- If the variable *days* is less than 14 and *act* isn't "u," the script writes an image tag for the new.gif icon.

- If the variable *days* isn't less than 14, the script writes an image tag for cyanball.gif.

The table cell preceding each menu choice contains another Script component, the first of which appears at the bottom of Figure 13-11. These scripts are one line each, as in

```
newicon("Aug 31, 1999", "a")
```

This statement runs the *newicon* routine with Aug 31, 1999, as *effDate* and "a" as *act*. The appropriate icon will appear in place of each such JavaScript statement when the browser displays the Web page.

The last Script component on the page displays the current date. It consists of the following two statements, which use concepts explained earlier in this section.

```
today = new Date();
document.write (today);
```

Function to compare date
and display correct icon

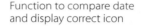

FIGURE 13-11.

Here's the Web page shown in Figure 13-10 as it appears in Front-Page's HTML view.

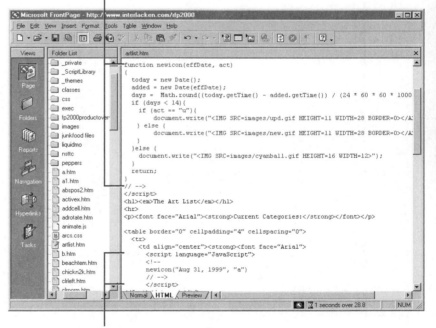

Call function with item's
effective date and type of update

Creating Web Pages

Coding Example 3: Responding to Events

Figure 13-12 shows a simple Web page that responds to events. The Web visitor selects one of the radio buttons and then clicks the Jump button to display the corresponding Web page.

> **NOTE**
>
> What Microsoft calls option buttons, the World Wide Web Consortium calls radio buttons.

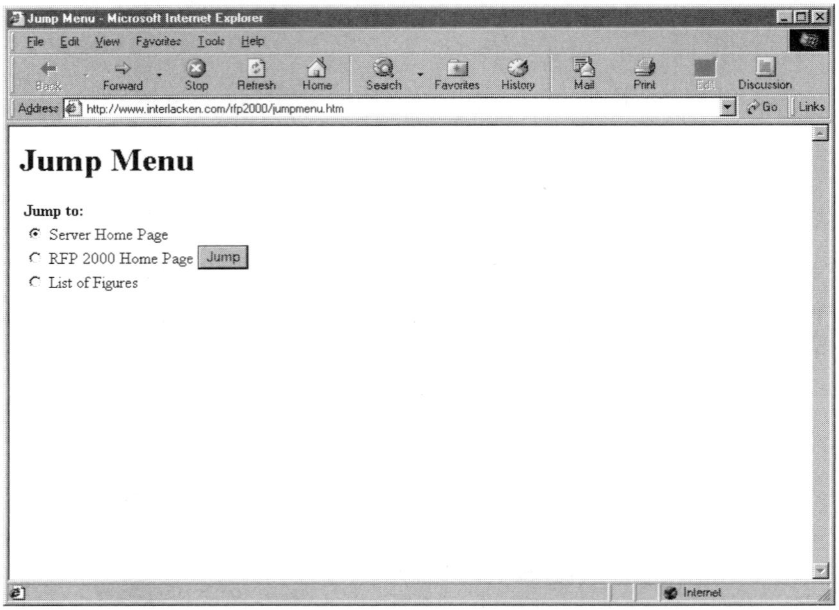

FIGURE 13-12.

Clicking this Jump button runs a script that creates a hyperlink to the specified Web page.

An odd JavaScript problem arises with radio buttons and drop-down lists: their values aren't available to browser-side scripts. You can access the value of a text box with the expression

```
text1.value
```

where text1 is the name of a text box. But you can't access the value of a radio button or drop-down list the same way; the expressions are valid, though the values are always blank.

For this reason, scripts can't directly read the value of a radio-button group. Instead the script must initialize some type of variable when the page loads, and then update that variable whenever the Web visitor clicks a radio button. This provides a usable value in all cases.

Figure 13-13 shows the Web page of Figure 13-12 open in FrontPage. The script near the top of the main window is in the head section. This is possible because the script has nothing to display, and in fact, it's desirable because it ensures the script runs before the body of the Web page loads. The line of code

```
nexturl = "/";
```

initializes the *nexturl* variable to "/". This is the same value assigned to *nexturl* when the Web visitor clicks the first (and default) radio button.

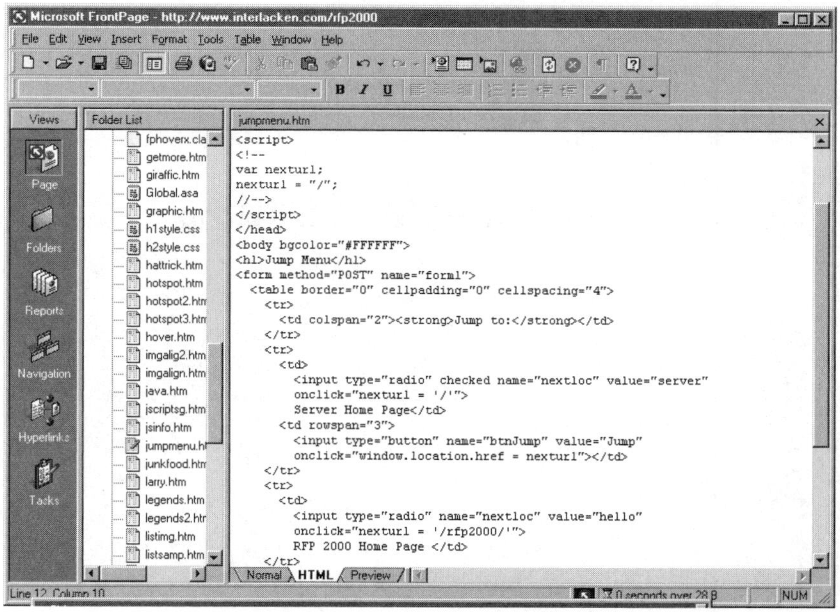

FIGURE 13-13.

Front Page Editor displays the Web page shown in Figure 13-12.

The HTML code for this button appears below.

```
<input type="radio" checked name="nextloc"
       value="server"
       onclick="nexturl = '/'">
```

Note the onClick attribute in line three. This tells the browser that every time the Web visitor clicks this button, the browser should run the JavaScript statement:

```
nexturl = '/'
```

Similar onClick attributes appear for the remaining two buttons, each, of course, assigning a different value to *nexturl*. The button's HTML contains an onClick attribute as well, but it specifies a different type of action. Here's the button's HTML:

```
<input type="button" name="btnJump" value="Jump"
       onclick="window.location.href = nexturl">
```

When the visitor clicks the Jump button, the browser sets its *window.location.href* value to the value saved in *nexturl*. This makes the browser load the relevant Web page.

Internet Explorer 4 recognizes a wide variety of events, and you can code them on any HTML tag. Netscape Navigator 4 recognizes fewer events, and only for hyperlinks and form elements. Hopefully, complications caused by these differences will decrease over time. In the meantime, exercise care and be sure to test with every browser you're concerned about.

Server-Side Scripting

The advantage of browser-side scripting is that it requires no special services or features on the Web server. The server delivers the script statements as part of the HTML with no special handling. The primary disadvantages are the uneven level of support among various browsers and the fact that no server-side resources are available.

Note also that in the previous section's second example, the date that determines the proper icon is the date on the Web visitor's computer. For some applications, lack of control over that date (or other environmental factors) may be a limiting issue. In addition, visitors can turn off browser-side scripting and render the routines useless.

An Introduction to Server-Based Processing

The first server-side components for the Web were CGI programs. CGI stands for common gateway interface. The term *gateway* in this case refers not to a network device, but rather to the fact that CGI programs provide a software gateway between Web pages and other services on the same server.

CGI programs are relatively inefficient. For each execution, the operating system must create an address space, start a process, load the program, run it, and then shut everything down. CGI programs get input data from environment variables, from the command line, and from data piped into standard input. They write HTML to standard output piped into the Web server, and the server transmits this HTML to the originating computer for display. In short, CGI programs greatly resemble MS-DOS command-line programs with console input and output.

Because CGI was the first server-side programming technology, almost all Web servers support it. The most common programming languages used for CGI scripts are Perl and C. In general, CGI programs don't interact with script languages.

⊗ CAUTION

Active Server Pages are available only on Microsoft Web servers. If your Web server uses different software, contact the server's administrator for information on alternative approaches.

To solve performance and flexibility problems of CGI, Microsoft and other developers invented ISAPI—the Internet Server Application Programming Interface. ISAPI programs run as DLLs (dynamic-link libraries), so only one copy needs to be in memory regardless of the number of visitors. ISAPI programs also run in the Web server's address space and therefore avoid the constant startup/shutdown memory overhead of CGI. For these performance reasons, most server-side utilities for Internet Information Server, Microsoft's flagship Web server, are supplied as ISAPI programs.

❓ SEE ALSO

For information about configuring Microsoft Web servers to run scripts see Chapter 16, "Installing and Configuring Your Web Server."

Another early problem with server-side scripting was that it required use of programming languages unfamiliar to many Windows users: languages such as C++ and Perl. Microsoft addressed this problem by developing a way to use VBScript as a server-side scripting language. Pages that use server-side VBScript are called Active Server Pages, and have an ASP file name extension.

If you don't administer your own Web server, you will probably need to contact the server administrator to get permission to run server-side scripts.

When the server gets a request for an ASP Web page, it processes the page, executes the server-side script, and sends only the results to the remote user. The results consist of plain HTML and not the original script statements.

⭐ TIP

There's no restriction against using server-side and browser-side scripts on the same page. The two script types are identified differently in the HTML, allowing the server-side script processor to pass browser-side script statements to the browser unmodified. Server-side scripts can even generate browser-side scripts by writing the necessary statements to the outbound HTML stream.

A third problem with server-side scripting is that running any sort of program on the Web server consumes more resources and involves greater security risks than delivering simple Web pages. For this reason, Web servers refuse to run scripts unless an administrator has specially marked the folder that contains them as *executable*. The administrator then limits updating of such directories to trusted individuals running trusted applications.

II

Creating Web Pages

Example: Changing Content

This section will illustrate a server-side solution to the problem posed in the second example in the previous section—the problem of displaying New! and Upd! icons for a specified period of time. This solution uses VBScript and the Active Server Pages feature of Internet Information Server. The results appear in Figure 13-14.

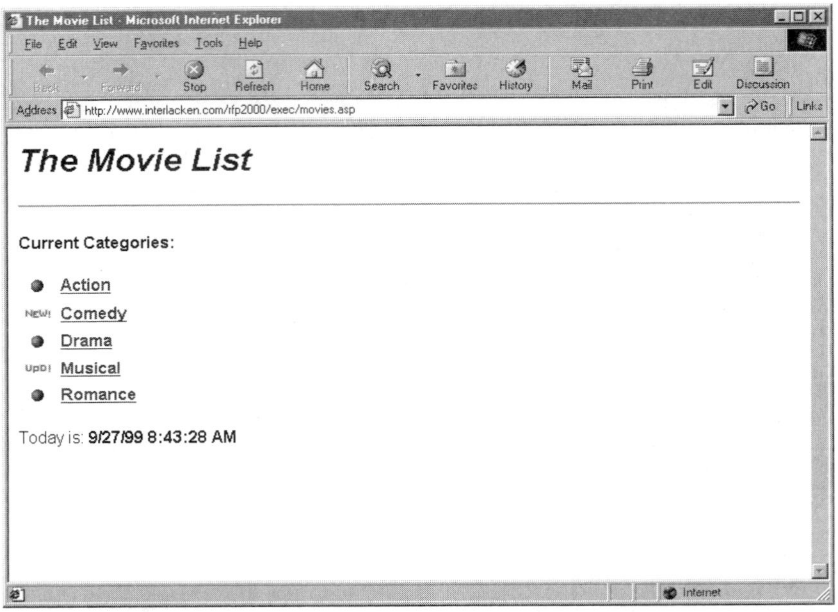

FIGURE 13-14.

This Web page is very similar to that in Figure 13-10 but uses server-side scripting. The file name extension is ASP rather than HTM, and the page resides in an executable directory.

Within the HTML, server-side VBScript statements can be marked either with the tags

```
<SCRIPT LANG=VBSCRIPT RUNON=SERVER> statements </SCRIPT>
```

or with percent sign tags

```
<% statements %>
```

Using the latter form, the code to set the first item's graphic is

```
1 <%maxdays = 14%>
2 <%if (now - #9/19/99# < maxdays) then%>
3   <img src="../images/new.gif">
4 <%else%>
5   <img src="../images/cyanball.gif">
6 <%end if%>
```

Four features of VBScript make this code somewhat simpler than the JavaScript version:

- The *now* function in VBScript returns the current date and time.

- Dates and times in VBScript are stored as whole numbers for days and fractions of a day for time—6:00 AM is 0.25, 12:00 noon is 0.5, and 6:00 PM is 0.75, for example. Subtracting two dates immediately provides the difference in days.

- VBScript directly supports date values. Anything enclosed in pound signs (#) is considered a date.

- VBScript supports a document.write command as JavaScript does, but it also supports HTML code interspersed within if-then-else statements.

Given all this, line 1 in the listing above defines a variable that gives the cutoff period in days: 14. Line 2 subtracts the date 9/19/99 from the current date, giving the difference in days, and then compares the difference to the cutoff period. Line 3 is ordinary HTML that the server transmits to the browser only if the *if* condition is true—that is, only if 9/19/99 is within 14 days of the current date.

Line 4 is an *else* statement that negates the *if* statement on line 2. Line 5 is ordinary HTML that the server transmits to the browser only if the *if* condition on line 2 is false. Line 6 terminates the *if* condition.

The code on lines 2 through 6 can be repeated to generate the bullet for each item in the jump list. Since there's less code to repeat than in the JavaScript example, it isn't so tempting to create a procedure. Not creating a procedure also avoids the complexity of passing the item date and the add-or-update indicator as arguments. The date and icon (New! or Upd!) can simply be hard-coded.

Figure 13-15 shows the Web page of Figure 13-14 open in FrontPage. Line 1 from the listing above resides in the head section and doesn't appear in WYSIWYG view. Each category row begins with three VBScript components containing the *if, else,* and *end if* statements from lines 2, 4, and 6, respectively. Lines 3 and 5 of the listing appear as ordinary HTML, which accounts for the appearance of the graphic bullets.

Figure 13-16 shows the same Web page open in HTML view. You can see the maxdays = 14 statement just before the </head> statement, and two of the *if-else-end if* sequences that control the bullets.

FIGURE 13-15.

The Web page of Figure 13-14 is open in FrontPage, showing the three VBScript components preceding each category item. These contain *if, else,* and *end if* statements so that only one icon appears on display.

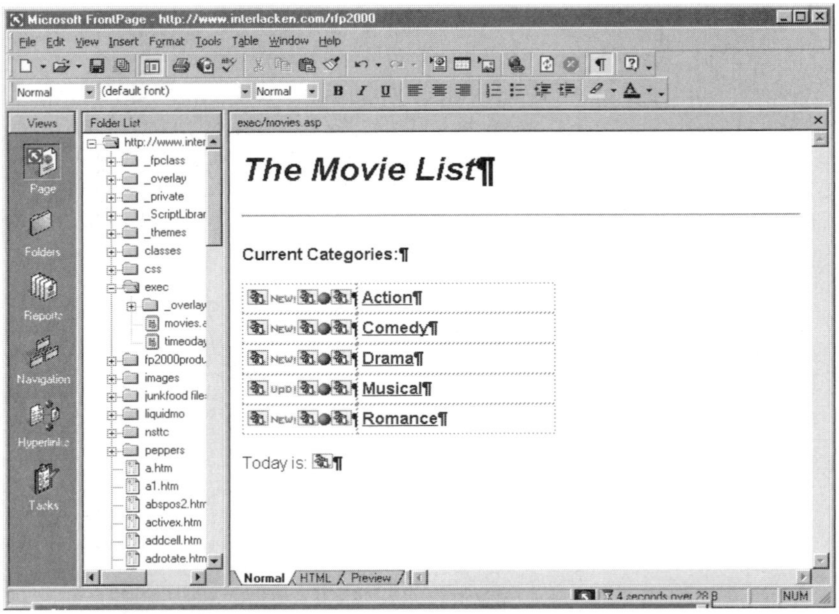

FIGURE 13-16.

Here are the contents of the first VBScript component in row 1, column 1 of the category table in Figure 13-15.

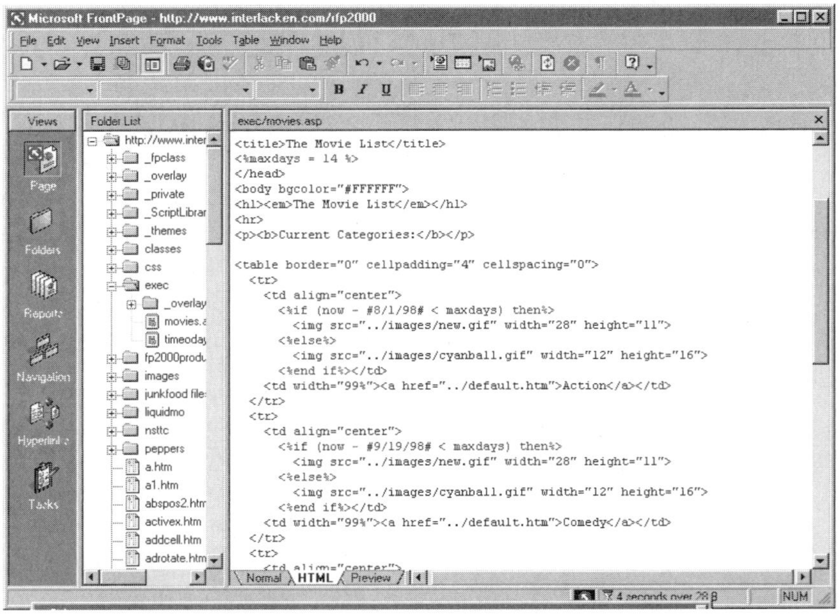

To add additional categories, the Web page author would copy a set of three VBScript components and two icons from an existing row, double-click the first icon to set the date, and change the icon file name to *new.gif* if necessary. To flag a category as updated, the author would change the icon file name to *upd.gif* if necessary and then double-click the first component to reset the date.

The last Script component on the page displays the current date. The code required to do this is quite simple.

```
<% = now %>
```

Within an Active Server Page—a page that contains a server-side script—an equal sign (=) at the beginning of a script line is equivalent to document.write. That is, it evaluates the rest of the line and inserts it into the HTML stream. Type conversion is automatic in VBScript, so <% = now %> converts the current date and time to text and inserts the text into the outgoing Web page.

There are three primary advantages to server-side scripting:

■ Browser compatibility issues are eliminated. There's no worry about whether your script will run on all browsers; you need to verify only that it runs on your server.

■ Server-side resources are available. Although these features are not demonstrated here, server-side scripts can read and write files, query and manipulate databases, and make use of other resources on the Web server.

■ Control is greater. All Web visitors receive information on the same basis—the server's date, for example—and visitors never see script code. Visitors can't turn off the script in their browsers either.

The chief disadvantages of server-side scripting are that your server must support it and your Webmaster must let you use it. Initially, only Micro-soft Internet Information Server for Windows NT Server and Microsoft Personal Web Server supported Active Server Pages. Furthermore, Active Server Pages must reside in an executable directory and, for security reasons, many server administrators tightly control access to such directories.

Using Microsoft Script Editor

In previous versions of FrontPage, opening a Script component produced a simple dialog box that displayed script code in a text box. You could type in code and use the keyboard commands for cut, copy, and paste,

Creating Web Pages

but this was no code editor *extraordinaire*. There was also a Script Wizard that in theory simplified code creation, but that in fact no one could figure out.

In FrontPage 2000, Microsoft has abandoned both these approaches and instead supplied a full-bore, state-of-the-art code editor called Microsoft Script Editor. There are two ways to start Script Editor:

- Open any script icon by double-clicking it, by selecting it and pressing Alt+Enter, or by selecting it and choosing Properties from the Format menu. When the dialog box in Figure 13-9 on page 427 appears, click Yes.

- Choose Macro from the Tools menu, then Microsoft Script Editor (pressing Shift+Alt+F11 is equivalent).

Either method produces the window shown in Figure 13-17.

Expand these icons to view Web page events and objects.

Project explorer window shows files used in current session.

FIGURE 13-17.
This is Microsoft Script Editor, an advanced development environment for Web coding.

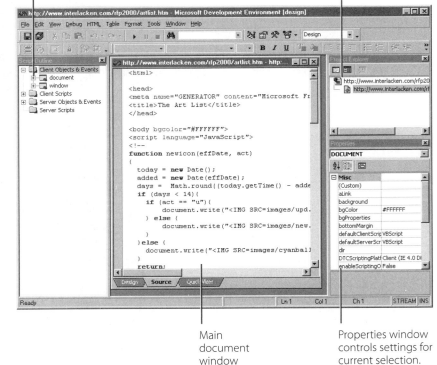

Main document window

Properties window controls settings for current selection.

Script Editor is a power tool for working with Web pages as lines of code. Working with code is probably something you hoped to avoid when you bought FrontPage, so this section will just provide an overview. If you're a coder at heart, a coder in hiding, or in fact any sort of coder at all, this will probably be enough to get you started.

Strictly speaking, Script Editor isn't part of FrontPage; it's a tool developed separately for use in various Microsoft products. Don't be surprised when Script Editor and FrontPage have different ways of doing things.

Main Document Window

The large center area in Figure 13-17 is the main document window. This is where the code for your Web page appears. You can modify the code by typing, by using the Edit menu, by using the normal keyboard shortcuts, and in other ways we'll see later.

Source code in the document window is color coded: tag names are dark red, attribute names are bright red, attribute values are blue, and so forth. You can change the source code color scheme, font, and size after choosing Options from the Tools menu, then Text Editor, then Font And Colors.

Note the three tabs at the bottom of the window. Of these, only two work:

- The **Design** tab displays a graphical design view of the current document, and this is the tab that doesn't work. When Script Editor is bundled with Office applications like FrontPage, it depends on the host application for graphical design view. In other words, use FrontPage, not Script Editor, for WYSIWYG editing.

> **NOTE**
>
> If Script Editor appeals to you and you want the Design tab to work, consider purchasing Microsoft Visual InterDev.

- The **Source** tab displays your HTML code. This is the default view.
- The **Quick View** tab uses Internet Explorer to display your Web page in a preview window.

Project Explorer Window

The Project Explorer shows the files that make up the current Web page. As you might expect, there's usually only one file listed here—your HTML or ASP file. This window appears in the upper-right corner of Figure 13-17.

The Properties window, located just below the Project Explorer, is more interesting. This window displays a property sheet for most Web-page elements you select in the main document window. If no properties are available for a given element, the Properties window applies to the document as a whole.

Properties Window

Figure 13-18 zooms in on the Properties window. There are three views, corresponding to the three toolbar icons: Alphabetic, Categorized, and Property Pages. The box above the toolbar indicates that a <TD> (table detail) tag is selected in the main window. The property list below the toolbar includes only those properties appropriate to the type of tag.

FIGURE 13-18.

The Properties window displays settings appropriate to the item selected in the main Script Editor window. This figure shows the three views corresponding to the three toolbar icons.

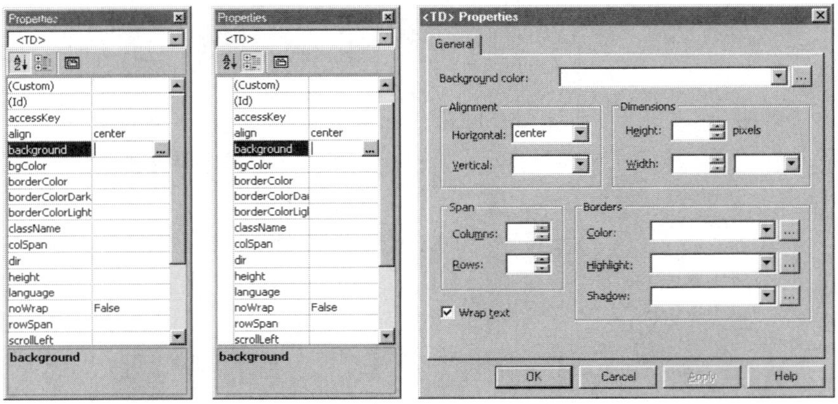

- **Alphabetic** view lists the element's properties in alphabetical order.

- **Categorized** view lists the same properties, but grouped by category. In practice, all Web-page properties fall into the same category—Misc—so that sorting them by category accomplishes nothing.

- **Property Pages** are dialog boxes that provide another view of the same properties. In general, these are not the same dialog boxes FrontPage uses.

To set property values in Alphabetic or Categorized view, first select the property name and then enter the value. You can enter most values by hand, and many by drop-down list or dialog box. If a drop-down list is available, a drop-down button will appear when you select the property name. If a dialog box is available, then an ellipsis button will appear.

Figure 13-19, Figure 13-20, and Figure 13-21 show the three tabs on Script Editor's color dialog box.

FIGURE 13-19.

Within Script Editor's Color Picker dialog box, the Named Values tab selects colors recognizable to browsers by name.

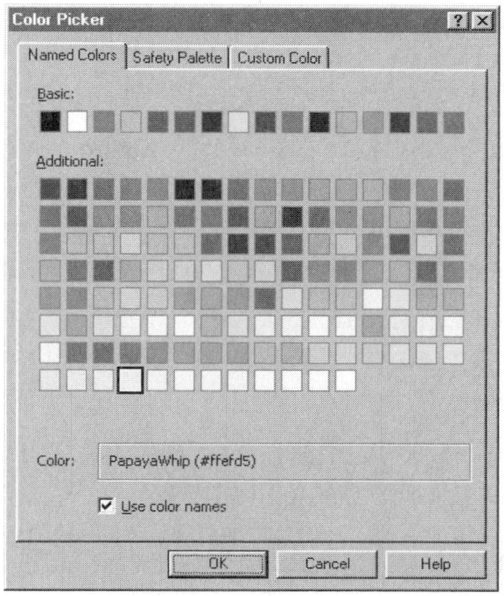

FIGURE 13-20.

The Safety Palette tab selects colors that browsers can display without dithering or substitution on 256-color display systems.

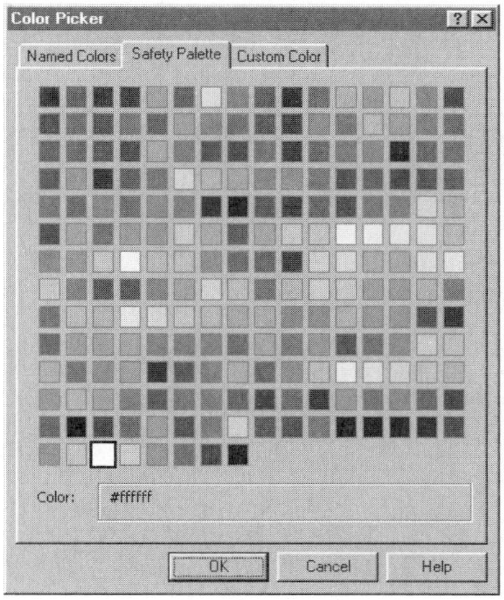

- The Named Colors tab (shown in Figure 13-19) displays the colors most browsers recognize by name. Most browsers recognize bgcolor="PapayaWhip" as equivalent to bgcolor="#FFEFD5" for example. The Named Colors tab shows all colors for which such an equivalence exists.

  The origin of this list of colors seems lost in antiquity. You might think the named colors are better supported in some way than other colors, but if so, you'd be wrong. The Safety Palette colors (also called the Safe Colors) are really the best supported, and very few of those have browser-recognized names.

SEE ALSO

For more information about safe colors, see "Achieving Accurate Rendition—Safe Colors," page 102.

■ The Safety Palette tab shown in Figure 13-20 displays the 216 safe colors first discussed in Chapter 4, "Getting Started with Web Pages." Color arrangement is roughly by hue: blue at the top, then magenta, red, yellow, green, cyan, and back to blue at the bottom.

■ The Custom Color tab appears in Figure 13-21. This is nothing more than another RGB color picker with sliders for the three colors and a preview box.

Unfortunately, Script Editor has no HSB color picker and no way to pick combinations of colors in unison.

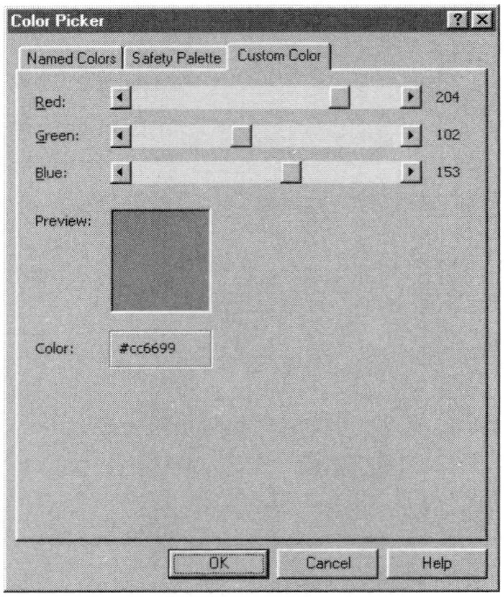

FIGURE 13-21.

The Custom Color tab specifies colors in terms of Red, Green, and Blue components.

Script Outline Window

This window displays a list of all events and scripts in the current Web page. It appears along the left edge of Figure 13-17. There are four collapsible lists.

■ **Client Objects & Events** contains a list of all major objects in the Web page and, subordinately, a list of events and child objects. Double-clicking an event jumps to the existing script routine that handles it, or creates a new, empty one.

- **Client Scripts** contains an entry for each <SCRIPT> tag in the Web page. Opening any of these entries displays a list of functions defined within the scope of that tag, and double-clicking one of those functions displays it in the main document window accordingly.

- **Server Objects & Events** contains a list of objects and events similar to the Client Objects & Events list, but for Active Server Pages.

- **Server Scripts** contains a list of scripts similar to that for Client Scripts. These, however, are Active Server Page scripts.

HTML Outline Window

HTML Outline displays a condensed, structured diagram of the elements in your Web page. When you click an element in the outline, Script Editor highlights and positions its code in the main editing window.

This window doesn't appear by default; to display it, choose Other Windows from the View menu, then Document Outline. As shown in Figure 13-22, the HTML Outline and the Script Outline share the same window. Use the tabs at the bottom to select between them.

FIGURE 13-22.
The HTML Outline window shows the structure of your Web page in terms of HTML elements. Selecting an item in the outline windows positions and selects the corresponding code in the main document window.

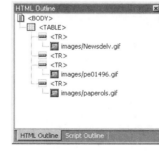

Toolbox Window

The Script Editor toolbox is a source of generic elements you can add to your Web page by dragging. It appears in Figure 13-23. To display the toolbox, choose Toolbox from the View menu.

To add any element in the toolbox to your Web page, drag it from the toolbox to wherever in your HTML the element should appear.

Script Editor's HTML menu offers additional tags you can insert. Set the insertion point where you want the element to appear, then choose the element type from the HTML menu.

Creating Web Pages

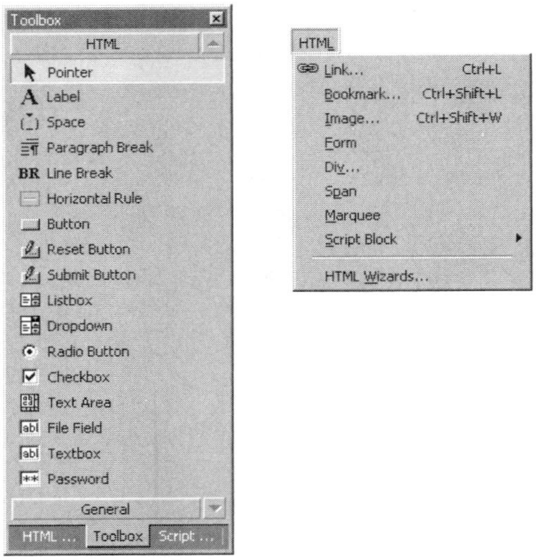

FIGURE 13-23.

The Script Editor tool-box provides a selection of Web-page elements you can drag into your Web page. The HTML menu, pictured at the right, inserts additional types of elements.

Either way, Script Editor will insert only a basic set of tags and attributes. You'll need to fill in attribute values by hand or by using the Properties window.

Editing Script Code

As interesting as all these HTML editing features may be, Script Editor's major strength lies in entering and debugging script code. Figure 13-24 shows an example of code completion, a major advance in code editing.

FIGURE 13-24.

Whenever you type a period after the name of a known object, Script Editor presents a list of valid properties and methods. Here, the developer is choosing the document object's write method.

Code completion kicks in whenever you type a period and the text preceding the period is the name of an object known to Script Editor. Instantly, Script Editor displays a drop-down list of that object's valid properties and methods. If you type additional characters, Script Editor positions the drop-down list accordingly. Pressing the Tab key enters the complete property or method name.

Figure 13-25 shows the same line of code, somewhat further developed. In Figure 13-24 the Web designer chose *write* as the desired method, and in Figure 13-25 the designer will choose the *lastModified* property.

FIGURE 13-25.

This example shows selection of an object property— document.lastModified.

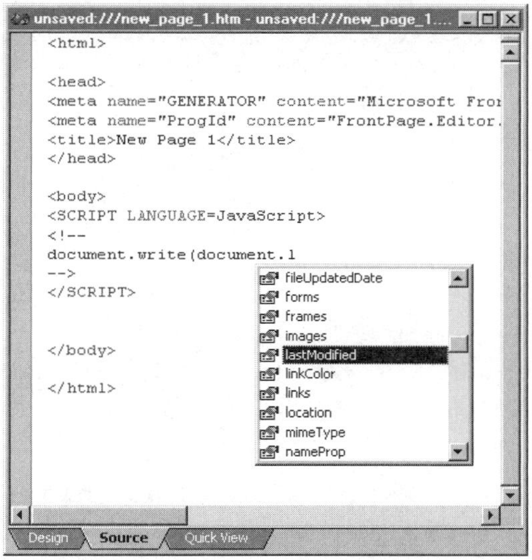

II

Creating Web Pages

Debugging with Script Editor

The most impressive feature Script Editor has to offer is its ability to debug browser scripts and Active Server Pages interactively. This means you can start a script, let it run one line at a time, inspect variables and objects as the script progresses, set breakpoints, and generally poke around while the script is running.

Figure 13-26 shows Script Editor debugging a simple script. The highlight shows the current statement, and the Locals window shows the values of all current local variables (local to the script in the current browser window, that is).

Here's what's happened so far:

1 The Web designer opened the file *pargloop.htm* in Page view.

2 The designer chose Macro from the Tools menu, then chose Microsoft Script Editor.

3 The designer pressed F11 to load the Web page into the browser, execute the first line of script code, and highlight it in the main document window. That line was:

```
Cnt = 1;
```

4 Each time the designer pressed F11, Script Editor executed the next sequential line of code.

FIGURE 13-26.

Here, Script Editor is single-stepping though a browser script written in JavaScript. The highlighted statement is the next to be executed, and the value of Cnt—in the Locals window—shows this is the fifth iteration through the while loop.

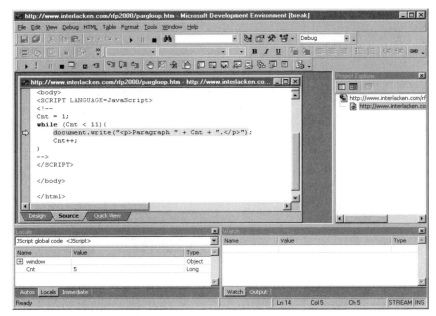

The Locals window shows the values of all current, local variables—that is, of all variables available to the current script procedure. In this case there's only one, Cnt, and its value is 5.

Clicking the Immediate tab (at the bottom of the Locals window) displays the Immediate window. Here you can enter any valid script statement, and Script Editor will execute it—immediately. For example, you could type:

```
Cnt=3;
```

and when you return to the Locals window, the value of Cnt will be 3.

Features like this are great for figuring out why your script is doing what it's doing, or not doing what you think it should. Repeatedly pressing the F11 key quickly becomes boring and mundane, however, especially for long and complex scripts. In such cases, it's usually preferable to press the F5 key, which runs the script continuously, having first set a breakpoint to stop the script where a suspected problem exists.

A breakpoint flags a script statement so that whenever it's about to be executed, execution of the entire script stops. To set a breakpoint, select the statement in Script Editor and then choose Insert Breakpoint from the Debug menu. Script Editor will flag the statement by placing a red dot in the left margin of the document window, and it will halt execution whenever that statement is about to execute. You can flag as many statements as you want as breakpoints.

TIP

> You can also set and remove breakpoints by double-clicking the left margin of the main document window.

To cancel a breakpoint, select the statement and then choose Remove Breakpoint from the Debug menu. To leave the breakpoint defined but ignore it, choose Disable Breakpoint. To cancel all breakpoints, choose Clear All Breakpoints.

Script Editor is a remarkably full-featured and complex application with advanced features not limited to those described here. Describing it completely would require a book this size, with no space left for FrontPage. Hopefully, though, this introduction will be enough to get you started.

Using the Visual Basic Editor

Previous sections have shown how FrontPage 2000 supports both scripts that run on the Web visitor's browser and scripts that run on the Web server. These are great and useful features, but what about scripts that run macros and otherwise control FrontPage?

Like other Office 2000 applications, FrontPage now supports Visual Basic for Applications (VBA). This is a fairly large subset of the full-blown Visual Basic programming environment, complete with capabilities to develop and debug code, display custom dialog boxes, and use both its own properties, methods, and events and those of the host application (FrontPage).

Visual Basic for Applications is a large and full-featured application in its own right, and again, describing it completely in a book this size would leave no room for FrontPage. This section provides only a brief overview.

Figure 13-27 shows the VBA development environment, which you can invoke either by choosing Macro from the Tools menu, then Visual Basic Editor, or by pressing Alt+F11.

FIGURE 13-27.

This is the Visual Basic for Applications (VBA) development environment. VBA adds a macro facility to FrontPage.

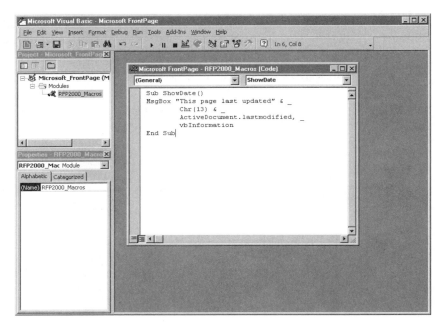

The Project window in the upper-left corner shows the modules, forms, and class modules currently defined to VBA. A module is simply a file containing VBA source code, usually within functions or subroutines. A form is a custom-designed dialog box or window. A class module contains object-oriented code that interacts with other modules through properties, methods, and events.

The Properties window shows the properties of the currently selected object. The RFP2000_Macros module has only one property, its name. Objects like dialog boxes and form elements are considerably more interesting, with dozens of properties.

NOTE

In the context of VBA, forms are Windows dialog boxes, and form elements are controls on those boxes. There is no relevance to HTML forms.

The main document window in Figure 13-27 defines a subroutine named *ShowDate*. The routine contains a single statement, namely:

```
Msgbox "This page last updated" & _
        chr(13) & _
        ActiveDocument.lastmodified, _
        vbInformation
```

The Msgbox command displays a standard Windows message box. The ampersands (&) join strings of text together, and the underscore characters (_) indicate line continuations. The expression ch(13) means ASCII character 13, the carriage return.

The expression *ActiveDocument.lastmodified* obtains information from FrontPage. *ActiveDocument* is a generic object that refers to the document currently open in FrontPage. The *lastmodified* property is the date and time that document was last saved.

The expression vbInformation is a constant built into VBA. It always contains the value required to display an information icon when the message box appears. VBA includes the same sort of code completion features as Script Editor; typing ActiveDocument and a period displays a drop-down list of methods and properties from which you can choose lastmodified. You could locate the vbInformation constant the same way; it appears after you type the comma that precedes it in the code.

To run the macro, return to FrontPage, again choose Macros from the Tools menu, and then choose Macros. The results appear in Figure 13-28. You can also display this dialog box by pressing Alt+F8.

FIGURE 13-28.

This dialog box runs VBA macros within FrontPage.

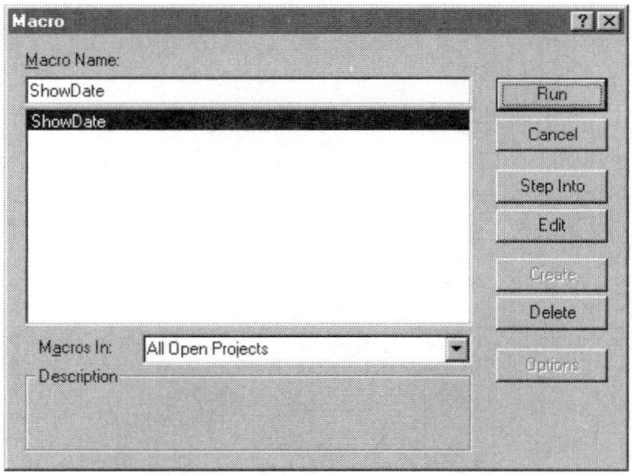

To run a VBA macro, select it in the Macro Name list and then click Run. Figure 13-29 shows the results.

If you use a VBA macro frequently, you may wish to create a menu command or toolbar button that runs it. To learn about doing this, see "Moving and Inserting Commands" on page 454.

FIGURE 13-29.

A VBA macro displayed this informational message, based on information FrontPage supplied programmatically.

In Summary...

Although FrontPage makes great efforts to let you develop Web pages without learning to code, it offers outstanding facilities to work with code should you wish to do so. Working with code is particularly appropriate for writing scripts and other sorts of program code that interacts with your visitors.

The next chapter describes ways that you can customize your copy of FrontPage.

CHAPTER 14

Customizing Your Copy of FrontPage

No two people arrange their living room the same way, and the same is true for software. The more we use a piece of software, the more we want to rearrange and reconfigure it. Fortunately, Microsoft FrontPage has plenty of options in this regard. (I have yet to meet a piece of software that arranges its own living room but who knows; maybe next release.)

This chapter describes how you can customize menus and toolbars, customize overall settings and preferences, and customize the way FrontPage creates your Web pages. FrontPage can customize the way it handles FrontPage Webs as well, but that's covered later in Chapter 19, "Working with FrontPage Webs."

Customizing Menus and Toolbars

 Reorganizing menus and toolbars ranks among the most popular Front-Page customizations. Everyone has their favorite commands they want placed at their fingertips, and just as many shunned commands they never use. FrontPage accommodates these preferences with quite a bit of flexibility.

Positioning Menus and Toolbars

Did you ever notice how some commands are never where you look for them? Unfortunately, everyone's taste in this matter seems to differ, so there's no one configuration that satisfies everyone. The alternative, which FrontPage supports, is to let each Web author rearrange the menus.

To control the toolbars FrontPage displays, choose Toolbars from the View menu. On the resulting submenu, selecting a checked toolbar hides it, and selecting an unchecked toolbar displays it.

> Some toolbars appear only when a suitable object is selected. The Picture toolbar is a case in point.

Like other Office 2000 applications, FrontPage has *dockable* menus and toolbars. This means there are five places you can put any menu or toolbar: the four main window edges and floating.

Undocking a toolbar or menu bar is easy: just grab it with the mouse and drag it away from the edge of the window. You have to grab it where there's no button or menu command, though, and the easiest way to do that is to grab one of its divider bars. Every menu bar or toolbar has at least one divider bar; it's at the far left of the object.

As you drag the bar around, the mouse pointer will take on its usual Move shape. When you drag the mouse pointer near a window edge, the dragging outline snaps into place along that edge. If you drop the bar anywhere else, it floats freely around the screen.

Figure 14-1 shows FrontPage with a very unusual menu and toolbar placement. Each of the four window edges has toolbars along it, the main menu bar is floating, and the DHTML Effects toolbar is also floating. As stated, there's no accounting for taste.

One more thing to notice about Figure 14-1 is that some toolbars are truncated. Along the top of the window, for example, both the Standard and Formatting toolbars are shortened. When this happens, two angle brackets >> appear at the right end of the toolbar's visible portion. Clicking that part of the toolbar displays the additional buttons.

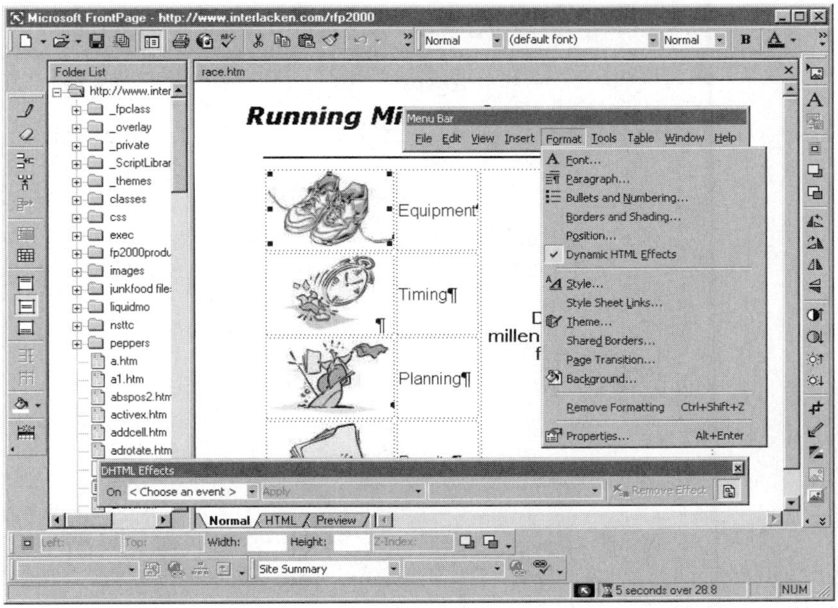

FIGURE 14-1.

This unusual menu and toolbar configuration demonstrates the flexibility of Front-Page's user interface.

Displaying and Creating Toolbars

FrontPage is highly flexible in the way it presents commands; you can add, rearrange, or delete menu options, toolbar buttons, and entire toolbars at will. To begin, choose Customize from the Tools menu. The dialog box shown in Figure 14-2 will result. Note the three tabs labeled Toolbars, Commands, and Options.

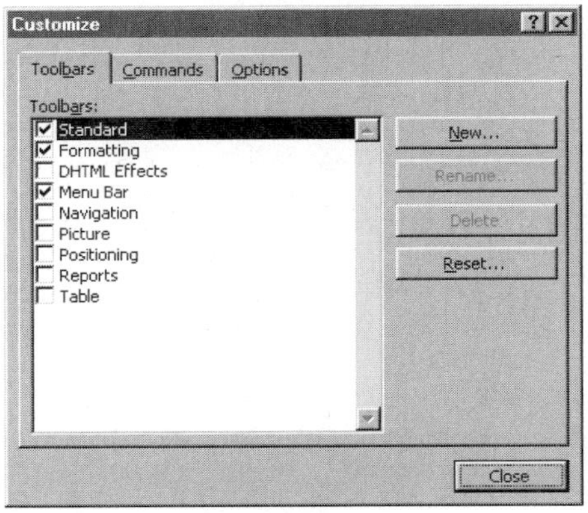

FIGURE 14-2.

The Customize Toolbars tab displays a list of current toolbars, along with check boxes to hide or reveal one. The New, Rename, and Delete buttons apply to custom toolbars only.

A word of caution is warranted here: anytime the Customize dialog box is displayed, other menus and toolbars don't act in the normal way. FrontPage leaves its normal operating mode far behind and enters a sort of drag-and-drop menu rearrangement mode. This is very cool and intuitive once you understand it, but please read the material presented here before you play.

The Toolbars tab displays a listing of currently defined toolbars. Turning the leading check boxes on and off displays or hides each toolbar, respectively. This is perfectly equivalent to choosing Toolbars from the View menu except that, as mentioned, you shouldn't try to use any menus or toolbars when the Customize dialog box is on display.

To create a new toolbar, destined to contain your favorite combination of commands, simply click the New button. FrontPage will prompt you for the new toolbar's name, and then add it to the Toolbars list. The check box will initially be turned on, and the toolbar will be visible, although of course it won't have any buttons yet.

To rename a custom toolbar, select it, and then click the Rename button. To delete a custom toolbar, select it and click the Delete button. These options aren't available for built-in FrontPage toolbars, though.

The Reset button applies only to built-in FrontPage toolbars, and it sets them back to their original, default settings.

Moving and Inserting Commands

Whenever the Customize dialog box is displayed, you can move menu and toolbar commands around at will just by dragging and dropping. If you drag a toolbar icon from one toolbar to another, for example, it'll remain wherever you drop it. The same procedure works for menu options; just drag them wherever you want them to be. To copy a menu choice or toolbar button, hold down the Ctrl key while dragging it. To delete a menu or toolbar option, drop it somewhere no toolbar or menu exists.

> To drag a command onto a menu, you may have to drag it *through* the menu bar command. Holding down the mouse button, first drag the command to the menu bar text and then, continuing to hold down the mouse button, drag downward to open the menu and drop the command.

To add commands from a centralized list, choose the Commands tab and drag from there. The Commands tab appears in Figure 14-3.

FIGURE 14-3.

The Commands tab provides a source of commands you can drag onto menus or toolbars without removing them elsewhere.

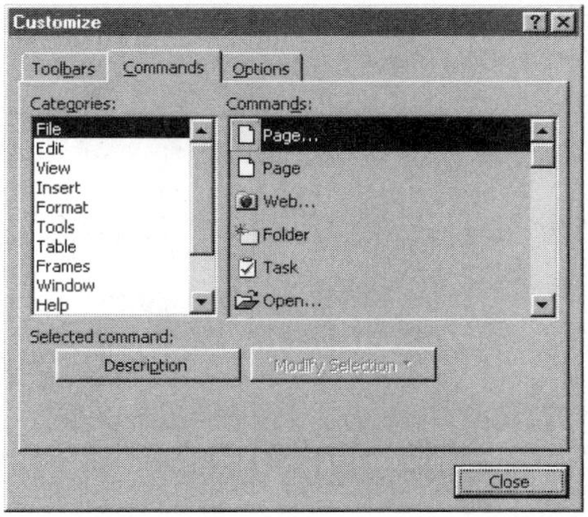

The Categories list controls which group of commands appears in the Commands list to its right. Although the category names are the same as those of the default FrontPage menus, this is only to help you locate commands. Both lists are read-only.

- You *don't* update the actual menus by updating the Customize Commands tab.

- Rearranging the menus *doesn't* rearrange the categories in the Customize Commands tab.

To add a command to a toolbar or menu, locate it in the Commands list, and then drag it to the location you want. For example, here's the procedure to add an Exit icon to the Standard toolbar.

1 Select Customize from the Tools menu.

2 On the Toolbars tab, make sure the check box for Standard is turned on.

3 On the Categories tab, choose File in the Categories list, and then find Exit at the end of the Commands list.

4 Drag the Exit command out of the Commands list, out of the Customize dialog box, and onto the Standard toolbar.

5 Drop the Exit command where you want it to appear on the toolbar.

To drag a command onto a menu, single-click the menu and let it remain displayed just before step 4.

II

Creating Web Pages

To assign a macro as a menu choice:

1 Drop down the desired menu.

2 Choose Macros from the end of the categories list.

3 Drag Custom Menu Item into position on the menu.

To assign a macro to a toolbar:

1 Choose Macros from the end of the categories list.

2 Drag Custom Button into position on the desired toolbar.

In either case, continue by right-clicking the new item, choosing Assign Macro, and then modifying the item as described in the next section.

Modifying Commands

To modify the effect of a menu choice or toolbar button, first right-click it whenever the Customize dialog box is open. This will produce the pop-up menu shown in Figure 14-4.

FIGURE 14-4.

This pop-up menu modifies menu choices and toolbar buttons in Customize mode.

Here's what each menu choice does.

■ **Reset** restores the command to its original settings.

■ **Delete** removes the command from the menu or toolbar.

- **Name** specifies the text that identifies the command. Preceding any letter or number with an ampersand (&) makes that character the Alt hot key. (That is, it designates the underlined character in the menu text.)

- **Copy Button Image** copies the command's current icon to the Clipboard.

- **Paste Button Image** pastes the current Clipboard image, making it the current command's icon.

- **Reset Button Image** restores the command's icon to its original appearance.

- **Edit Button Image** displays the current icon image as a 16x16 array of pixels you can edit.

- **Change Button Image** displays a selection of common icon images. Clicking any of these images makes it the icon for the current command.

- **Default Style** means the icon and command name will appear as configured for the rest of FrontPage.

- **Text Only (Always)** means the command will always appear by name, and never by icon.

- **Text Only (In Menus)** means the command will always appear as text in menus, but possibly as an icon in the case of toolbars. (This means the command may change from text to an icon when you drag it from a menu to a toolbar.)

- **Image And Text** means both the icon and the command name will appear.

- **Begin A Group** means FrontPage should display a dividing bar above the menu choice or before the toolbar button.

SEE ALSO
For information about writing FrontPage macros, see "Using the Visual Basic Editor," page 447.

- **Assign Macro** associates a Visual Basic for Applications (VBA) macro with the toolbar button or menu choice.

Choosing Assign Macro displays the dialog box shown in Figure 14-5. Choose the macro you want to execute, and then click OK.

Creating Web Pages

FIGURE 14-5.

This dialog box associates a VBA macro with a custom menu choice or toolbar button.

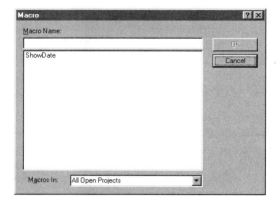

Toolbars, as it turns out, are literally overflowing with pop-up menus. The one pictured in Figure 14-6 appears when you right-click any toolbar, and the Customize dialog box is *not* on display. Turning any check box on or off displays or hides that toolbar, and choosing Customize displays the Customize dialog box just as if you'd chosen Customize from the Tools menu.

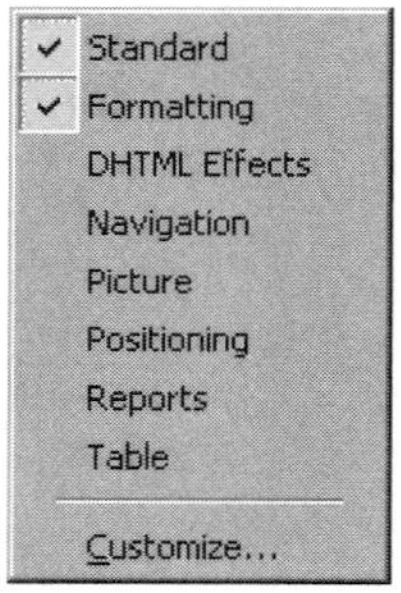

FIGURE 14-6.

This pop-up menu appears when you right-click a toolbar and you're not in Customize mode. The check boxes display and hide toolbars.

The last toolbar menu appears when you click the More Buttons choice at the right of any built-in toolbar, and then choose Add Or Remove Buttons. This produces a display like that of Figure 14-7.

The check boxes in front of each toolbar command control whether or not that command appears on the toolbar. Note, however, that turning off any of these check boxes doesn't delete the command from the toolbar; it merely hides it from display. The Reset Toolbar choice restores the original toolbar setup.

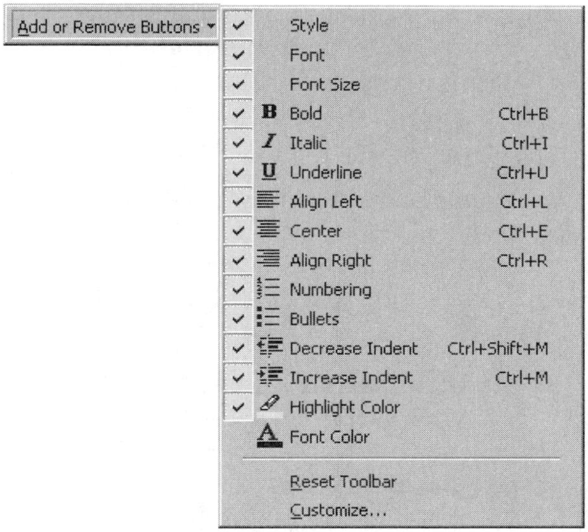

FIGURE 14-7.
This menu appears only for toolbars built into FrontPage. The check boxes hide or reveal toolbar commands without actually deleting or adding them.

Add or Remove Buttons ▾	✓	Style
	✓	Font
	✓	Font Size
	✓ **B**	Bold	Ctrl+B
	✓ *I*	Italic	Ctrl+I
	✓ <u>U</u>	Underline	Ctrl+U
	✓	Align Left	Ctrl+L
	✓	Center	Ctrl+E
	✓	Align Right	Ctrl+R
	✓	Numbering
	✓	Bullets
	✓	Decrease Indent	Ctrl+Shift+M
	✓	Increase Indent	Ctrl+M
	✓	Highlight Color
		Font Color
		Reset Toolbar
		Customize...

Customizing Additional User Interface Options

The third and final tab on the Customize dialog box controls various high-level options related to the FrontPage user interface. To display this dialog box, choose Customize from the Tools menu, and then click the Options tab. The same dialog box appears in Figure 14-8.

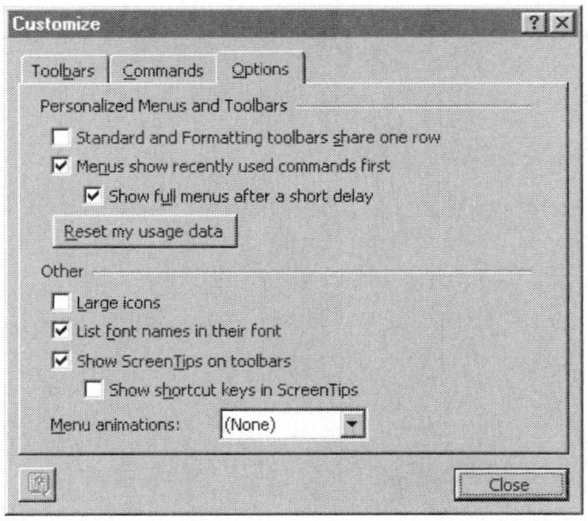

FIGURE 14-8.
These options control overall aspects of the FrontPage interface.

Customize ? X

Toolbars | Commands | Options

Personalized Menus and Toolbars
☐ Standard and Formatting toolbars share one row
☑ Menus show recently used commands first
☑ Show full menus after a short delay
[Reset my usage data]

Other
☐ Large icons
☑ List font names in their font
☑ Show ScreenTips on toolbars
☐ Show shortcut keys in ScreenTips
Menu animations: (None) ▾

[Close]

II

Creating Web Pages

- **Standard And Formatting Toolbars Share One Row.** Check this box if you want the Standard and Formatting toolbars displayed next to each other in a single row. This saves screen space at the expense of not showing the entire toolbar. To access the truncated part of any toolbar, click the >> icon at its right.

- **Menus Show Recently Used Commands First.** Check this box if you want Office 2000 Personalized Menus in effect. This feature counts how often you use each menu choice and then, after building up a history, displays menu choices in order from most used to least used.

- **Show Full Menus After A Short Delay.** Choose this option if you want menus to appear in two phases. The first phase displays only the most commonly used choices. The second phase takes effect after you wait a few seconds or click the bottom of the menu, and it displays all the menu choices. For an example, refer to Figure 14-9.

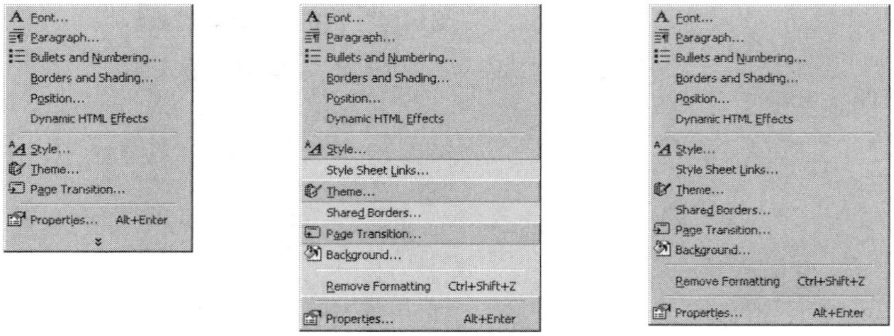

FIGURE 14-9.
FrontPage can optionally display menu choices in two phases: first, with only the most frequently used command, and then with all commands. It can also revert to traditional, single-menu mode.

- The leftmost menu illustrates phase one with Show Full Menus After A Short Delay in effect.

- The center menu shows phase two, which appears after you wait a few seconds or click the down arrows at the bottom of the menu. The less-used choices now appear.

- The rightmost menu doesn't have Show Full Menus After A Short Delay in effect. In short, it's the ordinary type of menu you've been using since the start of Windows.

- **Reset My Usage Data.** Click this button to erase the counts of how often you use each menu choice. This resets menus to their original appearance.

■ **Large Icons.** Check this box to display toolbar icons at twice their normal size. This may be desirable if you have a very high screen resolution, if you're visually impaired, or if you just like big icons.

■ **List Font Names In Their Font.** Check this box if you want the Font selector on the Formatting toolbar to display each font name in its own font. This means the font name Arial will appear in Arial, the font name Courier New will appear in Courier New, and so forth. (Symbol fonts are an exception; for these, FrontPage displays the font name in ordinary type and then shows the symbols corresponding to the first few characters in the alphabet.)

■ **Show ScreenTips On Toolbars.** Check this box if you want ScreenTips (little yellow boxes of text) to appear whenever the mouse pointer hovers over a toolbar button for more than a few seconds. This is very useful when you're unsure about the function of a given button. Resting the mouse pointer over the button displays a description.

■ **Show Shortcut Keys In ScreenTips.** Check this box if, when a toolbar ScreenTip appears, you want it to include the button's keystroke equivalent.

■ **Menu Animations.** Select the way you want pull-down menus to appear.

- **(None).** Choose this option to have menus appear all at once, as they have since the beginning of Windows.

- **Random.** Choose this option if you want menus to appear with a random choice of the next two methods.

  Unfold. Choose this if you want menus to appear with a top-to-bottom motion.

  Slide. Choose this if you want menus to appear from the upper-left corner and grow toward the lower right.

Customizing Program Options

The Options choice on the Tools menu controls the global operation of FrontPage on your computer. The three tabs on the Options dialog box are General, Configure Editor, and Reports View.

II

Creating Web Pages

Controlling General Options

Figure 14-10 displays the General tab.

The General tab contains the following options, which you can set by turning each box on or off:

- **Open Last Web Automatically When FrontPage Starts.** If this option is turned on, starting FrontPage will open the Web that was open when you last closed FrontPage.

- **Check If Office Is The Default Editor For Pages Created In Office.** If this box is on, every time you start FrontPage it will verify that file types belonging to Microsoft Office applications are, in fact, associated with those applications.

- **Check If FrontPage Is The Default Editor For Pages.** Turning on this option tells FrontPage, every time it starts, to verify that it's registered as your standard editor for Web pages.

- **Show Status Bar.** If this box is checked, FrontPage will display a status bar along the lower edge of the FrontPage window. If it's off, the lower edge will be an ordinary window border.

- **Warn When Included Components Are Out Of Date.** If this option is turned on, FrontPage will inform you if any included components are out-of-date. If an out-of-date condition occurs, use the Recalculate Hyperlinks command from the Tools menu of FrontPage.

- **Warn When Text Index Is Out Of Date.** If this option is turned on, and you open a Web whose text index is out-of-date, FrontPage will notify you and ask whether to recalculate the index.

- **Warn Before Permanently Applying Themes.** With this option turned on, FrontPage will display an *Are You Sure?* dialog box before permanently applying a theme to a site. Note that applying a theme overwrites existing formatting in your Web pages, with no possibility of Undo.

- **Proxy Settings.** If your network is connected to the Internet (or some other network) through a proxy firewall, click this button to verify your computer's firewall settings.

> **NOTE**
>
> FrontPage uses the same software, and therefore the same proxy settings, that Internet Explorer uses for connecting to the Internet. Therefore, if Internet Explorer can get to the Internet, so can FrontPage and vice versa.

> **NOTE**
>
> A proxy firewall receives HTTP requests from client computers on a local network, satisfies the requests using an outside network, and then sends the responses back to the client computer. This allows *inside* computers to access *outside* resources, but prevents *outside* computers from accessing *inside* resources. Consult your network administrator to determine what settings are required at your site.

Configuring External Editors

You can configure FrontPage to invoke the editor of your choice for any given file type. Doing so minimizes the need to recalculate hyperlinks and, at the same time, builds a more integrated environment. The procedure is as follows:

> **TIP**
>
> If you double-click an image in Page view and get the message, "No picture editor is configured," it's probably because Configure Editors has no editor associated with the image type (GIF or JPG).

1 Choose Options from the Tools menu.

2 Choose the Configure Editors tab to display the dialog box shown in Figure 14-11. The list box shows each currently defined file type and its associated editor.

II

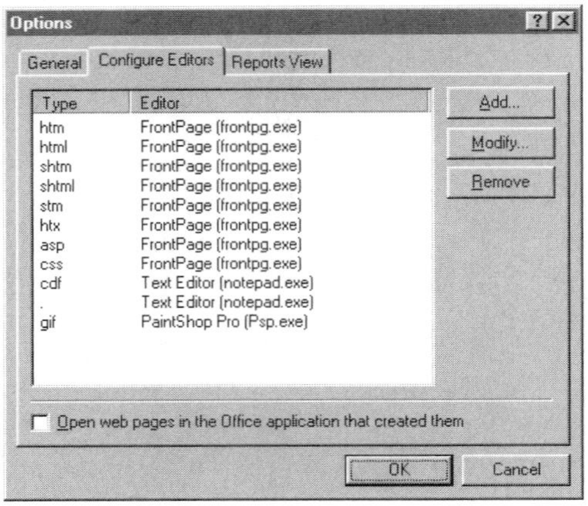

FIGURE 14-11.

FrontPage can associate a different editor with each file name extension.

- **Add** displays a dialog box for adding a file type and its associated editor.

- **Modify** displays a similar dialog box that alters the editor associated with the currently selected file type.

- **Remove** deletes the editor association for the currently selected file type.

Figure 14-12 shows the dialog box for adding an editor association. Use the controls in this window as follows:

- **File Type** specifies the file name extension associated with the editor. There can be only one editor associated with a given file type. You can't, for example, define two GIF entries to give yourself a choice of image editors. See the sidebar "A Bug in the Alphabet Soup?" on page 466.

- **Editor Name** gives the editor's name in words.

- **Command** specifies the name and, if required, the path to the editor's application file, which would normally be an EXE file.

- **Browse** locates the editor's application file.

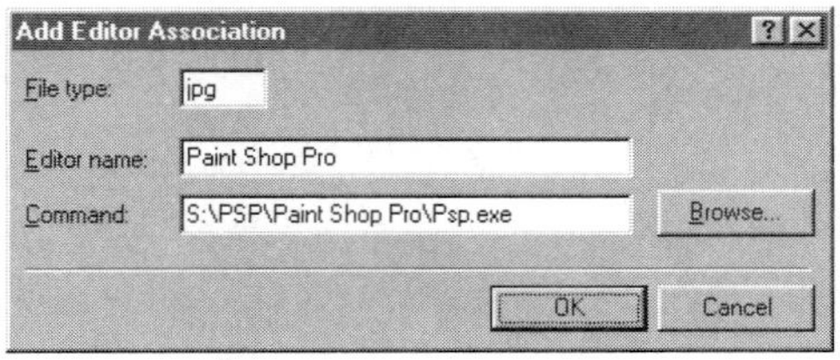

FIGURE 14-12.

This dialog box associates an editor with a file type.

When you double-click a file in FrontPage or use the Edit button in a dialog box, FrontPage honors the normal file association. To choose a secondary editor (one defined on a wildcard entry), right-click the file in FrontPage and choose Open With from the pop-up menu. Front-Page will present the dialog box shown in Figure 14-13, so you can open the file with the editor of your choice.

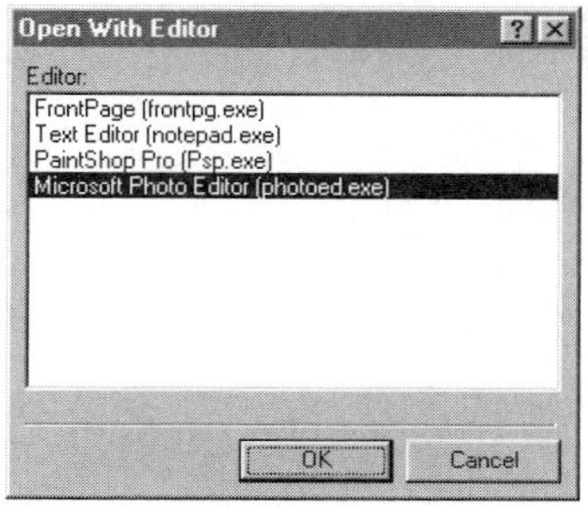

FIGURE 14-13.

Right-clicking a file in FrontPage and choosing Open With produces a list of program choices such as this.

When FrontPage opens a file with any editor other than FrontPage it-self, it follows this six-step process:

1 Copies the file to a temporary area.

2 Notes the temporary file's size and date stamp.

3 Launches the editor, passing it the name and location of the temporary copy.

4 Watches for the editor to terminate.

5 Compares the size and date stamp of the temporary file to that of step 2.

6 If the comparison in step 5 is unequal, imports the updated file from the temporary area to the FrontPage Web.

There are two reasons for this process. First, it's unlikely that the external editor can read and save files via HTTP as FrontPage does. Second, importing the updated temporary file triggers a limited hyperlink recalculation and keeps all FrontPage indexes, cross-references, and FrontPage components up-to-date.

Be aware, however, that until FrontPage imports the modified page, no changes will be visible in FrontPage or in your browser. The File Save command in the external editor updates only the temporary copy; FrontPage doesn't import the copy until the editor terminates.

II

Creating Web Pages

The last option in the Configure Editors tab (Figure 14-11) is the check box titled Open Web Pages In The Office Application That Created Them. If this box is turned on, and you open a Web page created by another Microsoft Office application, FrontPage will pass the document over to that application rather than editing the page itself. If the box is off, Front-Page will open all such Web pages itself.

A Bug in the Alphabet Soup?

FrontPage exhibits a curious behavior when displaying the Open With Editor dialog box shown in Figure 14-11. Any editor associated with a wildcard file extension, such as *gi?*, is always listed, regardless of the currently selected file type. This may be a bug but, even so, it's a convenient one; it means you can add as many editors as you like, regardless of file type, by specifying extensions containing an asterisk or question mark wildcard character: *gi*, g?f, ht*, do?, tx?,* and so forth.

The only downside to making very many wildcard entries is that you'll have a long and confusing list to sort through every time you use the Open With command.

Customizing Reports View

The Reports View tab pictured in Figure 14-14 controls five settings relative to Reports view.

- **"Recent" Files Are Less Than xxx Days Old.** The value of xxx determines which files appear in the Recently Added Files report.

- **"Older" Files Are More Than xxx Days Old.** The value of xxx determines which files appear in the Older Files report.

- **"Slow Pages" Take At Least xxx Seconds To Download.** The value of xxx specifies the download time that qualifies a Web page for inclusion on the Slow Pages report.

- **Assume Connection Speed Of.** To compute total download time, FrontPage will divide the total number of bytes for a Web page and all its constituent files by this connection speed.

NOTE You can also view the download time in Page view; it appears at the bottom of the main FrontPage window, near the right edge of the status bar. Clicking that area provides another way to change the assumed connection speed.

■ **Display Gridlines When Viewing Reports.** If turned on, this option tells FrontPage to draw row and column gridlines whenever it displays reports.

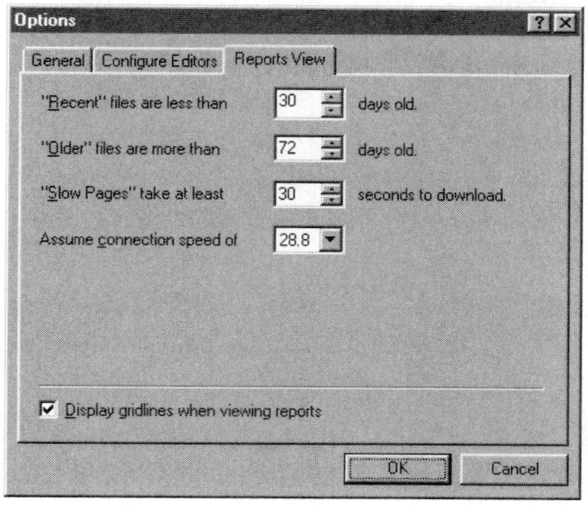

FIGURE 14-14.
This tab on the Page Options dialog box controls how FrontPage creates thumbnail images.

Customizing Page-Creation Options

This section describes the seven tabs that appear within the Page Options dialog box. To display this box, select Page Options from the Tools menu.

General

Figure 14-15 shows the first tab on the Options dialog box, namely the General tab. The first two options work like this:

■ **Use DIV Tags When Positioning.** If this option is turned on, FrontPage will use DIV tags, as opposed to other means, for positioning Web-page elements.

■ **Surround Form Fields With FORM Tag.** If this option is turned on, and you insert a Form field outside the bounds of any HTML form, FrontPage will surround the new form element with a new HTML form.

Regarding the second option, form fields originally had no use outside an HTML form, and at least through version 4, Netscape Navigator ignores them. Now that form fields can interact with scripts, however, form fields outside HTML forms do have a use, and surrounding them with form fields can be a nuisance. The Surround Form Fields With FORM Tag option gives you a choice between Netscape compatibility (option box on) and simpler HTML (option box off).

II

Creating Web Pages

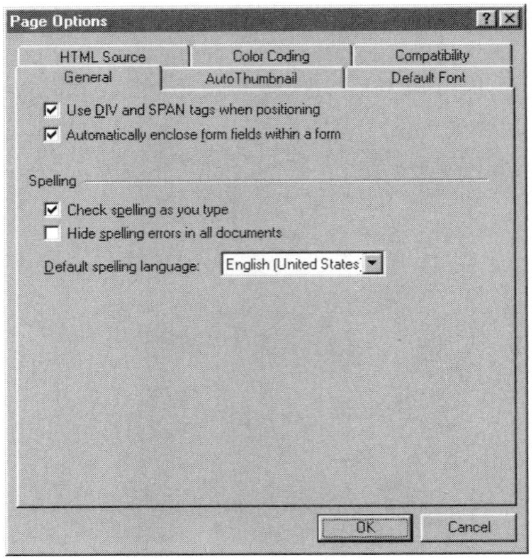

FIGURE 14-15.

The General tab controls two settings that don't logically belong elsewhere.

The options below the Spelling divider control the FrontPage spelling checker. For a full explanation of their use, see "Checking Spelling," page 121.

② SEE ALSO

For more information about creating thumbnail images, see "Creating Thumbnail Images" page 192.

AutoThumbnail

The AutoThumbnail tab controls creation of thumbnail images. This tab appears in Figure 14-16.

- **Set** controls the size of the thumbnail images. You should specify both a sizing strategy and a measurement. The sizing strategies are:

  - **Width.** FrontPage will make all thumbnail images the same specified width and calculate a height proportional to that of the full-size image.

  - **Height.** FrontPage will make all thumbnail images the same specified height and calculate a width proportional to that of the full-size image.

  - **Shortest Side.** FrontPage will make the shortest side of each thumbnail image the same specified size, and make the longest side proportional to that of the full-size image.

  - **Longest Side.** FrontPage will make the longest side of each thumbnail image the same specified size, and make the shortest side proportional to that of the full-size image.

FIGURE 14-16.

This tab on the Page Options dialog box controls how Front-Page creates thumbnail images.

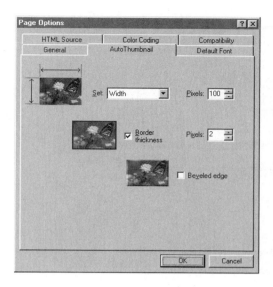

- **Pixels.** This field specifies the fixed size applied to the edge chosen above.

- **Border Thickness.** Turning this box on tells FrontPage to create borders around each thumbnail image. The Pixels box controls the border width.

- **Beveled Edge.** Turning this box on instructs FrontPage to create bevels around the edge of each thumbnail image.

Default Font

This tab specifies the character set and font FrontPage displays in the absence of any specifications within a Web page. These specifications don't appear in the HTML, and thus have no effect whatsoever on what your Web visitors see. Figure 14-17 shows the available options.

- **Language (Character Set)** controls the national language character set used to display text.

- **Default Proportional Font** specifies the font used for displaying most text.

- **Default Fixed-Width Font** specifies the font used for fixed-character-width text—text formatted, for example, with the <PRE> (Formatted) HTML tag.

Creating Web Pages

FIGURE 14-17.

The Default Font tab controls the way Front-Page displays text when the Web page itself provides no guidance.

HTML Source

This tab controls the formatting of HTML source code. For a full explanation of its use, see "Personalizing HTML Format," page 415.

Color Coding

When FrontPage displays code in HTML view, it displays different types of code in different colors. The Color Coding tab, which appears in Figure 14-18, specifies those colors.

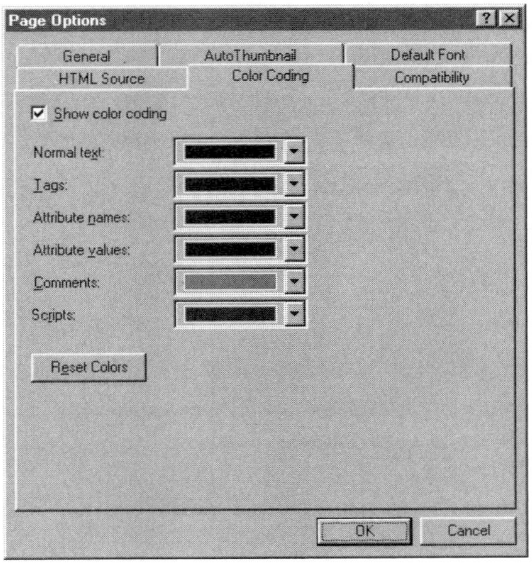

FIGURE 14-18.

This tab controls the color of source code FrontPage displays in HTML view.

- **Show Color Coding** controls whether or not HTML view displays code in color. If the box is turned off, the code appears in black and white. If it's turned on, the code appears in color.

- **Normal Text** controls the color of normal text. Clicking the drop-down button initiates the normal series of FrontPage color dialog boxes.

- **Tags** controls the color of angle brackets and identifiers for HTML tags.

- **Attribute Names** controls the color of HTML attribute identifiers.

- **Attribute Values** controls the color of HTML attribute values.

- **Comments** controls the color of HTML comments.

- **Scripts** controls the color of script statements.

- **Reset Colors** returns all HTML code colors to their original values.

This tab has no effect on any colors your Web visitors see. Changing the Normal Text value, for example, has no effect on the text in Web pages your visitors see.

Compatibility

This tab specifies the technologies available in your production Web environment, and then dims any FrontPage options that wouldn't be compatible. The tab appears in Figure 14-19.

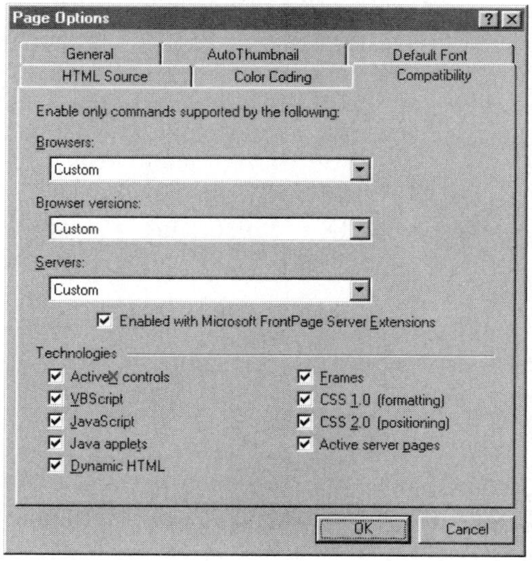

FIGURE 14-19.

With this tab you can specify the technologies you want your site to support. FrontPage then dims all options that would be incompatible.

- **Browsers.** Choose which browsers you want your site to support. The choices are Internet Explorer only, Netscape Navigator only, Both, and Custom.

- **Browser Versions.** Choose which version of the chosen browser you want your site to support.

- **Servers.** Specify what kind of Web server delivers your Web pages to your visitors. The choices are Microsoft Internet Information Server and Custom.

- **Enabled With Microsoft FrontPage Server Extensions.** Turn this box on if the FrontPage Server Extensions are installed on the server that delivers your Web pages to your visitors. Otherwise, turn it off.

- **Technologies.** Beneath this heading appear nine technologies you can choose to support or not. The list appears in Figure 14-17. To support a technology, turn the option box on; otherwise, turn it off.

> **NOTE**
>
> Some choices under the Technologies heading may be dimmed because of browser and server choices you made earlier in the dialog box.

In Summary...

The material in this chapter proves that FrontPage is as flexible as it is powerful. A plethora of configuration options ensures you can configure FrontPage to suit your preferences and style of working.

This chapter concludes the portion of this book that deals primarily with creating single Web pages. Part III, which begins with the next chapter, discusses Web-server configuration, and then Part IV explains FrontPage Webs—the key to managing Web sites as sets of interrelated pages and files.

Managing a Personal Web Server

CHAPTER 15

Looking at the Web— Inside Out

I n all probability, your interest in Microsoft FrontPage reflects a distinct lack of interest in computer networking. Nevertheless, publishing in any medium—whether print, broadcast, or online—requires a certain knowledge of that medium's technology, strengths, limitations, and mind-set. To become proficient in publishing to the Web requires at least a basic understanding of how the Web works.

In this chapter, we broadly review the structure of the World Wide Web. While making no claims of comprehensive coverage, the material that follows provides an overview of the Web's core technologies. Later chapters will use this information to discuss managing specific Web servers.

If you're an old hand at Web communication, you may wish to skip ahead to Chapter 16, "Installing and Configuring a Web Server," or treat this chapter as a review, or place it at the bottom of your bird cage. If you're a beginner, proceed in confidence that no arcane syntax or hexadecimal codes lie in waiting. (Well, maybe a little....)

Relationships Between Browsers and Servers

Like most Internet applications, the Web is a client/server system. The clients are machines where Web visitors submit commands and view responses using software called a *browser*. Microsoft Internet Explorer and Netscape Navigator are the most popular browsers. The servers typically are located some distance from the visitors, service simultaneous requests from multiple visitors, and have no need for a keyboard, mouse, or monitor other than for system administration.

In one sense, a server is any computer that runs applications or provides services on behalf of other computers. One such computer can provide any number of applications or services (provided, of course, that it doesn't run out of memory, disk, CPU power, or other resources). The application that delivers pages on the World Wide Web is called an *HTTP server*. HTTP is the HyperText Transfer Protocol.

> **NOTE**
>
> The term *server* is a bit ambiguous. Sometimes it refers only to the hardware, sometimes to a specific piece of background software, and sometimes to the combination of all hardware and software on a machine. Because this is a book about the Web, the term *server* will mean all the hardware and software required to service HTTP requests—that is, requests to deliver Web pages.

Another distinction between clients and servers is that clients generate requests and servers provide responses. Obviously, the client must formulate its requests and submit them in a way the server understands. Likewise, the server must formulate its responses in a way the client can deal with. The rules governing these interchanges are called *protocols*.

> **NOTE**
>
> A protocol is nothing more than a way of acting. Life is full of little protocols, such as the conventions we use to avoid bumping into people on sidewalks, in hallways, and when entering and leaving elevators. If an individual (or computer) acts outside established protocols, interaction with others will generally fail.

There are millions of computers on the Internet, and they interact in quite a variety of ways. As a result, many different Internet protocols are used. People can hardly talk about anything on the Internet without talking about protocols. Protocols govern how telephone numbers must be dialed, how modems link to each other, how dial-up networking software negotiates settings and logs onto the network of an Internet service provider (ISP), and how machines on a local network (or intranet) communicate via Ethernet. There are hundreds more protocols, but fortunately most of them can be ignored in a discussion of browsers and HTTP servers.

The two most important protocols involved in Web browsing are HTTP and TCP/IP. Later sections in this chapter describe both protocols.

Understanding TCP/IP

? SEE ALSO

If your working environment doesn't include a TCP/IP network, you may decide to use a disk-based Web for development rather than a Web server. See "Publishing to a Disk-Based Web," page 807.

All communication on the Internet uses a group of protocols collectively called Transmission Control Protocol/Internet Protocol (TCP/IP). For any sort of Internet client and server to communicate, both must be running TCP/IP and have an active network link between them.

Browsers and HTTP servers always communicate by TCP/IP. This means each computer running these applications needs working TCP/IP software, configured with an *IP address*. IP addresses are four bytes long, with the value of each byte typically stated as a decimal number; for example, 192.168.180.2 is a typical four-byte IP address.

⭐ TIP

> TCP/IP software usually comes with operating systems, and not with browsers or HTTP servers. To install TCP/IP on most versions of Windows, open Control Panel, then Network, then Add, then Protocol. Select TCP/IP and then follow the prompts.

Period Speech

In the interest of brevity, technical people often refer to punctuation marks using the following shorthand terms.

period	.	dot
exclamation point	!	bang
slash	/	whack
backslash	\	hack
ampersand	&	amper
parentheses	()	paren
asterisk	*	star

III

Managing a Personal Web Server

If you connect to the Internet by dial-up link, your PC probably has no assigned IP address. Instead, software at your Internet service provider assigns a temporary address every time you dial in. HTTP servers, browsers, and applications like FrontPage can use this temporary address to connect to Web servers on the Internet or on your local machine, but once you disconnect, the IP address disappears and even a Web server on your own PC becomes inaccessible. Some Internet service providers will provide a permanent, or *static,* IP address for an additional fee.

If your PC is on a campus or enterprise LAN (local area network), your network administrator has probably assigned the PC an IP address. For this discussion, it makes little difference whether the administrator assigned your address manually or via an automated network service, or whether the administrator configured your network software personally or simply provided instructions. If your PC has an IP address, FrontPage can communicate with Web servers also running on your PC or elsewhere on the network.

! WARNING

It's absolutely critical that no two computers on the same network have the same IP address. Duplicate IP addresses prevent both computers from working and lead to other network problems as well. Never give your computer an IP address you guessed at, chose randomly, or copied from someone else's computer.

Regardless of type, servers are usually situated on local area networks and generally have administrator-assigned IP addresses. Administrators also publicize the server's IP address by assigning an easy-to-guess, easy-to-remember name and providing lookup through a globe-spanning network service called the Domain Name System (DNS).

Talking to Yourself—The Loopback Address

Whenever you have trouble connecting from a client to a server, both running on the same computer, try using 127.0.0.1 or the name *localhost*. These are special values that mean *myself* on every computer running TCP/IP.

The number 127.0.0.1 is a special IP address—called the *loopback address*—that always refers to the local machine. If you're running a Web server and a client (that is, FrontPage or a browser) on the same machine, the client can access the local Web server by connecting to 127.0.0.1. This can be extremely convenient if you don't know your IP address or if it changes frequently (for example, each time you dial into your Internet service provider). In most cases, the name *localhost* is synonymous with 127.0.0.1.

Port Numbers

When a single server provides several TCP/IP services, clients need a way to identify which of these services they wish to use. Port numbers provide such a method.

When a TCP/IP service starts up, it registers with the local machine's network software and asks to receive all traffic directed to certain ports. The network software then forwards all incoming traffic on those ports to that service.

If a service requests a port that's already in use, it receives an error code. Allowing two services to register the same port would be ambiguous; the network software would again be unable to identify which service should receive traffic arriving on that port.

By default, HTTP servers listen on port 80. This is also the default port number in an *http://* URL. If a system administrator wants to run several kinds of Web-server software at the same time on the same machine, the administrator must configure each piece of software to listen on a different port number, and visitors must specify the same port numbers in their URLs. For instance,

> *http://www.pfew.com*

will access an HTTP server on port 80, and

> *http://www.pfew.com:8080*

will access an HTTP server on port 8080. Port 8080 is a common choice for Web servers running on computers where port 80 is already in use.

Building a Private TCP/IP Network

If you have more than one computer in your home or office, connect them together! This makes it easy to share printers and data among your computers, and you can even set up your own intranet.

The complete details of setting up a small LAN are beyond the scope of this book, but generally it involves these steps:

1 Install a network card in each machine, and then connect the cards to each other with suitable wiring. Ethernet network cards cost less than $100, and hubs to connect them are just as cheap.

2 Install the driver software for your network card. Windows 95, Windows 98, and Windows NT include all the software you need for a wide variety of network cards.

⭐ **TIP**

The Plug and Play features of Windows 95 and Windows 98 will usually detect the new network card, prompt you for the necessary disks and CDs, and walk you through the installation. If not, open the Control Panel's Network applet, click Add, and choose Adapter.

3 When the network setup program prompts you for protocols, be sure to choose TCP/IP.

4 Give each machine an IP Address from Table 15-1. Unless you need to connect more than 255 computers, this means choosing 192.168.*xxx*.*yyy* where

- All the machines have the same *xxx* number between 1 and 254.

- Each machine has a different *yyy* value between 1 and 254.

5 Assign a Subnet Mask of 255.255.255.0.

6 Leave the Default Gateway, DNS, and WINS dialog boxes blank.

⭐ **TIP**

Unless you've installed network cards, cabling, and software before, get help from someone with experience or from another book. The material presented here is only an overview.

TABLE 15-1. Private Network IP Addresses

Class	From IP Address	To IP Address	Subnet Mask	Maximum Computers per Network
A	10.0.0.1	10.255.255.255	255.0.0.0	16,581,375
B	172.16.0.1	172.31.255.255	255.255.0.0	65,025
C	192.168.0.1	192.168.255.255	255.255.255.0	255

▷ **NOTE**

Private IP addresses are assigned by an Internet standard called RFC 1597.

❓ **SEE ALSO**

For more information about proxy servers, see "Proxy Servers and GET Requests," page 484.

Private network IP addresses aren't valid on the Internet; you can use them only to connect private networks for a home or small business. No conflict results if machines on the private network occasionally dial into an Internet service provider, or if you later connect the private network to the Internet using software called a *proxy server*.

There's one more step in setting up a private TCP/IP network, namely setting up a *hosts* file so the computers can find each other by name. The section titled "Using a *hosts* File," page 482, explains.

Server Names and the Domain Name System

Because IP addresses are difficult to remember and subject to change, Internet authorities (such as they are) invented the Domain Name System—DNS. Essentially, DNS is an online, distributed database that translates easily remembered names such as *www.intel.com* and *ftp.microsoft.com* to IP addresses. When your browser, for example, tries to open the URL

> *http://www.microsoft.com/frontpage*

it actually begins by using DNS to translate *www.microsoft.com* to an IP address. The browser then connects to the IP (numerical) address and not to the DNS name.

Like most Internet applications, DNS is a client/server system. The client software is called a *resolver* and, in the case of Windows, it's part of the TCP/IP software that comes with the operating system. *Name resolution* is the process of translating computer names to IP addresses, and vice versa.

A DNS server usually resides centrally on a network and contains the databases that allow DNS to work. When a Web visitor requests a connection to a named host, the visitor's computer sends the name to the local DNS server, and with any luck the DNS server responds with the corresponding IP address. If the local DNS server can't resolve the request, it might contact additional DNS servers until it can.

TIP

Your Internet service provider or information services department will normally provide a DNS server for you to use. Your TCP/IP software may get the DNS server's IP address when you dial in or connect to the network; otherwise, you may need to enter it manually. Contact your service provider or system administrator if you need assistance using DNS.

Each dot (period) in a DNS name normally indicates a different database and possibly a different machine. If your network software asks your local DNS server for the IP address of *www.microsoft.com*:

1   The local server first contacts a root DNS server that knows all the COM entries in the world.

III

Managing a Personal Web Server

2 The root server provides the names and IP addresses of all DNS servers in the *microsoft.com* domain.

3 Your local server would contact one of the *microsoft.com* DNS servers to get the IP address for *www.microsoft.com*.

The inner workings of DNS really aren't important for Web authoring. However, if someone asks you for your DNS name, you should know what they're talking about. You'll also need to understand a little about DNS so that you can ask your Internet service provider or network administrator to establish a name for your server, as well as to understand the error messages you'll get if DNS isn't working.

Using a *hosts* File

It's common in small environments—such as home and small office networks—to have small Web servers not included in any DNS server's database. To permit accessing such servers by name rather than IP address, you can provide name-to-IP-address translation using a hosts file. This is a simple text file named *hosts* (with no extension) and located in the following folders:

- **Windows 95** and **Windows 98:** the Windows folder (that is, c:\windows)

- **Windows NT:** <systemroot>\system32\drivers\etc. (where <systemroot> is typically c:\winnt)

You can create this file using any simple ASCII editor, such as Notepad. Each line in the file contains an IP address, one or more spaces, and a computer name. After saving the file in the correct location, you should find that your computer translates the entered names to corresponding computer names as if they were in DNS.

⭐ **TIP**

> If you use Save As to save the hosts file with Notepad, be sure to enclose the file name—hosts—in quotes ("hosts"). Otherwise, Notepad will add a TXT extension and the file won't work.

The primary disadvantage of hosts files is that each computer needs its own copy of the file. Keeping all these files up-to-date becomes unwieldy in large environments.

HyperText Transfer Protocol—
A Simple Concept

Using Web browsers like Internet Explorer to retrieve and view Web pages is generally a pleasant and easy experience. The data you see, however, is obviously stored somewhere else on the network, and your browser retrieves it using a relatively hidden transfer mechanism. In the case of the World Wide Web, the data comes from a Web server and the transfer mechanism is HyperText Transfer Protocol—HTTP.

Like so many other technologies, HTTP started out simple and later grew to be complicated. As originally conceived:

1 The browser opened a connection to the computer and port specified in the desired Web page address.

2 The browser transmitted the word GET followed by a space, a folder path, an optional file name, and a carriage return (equivalent to pressing Enter). A typical GET request, for example, was

```
GET /sports/hockey/standings.html
```

3 The server sent back a status code, a file type indicator, a blank line, and the contents of the requested file.

4 The server then closed the connection.

Notice that the GET command in the previous paragraph contains less information than a normal URL. The corresponding URL might have been

http://www.nws.com:80/sports/hockey/standings.html

SEE ALSO
For an explanation of port numbers, see "Port Numbers," page 479.

where *http* specifies the protocol, *www.nws.com* is the name of the Web server, and *80* is a port number on that server. The browser uses the information in *http://www.nws.com:80* for connecting to the Web server, and it transmits the rest as a command to locate and deliver the file—that is, as the GET request shown above.

The file standings.html probably contains HTML and might call for additional files. If so, the browser retrieves each additional file by issuing another GET request. The server handles all ordinary GET requests identically, regardless of file type. The job of assembling multiple files and formatting the finished page falls entirely to the browser.

III

Managing a Personal Web Server

Proxy Servers and GET Requests

There's one instance where a browser sends out GET requests containing the remote host name and port number: that is, when it uses a proxy server.

For security reasons, many organizations provide access to external Web sites only through a proxy server. A proxy server is simply a relay agent that retrieves Internet Web pages for people at that site but prevents Internet visitors from accessing the site's internal resources. To use a proxy server, each browser must be configured to do both of the following:

- Send all GET requests to the proxy server and not to the host specified in the URL.

- Include the full URL, including the server name and port, in all GET requests.

Essentially, the browser sends the proxy server GET requests containing host names. The proxy server then connects to the named host and sends a GET request with the host name removed. With or without a proxy server, the remote Web server receives GET requests not containing its host name.

Nowadays, in addition to the basic GET request, browsers transmit *headers* that convey additional information about the connection. In the recording below, for example, the browser indicates what kinds of files it can accept, what human language it prefers (English), the size and color depth of the Web visitor's screen, the visitor's operating system and CPU type, the name and version of the visitor's browser, the computer name the browser is trying to contact, and an indication that the browser is willing to use the same connection for several transfers rather than opening new connections for each file.

```
GET / HTTP/1.0
Accept: image/gif, image/x-xbitmap, image/jpeg,
image/pjpeg, */*
Accept-Language: en
UA-pixels: 1024x768
UA-color: color8
UA-OS: Windows 95
UA-CPU: x86
Visitor-Agent: Mozilla/2.0 (compatible; MSIE.3.0;
  Windows.95)
Host: www.interlacken.com
Connection: Keep-Alive
```

HTTP and Stateless Connections

The greatest limitation of HTTP connections is that they are *stateless*. This means that the connection is closed immediately after a page is transmitted, and the server retains no useful memory of it. This becomes a real nuisance when a single transaction requires several Web pages to complete. Suppose, for example, that a Web visitor brings up the first Web page, submits some information, and gets a second screen prompting for more data. When the visitor submits the second page, the server has no memory of what transpired on the first.

There are three common solutions to this dilemma:

- Have the server write all the data about a transaction out to each Web page, and have the browser transmit it back with every transaction. This usually involves an invisible form field for each item of data.

- Have the server and browser exchange transaction data as cookies. Cookies are data fields that the browser and server exchange by means of special HTTP headers. Cookies may apply to a specific Web page, folder, or site, but cookies from one site can never be sent to another.

- Have the server keep transaction data in a file or database record designed for that purpose. Transmit a transaction identifier to and from the server using hidden form fields, path data, query strings, or a cookie.

By default, cookies reside in the browser's memory and disappear when the visitor closes the browser. However, a Web page can specify that its cookies should be saved persistently in a special file on the visitor's hard disk. Once cookies exist for a given Web page, folder, or site, the browser transmits them with every request to that location until the cookies expire. The server specifies an expiration date every time it sends the cookies.

In response to the previous GET request, the server responded with the following headers. They indicate the status code "200 OK," the name and version of the Web-server software, the willingness to reuse connections, the date and time, the file type "text/html," the ability to supply a byte-numbered portion of a page, the date the returned page was last modified, and the length in bytes of the returned page.

```
HTTP/1.0 200 OK
Server: Microsoft-IIS/4.0
Connection: keep-alive
Date: Sun, 03 Nov 1998 22:41:10 GMT
Content-Type: text/html
Accept-Ranges: bytes
Last-Modified: Sun, 03 Nov 1998 03:50:15 GMT
Content-Length: 5574
```

III

Managing a Personal Web Server

A second type of request, POST, is often used by Web pages containing HTML forms. The POST method uses additional HTTP headers to transmit all the names and values from an HTML form. This provides more flexibility and data-handling capacity than using the GET method with a query string.

A complete explanation of HTTP headers is beyond the scope of this book, but Web designers should be aware that browsers and Web servers exchange a variety of information about themselves during each request. Information supplied by the browser, for example, can be used on the server to customize the server's response.

Secure Sockets Layer (SSL)

Security is always a concern on the Web, especially for activities that involve transfer of money, exchange of credit card number or bank accounts, or other financial transactions. Both parties in any such transaction want such data encrypted so no one else can tap into the communication, modify the transaction to suit their own purposes, duplicate the transaction, or capture the data for later (and presumably fraudulent) use.

Secure Sockets Layer (SSL) provides the type of encryption required on the Web. SSL works like this:

1 The Web visitor submits a URL—perhaps by clicking a hyperlink or form button—with a protocol identifier of https.

2 The browser contacts the Web server on port 443.

3 The browser and server negotiate an encryption key for the current session. This key includes factors specific to the Web visitor's computer, such as its IP address, that make it very unlikely any other computer would get (or guess) the same key.

4 Once the encryption key is agreed to, all communication (using https URLs) between that browser and server will be encrypted using that key.

- The browser sends the encrypted data to the SSL service on port 443.

- The SSL service decodes the transmissions and forwards it internally to the requested server and port.

- The SSL service receives the Web server's response, encrypts it, and transmits the results to the browser.

- The browser decrypts and displays the results.

Note that the client software—the browser or FrontPage, for example—always initiates SSL communication. In addition, the Web server must support SSL and be properly configured to use it.

Server Home Folders

It's hard to imagine a case where any server administrator would want to make a Web server's entire file system available to everyone on the World Wide Web. Web servers therefore assign a *home folder* as the starting point for all GET requests. The term *home folder* is used interchangeably with any of the following: *home directory, root folder, root directory, HTTP root, document root,* and *home root.* If the server's home folder was

```
H:\inetpub\wwwroot
```

and the server received

```
GET /sports/hockey/standings.html
```

it would actually look for and deliver the file

```
H:\inetpub\wwwroot\sports\hockey\standings.html
```

Virtual Folders

For one reason or another, it's frequently convenient to view data as though it resided within a server's home folder even though it doesn't. The data might reside on a different drive letter for space management or historical reasons, for example, or it might reside on another machine. *Virtual folders* solve this dilemma by making folder locations outside the server's home folder appear to be within it.

Suppose, for example, a site kept its local announcements in a folder at

```
I:\sitenews
```

but its server home folder was

```
H:\wwwroot
```

The server administrator could define a virtual folder called /news that represented I:\sitenews. If the server then received

```
GET /news/default.html
```

it would look for and deliver

```
I:\sitenews\default.html
```

rather than

```
H:\wwwroot\news\default.html
```

CAUTION

Don't assign your computer's root directory as your Web server's root directory. This makes the entire content of your computer accessible to anyone on the same network. And, if you're on the Internet, that's a lot of other computers.

III

Managing a Personal Web Server

A frequent reason for setting up virtual folders is security. An administrator may feel more confident of a system's security by physically locating important files outside the server's home folder. In addition, many Web servers use virtual folders to implement folder-level security provisions. Any folder-level settings used by the Web server but not by the local file system usually reside in virtual folder definitions.

Virtual Servers

Contrary to popular belief, no law of nature dictates that all Web sites have DNS names beginning with *www* and ending in *com*. Nevertheless, this is what most Web surfers now expect, and it creates problems for large and small sites alike.

For large Web sites, problems arise building servers powerful enough to handle hundreds (or thousands) of incoming requests per second. The solution is normally to keep upgrading hardware and software, or to set up additional servers for menu choices one or two levels removed from the home page.

For small Web sites, the problem is the cost of building a separate server, even if the number of hits per day is small or moderate. The obvious solution is locating several small Web sites on one server, but the site owners want direct, custom names like *www.cats.com* and *www.dogs.com*, not *www.provider.com/~cats* and *www.provider.com/~dogs*.

Virtual servers provide an elegant solution to this common dilemma. An administrator sets up a different DNS name and IP address for each Web site, and then configures the one computer's network software to respond to several such addresses. Finally, the administrator configures the Web server software to access a different home folder, depending on which IP address the Web visitor specified. This allows different DNS names like *www.cats.com* and *www.dogs.com* to access different home folders on the same physical server.

> ⭐ **TIP**
>
> To display the dialog box that makes a Windows NT computer respond to more than one IP address, open the Windows NT Control Panel, double-click Network, click the Protocols tab, select TCP/IP Protocol, click the Properties button, click the IP Address tab, and then click the Advanced button.

Server-Side Programming

Delivering prewritten Web pages is quite a useful function, but generating pages on the fly offers considerably more flexibility. Generating

? SEE ALSO

FrontPage provides a number of server-side programming features that don't require programming knowledge on your part. For more information, see Chapter 21, "Using Server-Side FrontPage Components," and Chapter 22, "Accessing Databases with FrontPage."

pages on the fly does require custom programming, but it means the same URL can produce different results depending on the date, the time, the type of browser, or any other information available to the Web server. The same technologies can also process input from HTML forms and display database data.

Here are some popular ways to deliver Web pages customized by programming.

- **CGI—common gateway interface.** When the remote user clicks a hyperlink or a form button, the associated URL identifies not a file the server should transmit, but a program the server should run. Such programs typically receive input from HTML forms or from data appended to the URL, and as output they generate HTML for delivery to the remote user. They can also update files or databases on the server, send mail, and perform other useful functions.

- **ISAPI—Internet Server Application Programming Interface.** This approach is similar to CGI in function but implemented differently. ISAPI programs are dynamic link libraries (DLLs) that the operating system needs to load only once for any number of executions. By contrast, CGI programs are EXE files that must be loaded, initialized, run, and unloaded for each incoming request. The visitor submits a URL containing the name of the DLL.

- **ASP—Active Server Pages.** Unlike CGI and ISAPI, Active Server Pages consist of ordinary HTML intermixed with program code. The Web server interprets and executes the program code as it delivers the Web page. Web pages containing server-side scripts have the file-name extension ASP.

  Programmers usually create code for Active Server Pages using simple script languages such as JavaScript and VBScript. These languages can then invoke services from built-in server functions, ActiveX controls, Java applets, and other objects.

Because of the damage an errant or mischievous program can inflict, server-side programming raises significant security concerns. No Webmaster or system administrator wants visitors interfering with normal operation or tampering with content. For this reason, most Web servers are configured to execute only programs in specially designated folders. Administrators then allow just a few trusted individuals to place programs there.

III

Managing a Personal Web Server

MIME Types and Other Curiosities

The GET response on page 485 includes the following line in the HTTP headers:

```
Content-Type: text/html
```

The string text/html is a MIME file-type code that indicates the type of data that will follow. MIME stands for Multipurpose Internet Mail Extensions and, as you might expect, was first defined as a way to handle e-mail attachments. The MIME type simply provides a system-independent way to indicate the format of a file; mail programs use it to launch an appropriate viewing program when file attachments arrive with electronic mail. It makes sense to use the same MIME-type associations for viewing Web files as well.

The Web doesn't use file-name extensions to identify file types sent between computers, because not all operating systems support them. The Macintosh is a case in point. Instead, Windows-based Web servers usually have a table that translates file-name extensions to MIME types, and browsers use local MIME tables to select appropriate viewer programs. If you run into problems with Web content appearing incorrectly or prompting the Web visitor for a download location, investigate the MIME tables on both the server and the client.

Figure 15-1 shows the Windows dialog box for configuring MIME types. To display it, choose Options from any Windows Explorer menu, and then click the File Types tab. Each file type in the resulting table has associations with one or more file extensions, a MIME type, and a program capable of opening the file.

- To display the Edit File Type dialog box, select the Registered File Type and then click Edit.

- To display the Action For Type, select an entry from the Actions list and then click Edit.

The flip side—some would say the server side—of MIME configuration appears in Figure 15-2. This is the dialog box that controls the MIME types that Internet Information Server 4.0 transmits. The server translates each file name extension to a MIME type, and the browser uses these MIME types in deciding how to handle the file.

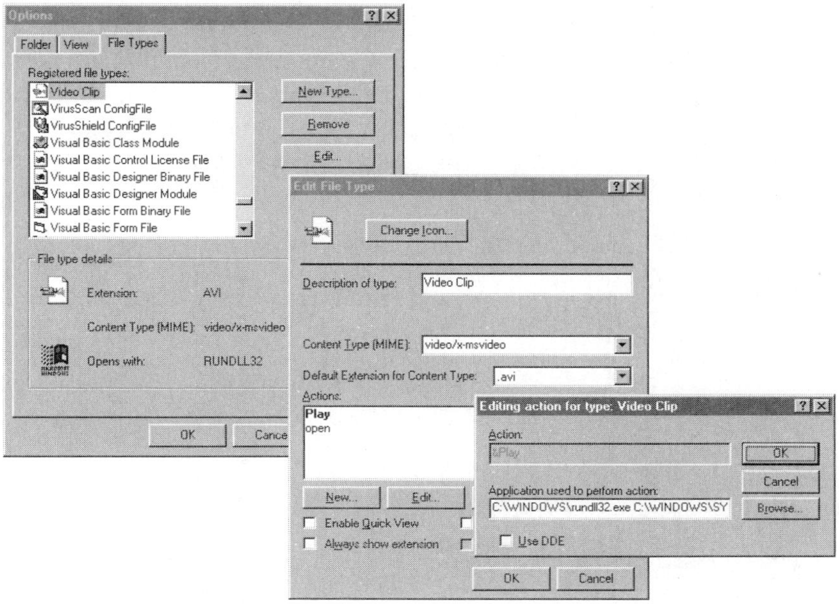

FIGURE 15-1.

Web servers identify file types with MIME Content Type codes. The browser uses this information to invoke the proper viewing program.

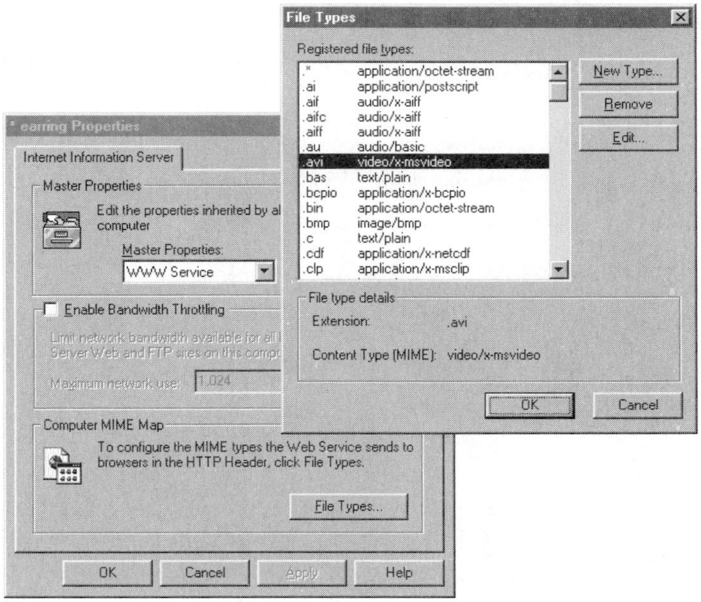

FIGURE 15-2.

This is the dialog box that configures MIME types transmitted by Internet Information Server.

Using a Proxy Server

Here are the steps required for configuring Internet Explorer 4, Internet Explorer 5, and FrontPage 2000 to use a proxy server. You can safely ignore them if your environment doesn't include a proxy server. If it *does* contain a proxy server, contact your network administrator or help desk for exact settings.

1 The first step varies depending on your current application.

- In Internet Explorer 4, choose Internet Options from the View menu.

- In Internet Explorer 5, choose Internet Options from the Tools menu.

- In FrontPage 2000, choose Options from the Tools menu, then click the Proxy Settings button.

2 When the Internet Options dialog box appears, take one of these actions depending on which browser is installed on your system.

- For Internet Explorer 4, click the Connection tab. The display of Figure 15-3 will result.

- For Internet Explorer 5, first click the Connections tab, and then click the LAN Settings button. Figure 15-4 shows the result.

FIGURE 15-3.

To configure a proxy server in Internet Explorer 4, use the Proxy Server section of its Connection tab.

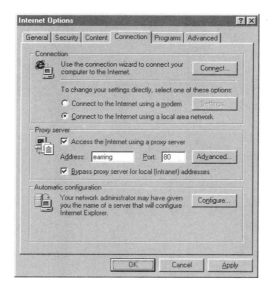

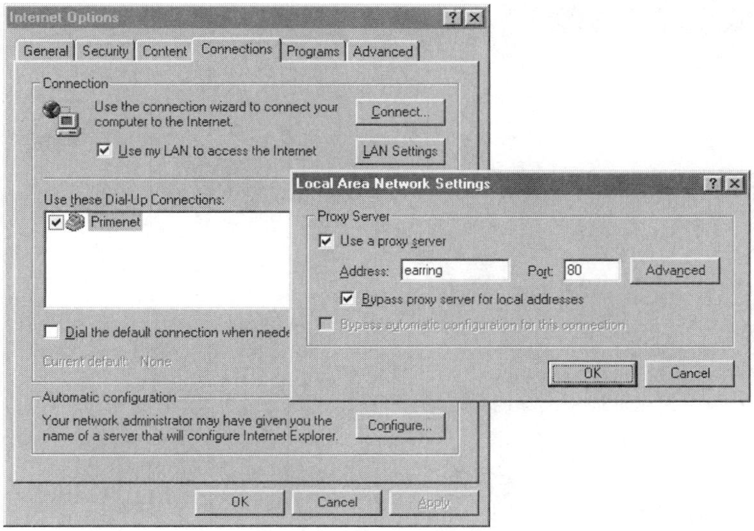

FIGURE 15-4.

To configure a proxy server in Internet Explorer 5, click the LAN Settings button in the Connection tab.

3 Turn on the check box titled Use A Proxy Server (or Access The Internet Using A Proxy Server).

4 In the Address field, specify the proxy server's name or IP address.

5 In the Port field, specify the proxy server's port number (usually 80).

6 To not use the proxy server for computers on your local network, turn on the box titled Bypass Proxy Server For Local Addresses. Your Internet service provider, system administrator, or help desk can tell you if this setting is required in your environment.

7 If your environment requires additional settings, click the Advanced button. This displays the Proxy Settings dialog box shown in Figure 15-5.

8 The Servers section of the Proxy Settings dialog box works like this:

- If the box titled Use The Same Proxy Server For All Protocols is turned off, the settings for HTTP apply to all protocols. This is the default.

- If the same box is turned on, you can specify a different proxy server, a different port, or both for each listed protocol.

9 The Exceptions section optionally contains a list of servers for which connecting through the proxy server isn't appropriate. As you enter the list, place a semicolon between each computer name. Again, contact your network support staff for settings.

III

Managing a Personal Web Server

⭐ **TIP**

The need for proxy-server settings is much more common if your PC is connected to a large organizational network. Dial-up Internet accounts generally don't involve proxy servers.

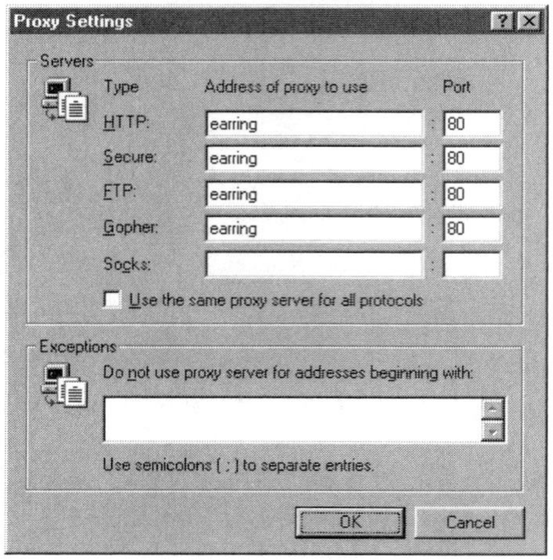

FIGURE 15-5.

Clicking the Advanced proxy server button in Figure 15-3 or Figure 15-4 provides more granular control over proxy server usage.

HyperText Markup Language

❓ **SEE ALSO**

For more information about HTML and text formatting, see "HTML Basics," page 408.

HTML, or HyperText Markup Language, arose from an earlier format called Standard Generalized Markup Language (SGML). SGML had been a fixture in the technical publishing industry for years because of its ability to assemble uniform documents from the writings of many contributors. This was possible because the contributors submitted only plain text intermixed with style codes that indicated headings, captions, bulleted and numbered lists, and other structural elements. Publishing specialists then chose fonts, margins, and other aspects of page layout independently from the original authors.

The first use of HTML was to publish technical papers at the European Laboratory for Particle Physics in Geneva, Switzerland. The technical contributors there were familiar with SGML, so HTML was designed along the same principles—plain ASCII text marked up with ASCII style codes. This produced documents like the one in Figure 15-6.

As use of the Web grew beyond the scientific community and entered the mainstream community, Web-page creators wanted to match the appearance of other high-visibility mass media. Browser manufacturers sought market share by adding markup tags that would appeal to these creators, and the result has been pages such as that shown in Figure 15-7.

FIGURE 15-6.

This is HTML doing what its inventors intended—displaying simple text documents.

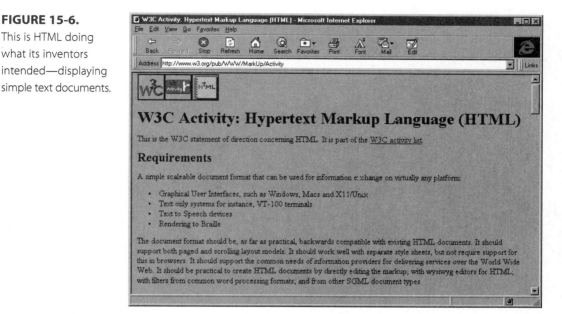

FIGURE 15-7.

Complex Web pages test the limits of HTML's capabilities.

III

Managing a Personal Web Server

The creator of a page like the one in Figure 15-6 has very little control over paragraph formatting, font selection, page width, or line endings. The creator *can* specify paragraph styles such as <H1> for Heading Level One and font styles like <B> for Bold, but the Web visitor's browser and computer system control the typeface, point size, and color used for each style. There are no controls for paragraph indentation, line spacing, or margins. Everything is flush left (left-aligned).

 SEE ALSO

For more information about frames, see "Creating and Editing Frames," page 261.

By contrast, the page shown in Figure 15-7 is divided into *frames* and makes considerable use of graphic images, even as the text within each frame follows the same rules as the text in Figure 15-6. The limitations of HTML tempt many Web creators to make each page a single large graphic, but this usually results in unacceptably long download times for visitors who access the Web by modem.

SEE ALSO

For more information about tables, see "Creating and Editing Tables," page 230.

The original HTML specification provided no means for placing text, images, or other objects spatially on the page; contents flowed left-to-right, top-to-bottom, and were left-aligned only. Frames provide a way to divide a page into areas and control each area, but *tables* provide an additional technique for *x-y* positioning.

Figure 15-8 shows a Web page that uses tables to organize six topics into a three-column by two-row grid. A second table ("Island Excursions"), near the bottom of the figure, has four columns. The first two columns contain bulleted items, the third provides white space, and the last provides some unbulleted hyperlinks. Note that the heading for the first two columns spans both of them.

FIGURE 15-8.

This page uses HTML tables to arrange information horizontally and vertically.

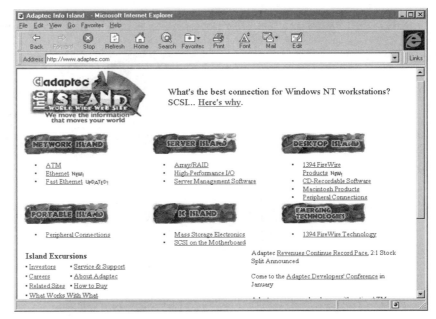

HTML Forms

(?) SEE ALSO

For more information on HTML forms, consult Chapter 10, "Creating and Using Forms."

Forms created in HTML provide a limited *graphical user interface (GUI)* that's useful for constructing data-entry screens. Figure 15-9 shows FrontPage creating such a form. Note the use of an HTML table to arrange the field titles and form.

Each element within the form has a name assigned by the Web designer plus a value assigned by the Web visitor. When the visitor clicks the Submit button in the form, the browser sends the name and value of each field to a program on the Web server. The server program uses the form data to send mail, update a database, or perform some other action.

(X) CAUTION

Radio (option) buttons are the only form elements where duplicate names are valid. Normally, each element in the form must have a unique name.

Figure 15-9 shows the configuration of a radio button (or option button). The value in the Group Name box (*location,* for example) identifies all option buttons in the same group; selecting one button deselects all other buttons with the same Group Name identifier. The Value box specifies the string transmitted to the server if the form is submitted with this button selected. The Initial State button controls whether this button is selected when the form is first displayed. The value in the Tab Order box optionally indicates the sequence this button occupies as the visitor tabs from one form element to another.

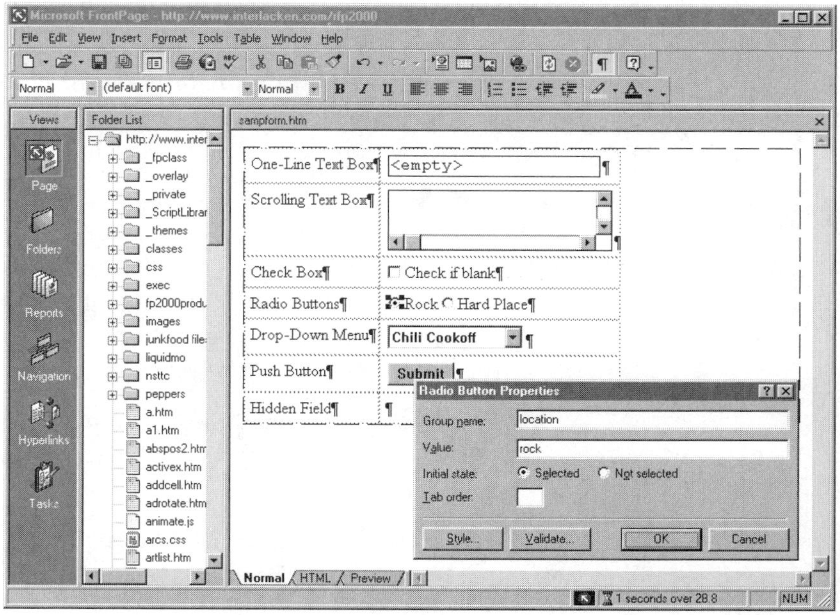

FIGURE 15-9.

FrontPage Editor provides a graphical way to easily construct HTML forms.

A single Web page may contain any number of HTML forms. If there are several forms on a single page, the only elements transmitted are those in the form whose Submit button was clicked.

What Activating the Internet Is All About

During the first few years of the Web's existence, most activity consisted of publishing information in fixed HTML pages and building hyperlinks. What was termed progress consisted of getting HTML to render more and more attractive pages—a challenging task both technically and artistically. This kind of progress hasn't reached its zenith and probably never will, but a second challenge has arisen: that of making pages respond more interactively than simple hyperlinks ever can. Microsoft calls providing this kind of interactivity "activating the Internet."

The software foundation for activating the Internet has four layers:

- HTML provides basic page layout and presentation.

- Scripts provide simple application logic and coordinate interaction among other components. Script languages typically require no compilation, no declaration of variables, and no installation. They are comparable to macro languages in applications. On the Web, scripts typically reside within the HTML files of pages they affect. The script may execute either on the server, just before the HTML gets transmitted, or on the browser. Browser scripts can execute as the page loads, later as timers go off, or as visitors operate controls on the Web page.

- Components usually provide more complex or intricate services than scripts. Programmers write them in rigorous, compiled languages such as C++, Java, and Visual Basic. Because of the development time required, it usually isn't practical to write component objects for a single Web page. Well-written components are versatile, fast, and designed to be used by scripts or other components.

- The operating system and services provide basic functions such as file input and output, database management, and network communication.

These layers are arbitrary and, in practice, the lines between them sometimes blur. Nevertheless, they provide a useful model. Components and services provide a way to implement functions of any complexity in a reusable way. Scripts and basic HTML provide ways to complete jobs in hours rather than days or months.

In Summary...

This chapter presented an overview of the way the World Wide Web and various related protocols work. It also provided some high-level guidance for setting up your own local network.

The next chapter addresses the process of installing a Web server, be it on your home network, your company's intranet, or the full global Internet itself.

Managing a Personal Web Server

CHAPTER 16

Installing and Configuring a Web Server

This chapter describes how to install and administer a Microsoft Web server on your Windows 95, Windows 98, or Windows NT 4.0 computer. Installing and managing Web servers is normally a task for professional system administrators, but there are several reasons you might do it yourself.

1 You *are* the professional system administrator.

2 You're working in a highly decentralized environment.

3 You need a Web server for testing processes that only run within a Web-server environment.

The FrontPage Server Extensions are a set of programs designed to run on a Web server. When the FrontPage desktop software creates HTML for the features listed below, it assumes the server extensions will be present when remote users visit your site.

■ **Hit Counter** is a process that counts and displays how often Web visitors access a given page.

■ **Search Form** provides full-text search capability for the pages on your site.

- **Save Results,** which accepts data from an HTML form and then saves it for later use in a file or database on the server or by sending it as mail.

- **User Self Registration,** a process whereby users must identify themselves before accessing certain parts of your site.

- **Discussion Sites,** which collect and organize comments from your Web visitors.

- **Database Access,** which queries and updates databases based on HTML forms.

- **Confirmation Field,** a component that shows Web visitors the results of their input.

Chapters 21 and 22 describe these features in detail, but using them requires a FrontPage Web hosted on a Web server. Chapters 18 and 19 describe how to create and manage such a Web, and Chapter 17 describes how to install the requisite FrontPage Server Extensions. Of course, you can't install the extensions without a Web server to put them on, so here we are.

If your situation is one of the following, you may safely decide to skim or skip this chapter and the next:

- You have no interest in the features listed above.

- Your production Web server (the one your Web visitors will access) won't have the FrontPage Server Extensions installed.

- You plan to use at least one of the features listed above, but don't plan to test those pages before uploading them to your production Web server.

- Your responsibilities mainly involve content development, and someone else administers the Web server you plan to use for testing.

Choosing and Configuring Your Web Server

Choosing Web servers is a major site-planning decision. If your site uses server-side processing, you'll probably want two Web servers: one for access by your Web visitors and another for designing and testing pages before making them public. These will be your production and test Web servers, respectively.

? SEE ALSO
For information about deciding how many Web servers you need, and where, see "Organizing Your Web Server Environment," page 77.

In almost every case, it makes sense for these two servers to be as similar as possible. Otherwise, what works in test may not work in production, and vice versa. The more dissimilar the servers, the greater this problem may be.

Microsoft provides Web servers for Windows 95, Windows 98, Windows NT Workstation, and Windows NT Server. Personal Web Server (PWS) 4.0 is available for Windows 95 and Windows 98. Windows NT 4.0 Server uses Internet Information Server (IIS) 4.0. Personal Web Server for Windows NT 4.0 Workstation is basically a limited version of IIS.

New releases of Microsoft Web servers don't appear simultaneously with those of FrontPage, nor those of the various Windows operating systems. This book deals primarily with IIS 4.0, which is part of the Windows NT 4.0 Option Pack. If a newer version exists when you start your installation, by all means use it. Note that PWS is also available on this Option Pack and can be installed on current Windows operating systems.

W ON THE WEB

You can download the Windows NT 4.0 Option Pack from Microsoft's Web site at *http://www.microsoft.com/ntserver/all/downloads.asp*.

Before installing any of these servers, first remove any existing Web servers by using the Add/Remove Program options in the Windows Control Panel. If you want to preserve your existing content, be sure to note the existing software's HTTP root folder.

It's also a good idea here to check your computer's name. Right-click Network Neighborhood, choose Properties from the pop-up menu, and then click the Identification tab. The dialog box shown in Figure 16-1 will appear. If the Computer Name field contains any spaces, punctuation, or special characters, remove them. You'll have to reboot after any change of computer name.

Finally, before installing the Windows NT 4.0 Option Pack on any computer, you must first install Internet Explorer 4.0 or above. If you're running Windows NT 4.0 Workstation or Server, you'll also need to have Windows NT Service Pack 3 or 4 installed on your machine.

III

Managing a Personal Web Server

FIGURE 16-1.
This dialog box shows the computer's name. Remove any spaces, punctuation, or special characters before installing Web-server software.

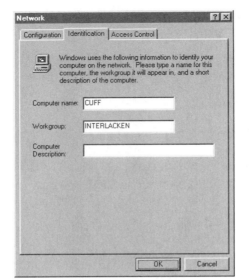

Microsoft Personal Web Server for Windows 95 and Windows 98

If you need a personal or workgroup Web server that runs under Windows 95, Windows 98, PWS is an excellent choice.

Installation

⊗ **CAUTION**
Microsoft Personal Web Server for Windows 95 and Windows 98 is meant for individuals or small workgroups developing and testing Web pages. Capacity, security, and licensing restrictions make it unsuitable as a high-volume production Web server.

To begin installing the Web server, insert the Windows NT Option Pack CD into your CD-ROM drive and wait for a splash screen to appear in Internet Explorer. When it does, click the Install option. If prompted for security reasons whether to run setup.exe, click Yes. If for any reason the splash screen doesn't appear, just run setup.exe from the CD's root folder. When the introductory screen in Figure 16-2 appears, you're on your way. Click Next.

Consent to the End User License Agreement, and then when the choice presented in Figure 16-3 appears, click Custom. (No great harm will come if you choose Typical, but Custom reveals more about what's going on and avoids some extra steps later.)

Figure 16-4 shows the next screen you'll see, modified slightly to display all available options at one glance. The choice of components in this figure includes two modifications to the default selections:

- Front Page 98 Server Extensions is turned off because we'll install the FrontPage 2000 Extensions in the next chapter.

- The options for PWS are modified to install all the documentation. To make this choice, select Personal Web Server (PWS), then click the Show Subcomponents button and choose Documentation.

FIGURE 16-2.

This screen signifies that setup for Microsoft Personal Web Server is underway.

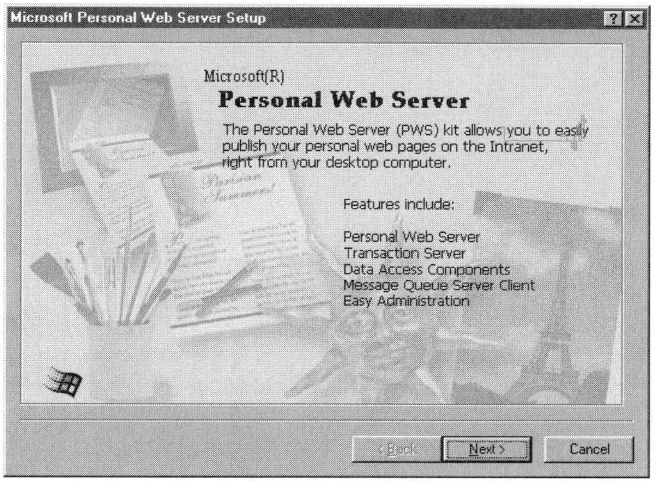

FIGURE 16-3.

To get the most information out of Setup, choose Custom when this screen appears.

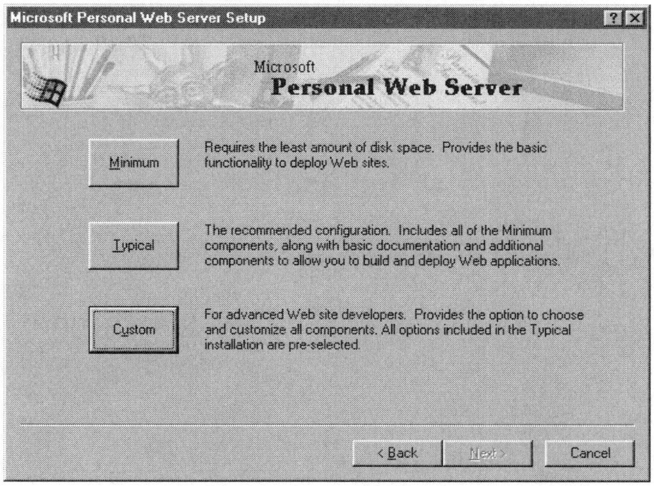

After verifying the components to install, click Next and receive the prompt shown in Figure 16-5. This is where you specify the Web server's HTTP root folder on your hard disk (that is, the location on your disk that corresponds to the URL "/"). If this is the first time you've installed

PWS, accept the default or, if you prefer, change the drive letter to another one that's more convenient. If you want to reuse the HTTP root folder from a previously installed Web server, enter its location in the WWW Service text box.

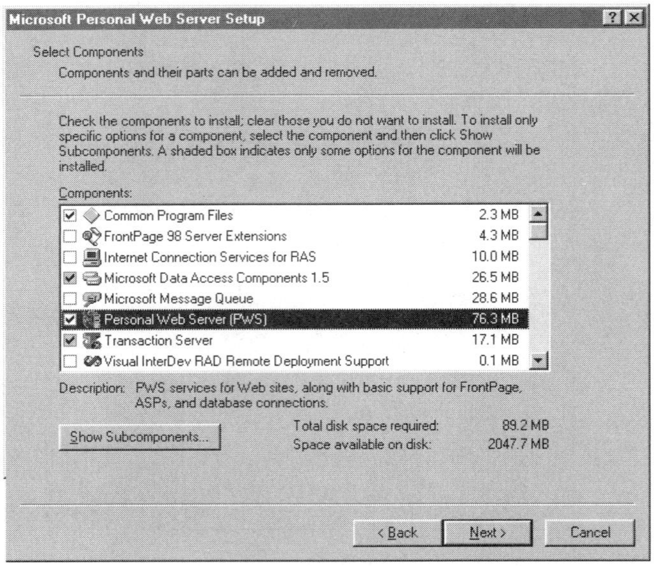

FIGURE 16-4.

FrontPage 98 Server Extensions is turned off in preference to installing the FrontPage 2000 extensions later.

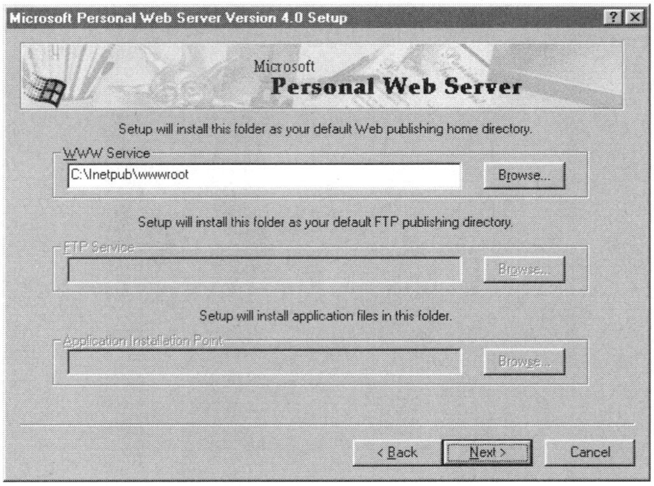

FIGURE 16-5.

Specify your Web server's HTTP root folder here.

There's no point in installing the FrontPage 98 Server Extensions at this point, because we'll install the FrontPage 2000 extensions later. PWS 4.0 for Windows 95 and Windows 98 doesn't include an FTP service, so you can't specify an FTP root folder. In addition, Setup will always install the Web server programs at C:\Windows\System\InetSrv (assuming C:\Windows is your Windows directory).

Setup will next display a screen that specifies where to install Microsoft Transaction Server. Accept the default unless the suggested drive is short of disk space and you have another drive available; in that case, only change the driver letter. Click Next.

At this point, Setup will copy all the PWS files to your hard disk and then suggest rebooting your PC. Accept this reboot and then, when the system comes back, wait for the installation to complete.

Configuration

To configure the server, click Start, then Programs, then Microsoft Personal Web Server, then Personal Web Manager. The dialog box shown in Figure 16-6 will appear.

FIGURE 16-6.
This application controls most aspects of PWS's operation.

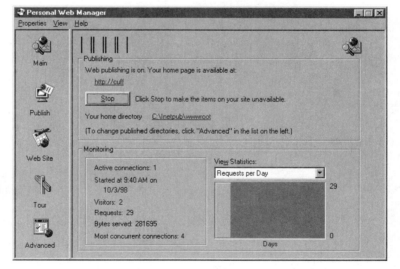

CAUTION
Configuring a Web server doesn't add the computer's name to DNS, and therefore doesn't make it available by name to other computers on the same network. If this presents a problem, either get your computer's name and IP addresses defined in DNS or update the hosts file on each computer that needs to access yours.

Clicking the Main icon in Figure 16-6 displays the options shown. Immediately after installation, the Web server probably won't be started, so click the Start button in the dialog box to get it going. This will change the button's caption to Stop, as shown in Figure 16-6.

Note the URL, *http://cuff,* just above the Stop button. This is the Web server's URL. Clicking it starts Internet Explorer and displays your home page. Figure 16-7 shows the default home page. Note that the URL shown in Figure 16-7 isn't *http://cuff*. This happened because the server's true home page performs a redirection.

FIGURE 16-7.

This is the PWS default home page.

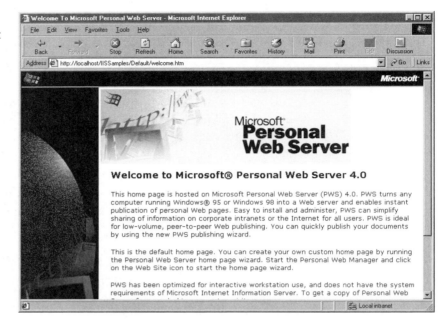

? SEE ALSO

For more information about virtual folders, see "Virtual Folders," page 487.

The Publish icon in Personal Web Manager runs a rather convoluted process that copies files into a virtual folder called WebPub. For Front-Page users, it's best to ignore this facility and use FrontPage's Import functions instead.

Clicking the Web Site icon starts the Home Page Wizard as shown in Figure 16-8. This presents a series of prompts for choosing a visual style for your page (that is, a theme, but not a FrontPage Theme) and specifying, by filling in the blanks, what information should appear on your home page. Figure 16-9 shows a home page created by the Home Page Wizard.

The Home Page Wizard merits a word of caution here: any home pages it creates are sometimes interesting and often attractive, but they're not the sort of pages FrontPage works with easily. The wizard doesn't create the home page as a single file, for example; instead, it assembles the home page by combining multiple files and saved values on the fly each time someone requests the page. Because of that, you'll probably want to create your home page directly in FrontPage.

The Home Page Wizard also offers to construct a guest book and a drop box for your site. Again, feel free to use these but don't think of them as part of FrontPage or expect FrontPage to provide more than generic support for them.

Once the home page is built, the Web Site icon displays options to edit the home page, view the guest book (if you created one), and open your drop box (again, if one exists).

FIGURE 16-8.
Clicking the Web Site icon starts the Home Page Wizard.

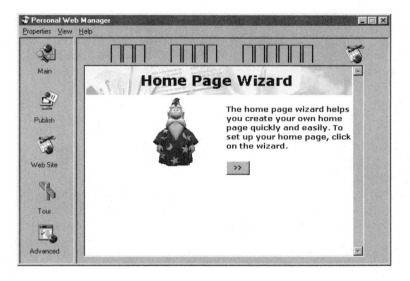

FIGURE 16-9.
This is a typical home page built by the Home Page wizard.

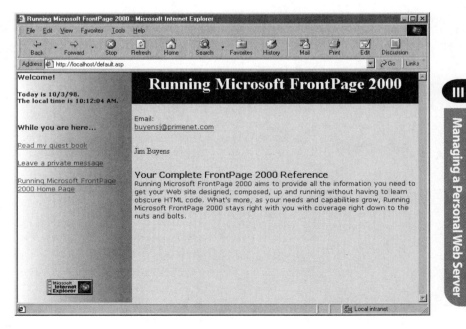

The Tour icon presents a brief tutorial for PWS.

Clicking the Advanced icon displays the following options, as shown in Figure 16-10:

- **Virtual Directories** displays a list of virtual directory mappings currently in effect.

- **Enable Default Document,** if turned on, tells PWS to look for and deliver Web pages with predefined file names whenever it receives a GET request that lacks a file name. The Default Document(s): box specifies the list of file names, in order, separated by commas.

  If PWS is configured as shown in Figure 16-10, and it receives a GET request such as "/" or "/IISHELP/" with no file name, it will search the corresponding folder first for a file named Default.htm, and then for a file named Default.asp.

FIGURE 16-10.
Clicking the Advanced icon displays the most detailed and technical PWS settings.

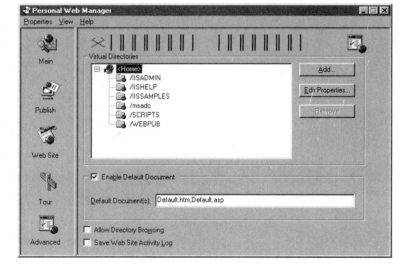

> **NOTE**

When creating a server-based Web, FrontPage determines the server's default document name, and names the Web's home page accordingly. For new disk-based Webs, FrontPage always uses the name index.htm. You can avoid considerable confusion by using the same default document name everywhere.

- **Allow Directory Browsing** specifies what will happen when a Web visitor submits a GET request with no file name, and no default document exists.

  - If the box is turned on, the Web visitor gets a clickable list of files and folders that *do* exist.

  - If the box is turned off, the Web visitor gets an Access Denied error.

- **Save Web Site Activity Log,** if turned on, tells the Web server to record a log of all incoming requests. The log appears in the directory: C:\Windows\System\LogFiles\W3SVC1\ and has the file name ncyymm.log, where yy is the two-digit year and mm is the month.

SEE ALSO

For more information on virtual directories, see "Virtual Folders," page 487.

To add a virtual directory, click the Add button. To modify or remove one, first select it and then click Edit or Remove. Removing a virtual directory doesn't actually delete the folder or its files; it only removes the virtual directory definition.

Figure 16-11 shows the dialog box for adding or editing a virtual directory entry. It has the following options:

- **Directory** specifies a physical directory location anywhere on your disk.

- **Alias** specifies the directory Web visitors will use to access the physical directory.

- **Access** specifies the mode in which Web visitors can access this directory.

  - **Read** means Web visitors can retrieve Web pages and other files in the ordinary way.

SEE ALSO

For a review of the terms CGI and ISAPI, see "Server-Side Programming," page 488.

  - **Execute** means Web visitors can execute programs residing in the virtual directory. In general, these would be CGI programs (with EXE file name) extensions, or ISAPI programs (with DLL file name extensions).

  - **Scripts** means that Web visitors can run Web pages that contain server-side scripting.

III

Managing a Personal Web Server

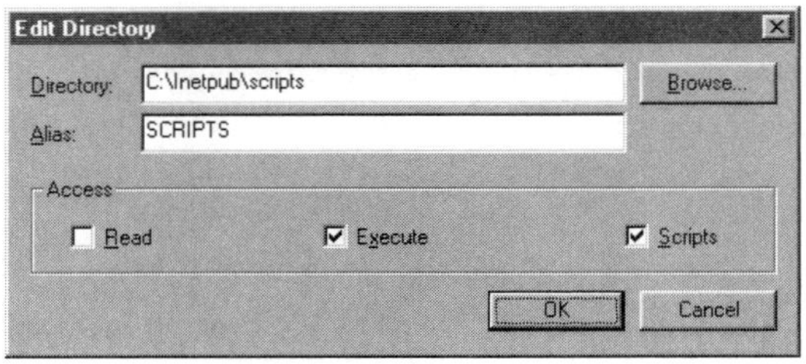

FIGURE 16-11.

This is the dialog box for adding or modifying a PWS virtual directory entry.

The difference between Execute and Scripts can be confusing. Execute permissions means Web visitors can specify the name of an EXE or DLL file in their URL, and the Web server will run that file as a CGI or an ISAPI program, respectively. (Of course, the program must physically reside within the virtual directory's physical tree.)

Scripts permission means that Web visitors can run Web pages processed by another program on the server. ASP pages provide an example of this. The fact that a script inside an ASP page runs indirectly—an intermediate program interprets and runs the script—provides a level of isolation between the script and the total resources of the computer. This makes script files somewhat more secure than CGI or ISAPI programs.

It's good practice *not* to authorize Read access to virtual directories having Execute or Script permissions. This provides a measure of protection against Web visitors downloading script code or programs you don't want them to have.

Security

The preceding material has already touched on two aspects of Web-server security: limiting the HTTP root folder to only a subset of your disk and limiting Read, Execute, and Script permissions assigned to virtual directories.

Administering user security for the Windows 95 or Windows 98 versions of PWS involves no complicated security issues. The reason for this is simple: there's no user security at all.

Unlike Windows NT, the Windows 95 and Windows 98 operating systems themselves don't have built-in security subsystems. Rather than implement a new security system different from Windows NT, the PWS designers kept things simple and avoided the issue. The result is that any changes you can make to your Web server through Internet Explorer (or through a server-based FrontPage Web), others on the same network can make as well.

SEE ALSO
For more information on installing, configuring, and managing Windows NT in general or IIS in particular, consult the product documentation, Microsoft's Web site at *http://www.microsoft.com,* or books dedicated to these topics.

The seriousness of this varies depending on your situation. If yours is a home- or small-office PC that only occasionally dials into the Internet, then your machine is at risk only while dialed in, and even then your PC doesn't have a DNS name, and no one knows what your IP address is. If, on the other hand, your machine is permanently connected to a large heterogeneous network, such as a university or the Internet itself, your risk would be considerably greater. In any event, you can reduce your exposure by running the Web service only when you're using it.

If lack of security is an issue, a move to Windows NT Workstation or Server may be in order. There was never a lock built that can't be picked, but Windows NT's security is light years ahead of Windows 95 and Windows 98.

Internet Information Server for Windows NT Server

The flagship of Microsoft's Web server line is Internet Information Server (IIS). This is an extremely powerful, commercial-grade Web server suitable for a wide range of production environments. IIS runs on Windows NT Server, and thus on a variety of processors.

If you want your FrontPage environment or your server environment to be 100 percent Microsoft, IIS should be your production Web server. The various Web servers tend to leapfrog one another in terms of features and performance, but IIS is perennially near the top. IIS's large installed base ensures a wide variety of third-party add-ons, and Microsoft is a leader in bringing new technologies to its server. Finally, IIS ships at no extra charge with every copy of Windows NT Server.

IIS can also be installed on Windows NT Workstation, although, in a strange twist of nomenclature, it changes its name to Microsoft Personal Web Server. Don't be fooled by the name change, though. What you're running on NT Workstation is IIS, and not the same PWS software that runs on Windows 95 and Windows 98. The Windows NT Workstation version of IIS does have some restrictions, however:

- There's no support for virtual servers.
- You can't selectively grant or deny access based on a Web visitor's IP address.
- You can't control total bandwidth allocated to Internet services.
- Microsoft Index Server (a text searching tool) isn't available.

- Licensing prohibits more than 10 different IP addresses from connecting to a Windows NT Workstation in any 10-minute period.

> NOTE

> If Web services running on Windows NT Workstation seem attractive, consider that not all FrontPage authors need their own copy of Windows NT Workstation running a Web server. It's perfectly acceptable—and frequently desirable—to set up one NT Workstation Web server per small workgroup, especially in collaborative environments.

These restrictions conform to Windows NT Workstation's pricing and positioning as a single-user desktop operating system. Windows NT Workstation's machine-to-machine connectivity is intended for small workgroups, not for large enterprises or the world.

Installation

You can install IIS when you first install Windows NT Server, but it's usually best to bypass this option and install IIS later. There are two reasons for this:

- During initial setup, the only drive letter available is the system drive. Installing IIS after initial setup provides more flexibility in drive assignment (assuming, of course, you manage disk space by allocating drives to specific applications).

- The version of IIS contained on the Windows NT setup CD may not be current. New releases of IIS appear much more frequently than new releases of Windows NT.

The procedure for installing IIS 4.0 on Windows NT Workstation or Server follows the same general approach described earlier in this chapter for the Windows 95 and Windows 98 Personal Web Servers. Insert the CD and choose Install from the splash screen, or run setup.exe from the CD's root directory. Cosmetics aside, setup will proceed as before until you get to the Select Components screen pictured in Figure 16-12.

The figure is actually a composite; the Components list is artificially lengthened to show the full list of options in one screen shot. The key component, from the viewpoint of installing a Web server, is of course IIS. You'll almost certainly want to install the Data Access Components, which provide database connectivity, and Transaction Server, of which IIS is a user. You'll also need the Common Files package. You can get descriptions for the other components by single-clicking them and looking underneath the Components list.

FIGURE 16-12.
The Windows NT
Option Pack offers con-
siderably more compo-
nents when installed
on Windows NT Server
than it does on Win-
dows 95 or Windows
98. Compare this dis-
play to Figure 16-4.

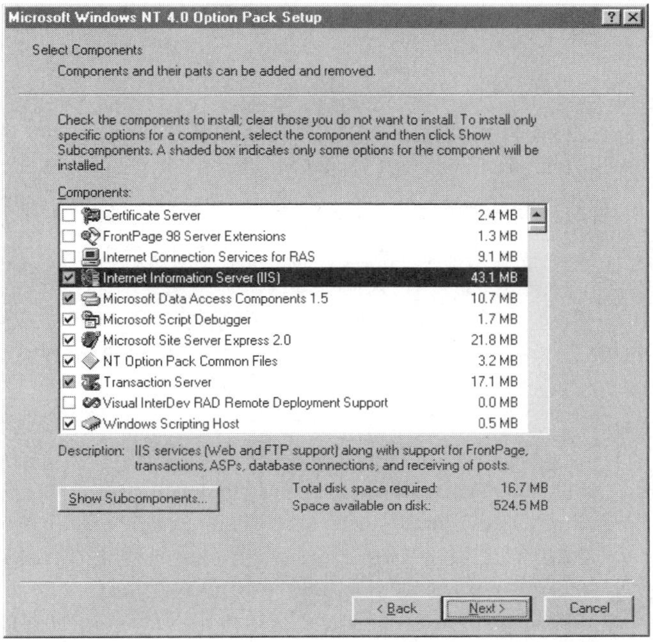

Selecting Internet Information Server (IIS) and clicking Show Subcomponents displays the dialog box shown in Figure 16-13, which is another composite modified to show all the subcomponents at once.

FIGURE 16-13.
The IIS choice in Figure
16-12 includes these
subcomponents.

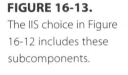

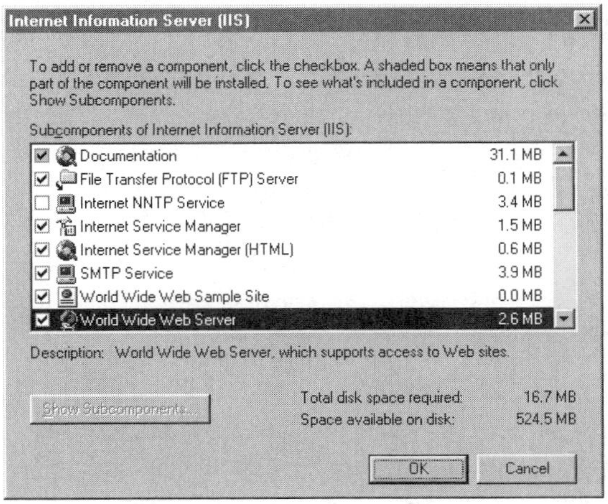

Of the listed components, you should of course install the World Wide
Web server and, to permit configuration, the Internet Service Manager.

Unless disk space is incredibly scarce, installing the documentation and World Wide Web Sample Site is probably a good idea. The Internet Service Manager (HTML) supports remote administration through HTML forms.

The option to install the following components is entirely yours: File Transfer Protocol (FTP) Server, Internet NNTP Service (an Internet Newsgroup server), and SMTP Service (for sending and forwarding Internet mail).

> The Option Pack's Simple Mail Transfer Protocol (SMTP) service is suitable for sending mail and transferring it between servers, but not for delivering mail to individual users. That would require a Post Office Protocol (POP) server or an Internet Message Access Protocol (IMAP) server, neither of which the Option Pack includes.

The Option Pack setup will prompt you for various file locations, using dialog boxes similar to Figure 16-5. You'll probably want to keep the suggested path names but change the driver letters, first, to keep things off the Windows NT system drive, second, to isolate data files from software areas, and third, to segregate applications with possible rapid disk growth from others that would be adversely affected.

When setup is complete, it will ask you to reboot the computer so it can complete the installation. After the system comes back up and the installation is complete, you're ready to configure your Web server.

Configuration

To configure IIS on either Windows NT Workstation or Server, you'll need to open Internet Service Manager, a utility that's installed with IIS. Click Start, Programs, Windows NT Option Pack, Microsoft Internet Information Server, and then Internet Service Manager. This will produce the window shown in Figure 16-14. As usual, clicking a Plus icon expands an item, and clicking a Minus icon collapses one. In the figure, the items Internet Information Server and Earring are both expanded. Earring is the server's computer name.

> The application shown in Figure 16-13 is actually Microsoft Management Console, a general purpose interface for managing Windows NT services. The capability to administer individual services comes from so-called snap-in modules, each of which appears as a first-level item under Console Root. To administer listed services running on other machines, right-click the service name and choose Connect from the pop-up menu.

FIGURE 16-14.

Internet Service Manager is a snap-in module for Microsoft Management Console.

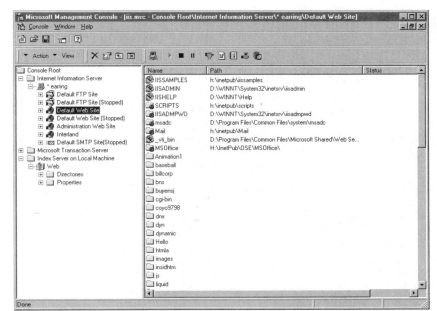

You can configure IIS settings at three levels: the entire machine, an individual Web server, or an individual folder. Settings established at more general levels also apply to more specific ones, unless overridden.

Keep this in mind as you read the following sections. You can apply most of the dialog boxes at the computer level, at the Web-server level, or at any directory within a server's document tree. To display or modify properties at any level, find the item in Microsoft Management Console, right-click it, and then choose Properties from the pop-up menu.

To create a new virtual directory, right-click the folder's parent location, choose New from the pop-up menu, and then choose Virtual Directory.

SEE ALSO

For information about the Server Extensions tab in this and subsequent dialog boxes in this chapter, see Chapter 17, "Understanding the FrontPage Server Extensions."

Configuring Master Properties

Figure 16-15 shows the dialog box that results from right-clicking a computer entry listed below Internet Information Server and then choosing Properties. Here are some of the options you can choose:

■ The **Master Properties** list box itemizes services available for configuration. The choice to configure the IIS Web server is, of course, WWW Service. To proceed with configuration, click the Edit button.

■ The **Enable Bandwidth Throttling** option, if turned on, sets a maximum on the amount of bandwidth Internet services can consume.

■ The **Computer MIME Map** frame configures the assignment of MIME types to file name extensions. Clicking File Types displays the dialog box shown previously in Figure 15-2.

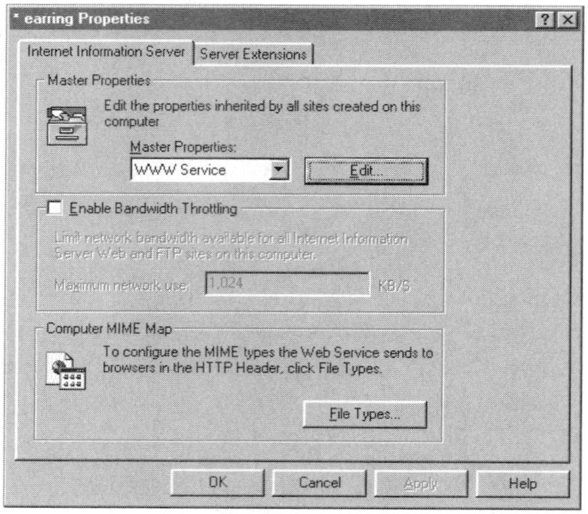

FIGURE 16-15.
This is the IIS Properties dialog box for a computer named Earring.

Configuring Site Level Options

Selecting WWW Service and clicking Edit produces the multi-tabbed dialog box that appears in Figure 16-16. Various options will be enabled or dimmed depending on the context, but here's a run-down of the complete set:

■ **Web Site Identification** controls the server's worded and network identities.

• **Description** gives the IIS server a name that serves as documentation and appears in various configuration dialog boxes.

• **IP Address** specifies the IP address a virtual server should respond to. Recall that for virtual servers, the computer responds to more than one IP address and uses a different server configuration accordingly.

• **TCP Port** specifies the port number on which the server will operate.

• **SSL Port** specifies the port number on which the server will accept Secure Socket Layer (SSL) transmissions.

🟠 TIP

To create a new virtual server, right-click the computer entry under Internet Information Server, choose new from the pop-up menu, then choose Virtual Server.

■ **Connections** sets limits on the number and duration of network connections.

- **Unlimited** sets no maximum on the number of simultaneous connections the server will try to accommodate.

- **Limited To** controls the number of simultaneous connections the server will allow. In extremely busy environments, it may be better to turn away some connections than to provide substandard service to everyone who connects. Browsers will usually retry refused connections.

- **Connection Timeout** is the number of seconds the server will wait for network responses.

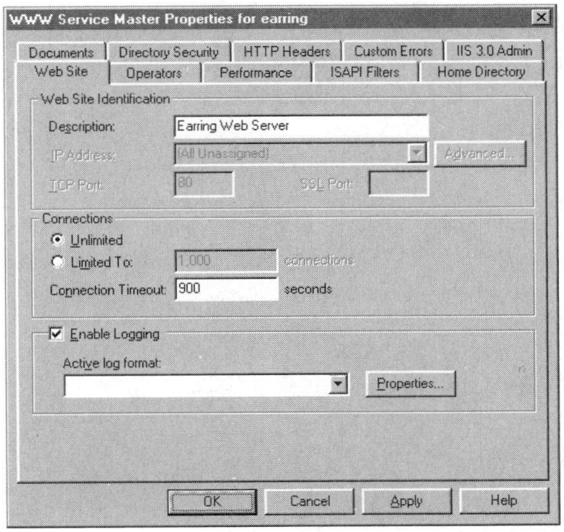

FIGURE 16-16.
The Web Site tab configures the most general options for a default or virtual server.

Authorizing Web-Server Operators

The Operators tab, shown in Figure 16-17, controls who may administer this IIS installation or virtual server. Clicking the Add button displays the normal Windows NT Add Users And Groups dialog box, which, in this context, selects additional operators. To remove an Operator entry, first select it and then click Remove.

III

Managing a Personal Web Server

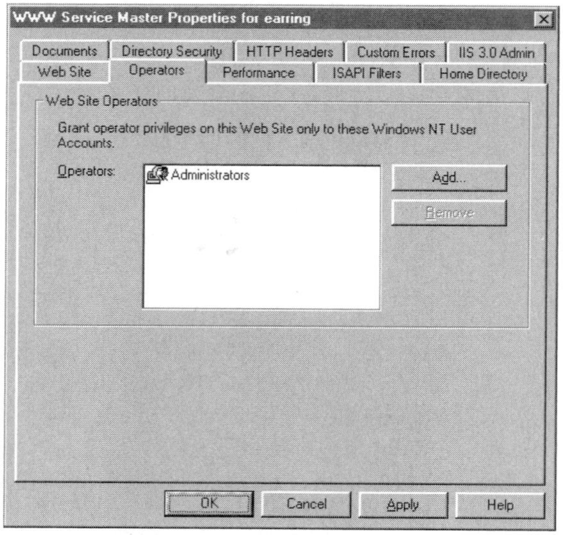

FIGURE 16-17.

The Operators tab controls which users and groups can administer the current Web server.

Configuring Performance Settings

The Performance tab appears in Figure 16-18. The slider in the Performance Tuning frame indirectly controls the amount of RAM IIS will allocate to the current site. The more hits you tell IIS to expect, the more RAM it will allocate to the current server (at the expense, of course, of other processes on the same computer).

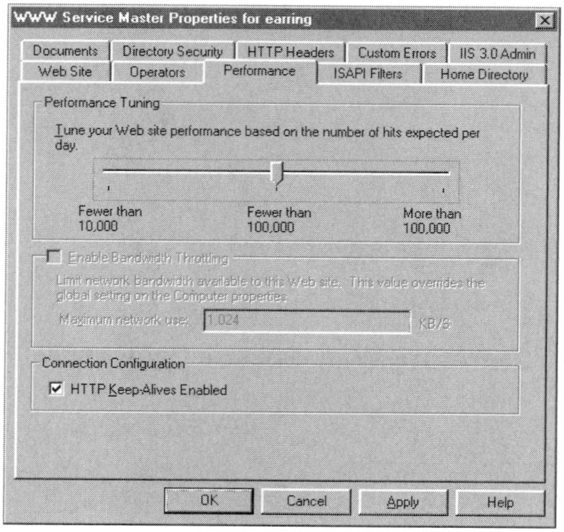

FIGURE 16-18.

The Performance tab provides controls that optimize Web-server performance.

The Enable Bandwidth Throttling option, if turned on, sets a maximum on the amount of bandwidth Internet services can consume. This setting repeats at various levels to control bandwidth allowed at each level.

The HTTP Keep-Alives Enabled setting, if turned on, permits browsers to request multiple files over the same TCP/IP connection. This is beneficial for both browsers and servers because opening a new connection for each file consumes more resources.

Configuring ISAPI Filters

Figure 16-19 shows the ISAPI Filters tab. An ISAPI filter is installed as part of the Web server, taking action based on requests, responses, and other events to which it's programmed to respond. Basically, it modifies or extends the Web server's actions.

FIGURE 16-19.
ISAPI filters are programs that hook into the Web server and modify its behavior.

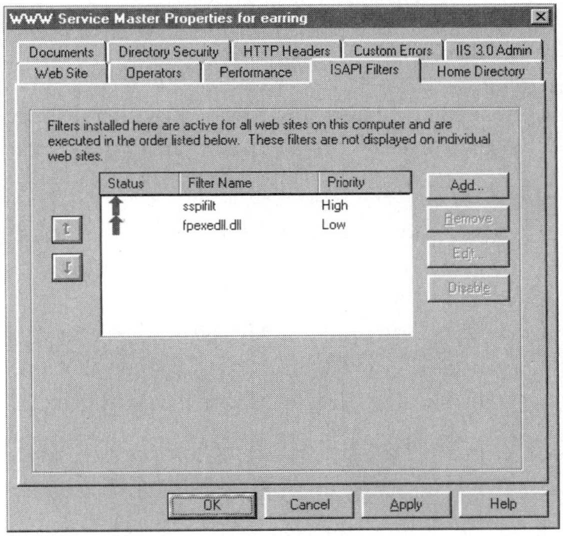

You can add, remove, modify, or disable ISAPI filter definitions by using the buttons provided, but doing so is extremely unusual. Most ISAPI filters are components of larger software packages installed and removed by setup programs. However, if you suspect a certain filter is causing a problem, you might want to temporarily disable it.

III

Managing a Personal Web Server

Configuring Home Directory Settings

The Home Directory tab, shown in Figure 16-20, controls the location and other options for a server's HTTP root directory. The first option, at the top of the box, controls where the server's content should come from. The options are:

- **A Directory Located On This Computer** is by far the most common option. This indicates how the URL "/" corresponds to a location in the server's local file system. Click the Browse button to choose the proper location.

- **A Share Located On Another Computer** means the Web server will deliver content physically located on another computer and accessed by file sharing. When you select this option:

  - The Local Path box changes to a Network Directory box, where you should enter a \\<server>\<sharename> path to the desired file server.

  - The Browse button changes to Connect As. Click this button to specify a username and password that allows access to the specified files.

- **A Redirection To A URL** means that instead of delivering content, the server will redirect any requests to another server. This can be a temporary redirection to another server, a temporary redirection to a subordinate folder, or a permanent redirection. You can specify exact URLs for these redirections or build them symbolically from components of the incoming URL.

  This option is most useful after you've moved content to another location or server.

> **NOTE**
> When notified of a permanent redirection, some browsers update stored locations such as those in a Favorites menu.

The remaining options apply only if you chose A Directory Located On This Computer or A Share Located On Another Computer.

- **Access Permissions** controls whether or not Web visitors can read items in this folder, and whether or not they can write to them.

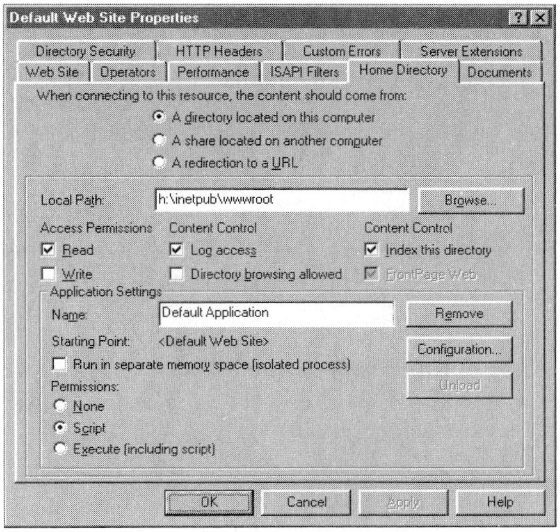

FIGURE 16-20.

The Home Directory tab controls the starting point for Web pages and other files in a Web server.

> **SEE ALSO**
>
> For more information about server-based FrontPage Webs, see Chapter 18,"Creating and Managing Front-Page Webs." For more information about the FrontPage Server Extensions, which make server-based Front-Page Webs possible, see Chapter 17,"Understanding the FrontPage Server Extensions."

- **Content Control** provides options related to managing the server's content.

  - **Log Access,** if turned on, extends a log file by one record for each request the server receives.

  - **Directory Browsing Allowed** specifies what happens when a Web visitor submits a GET request with no file name, and no default document exists. If the box is turned on, the Web visitor gets a clickable list of files and folders that *do* exit. If the box is turned off, the Web visitor gets an Access Denied error.

  - **Index This Directory** means that Microsoft Index Server will maintain a full text index of documents in the directory tree starting at this location.

  - **FrontPage Web,** if turned on, indicates that this folder is the start of a server-based FrontPage Web.

- **Application Settings** controls the settings for a Web *application*. An application starts at a specified Web folder and includes all folders within it, except folders and subfolders defined as part of *another* application. All files within an application space share certain executable program settings and certain kinds of state data. The settings include those below.

- **Name** specifies the application's identity in words. This is essentially documentation.

- **Configuration** displays an editable list associating file name extensions with programs that process them. For example, this list usually associates the extension ASP with the Active Server Page interpreter.

- **Run In Separate Memory Space,** if turned on, runs the application in its own memory space, separate from that of the Web server. This increases performance and decreases problems following an application failure, but consumes more system resources.

- **Permissions** controls the way Web visitors can access the folder. Read means Web visitors can retrieve Web pages and other files in the ordinary way. Execute means Web visitors can launch executable programs residing in the directory. Scripts means that Web visitors can run Web pages that contain server-side scripting.

Configuring Document Options

Figure 16-21 illustrates the Documents tab. The check box Enable Default Document controls whether IIS will look for a certain file name when someone submits a URL without one. This situation occurs when, for example, a user submits a URL such as *http://www.microsoft.com/*. If Enable Default Document is turned on, the server will switch to the directory specified in the URL and then search for the given default document names in the order specified. Use the Add and Remove buttons to insert and delete file names from the list. Use the Up and Down buttons to change a selected name's position.

If the check box titled Enable Document Footer is turned on, the Web server will append a specified file to every Web page it delivers. This is useful for appending page footers to every page within a certain tree. The Browse button locates that file.

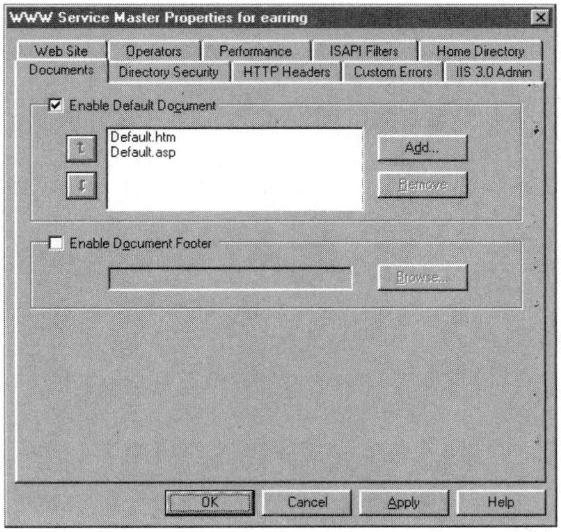

FIGURE 16-21.

This property tab configures two optional settings: the default document name and a document footer.

Configuring Directory Security

The Directory Security tab, shown in Figure 16-22, controls three security settings:

- **Anonymous Access and Authentication Control** controls the use of login accounts required for accessing Web pages.

- **Secure Communications** manages the digital certificates (electronic credentials) used for secure communication over networks such as the Internet.

- **IP Address and Domain Name Restrictions** configures rules that restrict access based on the Web visitor's IP address. For example, all or part of a Web server can be restricted to Web visitors with IP addresses belonging to a given enterprise.

User-level control of Web access works like this: when a visitor first accesses an IIS site, IIS tries to access the requested file name using a so-called *anonymous* account. This is a user account, typically named IUSR_<computername>, that has no privileges other than accessing unrestricted Web content. If the NT File System (NTFS) is coded so the anonymous account has access, the Web server delivers the content. If

NTFS permissions *don't* grant access to the anonymous account, the Web server sends an Access Denied status code.

⭐ **TIP**

> Always use the NTFS file system on every drive of any computer used for Web access. Using the FAT file system, which has no built-in security, is just too risky.

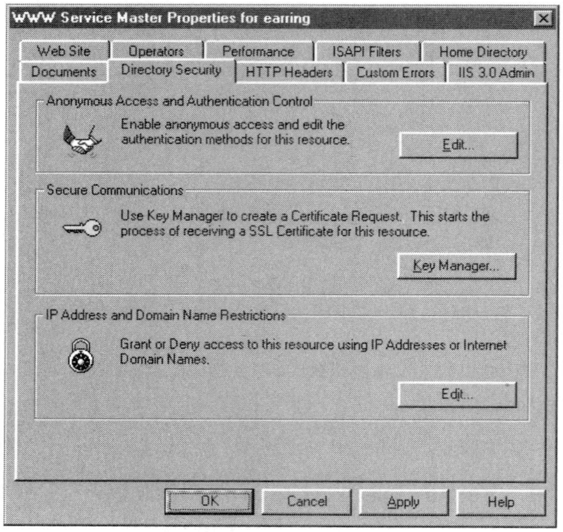

FIGURE 16-22.

This tab configures the login account used for anonymous access, the keys used for secured communications, and access restrictions based on the Web visitor's IP address.

When the Web visitor's browser gets the Access Denied status code, it prompts its user for another user name and password and then, when the visitor presses enter, it transmits those values along with the original request.

If the submitted user name is the name of a valid Windows NT logon account, and if the submitted password is correct, the Web server tries using that account to access the requested file. If NTFS grants access, the Web server delivers the page. In any other case, the Web server again transmits the Access Denied status code.

Once a Web visitor gets a user name and password to work, the browser transmits those values on *every* subsequent request to the same server. This continues until access again fails (presumably because permissions on another area of Web content are different) or until the visitor terminates the browser program.

Figure 16-23 shows the dialog box that results from clicking the Edit button for Anonymous Access And Authentication Control in Figure 16-22.

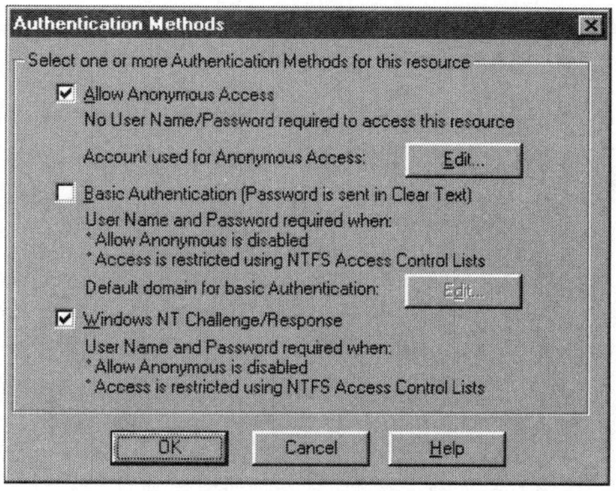

FIGURE 16-23.
This dialog box controls the use of Windows NT user accounts for secure Web-page access.

FIGURE 16-23.
This dialog box controls the use of Windows NT user accounts for secure Web-page access.

This dialog box exposes three more options:

- **Allow Anonymous Access,** if turned on, instructs IIS to determine whether the Anonymous account has access to a file before prompting the remote user for a user name and password. If the anonymous account has access to the requested file, no user name/password prompting will occur. If the anonymous account doesn't have access, IIS will prompt the remote user for a user name/password combination that does.

  The Edit button selects the anonymous account.

- **Basic Authentication,** if turned on, instructs IIS to accept unencrypted passwords from remote users. Unencrypted passwords are a security risk because others on the network can capture, decipher, and use them without proper authority. Unfortunately, this is the only authentication scheme many Web browsers support.

  The Edit button identifies the Windows NT Domain used for authenticating user name/password combinations.

- **Windows NT Challenge/Response,** if turned on, indicates that IIS should verify passwords using a very secure process also used for network logins to a Windows NT server. As of this writing, Internet Explorer was the only browser that supported this option.

> **NOTE**

If Basic Authentication and Windows NT Challenge/Response are both enabled, IIS will use Windows NT Challenge/Response if possible and Basic Authentication otherwise.

III

Managing a Personal Web Server

Configuring HTTP Headers

Figure 16-24 shows the HTTP Headers tab, which controls different kinds of information delivered with your Web pages.

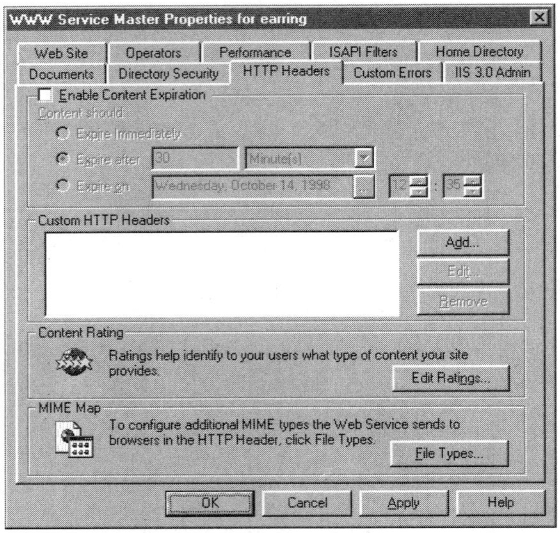

FIGURE 16-24.

HTTP headers transmit informational data about your Web pages.

- **Enable Content Expiration,** if turned on, controls content caching on the Web visitor's browser. This pertains only to files received from your site, and only from within the directory tree where you define the setting. There are three possible approaches:

  - **Expire Immediately** means the browser shouldn't cache the content at all.

  - **Expire After** means the browser shouldn't cache the content longer than the specified interval.

  - **Expire On** means the browser shouldn't cache content beyond the specified date and time.

SEE ALSO

For more information about HTTP headers, see "HyperText Transfer Protocol—A Simple Concept," page 483.

- **Custom HTTP Headers** consist of strings you supply entirely by hand. Use the Add, Edit, and Remove buttons to modify the list.

- **Content Rating** displays a dialog box where you can rate your site's content in terms of Violence, Sex, Nudity, and Language. Web visitors can then set their browsers to accept or exclude pages based on these settings. These settings can assure your visitors there's nothing objectionable about your site or, if your site contains potentially objectionable content, possibly lessen your liability.

- **MIME Map** displays a list of file name extensions and corresponding MIME types that override those set at the computer level (that is, those set in Figure 16-15 on page 518).

Customizing Error Displays

The Custom Errors tab, which appears in Figure 16-25, controls the format of standard-error messages your visitors receive. Basically, there's a Web page for each standard error. It's usually better to click the Edit properties button and specify a different page than to modify the default error message pages.

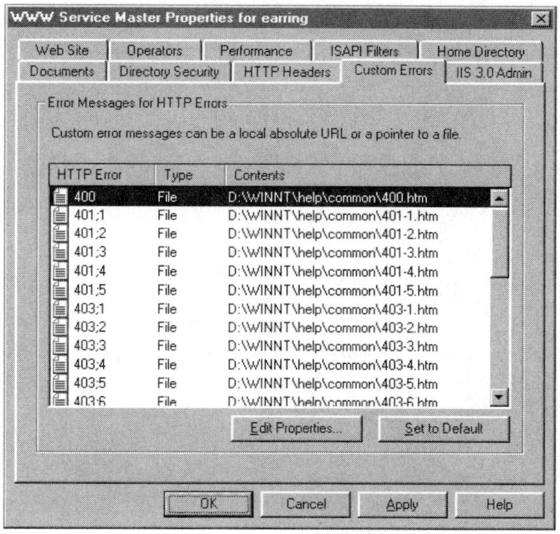

FIGURE 16-25.
This tab specifies the Web page the server will send in the event of each standard error.

Configuring IIS 3.0 Administration

The last properties tab, shown in Figure 16-26, pertains to administering an IIS 4.0 site remotely with the Internet Service Manager supplied with IIS 3.0. Because IIS 4.0's configuration is so much more flexible than IIS 3.0's, the IIS administration tools can only administer one designated server: that is, the default server or one virtual server. This tab specifies which server.

III

Managing a Personal Web Server

FIGURE 16-26.

This property tab specifies the one IIS 4.0 Web server that IIS 3.0's Internet Service Manager can remotely access.

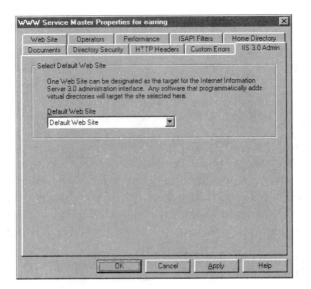

Using a Non-Microsoft Web Server

The FrontPage Server Extensions are designed to minimize differences among Web servers. Assuming FrontPage Extensions (described in the next chapter) are available for the target server, and the server administrator has installed them, Web page authors shouldn't have to concern themselves greatly about which Web server is in use. For programmers and administrators, however, the differences aren't nearly as transparent.

Regardless of the type of Web server in use, authors will need to learn the default document name. This name is default.htm on most Microsoft servers and index.html on most others, though local configurations can vary in either case.

Security is another area where no two servers tend to be alike. Web authors, Web administrators, and system administrators will need to learn how security works on each server—target and development—and must control access on each machine appropriately.

Each Web server tends to provide a slightly different environment for running programmed elements such as CGI programs, ISAPI programs, server-side includes, and server-side scripts. Different versions of such tools are usually required for each different Web server, and few are available for all. This variance also affects programs you or others at your site may write; in general, without modification they won't be portable from one type of server to another.

If FrontPage extensions aren't available for the target Web server or aren't installed, authors will have to publish Webs manually or using the Web Publishing Wizard. In addition, browse-time services provided by the extensions obviously won't be available—services such as search and server-side form-field validation.

If the FrontPage extensions on a server aren't up-to-date, you'll get various errors when authoring and publishing. The best solution is to upgrade the extensions. If that isn't possible, do as much work as possible on a server that has up-to-date extensions, and then publish the results to the out-of-date server later. Before using any browse-time features, test them on the outdated server to determine whether they work as expected.

The more active services you expect from your Web server, the more difficult mixed server environments will be. If at all possible, use the same server or at least the same family of servers for development, testing, and production.

Other Windows Web Servers

All Web servers must, by definition, implement the hypertext transfer protocol similarly. This means that virtually all Web servers deliver simple Web pages the same way, transparently to Web authors.

As just stated, differences are more pronounced with respect to executables, such as CGI, ISAPI, and server-side scripts. Before using any of these facilities, verify that your target Web server supports them.

Web Servers on Non-Microsoft Operating Systems

All the cautions mentioned in the previous section apply as well to Web servers operating in a non-Windows environment. In addition, such servers raise issues involving non-Windows file systems.

Unix file systems are usually case-sensitive, limited to 32 characters per file name or folder name, and subject to different restrictions on file name characters. This means, among other things, that a URL for Index.html will not retrieve a file named index.html; instead, the server will return a Not Found message. The best policy, therefore, is to limit file names and folder names, both in the file system and in URLs, to lowercase letters and numbers only.

Some executables will run on more than one Windows Web server, but virtually none will run on both Windows and non-Windows systems. Most executables are completely nonportable between Windows and

III

Managing a Personal Web Server

Unix, even on the same hardware. If Windows-based authors need to invoke Unix-based server-side programs, they'll have to work carefully from the documentation and, in the best of circumstances, test their results in an environment closely resembling production.

In Summary...

This chapter described in some detail how to install and configure the Microsoft Web servers designed for Windows 95, Windows 98, and Windows NT and supplied with the Windows NT Option Pack. This information will be valuable if you need to set up your own production Web server on the Internet, a production intranet server, or a test and development server for yourself or your workgroup.

The next chapter will discuss installing the FrontPage Server Extensions, which make server-based FrontPage Webs possible and which fully support all the features of Web pages created with FrontPage.

PART IV

Using FrontPage Webs

CHAPTER 17

Understanding the FrontPage Server Extensions

From one perspective, a FrontPage Web is any collection of HTML pages and support files that FrontPage admin-ministers as a unit. A FrontPage Web begins at a certain folder, either on your disk or on a Web server, and includes all files within that folder and any subfolders. Once you de-clare such an area to be a FrontPage Web, FrontPage starts managing that area as a single body of content.

FrontPage, however, lives intimately on the Web. Not only can it create and manage Web content on your local disk; it can also function as a Web-based, client/server authoring system. In this second mode, FrontPage has processing components on both Web clients and Web servers, and these components communicate via Web protocols.

In client/server mode, the FrontPage desktop software acts as the client, and the FrontPage Server Extensions, running on your Web server, provide the complementary server processes. The FrontPage Server Extensions also provide the software for certain FrontPage components that run on the Web server when remote users visit your site.

This chapter will first describe the extensions in a bit more detail, and then explain how to obtain and install them. If your involvement with FrontPage involves only page creation and someone else administers your Web servers, you can safely skip all but the first section. However, if you manage Web servers for others—even a personal Web server for yourself—this chapter will get you started with the server side of FrontPage processing.

Understanding Disk-Based Webs

Itself a denizen of the Web, FrontPage requires the presence of a Web server to deliver its full complement of features. There may be cases, however, when a Web server isn't available—not even a personal Web server operating on your own computer. Some possible reasons include the following:

- You find configuring your own Web server impractical.

- Your computer isn't on a TCP/IP network and has no IP address.

- You have access to a Web server, but for some reason FrontPage Server Extensions can't be installed. The extensions might not be available for the particular server and platform, for example.

- You notice that performance is inadequate when you're running a personal Web server.

Fortunately, FrontPage can provide most of its features in a completely serverless environment called a *disk-based Web*. Instead of having a Web server read and write files on the server's local disk, FrontPage simply reads and writes the files directly, using either your computer's local hard disk or space on a network file server.

TIP

> If two Web pages belong to the same body of content and share the same administrative control, put them in the same Web. If they're significantly different in terms of content or control, put them in separate Webs.

You can create a disk-based Web in a location where HTML files already exist, but FrontPage will "webify" that location by adding its own folders and files. To keep your original location clean, first create a new disk-based Web in a different location and later import the existing content. You can create one FrontPage Web inside another, but the two Webs become separate bodies of content. No file or folder can belong to more than one Web.

Before FrontPage converts any folder to a disk-based Web, it displays the confirmation prompt shown in Figure 17-1.

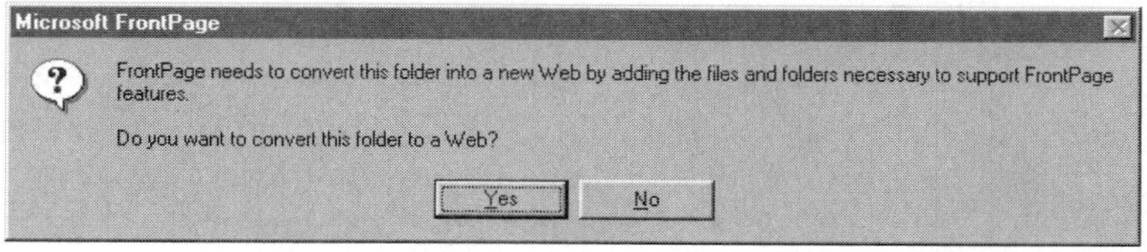

FIGURE 17-1.

This dialog box prompts for confirmation before FrontPage converts an ordinary disk folder to a disk-based FrontPage Web.

You can publish a disk-based Web to another disk-based Web or to a real Web server. Likewise, you can publish a real FrontPage Web to a disk-based Web. Simply specify the correct location, whether Web server or disk, when you open the source Web and also when you specify the target Web.

SEE ALSO

For more information on Web publishing, see Chapter 24, "Publishing Your FrontPage Web."

A disk-based Web has no way to run CGI or ISAPI programs. Such programs provide dynamic services, at either authoring time or browse time. They're designed to run in a Web-server environment, and can't run without one, so the following FrontPage features won't work on a disk-based Web:

■ Confirmation Field component

■ Discussion Group component

■ Form Results component

■ Registration component

■ Search component

■ Server-side scripts (Active Server Pages)

■ Any other user-written, shareware, or commercial server-side programs

Using a disk-based Web doesn't prevent you from creating Web pages using these features; it only prevents you from running or testing them. Still, this is a significant list of features to lose. In addition to these restrictions, disk-based Webs have no security features at all; anyone with at least read permission to the disk-based Web's file area has access.

Despite their restrictions, disk-based Webs are now the recommended environment for new FrontPage users and for anyone who doesn't plan to use the components listed above. If ordinary Web pages, perhaps enhanced with browser scripts, are all you plan to create, disk-based Webs are perfectly adequate. If you need more, you can always advance to a server-based Web.

Understanding Server-Based Webs

If you decide the restrictions of a disk-based Web are unacceptable, server-based FrontPage Webs provide the answer. With a server-based Web, all your Web files physically reside on a Web server equipped with the FrontPage Server Extensions. This is exactly the environment where all FrontPage features for authoring, browse-time processing, and site management are fully supported.

The primary disadvantage of server-based Webs is their complexity. Most users of desktop software aren't experienced Web-server administrators and moreover, have no desire to become so. This is why Microsoft has positioned disk-based Webs for beginning and intermediate Web authors while recommending server-based Webs for advanced Web developers.

Server-based Webs are client/server environments. The client is the FrontPage desktop software, the server is the Web server running the FrontPage Server Extensions, and the two communicate entirely by HTTP. When the client needs to read files from the server, it does so just like a browser. When the client needs to upload files or send commands, it transmits the data to CGI or ISAPI programs on the server, just as browsers submit HTML forms. The server-based programs then update the requested files or settings.

A server-based Web can reside anywhere a Web server can reside: on your own PC, on another PC in your office or work group, on a corporate intranet server, or anywhere on the Internet. If you can browse a server's Web pages, you can author its FrontPage Webs (subject, of course, to logon security).

The FrontPage Server Extensions contain the software that makes server-based Webs possible. The process of enabling server-based Webs is therefore the process of installing and configuring the server extensions.

Server-Extension Functions

The FrontPage Server Extensions provide four kinds of services:

- **Browse-time services.** Features like text search and server-side, form-field validation obviously require programs that run on the server not when the developer creates or uploads the page, but every time a Web visitor submits a request. The FrontPage Server Extensions provide this programming in a standard way.

- **File and folder access.** When you open a page in FrontPage, it can retrieve any necessary files not only by reading a local file system, but also by opening an HTTP connection over the network. This pertains to the data files for the Task list, Navigation view, and Text indexes as well.

At some point, however, the needs of FrontPage exceed the capabilities of standard Web servers. FrontPage needs to create, replace, rename, move, copy, and delete files on the server based on commands received from the client—that is, from FrontPage. The FrontPage Server Extensions provide the server-side software for these client/server functions.

Compared to local file access or traditional file sharing, using Web protocols for file handling may initially seem awkward. Consider, however, that many Web developers lack facilities for local file sharing but do have Web connectivity. In this environment, using Web protocols and Server Extensions indeed makes sense.

- **Security services.** The ability of remote users to add, update, delete, and reorganize files and folders carries with it the necessity to differentiate between authorized and unauthorized users. The FrontPage extensions not only provide and configure these services, but also provide network interfaces for configuring security via the FrontPage client.

- **Background services.** The FrontPage Server Extensions also provide a number of content services that run in the background on the server. Choosing Recalculate Hyperlinks from FrontPage's Tools menu, for example, brings up the dialog box shown in Figure 17-2, advising the Web author that FrontPage is about to launch a server-side process.

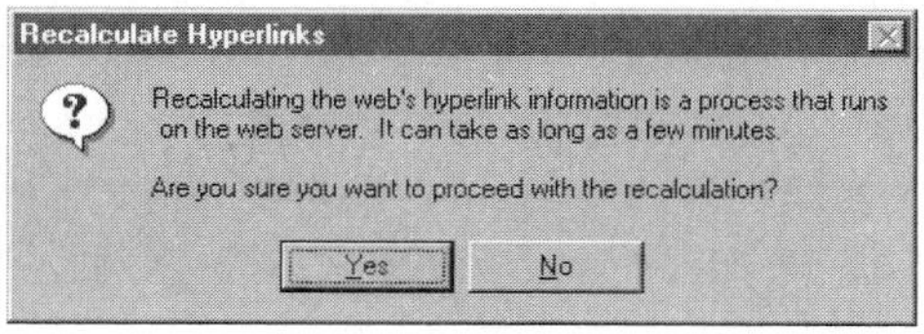

FIGURE 17-2.

FrontPage clients can initiate server-side processes installed by FrontPage Server Extensions.

Despite running with different Web servers and on different operating systems, each implementation of the FrontPage Server Extensions provides the same services and application protocols. This allows FrontPage and other clients to use the FrontPage Server Extensions in a platform-independent way.

Server Extensions Documentation

The FrontPage Server Extensions come with detailed documentation in HTML format. If you choose to install the Server Extensions Resource Kit, the setup program will copy these files to your local disk. You can locate the Server Extensions Resource Kit on your hard disk or CD by running a file search for the folder name *serk*. If you find multiple *serk* folders, examine the directory paths and choose the one that corresponds to your preferred language. The folder name *enu*, for example, means US English; *deu* means Deutsche (German) and so forth.

You can view the Server Extensions Resource Kit documentation directly, by opening its file location in your browser, or by publishing it to your Personal Web Server. To view it from your Web server, first copy the *serk* folder to a folder on your Web server disk (if *Setup* hasn't already done so), and then define a virtual folder that points to the *serk* folder on your disk.

Installing the FrontPage Server Extensions

The procedure for installing the FrontPage extensions varies somewhat, depending on the Web server, the operating system, and the server extension version. In general, though, there are four steps:

1   Install the server's operating system and the Web-server software.

For purposes of this book, we'll assume this work is already done and tested. That is, the hardware is complete, the operating system is stable, and the Web server is delivering pages and performing other functions normally.

2   Install the FrontPage Server Extension software.

If you're running a Windows-based Web server and install the FrontPage client on the same machine, FrontPage Setup will usually copy the FrontPage Server Extensions onto the computer and, coincidentally, perform step 3 on the default Web server.

For machines not running Windows, machines running Web servers FrontPage Setup doesn't detect, and machines where the Web server got installed after the FrontPage client, obtain the FrontPage extensions as described in the sidebar "Obtaining FrontPage Server Extensions," page 542, and then run the accompanying setup program.

3 Convert any desired real or virtual Web servers to FrontPage Webs.

Installing the Server Extension software and creating FrontPage Webs are two separate but related operations.

- Installing the Server Extensions provides a set of installation and administration utilities, and provides a master source of software for individual FrontPage Webs. This task is step 2, above.

- Creating a FrontPage Web means copying three programs into a Web server's file space, initializing various configuration files, and indexing any existing content. This is the current step 3.

CAUTION

If the Web server has a large body of existing content, indexing it can take a long time.

Most Web-server software allows one computer, responding to multiple IP addresses, to deliver different content for each of those addresses. Each such arrangement is called a *virtual server*. For each such server, you are perfectly free to install the FrontPage Server Extensions or not.

In virtual-server environments there's usually one server—called the *default server*—that responds to any IP address not associated with a specific virtual server. Installing the FrontPage Server Extensions on such a computer usually converts the default server to a FrontPage Web; that is, it automatically performs step 2 for the whole server and step 3 for the default Web server. For the remaining virtual server, you'll need to install the FrontPage extensions by issuing a command.

4 Create subwebs within the root Webs from step 3.

When you first install the FrontPage extensions on a Web server, FrontPage considers the server to be one large body of content—one Web—called the root Web. Very seldom, however, is this appropriate. Most Web servers contain multiple bodies of content, each with its own set of authors and administrators. The solution is to segregate each body of content into its own folder, and then designate those folders as FrontPage Webs in their own right. Because these Webs remain physically subordinate to the root Web, they're often called *subwebs*.

The root Web is so called because it begins at the Web server's HTTP root directory—that is, at the URL "/". All other Webs on that server are subwebs that reside within the root Web or within other Webs, nested to any level.

(?) SEE ALSO

For more information about the Office Server Extensions, see "The Microsoft Office Server Extensions," page 601.

Obtaining FrontPage Server Extensions

There are four ways to obtain and install the FrontPage Server Extensions. The method you use depends on your Web server's operating system and software.

- **Delivered with FrontPage.** The FrontPage CD provides Server Extensions for most Windows-based Web servers. Running Setup from the CD will normally detect any Web servers on the same machine and install the appropriate extensions.

- **Delivered with the Office Server Extensions.** Beginning with Microsoft Office 2000, the Microsoft Office applications now have their own set of Web-server extensions. The Office extensions, however, are an extension of the FrontPage extensions. Installing the Office Server Extensions is therefore tantamount to installing the FrontPage extensions plus additional applications.

- **Delivered with Web Server Software.** Some Web servers include FrontPage Server Extensions on their distribution disks. Check your product documentation for availability and instructions.

- **Downloaded from Microsoft.** Many FrontPage Server Extensions are available from Microsoft's Web site at http://www.microsoft.com/frontpage/wpp. Even if you obtain FrontPage Server Extensions from another source, it's usually worthwhile to check the Microsoft site for a newer version.

In previous versions of FrontPage, all subwebs had to reside in the root folder of the root Web. This is no longer the case; you can now define subwebs at any point in the server's directory tree and also, you can nest one subweb inside another with no restriction other than path length on the level of nesting. Creating a subweb requires the parent administrator account and password.

If you installed your own Web server, you'll have chosen its root Web administrator name and password during the installation. If you're using a shared or centralized Web server, the server's administrator probably controls the root Web and performs whatever tasks require the root Web password.

If the server supports multiple groups or customers, it's usually best to create a separate FrontPage Web for each one. If one physical server supports multiple virtual Web servers, the virtual servers can be FrontPage-extended or not in any combination. In addition, the system administrator can delegate administration of each virtual server to its owner.

To install the FrontPage Server Extensions and the Office Server Extensions on a Windows NT Server, insert Office 2000 Premium Disk 3 and choose Install Microsoft Office Server Extensions from the splash screen. If the splash screen doesn't appear, run setupse.exe from the root directory of Disk 3.

To install the FrontPage Server Extensions on Windows 9x, Windows NT Workstation, or Windows NT Server, follow these steps:

1 Run the Office 2000 Premium setup from Disk 1.

2 When the setup wizard gets to the Ready To Install panel, Choose Customize.

3 When the wizard displays the Selecting Features panel, expand the choice Microsoft FrontPage For Windows and set the following options to Run From My Computer:

- Server Extensions Resource Kit

- Server Extension Admin Forms (provided that you want to administer the extensions via your browser)

TIP

When you are installing the FrontPage extensions on a Windows NT Server, you probably don't want to install any desktop applications. Therefore, when the Selecting Features panel appears, first set each application in the list to Not Available and then set Server Extensions Resource Kit to Run From My Computer.

Software Platforms and Availability

The FrontPage Server Extensions are available for all popular Web-server software on all popular platforms. Table 17-1 lists those supported at the time of this writing.

As you might expect, versions of the Server Extensions for various servers and operating systems tend to appear at intervals rather than all at once. To check the current availability of FrontPage Server Extensions for your environment, browse Microsoft's Web site at:

http://www.microsoft.com/frontpage/wpp

TABLE 17-1. **Web Server Availability for FrontPage Server Extensions**

Provider	Web Server	Operating System
Apache Project	Apache	Unix, Linux
Microsoft	Microsoft Personal Web Server	Windows 95, Windows 98
Microsoft	Internet Information Server	Windows NT
NCSA	NCSA	Unix
Netscape	Netscape Web Servers	Unix, Windows
O'Reilly	WebSite	Windows

FrontPage Server Extension Administration Tools

Microsoft provides five tools for creating, deleting, and otherwise administering server-based FrontPage Webs. No one tool provides all capabilities in all situations, but you should view this as reasons for multiple tools to exist, and not as a deficiency of any one tool. The five tools are:

- **The FrontPage Desktop Software** can configure most aspects of a FrontPage Web, and it can create subwebs as well.

- **The FrontPage MMC Snap-In** is a graphical user interface program that administers the FrontPage Server Extensions. However, the snap-in runs only on Windows operating systems, and it can't administer server extensions on a remote computer.

> **NOTE**
>
> The FrontPage MMC snap-in replaces the FrontPage Server Administrator program supplied with previous versions of FrontPage.

- **HTML Administration Forms** are HTML forms that administer the FrontPage Server Extensions from a Web browser.

- **The Fpsrvadm Utility** is a command-line program available not only on Windows, but also on various Unix operating systems. This can be useful if you want to perform FrontPage operations on a timed basis, on Unix where GUI FrontPage tools aren't available, or if you just prefer working at the command line. Fpsrvadm is installed as part of the FrontPage Server Extensions, and it only administers extensions on the local computer.

- **The Fpremadm Utility** is a command-line program that administers the FrontPage extensions on a remote computer. Fpremadm can administer extensions running on any operating system—even Unix—but the program itself only runs on Windows 95, Windows 98, Windows NT Workstation, and Windows NT Server. Installing the FrontPage Server Extensions installs Fpremadm as well.

ON THE WEB

For more information about administration utilities for server-based Webs, refer to the FrontPage Server Extensions Resource Kit at http://www.microsoft.com/frontpage/wpp/serk

SEE ALSO
For information about using FrontPage desktop software to configure a server-based Web, see Chapter 18, "Creating and Managing FrontPage Webs."

The tools inside the FrontPage desktop software deal mostly with configuration and administration of existing FrontPage Webs, with creation of subwebs, and, of course, with creation of content. You can't install the Server Extensions or add them to a virtual server using the FrontPage client.

The remaining four tools deal primarily with installing the extensions, adding them to new virtual servers, and creating subwebs. In short, they're devoted to system management rather than content creation. The remainder of this chapter will review each of these tools in turn.

Administering the FrontPage Extensions from Microsoft Management Console

Microsoft Management Console (MMC) is a general purpose utility that integrates administration of various system services into a single graphical framework. Applications that use MMC generally install a copy along with their own software: Internet Information Server and Microsoft Personal Web Server for Windows NT Workstation both install MMC, for example. You can also download MMC from Microsoft's Web site.

ON THE WEB

To obtain the most recent version of Microsoft Management Console, browse http://www.microsoft.com/management/mmc

Figure 17-3 shows a typical MMC display. The large pane at the left displays a hierarchy of service types, computers, and service-related resources within each computer. This is the *console tree*, and selecting any item within it establishes a context for any commands you issue. The commands themselves are located on context-sensitive menus displayed either by right-clicking the object in the console tree, or by selecting the object and then clicking the Action toolbar button.

FIGURE 17-3.

Microsoft Management Console displays its console tree in the left pane and details in the right. To issue commands, either right-click an icon or select an icon and then click the Action toolbar button.

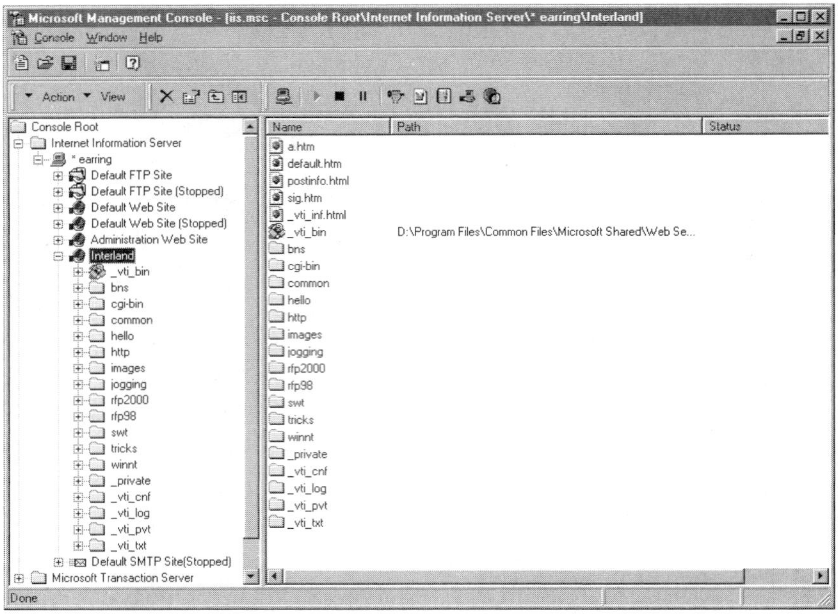

Software modules called *snap-ins* provide the capability to administer a particular service. Internet Information Server and the FrontPage Server Extensions both provide snap-ins. When both are present, the FrontPage snap-in operates as a component of the IIS snap-in. This will become clearer as we examine individual features.

To administer the FrontPage 2000 extensions installed on Microsoft Personal Web Server for Windows 95 or Windows 98, click Start, then Programs, then Microsoft Office Tools, and then Server Extensions Administrator.

Finding FrontPage MMC Snap-In Components

On Windows NT, FrontPage commands appear at three locations in the Microsoft Management Console tree.

- **New Menus** displayed by suitable icons in the console tree (such as a Web server or folder) provide commands that add FrontPage components. These commands create new Webs, add new administrators, and so forth.

- **Task Menus** displayed by suitable icons in the console tree provide commands that work on installed FrontPage components. These include, for example, commands to check and fix, remove, and upgrade the FrontPage Server Extensions.

- **The Server Extensions Tab** modifies detailed server-extension settings such as e-mail options and security settings.

On PWS for Windows 95 and Windows 98, right-click the computer name under FrontPage Server Extensions and look for these commands:

- Clicking New and then Web installs the FrontPage Server Extensions.

- Clicking Task and then Check Server Extensions validates that the server extensions are installed correctly.

- Clicking Properties displays the Server Extensions tab shown later in Figure 17-10.

Using the MMC New Menu

Figure 17-4 shows MMC displaying the New menu for a virtual Web server. (On Windows 95 and Windows 98, the virtual Web Server's name is `/LM/W3SVC/1:`.) Here are the commands applicable to FrontPage.

- **Server Extensions Web** creates a FrontPage subweb: that is, a FrontPage Web that resides within the selected server's root Web.

- **Server Extensions Administrator** adds a specified Windows NT user or group to the list of administrators for the given FrontPage Web (the root Web, in this instance).

Choosing Server Extensions Web runs a wizard that starts by displaying the dialog box shown in Figure 17-5.

- **Directory Name** specifies the new Web's file system name. This is also the path name that appears in the Web's URL.

- **Title** gives the Web a name in words. This is for human identification and documentation.

On Windows NT systems, clicking the Next button displays the dialog box shown in Figure 17-6, which initializes access control for the new Web.

- **Use The Same Administrator As The Parent Web** means this Web won't have a different list of administrators than the Web that contains it.

- **Use A Different Administrator For This Web** means this Web will have its own list of administrators. If you choose this option, you must also specify the name of a Windows NT user or group that will initially serve as the administrator. You can add additional administrators after the Web exists.

■ **Create Local Machine Groups,** if turned on, tells the Wizard to create Windows NT security groups for the basic kinds of FrontPage users. Later, you can add users to these groups with the Windows NT User Manager program. If you specify this option, you must also specify a Basic Group Name. This serves as a prefix for all groups the Wizard creates.

Clicking the Next button, and then Finish, completes creation of the new FrontPage Web.

The Server Extensions Administrator choice displays the dialog box shown in Figure 17-7. Enter the new administrator's user name, then click OK.

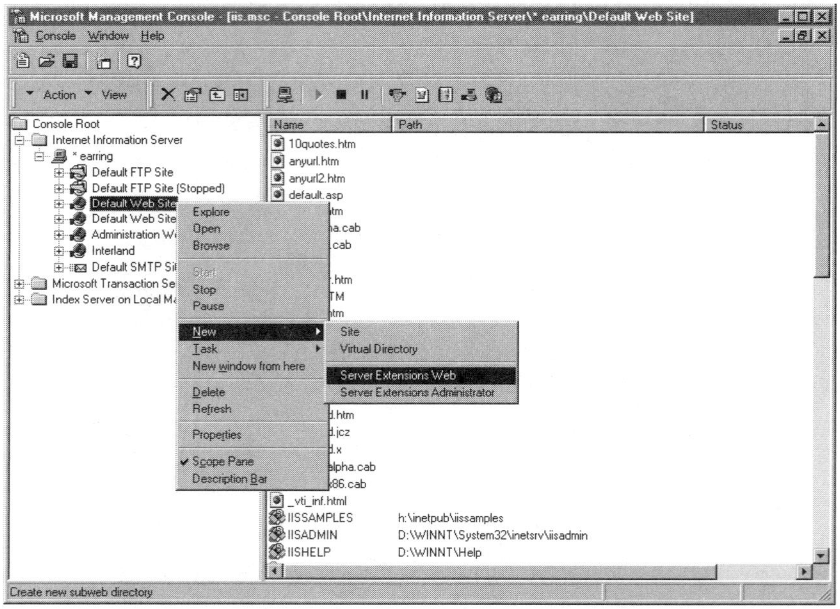

FIGURE 17-4.

The New menu adds FrontPage resources to a Web-server environment.

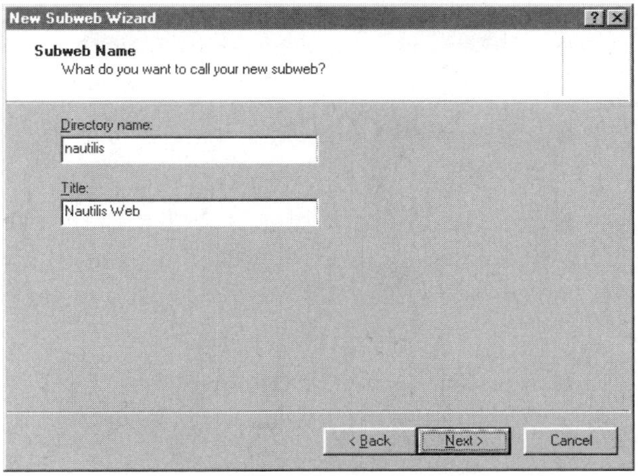

FIGURE 17-5.
MMC's New Subweb Wizard begins by prompting for the new Web's directory and textual names.

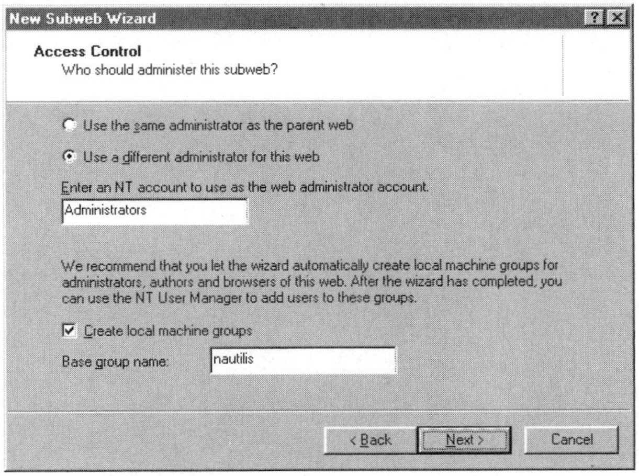

FIGURE 17-6.
With this dialog box the New Subweb Wizard prompts for initial security settings.

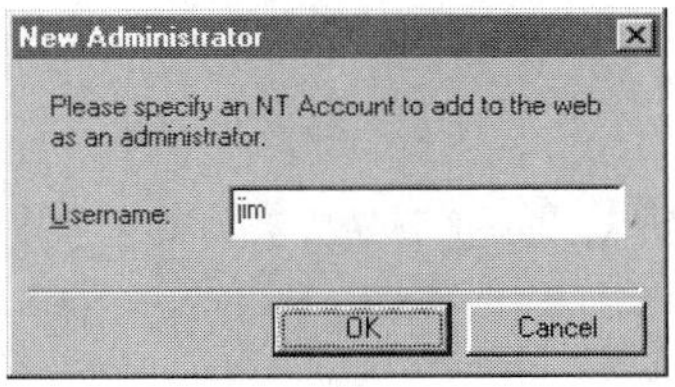

FIGURE 17-7.
Choosing Server Extensions Administrator in MMC displays this dialog box, which adds an administrator to the selected FrontPage Web.

Using the MMC Task Menu

In Figure 17-8, the administrator has right-clicked the console tree icon for an existing Web server and chosen Task. This reveals the following commands applicable to FrontPage.

- **Check Server Extensions** examines the FrontPage Web and corrects any incorrect software files, configurations, or security settings.

- **Open With FrontPage** starts the FrontPage desktop software and opens the selected Web.

- **Recalculate Web** rebuilds all FrontPage indexes and crossreferences. This is equivalent to opening the Web with the FrontPage desktop software and then choosing Recalculate Hyperlinks from the Tools menu.

- **Remove Server Extensions** removes all FrontPage components from the selected Web.

FIGURE 17-8.
The Task menu provides commands that control existing FrontPage components.

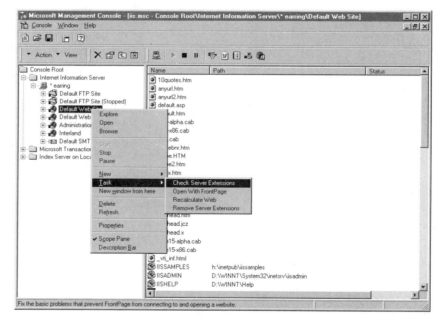

Using the MMC Server Extensions Tab

On Windows NT, right-clicking a default or virtual server and choosing Properties displays the multi-tabbed dialog box shown in Figure 17-9. Chapter 16, "Installing and Configuring a Web Server," discussed most of these tabs, but deferred discussion of FrontPage options until this section.

In this figure, note the dimmed check box titled FrontPage Web. This is a carryover from the FrontPage 98 Server Extensions, where it installed or removed the extensions from a given server. It has no purpose when the FrontPage 2000 Server Extensions are installed.

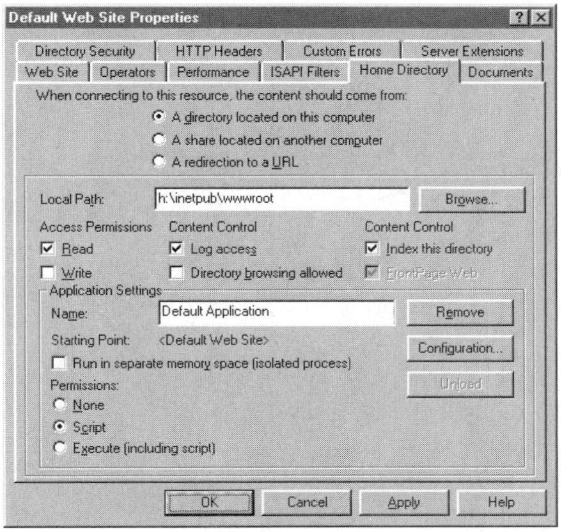

FIGURE 17-9.

The Home Directory tab on a Web server's property sheet contains a FrontPage Web check box. If the FrontPage 98 Server Extensions are installed, this check box installs or remove them.

Figure 17-10 shows the Server Extensions tab of a Web server's MMC property sheet. This is the *only* Web Site Properties tab that appears on Windows 95 and Windows 98 machines. It presents the following options:

- **Enable Authoring,** if checked, permits making changes to the Web with FrontPage and other programs that use the extensions. If the box isn't checked, the Web is secure from changes.

SEE ALSO

For more information about version control, see "Page-Level Check In / Check Out," page 658.

- **Version Control** specifies whether Check-in and Check-out are required for this Web. This setting is also configurable using the FrontPage desktop software.

- **Performance** selects one of several performance modes, depending on average daily volumes. Choosing Use Custom Settings and clicking the Settings button permits fine tuning.

- **Client Scripting** selects the scripting language FrontPage will use when creating scripts that will run on the browser. This setting is also configurable using the FrontPage desktop software.

- **Options** controls two groups of settings configurable only at the server.

  - **Specify How Mail Should Be Sent** specifies the name of the mail server, the From address, and other details required for server-based processes to send data as mail. Click the Settings button to display the available options.

- **Configure Office Collaboration Features** configures the Office 2000 Server Extensions. Click the Administer button to display the available options.

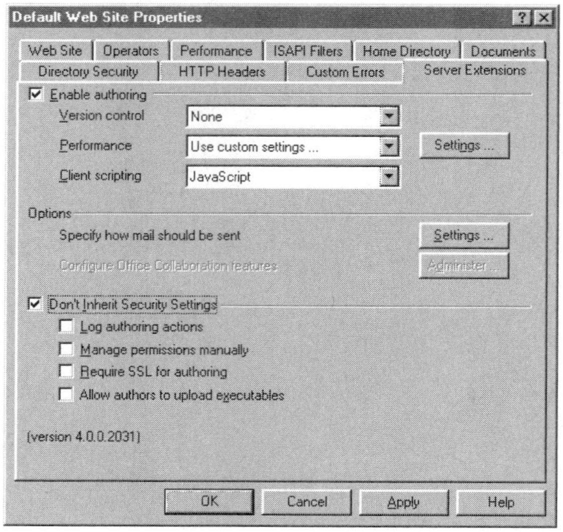

FIGURE 17-10.
The MMC property sheet for a default or virtual Web server has this Server Extensions tab.

- **Don't Inherit Security Settings,** if turned on, indicates that this Web shouldn't inherit security settings from its parent. If the box is turned off, the four settings below default to the parent Web's settings.

  - **Log Authoring Actions,** if turned on, tells the Server Extensions to keep a log of all authoring activity within a Web. This log includes the user name, Web name, remote computer name, and data pertaining to the specific operation. There's one log file per server, located in the root Web and named _vti_log/Author.log.

  - **Manage Permissions Manually,** if turned on, indicates system-assigned permissions can be overridden.

  - **Require SSL For Authoring,** if turned on, means that authoring activity will only be allowed when using encrypted communication (using Secure Sockets Layer) between client and server.

  - **Allow Authors To Upload Executables,** if turned on, means Web-page authors can upload executable programs—that is, programs with an EXE or DLL file name extension—and subsequently execute them on the server.

Clicking the Performance button (located under Enable Authoring) displays the dialog box shown in Figure 17-11. If a certain category of activity seems slow compared to expectations or other processes on the server, increasing its cache may provide an improvement. Conversely, decreasing cache size usually frees up resources for other uses. Here are the specific settings:

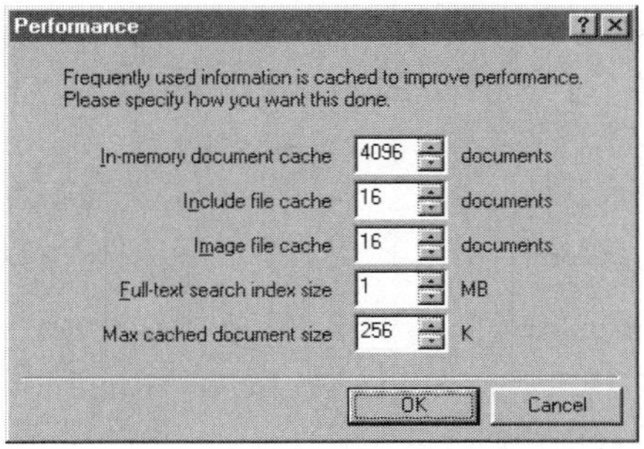

FIGURE 17-11.
The Performance dialog box fine-tunes caching and indexing thresholds.

SEE ALSO
For more information about including one Web file in another, see "Include Page," page 368.

SEE ALSO
For more information about the Text On GIF feature, see "Adding Text to Images," page 190.

SEE ALSO
For more information about the FrontPage Search component, see "Search Form," page 695.

- **In-Memory Document Cache** controls the number of documents whose property information, such as link maps and Web parameters, the Server Extensions will keep in memory. If the setting is 4096, the extensions will keep property information in memory for the 4096 most recently accessed documents.

- **Include File Cache** controls the number of files kept in memory for inclusion in other files. There might be header, footer, and copyright files widely included in a site's regular Web pages.

- **Image File Cache** controls the number of image files the Server Extensions keep in memory to create layered pictures in Web pages (that is, for the Text On GIF feature). Avoiding disk access to these files can speed up the Text On GIF feature.

- **Full-Text Search Index Size** controls the maximum size of a FrontPage full-text search index. If this isn't sufficient to index all files in a Web, some files won't be indexed. However, this setting doesn't affect text indexes used by Microsoft Index Server.

- **Max Cached Document Size** controls the maximum size of a document that can be stored in memory. This applies to any files that may be stored in a cache.

The button under Options titled Specify How Mail Should Be Sent displays the dialog box shown in Figure 17-12. It controls how the extensions send messages from a Web that uses mail-based features like the Save Results form handler. The options include:

- **Web Server's Mail Address** specifies the From e-mail address that appears in messages the Server Extensions send.

- **Contact Address** specifies the e-mail address users should write to if they have problems. This address appears in certain FrontPage error messages.

- **SMTP Mail Server** specifies the Internet mail server that will route messages to or from the remote users.

- **Mail Encoding** specifies the mail-encoding scheme used for your mail messages. The default is 8-bit encoding, which is very common. However, if your Web visitors require some other encoding scheme, you can specify it here.

- **Character Set** specifies the set of characters used in e-mail messages the extensions send. Each character set corresponds to the alphabet of a natural language.

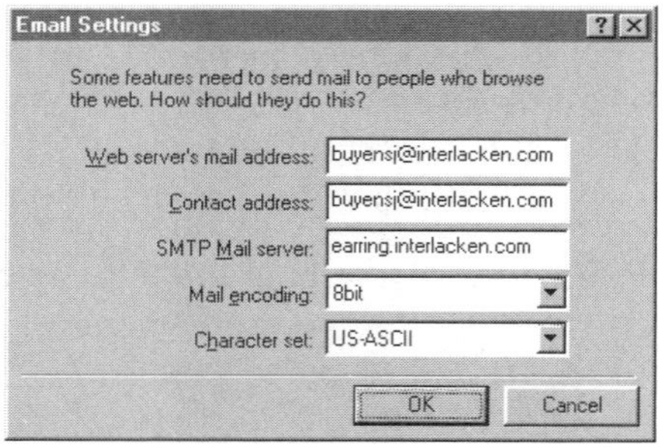

FIGURE 17-12.

The Email Settings dialog box controls how the Server Extensions send mail.

Administering the FrontPage Extensions with Web Pages

The FrontPage 2000 Server Extensions include a series of Web pages that can remotely install and administer the extensions using a standard Web browser. Collectively, they're called the FrontPage 2000 HTML

Administration Forms. Setting up the extensions copies these pages onto your Web server's hard disk, typically at a location such as:

```
C:\Program Files\Common Files\Microsoft Shared\
Web Server Extensions\version4.0\admin\isapi
```

Such locations can be tiresome to navigate, so you might find it easier just to search your disk for the HTML Administration Form home page, namely *fpadmin.htm*.

Because of possible security implications, installing the extensions doesn't make these forms available by default. To make them available for administering a specific server, you must set up—on that server—an executable virtual directory pointing to their physical location. In addition, make *sure* the Web server's security features keep unwelcome visitors away from the Administration Forms. If you don't, the results can get ugly.

Installing the FrontPage Server Extensions on a New Virtual Server

Figure 17-13 shows the first option available using the HTML Administration Forms: adding the FrontPage extensions to a new virtual server. Note the URL in the browser's Address field; this will always point to the HTML Administration Forms' virtual directory on the machine you wish to administer. All form elements within the HTML forms point to locations within that server.

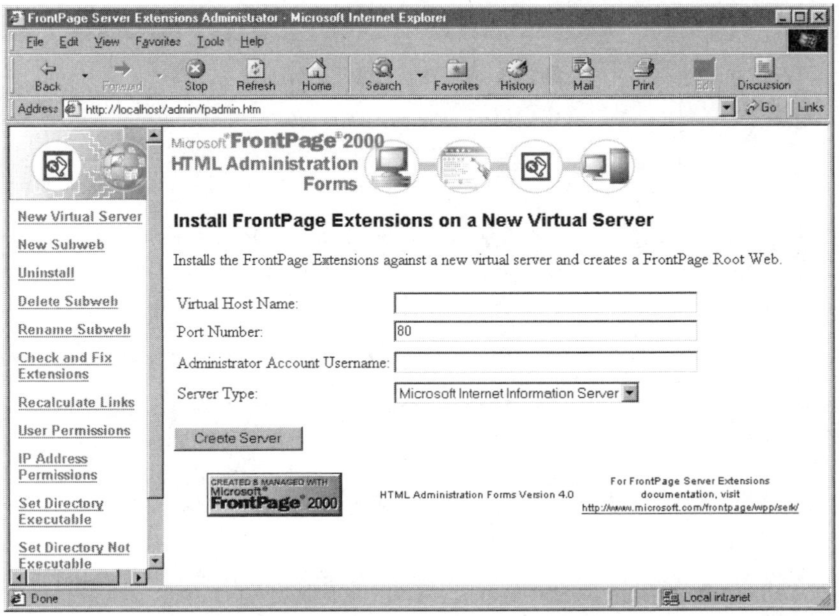

FIGURE 17-13.
The first FrontPage HTML Administration Form adds the Server Extensions to a new virtual server.

No one, not even an administrator, can initially add the FrontPage Server Extensions to a server over the network. Installing the software initially and creating the first root Web requires being at the server console. The function described here adds the extensions to the second, third, and subsequent Web servers on a computer.

This form presumes that an administrator—using some other process—has defined a new virtual server on the target machine, and wants the FrontPage Server Extensions to be active on that virtual server. The following entries are required.

- **Virtual Host Name.** Identify the virtual server that should have the FrontPage Server Extensions installed. The required notation depends on the Web server software.

- **Port Number.** Enter the port where the virtual server listens.

- **Administrator Account Username.** Identify the initial root Web administrator. If the Web server is IIS, you can specify either a Windows NT user account name or a Windows NT group name, and you can prefix it with a Windows NT domain name (using domain\user name notation).

Clicking Create Server will install the FrontPage Server Extensions and create a root Web.

Installing the FrontPage Server Extensions on a New Subweb

This function creates a new FrontPage Web on a server that already has the FrontPage extensions installed. To begin, click New Subweb to display the Web page shown in Figure 17-14. Here's what the input fields do:

- **Virtual Host Name.** Identify the virtual server where the new subweb will reside. The required notation depends on the Web server software.

- **Port Number.** Enter the port where the virtual server listens.

- **Web Name.** Specify the URL path to the new subweb's root folder, such as /newweb or /myoldweb/newweb. If the path contains more than one folder name, all but the last must already exist.

- **Administrator Account Username.** Identify the initial root Web administrator. If the Web server is IIS, you can specify either a Windows NT user account name or a Windows NT group name, and if necessary you can prefix it with a Windows NT domain name (using domain\user name notation).

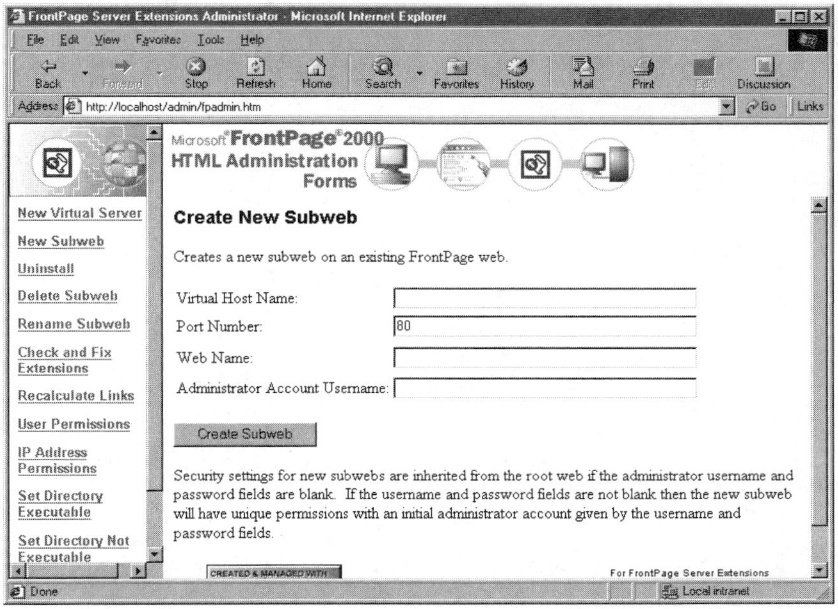

FIGURE 17-14.
This form creates a new FrontPage Web on a server that already has the FrontPage extensions installed.

Clicking the Create Subweb button creates the subweb and installs the FrontPage Server Extensions. If Administrator Account Username is blank, the new Web will inherit permissions from its parent.

To change subweb security, use the User Permissions and IP Address Permissions forms.

Removing the FrontPage Server Extensions from a Virtual Server

This function removes the Server Extensions from a virtual server. This disables all FrontPage authoring, disables all FrontPage browse-time processing, such as hit counters and Save Results processors, and deletes all FrontPage configuration data. Content files, such as Web pages and image files, are unaffected. To proceed, choose the Uninstall option and receive the display shown in Figure 17-15.

- **Full Uninstall.** Choose Yes to remove not only the identity of the FrontPage Web, but all information about its contents. Choose No to retain FrontPage content information.

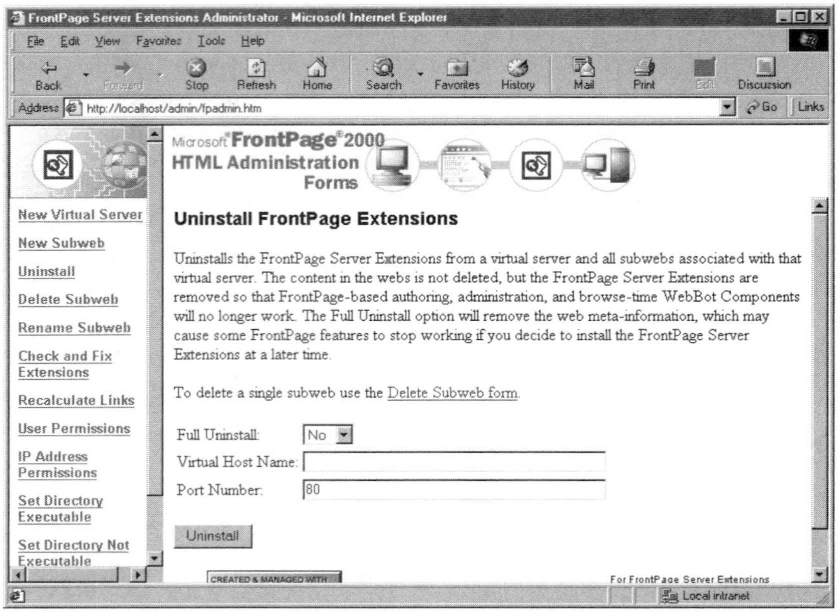

FIGURE 17-15.

This screen removes all FrontPage authoring capability, browse-time services, and configuration data from a virtual Web server.

- **Virtual Host Name.** Enter the virtual server's name.

- **Port Number.** Enter the virtual server's port.

Clicking Uninstall will remove the extensions from that server.

Uninstalling the server extensions from a virtual server's root Web will uninstall the Server Extensions from not only the root Web but also from any subwebs that were present beneath the root Web.

Deleting a Subweb

This form deletes a FrontPage subweb and all its contents, including Web pages and image files. To begin, choose Delete Subweb to display the Web page in Figure 17-16.

- **Virtual Host Name.** Enter the virtual server's name.

- **Port Number.** Enter the virtual server's port.

- **Web Name.** Specify the URL path to the subweb's root folder.

This form provides the only way to delete subwebs on NCSA, Apache, and CERN Web servers. You can't delete the root Web using this command; doing that requires the Uninstall form.

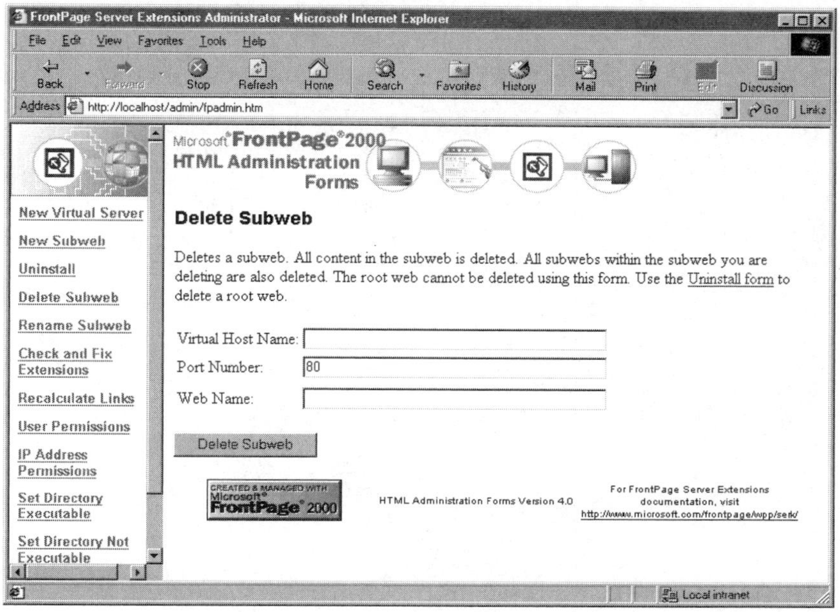

FIGURE 17-16.
This form deletes a subweb and all its contents.

Renaming a Subweb

The next FrontPage HTML Administration Form changes the name of a subweb. The new name takes effect immediately, changing the URL that Web authors, Web visitors, and hyperlinks in other pages need to use. To begin, choose Rename Subweb and examine the form shown in Figure 17-17.

- **Virtual Host Name.** Enter the virtual server's name.

- **Port Number.** Enter the virtual server's port.

- **Web Name.** Enter the subweb's current name.

- **New Web Name.** Enter the new subweb name.

Clicking the Rename Subweb button renames the Web. This is the only way to rename subwebs on NCSA, Apache, and CERN Web servers.

Checking and Fixing the FrontPage Server Extensions on a Virtual Server

Checking and fixing Server Extensions replaces missing FrontPage directories and files, ensures all FrontPage executables are present and have correct permissions, and removes lock files. To initiate this process, choose Check And Fix Extensions, which displays the Web page shown in Figure 17-18.

FIGURE 17-17.

This form renames a subweb, in effect changing the path portion of its URL.

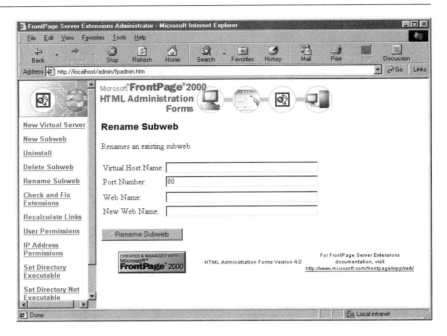

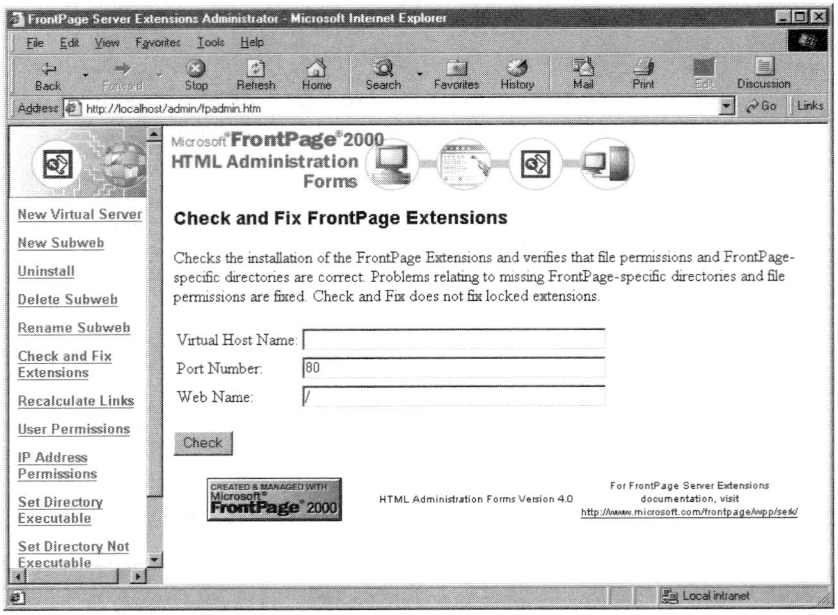

FIGURE 17-18.

The Check and Fix form runs a process that detects and corrects various problems in a FrontPage Web.

- **Virtual Host Name.** Enter the virtual server's name.

- **Port Number.** Enter the virtual server's port.

- **Web Name.** Enter the subweb's name.

Clicking the Check button initiates the process.

Use this process if you suspect a Web isn't working properly because of software problems.

Recalculating Hyperlinks on the Root Web or a Subweb

This function recalculates and repairs all internal hyperlinks in the specified FrontPage Web. It also refreshes pages in Include Page components, regenerates components like Search Forms and Navigation Bars, reapplies page borders, resets permissions on form-handler-results pages, and regenerates text indexes. Its administration form appears in Figure 17-19. The following fields are required.

- **Virtual Host Name.** Enter the virtual server's name.

- **Port Number.** Enter the virtual server's port.

- **Web Name.** Enter the subweb's name, or "/" for the root Web.

FIGURE 17-19.
The Recalculate Links function synchronizes the components of a FrontPage Web.

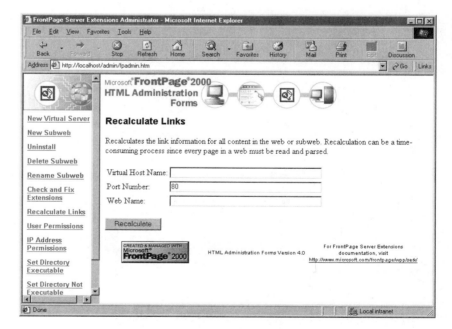

Use this process if you suspect a Web isn't working properly because of inconsistencies in content or FrontPage indexes.

Changing Permissions for a User

If your Web server supports user-level access control, the form pictured in Figure 17-20 grants and revokes access to individual users. After displaying the form, enter this data.

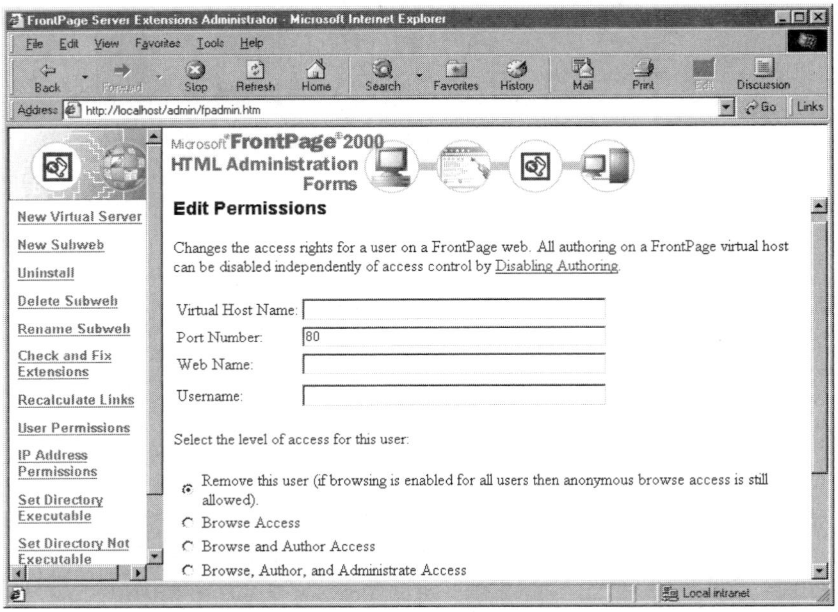

FIGURE 17-20.

This HTML form modifies permissions for a user already known to the Web server.

- **Virtual Host Name.** Enter the virtual server's name.

- **Port Number.** Enter the virtual server's port.

- **Web Name.** Enter the subweb's name, or "/" for the root Web.

- **Username.** Identify a user whose permissions require change.

- **Select The Level Of Access For This User:** Choose one of the following.

  - **Remove This User** revokes any existing permissions for the named user.

  - **Browse Access** permits the named author to browse this Web.

  - **Browse And Author Access** permits the named user to browse this Web and to change its content.

- **Browse, Author, and Administrate Access** permits the named user to browse this Web, change its content, and modify its configuration.

To make the change take effect, click the Change Permissions button that appears below the visible part of the figure. This form can only modify the FrontPage permissions of a user already known to the Web server. It can't add users, delete users, or change passwords.

Changing Permissions for a Computer

To control client-mode access from one or more computers, choose IP Address Permissions to display the form shown in Figure 17-21. Here are the input fields.

- **Virtual Host Name.** Enter the virtual server's name.

- **Port Number.** Enter the virtual server's port.

- **Web Name.** Enter the subweb's name, or "/" for the root Web.

- **IP Address.** Enter the IP address of the computer or group of computers whose access you wish to modify. You can use the asterisk character (*) as a wildcard, as in 192.168.180.*.

- **Select The Level Of Access For This IP Address Mask:**

  - **Remove This Mask** removes any special rights or restrictions granted the IP address.

  - **Browse Access** permits computers with matching IP addresses to browse this Web.

  - **Browse And Author Access** permits computers with matching IP addresses to browse this Web and to change its content.

  - **Browse Author And Administrate** permits computers with matching IP addresses to browse this Web, change its content, and modify its configuration. (This option is below the visible portion of Figure 17-21.)

To make the changes take effect, click the Change Permissions button (which once again is below the visible portion of the figure).

Setting a Directory Executable or Not Executable

The choices Set Directory Executable and Set Directory Not Executable control whether the Web server should run scripts and programs residing in a specified Web folder. Figure 17-22 and Figure 17-23 show the two corresponding forms. In both cases the input fields are the same.

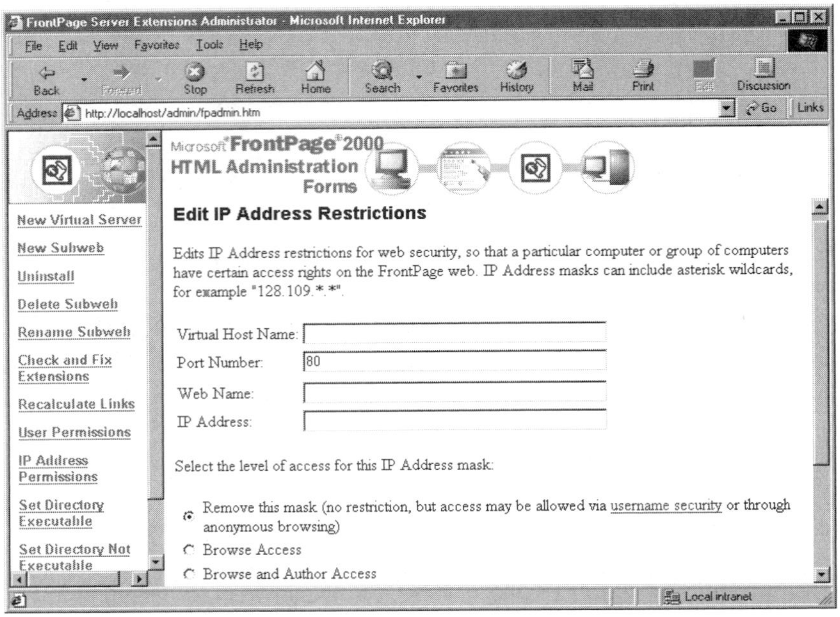

FIGURE 17-21.

This form uses client computer IP addresses to allow or disallow various kinds of access to a FrontPage Web.

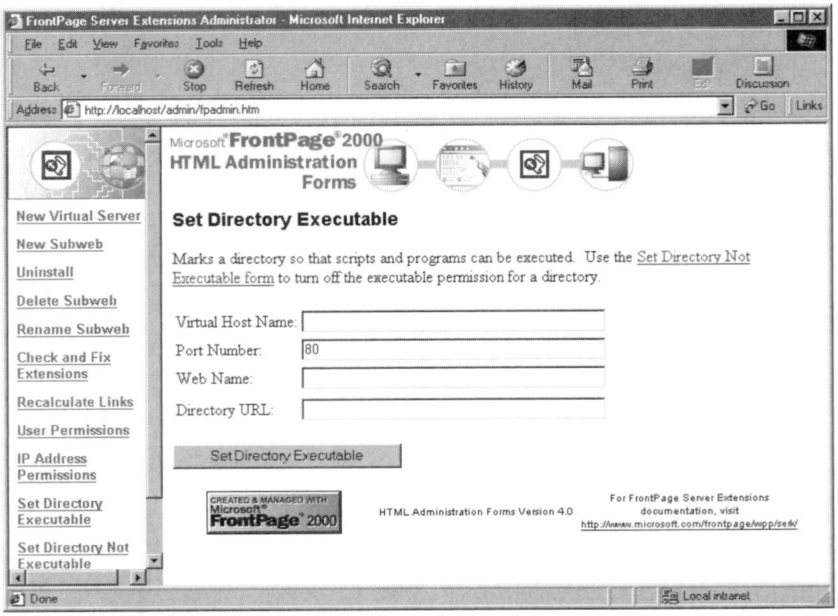

FIGURE 17-22.

This administration form marks a Front-Page Web directory as executable.

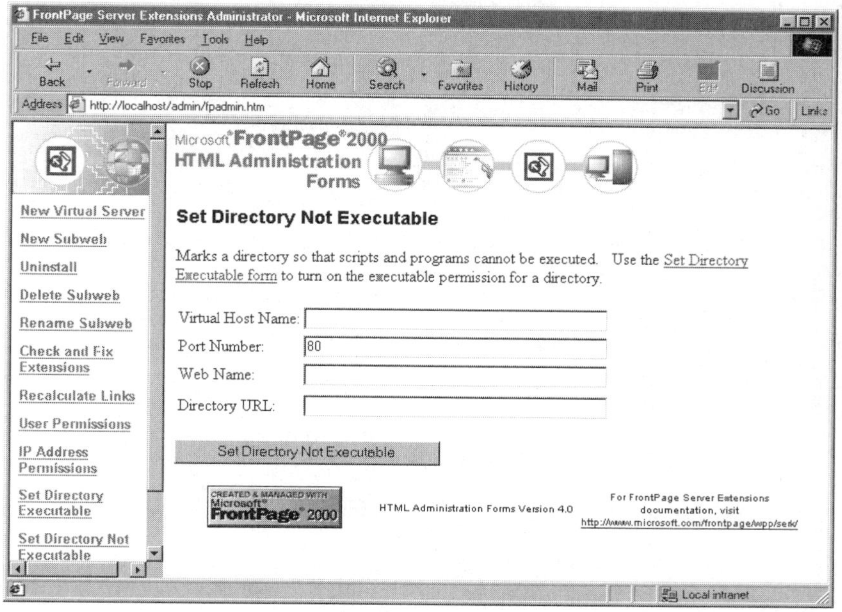

FIGURE 17-23.

This form marks a FrontPage Web directory as not executable

- **Virtual Host Name.** Enter the virtual server's name.

- **Port Number.** Enter the virtual server's port.

- **Web Name.** Enter the subweb's name, or "/" for the root Web.

- **Directory URL.** Enter a URL relative to the start of the FrontPage Web.

Clicking the Set Directory Executable button (Figure 17-22) or the Set Directory Not Executable button (Figure 17-23) makes the change take effect. This is the only FrontPage method that makes directories executable or not on NCSA, Apache, or CERN Web servers.

Enabling and Disabling Authoring on a Virtual Server

These two forms control whether or not the FrontPage extensions will accept changes to any Web on a given server. If you choose Enable Authoring, the form shown in Figure 17-24 will result. Choosing Disable Authoring displays the form in Figure 17-25.

- **Virtual Host Name.** Enter the virtual server's name.

- **Port Number.** Enter the virtual server's port.

Clicking the Enable Authoring or Disable Authoring button permits or inhibits changes to the root Web and all subwebs on the given server.

FIGURE 17-24.

This form instructs the FrontPage extensions to accept changes to a Web.

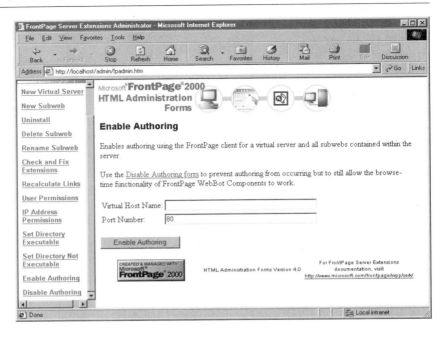

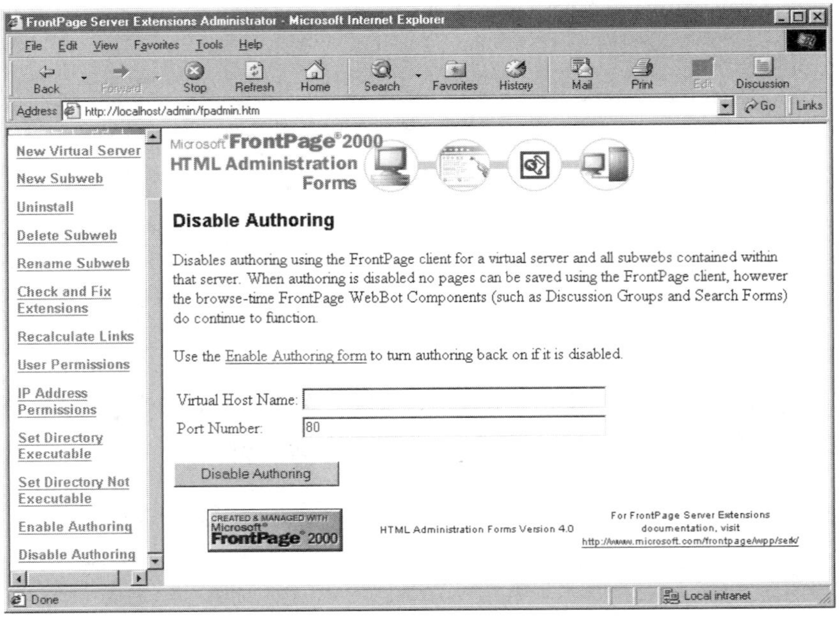

FIGURE 17-25.

This form instructs the FrontPage extensions to reject all attempted changes to a Web.

Administering the FrontPage Extensions from the Command Line

In addition to the Windows-based FrontPage MMC plug-in and the Web-based FrontPage HTML Administration Forms, FrontPage also provides a command-line administration program called fpsrvadm.exe. This can be useful for performing operations in batch files or on a timed basis. It's also the only method for installing the FrontPage Server Extensions on Unix-based systems.

Table 17-2 summarizes the command-line switches for fpsrvadm.exe. For more information about the fpsrvadm.exe program and its options, consult the *admin.htm* page in the Server Extensions Resource Kit.

TIP

The program fpsrvadm.exe also has a prompted mode. Simply enter *fpsrvadm* with no switches at the command line.

TIP

For examples of typical commands, search FrontPage Help for the string *command line version* or type *fpsrvadm -h* at the command line.

The fpsrvadm.exe program has no remote administration capabilities; you must run it on the computer hosting the target Web. A version of fpsrvadm comes with the FrontPage extensions for each supported operating system.

The HTML administration forms provide remote administration of the Server Extensions regardless of the operating system. However, if you require remote administration from a command-line interface, the fpremadm utility fits the bill.

The fpremadm utility runs the same server-side programs as the FrontPage HTML Administration Forms, but it does so from the command line. Because of this approach, fpremadm won't work unless you enable those forms as described earlier in this chapter.

The command-line switches for fpremadm are the same as those described for fpsrvadm, plus three new switches described in Table 17-3. Although it can administer FrontPage Webs on any supported operating system, the fpremadm program itself only runs on Windows. There's no Unix version.

TABLE 17-2. **Command-Line FrontPage Server Administrator Switches**

Switch	Abbreviation	Argument	Function
-help	-h	N/A	Displays a help screen summarizing command-line syntax.
-operation	-o	install	Installs the FrontPage extensions.
		upgrade	Upgrades existing FrontPage extensions to match the current version of FrontPage.
		uninstall	Removes the FrontPage extensions from a virtual Web server.
		fulluninstall	Completely removes the FrontPage extensions from a computer.
		check	Verifies proper installation of the FrontPage extensions.
		create	Creates a new FrontPage Web.
		merge	Converts a FrontPage Web into an ordinary folder in its parent Web.
		delete	Deletes a FrontPage subweb.
		rename	Renames a FrontPage subweb.
		setDirExec	Specifies that a directory can contain executable scripts or programs.
		setDirNoExec	Specifies that a directory cannot contain executable scripts or programs.
		security	Adds to or removes administrators, authors, or end users from a Web. Sets IP address restrictions.
		chmod	On Unix only, chowns and chmods the FrontPage folders, Server Extension files, and Web content to a Unix username and groupname.
		enable	Enables authoring.
		disable	Disables authoring.
		recalc	Recalculates links for the specified Web.
		putfile	Adds a file to the specified Web. -web specifies the Web. -destination specifies the relative URL. -filename specifies the file.
		recalcfile	Recalculates links as if the specified file had changed. -destination or -filename specifies the file.

(continued)

TABLE 17-2. *continued*

Switch	Abbreviation	Argument	Function
-port	-p	nnnn	The port on which the server is running. If virtual servers exist, specify them as hostname:port or ipaddress:port. For some operations, such as recalc, this switch can be specified as all.
-web	-w	web name	The name of the FrontPage Web. Specify "" for the root Web.
-type	-t	apache apache-fp apache-manual-restart cern cern-manual-restart ncsa ncsa-manual-restart netscape netscape-manual-restart	The server type.
-servconf	-s	server config file	The name of the server's configuration file. The default location is the folder where the server is installed plus conf/httpd.conf (for NCSA or Apache) config/httpd.conf (for CERN) config/magnus.conf (for Netscape)
-multihost	-m	hostname	The name of a virtual server configuration. This can be either a fully qualified DNS or an IP address.
-username	-u	username	The administrator username. This is required if -operation is install or security.
-password	-pw	password	The administrator password. This is required if -operation is install or security.
-ipaddress	-i	IP address	Specifies IP addresses administrators may use. FrontPage will accept administrator functions only from matching addresses. The asterisk wildcard can be used in any of the IP addresses' four parts; for example, 143.45.*.*.

(continued)

TABLE 17-2. *continued*

Switch	Abbreviation	Argument	Function
-access	-a	remove/ administrators/ authors/users	The type of FrontPage Web access being granted.
-destination	-d	destination url	The destination URL for a document in a FrontPage Web on the server. This address is relative to the Front-Page Web specified with -web.
-filename	-f	filename	The full pathname of a file on the server machine.
-xUser	-xu	Unix username	A Unix account name.
-xGroup	-xg	Unix group	A Unix group name.
-noChown/Content	-n	yes	Chowns only FrontPage _vti folders and no user content.

TABLE 17-3.   Switches for Remote Administrator via fpremadm

Switch	Specifies
-targetserver	The full URL of the server-side administration script. This will begin with http:// and end with either fpadmdll.dll (for IIS and PWS) or fpadmcgi.exe (for all other Web servers). Example: http://<server name>/<path>/fpadmcgi.exe
-adminusername	A user name that permits access to the *targetserver* URL.
-adminpassword	The password that corresponds to the *adminusername* account.

In Summary...

This chapter introduced the FrontPage Server Extensions as the server side of a client/server, Web-authoring environment. The FrontPage desktop software, of course, provides the client. The Server Extensions also provide a variety of browse-time services FrontPage assumes will be present when it creates the HTML for certain features.

Of five tools for administering FrontPage Webs—and the Server Extensions that support them—this chapter discussed four. The next chapter will discuss the fifth such tool: FrontPage itself.

Creating and Managing FrontPage Webs

A Microsoft FrontPage Web is any collection of Web pages, image files, and other components it makes sense to treat as a unit. Letting FrontPage manage and coordinate all the relationships among such files provides incredible benefits of speed and accuracy.

The previous chapter discussed creating simple disk-based Webs, creating more complex server-based Webs, and managing the software that makes server-based Webs possible. This chapter explains how to create Webs in the FrontPage desktop software, which may be the easiest approach of all. Not only can FrontPage initialize Webs, it populates them with content as well.

Initializing a FrontPage Web

To create a new FrontPage Web, first choose New from the File menu, and then select Web. The dialog box of Figure 18-1 will appear.

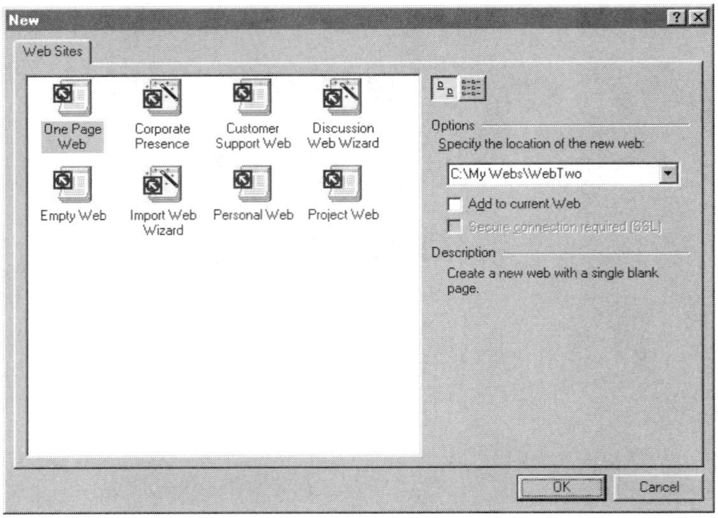

FIGURE 18-1.
To create a new Web, choose the initial content you want, specify an HTTP or disk location, and then click OK.

The large area at the left of Figure 18-1 lists the types of initial content FrontPage can supply. As you select each choice on the left, FrontPage provides relevant information under the Description heading on the right. Table 18-1 summarizes these choices.

Complete the following fields, as appropriate, under the Options heading:

■ **Specify The Location Of The New Web.** Indicate where you want the new Web to reside. Two types of locations are valid.

● To create the new Web on a local disk or file server, enter a drive letter and folder name. If any of the folders you specify don't exist, FrontPage will create them.

Example: C:\My Webs\creating\new\web
This would work even if the *creating, new,* and *web* folders didn't exist.

● To create the new Web on a Web server, enter an existing Web's URL, plus any intermediate folders, plus one new or existing folder.

Example: http://www.interlacken.com/creating/new/web
This would work only if the *creating* folder and the *new* folder already exist.

> **NOTE**
>
> All Web servers running the FrontPage Server extensions contain at least one FrontPage Web: the *root Web*. The root Web's URL is http://<servername>/. You can create additional Webs—called *subwebs*—directly within the root Web or within another subweb.

- **Add To Current Web.** Turn this box on if you don't want to create a new Web, but you want the new content added to an existing Web.

- **Secure Connection Required (SSL).** Turn this box on if you specified a Web-server location, and that server requires Secure Sockets Layer (SSL) communication for authoring.

You can name the Web anything that's valid as a folder name on your disk or Web server, but the following restrictions will minimize later problems.

- Use only lowercase letters or numbers.

- Don't use any spaces or special characters.

- Create a name that's meaningful, but no longer than 8 or 10 characters.

> You should choose a Web name, folder names, and file names for your Web that are valid on any server that will host it. This is one reason to avoid special characters, spaces, and uppercase letters when choosing these names.

TABLE 18-1.   New FrontPage Web Templates and Wizards

Template or Wizard	Description
Corporate Presence	A comprehensive Internet presence for your organization.
Customer Support Web	A Web for providing customer support services.
Discussion Web Wizard	A discussion group with threads, a table of contents, and full-text searching.
Empty Web	A Web with nothing in it.
Import Web Wizard	A Web populated with content from an existing location. FrontPage prompts for the existing location, then copies its content into the new Web.
One Page Web	A Web containing only a blank home page.
Personal Web	A personal Web, with pages for your interests, photos, and favorite Web sites.
Project Web	A Web for a project team; it includes Web pages for the project members, status reports, the project schedule, an archive area, and ongoing discussions.

At this point, FrontPage will begin building your Web. If it's a server-based Web, FrontPage might prompt you for the parent Web's administrator name and password. Figure 18-2 illustrates this dialog box.

FIGURE 18-2.
To create a FrontPage Web on a Web server, you'll need the parent Web's administrator name and password.

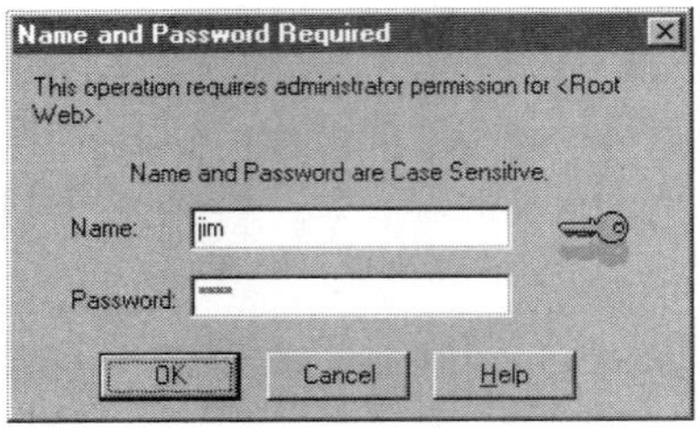

If FrontPage doesn't prompt for root Web account information, it means your credentials are already established. Microsoft Internet Information Server and Microsoft Personal Web Server for Windows NT, for example, won't prompt for a root Web password if you're already logged onto the Windows NT system as an administrator.

If you chose to import an existing Web or use a wizard, FrontPage will now prompt you for additional input. Figure 18-3, for example, shows one screen from the Corporate Presence Web Wizard. Answer the questions to the best of your ability, but don't agonize; you can always delete the new Web and start over. In fact, you *should* expect to delete the new Web and start over several times until you get the results you want.

FIGURE 18-3.
This is a prompt from the Corporate Presence Web Wizard. Your answers will determine the initial content of the new Web.

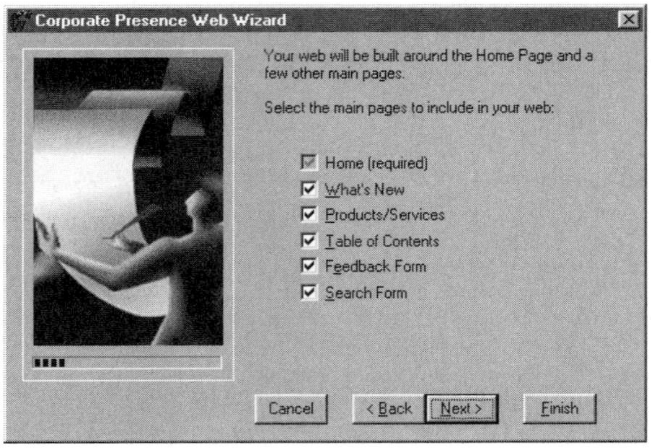

When FrontPage finishes building the new Web, it displays it in FrontPage, as shown in Figure 18-4.

FIGURE 18-4.

FrontPage Explorer will display a new FrontPage Web like this. The drive letter and folder-path location mark this as a disk-based Web.

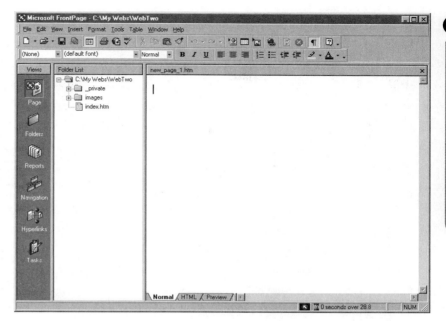

For information on the following topics, see: "Templates," page 665; "Themes," page 668; "Navigation Bars," page 671; "Substitution," page 680; and "Include Page Components," page 682.

Creating a project Web, for example, produces the 23 generic Web pages shown in Figure 18-5. The Web's name is C:\My Webs\baseball. Figure 18-6 shows another unmodified page from the baseball project Web: the Discussions page.

The difference between wizards and templates lies in their degree of automation. While a template is relatively static and preformatted, a wizard prompts you for local information and then custom-builds your site accordingly. The Corporate Presence Wizard, for example, displays 15 pages of prompts that affect the resulting site. While detailed discussion of these wizard prompts is beyond the scope of this book, the prompts are fairly obvious, and there's on-screen Help for each. The Corporate Presence Wizard prompts you for information such as company name, company address, color scheme, and background. It also presents lists of pages you can choose to generate or not.

- Note in Figure 18-7 that the Corporate Presence Wizard has created Web Parameters for changeable information and Task list items reminding you to finish the generated pages.

- Figure 18-8 shows FrontPage displaying the Corporate Presence home page that Explorer generated; note the boilerplate text suggesting information you should enter under each heading. This

Web's appearance resulted from specifying the Value Added theme while running the wizard, but themes can be changed at will from Themes view in FrontPage.

FIGURE 18-5.

All the pages in this Web resulted from choosing the Project Web template.

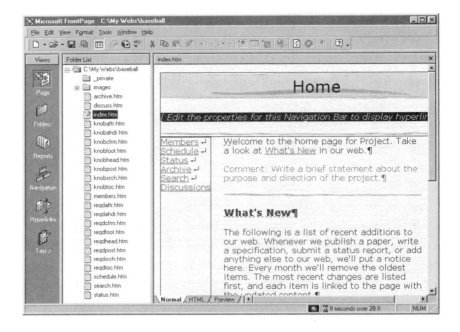

FIGURE 18-6.

This is a typical Discussions page in a new FrontPage project Web.

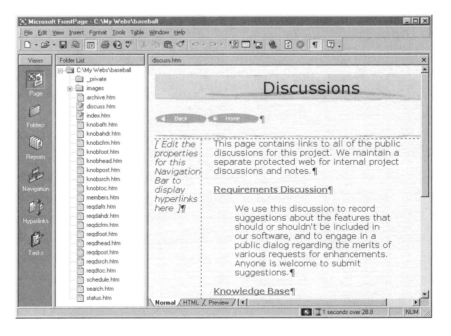

- Figure 18-9 shows the Navigation view of the Corporate Presence Web. The wizard prompted the Web's creator for the number of press releases, products, and services. The Feedback, Contents, and

FIGURE 18-7.

The FrontPage Corporate Presence Wizard built this Web.

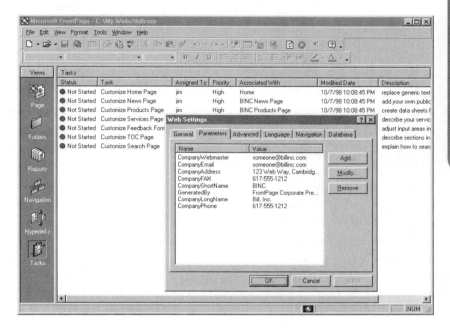

FIGURE 18-8.

FrontPage is ready to modify the default Corporate Presence home page. Boilerplate text suggests typical content.

Search pages aren't actually part of the hierarchy; they're peers at the Web's top level and, by virtue of a navigation bar included in a shared border, have links available from every page in the Web.

FrontPage's wizards for creating a new Web can produce so many unique variations that describing them all is impossible. The best advice is simply to try them and judge the results for yourself. Create, decide, delete, and re-create until you have the starting point you want, and then begin your own modifications.

FIGURE 18-9.

This is the Navigation view of a Corporate Presence Web.

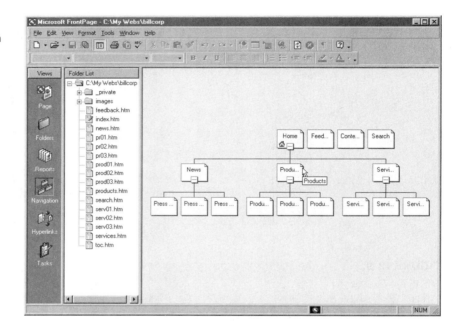

FrontPage and the File System

Within the root Web, FrontPage maintains information not only about the root Web itself, but also about each normal FrontPage Web. In addition, each normal Web maintains indexes and other information about itself. You should be extremely cautious about moving, renaming, or otherwise updating file areas under control of FrontPage.

Once you make a folder a FrontPage Web, you should use FrontPage for making changes whenever possible. If you add, change, or delete any content files without going through FrontPage, be sure to later open the Web with FrontPage and choose Recalculate Hyperlinks from FrontPage's Tools menu.

Never use Windows Explorer or any other programs to update FrontPage system files or folders. This might create situations that are very difficult to recover from.

Importing an Existing Web

The Import command on FrontPage's File menu doesn't create a new Web; its purpose is adding files to an existing Web. To create a new FrontPage Web from an existing Web, follow the instructions on the next several pages.

Creating new FrontPage Webs is relatively straightforward, but converting an existing Web site to FrontPage is perhaps a more common task. This is especially true for new FrontPage users, who frequently have an existing body of work. FrontPage 2000 provides an Import Wizard that builds a new FrontPage Web from existing content; its ease of use, however, depends greatly on how the existing pages are organized.

The following sections will describe three scenarios for initializing a new Web with existing content.

1 Initializing a new Web with files from a file-system folder.

2 Initializing a new Web with files from a Web server.

3 Converting a folder to a Web.

Initializing a New Web from a File System Folder

To learn about adding individual files to a FrontPage Web, see "Importing Web Pages," page 585.

Having FrontPage create a blank or standardized Web provides a good start for new projects, but converting existing Web sites to FrontPage is equally important, especially for new FrontPage users and clients. Front-Page therefore provides an Import Web Wizard that creates new Webs from existing file-system folders and existing sites. To initialize a new Web with existing content from disk:

1 Choose New from the File menu, and then choose Web. This displays the dialog box previously shown in Figure 18-1.

2 Select the Import Web Wizard icon.

3 Specify a folder location in the box titled Specify The Location Of The New Web (under Options). As in the previous section, this should be either a drive letter and folder combination, for locations on your local disk, or an HTTP URL, for locations within an existing server-based Web.

4 Click OK.

5 If you specified a location within an existing server-based Web, FrontPage may prompt you for that Web's administrator name and password.

6 FrontPage displays the Import Web Wizard dialog box shown in Figure 18-10, asking you for the location of your existing Web files. Because this example assumes that you're importing files from a local computer or network, choose the first option (From A Source Directory…).

- Specify the file location by typing it in the Location text box or by using the Browse button.

- To import files in the specified source folder only, leave the Include Subfolders box blank. To import all folders contained within the source folder, turn on the box.

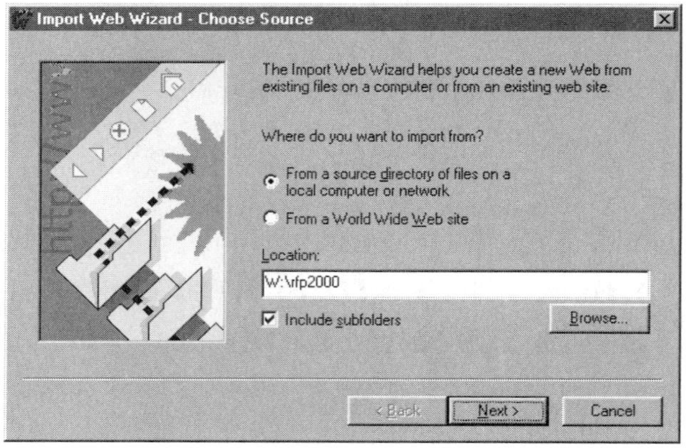

FIGURE 18-10.

FrontPage can populate a new Web with files from a local disk location or from a remote Web site.

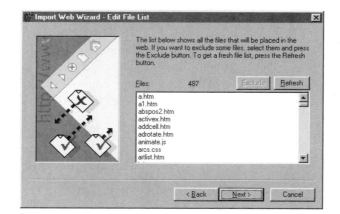

7 The wizard next displays the Edit File List dialog box shown in Figure 18-11. Here you can exclude any files from the existing Web that aren't necessary for the new FrontPage Web. After making your selections, click the Next button.

FIGURE 18-11.

You can choose which files are imported into your new FrontPage Web.

8 Click the Finish button on the final dialog box.

When the import process is complete, you'll have a new FrontPage Web that contains all your former pages. You might also have a mess. Unless you've been extraordinarily meticulous in the past, you'll probably discover many cases of inconsistent file names, missing page titles, and files not residing in the most logical location. Repairing these problems is the subject of the section, "Planning and Managing Folders," page 624.

Initializing a New Web from Another Web Server

The best way to copy a Web from one server to another is by using the Publish FrontPage Web command. This requires that both servers have the FrontPage Server Extensions installed. If they do:

If the content for your new FrontPage Web already resides in the desired server's root Web, skip to the next section in this chapter.

1   Open the existing FrontPage Web in FrontPage.

2   Choose Publish FrontPage Web from the File menu.

3   Specify the Destination Web Server and the FrontPage Web.

4   Click OK.

For more information about Web publishing, see Chapter 23, "Publishing Your FrontPage Web."

If the server hosting the source Web doesn't have the FrontPage Server Extensions, proceed as follows:

1   Start the Import Web Wizard using steps 1 through 4 on page 579.

2   When FrontPage displays the Choose Source dialog box shown in Figure 18-10, choose From A World Wide Web Site.

3   The dialog box changes to that shown in Figure 18-12.

   ■ In the Location text box, specify the URL of the site's home page.

   ■ Turn on the check box titled Secure Connection Required (SSL) if the source Web server requires a secure connection.

When importing from a Web location that doesn't have the Front-Page Server Extensions, FrontPage determines what pages to retrieve based on an analysis of hyperlink links. This means it won't download orphan pages—pages never referenced in the site's HTML.

4   Click the Next button.

5   The Choose Download Amount dialog box shown in Figure 18-13 optionally limits the amount of material added to the new Web.

   ■ To limit the depth of retrieval, turn on the check box titled Limit To This Page Plus and specify the maximum number of levels between an imported page and the home page. Specifying 1, for example, means FrontPage will import the home page and any files referenced on it. Specifying 2 means

FrontPage will import the home page, any files referenced on it, plus any files referenced on those pages.

> When determining which Web files to download, FrontPage ignores hyperlinks and other references external to the requested site. That is, FrontPage imports files only from the requested site, and not from other sites it may refer to.

Honor copyright restrictions whenever you import pages or images from the World Wide Web.

- To limit the number of bytes downloaded, turn on the Limit To check box and specify the maximum number of kilobytes.

- To download text and image files only, turn on the box titled Limit To Text And Image Files. This imports Web pages and graphics, but skips content such as ZIP files and executables.

6 Click the Next button and then click the Finish button on the final dialog box.

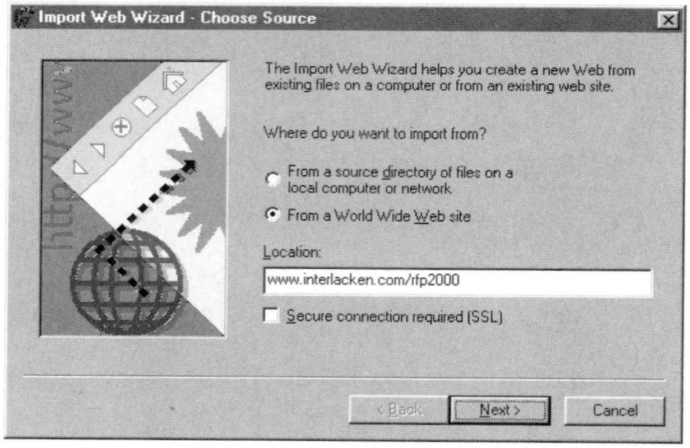

FIGURE 18-12.
FrontPage presents this dialog box for populating a new Web with files from a remote Web site.

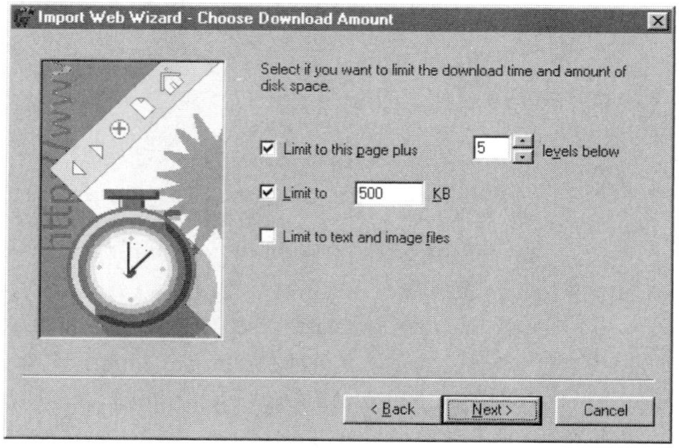

FIGURE 18-13.
FrontPage provides three ways to avoid excessive downloading when importing an existing Web site.

Converting a Folder to a Web

As FrontPage Webs grow in size and complexity, it often becomes apparent that what started as an ordinary folder deserves to become a full FrontPage Web. This breaks your content into more manageable units, both in terms of data volume and administrative responsibility, and it sets bounds on FrontPage functions that process an entire Web.

To convert a folder in an existing Web to a full FrontPage Web of its own:

1 Open the existing Web in FrontPage.

2 Right-click the existing folder.

3 Choose Convert To Web from the pop-up menu.

4 When the confirmation prompt shown in Figure 18-14 appears, click OK.

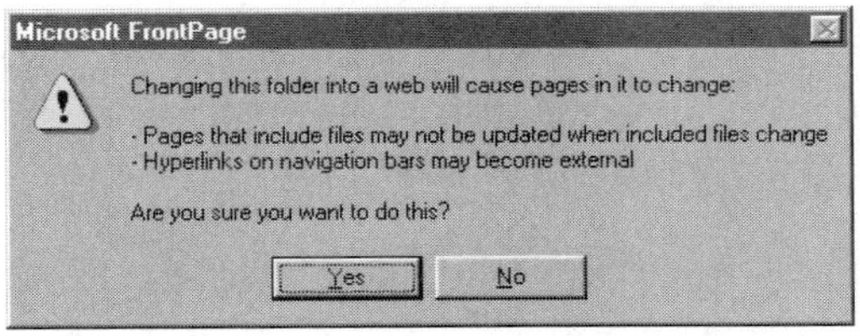

FIGURE 18-14.

This prompt warns you that making a new Web out of a folder in an existing Web severs ties between the converted folder and the existing Web.

Recall that no file or folder can belong to two Webs, even if one Web physically resides within another. This explains the confirmation prompt in Figure 18-14. Suppose, for example, that the Web page default.htm has a hyperlink to the page products/hardware.htm.

- If these pages are in the same Web, renaming products/hardware.htm to products/drygoods.htm would update the hyperlink in default.htm.

- If you converted the products folder to a FrontPage Web and *then* renamed hardware.htm to drygoods.htm, FrontPage *wouldn't* update the hyperlink in default.htm, because the two files would then be in different Webs.

The second part of the prompt reminds you that for each file included in the new Web, any references from the old Web will become *external* (that is, those references will now point to locations outside the old Web).

Converting a folder to a Web can be a relatively major change. Planning is the key. Here are some things to consider:

- Organize your content *before* creating the new Web, while FrontPage can still fix hyperlinks as you move things around.

Make sure your content is clearly and logically divided between the old and new areas.

■ Don't forget to organize images and other files as well as Web pages. Create an *images* folder inside the folder before converting it, and then move or copy any required images into that images folder. Again, do this while FrontPage can still fix hyperlinks for you.

If the existing FrontPage Web is server-based and administered by Microsoft Management Console (MMC), you can also convert folders to Webs in MMC. Expand the console tree until you find the desired folder, right-click, and choose Configure Server Extensions.

Converting a Web to a Folder

Just as you can convert folders into FrontPage Webs, you can also convert FrontPage Webs back into ordinary folders. There is, however, one significant catch: any Web you convert to a folder must already reside within another Web. That is, you can convert a subweb into a folder in its parent Web, but you can't convert a root Web into something dangling in space. Here's the procedure.

1 Open the Web that contains the subweb you want to convert.

2 Locate the subweb in the FrontPage Folder list.

3 Right-click the subweb's icon, and then choose Convert To Folder from the pop-up menu.

4 When the confirmation prompt in Figure 18-15 appears, click Yes to proceed.

FIGURE 18-15.

This prompt warns that converting a FrontPage Web to an ordinary folder discards any information unique to that Web.

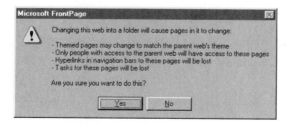

The warning reminds you that when the subweb loses its identity, it also loses its unique security, its Navigation view data, and its task list. Furthermore, if you've applied a theme to the entire parent Web, that theme may now apply to pages in the converted Web as well.

Importing Web Pages

Adding existing Web pages, images, and other files to a FrontPage Web is a common requirement. FrontPage calls this process *importing* and can perform it at the file or folder level. There are two methods: the menu method and the drag-and-drop method.

> FrontPage can import pages accessible on a local disk or through Windows file sharing, but it can't import individual pages accessible only via HTTP. To import pages available from an intranet or the World Wide Web, open them in Page view and then save them to the current Web.

Importing files with menus is a two-step process. First you must build a list of files to import, and second you must actually import them. To build the list:

1 Open the receiving Web with FrontPage.

2 Select the Web folder you expect to receive the most files.

3 Choose Import from the File menu. This will display the Import File To FrontPage Web dialog box, shown in Figure 18-16.

FIGURE 18-16.
Use this dialog box to build a list of items to import.

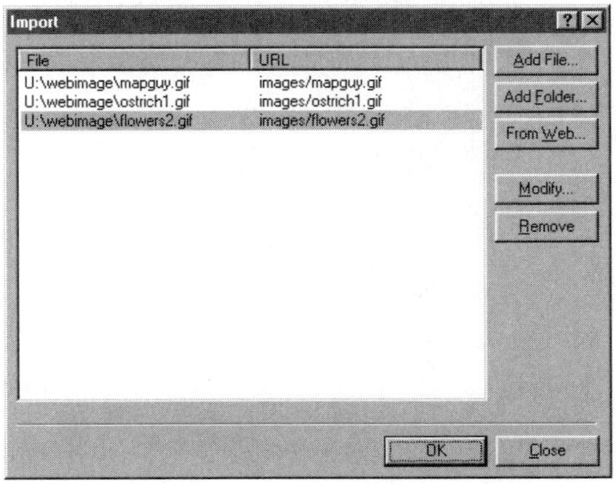

4 Depending on what you wish to import, choose *any* of these:

- To add individual files, click the Add File button. When the Add File To Import List dialog box appears, find the files you want to import and then click Open. FrontPage will add the selected files to the import list shown in Figure 18-16.

- To add all the files in a given folder (and all its subfolders), click the Add Folder button. When the Browse For Folder dialog box opens, locate the desired folder and click OK. FrontPage will add all the files in the selected folder, including subfolders, to the import list.

- To add a group of related files from an intranet or World Wide Web site, click the From Web button. You will be prompted for the URL and will be able to select how many levels of the Web will be imported, limit the total size of pages imported, or choose to limit the import to text and image files.

5   Normally, FrontPage imports all files to the current folder in Front-Page. To change the destination of an individual file, select the file and click Edit URL. (You won't have this option if you're importing a Web.) When the Edit URL dialog box (shown in Figure 18-17) appears, change the displayed destination and click OK.

FIGURE 18-17.

Use the Edit URL dialog box to change the planned destination of an imported Web file.

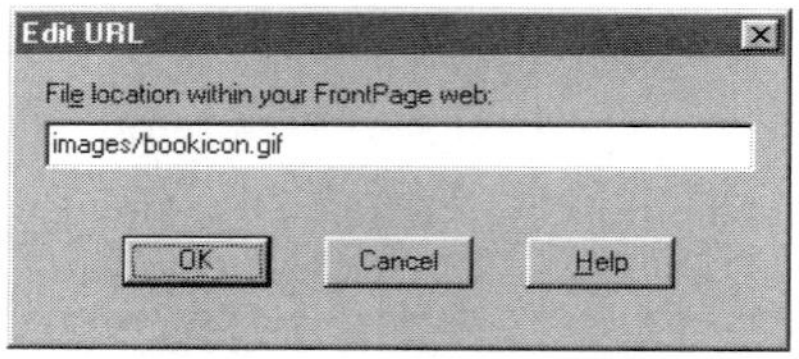

6   To remove a file you've placed on the import list, select it and click the Remove button.

When you're ready to import the files in the list, click OK. To abandon or postpone importing, click the Close button. FrontPage will remember the import list. To import the list later, until you close the current Web, choose Import from the File menu before closing the current Web.

To import Web files using a drag-and-drop operation:

1   Open the receiving Web with FrontPage.

2   Use Windows Explorer to locate the files or folders you want to import.

3   Drag the files or folders from Windows Explorer to the desired destination in FrontPage.

To copy content between two FrontPage Webs, open both Webs in FrontPage and then drag the desired content between the two Front-Page windows.

Imported pages frequently contain incorrect or nonstandard HTML, especially if they were previously maintained by hand. Front-Page might interpret these questionable elements differently than a browser. Keep the original files until you view the imported versions in FrontPage, save them, and review the results with your browser. If more than minor cleanup is needed, you might want to correct the originals and reimport them.

Of course, you can also move content into, out of, and among FrontPage Webs using the Web Folders feature that comes with Office 2000. The default drag operation is Copy as long as the source and target locations are on different drives, on different servers, or on one drive and one server. If both locations are on the same drive or server, the default operation is Move. You can reverse these defaults by holding down the Ctrl key while dragging, but it's often less confusing to drag with the right mouse button instead.

> After you drag and drop something with the right mouse button, Windows displays a pop-up menu asking whether to move, copy, or cancel.

Importing vs. Copying—What's the Difference?

If your FrontPage Web resides on a local disk or file server, copying files into the Web file area with Windows Explorer or the command prompt might seem quicker and easier than importing them with FrontPage. The difference is this: when FrontPage imports a Web file, it copies the file into place and also updates all the necessary FrontPage indexes and cross-reference files. Externally copying the files into place doesn't perform the FrontPage updates. To restore a FrontPage Web to consistency after an external process has changed it:

1 Open the Web with FrontPage.

2 Choose Recalculate Hyperlinks from the Tools menu.

Configuring Your FrontPage Web

Before starting to work on your Web, you may wish to review the FrontPage options that control your work environment.

Reviewing Web Settings

The Web Settings command on the Tools menu of FrontPage governs settings for the current FrontPage Web. There are six tabs on the Web Settings dialog box: General, Parameters, Advanced, Language, Navigation, and Database.

Controlling General Web Settings

Figure 18-18 displays the General Web Settings tab. There are two configurable options.

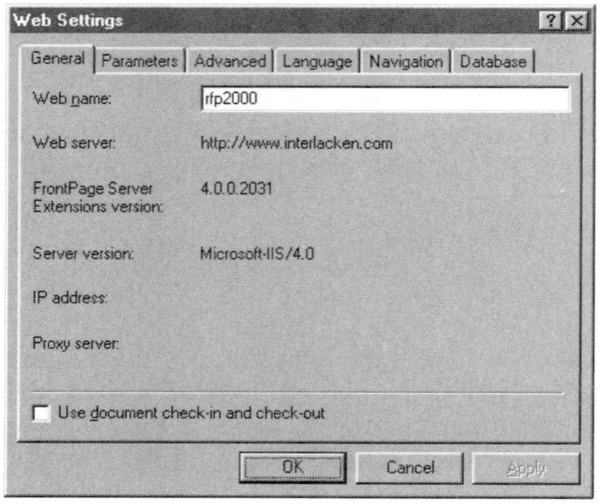

FIGURE 18-18.

The General Web Settings tab specifies the Web's textual name and controls document check-in and check-out.

- **Web Name** specifies the identity of the current Web. To rename a Web, you must be an administrator of its parent Web.

For more information about source-code control, see "Page-Level Check In/Check Out," page 658.

- **Use Document Check-In And Check-Out** governs the use of source-code control for the current Web. If the box is turned on, FrontPage will insist that you check out (that is, take control of) any file you want to edit. FrontPage will then prevent anyone else from checking out or modifying the file until you check it in (that is, relinquish control of it).

The General tab also displays the Web server's URL, the version number of the FrontPage extensions on that server, the name and version of the Web server itself, and the name (if any) of the proxy server in use.

Controlling Web Parameters

For more information about the Substitution FrontPage component, see "Substitution," page 680.

The Parameters tab displays a list of Web parameters or variables and their current values. After defining these variables once here, you can use them in any number of Web pages by choosing Substitution from the Component command of FrontPage's Insert menu. The Parameters tab appears in Figure 18-19.

- **Add.** To define an additional variable, click the Add button, enter the desired name and value, and then click OK.

- **Modify.** To change the value of a variable, first select it in the list, and then click the Modify button. When the prompt appears, make your edits and then press OK.

- **Remove.** To remove a variable, select it and then click the Remove button.

FIGURE 18-19.
You can define any number of variables from the Parameters tab in FrontPage's Web Settings dialog box.

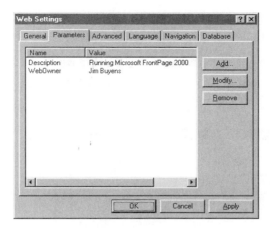

Controlling Advanced Web Settings

The Advanced tab, pictured in Figure 18-20, controls settings relative to scripting languages, display of hidden directories, and temporary files.

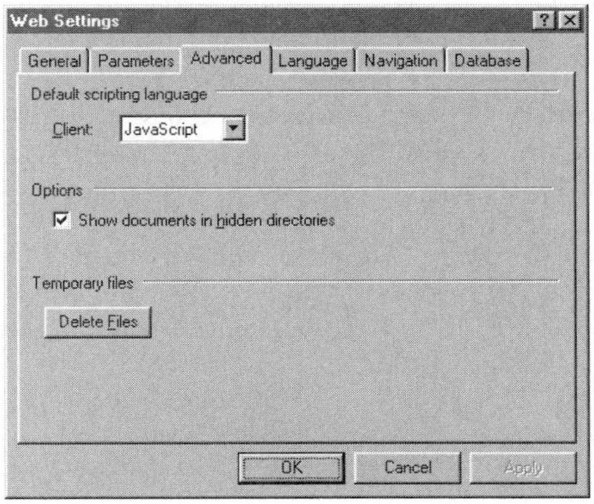

FIGURE 18-20.
The Advanced tab of the Web Settings dialog box contains settings for client scripting language, display of hidden directories, and cleanup of temporary files.

- **Default Scripting Language: Client.** This setting controls the programming language FrontPage will use to generate script code that runs on the Web visitor's browser. As of version 4, both Microsoft Internet Explorer and Netscape Navigator supported JavaScript, but only Internet Explorer supported VBScript.

- **Show Documents In Hidden Directories.** Turning this box on tells FrontPage to display files in hidden folders. Such folders contain system information and files generated by FrontPage. They usually have names beginning with an underscore.

■ **Delete Files.** Click this button to delete any temporary files that are no longer in use.

Controlling Language Settings

The Language tab controls natural language defaults for your Web. It appears in Figure 18-21.

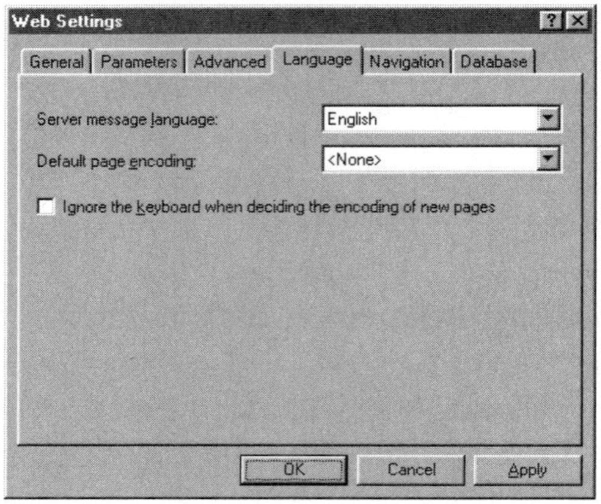

FIGURE 18-21.

The Language tab of the Web Settings dialog box controls whether server error messages will appear in English or another available language, as well as the default character set for saving pages.

■ **Server Message Language.** This setting controls the language used for sending error messages from the FrontPage Server Extensions to the Web browser. Match this setting to your audience.

■ **Default Page Encoding.** FrontPage will use the character set specified here for all new Web pages it creates.

> To override the default HTML Encoding setting for individual pages and use a different character set, open each page in FrontPage, choose Page Properties from the File menu, and then edit the HTML Encoding settings on the Language tab.

■ **Ignore The Keyboard When Deciding The Encoding Of New Pages.** Turning this box on tells FrontPage not to consider the current keyboard language—specified under Control Panel, Keyboard—when initializing the language setting for new Web pages.

Configuring software to accept different natural languages is only half the battle; you also need to configure your keyboard for typing the necessary characters. The Keyboard icon in the Windows Control Panel configures natural language settings for keyboards. This of course begs the further question of getting a keyboard with the necessary keys and key caps, but that's a hardware issue.

Understanding Web Pages and Language Encoding

Because the Web is world-wide, it must accommodate the character set of every written language on Earth. Yet, because the Web is bandwidth-constrained, it uses single-byte character sets.

A single-byte character set provides only 256 different codes, which isn't nearly enough to represent all the characters in all the languages on Earth. As a result, each language uses the 256 codes in its own way. To display a Web page properly, a browser must know what character set its author intended. The following HTML, for example, indicates the US/Western European character set.

```
<meta http-equiv="Content-Type" content="text/html;
charset=iso-8859-1">
```

The Default Page Encoding setting in FrontPage specifies the character set FrontPage will assign to new pages created in the current Web. You can also modify HTML Encoding for individual pages by using the Language tab of the Page Properties dialog box in FrontPage. The setting for most Western languages is US/Western European.

Specifying an HTML Encoding value causes some browsers to display the resulting Web pages twice, as if they notice the charset= parameter on the first pass and then apply it on a second. To avoid this behavior, specify HTML Encoding = <none>. Specifying <none>, however, implies complete trust that the default character set on the remote user's browser will display your page correctly.

For more information about Navigation bars, see "Working with Navigation View," page 639, and "Navigation Bars," page 671. For more information about using FrontPage to create database applications, see Chapter 22, "Accessing Databases with FrontPage."

Configuring Other Web Settings

The Navigation tab specifies the titles FrontPage will use for four standard Navigation bar entries: Home page, Parent page, Previous page, and Next page.

The Database tab lists and configures named connections between your Web pages and databases that reside on the Web server.

Controlling Web Security Through FrontPage

Security is a constant concern on the Internet. Most Web sites allow any and all to visit, but restrict editing and administration to a few authorized individuals.

FrontPage supports these requirements with an intuitive, built-in security model involving user names, passwords, and three levels of access.

■ **Browse** allows Web visitors to access the Web with browsers such as Internet Explorer, but not to open it with FrontPage or to make changes.

■ **Author And Browse** allows FrontPage users to open the Web and change its content, but not to modify Web settings or permissions.

■ **Administer, Author, And Browse** permits assigned users to change content, settings, and permissions.

FrontPage depends largely on your Web server's security functions for control. Security commands issued within FrontPage communicate with FrontPage software on the server and instruct it to implement the required settings. Working though FrontPage isolates Web authors from many of the security differences among Web servers.

If during Setup, FrontPage installs or detects a Web server on the local machine, it adds the FrontPage Server Extensions to the default Web server and initializes various settings, including security. Later, if required, you can reinstall the Server Extensions manually. You might need to do this if:

■ You've changed your Web-server software.

■ You need to change settings.

■ You want to install, upgrade, remove, or check the FrontPage Server Extensions.

Installing FrontPage Server Extensions, initializing security, and creating new FrontPage Webs are usually tasks done by a system administrator—someone responsible for the overall stability and performance of the server. If you're running a personal Web server, this is probably as far as you'll go by way of security. It's like being the president, chief engineer, and janitor of a one-person company.

In a multi-user environment, however, the system administrator usually turns ongoing maintenance over to the new Web's owner. The owner then designates any additional administrators and authors.

To change permissions via FrontPage on a particular Web server, you must open the applicable FrontPage Web *on that server*. This requires the presence of the FrontPage Server Extensions. If the extensions aren't installed, you or an administrator will have to control permissions using the server's native security system.

Updating a Web's permissions on your authoring machine and then publishing your Web to a production server doesn't affect security on the production server. This is because, in most scenarios, security on the two servers *ought* to be different. You may be an administrator of your personal Web server, for example, but only an author (allowed to change content but not permissions) on the production server. In a shared development environment, many Web authors could have permission to update the group's authoring server, though only the project leader or librarian might have rights to publish content on the production server.

Administering Web-Level Security

To change permissions for an existing Web, the Web's administrator opens the Web in FrontPage and then chooses Security from the Tools menu, and then Permissions. This displays the dialog box shown in Figure 18-22. The tabs available will vary, depending on the capabilities of the Web server and the installed FrontPage Server Extensions.

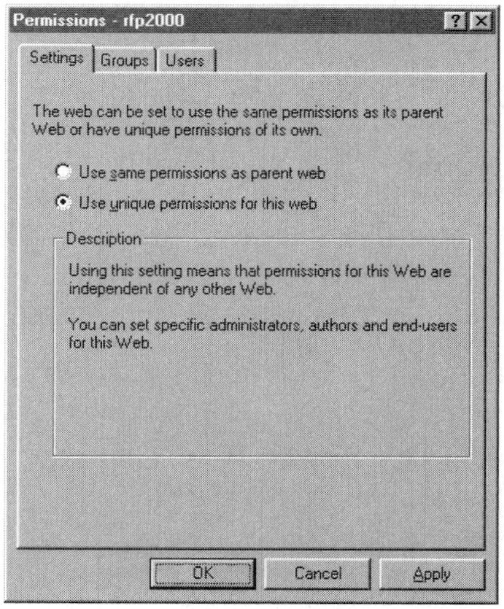

FIGURE 18-22.

The Permissions dialog box in FrontPage lets administrators establish permissions for the current Web that differ from those of the root Web.

The Permissions choice on the Tools menu will be disabled for servers having no security in effect, or for those whose security isn't configurable through the FrontPage Server Extensions.

The Settings tab controls whether the current Web will use the same permissions as the root Web or unique permissions of its own. While new Webs always inherit permissions from the root Web, this is seldom appropriate for ongoing use. In all but the simplest environments, different people will maintain the root Web and subordinate Webs. Therefore, after creating a new Web, the root Web administrator will generally activate unique permissions so that the appropriate users or groups can begin setting their own permissions and creating content.

Choosing the option Use Unique Permissions For This Web and clicking Apply unlocks the remaining tabs on the dialog box. These might include Users, Groups, and Computers, depending on the Web server.

Controlling User-Level Web Access

There are two major variations for the Users tab: one for Web servers that use a Windows NT User Account Database and another for servers that maintain Web-specific user lists. Microsoft Internet Information Server and its cousin—Microsoft Personal Web Server for Windows NT Workstation—take this approach. Most other Web servers use Web-specific user lists.

The dialog box shown in Figure 18-23 depicts the Users tab for Microsoft's Windows NT-based Web servers.

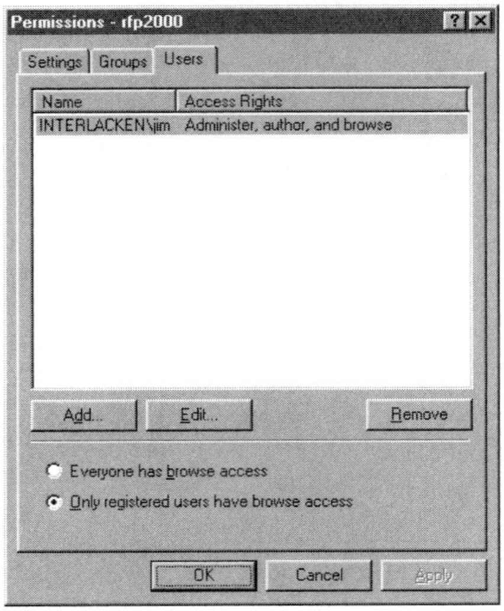

FIGURE 18-23.

This Users tab is typical for Webs running on servers that support Windows NT security.

The list box at the top of the Users tab shows which users have per-mission to access the current FrontPage Web and tells what activities are permitted. To begin adding a user to the list, bring up the dialog box in Figure 18-24 by clicking the Add button.

For more information about Windows NT domains and the vari-ous roles Windows NT servers can play in them, consult a book about Windows NT Server.

If the server supports multiple User Account Databases, the drop-down list titled Obtain List From can retrieve user names from the database you want. In Figure 18-24, for example, INTERLACKEN is the name of the Windows NT domain, and the Names box lists users in that domain.

- If the Web resides on a standalone Windows NT workstation or server, the Obtain List From box will contain the standalone machine's computer name.

- If the Web resides on a Windows NT primary or backup domain controller, the Obtain List From box contains the name of the Windows NT domain and the names of any other Windows NT domains that domain is permitted, by trust relationships, to trust.

- If the FrontPage Web resides on a standalone Windows NT server or Windows NT workstation that's a *member* of a Windows NT domain, the Obtain List From box includes entries for the stand-alone server or workstation, plus the domain name, plus the names of other domains permitted to trust.

If you log in to a Windows NT domain, operate a Microsoft Web server in the same domain, and open a FrontPage Web on that server, FrontPage will automatically use the current login account to log in to the FrontPage Web.

FIGURE 18-24.

This dialog box grants users with Windows NT accounts access to a FrontPage Web.

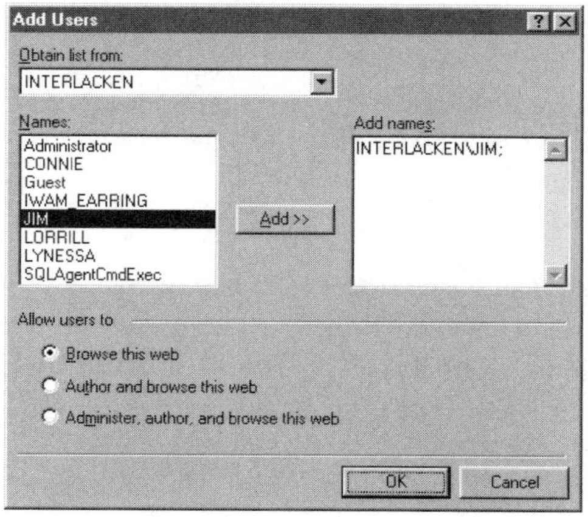

Password-protected Web pages are accessible only if the browser and Web server use the same authentication scheme. If the server and browser come from different providers, they might not reveal their security algorithms to each other for security reasons. If you have trouble getting valid passwords accepted, change or add authentication schemes until you find a compatible set.

To continue granting Web access to an existing Windows NT user, follow these steps:

1 In the Add Users dialog box (Figure 18-24), select a user within the Names list and then click the Add button. You can also add users by double-clicking their entries in the Names list.

2 Select the most appropriate privilege in the Allow Users To section.

3 Click OK.

You can add as many users as you like before clicking OK, but they all receive the same permissions. To give various users different permissions, close and reopen the dialog box. FrontPage can't create, modify, or delete Windows NT users, nor can it change passwords. These are functions provided in Windows NT User Manager.

To change permissions for a user already listed in the Users tab (Figure 18-23), first select the user and then click the Edit button. This displays the Edit Users dialog box shown in Figure 18-25, where you can change a group's level of access. Clicking the Remove button on the Users tab deletes permissions for the currently selected user.

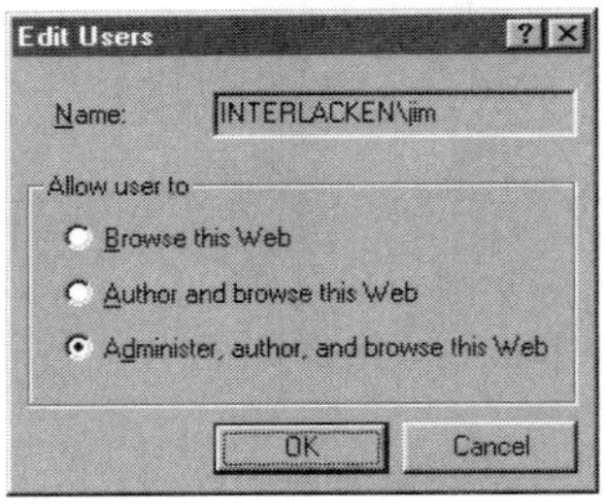

FIGURE 18-25.

This dialog box adds existing Windows NT users to the list of those permitted to access the current FrontPage Web.

Note the following options at the bottom of the Users tab (Figure 18-23):

■ **Everyone Has Browse Access** means that anyone with network access to your Web server can browse it, using programs such as Internet Explorer or Netscape Navigator.

■ **Only Registered Users Have Browse Access** means that Web browsing is available only to authorized users and to members of authorized groups. To verify authorization, the Web server will prompt visitors for a qualifying user name and password.

Most non-Microsoft Web servers have Web-specific user lists that are quite distinct from the operating system's list of login accounts. This avoids the security concerns of granting Web users system-wide login accounts, but it also means that people needing both types of access will have to remember an additional user name and password.

In many of these cases, you can maintain Web-specific user lists directly from within FrontPage. The Users tab and the Add Users dialog box take on the appearance shown in Figure 18-26.

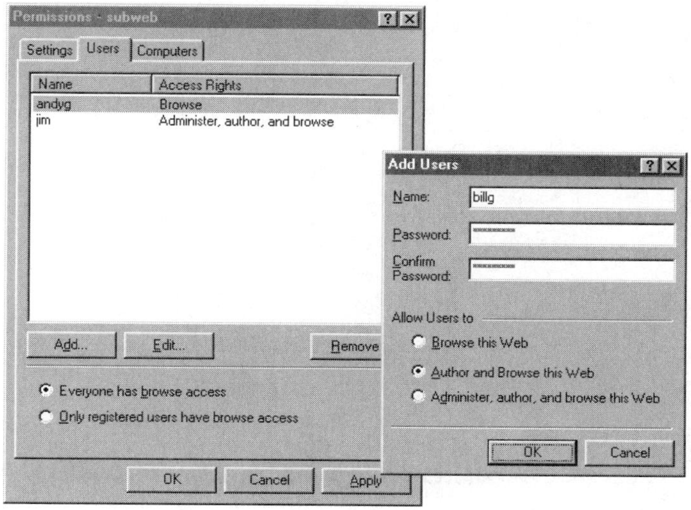

FIGURE 18-26.

These dialog boxes appear for Web servers that maintain their own user databases.

Clicking the Add button in Figure 18-26 brings up the Add Users dialog box shown. Enter the new user name, enter the new password twice, specify the level of access, and then click OK.

Controlling Web Access by Group

Groups are simply collections of users granted identical security privileges. Grouping all users in a certain department, in a certain job classification, at a client site, or in some other category makes it easy to grant or revoke privileges for the whole group. Granting privileges by group also eases maintenance as individuals enter and leave the group; rather than updating security in many different locations, you need only update the group's membership.

Support for groups varies from one Web server to another, as does the ability to create, delete, and modify groups from within FrontPage. In Figure 18-27, the Web server is Microsoft Internet Information Server and the groups listed are those in the Windows NT server's domain. The Windows NT User Manager tool creates, modifies, and deletes these groups. Other Web servers maintain groups in their own way, and might permit maintenance via FrontPage. The Add, Edit, and Remove buttons in Figure 18-27 work very much as they do in the Permissions dialog box shown in Figure 18-23 on page 594.

Controlling Web Access by Network Address

Some Web servers can control access based on a remote user's IP address. Because IP addresses are typically assigned to organizations in blocks, granting or denying access based on IP address can provide a form of security broadly grounded in organizational membership.

The Computers tab shown in Figure 18-28 controls access to a Front-Page Web based on the IP address. This tab is available only for Web servers that support this feature.

To provide Web access for a given computer, click the Add button, enter the computer's IP address in the IP Mask field, choose the level of access, and then click OK. The access levels work the same as those for users and groups, except, of course, that you can exercise no direct control over who might be sitting at the computer with the given IP address.

To control access for a range of IP addresses, enter asterisks (*) in one or more boxes in the IP Mask field. In Figure 18-28, the Web server will allow browsing by all users having IP addresses 192.168.180.0 through 192.168.180.255.

The Edit button in the Permissions dialog box shown in Figure 18-28 modifies the permissions of an existing IP address entry. The Remove button just to its right deletes the selected entry from the list.

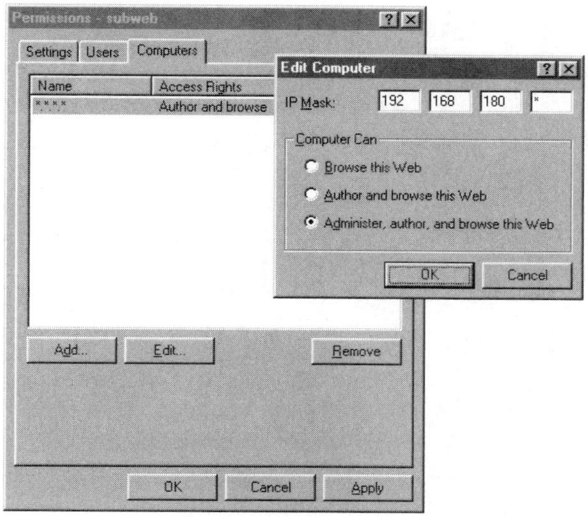

FIGURE 18-28.

The Computers tab grants or limits Web access based on IP address.

Securing Web-Page Delivery with IIS

In addition to storing file and folder information, the Windows NT File System (NTFS) stores *access control lists* (ACLs) that specify which users can access a given file or folder, as well as what permissions they have. If a file's ACL doesn't authorize a user to perform an operation, NTFS blocks the attempt and returns an error message.

When retrieving pages for Web delivery, IIS normally accesses the file first with an anonymous account. If that access succeeds, IIS delivers the page. If it fails, IIS prompts the Web visitor for another user name and password. If the visitor responds with a user name and a password that have access, IIS delivers the requested page. If not, IIS repeats the prompt.

FrontPage establishes the following NTFS permissions for the various FrontPage access levels.

- **Browse This Web.** Users and groups at this access level have Read permissions in the Windows NT file system.

- **Author And Browse This Web.** Users and groups in this category have Change permissions in NTFS.

- **Administer, Author, And Browse This Web.** Web administrators have Full Control permissions over their Web files; they can update both files and permissions.

It's best to use FrontPage, rather than native Windows NT dialog boxes, to set permissions for FrontPage Webs. This avoids problems caused when Front-Page finds permissions in an unexpected state.

Administering Folder-Level Security

Using FrontPage 2000, the administrator of a FrontPage Web can now control access to individual folders within a Web. To do this, locate the folder in FrontPage, and then either select the folder and choose Properties from the Edit menu, or right-click the folder and choose Properties from the pop-up menu. The dialog box shown in Figure 18-29 will appear.

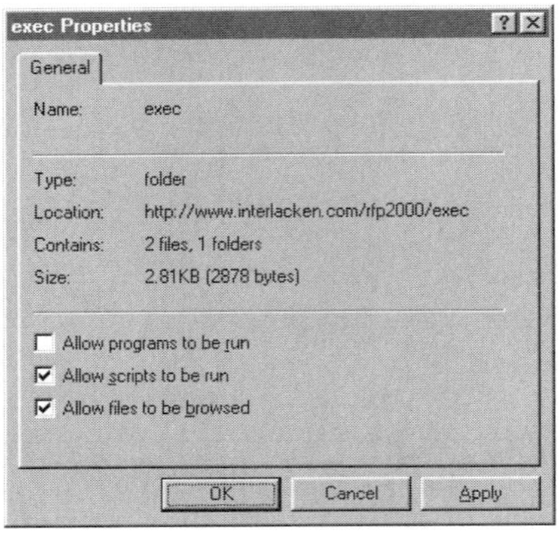

FIGURE 18-29.

The folder Properties window in FrontPage controls execute and browse access for the selected folder.

⑦ SEE ALSO

For more information about choosing, configuring, and administering a FrontPage Web server, see Chapter 16, "Installing and Configuring Your Web Server."

- **Allow Programs To Be Run,** if turned on, allows the Web server to run executable programs in the selected folder. These primarily include CGI and ISAPI programs, which, on Windows, usually have EXE or DLL file name extensions.

- **Allow Scripts To Be Run,** if turned on, allows the Web server to run scripts from the selected folder. The difference here is that scripts aren't executable in themselves; they're interpreted by other programs—script processors—authorized and approved by the server administrator. This provides an extra layer of control and security. Two common script types are Active Server Pages and Perl programs.

- **Allow Files To Be Browsed,** if turned on, permits file access from Web browsers. Turn this option off to prevent ordinary remote users from accessing the folder. This option will be absent from Web servers that don't support it, such as FrontPage Personal Web Server for Windows 95 and Windows 98.

Setting these options modifies the security settings on your Web server. If your server's system administrator hasn't granted you permissions to do this, the commands will fail. Contact the system administrator for assistance.

IV

Using FrontPage Webs

Security administration is a complex, critical, and judgmental task. It always involves tradeoffs among the degree of protection, ease of administration, and ease of access for authorized users. There are no universal answers or pat solutions—but FrontPage at least provides a start.

Deleting a FrontPage Web

To delete a FrontPage Web:

1 Open the parent Web—that is, the Web that contains the Web you want to delete.

2 Locate the obsolete Web in the Folder List and select it.

3 Choose Delete FrontPage Web from the File menu (or right-click the obsolete Web and choose Delete from the pop-up menu).

4 Click Yes in the resulting Confirm Delete dialog box.

WARNING

Deleting a FrontPage Web deletes absolutely everything it contains—Web pages, images, text files, FrontPage system files, and all folders. If you want to save the Web pages, images, and other content, back them up before deleting the FrontPage Web.

The Microsoft Office Server Extensions

Office 2000 includes its own set of Web-server extensions, which provide seven applications unique to Office. Two of these applications involve both traditional Office applications and the Web, four involve only the Web, and one is a background process on the Web server. The two applications that involve traditional Office applications are:

■ **Web Discussions.** After an Office 2000 user has saved a document to a Web server as HTML (and recall: this is an integrated, one-step process), Web visitors browsing that document can make comments using a *discussion toolbar*. The Office extensions store these comments as separate files on the Web server and then, when the Office 2000 user opens the document, all the comments appear seamlessly merged.

- **Web Subscriptions.** With this feature, both Office 2000 users and Web visitors can ask to be notified whenever a specified document or folder changes. The Office Server Extensions detect such changes and send the notifications by e-mail.

The following applications involve only the Web server and a browser.

- **Start Page.** This feature provides a home page for accessing the remaining applications.

- **Enhanced Directory Page.** This enhances the normal display Web visitors get when browsing a directory with no default document.

- **Search Page.** This is a special Search tool tailored for Microsoft Office documents.

- **Administration Tool.** This Web-based tool provides control over the preceding applications.

The background application is a database server that keeps track of all the activity described above.

- **Workgroup Database.** Providing Office Server Extensions functionality requires a database to keep track of activity data, indexes, and settings. This can be either a Workgroup database supplied as part of the extensions, or a database residing on Microsoft SQL server.

The clients for these features are either a browser (for the Web-based tasks) or standard Office 2000 applications (for document creation and retrieval). The server-based software comes in a package Microsoft calls *The Microsoft Office Server Extensions*. The Office Server Extensions consist of the FrontPage Server Extensions, plus a collection of Active Server Pages and ActiveX controls, plus the workgroup database server. In effect, the Office Server Extensions are an extension to—and require the presence of—the FrontPage Server Extensions.

The Office Server Extensions require Windows NT Server 4.0 (or above) and Internet Information Server 4.0 (or above). As such, installation is a job for the server administrator. The setup files may be present in an /OSE folder on the Office 2000 CD, or they may be downloaded from Microsoft's Web site.

Notably, and just to make life complicated, the Web Folders feature that comes with Office 2000 *doesn't* require the Office Server Extensions. Because the Web Folders feature is only a file transfer mechanism, it requires only the FrontPage Server Extensions.

Figure 18-30 illustrates the Web Folders feature. Basically, it uses the familiar Windows Explorer interface to display the content of server-based FrontPage Webs and of course, you can move, copy, rename, and open files in all the usual ways.

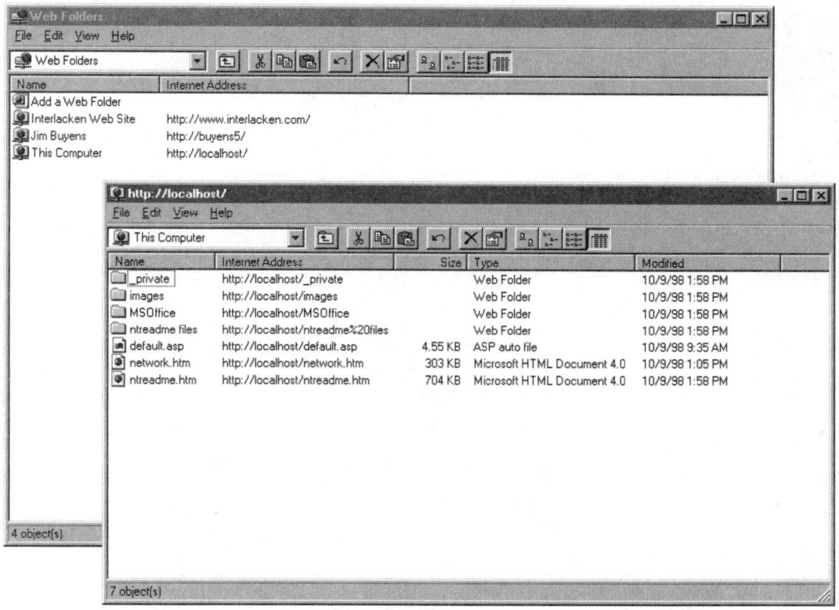

FIGURE 18-30.

Office 2000's Web Folders feature provides drag-and-drop desktop access to server-based FrontPage Webs.

Initially, Web Folders appears as a simple icon under My Computer. Double-clicking Web Folders displays an Add Web Folder icon that, if double-clicked, prompts you for the names of Web servers to display in the future.

TIP

If you're a frequent user of Web Folders, you may find it convenient to have a Web Folders icon on your desktop. To set this up, first open My Computer, and then drag the Web Folders icon onto your desktop.

Using the Office Server Extensions from Word 2000

Figure 18-31 shows Microsoft Word 2000 saving a document into a server-based FrontPage Web. This is old stuff, previously covered in Chapter 5, "Adding and Formatting Text," but it's the starting point for using the Office Server Extensions. In case you forgot, here's the procedure for saving a Word document into a FrontPage Web: choose Save As HTML from the File menu, and then click Web Folders in the Save As box.

FIGURE 18-31.

Word 2000 can save documents directly into a FrontPage Web.

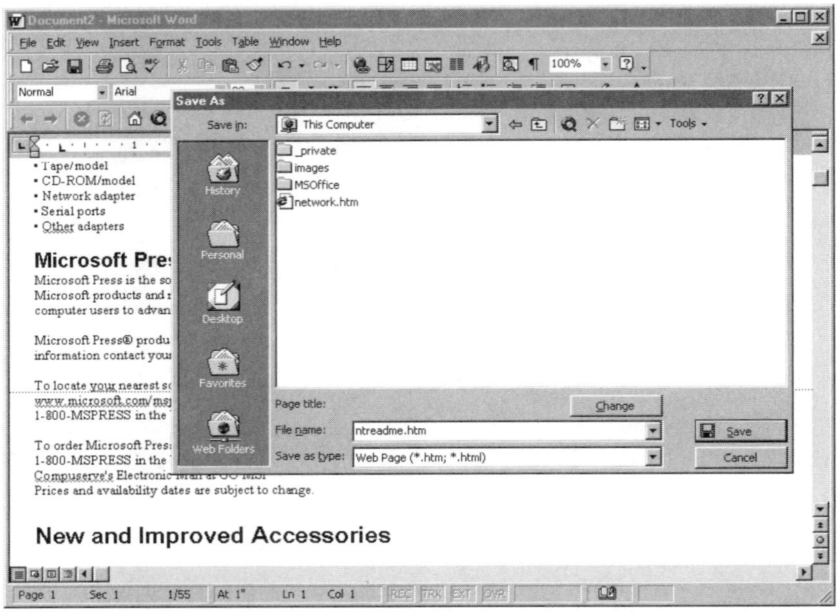

Once your document is on the Web server, choose Online Collaboration from the Tools menu, and then select Web Discussions. This initiates discussions on the document and displays the Discussions toolbar seen at the bottom of Figure 18-32.

> **NOTE**
>
> Within the Web Discussion feature, Microsoft calls each comment a discussion.

With the Discussions drop-down menu, at the left of the toolbar, you can insert a discussion, refresh the display of existing discussions, filter discussions, print discussions, and set discussion options. The five icons next from the left insert discussions in the document, insert discussions about the document, jump to the previous discussion, jump to the next discussion, and toggle display of general discussions.

Clicking the Subscribe button displays the dialog box seen in Figure 18-33. Here you can subscribe to change notices on the current document or on any document in a specified folder (subject to filters), set notification criteria, specify your e-mail address, and indicate how long the Server Extensions should accumulate changes before sending them.

FIGURE 18-32.

The Discussion toolbar at the bottom of this window controls Web Discussions and Web Subscriptions.

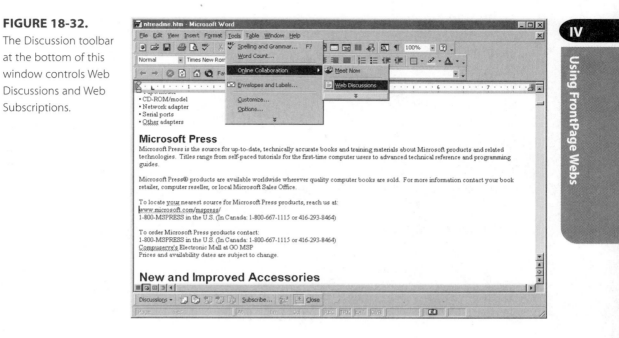

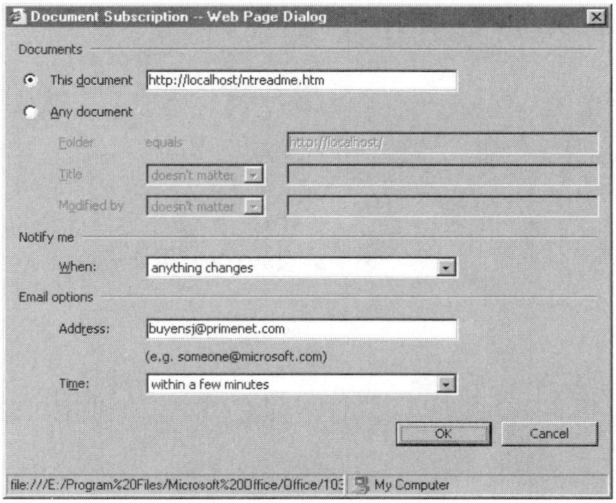

FIGURE 18-33.

This dialog box subscribes an e-mail user to change notifications for a given document or folder.

Figure 18-34 shows the same document being discussed in Internet Explorer. The Web visitor first opened the document location specified in Figure 18-31, then chose Discussions from the View menu. This displayed the Discussions toolbar that's visible at the bottom of the figure. Clicking the Insert Discussion icon on the Discussions toolbar displayed a "sticky note" icon each place a discussion could be inserted. The Web visitor double-clicked one of these icons to display the Enter Discussion Text dialog box and, in the figure, has just typed the text. Clicking OK submits the discussion text and displays it as shown in Figure 18-35.

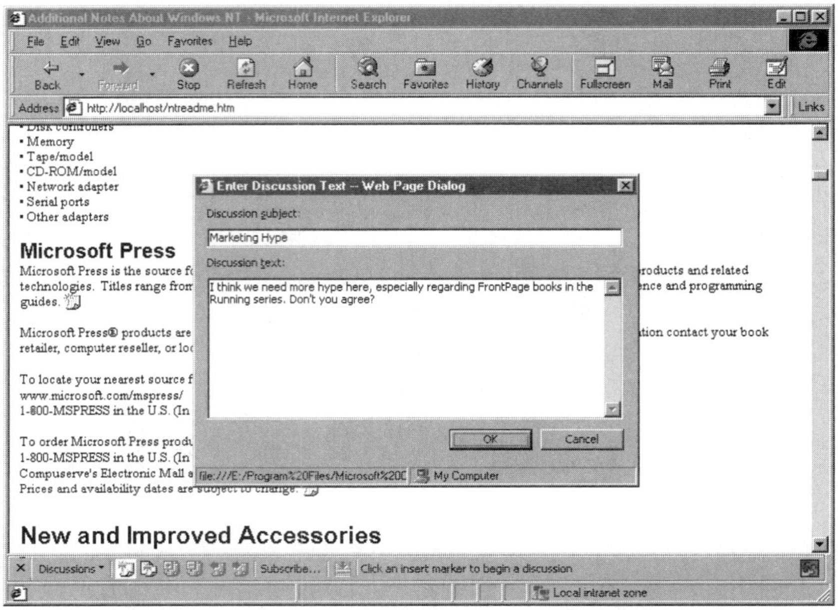

FIGURE 18-34.

After displaying the Discussions toolbar, Internet Explorer can accept discussion text and subscribe Web visitors for change notification.

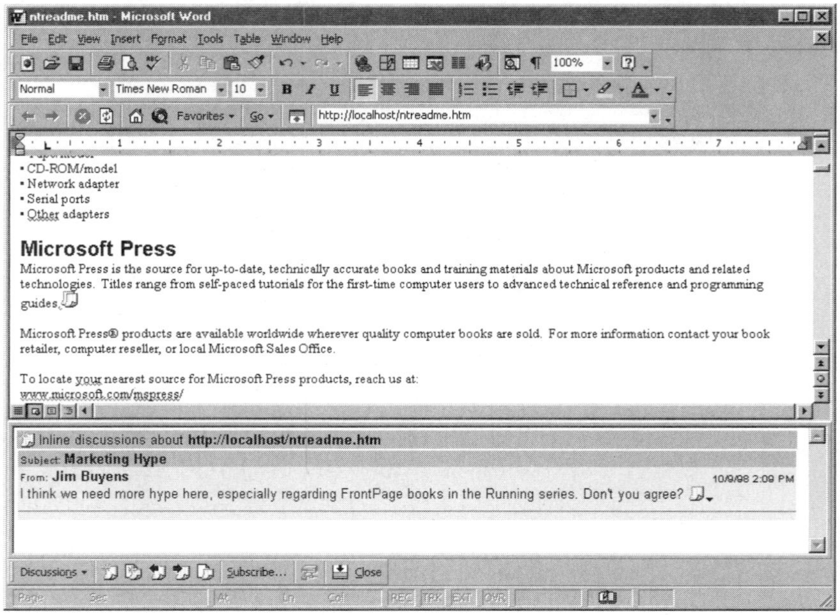

FIGURE 18-35.

Internet Explorer displays discussions inline with document text.

> **NOTE**
>
> Browser users can also subscribe to change notices for discussion documents. Clicking the Subscribe button in Figure 18-34 displays the same dialog box as clicking the Subscribe button in Word 2000 (seen in Figure 18-33).

Discussion text also appears—in almost identical format—when the original Web visitor opens the HTML file in Word. In fact, all discussion text from all visitors gets merged seamlessly into place. Figure 18-36 shows what this looks like.

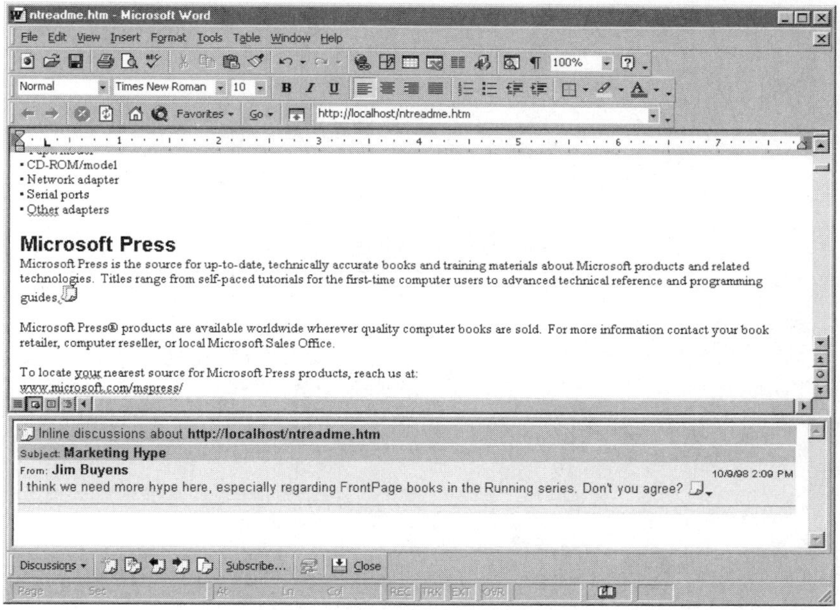

FIGURE 18-36.

Word 2000 merges all Web Discussion text and displays it in place.

Given that Internet Explorer uses a special toolbar for handling Web Discussions and Web Subscriptions, you might wonder about Netscape Navigator support. Navigator doesn't have a Discussions toolbar, but the Office Server Extensions do their best to emulate one using framesets. Figure 18-37 provides an example; note the emulated toolbar at the bottom of the window and the Document Subscription dialog box displayed as an HTML form.

Figure 18-38 shows a typical change notification message. Note that a single message can report multiple changes; the notification process periodically scans a database and combines all notifications to the same recipient.

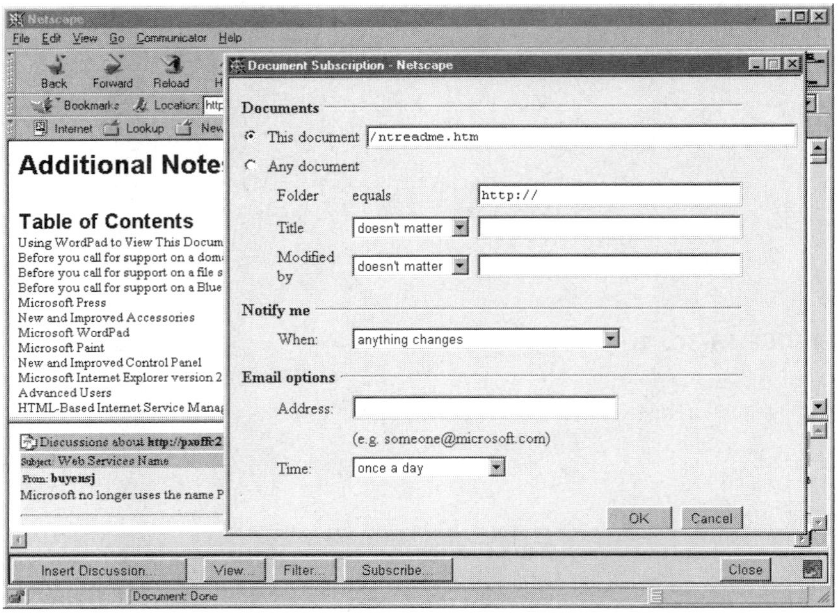

FIGURE 18-37.

The Office Server Extensions use standard HTML to communicate with Netscape Navigator visitors.

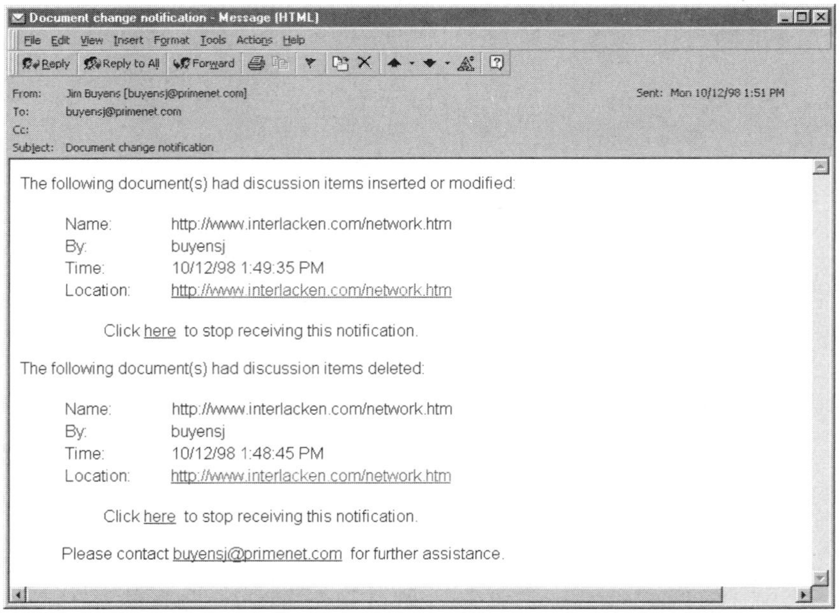

FIGURE 18-38.

This is a notification message generated by the Office Server Extensions.

Using Web-Based Office Server Extension Features

The Office extensions also support a number of purely Web-based features, normally accessible from a Start Page located at *http://<servername>/ msoffice/*. Figure 18-39 illustrates this page.

FIGURE 18-39.

The Office Server Extensions Start Page provides the starting point for purely Web-based functions.

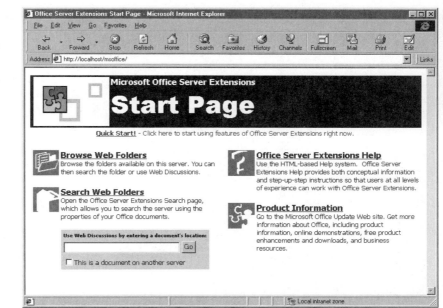

Clicking Browse Web Folders displays a listing like the one in Figure 18-40 provided, of course, that directory browsing for the given directory is turned on. Notice the Search option, the Filter On Name option, the customized file icons, the Last Accessed dates, and the Date Created values, none of which appear in normal directory browsing lists. Note the contents of the browser's Address box as well: you can display this type of listing for any permitted folder on your server just by modifying the *URL=* value.

Clicking the Search Web Folders hyperlink in Figure 18-39 displays the Search Web Folders page shown in Figure 18-41. Clicking the Search button in Figure 18-40 does the same.

The Search Web Folders page is just a front-end for Microsoft Index Server, a text-search engine that's installed by default as part of IIS 4.0. This version, however, provides more options than the default Search page supplied with Index Server, and more options than the default

FrontPage Search form as well. Note in particular the Search By Property section, which searches for properties you set in Office 2000 applications (usually by choosing Properties from the File menu).

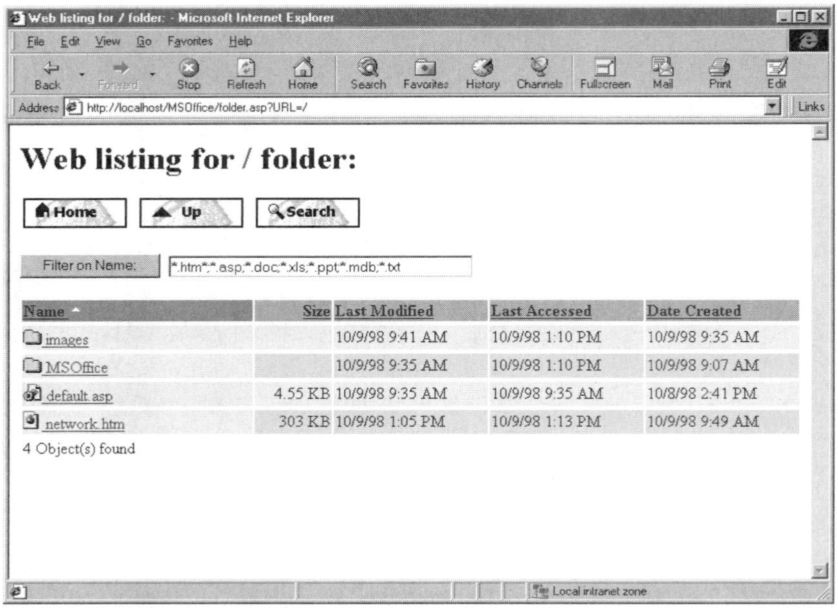

FIGURE 18-40.

This directory listing provides a Search button, file name filters, and column sorting—all enhancements over the standard Web-server directory displays.

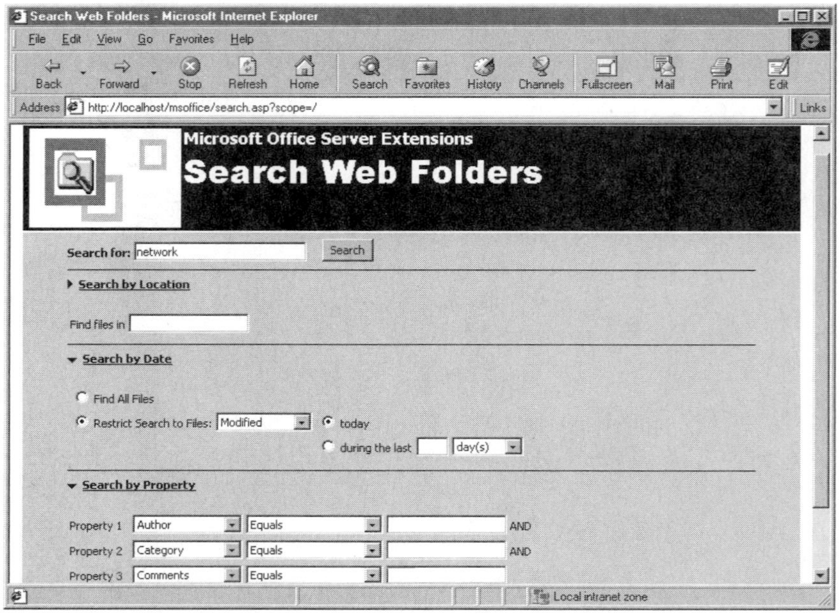

FIGURE 18-41.

This Search Web Folders page locates documents on an Office-extended Web server.

To display this Search page from any hyperlink, enter the URL *http:// <servername>/msoffice/search.asp?scope=/*. To search less than the entire server, specify a directory path as the *scope=* value.

Administering the Office Server Extensions

Web pages provide the most universal way to administer the Office Server Extensions. To display the Administration Home Page, browse the URL *http://<servername>/msoffice/msoadmin/*. The Web page shown in Figure 18-42 will result.

FIGURE 18-42.

This Administration Home Page controls the Office Server Extensions.

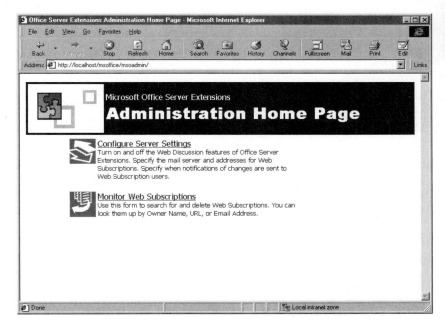

Clicking the hyperlink Configure Server Settings displays the Web page shown in Figure 18-43 and Figure 18-44. Note that these figures show the top and bottom of the same Web page. As you might expect, there are two categories of options: Web Discussions and Web Subscriptions. The options for Web Discussions are at the top of the page, and thus appear in Figure 18-43.

- **Web Discussions Are** provides a master on-off switch for Web Discussions.

- **Allow Web Discussions On** controls discussion of documents located on other servers.

FIGURE 18-43.

This Web page administers the Web Discussions and Web Subscriptions features of the Office Server Extensions.

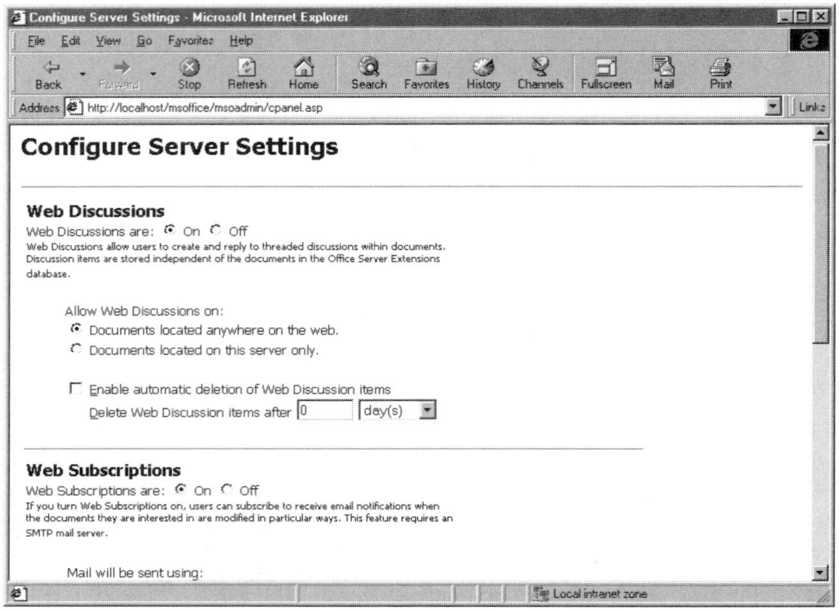

FIGURE 18-44.

This is the bottom half of the Web page shown in Figure 18-43.

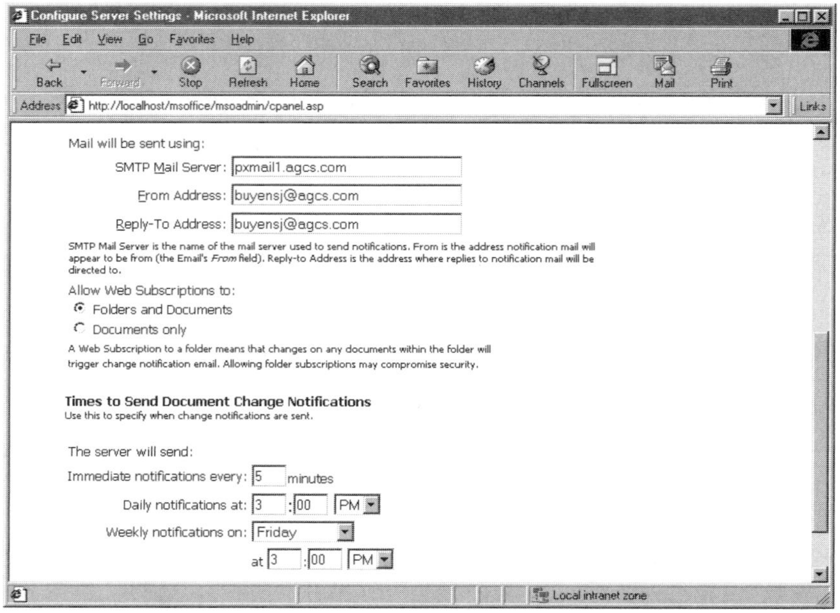

IV

- **Documents Located Anywhere On The Web,** if turned on, indicates that this server may record discussions about documents residing on other servers.

- **Documents Located On This Server Only,** if turned on, means the server will only accept discussions for documents on the same server.

NOTE

To host discussions on one server about documents on another, first open the document and then, on the Discussions toolbar, choose Discussion Options from the Discussions drop-down list. Finally, use the box titled Select A Discussion Server to select the server that will record discussion items.

- **Enable Automatic Deletion Of Web Discussion Items,** if turned on, indicates that the Office Server Extensions should delete discussion items beyond a specified age.

The Web Subscriptions options occupy the lower portion of the Configure Server Settings Web page, and thus appear in Figure 18-44. They are:

- **Mail Will Be Sent Using** controls settings that pertain to mail delivery and addressing.

  - **SMTP Mail Server** specifies the network name of the Simple Mail Transport Protocol (SMTP) mail server that the Office Server Extensions will use for sending mail.

  - **From Address** specifies the e-mail address that will appear as the sender of all change notifications.

  - **Reply-To Address** specifies the destination of mail created when subscribers respond to a change notification by using their mail program's Reply button.

- **Allow Web Subscriptions To** controls the permissible scope of change notification subscriptions.

  - **Folders And Documents,** if turned on, means subscribers can sign up for individual documents or for any document in a given folder.

  - **Documents Only,** if turned on, means subscribers can sign up for individual documents only.

■ **Times To Send Document Change Notifications** controls when the Office Server Extensions will send change notifications.

- **Immediate Notifications Every** controls how often the extensions send mail to subscribers who requested notification within a few minutes of any change.

- **Daily Notifications At** controls when the extensions send mail to subscribers who requested daily change notification.

- **Weekly Notifications At** controls when the extensions send mail to subscribers who requested weekly change notification.

> **NOTE**

The Office Server Extensions send change notifications summarized by interval, not one-by-one as they occur.

The Monitor Web Subscriptions page, shown in Figure 18-45, displays current subscriptions for all Web visitors or for any specific visitor. The Delete button at the bottom cancels the currently selected subscription, and the Delete All button deletes all those displayed.

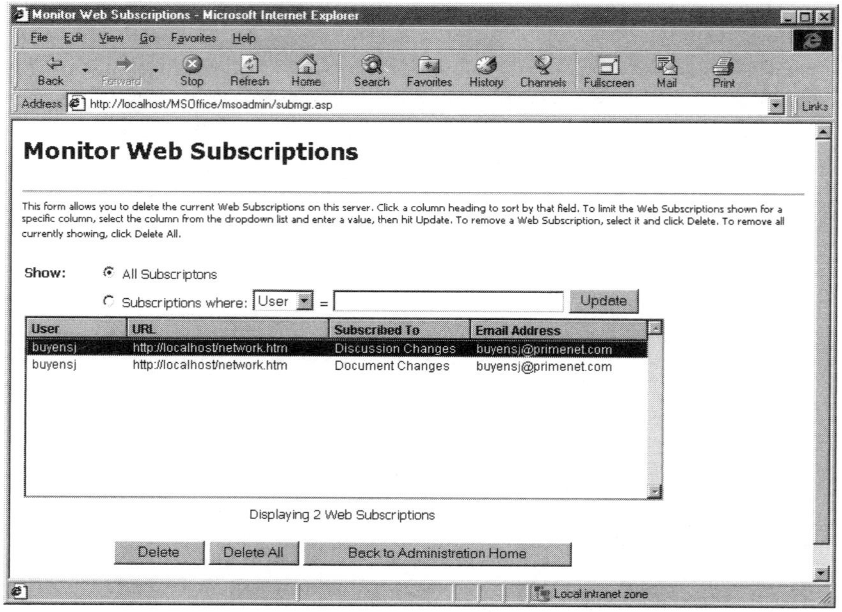

FIGURE 18-45.
The Monitor Web Subscriptions page displays current subscriptions and provides a way to administratively delete obsolete ones.

In Summary...

This chapter and the last provided considerable detail on the process of installing and configuring FrontPage Webs. The payoff begins in Chapter 19, which explains many of the FrontPage features that help you manage your Web pages.

Working with FrontPage Webs

Microsoft FrontPage is the control point for managing your Web. From here you can not only edit Web pages, but organize files and folders, keep track of pending tasks, record assignment and review of individual files, control which files are published to your production server, and take ownership of files so others can't change them while you do.

FrontPage also provides a variety of views and reports that help you manage your site. It lists, summarizes, and filters all the files in your Web, highlighting new files, old files, slow pages, broken hyperlinks, and so forth. FrontPage can even document your Web's structural hierarchy and automatically manage the hyperlinks among your pages.

In short, FrontPage treats your Web as an organized and highly interrelated set of files and provides site-level tools no text editor can match. Learning to use these tools is well worth the effort.

Opening a FrontPage Web

The first step in working with a FrontPage Web is to open it. There are several ways to do this.

? SEE ALSO
For an explanation of the Open Web view and toolbar icons, see the topic, "Opening a Page from Page View," page 84.

- Choose Open Web from the File menu, locate the Web in the resulting Open Web dialog box, and then either double-click it or select it and click the Open button. This will display the dialog box shown in Figure 19-1.

  - To locate a disk-based Web, use the History, My Documents, Desktop, or Favorites icon.

  - To locate a server-based Web, use the Web Folders icon.

    The first time you try to open a server-based Web, its server may not appear in the Web Folders list. FrontPage can't display a list of Web servers in your environment, because your environment might be the entire Internet! If the folder you want doesn't appear in the Web Folders list, just type its URL and then click Open. This both opens the Web and adds it to the list for next time.

FIGURE 19-1.
The Open Web dialog box is very similar to the Open File dialog box shown in Figure 4-3 on page 85. Rather than opening a single file, however, this box opens a group view of many files.

? SEE ALSO
For information about opening individual files in FrontPage, see the topic, "Opening a Page from Page View," page 84.

- Open a Web page that resides in a FrontPage Web. FrontPage will open both the specified file and the Web that contains it.

- Choose Recent Webs from the File menu. If the Web you want to open appears in the list, simply select it.

- Locate the Web within the Folder List of another Web and double-click it. Right-clicking and choosing Open from the pop-up menu accomplishes the same thing.

IV

Using FrontPage Webs

Opening a regular folder in FrontPage displays that folder's contents in the same window. Opening a FrontPage Web creates a new window displaying that Web.

In the case of server-based Webs residing on servers that support user level security, FrontPage may prompt you for a user name and password. Enter whatever values the Web administrator has established.

> **NOTE**

> In folder listings, the icon for a FrontPage Web looks like a folder with a globe on it. This visually distinguishes FrontPage Webs from regular folders.

Figure 19-2 shows a FrontPage Web open in FrontPage. Below the toolbars appear three distinct frames.

FIGURE 19-2.

FrontPage displays an open Web in three main panes. From left to right, these are the Views Bar, the Folder List, and the Document window.

Views Bar   Folder List   Document Window

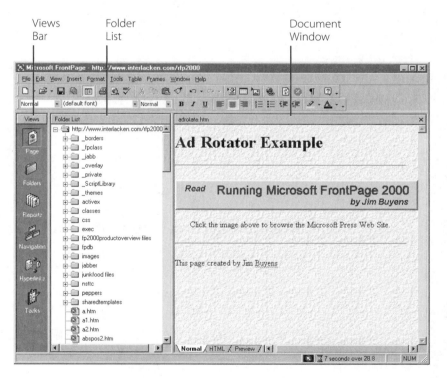

- **Views Bar** icons display any of six views in the document frame.

    - **Page** displays Web pages in WYSIWYG view for editing.

    - **Folders** displays a tabular list of files in the Web organized by folder.

- **Reports** displays an assortment of tabular listings useful for site management.

- **Navigation** graphically displays the logical hierarchy of a Web.

- **Hyperlinks** graphically displays files in a Web, organized by hyperlink reference.

- **Tasks** displays a list of reminders to complete or correct pages.

■ **Folder List** displays the Web contents as a folder tree.

■ **Document Window** displays the document, report, or work area selected by the Views bar.

To hide or view the Views bar, choose Views Bar from the View menu. To hide or view the Folder List, choose Folder List from the View menu.

Because the Views bar and the document window are tightly linked, and because the Folder List applies to four of the six views, we'll discuss the Folder List first.

Working with Web Folder Lists

The Folder List appears whenever a FrontPage Web is open; it occupies the middle pane of the main FrontPage window and provides access to all files and folders in the Web. In addition to providing information, the Folder List has two main uses: manipulating the files and folders in the Web, and opening files with the appropriate editor.

Manipulating Files and Folders

The center pane in Figure 19-2 shows a typical Folder List. All the normal Windows Explorer commands work as expected.

■ To open a collapsed folder, double-click it or click the preceding plus-sign icon.

■ To collapse an open folder, double-click it or click the preceding minus-sign icon.

■ To load the Clipboard with a file to be copied, press Ctrl+C, press Ctrl+Insert, or choose Copy from the Edit menu.

■ To load the Clipboard with a file to be moved, press Ctrl+X, press Shift+Delete, or choose Cut from the Edit menu.

IV

Using FrontPage Webs

- To complete a move or copy operation, highlight the desired folder, and then press Ctrl+V or Shift+Insert or choose Paste from the Edit menu.

- To move a file from one folder to another, drag that file over that folder's icon, and then drop it.

- To copy a file from one location to another, hold down Ctrl while dragging it to that location.

- To move or copy a file or folder and control the operation from a pop-up menu, drag the file or folder with the right mouse button.

- To rename a file or folder, either select it and press F2 or right-click it and choose Rename from the pop-up menu.

- To delete a file or folder, select it and press Delete, select it and choose Delete from the Edit menu, or right-click it and choose Delete from the pop-up menu.

⭐ TIP

> To copy or move a file to another folder, paste or drop it on that folder's icon.

You can also cut, copy, and drag files to transport them between two Webs and between a disk location and a Web. However, the following special precautions apply.

- You can only copy files into or out of a Web. There is no facility for moving a file (that is, for copying a file and then deleting the original).

- You can't copy or drop files or folders onto a Web folder displayed in a parent Web. To copy between Webs, you must open each Web in a separate FrontPage window.

- When you drag or copy a file out of a Web and into Windows, Windows creates an Internet Shortcut to the file. Clicking this shortcut launches your browser and displays the file.

  Note that you can't copy a file from a FrontPage Web to a physical location on your disk by dragging it out of FrontPage Folder List or view. However, there are two other ways of doing this.

  - Open the file in Page view, choose Save As from the File menu, and specify a location on your hard disk.

- Open the My Computer icon on your desktop, Open the Web Folders icon, open the FrontPage Web that contains the file you want, and then drag the file into Windows Explorer. To control the effect of the dragging operation, drag with the right mouse button.

Figure 19-3 shows the pop-up menus you'll receive after right-clicking a file, a folder, and a subweb icon in the Folder List.

FIGURE 19-3.

Right-clicking a Folder List file, folder, and subweb produces these pop-up menus, respectively.

Individual File

Ordinary Folder

Subweb Folder

⑦ SEE ALSO

For more information about conversion between folders and Webs, see, "Converting a Folder to a Web," page 583, and "Converting a Web to a Folder," page 584.

Note the Convert To Web option on the Folder pop-up menu and the Convert To Folder option on the Web menu. These are reciprocal operations but, as explained in Chapter 18, both operations alter or discard Web-related data. After converting a folder to a Web, converting the same Web back to a folder may not restore all the files and FrontPage indexes back to their original condition.

Whenever you move or rename files in FrontPage, FrontPage will automatically correct all hyperlinks, image tags, and other references in the same FrontPage Web. Suppose, for example, that 23 pages in your Web use an image called cyanball.gif. For some reason, you decide to rename the file from cyanball.gif to cyandot.gif, and do so in FrontPage. FrontPage will update all 23 Web pages so that they reference cyandot.gif rather than cyanball.gif. FrontPage will also warn you before deleting a file used by other files in your Web.

FrontPage's Import command on the File menu adds an external file to the current FrontPage Web folder. If the FrontPage Web isn't on the local machine, the Import command will copy the file across the network. The Import command also updates FrontPage with appropriate file information, an operation that wouldn't occur if you simply copied the file to the Web's physical location by some other method.

CAUTION
FrontPage can't correct
references from outside
your Web to files within
it. First, this would re-
quire searching the
entire Internet. Second,
even if FrontPage *could*
locate such references,
you probably wouldn't
have the authority to
update them. You can
minimize this problem
by organizing related
Web pages into the
same Web.

The Add Task option creates a Tasks entry for the selected page. The section titled "Working with Task View," page 650, discusses this feature in detail.

Opening Files

Double-clicking any file in Folder List opens that file using the appro-priate editor. Unfortunately, FrontPage's idea of what constitutes an appropriate editor may be different from yours, and this can lead to confusion. Here's how FrontPage chooses an editor.

- Normally, FrontPage will open Web-page files—identified by file name extensions like htm, html, and asp—in FrontPage (that is, in Page view).

- For Web-page files saved by other Office 2000 applications, Front-Page will open them in that application. You can tell what appli-cation FrontPage will invoke by looking at each file's icon. Figure 19-4 shows examples of htm files saved by PowerPoint, Excel, and FrontPage.

TIP

If you want FrontPage to open all Web pages in Page view, regardless of the application that created them, choose Options from the Tools menu, choose the Configure Editors tab, and turn off the check box titled Open Web Pages In The Office Application That Created Them.

SEE ALSO
For more information
about the Configure
Editors tab, see "Con-
figuring External Edi-
tors," page 463.

- For other kinds of files, FrontPage first tries looking up the file-name extension in a list of configured editors. To configure this list, choose Options from the Tools Menu, then choose the Con-figure Editors tab.

- If all else fails, FrontPage chooses an editor by using Windows file associations; that is, it uses the same program Windows would use if you double-clicked the same type of file in Windows Explorer.

There are three ways to override FrontPage's normal choice of editors. First, if the application you want to use has a Web Folders choice in its File Open dialog box, you can simply start the application and open the file you want. Second, you can right-click the file in any Folder List or view, and then choose Open With from the pop-up menu. If the application you want doesn't appear in the resulting dialog box, add it to the Configured Editors list just described. Third, to open a Web page with the current Office 2000 application, locate it using the File Open dialog box, click the drop-down button just right of the Open button, and then choose the Open With option you want.

FIGURE 19-4.

FrontPage detects which Office application created a Web file, displays a corresponding icon, and opens files with the same application.

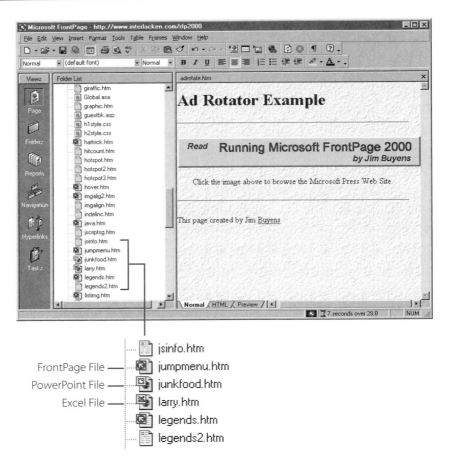

Planning and Managing Folders

Other than the hidden folders used by FrontPage, there are no requirements and no limits on the number of folders your Web can use. Most sites use folders to segregate and categorize their content, but the extent of such use is a matter of judgment and preference.

When a FrontPage wizard or template creates a site, it normally places all HTML files in the root folder of the current Web and all images in an /images folder. There are several good reasons for having an /images folder.

■ At most sites, HTML files require more structure and management than image files. Keeping all the images in one folder reduces clutter and makes it easier to manage folders of Web pages.

- Many images are stock items used on several pages. Keeping all images in one folder makes it easy to locate and use stock images when creating new Web pages.

- Most browsers cache Web files to eliminate unnecessary downloads. If you store the same image in two different folders, however, the browser has no way of knowing the two images are identical, and it downloads them *both*. Keeping all images in one folder eliminates duplicate downloads.

It's often a good idea to put all pages for a given topic in one folder, and to name the topic's home page with the server's default page name. Subtopics can then be nested in subordinate folders to form a topical tree. This keeps individual folders small enough to be reviewed at a glance and also provides a navigational aid for users. When Web visitors see a URL like

```
http://www.wizards.com/products/magic/wands.htm
```

they expect that shortening it to

```
http://www.wizards.com/products/magic/
```

will bring up a Magic Products home page, and that shortening this further to

```
http://www.wizards.com/products/
```

will produce a Products home page.

This isn't to say that every page—or even every menu page—should reside in its own folder. This is poor practice. It's also poor practice, however, to locate all pages in a large site in a single folder. The organization you choose depends on the structure of your content, but there *should* be organization of some kind.

Folder names are again a matter of preference, but long dual-case names containing special characters usually create more problems than clarity.

- Users do sometimes type URLs by hand—perhaps copying them out of magazines—and long names are simply hard to type. Folder names are limited to 32 characters on Unix Web servers, and to 8 on Windows 3.1 systems.

- Dual-case names create confusion because some systems (particularly Unix) are case-sensitive and others (such as Windows) are not. To Unix, /Potions and /potions are two completely different folders: as different as /potions and /notions. To a Windows Web server, however, /Potions and /potions mean the same thing. Always using lowercase avoids such confusion.

■ Many special characters, even though acceptable as folder names, require special encoding when used in URLs. The coding consists of a percent sign followed by the hexadecimal value of the character's ASCII code. If you create a folder name containing a space, for example, you'll have to represent the space as %20 in all URLs—ungainly and hard to fathom.

Working with FrontPage Views

FrontPage provides six views of the currently open Web: to select a particular view, click its icon in the Views bar or choose the desired view from the View menu. The following views also display the Folder List described in the previous section: Page, Folders, Navigation, and Hyperlink.

The following sections explain each view and give examples of its use.

Working with Page View

Page view is the part of FrontPage that provides WYSIWYG editing of Web pages. Part II of this book, "Creating Web Pages," provides extensive detail about using this feature. In addition, the following operations are available whenever a FrontPage Web is open.

■ Double-clicking an HTML file in the Folder List opens it in Page view.

■ Dragging any file from the Folder List and dropping it onto an open Web page creates a hyperlink from the open page to the dragged file.

■ If Page view has no document open, dragging an HTML file from the Folder List and dropping it on the document pane's background opens that file.

■ A number of FrontPage components and development features are available only for pages in a FrontPage Web. The remaining chapters in this book are largely devoted to these topics.

Working with Folders View

Folders view, shown in Figure 19-5, provides a way to view or manage the physical arrangement of files and folders that make up your Web. It also displays properties such as file date and file size.

Folders view supports all the cut, copy, paste, and drag and drop features described in the previous section for the Folder List. The difference is in the display; Folders view presents a tabular view of one folder at a time.

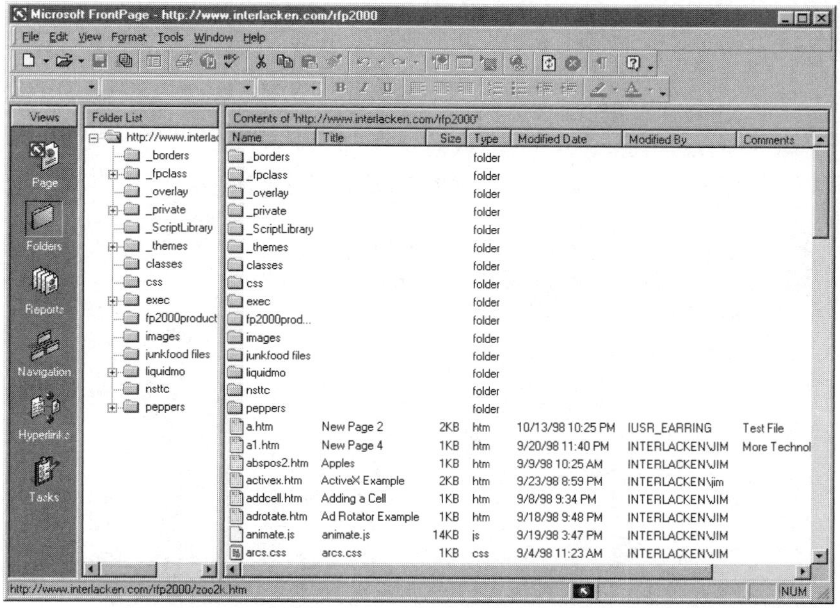

FIGURE 19-5.

FrontPage Folders view displays the physical location of pages in a site.

To display the contents of a specific folder, either select it in the Folder List or double-click it in the document window.

To sort the Folders view listing on any column, click its column heading. Repeatedly clicking the same column heading switches between ascending and descending sequence.

Referring again to Figure 19-5, note the Title column in the right pane. For Web pages, FrontPage obtains this from the HTML itself. To update the title of a Web page, you must:

1 Open the Web page in Page view. (Double-click the file name, or right-click it and select Open, or select the file name and then choose Open from the Edit menu.)

2 Choose Properties from the File menu.

3 Choose the General tab.

4 Update the Title field.

5 Click OK.

6 Save the file.

To update the title of a non-HTML file: right-click it, choose Properties from the pop-up menu, choose the General tab, update the Title field, and click OK. Figure 19-6 illustrates this. You can bring up the same dialog box by right-clicking the file and choosing Properties from the Edit menu.

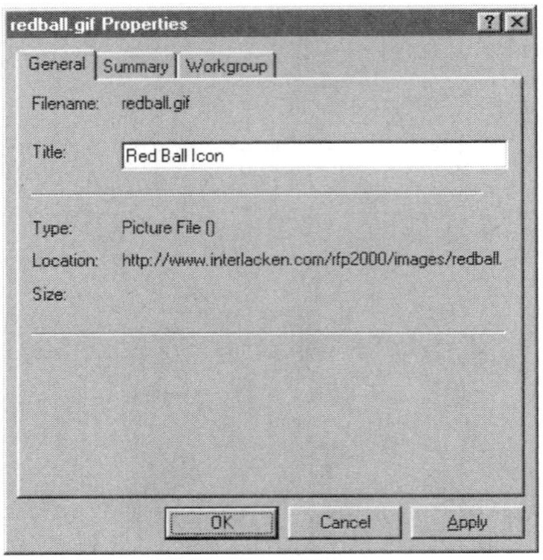

FIGURE 19-6.

For file types other than HTML, use the Properties command to update the file's title.

To change the comments for any type of file: right-click the file; choose Properties from the pop-up menu; and then choose the Summary tab shown in Figure 19-7. Finish by entering or updating the comments, then clicking OK.

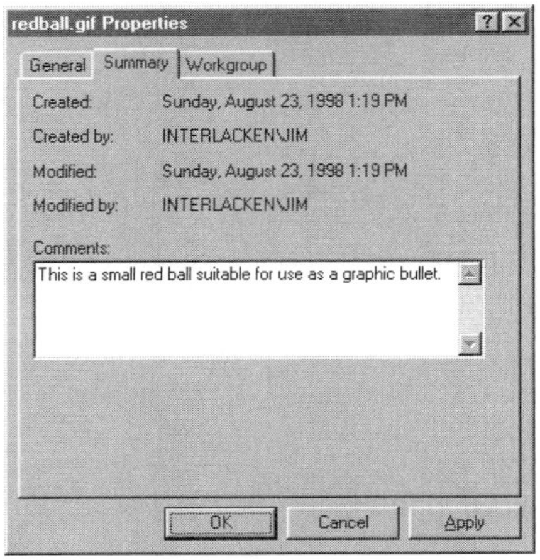

FIGURE 19-7.

This dialog box tab modifies the Comments field for a FrontPage Web file.

Working with Reports View

FrontPage provides 14 standard reports about the content of any Web. There are two ways to display any desired report. First, choose Reports from the View menu, and then choose the report. Alternatively, choose Toolbars from the View menu, then select Reports, then choose the report you want from the Reports toolbar. Table 19-1 describes the Reports toolbar.

Figure 19-8 shows the Recently Changed Files report, which is fairly typical in appearance. The horizontal and vertical scroll bars let you move around the list at will, and clicking the column headings sorts the report on any field you like. Right-clicking any line displays a pop-up menu with the usual choices: Open, Open With, Cut, Copy, Rename, Delete, Add Task, and Properties. Double-clicking any line is the same as right-clicking and choosing Open.

The Rename command, which is also accessible by pressing F2, pertains to the Name column. Fields in other columns may also be editable; the procedure is first to select the line you want to modify, and then to single-click the field you want to modify. If the field is modifiable, FrontPage will display the field as an editable text box, a drop-down list, or another control as appropriate.

SEE ALSO

For an alternate description of Reports view, see "Reports View," page 45.

TABLE 19-1.   FrontPage Reports Toolbar

Icon	Description	Function	Menu Command
Recently Added Files	Report	Specifies which report to display in the document window.	View/Reports
30 days	Report Setting	Selects filter settings for some reports.	Tools/Options/ Reports View
(icon)	Edit Hyperlinks*	Displays a target hyperlink location and changes it in all or selected pages where it appears.	Right-Click/ Edit Hyperlink
(icon)	Verify Hyperlinks*	Checks the validity of a selected hyperlink location.	Right-Click/ Verify

* Applies to Broken Hyperlinks report only.

FIGURE 19-8.

The Recently Changed Files report is typical of the 14 reports FrontPage provides.

Name	Title	Modified Date	Modified By	Size	Type	In Folder
sampform.htm	Sample Form Page	10/2/98 9:15 PM	INTERLACKEN\jim	1KB	htm	
delivery.htm	Running Microsoft FrontPage 2000	9/30/98 9:19 PM	INTERLACKEN\jim	1KB	htm	
pe01496.gif	images/pe01496.gif	9/30/98 9:19 PM	INTERLACKEN\jim	39KB	gif	images
pargloop.htm	Paragraph Loop	9/27/98 11:00 PM	INTERLACKEN\jim	1KB	htm	
movies.asp	The Movie List	9/27/98 8:43 AM	INTERLACKEN\jim	2KB	asp	exec
jumpmenu.htm	Jump Menu	9/26/98 11:23 PM	INTERLACKEN\jim	1KB	htm	
artlist.htm	The Art List	9/26/98 10:08 PM	INTERLACKEN\jim	3KB	htm	
jsinfo.htm	Obtaining Real-Time Values in Jav...	9/26/98 9:21 PM	INTERLACKEN\JIM	2KB	htm	
figures.htm	Figured Web Pages	9/26/98 9:04 PM	INTERLACKEN\jim	11KB	htm	
jscriptsg.htm	JavaScript Page Footer	9/26/98 8:27 PM	INTERLACKEN\jim	1KB	htm	
timeday.asp	New Page 1	9/26/98 2:01 PM	INTERLACKEN\jim	1KB	asp	exec
sun.gif	images/sun.gif	9/26/98 1:40 PM	INTERLACKEN\jim	4KB	gif	images
alarm.gif	images/alarm.gif	9/26/98 1:39 PM	INTERLACKEN\jim	4KB	gif	images
saguaro.gif	images/saguaro.gif	9/26/98 1:37 PM	INTERLACKEN\jim	3KB	gif	images
gala.gif	images/gala.gif	9/26/98 1:33 PM	INTERLACKEN\jim	3KB	gif	images
activex.htm	ActiveX Example	9/23/98 8:59 PM	INTERLACKEN\jim	2KB	htm	
pppp.htm	The Society of Painters, Patchers,...	9/23/98 5:00 PM	INTERLACKEN\jim	2KB	htm	
default.htm	Home Page	9/23/98 4:49 PM	INTERLACKEN\jim	1KB	htm	
carpntr2.gif	images/carpntr2.gif	9/23/98 12:36 PM	INTERLACKEN\JIM	3KB	gif	images
carpntr1.gif	images/carpntr1.gif	9/23/98 12:33 PM	INTERLACKEN\JIM	4KB	gif	images
T_pueblo.gif	images/T_pueblo.gif	9/23/98 12:15 PM	INTERLACKEN\JIM	1KB	gif	images
Bearpnt.gif	images/Bearpnt.gif	9/23/98 12:11 PM	INTERLACKEN\JIM	2KB	gif	images
Cnstrwk1.gif	images/Cnstrwk1.gif	9/23/98 12:08 PM	INTERLACKEN\JIM	2KB	gif	images

CAUTION

To change the title of a Web page, you must open the page in Page view, choose Properties from the File menu, and then change the title on the General tab of the resulting dialog box.

To change the title of anything but a Web page, locate the file in any report or folder list, right-click it, choose Properties, and use the Title fields on the General tab. Alternatively, update the title fields directly in Reports view.

FrontPage may let you enter a new title for a Web page using this second procedure, but it won't be saved. For Web pages, the first method predominates.

Here are the 14 reports grouped by category. Table 19-2, on pages 632–633, itemizes the fields available in each report.

■ **Summary Reports** include reports that provide overall Web statistics.

  • **Site Summary** accumulates and reports various statistics about your Web, such as the number of files, their total size, and so forth.

■ **Content Reports** include reports that list Web pages and other files that meet various criteria.

  • **All Files** lists all files in a Web, regardless of folder.

  • **Recently Added Files** lists all files added to a Web within a given interval.

  • **Recently Changed Files** lists all files changed within a given interval.

  • **Older Files** lists files that haven't been updated within a given interval.

  • **Unlinked Files** lists files FrontPage believes may be unused.

  • **Slow Pages** lists Web pages whose total download time, including linked components, exceeds a configured amount.

- **Categories** lists all Web pages, including a column that shows assigned Category codes.

■ **Troubleshooting Reports** display errors that exist within your Web.

- **Broken Hyperlinks** reports links to files that don't exist and provides options for fixing them.

- **Component Errors** reports errors and inconsistencies involving FrontPage components. These can occur when, for example, you first configure the component correctly, and then later delete a required file.

■ **Workgroup Reports** displays the status of a Web that several people are developing together.

- **Assigned To** shows which pages are assigned to which developer.

- **Checkout Status** shows which files are checked out for update, and by whom.

- **Review Status** shows which pages are assigned for review, and any further status the reviewer has assigned.

- **Publish Status** shows which pages are approved for publication and which are held back.

In all reports but Site Summary, each line pertains to a file in your Web. Choosing Open means opening the file with its default editor. For Web pages, this is FrontPage's Page view. For everything else, it's whatever's configured under Tools, Options, Configure Editor.

The Site Summary report doesn't list individual files; it lists statistics tabulated from other reports. Double-clicking one of these lines jumps to the associated detail report.

Using the Site Summary Report

Figure 19-9 shows a typical Site Summary report. You can see at a glance that the Web currently has 478 files occupying 3,684 KB of disk space, that 217 of those files are pictures, and that eight Web pages exceed the configured maximum download time. The Description column explains the meaning of each line.

Using the Content Reports

Figure 19-10 shows the All Files report, probably the most typical in this group. It contains one line for every file in a FrontPage Web, regardless of the folder.

TABLE 19-2. Reported Fields by Report Type

	Site Summary	All Files	Recently Added Files	Recently Changed Files	Older Files	Unlinked Files
Name	X	X	X	X	X	X
In Folder		X	X	X	X	X
Title		X	X	X	X	X
Comments		X				
Type		X	X	X	X	X
Size		X	X	X	X	
Modified Date		X		X	X	X
Created Date			X		X	
Modified By		X	X	X	X	X
Count	X					
Size	X					
Description	X					
Download Time						
Status						
Hyperlink						
In Page						
Errors						
Review Status						
Assigned To						
Review Date						
Reviewed By						
Assigned Date						
Assigned By						
Category						
Publish						
Checked Out By						
Version						
Locked Date						

Slow Pages	Broken Hyper-links	Compo-nent Errors	Review Status	Assigned To	Cate-gories	Publish Status	Checkout Status
X		X	X	X	X	X	X
X		X	X	X	X	X	X
X	X	X	X	X	X	X	X
				X			
X		X	X	X	X	X	X
X						X	
X						X	
X	X						
X							
	X						
	X						
	X						
		X					
			X			X	
			X	X			
			X				
			X				
				X			
				X			
					X		
						X	
							X
							X
							X

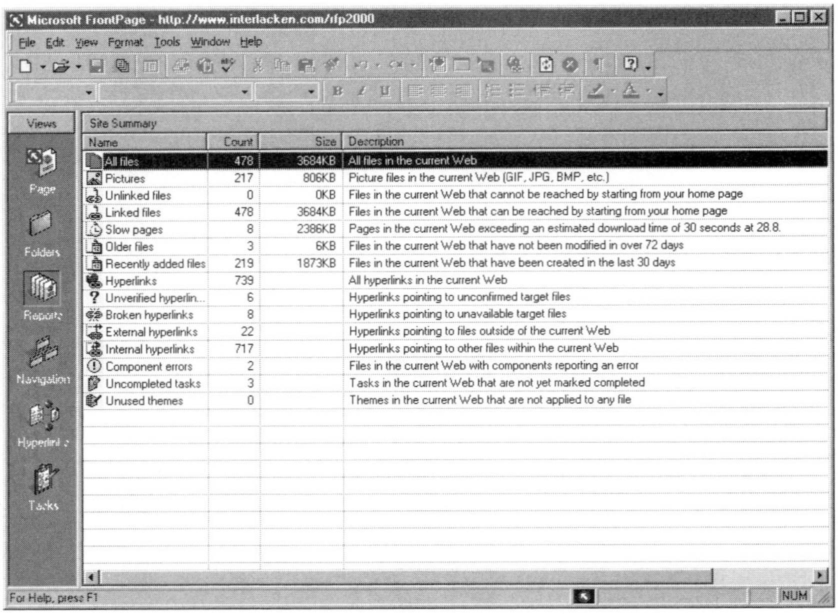

FIGURE 19-9.

The Site Summary report presents statistics concerning a FrontPage Web.

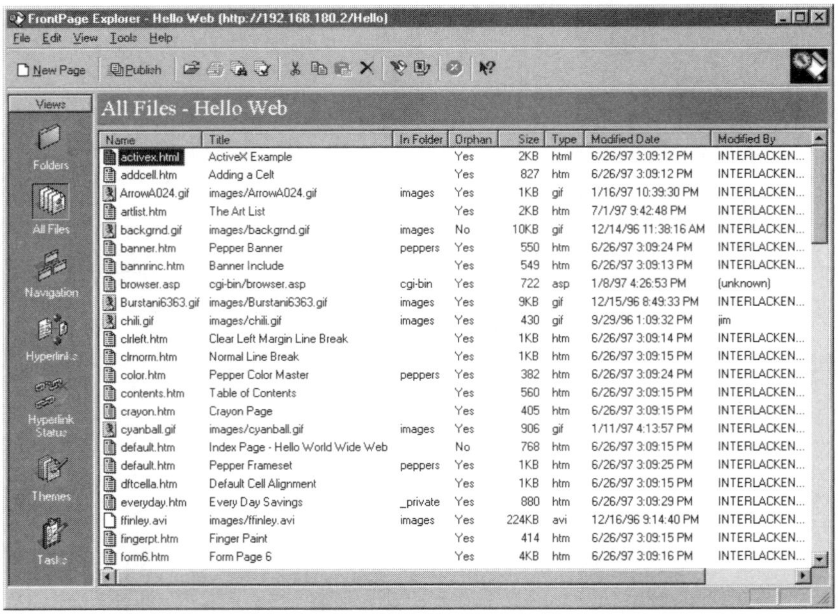

FIGURE 19-10.

The All Files report provides a single, alphabetical list of all files in a FrontPage Web, regardless of folder.

⑦ SEE ALSO

For more information on configuring default report settings, see the section titled, "Customizing Reports View," page 466.

The following reports are very similar to the All Files report, but each of them lists only those files meeting certain criteria. In addition, the column headings change slightly depending on the criteria.

- **Recently Added Files** lists files added to a Web within a certain number of days. To configure the default number of days, choose Options from the Tools menu, then click the Reports View tab. You can temporarily choose a different interval by using the Report Setting control on the Reports toolbar.

- **Recently Changed Files** is similar to Recently Added Files, but includes changed files as well as new ones.

- **Older Files** includes only those files no one has updated within a specified interval. It's a good idea to review such files periodically, to see if they've become stale or outdated.

- **Unlinked Files** lists files for which FrontPage can't find links in the current Web. Take care before deleting such files, however. They may be used by other Webs or by script code that FrontPage can't decipher.

⊘ NOTE

Some people call unlinked files *orphans*.

- **Slow Pages** involves calculating the total bytes required to display a Web page—including all components such as image files—and dividing this by a download speed. This produces an estimated download time. If the download time exceeds a threshold, the page appears in the Slow Pages report.

  - To configure the default download speed and threshold, choose Options from the Tools menu and then click the Reports View tab.

  - To override the default download speed, click the portion of the status bar just right of the FrontPage icon.

  - To override the default threshold, use the Report Setting control on the Reports toolbar.

★ TIP

To improve the download time for a Web page, decrease the number of images, decrease the size of the image files, or split a single, large page into multiple, smaller ones.

? SEE ALSO

For more information about using Categories, see "Categories," page 685.

Like the All Files report, the Categories report lists every file in the current Web. The Categories report, however, also shows a list of category codes assigned to each file. To change a file's category codes, right-click its line in any report or folder list, choose Properties, and then choose the Workgroups tab.

Using the Troubleshooting Reports

Broken hyperlinks are living proof that, left to itself, the universe *does* revert to random bits. Even if nothing within your Web changes during a certain interval, hyperlinks outside your site are sure to change and require correction. The Broken Hyperlinks report therefore checks and corrects all the hyperlinks within your Web.

Figure 19-11 pictures a typical Broken Hyperlinks report. Links among pages in your own Web normally won't appear unless they're broken. To display all internal hyperlinks, right-click a blank area in the Broken Hyperlinks report and choose Show All Hyperlinks from the pop-up menu.

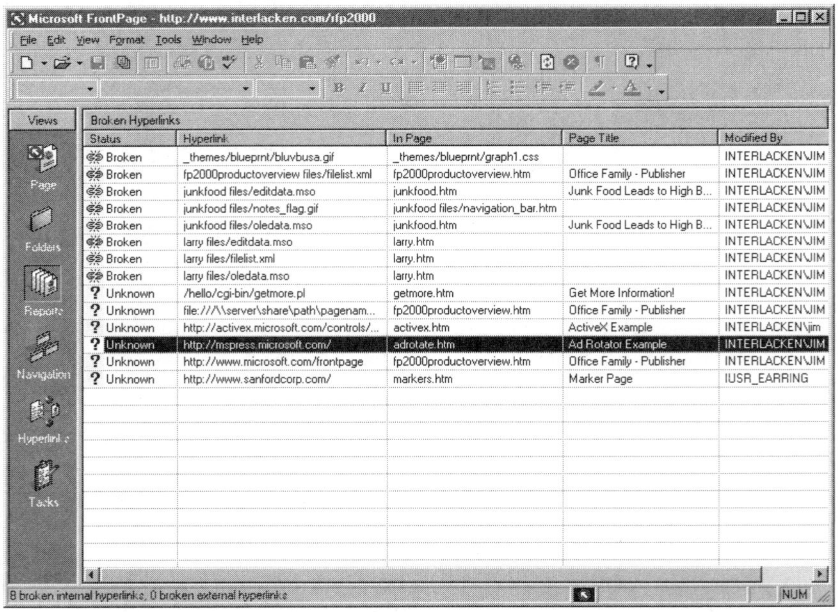

FIGURE 19-11.

The Broken Hyperlinks report shows the last known status of all hyperlinks in a Web. To reduce clutter, valid internal links normally don't appear.

FrontPage uses internal indexes for verifying hyperlinks among pages in the same Web. If you suspect these indexes might be out-of-date, you can refresh them by choosing Recalculate Hyperlinks from the Tools menu. The number one cause of corrupt indexes is changing a Web through means other than FrontPage.

To verify hyperlinks outside your Web, FrontPage attempts a connection to them. Therefore, make sure your connection to the Internet is working before you start the process.

- To verify a single hyperlink, right-click it and then choose Verify from the pop-up menu.

- To verify a group of hyperlinks, first select them, then right-click the selection, then choose Verify from the pop-up menu.

- To verify all hyperlinks in a Web, either click the Verify Hyperlinks button in the Reports toolbar, or right-click a blank line at the bottom of the report, and then choose Verify Hyperlinks from the pop-up menu.

Verifying a long list of hyperlinks can take a long time, especially if your Internet connection is slow or you have many bad links. Bad links usually show up as time-outs, and a lot of time-outs can consume a lot of time. (You might want to make a sandwich here or visit your relatives in Madagascar.)

When Verify Hyperlinks ends, the good links will be flagged with green check marks and the word "OK." Broken hyperlinks will have broken-link icons and the word "Broken." Right-clicking a broken link produces this pop-up menu.

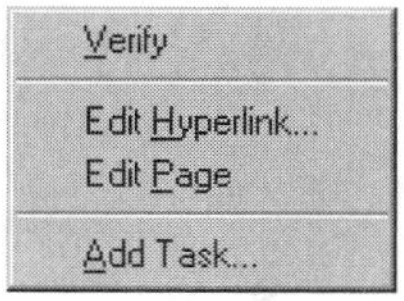

Figure 19-12 illustrates the dialog box for editing a hyperlink.

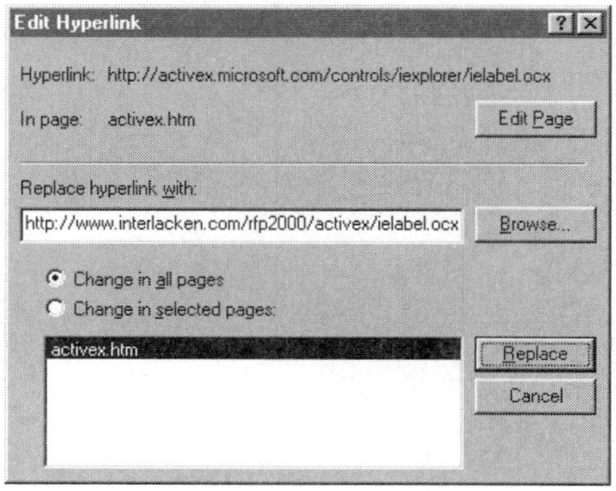

FIGURE 19-12.
The Edit Hyperlink dialog box can correct a broken hyperlink.

- The **Edit Page** button opens the current page for editing.

- The **Replace Hyperlink With** box specifies a corrected URL.

- The **Browse** button lets you search for a corrected URL using your browser. After locating the correct page, switching back to FrontPage will copy the browser's Address field into the Replace Hyperlink With box.

- **Change In All Pages** means that FrontPage will replace the broken hyperlink with the new one everywhere in your Web it appears.

- **Change In Selected Pages** means that FrontPage will make the replacement only on Web pages selected from the list shown.

- **Replace** makes your changes take effect.

Figure 19-13 shows an example of the Component Errors report. This report lists any errors or inconsistencies related to FrontPage components. Such errors tend to be quite rare because FrontPage creates all the HTML code by computer and won't let you make a mistake. Nevertheless, anything that can go wrong sooner or later will, and the Component Errors reports is here to tell you about it.

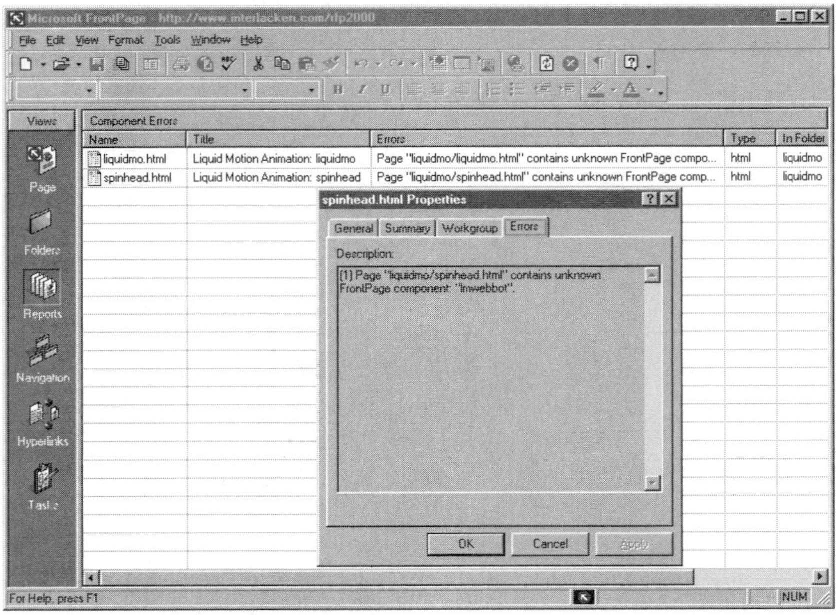

FIGURE 19-13.

The Component Errors report lists Web pages that have misconfigured FrontPage components.

If the Errors field is too long to fit on your screen, right-click the report line in question, choose Properties, and then click the Errors tab. As seen in the figure, this displays the full text.

The best way to repair a component error is normally to open the page in question and reconfigure the component using the normal FrontPage dialog boxes. An alternative is to simply display the Web page and see if it looks OK. If so, why worry? In Figure 19-13, another program (Microsoft Liquid Motion) has used a component of its own, one that FrontPage neither understands nor ignores. This requires no correction.

Using the Workgroup Reports

The Review Status, Assigned To, Publish Status, and Checkout Status reports are among FrontPage's workgroup features. The section "Group Authoring with Workgroup Features," on page 650, discusses these features in a unified way.

Working with Navigation View

Designers of most FrontPage Webs organize their pages in a logical hierarchy. The home page occupies the top position and presents several menu choices, each a Web page at the second level of the hierarchy. Pages at the second tier have child pages at the third, and so forth. As seen in Figure 19-14, Navigation view provides a way to record and organize this structure.

FIGURE 19-14.

Navigation view provides a way to record the logical structure of your Web.

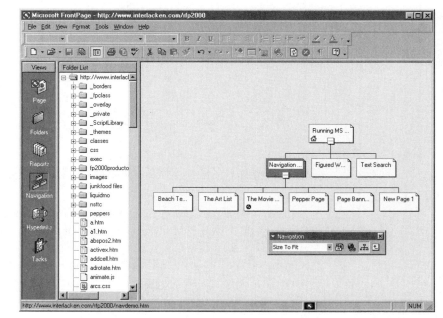

To learn about Naviga-
tion bars, see "Naviga-
tion Bars," page 671.

Using Navigation view has several advantages over other methods of drawing a site's logical structure.

- Navigation view, being electronic, is easier to revise than paper drawings.

- Integration with FrontPage means you can maintain content and structure seamlessly, using the same program.

- If you also use the Navigation Bar component of FrontPage, FrontPage will update the menus in your Web pages as you rearrange the view in FrontPage.

As you might suspect from their names, Navigation view and Navigation bars are highly related features. Navigation bars, pictured in Figure 19-15 appear in Web pages and provide hyperlinks Web visitors can use to traverse your site. A Navigation bar is a single FrontPage component that contains multiple links.

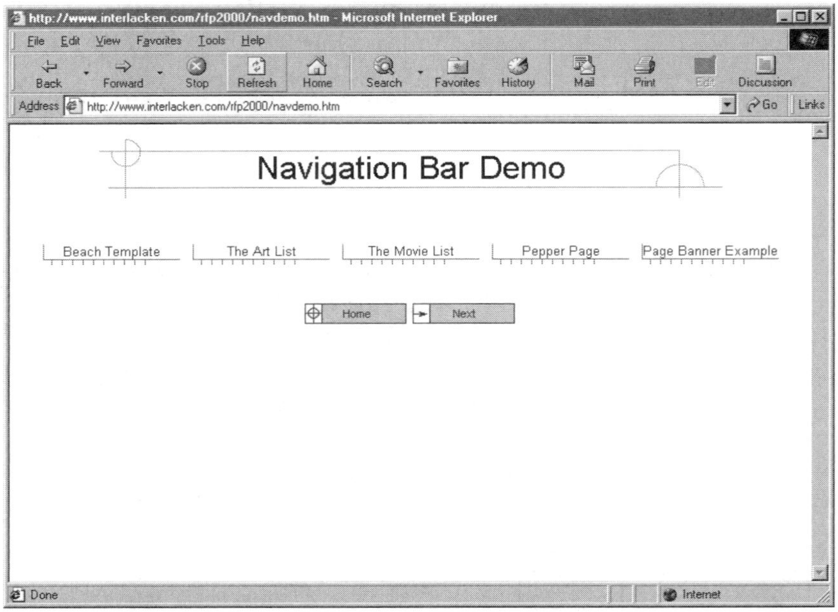

FIGURE 19-15.

FrontPage generates attractive Navigation bars like these based on the site structure you diagram in Navigation view.

You can insert Navigation bars and control their appearance while editing individual Web pages, but you can't configure the number or choices on the bar, their titles, or their destinations. Instead, you diagram your site in Navigation view and then let FrontPage create the appropriate links. The hyperlinks in Figure 19-15 were created not by direct editing, but from the diagram drawn in Figure 19-14.

Defining a Home Page in Navigation View

As happens so often in real life, the hardest part of using Navigation view is getting started. Specifically, this means getting FrontPage to recognize your home page as the top of the Navigation view hierarchy.

If Navigation view can't identify a home page, it displays the following message:

```
To create a Home Page, click New Page on the toolbar.
```

If you share the opinion that your Web doesn't yet contain a home page, the solution is simple: click the New Page button on the Standard toolbar (the second one in Figure 19-14). FrontPage will create a blank home page for you and place it at the top of your Navigation view hierarchy. Its file name will be your Web server's default page name, or, if you're not using a server-based web, index.htm.

If the Web *does* contain a home page, try choosing Recalculate Hyperlinks from the Tools menu. If a home page still doesn't appear, follow these steps:

1 Rename the existing home page file.

2 In Navigation view, create a new home page by clicking the New Page toolbar button.

3 Open both pages for editing.

4 Copy the entire contents of the old home page file.

5 Paste the contents into the new home page file.

6 Save the new home page file, and close both files.

7 Return to Navigation view and test for proper operation.

8 Test the new home page file, using a Web browser.

9 Delete the old, renamed file.

Your home page's file name should be the default file name for your Web server—that is, the file name your Web server substitutes when it receives a URL without a file name. If you have a server-based Web, FrontPage will, if possible, use the actual default file name for that server. Otherwise, it uses index.htm. If FrontPage creates a home page with the wrong file name for your server, simply rename index.htm to the correct name in the Folder List.

Confusion may result if your authoring and production Web servers have different default page names. For example, you might create Webs using a personal Web server whose default page name is default.htm,

? **SEE ALSO**

For information about creating redirection pages, see the sidebar "Taking Advantage of HTTP System Variables," page 100.

but publish them on a Unix Web server whose default page name is index.html. In such a case, create a redirection file with one file name and have it redirect requests to the other file name.

Adding Child Pages to Navigation View

Once Navigation view displays a home page, adding child pages is easy.

- If the pages already exist within your Web, simply drag them from the Folder List in the center frame and drop them under the appropriate parent in the document frame. As you drag files near prospective parents, FrontPage draws shaded lines suggesting a relationship. When the shaded line connects to the correct parent, release the mouse button.

★ TIP

If FrontPage won't draw shaded lines to a page that you drag from the files list, it's because that file already appears in the hierarchy. Each page in a Web can appear in the hierarchy only once.

- To create a new page and immediately define it as the child of another, right-click the parent page and then choose New Page from the pop-up menu. This is very handy when designing the initial structure of a Web.

  New pages created this way are just Navigation view entries and not physical files. As such, they don't appear immediately in the Folder List. However, when the screen is updated by choosing Apply Changes from the background pop-up menu, by switching to another view, by editing a page in FrontPage, or by closing the Web, the pages will be saved with file names and titles similar to their Navigation view names. Once a file is saved, you can change its file name using the normal Folder List commands.

- To create a physical file first and then add it to Navigation view, select anything in the Folder List, and then click the New Page toolbar icon. Continue by renaming the new page and then dragging it into position.

- To add a page outside the current Web to your hierarchy, right-click the page that will be its parent and choose External Link from the pop-up menu. This brings up the familiar Select Hyperlink dialog box seen in Figure 19-16. Locate or type the desired link, then click OK.

FIGURE 19-16.

Choosing External Link in Navigation view displays this dialog box for entering locations outside the current FrontPage Web.

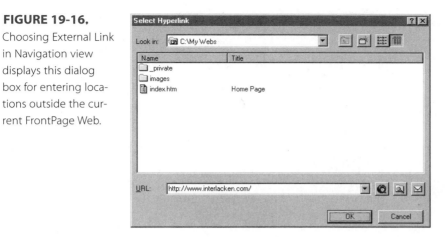

The only nodes that can have children in Navigation view are Web pages in the current Web. However, you *can* add external links, images, multimedia files, CGI programs, or anything you like as the *child* of a page in the current Web. Because of complications with Navigation bars, those other kinds of files can't be Navigation view parents.

Orphan pages are perfectly valid in Navigation view. If your Web has pages that don't fall within the hierarchy—pages like Search, Send Mail, and Contact Webmaster—you can drag them to the left and right of the home page, and they'll remain there without links. You can then create Navigation bars in FrontPage that list all pages at the top level.

 TIP

To view the file name of a page displayed in Navigation view, right-click its icon, and then choose Properties from the pop-up menu.

Rearranging pages is even simpler than adding them. In the main window, click the page you wish to move, hold down the mouse button while dragging, and then release it under the desired parent.

When you first add an existing page to Navigation view, FrontPage assigns a Navigation 'll want to shorten the Navigation view name. Page titles—assigned in FrontPage from the General tab of the Page Properties dialog box—are the strings that search engines and browsers use to identify the page. You'll probably want page titles to be fully descriptive of each page, and possibly to contain your company or site name as well. The Navigation view name, by contrast, frequently becomes the menu text displayed in navigation bars, and you'll likely want to keep this short.

Changing the Navigation view name of a Web page is quite simple.

1 Highlight the page's icon by clicking it in the main Navigation view window.

2 Choose Rename from the Edit menu, press the F2 key, or click the name.

⭐ **TIP**

In place of steps 1 and 2, you can right-click the page's icon and then choose Rename from the pop-up menu.

3 Type or revise the page's Navigation view name.

4 Press Enter or click anywhere outside the Navigation view name text box.

ⓧ **CAUTION**
Deleting a file from the Folder list always removes it completely from the Web. You can't undo this action.

To delete a page from Navigation view, do *one* of the following:

- Select the page and then choose Delete from the Edit menu.

- Select the page and press the Delete key.

- Right-click the page and choose Delete from the pop-up menu.

Following any of these actions, FrontPage will display a dialog box asking whether you want to remove the page just from Navigation view or to remove it completely from the Web. Make your choice and click OK.

To print a copy of the Navigation view structure, choose Print Navigation View from the File menu. To preview the printed appearance, choose Print Preview.

Controlling the Navigation View Display

As the size of your structure grows, you might find it convenient to hide the parts you aren't working on, or to view the diagram on a greater or lesser scale. You may even decide the diagram fits the screen better in left-to-right mode than in top-to-bottom. FrontPage has all these capabilities.

Collapsing and expanding the view works like this:

- To collapse (that is, to hide) the children of any page, click the minus icon on that page's lower edge. The children will disappear, but the icon will change to a plus. To display the children again, click the plus icon.

- To collapse the parent and peers of any page, either right-click the page and choose View Subtree Only from the pop-up menu, or select the page and click the View Subtree Only button on the Navigation toolbar. A View All icon will appear in place of the hidden pages. Table 19-3 describes the Navigation toolbar.

The same two commands toggle the display back to its former appearance, as does clicking the View All icon.

Right-clicking the background area in Navigation view displays the pop-up menu shown at the left of Figure 19-17.

FIGURE 19-17.
Right-clicking the Navigation view background and a Navigation view node produce these two pop-up menus.

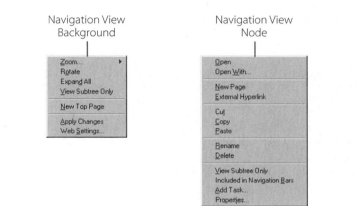

Navigation View
Background

Navigation View
Node

- **Zoom** controls the degree of magnification, as a percent of normal size. The Size To Fit option scales all visible pages into the main Navigation view window.

- **Rotate** toggles Navigation view between top-to-bottom and left-to-right display mode.

TABLE 19-3.   FrontPage Navigation Toolbar

Icon	Description	Function
Size To Fit	Zoom	Controls the degree of magnification.
	Portrait/Landscape	Switches the hierarchy display between top-to-bottom and left-to-right.
	External Link	Adds a child node that points to a location outside the current Web.
	Included in Navigation Bars	Toggles whether or not the currently selected nodes will appear in Navigation bars.
	View Subtree Only	Collapses or expands all nodes above, left of, or right of the current selection.

■ **Expand All** enlarges the view so that all pages in the structure are displayed. This has the same effect as clicking all the plus icons to show all the child pages.

■ **View Subtree Only** collapses or expands all nodes above, to the left of, or to the right of the current selection.

■ **New Top Page** creates a new orphan page as a peer of the home page.

■ **Apply Changes** saves the current Navigation view structure to disk. In so doing, it also creates empty Web pages for any nodes (other than External Hyperlinks) that don't have them.

? SEE ALSO

For information about the Web Settings dialog box, see "Configuring Your FrontPage Web," page 587.

■ **Web Settings** displays the same dialog box as choosing Web Settings from the Tools menu.

Right-clicking a Navigation view node produces the pop-up menu shown at the right of Figure 19-17. These commands work as follows:

■ **Open** opens the node using the standard editor configured for its file type.

■ **Open With** opens the node with an editor you select from a menu.

■ **New Page** creates a new node with the current node as its parent.

■ **External Hyperlink** creates a new node pointing to a location outside the current Web.

■ **Cut** copies the current selection and all its children to the Clipboard, and then removes it from the Navigation view.

■ **Copy** copies the current selection and all its children to the Clipboard.

■ **Paste** adds the current Clipboard contents to Navigation view, as the child of the currently selected node.

■ **Rename** changes the Navigation view name of the currently selected node. To rename the physical file, rename it in the Folder List.

> NOTE

Despite the fact that one defaults to the other, a Web page's title and its Navigation view name are two separate fields. Once both exist, changing one doesn't change the other.

■ **Delete** removes the node from Navigation view. A dialog box asks whether to delete the actual file or just remove it from Navigation view (and thus from all Navigation bars).

- **View Subtree Only** collapses or expands all nodes above, to the left of, or to the right of the current selection.

- **Included In Navigation Bars** toggles whether the current node appears in Navigation bars. The color of a node indicates its state: yellow if included in Navigation bars, gray if not.

- **Add Task** displays the New Task dialog box shown and described later in this chapter in Figure 19-20.

- **Properties** displays the Properties dialog box for the current node's Web page. This is the three-tabbed dialog box shown in Figure 19-6, Figure 19-7, and Figure 19-24.

Working with Hyperlinks View

Hyperlinks view, illustrated in Figure 19-18, provides an excellent picture of the hyperlink relationships among pages. It can be quite useful for working with complex or unfamiliar sites.

FIGURE 19-18.

FrontPage's Hyperlinks view charts the hyperlink relationships among the pages in a site.

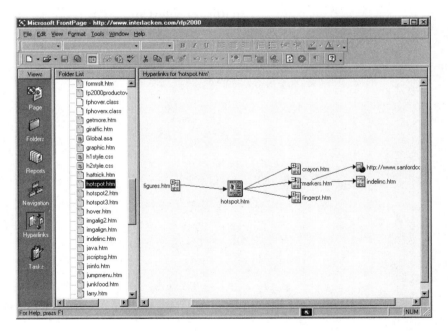

In Hyperlinks view, the document pane displays a chart of hyperlinks to and from a so-called *center page*. You can specify the center page either of two ways: first, by double-clicking it in the Folder list, or second, by right-clicking a page in the document pane and choosing Move To Center from the pop-up menu.

Whenever FrontPage displays a new center page, it also displays:

- All pages in the current Web with hyperlinks to the center page. These appear to the left of the center page, connected with arrows showing the direction of the link.

- All hyperlinks from the center page to any other page. These appear to the right of the center page, again connected by arrows.

Any page flagged with a plus icon has additional hyperlinks not displayed. Clicking the plus icon displays the additional links and changes the icon to a minus. Clicking a minus icon collapses the link display and changes the icon to a plus.

Hyperlinks view identifies items by either title or file name. This is controlled by the pop-up menu shown below, which appears whenever you right-click the document window's background. Choosing Show Hyperlink Titles toggles display of page titles rather than the file names shown in Figure 19-18.

```
Show Hyperlink Titles
Hyperlinks to Pictures
Repeated Hyperlinks
Hyperlinks Inside Page

Web Settings...
```

You can view the complete path and file name of items in either pane by right-clicking an item and choosing Properties from the pop-up menu. To see the file name of any item in the right pane, rest the mouse pointer over it; FrontPage will briefly describe the type of item and display its name:

```
Internal Hyperlink: indelinc.htm
```

By default, Hyperlinks view displays only hyperlinks from one Web page to another, disregarding duplicates. To toggle display of additional items, use these commands on the pop-up menu just shown.

- **Hyperlinks To Images.** Activating this option adds picture files to the Hyperlinks view display. Designating a picture as the center of Hyperlinks view displays all pages using that picture.

- **Repeated Hyperlinks.** Normally, if a page contains several links to the same target, Hyperlinks view displays only one of them. Activating this option shows all links, even duplicate ones.

■ **Hyperlinks Inside Page.** Many Web pages contain hyperlinks to internal bookmarks, typically so that clicking a menu choice scrolls the browser to a particular spot within a page. Hyperlinks view normally doesn't display such links, but with this option activated, it will.

Right-clicking a page in either pane produces a pop-up menu such as the following. Some choices might be dimmed or omitted, depending on the context.

```
Move to Center

Open
Open With...
Verify Hyperlink

Delete

Add Task...
Properties...
```

■ **Move To Center** designates the selected file as the center page in the right pane. This option doesn't appear for pages in the left pane, or when the selected page already occupies the center position.

■ **Open** starts the appropriate program to edit the selected page or file. Double-clicking the item accomplishes the same thing, as does choosing Open from the Edit menu. This option and the next are dimmed for links to pages located outside the current Web.

■ **Open With** presents a choice of command editors you can use to edit the selected file. The Open With command on the Edit menu is equivalent.

■ **Verify Hyperlink** validates a file or hyperlink outside the current Web by attempting to retrieve it. This option is dimmed for locations inside the current Web because, in that case, FrontPage has other means of verification.

■ **Delete** removes a page or file from the current Web. The Delete command on the Edit menu is equivalent.

■ **Add Task** opens the New Task dialog box, where you can enter a task that refers to the selected page.

■ **Properties** displays information about the selected file, such as its title and file name. You can also enter summary information about the page that might help you plan or maintain your Web.

New users are frequently enamored of Hyperlinks view, especially if they have existing Webs. They can use this view to analyze the Web pages they've been tediously building and maintaining by hand, producing attractive diagrams as a result. This can be heady stuff, but most users find Folders view and Navigation view more valuable for day-to-day work. Still, hyperlink analysis remains much like milk: we never completely outgrow our need for it.

Group Authoring with Workgroup Features

Server-based Webs and disk-based Webs residing on file servers both allow several people to work on the same Web at the same time. Far from being a problem, this is something FrontPage has special features to support.

- **Task View** maintains a list of pending work items for the current Web. FrontPage can create such tasks as part of other functions, associate these tasks with specific Web pages, and prompt for task status when a Web author saves the associated page.

- **Workflow Status And Reporting** records these items for each page in a FrontPage Web: Assigned To, Assigned By, Assigned Date, Review Status, Reviewed By, Review Date.

- **Page Level Control Over Publishing** provides a Publish/No Publish indicator for each file in a FrontPage Web. This is useful when some parts of a Web are ready for publication, but not others.

- **Page Level Check-In/Check-Out** reserves a file on behalf of one Web author so others can't make conflicting updates.

Although less powerful than full-scale, project-management and source-control systems, these features are highly integrated with FrontPage and provide all the functions many small projects need.

Working with Task View

Developing and maintaining your site involves a multitude of small, interrelated tasks. Changes made to one page require updates on another. New pages require links from others. Errors in spelling, missing images, and hyperlinks to nowhere require follow-up and correction. In short, you need a task list.

As shown in Figure 19-19, FrontPage provides an automated, highly integrated Task list. The FrontPage Task list provides several advantages over stand-alone, follow-up systems.

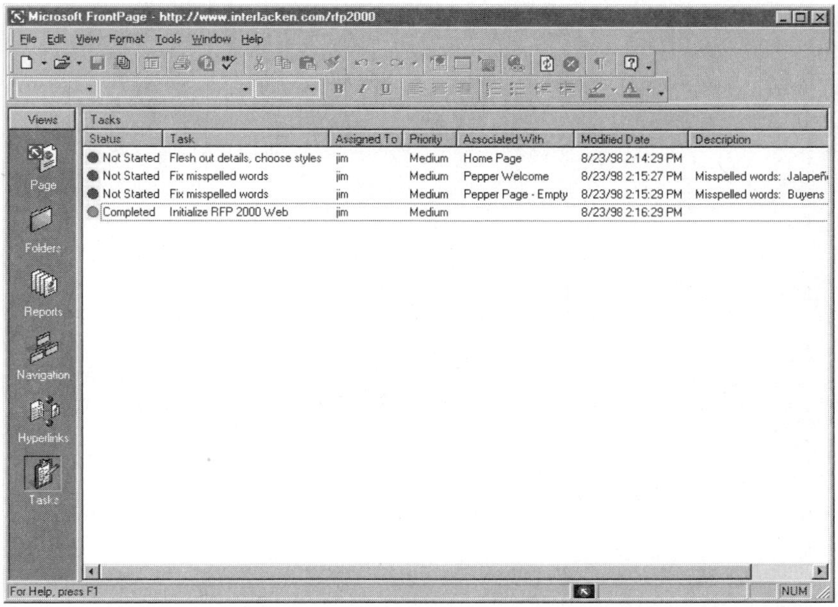

FIGURE 19-19.

The FrontPage Task list helps you remember unfinished tasks in a highly integrated way.

- FrontPage can add many tasks for you. These include:

  - Pages that contain spelling errors.

  - Pages with missing links.

  - New pages that need detail filled in.

- From the Task list, FrontPage can directly open pages associated with each task.

- When you open pages from the Task list and then save them, FrontPage will ask if those changes complete the task and, if they do, FrontPage closes the task.

The Task list column headings, as shown in Figure 19-19, are straightforward. Clicking any column heading sorts the list on that column.

FrontPage provides a variety of convenient ways to create tasks. To create tasks manually from Tasks view:

1   Choose New from the File menu, and then choose Task. Alternatively, right-click any blank area in the main Tasks view window and choose New Task from the pop-up menu.

2   The New Task dialog box shown in Figure 19-20 appears.

3   Enter a title in the Task Name box.

FIGURE 19-20.

Use this dialog box to create new tasks.

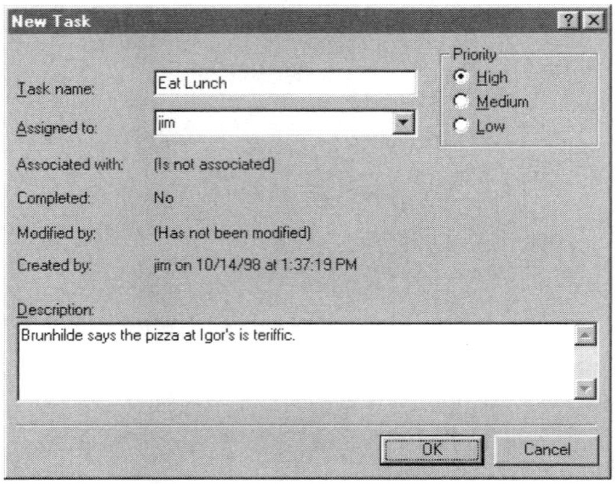

4   Select High, Medium, or Low priority.

5   Verify the Assigned To person.

6   Optionally, enter a comment in the Description box.

7   Click OK.

Note in Figure 19-20 that the Associated With field indicates no link. Creating a task directly from Tasks view has this effect. To manually create a task associated with a specific page, do *either* of the following:

■   Locate the page in another view, right-click it, and then choose Add Task from the pop-up menu. (To create a task linked to a hyperlink, create it from Hyperlinks view.)

■   Open the page in FrontPage and choose Add Task from the Edit menu.

The following FrontPage options also create Task list items:

■   In FrontPage, choose Spelling from the Tools menu and then re-view the Spelling dialog box in Figure 19-21. If you check Add A Task For Each Page With Misspellings, FrontPage will create a task for each page containing so much as a single misspelled word.

TIP

To spell check an entire Web, first display any view other than Page view, and then choose Spelling from the Tools menu.

■   When FrontPage creates a new page, it can either open the page immediately or create a blank page and a task reminding you to edit the page later. Figure 19-22 shows how a user might create a hyperlink to a new page.

FIGURE 19-21.

The FrontPage Spelling function can add pages with misspelled words to the Task list.

FIGURE 19-22.

FrontPage uses the New dialog box to create new Web pages. The option Just Add Web Task adds an entry to the Task list rather than opening the new page.

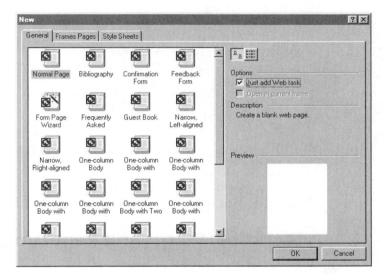

Right-clicking a task in Tasks view displays the pop-up menu shown below.

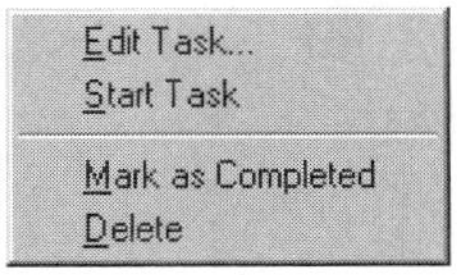

These commands work as follows:

- **Edit Task** displays the Task Details dialog box, which is similar to the New Task dialog box shown in Figure 19-20. Here you can modify the properties of a task. You can display the same dialog box by double-clicking the task you want to edit or by choosing Open from the Edit menu.

- **Start Task** opens the file with the appropriate editor, such as FrontPage for an HTML page.

- **Mark As Completed** changes the status of the task to Completed.

■ **Delete** removes a task from the list after you confirm your choice. Pressing the Delete key accomplishes the same result.

> **NOTE**
>
> Whenever you open a page using the Start Task command and then save it, FrontPage displays the message box shown in Figure 19-23 to ask if your changes satisfy the task's requirements. Clicking Yes indicates that your changes satisfy the task and instructs FrontPage to mark the task completed.

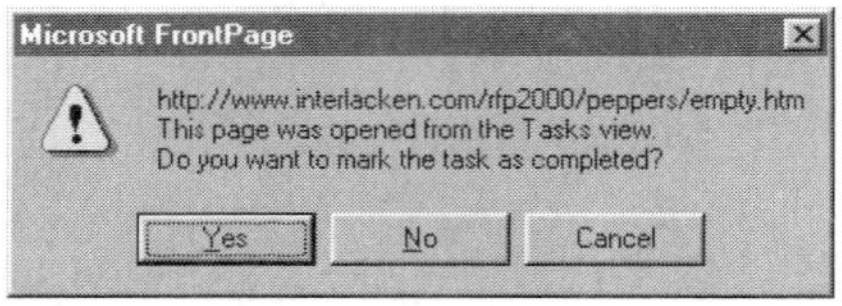

FIGURE 19-23.

This dialog box asks whether your changes to a Web page complete the page's remaining Task list items.

By default, the Task list displays only tasks that are Not Started or In Progress. To display completed tasks as well, choose Task History from the View menu or right-click a blank area in the main Task-list window and select Task History from the pop-up menu.

Workflow Status and Reporting

Task view records who's assigned to various tasks involving pages, but it doesn't show overall responsibility, overall status, review responsibility, or review status. FrontPage 2000 includes several new features related specifically to these areas.

Figure 19-24 shows the Properties dialog box for files in a FrontPage Web. To display this dialog box, right-click any file icon in a FrontPage view or Folder List, then choose Properties, and then choose the Workgroups tab.

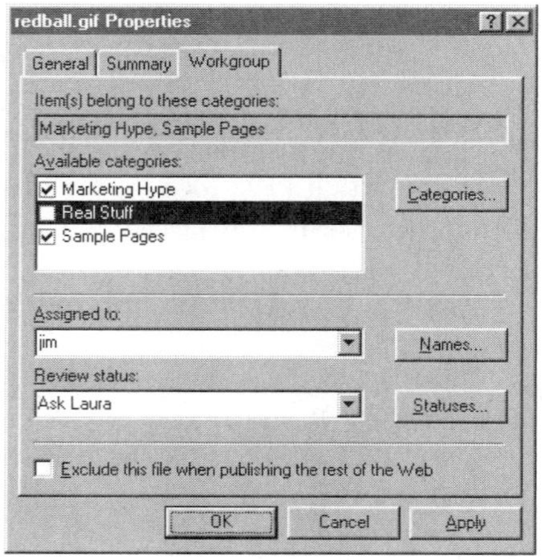

FIGURE 19-24.

The Workgroup tab on the File Properties dialog box specifies a file's assigned person and review status.

■ **Assigned To** specifies who's assigned to work on this file. You can either type the name by hand or select it from the drop-down list. Clicking the Names button displays the dialog box shown in Figure 19-25, which adds or deletes user names to or from the list.

Whenever it changes the Assigned To field for a file, FrontPage records the current user name, date, and time. This is where the Assigned Date and Assigned By columns in Figure 19-26 come from.

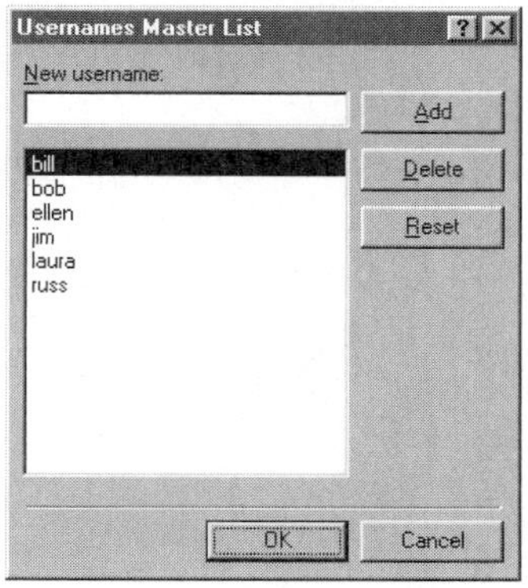

FIGURE 19-25.

This dialog box adds or removes names in the Assigned To drop-down list shown in Figure 19-24.

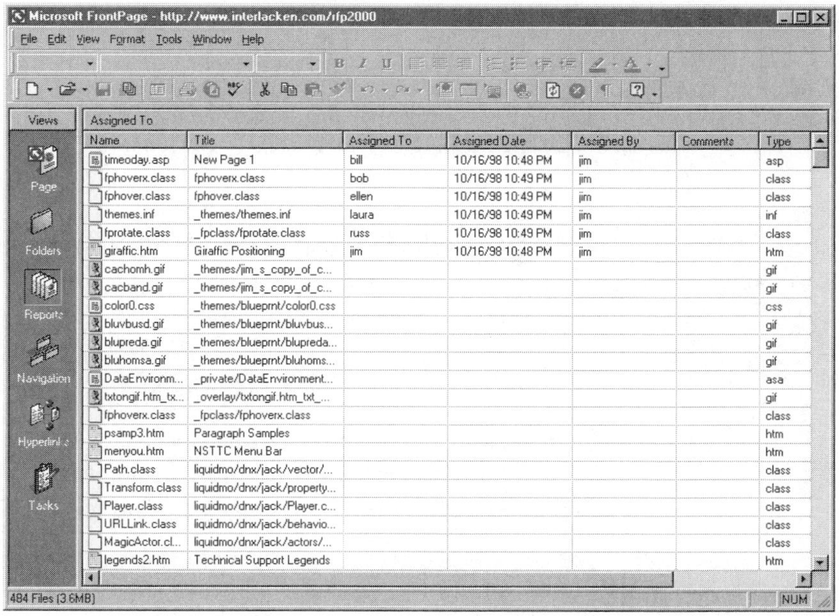

FIGURE 19-26.

The Assigned To report lists each file in a Front-Page Web, showing who is currently assigned, by whom, and when.

Figure 19-26, by the way, shows the FrontPage Assigned To report. To locate all files assigned to a specific person, click the Assigned To column heading and then scroll down to that name. You can also change the Assigned To field directly in this report by first selecting the correct line, and then single-clicking the Assigned To field.

■ **Review Status** records the results of the most recent review for each file in a Web. As with Assigned To, you can either type the Review Status or select it after clicking the drop-down list button. FrontPage records the given status, plus the current user name, date, and time.

Clicking the Statuses button in Figure 19-24 displays the dialog box shown in Figure 19-27. As with the Usernames Master List dialog box, you can add statuses, remove them, or reset the list.

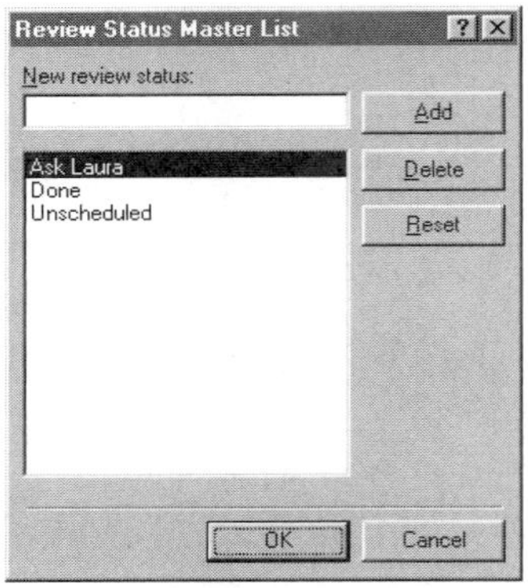

FIGURE 19-27.

This dialog box adds or removes values in the Review Status drop-down list shown in Figure 19-24.

Page Level Control Over Publishing

? SEE ALSO

For more information about the Publish feature, see Chapter 24, "Publishing Your FrontPage Web."

The check box titled Exclude This File When Publishing The Rest Of The Web, in Figure 19-24, prevents publishing the current file to another FrontPage Web or Web server. To prevent publishing of this file, turn the box on. To allow publishing, turn it off.

This feature doesn't affect your ability to import, move, or copy the given file, even among different FrontPage Webs or servers. It only affects operation of the FrontPage Publish feature.

The Publish Status report shown in Figure 19-29 shows which files are enabled and disabled for publishing. You can also update publishing status directly in this report. In the figure, an update is in progress where the drop-down list appears.

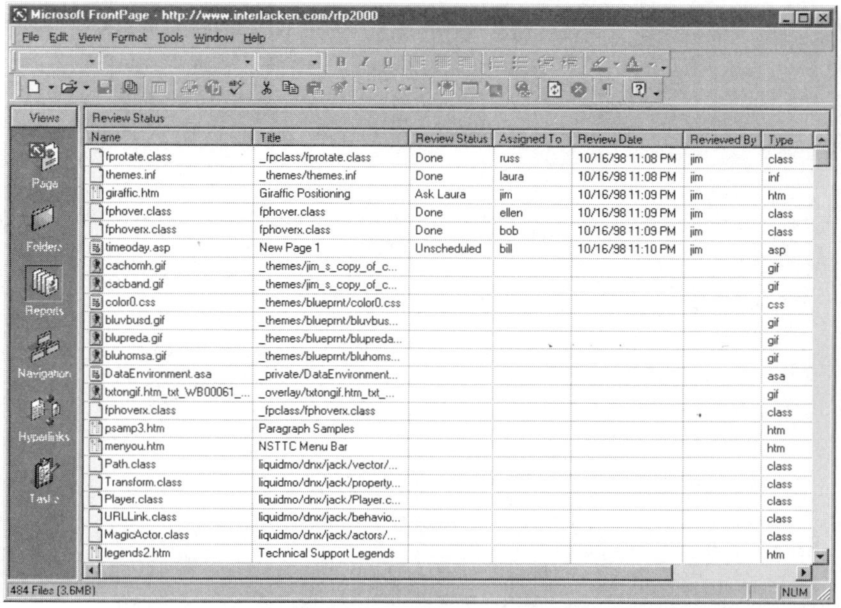

FIGURE 19-28.
The Review Status report lists status, reviewer, and date for each file in a FrontPage Web.

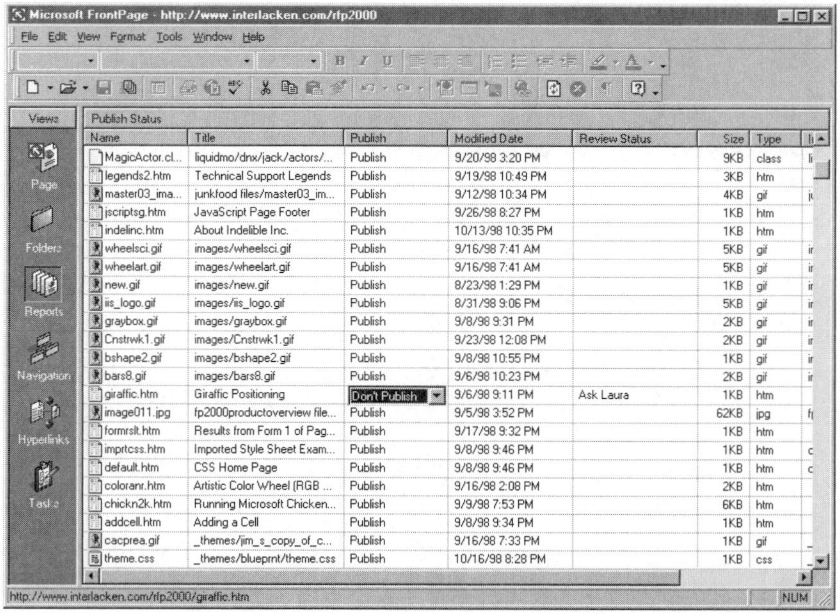

FIGURE 19-29.
The Publish Status report shows which pages in a Web are enabled or disabled from publishing to another FrontPage Web or server.

Page Level Check-In/Check-Out

When several people work on the same Web, there's always a chance that two people may start working on the same page at the same time. The result is a battle of dueling versions; whoever saves the file last overlays the first person's updates.

To compound the problem, changing a Web page can take days or weeks if the change is part of a general site upgrade or requires multiple approvals. Of course, that doesn't mean someone's going to keep the page open in FrontPage all that time, but it does mean that the Web author wants the file safe from update by other people during that interval.

Page Level Check-In/Check-Out provides an answer to this problem. Here's how this feature works:

- The Web's administrator turns on the Page Level Check-In/Check-Out feature.

- Before a Web author begins changing a file, he or she checks the file out: that is, takes ownership by using a right-click menu option. This does two things.

  - It prevents any other Web author from making changes to the file.

  - It saves a copy of the file for possible restoration.

- Once the file is checked out, it will show up as locked to other authors and administrators of the same Web. If they try to open the file, they'll get an error message with two options: either give up editing the file or open a read-only copy. They can save the read-only copy under another name, but they can't update the checked-out original.

- When the Web author who checked out the file is finished with any updates, he or she can take either of two actions.

  - Check the file in, which relinquishes ownership and deletes the backup copy.

  - Undo the checkout, which restores the backup copy (undoing all changes) and then relinquishes ownership.

The option that enables or disables Page-Level Check-In/Check-Out appears on the General tab of the Web Settings dialog box. To display it, choose Web Settings from the Tools menu, then click the General tab. Figure 19-30 provides an example.

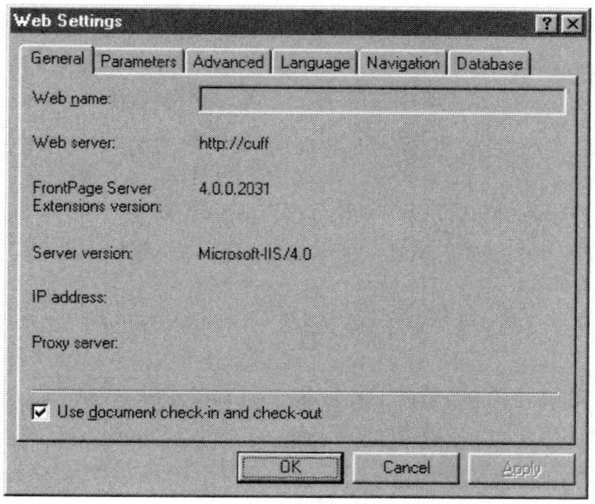

FIGURE 19-30.

The Use Document Check-In And Check-Out option in this dialog box enables and disables the use of source code control for a FrontPage Web.

TIP

Page Level Check-In/Check-Out is available only for disk-based Webs and for server-based Webs using the FrontPage 2000 Server Extensions. Older versions of the Server Extensions don't support this feature.

To activate Page Level Check-In/Check-Out, turn on the box titled Use Document Check-In And Check-Out. To disable it, turn the same box off. When you close the dialog box, FrontPage will need to recalculate hyperlinks.

TIP

The user name FrontPage uses for Check-In/Check-Out is normally the one that provides access to the FrontPage Web. For Webs with no user-level security, FrontPage uses your Windows user name.

Once Page Level Check-In/Check-Out is in effect, all FrontPage folder lists will display an icon in front of each file name.

- **Green Dot** means the file is available for checkout.
- **Red Check Mark** means the file is checked out to you.
- **Gray Padlock** means the file is checked out to someone else.

Figure 19-31 shows a typical FrontPage folder listing with Page Level Check-In/Check-Out in effect. All three icon types are visible. The Web author has right-clicked the file products.htm, and can use the Check-Out option on the pop-up menu to take ownership.

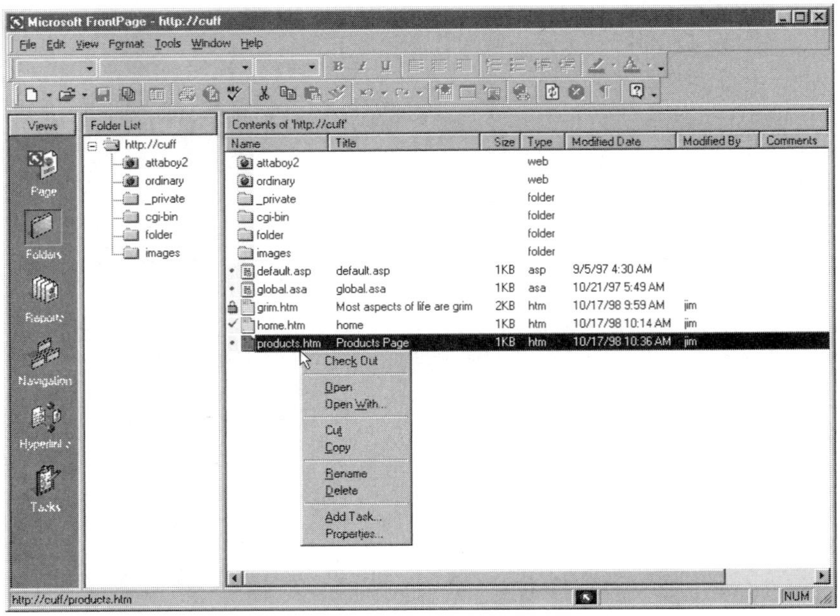

FIGURE 19-31.

With Page Level Check-In And Check-Out in effect, each file in a Web is either available for checkout (green dot), checked out to the current user (red check mark) or checked out to someone else (padlock).

If you try to open a file you haven't checked out, FrontPage presents the dialog box shown in Figure 19-32. Answering Yes checks the file out and then opens it. Answering No opens the file and permits saving it, but with no source code control in effect. (This might be acceptable for making quick, simple changes.) Answering Cancel abandons the edit.

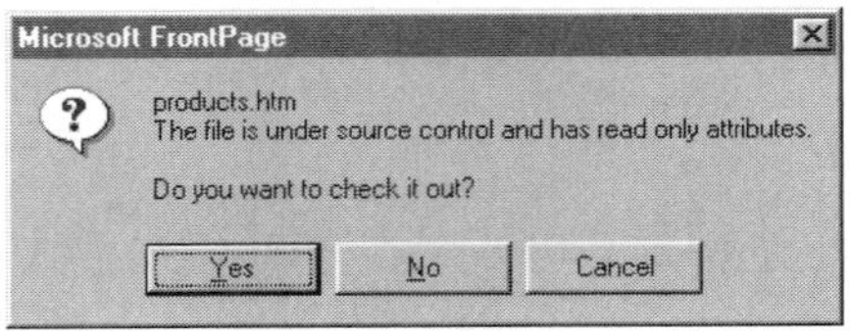

FIGURE 19-32.

FrontPage presents this choice when you try to open a file you haven't checked out.

If you try to open a file someone else has checked out, you'll receive the dialog box shown in Figure 19-33. Answering Yes opens the file despite the fact that user *mary* has checked it out, but won't let you update Mary's version. To save it, you'll have to use another file name. Answering No abandons the edit.

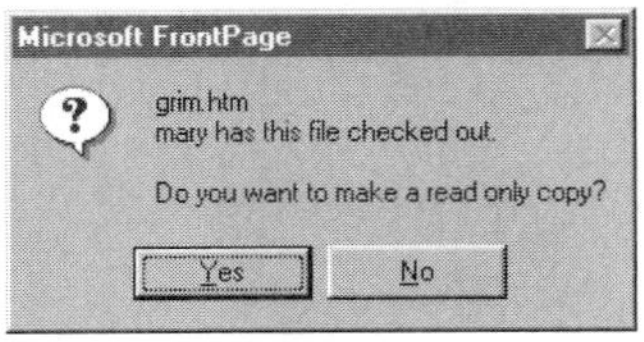

FIGURE 19-33.

FrontPage presents this choice when you try to open a file someone else has checked out.

Attempting to save a file that's checked out to someone else produces the dialog box shown in Figure 19-34. There are no real options here other than clicking the OK button, saving the file under another name, or talking to Mary and asking her to incorporate your change with hers.

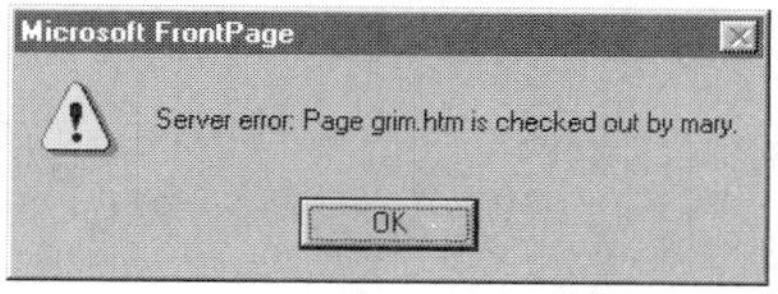

FIGURE 19-34.

FrontPage disallows any change to a file that's checked out to someone else.

The Checkout Status Report, shown in Figure 19-35, shows the Check Out status of every file in a Web. To find all files checked out by a specific person, sort the report by clicking on the Checked Out By column heading. To look for files that have remained checked out suspiciously long, sort the report by Locked Date.

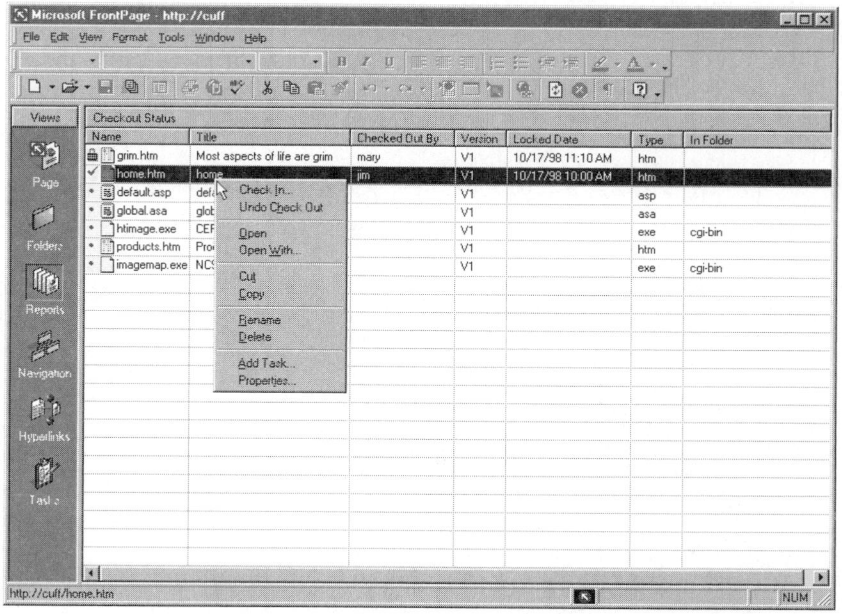

FIGURE 19-35.

The Checkout Status report shows who checked out each file in a Web, and when.

Figure 19-35 also shows the pop-up menu for a file checked out to the current user. Choosing Check-In relinquishes control of the file and deletes the backup copy taken at the time of check-out. Choosing Undo Check-Out restores the backup copy—in effect reversing all changes—and then relinquishes control.

There are two additional precautions related to creating and deleting files in a Web with Check-In/Check-Out in effect. First, creating a new file doesn't automatically check it out to you. If you want the file checked out, you have to do it yourself. Second, you can't delete a file checked out to anyone, even yourself. To delete a file checked out to you, first check it in and then delete it.

 NOTE

Even greater source-code control, including backout through multiple versions, is available by installing Microsoft Visual SourceSafe on a server-based Web.

In Summary...

This chapter explained how FrontPage views and reports give you control over your Web, and how its workgroup features help coordinate the activities of multiple Web authors working on the same project.

The next chapter reviews FrontPage features that control the content and appearance of multiple files, or even an entire Web, at a summary level.

Using Web-Based FrontPage Components

This chapter explains the FrontPage components that require a FrontPage Web in the authoring environment, but don't require the FrontPage Server Extensions on the production Web server. Such components require a FrontPage Web for authoring because they involve relationships among multiple pages or because they use other information that FrontPage stores in its Web indexes and configuration files. And, of course, whenever FrontPage deals with Web pages as an interrelated group, it deals with them as a FrontPage Web.

Here are the components that meet these criteria.

- **Templates.** In essence, these are the most useful blank pages you'll ever find. FrontPage lets you create any number of Web-page starting points, save them as templates, and then create new pages based on any desired template. You can save these templates either on your own PC for your own use, or in a FrontPage Web for access by other Web authors.

■ **Themes.** These are professionally designed color and style combinations that FrontPage can apply to an entire Web as well as to individual pages.

■ **Color Masters.** In FrontPage, you can configure any page to get its color scheme and background from another. By controlling the appearance of all pages in a site or topic through a single master page, you can fine-tune or totally redesign the site's color scheme at will.

■ **Navigation Bars.** These components automatically construct menus that link pages within a site. The structure entered in FrontPage's Navigation view provides the menu content.

■ **Page Banner.** This component displays the Navigation View title of the current page as text.

■ **Shared Borders.** FrontPage can apply a standard heading, footer, right edge, or left edge to every page in a Web or to selected pages. Each such border displays exactly the same content on every page so that changing a shared border on one page changes it everywhere. Note, however, that certain FrontPage components, with no change to their configuration, appear differently depending on the page in which they appear. The Navigation bar and Page Banner are two of these.

■ **Substitution.** FrontPage can store frequently occurring strings as Web Parameters, and then insert the parameter values wherever needed in your site. Later, if the information changes, you can modify it everywhere by changing the value of the Web Parameter in a single location.

■ **Include Page Components.** For longer and more complex page segments, FrontPage provides the ability to include one Web page in another. This means you can store any sort of repeating content in a small Web page, and then include that page wherever you want the content to appear. When it becomes necessary to change the content of the page segment, changing it once updates its occurrence in the entire Web. This is perfect for navigation bars, signature lines, and other elements that appear on many pages and need to be kept in sync.

■ **Table of Contents.** This component creates an indented, clickable table of contents based on hyperlink analysis, starting from a given page in the local Web.

■ **Category.** This creates a list of hyperlinks to pages in the same Web coded with given category codes. You specify these codes by right-clicking pages in Folder List or view, and then choosing Properties.

The following sections will describe how to add each of these components to pages in your Web. To change them, either double-click the existing component, right-click it and choose Properties, or select it and choose Properties from the Format menu.

If a Web-level component seems attractive for only portions of your Web, consider making those portions into a Web of their own. To do this is quite simple: just convert the desired portion into a single folder tree, right-click the starting folder, and choose Convert To Web from the pop-up menu.

Templates

Creating and using FrontPage templates is both easy and productive. Templates relieve page authors of repetitive tasks when creating new pages. To create a template:

1 Use any convenient method to create a Web page having the desired components and features. When in doubt, it's usually better to include optional page features than to omit them. Deleting features you don't need is easier than adding those you do.

2 With the page open in Page view, choose Properties from the File menu, click the General tab, and enter the template title in the Title field. This is the name you (or other Web authors) will later use to select the template.

3 Choose Save As from the File menu in FrontPage.

4 When the Save As dialog box appears:

  • Set Save As Type to FrontPage Template (*.tem). Figure 20-1 illustrates this action in progress.

  • Verify that the file name is acceptable.

  • Click the Save button.

5 When the Save As Template dialog box appears, enter or verify the following fields. Figure 20-2 shows the Save As Template dialog box.

  • **Title** is the name by which you or other FrontPage users will select the template.

- **Name** is the file name base used for saving the template files and folders.

- **Description** is any verbal explanation or notes.

- **Save Template In Current Web,** if turned on, saves the template in the current FrontPage Web. If the box is turned off, FrontPage stores the template on your hard disk.

6 Click OK to save the template.

FIGURE 20-1.

To save any Web page as a template, set Save As Type to FrontPage Template.

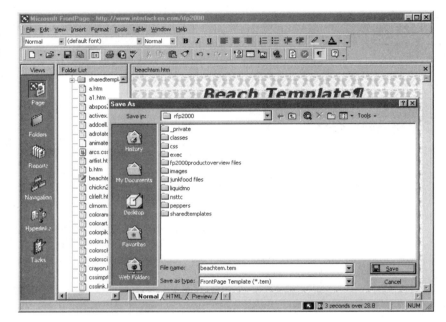

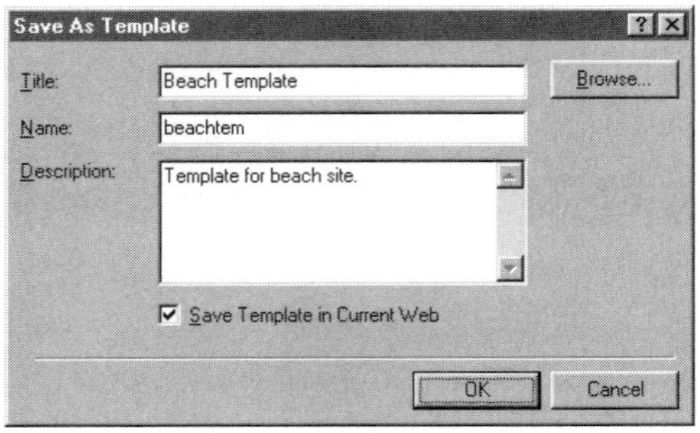

FIGURE 20-2.

Specify the template's name, description, and location when this dialog box appears.

 The ability to save templates in a FrontPage Web is new with FrontPage 2000. Saving templates in a Web instantly makes them available to all users of that Web, but *only* when creating pages *in that Web*. Saving a template to your disk makes it available only to you, but it's available no matter what Web you're using.

To create a new page using the template:

1 Choose New from the File menu, and then choose Page.

2 When the New dialog box shown in Figure 20-3 appears, choose the desired template on the General tab, and then click OK.

FIGURE 20-3.

FrontPage prompts for a template when creating new Web pages.

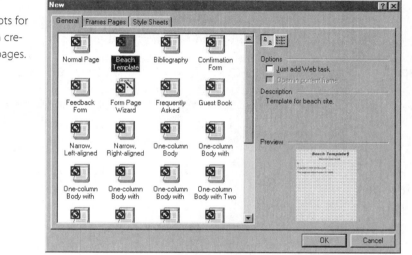

Changing a template doesn't change pages previously created from it; however, any variables, Include Page components, or color masters specified on a template will remain as such on created pages and provide global maintainability.

Distributing Templates Saved to Disk

Templates saved to disk consist of three files in a folder, usually located at:

```
C:\Windows\Application Data\Microsoft\FrontPage\
Pages\<template>.tem
```

where <template> is the name you specified when saving the template. The three files will be named <template>.dib, <template>.htm, and <template>.inf.

To distribute a template on disk to other users, copy the <template>.tem folder to a floppy disk or file server, and then have the other users copy it to their C:\Windows\Application Data\Microsoft\FrontPage\Pages\ folder.

Themes

? **SEE ALSO**

For more information about themes, see Chapter 9, "Using FrontPage Themes."

Chapter 9 discussed in some detail the use of themes on individual Web pages. This section presents two topics that apply to using themes in a FrontPage Web: default themes and distribution of themes.

Figure 20-4 shows the usual Themes window, this time displayed when a FrontPage Web is open. Note the All Pages choice in the upper-left corner, under the heading Apply Themes To. Choosing All Pages and clicking OK applies the selected theme, with one exception, to every page in the current FrontPage Web. The exception pertains to pages controlled by an individually applied theme; these remain unchanged.

FIGURE 20-4.

Choosing the Apply Theme To All Pages option applies the selected theme to every page in the current Web not already controlled by a theme.

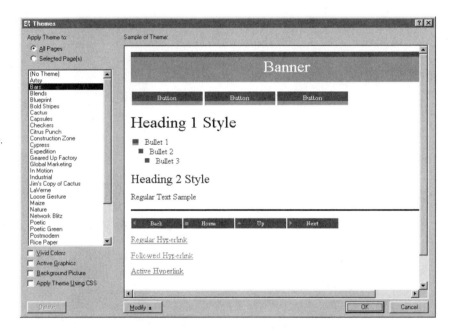

Applying a theme to all pages makes it the default theme for that Web. All existing pages will take on a uniform appearance, and any new pages will automatically use the specified theme as well.

To override a Web's default theme for certain pages, open those pages in Page view, choose Themes from the Format menu, and choose either the theme you want or (No Theme).

When a default theme is in effect for the current Web, you'll see it listed twice in the Themes window; once in its normal position and once at the top of the list, preceded by the string (Default). These choices may at first seem equivalent, but there's a difference. Choosing a theme from the main part of the list constitutes an override that won't be affected if someone later changes the Web's default theme. Changing the Web's default theme *will* affect any page configured with the (Default) theme entry.

Applying a theme to an entire Web is a somewhat irrevocable action. As indicated by the warning shown in Figure 20-5, the theme replaces all the fonts, colors, bullets, and lines in every page in the Web, with no possibility of undoing. You can remove the theme by applying the choice (No Theme) to All Pages, but this won't restore all the colors, fonts, and other formatting those pages used to have. Instead, these properties will revert to their HTML defaults.

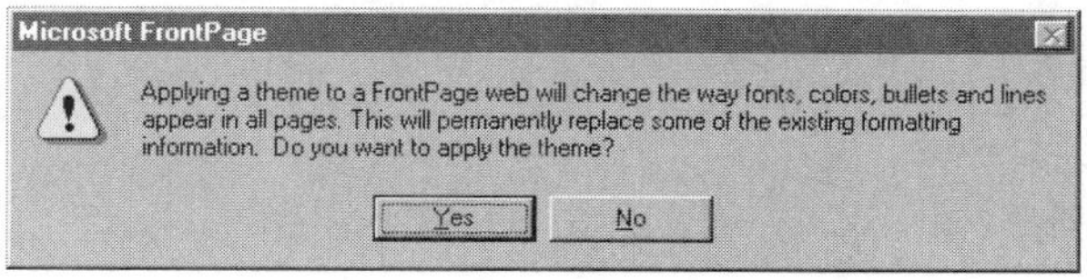

FIGURE 20-5.

This dialog box warns you that applying a theme to an entire Web overwrites formatting information that can't be restored.

Applying any theme to a Web—whether to individual pages or the entire Web—copies the theme into a hidden folder named, not surprisingly, _themes. This makes the theme available to anyone who opens that Web, and overrides any like-named themes on that user's hard disk. Distributing a theme to all users of a certain Web is therefore as simple as adding a page to that FrontPage Web, a page using that theme.

Distributing Themes Saved to Disk

Themes saved to disk consist of two files in a folder, usually located at:
    C:\Program Files\Common Files\Microsoft Shared\Themes\<theme>
where <theme> is the abbreviated name of the theme. The two files will be named <theme>.elm and <theme>.inf. To distribute a theme on disk to other users, copy the <theme> folder to a floppy disk or file server, and then have the other users copy it to their C:\Program Files\Common Files\ Microsoft Shared\Themes\ folder.

Color Masters

FrontPage can configure one Web page to use the background image and color scheme of another. If you key the backgrounds and color schemes of many pages off a single *color-master* page, you can change those aspects of the whole set in one stroke, simply by updating the master. This is similar to the global style management provided by Microsoft Word's Normal.dot file. A color master controls the following properties:

- Background Color

- Background Picture

- Text Color

- Hyperlink Color

- Visited Hyperlink Color

- Active Hyperlink Color

The color master itself is just an ordinary Web page; don't bother looking for a Create Color Master command or option. The color master could be your home page or any other page in your site, but administration will be easiest if you dedicate a simple page to this purpose only.

To create a color master:

1 In FrontPage, choose New from the File menu, then Page, then Normal Page. (Alternatively, click the New Page button on the Standard toolbar.)

2 Choose Properties from the File menu and select the Background tab.

? **SEE ALSO**

For assistance in choosing colors that will display clearly and accurately, see "Achieving Accurate Rendition—Safe Colors," page 102.

3 Specify the background image, background color, and text colors you want the entire set of pages to have, and then click OK.

4 Check the appearance of the page. If necessary, insert some text and a hyperlink so that you can see their colors.

5 Choose Save As from the File menu, specify a page title and a file name, and then click OK.

To have another page get its colors from the saved color master:

1 Open the page in FrontPage.

2 Choose Properties from the File menu, and then select the Background tab.

3 Choose the option Get Background Colors From Another Page.

4 Enter the URL of the color master, or click Browse to select it from the current Web. Figure 20-6 shows browsing in progress.

5 Click OK in the Page Properties dialog box to apply the changes.

Converting a set of existing pages to use a color master is somewhat tedious the first time—but no more tedious than changing the colors on all the pages by hand. The next color or background change, however, will be a snap.

If you use a color master when you create a template, all pages created from that template will automatically use that color master as well.

FIGURE 20-6.
You can control the appearance of many pages from one source by using the Get Background Information From Another Page option.

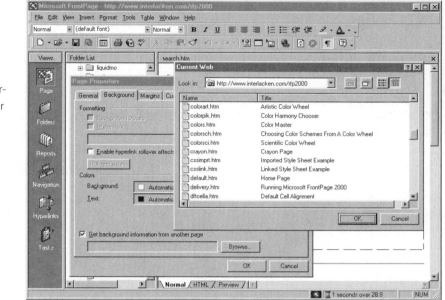

Navigation Bars

? SEE ALSO
To learn about entering the structure FrontPage uses to construct navigation bars, see "Working with Navigation View," page 639.

This component automatically creates and maintains menu bars (often called jump bars) that unify the pages in your Web. Using navigation bars requires first entering structure information in FrontPage's Navigation view, and then inserting and configuring one or more navigation bars in each Web page.

At first, navigation bars may seem to work backward. Most Web designers imagine a facility that draws structure charts based on hyperlinks, not a facility that creates hyperlinks from a structure chart. The problem with creating diagrams based on hyperlinks is that most Web pages contain too many convenience links. These are outside the Web's primary structure, and their presence obscures the true structure of the site. Constructing hyperlinks based on a diagram ensures that the user's view and the Navigation view are always in sync, and that all links and link titles throughout a site are consistent.

The first step in implementing navigation bars is to diagram your Web—or at least the main parts of it—in Navigation view. Once this is completed, you can add navigation bars in FrontPage by doing the following:

1 Open a page and place the insertion point where you want the navigation bar to appear.

2 Choose Navigation Bar from the Insert menu.

3 Make your choices in the Navigation Bar Properties dialog box shown in Figure 20-7.

4 Click OK.

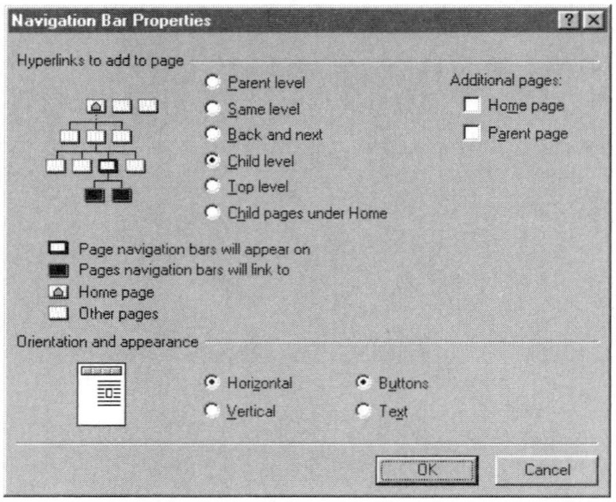

FIGURE 20-7.

This FrontPage dialog box configures the contents of a page's navigation bar. The menu choices will come from the Web's Navigation view structure.

Setting Navigation Bar Properties

FrontPage provides the dialog box shown in Figure 20-7 for controlling the content and appearance of navigation bars. The same dialog box applies for both creating new navigation bars and modifying existing ones.

■ **Hyperlinks To Add To Page.** You can apply only one of the following six choices to a single navigation bar. However, nothing prevents you from placing several navigation bars on the same page, each configured with different options.

  • **Parent Level** specifies that the navigation bar will contain hyperlinks to all pages one level higher than the current page, as positioned in Navigation view.

  • **Same Level** specifies that the navigation bar will list all pages at the same level as itself.

- **Back And Next** includes the two pages immediately left and right of the current page, and at the same level.

- **Child Level** includes all pages that have the current page as their parent.

- **Top Level** includes the home page and any others drawn at the same level.

- **Child Pages Under Home** includes all pages one level below the home page.

- ■ **Additional Pages.** You can include either or both of the following pages regardless of the choice you made above.

  - **Home Page** adds the home page to the navigation bar.

  - **Parent Page** adds the parent of the current page.

- ■ **Operation And Appearance.** These options control the appearance of the navigation bar.

  - **Horizontal** arranges the choices on the navigation bar as a single line of text.

  - **Vertical** arranges the navigation bar choices vertically, with each choice on its own line. You can choose either Horizontal or Vertical, but not both.

  - **Buttons** displays the navigation bar choices as graphical buttons.

  - **Text** displays the navigation bar choices as text. You can choose Buttons or Text, but not both.

FrontPage labels each option on the navigation bar with the title of the target page as it appears in Navigation view. This provides an incentive to keep the Navigation view names short but descriptive. To change the label appearing on a navigation bar, change the title of the target page in FrontPage's Navigation view.

The Navigation tab of the Web Settings dialog box, shown in Figure 20-8, contains options for setting the labels displayed for the home, parent, previous, and next pages. The default labels are, respectively, Home, Up, Previous, and Next. To globally apply your own labels, select Web Settings from the Tools menu, select the Navigation tab, and then type the text you wish to have displayed.

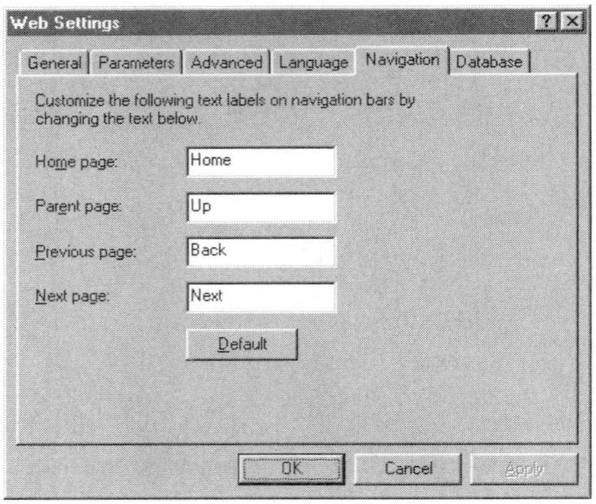

FIGURE 20-8.

The default navigation bar names for the Home, Parent, Previous, and Next pages can be globally customized here.

Figure 20-9 illustrates a horizontal text navigation bar. The bar appears between the two horizontal rules.

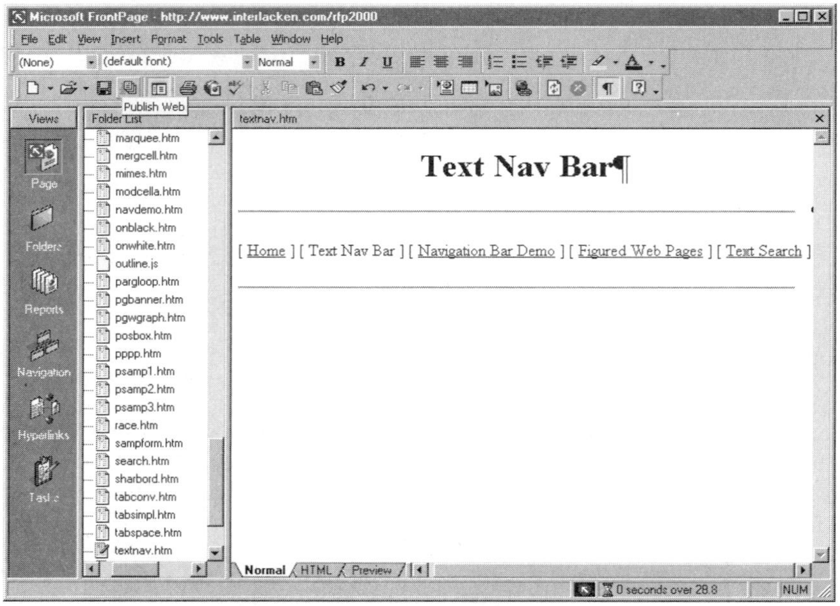

FIGURE 20-9.

This page includes a horizontal text navigation bar between two horizontal rules.

Figure 20-12, on page 678, shows a vertical navigation bar built using graphic buttons. FrontPage gets the button graphic from the Web page's theme. Graphic navigation bar buttons are a very popular feature, and they lead to two very common questions.

- Is there any way to generate graphic navigation bar buttons without applying themes to my Web pages?

SEE ALSO

For more information about the Text On GIF feature, see "Adding Text to Images," page 190.

■ Is there any way to set up links on a navigation bar without diagramming my site in Navigation view?

The answer in both cases is, "No." You can achieve similar results by using the Text On GIF feature, but not the same degree of automation.

Another common question is whether, after diagramming your site, there's any way to add navigation bars to all your pages automatically. In this case the answer is, "Yes, the Shared Border feature, described later in this chapter, can do exactly that." However, lest happiness overcome you, you'll still need to manually edit each page and take out your old, hand-coded navigation menus.

Page Banner

The Page Banner component performs a single function requiring very little configuration: It displays a page's Navigation view title.

The Page Banner component, the Navigation Bar component, and Navigation view all work together.

■ In Navigation view, you arrange your pages and give them names.

■ Navigation bars use the relationships and names from Navigation view to build menus that hyperlink among your pages.

■ The Page Banner component displays a page's Navigation view name as the heading of that page.

Using the Page Banner component has two advantages compared to just typing a heading into your Web page. First, it ensures that a page's visual heading contains exactly the same text as all navigation bar references to that page. This occurs because FrontPage bases both page banner text and all navigation bar text on the same source: the page's Navigation view title. Second, if your page uses themes, FrontPage can superimpose the page banner text over the theme's designated banner graphic.

Adding a page banner is a snap when you follow these steps:

1 Open the Web page in Page view.

2 Set the insertion point where you want the banner to appear, most frequently at the top of the page.

3 Choose Page Banner from the Insert menu. The dialog box shown in Figure 20-10 will result.

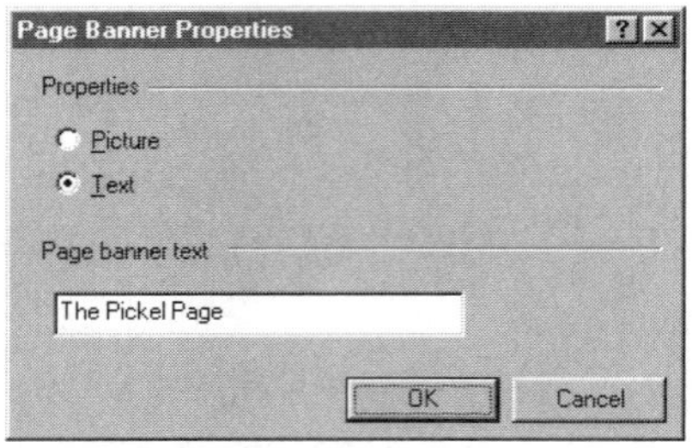

FIGURE 20-10.

This dialog box controls the appearance of a Page Banner compo- nent. The Picture option has meaning only on pages controlled by a FrontPage theme, and you can only specify page banner text for pages already entered in Navigation view.

4 Select Picture if the current page is controlled by a theme and you want the page banner text displayed over the theme's banner graphic.

5 Review the suggested page banner text, and correct it if necessary.

Initially, the Page Banner Text field will contain the current page's Navigation view title. Updating this text also updates Navigation view, and therefore all navigation bars pointing to this page. If the current page doesn't appear in Navigation view, FrontPage will ignore this field and the page banner will be blank.

6 Click OK.

The Page Banner component works only for pages you've diagrammed in Navigation view. You can insert Page Banner components even in Web pages not diagrammed in Navigation view, but instead of a page banner, FrontPage will display the message:

```
[Add this page in the Navigation view to display a
page banner here.]
```

If your Web page uses themes, the difference between an image banner and a text banner will be quite apparent. In Figure 20-11, the upper banner is an image while the lower one is text. Both banners display the title *Page Banner Example*.

⭐ **TIP**

> Just because a page banner appears as text doesn't mean it has to be plain. You can apply any and all FrontPage text formatting commands to textual Page Banner components.

If you like using themes but don't like diagramming your site in Navi- gation view, you might wonder if there's any other way to specify page banner text. There isn't.

To insert a page banner for every page in a FrontPage Web, activate shared borders (described in the next section) and place a Page Banner component in the desired border (most likely the top one). Of course, this won't remove any existing page headings, and it'll produce the error message noted above for any page not diagrammed in Navigation view.

The true power of the Page Banner component lies not in formatting page headings one by one, but rather in centralizing control of navigation bars and page headings through Navigation view. Although initially it might seem awkward to leave Page view and configure the page banner text in Navigation view, there's great power later on when changing a page's title once, in Navigation view, updates its page banner and all navigation bars.

FIGURE 20-11.

Page Banner Example appears first as an image and then as text.

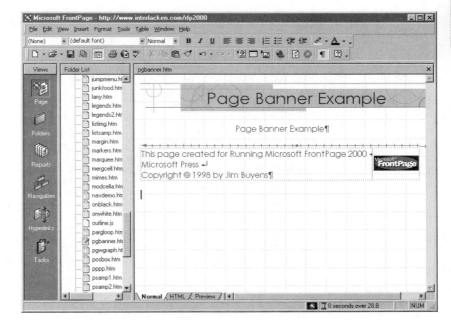

Shared Borders

This section discusses another FrontPage facility that standardizes content and appearance across an entire Web. *Shared borders* provide a way to insert standard content at the top, bottom, left, or right edges of any or all pages in the same Web.

Shared borders appear between your Web page's normal content and the top, left, right, or bottom edge of the browser window. You can put whatever you want inside the shared-border area, but the *same* content appears in the *same* border for *every* page in your Web. The bottom shared border for one page can't be different from the bottom shared border of any other page, for example. When Microsoft decided to call these borders shared, they weren't kidding!

A typical use of shared borders would include a Page Banner component in the top shared border, a Navigation Bar component in the left shared border, and copyright, contact, or date and time information in the bottom shared border. Figure 20-12 illustrates such a page.

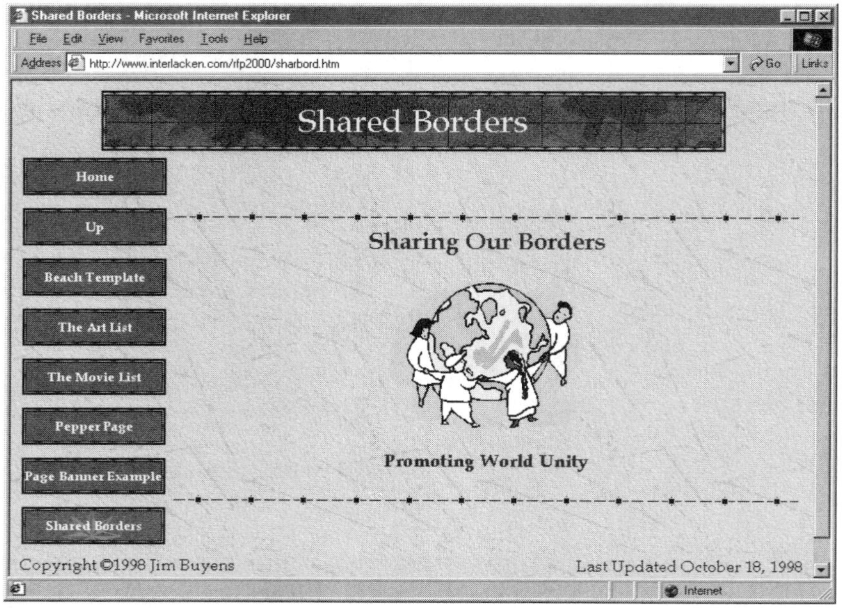

FIGURE 20-12.

This page uses a Page Banner component in the top shared border, a Navigation Bar component in the left shared border, and a Date and Time component text in the bottom shared border.

Note that a Page Banner or Navigation Bar component included in a shared border produces different results in each page where the shared border appears. The same is true for other components, such as Date and Time and Substitution, that display values stored outside the Web page itself.

 **SEE ALSO**

For more information about the Date and Time component, see "Date and Time," page 363.

For more information about the Substitution component, see "Substitution," page 680.

To apply shared borders, choose Shared Borders from the Format menu. This will display the dialog box shown in Figure 20-13, which controls these settings:

- **Apply To.** Choose All Pages to apply shared borders to an entire Web. Choose Current Page to override the Web's default for this page.

- **Top, Left, Right,** and **Bottom.** For each side of the page where you want a shared border to appear, turn on the corresponding box.

- **Include Navigation Buttons.** Turn on this box if you want FrontPage to include a Navigation Bar component within the shared border.

■ **Reset Borders For Current Page To Web Default.** Turn on this box if you want to remove all shared-border overrides to the current page.

FIGURE 20-13.

This dialog box controls the application of shared borders to any or all pages in a Web.

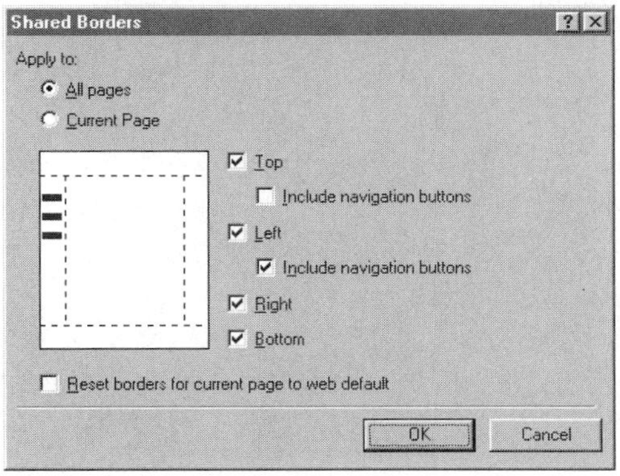

The first time you use shared borders in a Web, FrontPage will:

■ Create a folder called _borders.

■ Create Web pages called top.htm, left.htm, right.htm, and bottom.htm (or whichever of these you chose to use) within the _borders folder.

■ Surround the content of each existing Web page with an HTML table.

■ Include the top.htm, left.htm, right.htm, and bottom.htm files within the table cells along the corresponding borders.

Figure 20-14 shows FrontPage displaying the shared-borders page from Figure 20-12. The visible boundaries around each shared border disappear at browse time. You can edit information in the borders, but any changes will affect *every* page in the same Web that uses shared borders. That's the point of shared borders: to show zones of identical or self-customizing content on every page.

To override a Web's shared border settings for a specific page, first open it in Page view, and then choose Shared Borders from the Format menu. Make sure the Apply To choice is Current Page, then either:

■ Indicate which shared borders the current page should use.

    or

■ To return a page to its Web's default shared-border settings, turn on the box titled Reset Borders For Current Page To Web Default.

FIGURE 20-14.
Shared borders can provide standard content along the edge of any or all pages in a Web. The choice of edges is configurable.

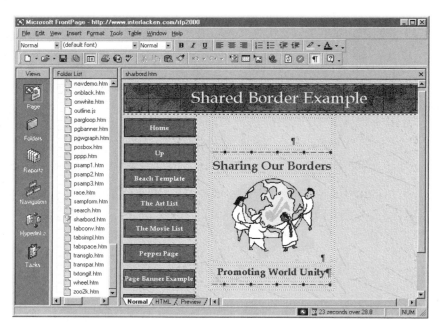

Substitution

? SEE ALSO
For details on setting up Web Parameters, see "Controlling Web Parameters," page 588.

Web Parameters are commonly occurring character strings you can establish centrally and then reference by name throughout a Web. Like included page segments, Web Parameters provide uniformity and eliminate redundant maintenance. If the value of a Web Parameter changes, you only need to update one place.

The Substitution component displays Web Parameter values in a Web page. You configure the component with the Web Parameter's name, and the component displays the parameter's value. Any text that will appear on multiple pages and be subject to occasional change is a candidate to become a Web Parameter.

To display Web Parameter values in a Web page:

1 Open the page in Page view.

2 Set the insertion marker where you'd like the Web Parameter value to appear.

3 Choose Component from the Insert menu, and then choose Substitution.

4 When the Substitution Component Properties dialog box appears, as shown in Figure 20-15, choose the Web Parameter you want to insert, and then click OK.

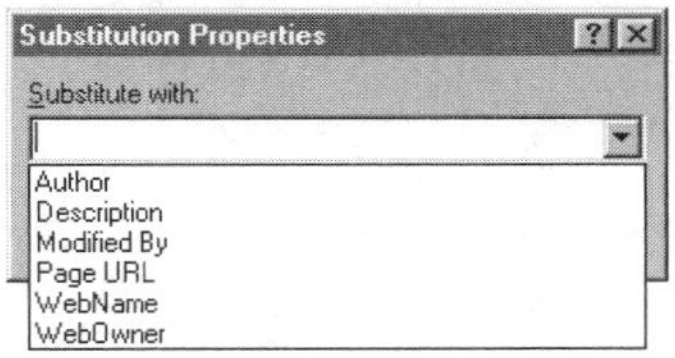

FIGURE 20-15.

The Substitution Component Properties dialog box lists all the Web Parameters you've defined in Explorer's Web Settings dialog box. (The OK and Cancel buttons are currently hidden by the drop-down list.)

After you click OK in Figure 20-15, FrontPage will insert a marker for the selected parameter. If you redefine the parameter later (from the Parameters tab of the Web Settings dialog box), FrontPage will update the value displayed on your Web pages everywhere the Web Parameter appears.

Note the four built-in Web Parameters shown in Figure 20-15: Author, Modified By, Description, and Page URL. FrontPage maintains these values on a page-by-page basis, as shown in Table 20-1. Only the Description field can be edited; it displays any comments entered on the Summary tab of a page's Properties dialog box invoked from Folder List or view. WebOwner, and WebName are user-defined Web Parameters.

Figure 20-16 shows a Web page with seven Substitution components. There's one component for each of the five built-in parameters plus two that display parameters configured under Tools, Web Settings: WebName and WebOwner.

TABLE 20-1.   Web Parameters Maintained by FrontPage

Substitution Name	FrontPage Property	Description
Author	Created by	The user name of the person who created the page.
Modified By	Modified by	The user name of the person who most recently modified the page.
Description	Comment	Comments entered in a page's Properties dialog box in Folder List or view.
Page URL	Location	The location of the page, as seen from a browser.

FIGURE 20-16.

FrontPage shows system-maintained Web Parameters as placeholders, but displays user-defined Web Parameters as values. Browsers show the final values in either case.

```
Microsoft FrontPage - http://www.interlacken.com/rfp2000
File  Edit  View  Insert  Format  Tools  Table  Window  Help

Heading 2   (default font)   Normal   B  I  U
```

Substitution Component Example¶

Web Parameter	Substitution Component Value¶
Author¶	INTERLACKEN\JIM¶
Description¶	[Description]¶
Modified By¶	INTERLACKEN\JIM¶
Page URL¶	http://www.interlacken.com/rfp2000/substitu.htm¶
vti_categories¶	Marketing\ Hype Real\ Stuff Sample\ Pages¶
WebName¶	Running Microsoft FrontPage 2000¶
WebOwner¶	Jim Buyens¶

Folder List: onwhite.htm, outline.js, pargloop.htm, pgbanner.ht, pgwgraph.ht, posbox.htm, pppp.htm, psamp1.htm, psamp2.htm, psamp3.htm, race.htm, sampform.ht, search.htm, sharbord.htm, substitu.htm, tabconv.htm, tabsimpl.htm, tabspace.ht, textnav.htm, transglo.htm, transpar.htm, txtongif.htm, wheel.htm, zoo2k.htm

Normal / HTML / Preview

? SEE ALSO

For more information about entering Description values, see "Working with Folders View," page 626.

The Substitution component for Description displays the placeholder [Description] in Figure 20-16 because the contents of the field are empty. In a browser, however, empty values display as blank.

The Description parameter displays a file's Comment property, as entered in Folder List or view. The Component Errors report lists all cases where Substitution components refer to missing or empty Web Parameters.

Include Page Components

The FrontPage Include Page component includes one Web page in another. This is a very useful feature for coding repetitive page segments once and using them on many pages. The concept is similar to that of boilerplate text in word processing.

? SEE ALSO

For more information about this topic, see "Include Page," page 368.

Chapter 11 described how to use Include Page components, but noted they work best when both the included page and the page that includes it reside in the same FrontPage Web. The reason is this: when you update an included page, FrontPage updates every page in the same Web that includes it. This is a very powerful feature, and it doesn't rely on special server features to make it work.

The same considerations apply to the Scheduled Include and Scheduled Image components. If everything involved with these components resides in the same Web, FrontPage can keep them working together smoothly. Otherwise, the task is yours.

Table of Contents

The Table of Contents component generates a clickable table of contents based on any starting page in your Web. The first level of entries consists of all hyperlink targets referenced in the starting page. Below each of these page entries, indented, are its hyperlink targets. This process continues through any number of levels. Each entry is a hyperlink to the page it represents.

The Table of Contents component lists only pages in the current Web. Hyperlinks to locations outside the current Web don't appear. Pages are identified by their titles, not by the hyperlink text or by their file names. To change a page's title, open it in Page view, Choose Properties from the File menu, and update the Title field.

You can create a table of contents either of two ways:

- Add a table of contents to any new or existing page. The process should by now be familiar.

    1 Set the insertion point.

    2 Choose Component from the Insert menu, and then choose Table of Contents.

- Create a new page using the Table of Contents template.

    1 Choose New from the File menu, and then choose Page.

    2 Select the Table of Contents template.

    3 Locate the table of contents in the new page, and then double-click it.

Both procedures display the Table of Contents Properties dialog box shown in Figure 20-17. The settings in this dialog box work as follows.

- **Page URL For Starting Point Of Table.** Identify the page whose hyperlinks will become first-level entries in the table of contents. To display an entire FrontPage Web, specify its home page.

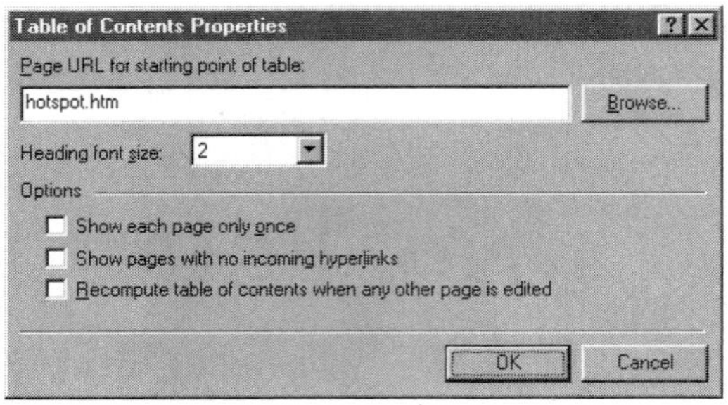

FIGURE 20-17.

This dialog box con-
figures the Table of
Contents component.

- **Heading Font Size.** Specify a heading style for the table-of-contents heading. Selecting 1 specifies the Heading 1 style, selecting 2 specifies the Heading 2 style, and so on. To omit the heading, specify None. The title of the starting-point page provides the heading text.

- **Show Each Page Only Once.** Turn this box on to prevent pages from appearing more than once in the table of contents. Turn it off if you want each page to appear under each page that has hyperlinks to it.

- **Show Pages With No Incoming Hyperlinks.** Turn this box on to display any orphan pages at the end of the table of contents. An orphan is a page that can't be reached by clicking any combination of your site's hyperlinks. If this check box is turned off, no orphan pages will appear.

- **Recompute Table Of Contents When Any Other Page Is Edited.** Turn this box on to make FrontPage re-create the table of contents every time a page in the Web changes. This can be time-consuming. If you'd rather re-create the table manually—by opening and saving the table-of-contents page—leave this box turned off.

A page containing the Table of Contents component appears twice in Figure 20-18—first in FrontPage and again in Internet Explorer. FrontPage shows only a mock-up of the actual table; to see the actual table, you must open the page with your browser.

Figure 20-18 reflects the Table of Contents settings shown in Figure 20-17. The page About Indelible Inc. appears three times because each of the other three pages hyperlink to it. Choosing Show Each Page Only Once would eliminate all but the first reference to About Indelible Inc. Turning on Show Pages With No Incoming Hyperlinks would extend the table with hyperlinks to all remaining files in the Web.

FIGURE 20-18.

The Table of Contents component appears in FrontPage as a mock-up. Browsing the page displays the actual content.

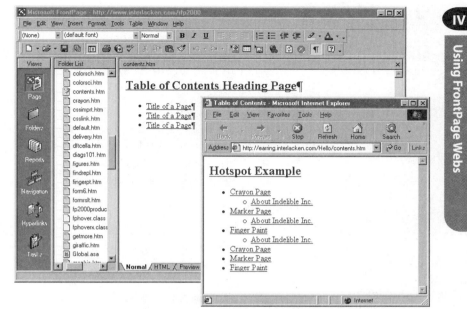

Not only are recursive hyperlinks possible on the Web, they're common. A *recursive hyperlink* is any pair of pages with links to each other, such as a home page hyperlinking to a topic page and that topic page hyperlinking back to the home page. To avoid infinitely nested entries, the Table of Contents component stops expanding hyperlinks for any page found subordinate to itself.

Approach this FrontPage component realistically. The concept of automatically creating a site table of contents is appealing, but few sites have pages so tightly organized that they automatically produce a well-organized table of contents. You may find that constructing a table of contents manually is easier than reorganizing your site so the Table of Contents component produces satisfactory results.

Categories

Navigation bars and the Table of Contents component are two very convenient ways to let FrontPage do the work of connecting pages in your Web. They both, however, take a rather structured, hierarchical view. Often, the pages you wish to group cut across other boundaries, and then you're back to maintaining lists of hyperlinks by hand. Fortunately, the new Categories component in FrontPage 2000 provides an alternative.

🗙 **CAUTION**

The Categories com-
ponent works only
with disk-based
FrontPage 2000 Webs
and with server-based
Webs using the
FrontPage 2000
Server Extensions.

Using the Categories component is a two-step process.

- First, you assign Categories codes to all like pages in your Web. You can define as many of these categories as you want, and you can assign zero, one, or any number of categories to any page in the same Web.

- Second, wherever you want a list of all Web pages in a certain category, insert a FrontPage Categories component. Tell the Categories component what categories to list and, when you save the Web page, FrontPage does the work of finding and listing all pages with matching categories.

To assign categories to a Web page:

1 Locate the page in any Folder List or view, then right-click it, and then choose the Workgroups tab. The dialog box shown in Figure 20-19 will result.

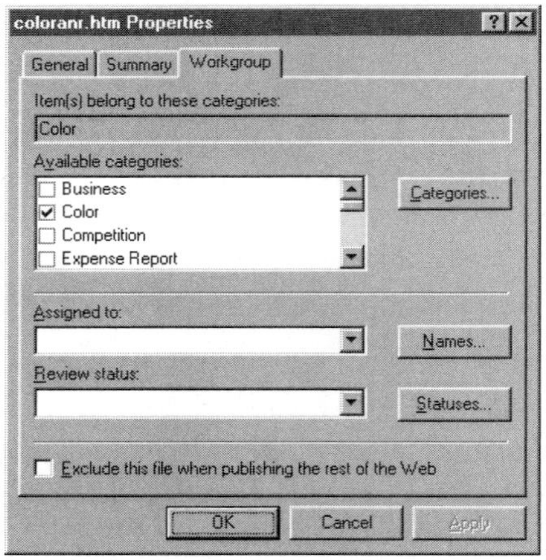

FIGURE 20-19.

To define categories
for a file, right-click
it in Folder List or
view, and then choose
Workgroups.

2 If the category you want to assign already exists, turn on its check box.

3 If you need to create a new category, click the Categories button to display the dialog box shown in Figure 20-20.

- To add a new category, type it in the New Category Box, and then click Add.

- To remove a category select it, and then click Delete.

- To undo all changes since opening the dialog box, click Reset.

- Click OK to save your changes and exit.

4 When all appropriate categories are turned on, click OK.

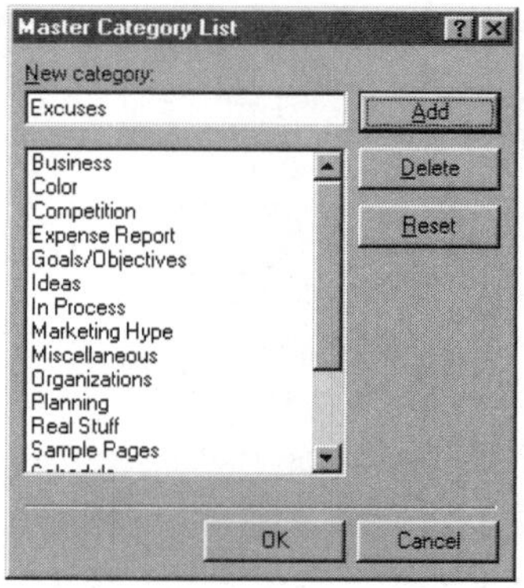

FIGURE 20-20.
Clicking the Categories button in Figure 20-19 displays this dialog box, where you can alter the list of valid categories.

To insert a FrontPage Categories component:

1 Open the Web page where you want it to appear.

2 Set the insertion point.

3 Choose Components from the Insert menu, and then choose Categories.

4 Figure 20-21 shows the resulting dialog box. Follow these instructions to configure each field.

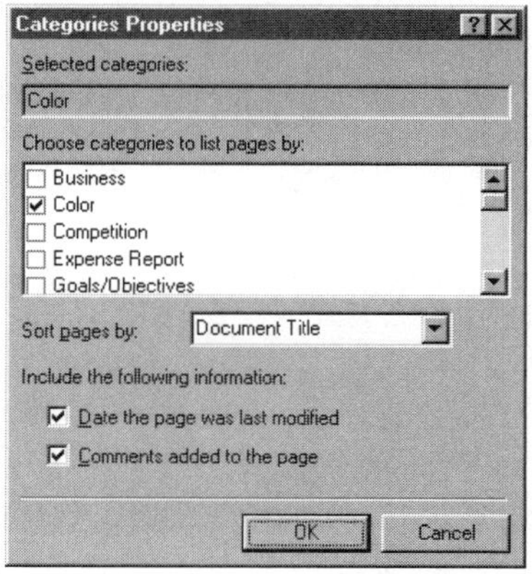

FIGURE 20-21.
The Categories component creates a hyperlinked list of all pages in a Web that are coded with given category codes.

- **Choose Categories To List Pages By.** Turn on the check box for each category you want included in the list of Web pages. If you turn on multiple boxes, a match to any one of them will include the page. For example, if you turn on both the Planning and the Waiting categories, the list will include any Web page coded Planning, Waiting, or both.

? **SEE ALSO**

The comments listed by the Categories component are those entered in Folder List or view. For more information about entering such comments, see "Working with Folders View," page 626.

- **Sort Pages By.** Indicate how you want the list sorted: by Title or Date Last Modified. Title sequence is ascending. Date Last Modified is most recent first.

- **Date The Page Was Last Modified.** Turn this box on if you want the list of matching pages to include the date someone last modified each page.

- **Comments Added To The Page.** Turn on this box if you want the list of matching pages to include comments made regarding each page.

As with the Table of Contents component, FrontPage displays only a mock-up of the finished Categories component. Figure 20-22 provides an example. Only saving the page and viewing it with your browser will display the actual list as it appears in Figure 20-23.

FIGURE 20-22.

Categories components appear as mock-ups when displayed in FrontPage.

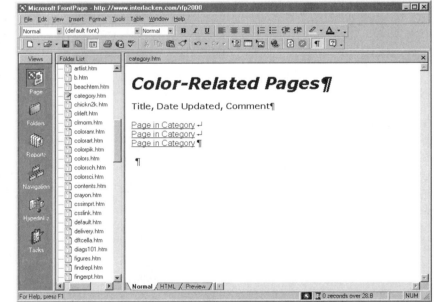

Categories components are great for displaying lists of Web pages selected by product line, responsible person, type of status report, or almost any sort of criteria you can imagine. Any time you need to select and list Web pages, doing so with category codes will almost certainly ease maintenance over time.

FIGURE 20-23.

Saved into a Web and displayed by a browser, Categories components appear as expected.

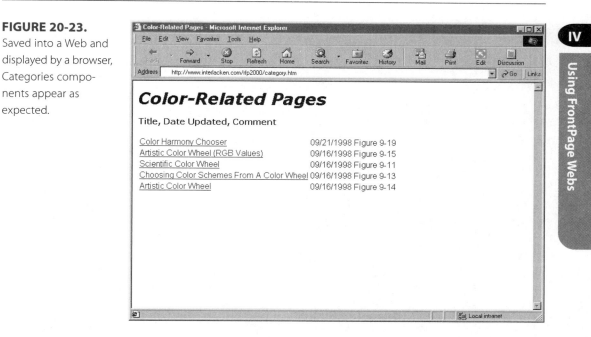

Simply changing the category code of a Web page may not update all the Categories components in the same Web. If you encounter this problem, run the Recalculate Hyperlinks command on the Tools menu.

In Summary...

Web-based components take advantage of FrontPage's built-in knowledge of the relationships among pages in a FrontPage Web. In a variety of ways, they centralize maintenance to a single point and update all required pages. This is not only easier but also more accurate than manually locating and updating all aspects of a change.

The next chapter will describe FrontPage components that require not only a FrontPage Web when you create or modify pages, but also the FrontPage Server Extensions when visitors browse your site.

CHAPTER 21

Using Server-Side FrontPage Components

This chapter describes Microsoft FrontPage components that run on the Web server when visitors access your site. In each case, the necessary server-side programs are part of the FrontPage Server Extensions. You configure these components by editing Web pages in FrontPage even though the components themselves reside and execute on the server.

- **Hit Counter** tabulates and displays how many times Web visitors access a page.

- **Search Form** adds an HTML form to the current Web page for entering and submitting text-search queries. At browse time, the form submits these queries and the Web server returns a clickable list of matching pages.

- **Save Results** converts data entered on an HTML form to a sequential file on the server or to electronic mail. The server-side file can be a text file suitable for input to a database or spreadsheet, Web pages available for immediate viewing, or both.

- **Registration** allows Web visitors to create their own accounts for access to FrontPage Webs.

- **Discussion Site** maintains a list of comments or messages about a certain topic and makes it available for browsing or searching.

- **Confirmation Page** verifies successful processing of submitted data by displaying the results back to the originator.

- **Confirmation Field** identifies where in a response page certain FrontPage components should echo input received from an HTML form.

Because these components use services of the FrontPage Server Extensions, they won't work unless the extensions are installed on your Web server. In addition, for reasons explained later, the Registration component doesn't work with Internet Information Server for Windows NT Server, Personal Web Server for Windows NT Workstation, or Personal Web Server for Windows 95 and Windows 98.

Chapter 22, "Accessing Databases with FrontPage," will describe how to create server-based database applications with FrontPage.

Hit Counter

Popularity is a common measure of success on the Web. The more often people on the Web visit your page, the more successful you're deemed to be. Most Web servers keep detailed activity logs that, in batch mode, permit intricate analysis of access patterns. Nevertheless, simple "hit counters" are a favorite way to measure activity against a given Web page—and to publicly brag (or moan) about the results. Hit counters involve three components.

- A count kept in a small file on the Web server. For FrontPage, this is a file in the _private folder of your Web.

- A program on the Web server that increments the count and creates a displayable version for output. For FrontPage, this is part of the FrontPage Server Extensions.

- HTML that triggers the server-side program and indicates where to insert the displayable output. This is what the Hit Counter component in FrontPage creates.

Figure 21-1 shows a page displaying a typical FrontPage-hit counter. The displayed count is actually an image whose source—rather than being a GIF or JPEG file—is a program that increments a count and generates data in GIF format. Each execution of the program increments the count by 1, until you reset the counter.

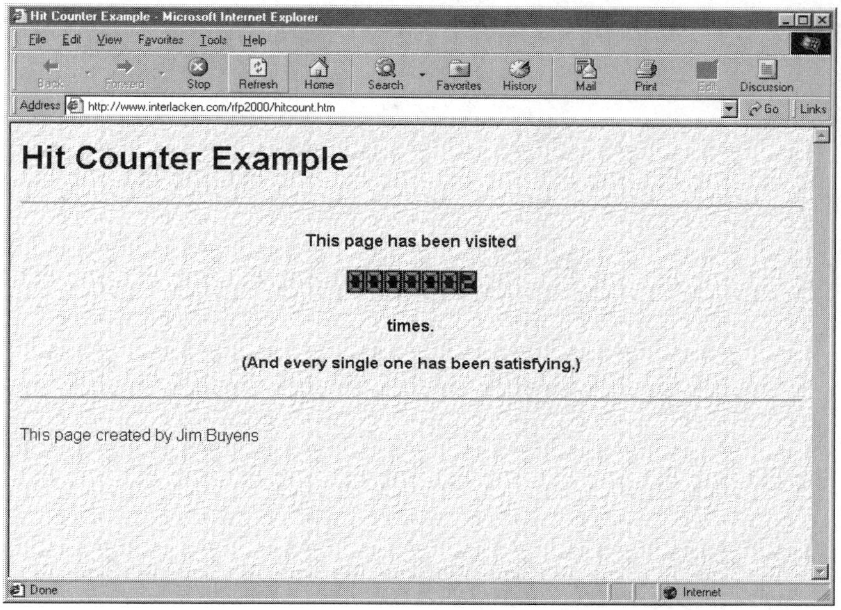

FIGURE 21-1.
It's easy to show Web-page activity using the FrontPage Hit Counter component.

Adding a hit counter to your page is simplicity itself. Open the page in FrontPage, choose Components from the Insert menu, and then select Hit Counter. The Hit Counter Properties dialog box shown in Figure 21-2 will result.

The fields on the Hit Counter Properties dialog box work as described below.

- **Counter Style** controls the style of digits that display the hit count. Select the option button of the style you prefer.

- **Custom Picture** specifies a digit style you designed or obtained yourself. Specify a file location relative to the root of your FrontPage Web, such as images/snapcnt.gif. This should be an image file containing the digits 0 through 9, in left-to-right order. The hit counter will use the left-most 10 percent of this image to represent 0, the next 10 percent to represent 1, and so forth. Obviously, the width of the image should be a multiple of 10 pixels.

- **Reset Counter To** sets the hit counter's starting value. To set a new start value, turn this check box on, specify the new starting count, and then save the Web page.

> **TIP**
>
> After resetting the counter to a new value, save the page, turn off Reset Counter To, and save again. Otherwise, FrontPage will keep resetting the counter every time the page is saved.

- **Fixed Number Of Digits** controls how many digits are displayed in the count. If the check box is turned off, FrontPage displays as many digits as necessary to represent the count without leading zeros. If the box is turned on, FrontPage always displays the number of digits you specify.

FrontPage doesn't display hit counters interactively in FrontPage; instead, as you can see in Figure 21-2, it simply displays the text *Hit Counter*. To see the hit counter in action, preview the page with your browser.

As usual, there are four ways to display the Hit Counter Properties dialog box for an existing hit counter:

- Double-click the Hit Counter component.

- Right-click the counter, and then choose FrontPage Component Properties from the pop-up menu.

- Select the counter, and then choose Properties from the Format menu.

- Select the counter, and then press Alt+Enter.

IV

Using FrontPage Webs

? SEE ALSO
For more information
about installing and
configuring the Front-
Page Server Extensions,
see Chapter 17, "Under-
standing the FrontPage
Server Extensions."

? SEE ALSO
For more information
about FrontPage Secu-
rity, see "Controlling
Web Security Through
FrontPage," page 592.

> NOTE

If the counter doesn't work, the problem usually lies on the Web server. Verify that all of the following are true:

■ The FrontPage Server Extensions are installed. If they aren't, ask your server administrator to install them. If you administer the Web server yourself—perhaps because you have Personal Web Server on your PC—try using the FrontPage Check And Fix function on the server or reinstalling the FrontPage Server Extensions.

■ Anonymous users have security permission to execute the Server Extensions, as well as to update the _private directory in your Web.

■ The hidden folder /vti_bin, in your Web, contains a program called fpcount.exe, and that folder is executable by anonymous users.

> In some versions of the FrontPage Server Extensions, the /vti_bin folder physically resides within each Web. For others, /vti_bin is a virtual directory that occurs only once on the Web server yet appears present within each Web at browse time.

Search Form

Text searching is one of the most common and popular means for Web visitors to find content on the Web. No matter how well organized a site's Web pages and menus, some visitors will always prefer entering a few keywords, reviewing a list of matching pages, and cutting to the chase. The FrontPage Search Form component provides a text search capability for FrontPage Webs.

The Search Form component searches only the local Web server, the current FrontPage Web, or one folder tree within a FrontPage Web. These restrictions aren't such a disadvantage as they might appear. First, if you've done a good job of organizing your Webs and servers, each Web represents a specific body of knowledge; searching that realm may well be a reasonable thing to do. Second, if the Webs belong to different clients, each client may prefer or even demand that search results stay within the client's own pages. Finally, if you want to search an entire group of servers, many other tools are available for that purpose.

There are two ways to provide search capability for a Web.

■ Add a Search Form component to any new or existing page. The process is much the same as for other FrontPage components.

  1 Set the insertion point.

2 Choose Components from the Insert menu.

3 Select Search Form.

■ Create a new page using the Search Page template.

1 Choose New from the File menu, and then choose Page.

2 Locate Search Page in the list of templates and wizards.

3 Double-click Search Page, or select it and click OK.

4 When the new page appears in FrontPage, locate the Front-Page component (an HTML form with a text box labeled Search For, like that shown in Figure 21-3), and double-click it.

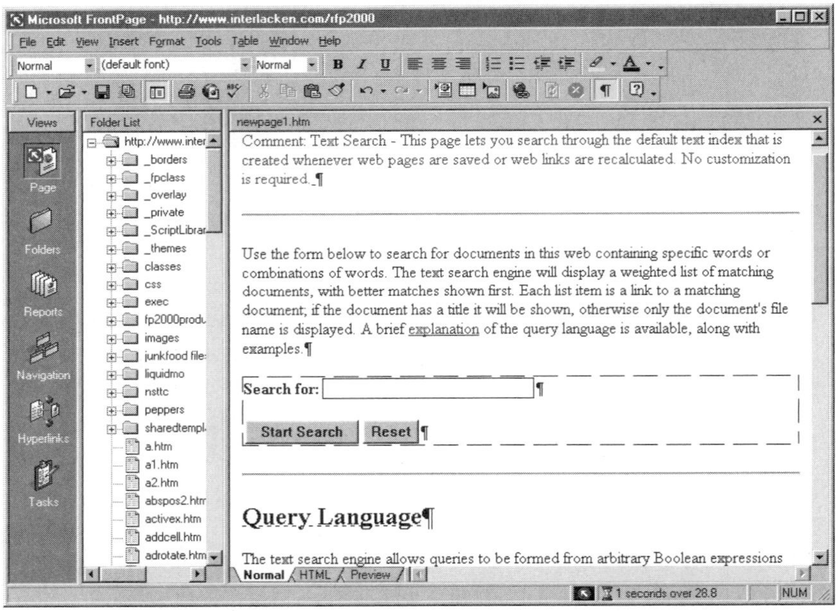

FIGURE 21-3.

The Search Page template produces a Web page like this. The Search Form component is the HTML form containing the Search For text box.

Following either procedure will open a two-tabbed dialog box named Search Form Properties. The first tab controls the appearance of the input form and appears in Figure 21-4.

■ **Label For Input** supplies the phrase that prompts for the keywords to locate.

■ **Width In Characters** specifies the width, in typical characters, of the text box provided for entering search terms.

■ **Label For "Start Search" Button** supplies a caption for the button that initiates the search.

■ **Label For "Clear" Button** supplies a caption for the button that reinitializes the search form.

FIGURE 21-4.
These settings control how a FrontPage search form appears to Web vistors.

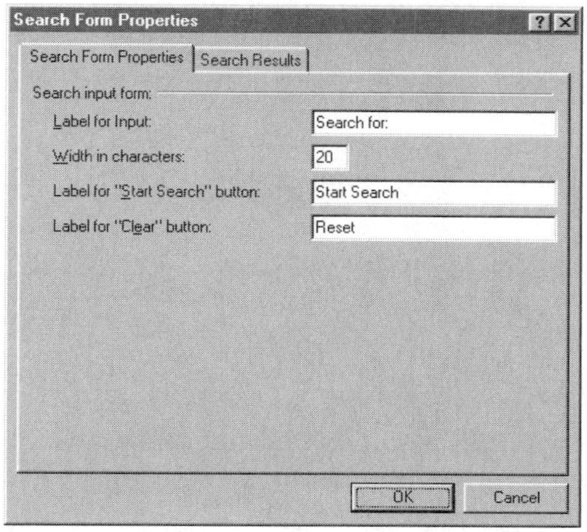

The second tab, Search Results, controls the presentation of items found in the search. There are two versions of this tab: one for Internet Information Server running with Microsoft Index Server and one for all other environments. Figure 21-5 shows the first version.

FIGURE 21-5.
This dialog box controls the format of search results when Microsoft Index Server is present.

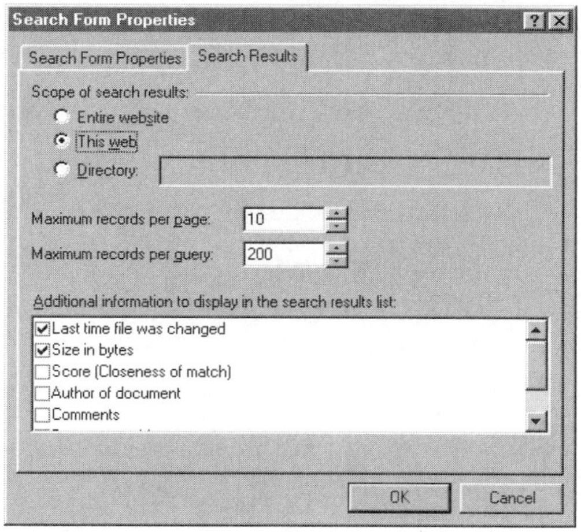

■ **Scope Of Search Results** sets the range of Web pages to search.

• **Entire Website** requests a search of the entire Web server where the FrontPage Web resides. This includes the root Web and all other Webs on the same server.

- **This Web** requests a search of the current FrontPage Web only.

- **Directory** requests a search of a single folder (plus its sub-folders) in the current FrontPage Web. Specify the folder in the text box provided.

■ **Maximum Records Per Page** limits the number of matching pages reported on one page of search output. The remote user must click a Next button to see each additional page of results.

NOTE

> Regardless of other settings, searches configured in FrontPage don't search hidden folders—those whose names begin with an underscore. Such folders aren't available for normal Web browsing.

■ **Maximum Records Per Query** limits the number of matching pages reported by an entire search.

■ **Additional Information To Display In The Search Results List** controls information presented with search results. Scroll down for more selections.

- **Last Time File Was Changed** displays the date and time that matched pages were last modified.

- **Size In Bytes** displays the size in bytes of each matching page.

- **Score** displays a number indicating match quality.

- **Author Of Document** displays the name of the person who created the document (if known).

- **Comments** reports any notes recorded with each matching file.

- **Document Subject** reports the name of matched documents in words. For Web pages, this is the title field. (This field and the next don't appear in the screen shot. To display them, scroll down the Additional Information… list box.)

- **Hit Count** reports the number of matching documents found.

In the absence of Microsoft Index Server, the Search Results tab looks like Figure 21-6.

■ **Word List To Search** can be either the keyword All, to search all pages in the current Web, or the name of a discussion group folder.

■ **Date Format** specifies the format for displaying file dates. This field will be dimmed unless the Display File Date box is turned on.

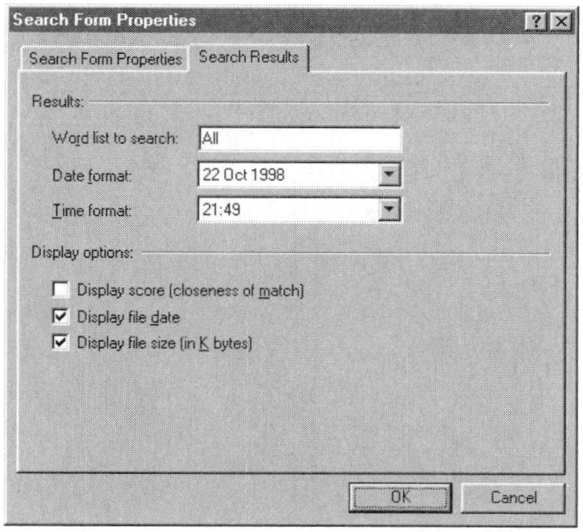

FIGURE 21-6.

This dialog box controls the format of search results not produced by Microsoft Index Server.

TIP

It's always best to use 4-digit year, alphabetic month, and 24-hour time formats on the Web. These are less confusing to international users. Depending on the country, 01/02/03 can be January 2, 2003, February 1, 2003, or February 3, 2001.

- **Time Format** specifies the format for displaying file times. This field will be dimmed unless the Display File Time box is turned on.

- **Display Score** displays a number indicating match quality.

- **Display File Date** displays the date and time that matched pages were last modified.

- **Display File Size** displays the size in bytes of each matching page.

Virtually all full-text search engines use a text index—a database of word locations—to satisfy queries. Scanning large numbers of files for every query would simply consume too much time.

Microsoft Index Server detects *all* file changes—whether made by FrontPage or other means—and updates its indexes as soon as the Web server has processing time available. This means text searches will always be up-to-date with little or no time lag.

If your Web doesn't use Microsoft Index Server, the Server Extensions use a text index that FrontPage updates incrementally whenever it saves Web pages, or *en masse* whenever it recalculates hyperlinks. Changing a FrontPage Web with tools other than FrontPage might therefore result in incorrect search results until someone runs the Recalculate Hyperlinks command.

Saving Form Results for Later Use

The FrontPage Save Results component receives data from an HTML form and then saves it on a Web server, sends it by electronic mail, or both. Save Results can format data as Web pages or simple ASCII text, build data files ready for importing into database or spreadsheet applications, or add information directly into databases.

The Save Results component absolutely requires presence of the FrontPage Server Extensions, both on the Web server you'll use for testing and on the server your visitors will use. If this is a problem, you'll have to get your system administrator to install the extensions, find another provider, or change your approach.

There are two ways to start using the Save Results component:

SEE ALSO
For more information about HTML forms, see Chapter 10, "Creating and Using Forms."

- Create a new Web page in FrontPage, specifying the Feedback Form template. This will create a working Save Results page you can modify to suit your requirements.

- Create or modify your own form, choosing and configuring the Send To option in the What To Do With Form Results section of the Form Properties dialog box.

Figure 21-7 shows a form created by the Feedback Form template and its form properties. The setting Send To File Name is the sole unique feature of pages created with this template; you can discard or modify anything else on the page. You can also choose this setting on existing forms or forms you create yourself.

TIP

To display the Form Properties dialog box shown in Figure 21-7, right-click anywhere on the form and select Form Properties from the pop-up menu.

SEE ALSO
For information about saving form results directly to a database, see "Using the Database Results Wizard," page 739.

To configure the Save Results component, click the Options button shown in Figure 21-7. This will display a dialog box with the following four tabs. Refer to the next four sections for screen shots and descriptions of each tab.

- **File Results** specifies the format and location of files that collect the form data.

- **E-Mail Results** specifies the format and destination of e-mail messages that transmit the form data.

- **Confirmation Page** optionally specifies a custom page that assures the Web visitor that the Web server has accepted the data.

- **Saved Fields** specifies which form fields to save.

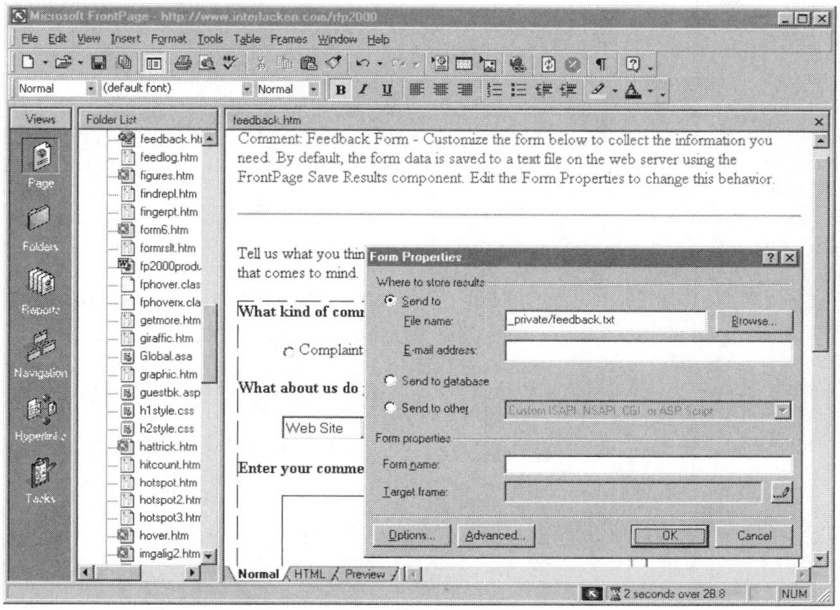

FIGURE 21-7.

The Feedback Form template creates a Web page that, using the Save Results component, accumulates data in files on the server.

Configuring File Results Options

The first Save Results configuration tab controls the format and location of text files that will accumulate the data. This tab appears in Figure 21-8.

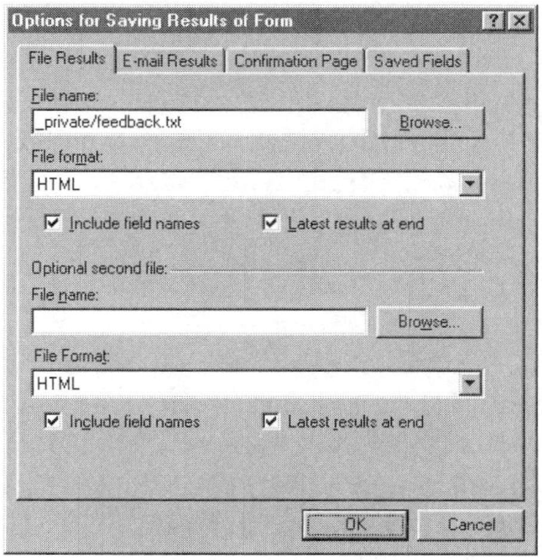

FIGURE 21-8.

This dialog box configures settings for the Save Results component.

Set the fields on the File Results tab as follows:

- **File Name.** Specify the name and location of the data-collection file.

- For locations within the current Web, specify a relative URL.

- For locations outside the current Web, specify a file name and folder in the server's file space. That is, specify a UNC or drive-letter path. If the file doesn't exist, the FrontPage Extensions will create it when the first data arrives.

If File Format (the next field) specifies an HTML option, use an HTM file name extension and a folder location that Web visitors can browse.

If File Format specifies text, use a TXT or CSV file name extension and locate the file in the _private folder of your Web. Be aware that the _private folder is hidden from Web browsers.

- ■ **File Format.** Choose a format for the results file. Table 21-1 lists the choices.

- ■ **Include Field Names.** Turn this box on to save both the name and value of each form field. If the box isn't checked, only the values are saved.

- ■ **Latest Results At End.** Turn this box on to append data to the end of a Web page. Turning the box off adds new data at the top of the page. FrontPage ignores this setting if the File Format isn't one of the HTML types; new data in such cases always appears at the end of the file.

In the section titled Optional Second File, specify the name, format, and other settings for a second file where the component will save results. This permits saving form results twice in different formats, such as HTML and comma-separated, or in two different file locations to reduce the risk of loss. Configure this section with the same four fields described above.

Figure 21-9 shows the effects of saving results with the HTML file-format setting. The Save Results component keeps appending form results to the same HTML page indefinitely in the manner shown. The identical data (numbered for clarity) appears on page 704 in the format Text Database Using Comma As A Separator. Note that the first data record contains field names rather than data; this is a common convention and very useful when performing spreadsheet and database imports.

TABLE 21-1.   Format Options for the Save Results Component

File Format	Description
HTML	The component will append the data to a Web page, formatting the data as normal text with each field on a new line. This is the default.
HTML definition list	As above, but the component will format the *name=value* pairs as a definition list.
HTML bulleted list	As above, but the component will format the data as a bulleted list.
Formatted text within HTML	As above, but the component will format the data as Formatted (monospaced) text.
Formatted text	The component will save a plain text file formatted for easy reading.
Text database using comma as a separator	The component writes all data values on one line, separating them with commas. This is useful for databases, spreadsheets, and other programs that can import the comma-separated values (CSV) format.
Text database using tab as a separator	As above, but tab characters separate the data values.
Text database using space as a separator	As above, but spaces separate the data values.

FIGURE 21-9.

Saving form results as HTML produces an ever-growing Web page formatted like this.

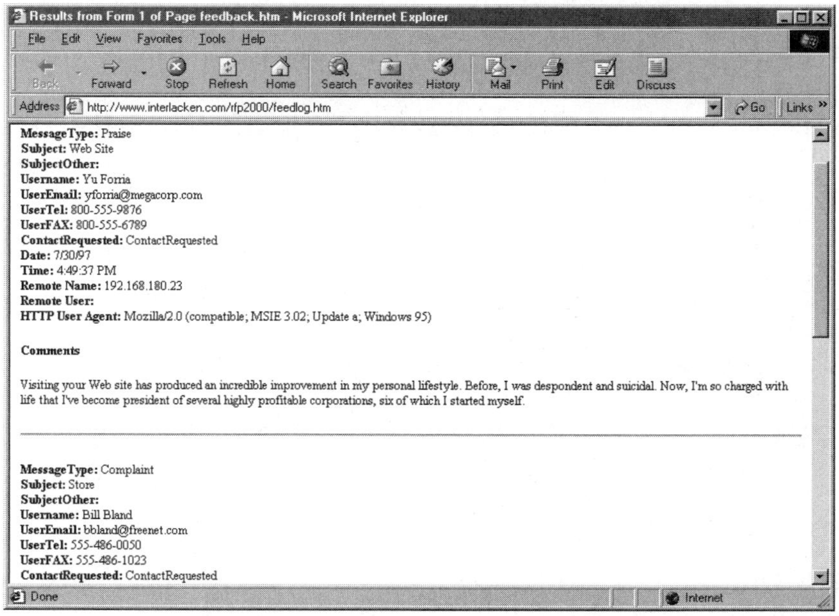

1 "MessageType","Subject","SubjectOther","Comments",
"Username","UserEmail","UserTel","UserFAX",
"ContactRequested","Date","Time","Remote Name",
"Remote User","HTTP User Agent"

2 "Praise","Web Site","","Visiting your Web site has
produced an incredible improvement in my personal
lifestyle. Before, I was despondent and suicidal.
Now, I'm so charged with life that I've become
president of several highly profitable
corporations, six of which I started myself.",
"Yu Forria","yforria@megacorp.com","800-555-9876",
"800-555-6789","ContactRequested","7/30/97",
"4:49:37 PM","192.168.180.23","","Mozilla/2.0
(compatible; MSIE 3.02; Update a; Windows 95)"

3 "Complaint","Store","","Your clerk overcharged me
on push pins last month. Please remit check for
$0.04 immediately.","Bill Bland",
"bbland@freenet.com","555-486-0050",
"555-486-1023","ContactRequested","7/30/97",
"4:57:49 PM","192.168.180.23","","Mozilla/2.0
(compatible; MSIE 3.02; Update a; Windows 95)"

4 "Suggestion","Employee","","Please get your
mechanic Otto to stop putting garlic by the
carburetor.","Vladimir Spinoza","vlad@casket.org",
"","","ContactRequested","7/30/97","5:09:44
PM","192.168.180.23","","Mozilla/2.0 (compatible;
MSIE 3.02; Update a; Windows 95)"

Configuring E-Mail Results Options

Figure 21-10 shows the E-Mail Results tab on the Options For Saving Results Of Form dialog box. Set the options as follows.

- **E-Mail Address To Receive Results.** Enter the e-mail address that will receive the mailed data.

- **E-Mail Format.** Select a data format for the mailed data. Formatted text is the most universally readable and is the default.

- **Include Field Names.** Turn on this box if you want to include field names in the message as well as field values.

  Fields in the E-Mail Message Header section control the subject line and Reply To address of the mailed data.

- **Subject Line.** This field is optional but recommended.

  - If the associated **Form Field Name** box is turned off, enter some text that will become the message's Subject line.

IV

Using FrontPage Webs

SEE ALSO
Saving form results as e-mail won't work unless your Web server's administrator has identified an SNMP mail server to the FrontPage Server Extensions. For more information about this configuration, see "Using the MMC Server Extensions Tab," page 549.

- If the box is on, enter the name of a form field; any data entered in that field then becomes the Subject of the message.

■ **Reply-To Line.** This field is optional; it adds a Reply To header to the message that transmits the form data. If the recipient of the form data replies to that message, the reply will be delivered to the address you specify here.

- If the associated **Form Field Name** box is turned off, enter the e-mail address of a person who will receive all such replies.

- If the box is on, enter the name of a form field. Any data entered in that field will then become the Reply-To address.

TIP

Saving results to a file and sending e-mail aren't mutually exclusive. If the need arises, the Save Results component can send mail as well as saving zero, one, or two result files.

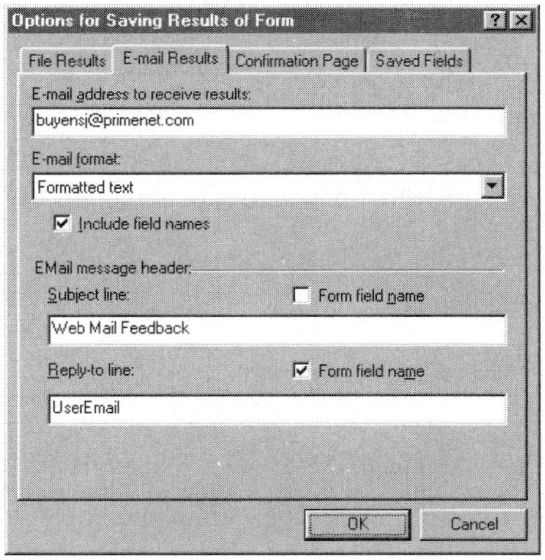

FIGURE 21-10.
Use this tab to send HTML form data as e-mail.

Options for Saving Results of Form

| File Results | E-mail Results | Confirmation Page | Saved Fields |

E-mail address to receive results:
buyensj@primenet.com

E-mail format:
Formatted text

☑ Include field names

EMail message header:
Subject line: ☐ Form field name
Web Mail Feedback

Reply-to line: ☑ Form field name
UserEmail

OK   Cancel

Configuring Confirmation Page Options

SEE ALSO
For advice about creating confirmation pages, see "Managing Confirmation Pages" on page 726.

Figure 21-11 shows the Confirmation Page tab of the Options For Saving Results Of Form dialog box. If the URL Of Confirmation Page field is blank, the Save Results component will generate a confirmation page like that shown in Figure 21-12. If this format isn't acceptable, you can design your own page and specify its URL on the Confirmation Page tab.

FIGURE 21-11.

The Confirmation Page tab specifies the URL of a custom confirmation page.

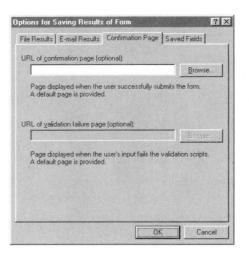

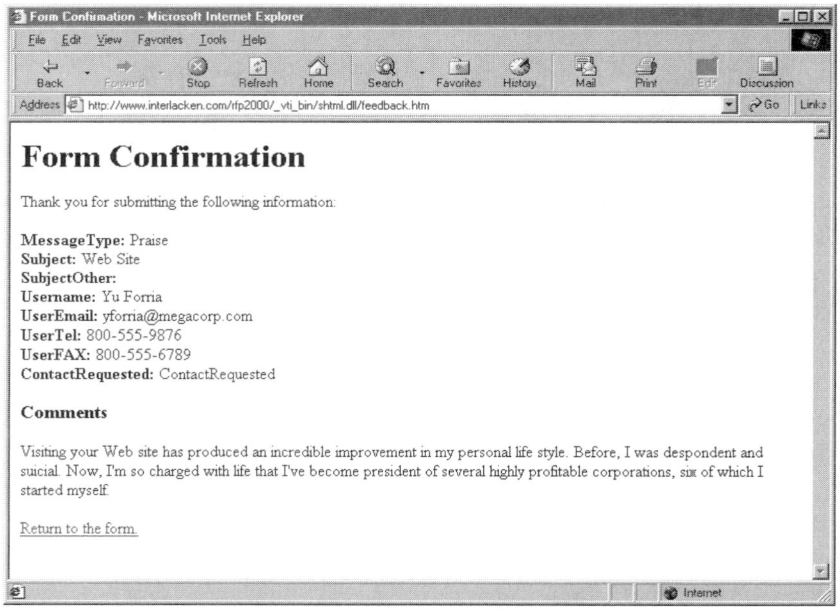

FIGURE 21-12.

By default, the Save Results component will generate form confirmation pages such as this.

? SEE ALSO

For advice about creating validation failure pages, see "Managing Confirmation Pages" lon page 726.

In some cases you can also specify the relative or absolute URL of a validation-failure page. The Save Results component will display this page if any submitted fields fail validation. If you don't specify a validation failure page, the Save Results component creates one on the fly.

Configuring Saved Fields Options

The fourth tab in the Options For Saving Results Of Form dialog box is titled Saved Fields and pictured in Figure 21-13.

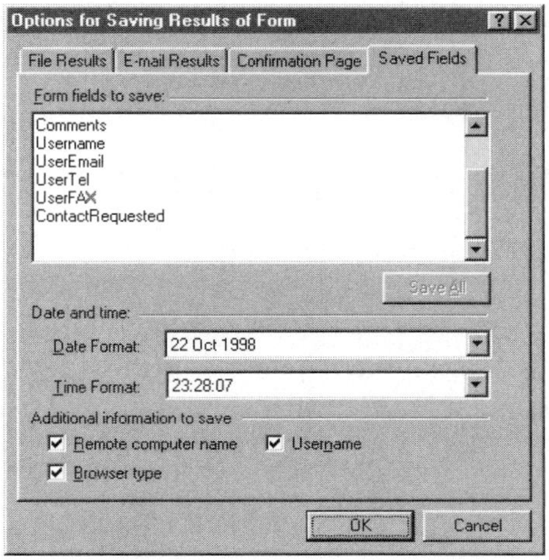

FIGURE 21-13.
Use the Saved Fields tab to control which HTML form fields and system fields the Save Results component will save.

The upper half of the Saved Fields tab specifies which fields to save and in what order. Clicking the button Save All lists all fields defined in the current form. To remove a field, select it by dragging the mouse, and then press the Delete key.

To reposition a field:

1 Select it (including the carriage return at the end), and then press Ctrl+X or Shift+Del to cut it.

2 Set the insertion point at the beginning of a line elsewhere in the list.

3 Press Ctrl+V or Shift+Ins to paste.

The remaining options record data not derived from the form itself. Activating any of these fields appends the relevant information to the form data.

- **Date Format.**   Choose (none) or a date format. If you specify a format, it will contain the date the user submitted the form.

- **Time Format.**   Choose (none) or a time format. If you specify a format, it will contain the time the user submitted the form.

- **Remote Computer Name.** Turn this box on to record the name of the computer that submitted the form.

- **User Name.** Turn this box on to record the name of the user who submitted the form. This data will be blank unless the Web page containing the form resides in a restricted Web and the user was prompted for both a name and a password.

- **Browser Type.** Turn this box on to record the type of Web browser used to submit the form.

Enabling User Self-Registration

The FrontPage Registration component lets Web visitors create their own accounts for Browse access to a FrontPage Web. An HTML form gathers the new user's name and password, plus any other desirable fields. The Registration component adds the user name and password to the Web's authentication database and uses the Save Results component to store submitted data for other uses.

A common use for the Registration component is requiring Web visitors to identify themselves before granting them access to a given Web. This supports any later follow-up you wish to perform and, combined with a log analysis tool, supports analysis of usage by individual.

There are two major restrictions that affect use of the Registration component.

1 The Registration form must be created, stored, and maintained in the root Web of the server that hosts the relevant FrontPage Web. Administrators of other FrontPage Webs can't configure the Registration component unless they're also administrators of the root Web.

NOTE

> A Registration form can't reside within the Web to which it provides access. Before registering, Web visitors have no access there!

2 The Registration component isn't supported for the following Web servers:

- Microsoft Personal Web Server for Windows 95 and Windows 98

- Microsoft Personal Web Server for Windows NT Workstation

- Microsoft Internet Information Server for Windows NT Server

The second restriction arises because the listed Web servers either have no user-level security or use a Windows NT User Account Database for user identification. If the Web server has no user security system, there's no way to block unregistered users. In the case of the Windows NT servers, allowing unknown Web visitors to create their own Windows NT accounts would be a major security breach.

To activate the registration component for a FrontPage Web on a supported server:

1 Open the server's root Web in FrontPage.

2 Choose New from the File menu, and then choose Page.

3 Select the User Registration template from the Page tab, and then click OK.

4 Choose Replace from the Edit menu, and then change all occurrences of the following string to the textual name of the Web that will have self-registration.

   `[Name of your sub web]`

5 Scroll to the bottom of the page and locate the HTML form pictured in Figure 21-14.

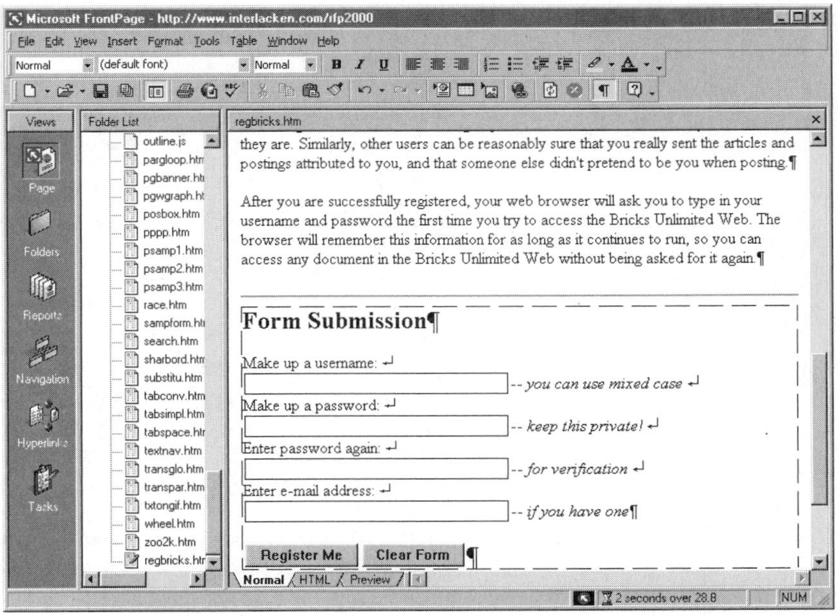

FIGURE 21-14.

This HTML form is the significant part of the Web page produced by the User Registration template.

6 Right-click anywhere in the form and choose Form Properties.

7 When the Form Properties dialog box appears, verify that the Send To Other option is turned on and set to Registration Form Handler. Clicking the Options button should then display the dialog box shown in the foreground of Figure 21-15.

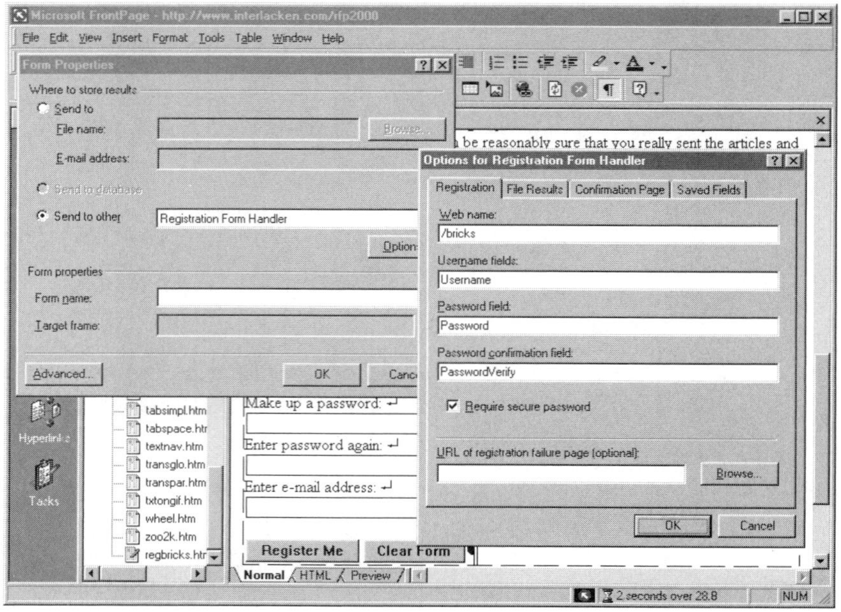

FIGURE 21-15.

This dialog box controls settings for the Registration form handler.

8 Enter or verify the following fields:

- **Web Name.** Enter the name of the FrontPage Web visitors will register to use. This must consist of a leading slash followed by the internal (short) name of the Web. Don't use a trailing slash or the Web's name in words.

- **Username Fields.** Enter the names of one or more form fields, separated by commas or spaces. The form handler will construct the user name by joining these fields. By default, the User Registration template creates a one-line text box named Username for this purpose.

- **Password Field.** Name the form field where the visitor enters a new password. The default text box is named Password.

- **Password Confirmation Field.** Name the field where the visitor retypes the new password to confirm it. The default text box is named PasswordVerify.

- **Require Secure Password.** Turn on to require that new passwords be at least six characters long and do not partially match the user name.

- **URL Of Registration Failure Page.** Optionally, enter the relative or absolute URL of a page the form handler will

CAUTION
If you rename the Username, Password, or PasswordVerify form elements, be sure to adjust the field names in the Registration Form Handler dialog box (Figure 21-15) as well.

display if it can't register the user for the FrontPage Web. You can hand-type the URL or click the Browse button to locate it.

9 If desired, use the File Results, Confirmation Page, and Saved Fields tabs to accumulate data about each registration in a Web page or text file. These tabs work exactly like the corresponding tabs in the Save Results component, described in the previous section.

TIP

> If you want the Save Results component to save the registration information within the Web visitors are registering for, be sure to specify the file location as a local file such as D:\FrontPage Webs\Content\hello_private\regdb.txt and not a relative URL such as hello/_private/regdb.txt.

10 Add any additional fields or make any desired changes to the Registration form or Web page.

11 Save the Web page in the root folder of the root Web. Each FrontPage Web supporting user registration will have its own registration page, so be sure to adopt a workable naming scheme such as *reg* followed by the Web name and then the HTM file name extension.

12 Open the FrontPage Web visitors will register for, logging in as an administrator.

13 Choose Permissions from the Tools menu.

14 On the Settings tab, select Use Unique Permissions For This Web and click Apply.

15 On the Users tab, select Only Registered Users Have Browse Access and click OK.

16 If the Web server permits configuring the Web page displayed in case of login failure, specify the registration page saved in step 11.

NOTE

> After you complete step 15, every Web visitor will need to enter a valid user name and password before accessing any page in the FrontPage Web.

SEE ALSO
For more information on security settings for FrontPage Webs, see "Controlling Web Security Through FrontPage," page 592.

Once you have Registration working, you can make further changes to the Registration page. However, you must have form elements for the user name, password, and password-confirmation fields, and you must also specify their names in the Registration Form Handler dialog box (Figure 21-15).

Creating and Managing Discussion Sites

A discussion site accumulates messages Web visitors submit through a special HTML form. The FrontPage Server Extensions:

■ Save each message as a Web page.

■ Build Next and Previous hyperlinks between pages.

■ Maintain an index page of all articles.

In some respects, Discussion Webs resemble Usenet newsgroups. Discussion Webs can also incorporate the Search component to locate articles containing specified text and the Registration component to identify Web visitors.

Creating a New Discussion Web

Here are the steps required to create a Discussion Web.

1 Open the Web where the Discussion Web will reside or, if you're creating a new Web, the desired parent Web. Log in as an administrator.

2 Choose New from the File menu, and then select Web. When the dialog box shown in Figure 21-16 appears:

• Choose Discussion Web Wizard.

• Specify a location for the Discussion Web, or click Add To Current Web. The FrontPage Server Extensions must be installed on any server you specify.

• Turn on the check box titled Secure Connection Required if the Web server at the given location requires Secure Socket Layer (SSL) communication.

⭐ **TIP**

> The short name of a Discussion Web must conform to the rules for naming folders on the system that hosts the Web. Pithy, intuitive names are usually better than verbose ones. You can provide a more descriptive name later.

3 When the Discussion Web Wizard displays the banner page shown in Figure 21-17, click Next.

FIGURE 21-16.
Use this dialog box to specify the server name and Web name of a new Discussion Web.

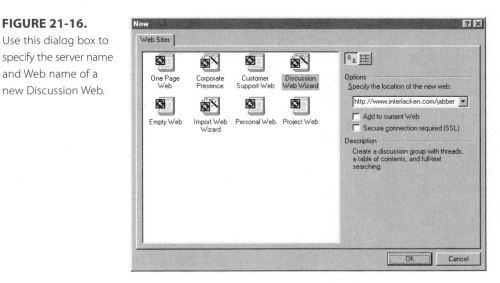

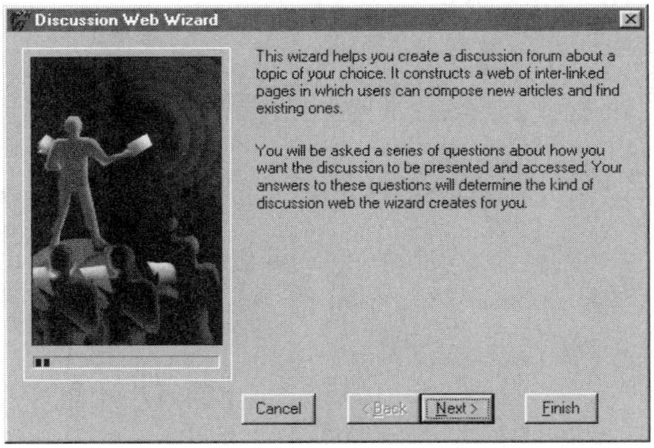

FIGURE 21-17.
Click Next after reading this banner page.

4   The second Discussion Web prompt appears in Figure 21-18. Select options for the discussion as follows.

- **Submission Form.** This option is mandatory. It provides the form for discussion participants to enter messages.

- **Table Of Contents.** Turn on this box if you want an index page containing hyperlinks to each message in the discussion.

- **Search Form.** Turn on this box to permit searching all messages for a word or phrase.

- **Threaded Replies.** Turning this box on lets participants create new top-level topics or replies to existing topics. Replies to any message will appear indented below it. Leaving this box turned off keeps messages in chronological sequence.

- **Confirmation Page.** Turn on this box if Web visitors should receive confirmation after posting discussion entries.

Click Next when your entries on this panel are complete.

FIGURE 21-18.
Choose the major features of your Discussion Web using this dialog box.

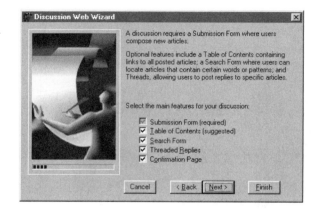

5   In the next dialog box, Figure 21-19, specify

- A descriptive name for the Discussion Web—the name of the Web in words.

- A name for the folder that will contain the posted messages. This is a folder within the FrontPage Web, and not the Web's root folder. The name must be two to eight characters long and begin with an underscore.

FIGURE 21-19.
Give the Discussion Web an external title and an internal folder name.

6 After clicking Next, use the prompt shown in Figure 21-20 to choose the fields you want on the input form. The Category and Product fields are drop-down list boxes. You can add additional fields later by editing the form directly in FrontPage. When satisfied with your entry, click Next.

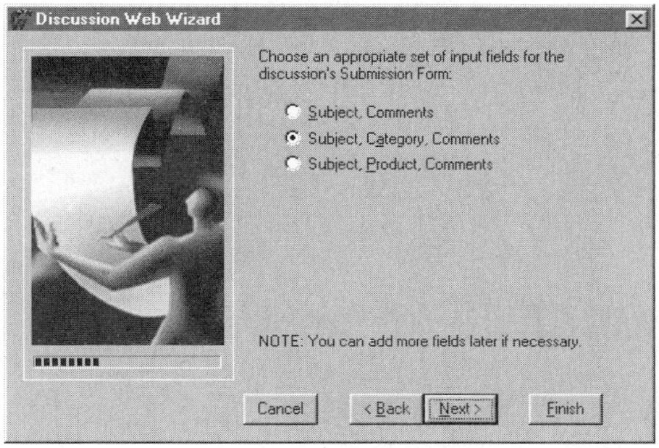

FIGURE 21-20.

Choose the fields you want included in the Discussion Web's message posting form.

CAUTION

Before choosing the Only Registered Users option, review the restrictions regarding self-registration described in "Enabling User Self-Registration," page 708.

7 Figure 21-21 shows the next prompt. If only registered visitors should access the discussion-group, choose Yes. Click Next to continue.

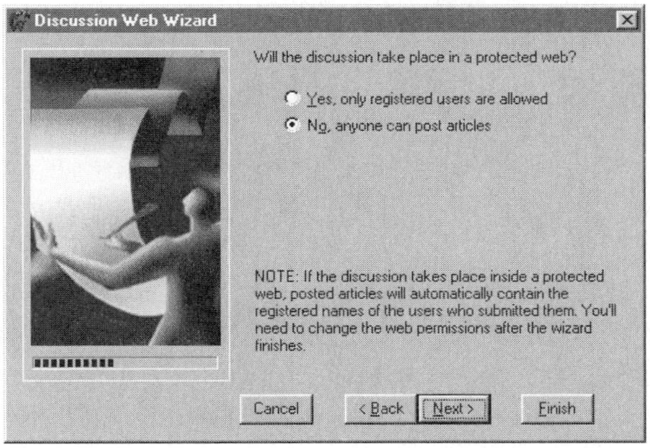

FIGURE 21-21.

Choose Yes to restrict the Discussion Web to registered visitors.

8 The next dialog box controls the order for displaying posted articles. See Figure 21-22. After choosing oldest to newest or newest to oldest, click Next to continue.

9 When the dialog box shown in Figure 21-23 appears, specify whether you want the discussion's table of contents to be the home page for the Discussion Web, and then click next.

FIGURE 21-22.

Specify here the order in which posted articles should appear.

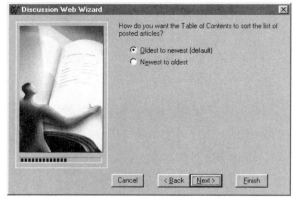

FIGURE 21-23.

Clicking Yes makes the table of contents the home page for the Discussion Web.

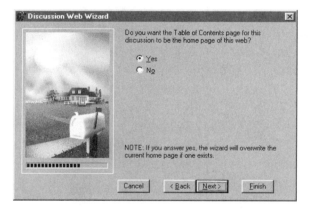

- If you're creating the discussion Web in a new FrontPage Web, it's probably best to choose Yes and make the table of contents page the home page for that Web.

- If you're adding the discussion Web to an existing Web, choosing Yes will overlay the Web's existing home page. To avoid this, choose No when this prompt appears.

10 If you chose in step 4 to have a search form, the prompt shown in Figure 21-24 will appear next. Choose the combination of fields a search of the discussion should report, and then click Next.

11 The Discussion Web Wizard uses the dialog box shown in Figure 21-25 to prompt for a theme. Clicking the Choose Web Theme button displays a standard theme preview dialog box for selecting the theme you want.

> **NOTE**
>
> You can change the theme used by a Discussion Web anytime from Themes view in FrontPage.

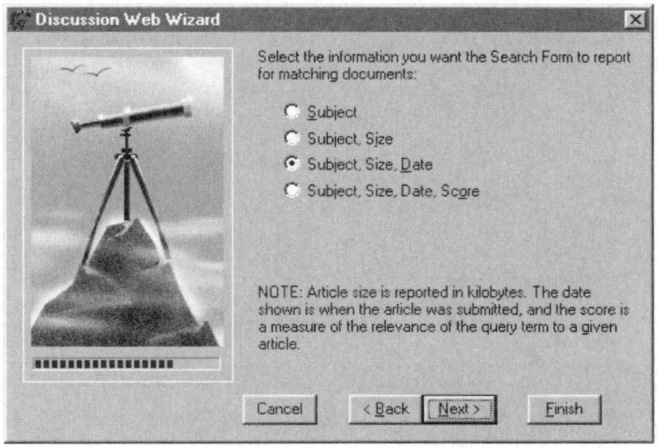

FIGURE 21-24.
Specify the result fields
a search of the discus-
sion should display.

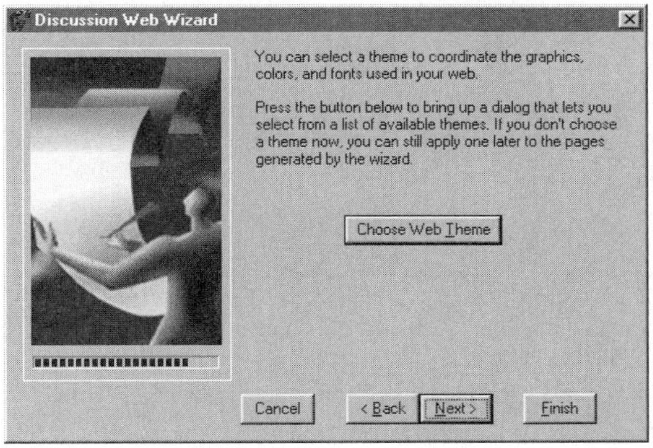

FIGURE 21-25.
Optionally set the theme
for a Discussion Web
using this dialog box.

12 Use the dialog box shown in Figure 21-26 to control use of frames. As you choose different settings in the Frame Options section, the diagram in the left of the window will change to show the resulting appearance. You can adjust the relative frame sizes by dragging their borders with the mouse.

13 Figure 21-27 shows the final dialog box displayed by the Discussion Web Wizard. There are no input fields—just a reminder that you can use the Back and Next buttons to review and modify any settings. The wizard saves nothing until you click the Finish button. When satisfied with your entries, click Finish and let the wizard create your Discussion Web.

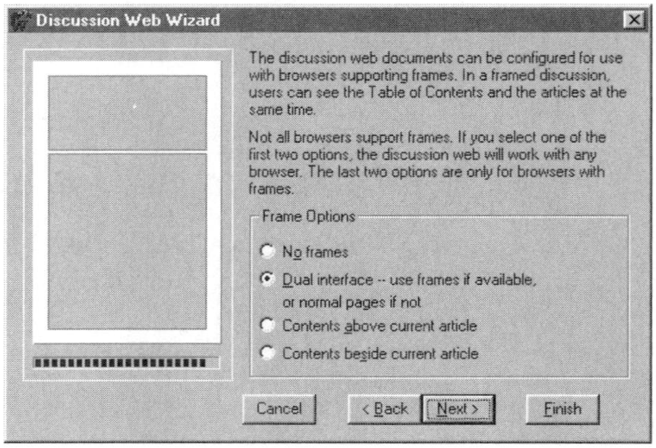

FIGURE 21-26.

Choose a frame design, or none, for the Discussion Web.

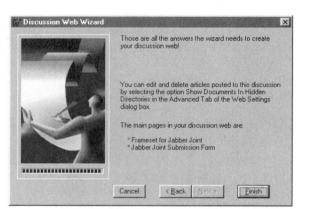

FIGURE 21-27.

Clicking the Finish button creates the Discussion Web. Use the Next and Back buttons to review your entries before clicking Finish.

? SEE ALSO

To check configuration of the self-registration page, add additional fields, or enhance data gathering, see "Enabling User Self-Registration," earlier in this chapter.

14 If you chose in step 7 to restrict the Web to registered visitors, FrontPage will create the Self-Registration Form shown in Figure 21-28. This form won't yet be saved.

To complete settings for the restricted Web, make FrontPage the active window.

- Verify that the new Discussion Web is the current Web.

- Choose Permissions from the Tools menu.

- Choose Use Unique Permissions For This Web, and then click Apply.

- Click the Users tab, select Only Registered Users Have Browse Access, and then click OK.

- Choose Save As from the File menu.

- When the Save As dialog box appears (as shown long ago in Figure 4-4, page 90), choose Web Folders, navigate to the root Web of the server that will host the Discussion Web, and save the page. If you have a naming convention for self-registration pages, follow it.

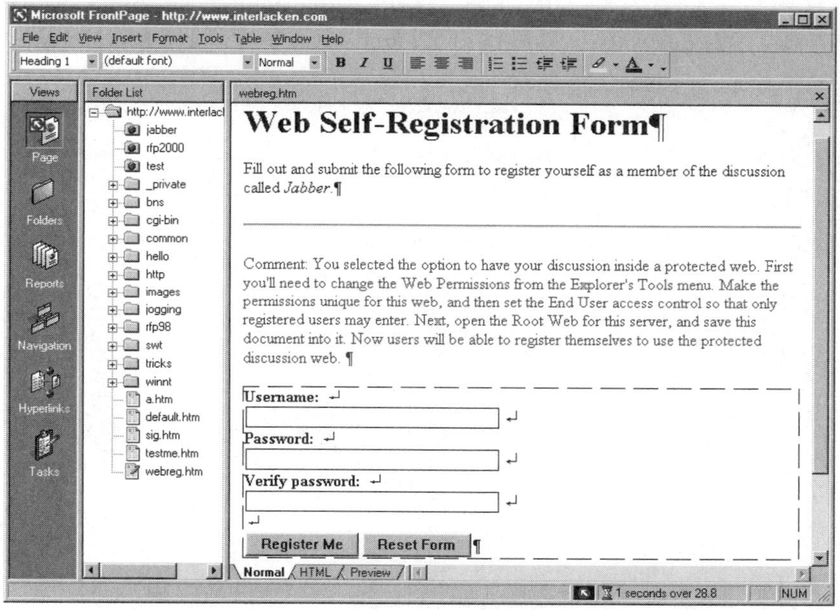

FIGURE 21-28.
FrontPage creates this registration page if you choose to restrict the Discussion Web.

Examining a New Discussion Web

Figure 21-29 shows a newly created Discussion Web named Jabber Joint. The root folder contains the following folders and files. (The prefix jabb_ will vary, depending on naming conventions within your Web.)

■ **_borders** contains any shared borders for this Web.

⭐ TIP

> Folders whose names begin with an underscore are normally hidden. To view documents in hidden folders, choose Web Settings from the Tools menu, choose the Advanced tab, and activate the setting Show Documents In Hidden Directories.

■ **_fpclass** contains Microsoft-supplied Java applets that FrontPage uses on certain Web pages.

■ **_jabb** is the folder that contains all the submitted articles.

- **_private** contains headers and footers included on various pages.

- **_themes** contains the Web's current theme.

- **images** is a folder designated for storing any images used within this Web.

- **Default.htm** is the home page for the Web. This is a frameset having the jabb_tocf.htm table of contents page and the jabb_welc.htm welcome page as frame sources. The name of the home page might vary based on your Web server's configuration.

- **jabb_cfrm.htm** is a confirmation page that provides feedback after a user contributes a message.

- **jabb_post.htm** is the form used for posting messages.

- **jabb_srch.htm** is the form that initiates a text search for messages.

- **jabb_toc.htm** is a table of contents page formatted for free-standing use.

- **jabb_tocf.htm** is a table of contents page formatted for use within the home page.

- **jabb_welc.htm** is a welcome page formatted for use within the home page.

FIGURE 21-29.

FrontPage displays a newly created Discussion Web.

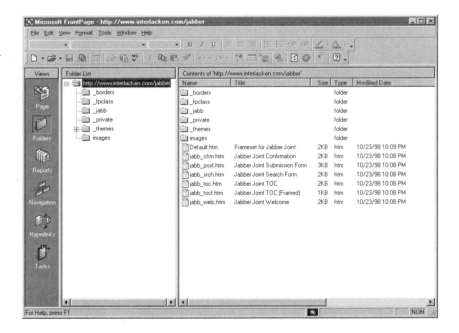

Figure 21-30 shows the default.htm frameset displaying the jabb_tocf.htm table-of-contents page in the top frame and the jabb_welc.htm welcome page in the lower. Indentations in the table of contents indicate *threading;* that is, responses to an article are indented under it.

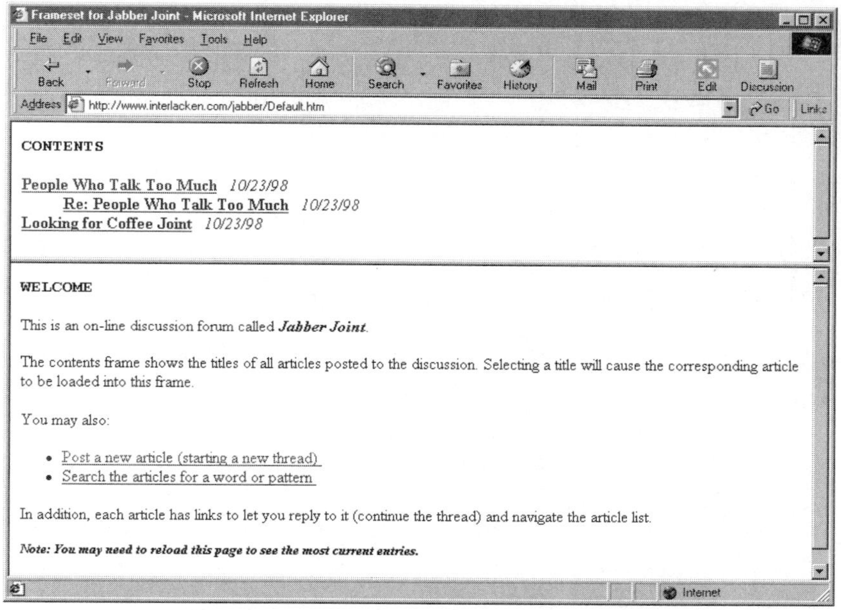

FIGURE 21-30.

The default frameset displays the discussion's contents at the top and a welcoming page below.

Clicking an article in the table of contents displays it as shown in Figure 21-31. The article frame includes a menu bar for displaying the table of contents, searching the entire discussion for words or phrases, posting a new article, posting a reply to the current article, jumping to the next or previous articles, or jumping to a higher article in the thread hierarchy. The discussion form handler constructs these pages from a combination of submitted data and included templates.

Figure 21-32 shows the discussion group submission form open in FrontPage. This page, like the others, provides more function than style. You'll almost certainly want to update the Category drop-down menu with meaningful choices, include a site logo, add hyperlinks to other pages, and so forth.

Enhancing Your Discussion Web's Appearance

The Discussion Web Wizard creates pages that—except for themes—are spartan at best. You'll almost certainly want to modify the styles, page layouts, and colors to make your Discussion Web distinctive and attractive. Be careful, though, to make cosmetic changes only.

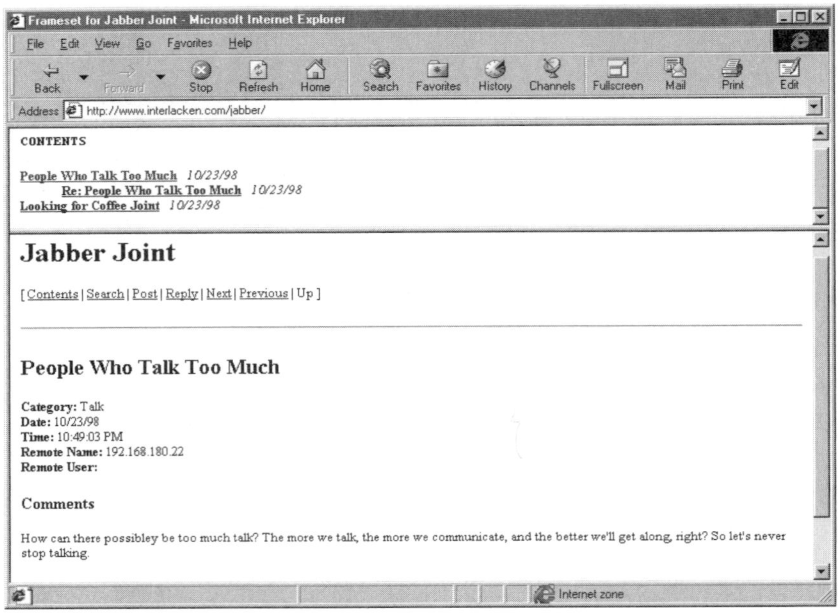

FIGURE 21-31.
Displaying an article with frames combines the table of contents with the article text and details.

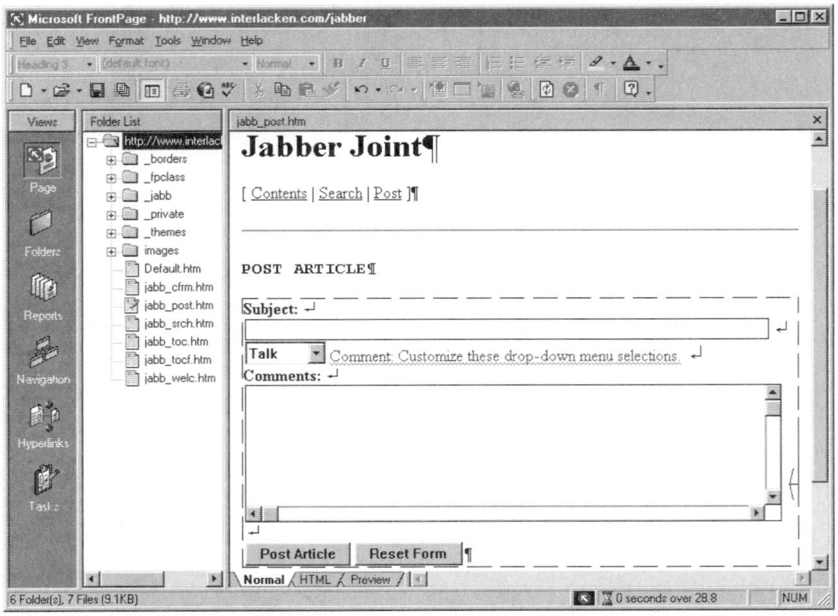

FIGURE 21-32.
FrontPage displays a Discussion Web's submission form.

- Take care not to delete or modify hyperlinks, form fields, or form properties involved in making the Discussion Web work. You can change the Category drop-down list to a radio button group, for example, but you must retain the element name Category.

- Don't delete any included sections. FrontPage will only include them again when it constructs future pages. Instead, change the content of the included sections.

- Because FrontPage makes frequent use of FrontPage components when constructing discussion group pages, view this as a help and work within the structure provided. The FrontPage components provide a degree of centralized control impossible with self-contained pages.

Modifying Discussion Web Properties

The submission form stores most operational settings for a Discussion Web. Submissions are, after all, a Discussion Web's primary update transactions. So, to view or modify the properties of an existing Discussion Web:

1 Open the Discussion Web's article submission page with FrontPage. To find it, look in Folders view for a file with the title Submission Form.

2 Right-click the HTML form on the submission page and choose Form Properties from the pop-up menu. Alternatively, double-click any push button in the form area, and then click the Form button on the Push Button Properties dialog box.

3 On the Form Properties dialog box, Send To Other should be turned on and the Discussion Form Handler should be specified as the location.

4 Click the Options button to display the properties of the Discussion Form Handler.

The dialog box for the Discussion Form Handler has three tabs. The first of these is the Discussion tab shown in Figure 21-33. Settings controlled by this tab include the following:

- **Title.** Supply a textual name for the discussion group. It will appear on article pages.

- **Directory.** Name the folder in the Discussion Web that will contain the article pages. This name must be two to eight characters long and begin with an underscore.

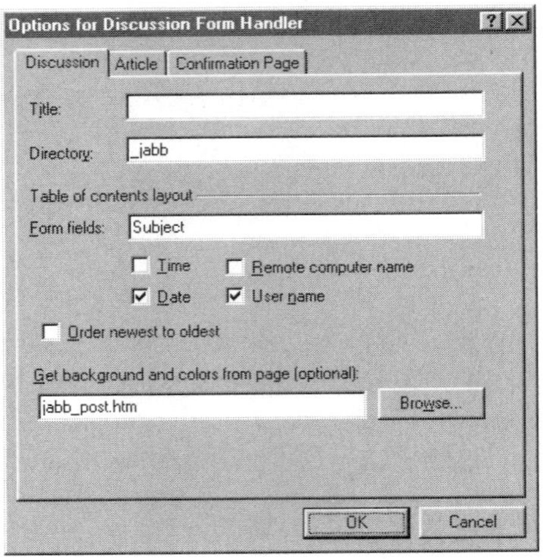

FIGURE 21-33.

This is the Discussion Form Handler's Discussion tab.

■ **Table Of Contents Layout.** Use this section to control which fields appear in the table of contents.

- **Form Fields.** Enter the names of one or more form elements, separated by spaces. Together, the content of these fields will become the article's subject in the table of contents.

- **Time.** Turn this option on if you want the table of contents to include the time the remote user submitted the article.

- **Date.** Turn this option on if you want the table of contents to include the date the remote user submitted the article.

- **Remote Computer Name.** Turn this option on if you want the table of contents to include the name or IP address of the submitting remote user's computer. Whether you get the computer's name or IP address depends on the configuration of your Web server. If you get the name, it may serve to identify the user's organization. IP addresses are considerably less interesting.

- **User Name.** Turn this option on if you want the table of contents to include the name of the remote user who submitted each article.

- **Order Newest To Oldest.** Turn on this option to make new postings appear at the beginning of the table of contents. If the option is off, new articles appear at the end.

⊗ CAUTION

The user name will be blank unless you set the Discussion Web's permissions to Only Registered Users Have Browse Access. To do so, choose Permissions in FrontPage's Tools menu and select Users.

- **Get Background And Colors From Page.** Specify the location of a Web page whose background color, background image, and text colors will apply to all pages in the Discussion Web. This setting is optional.

    - **Browse.** Click to select the background and colors page from the current Web.

The Article tab of the Discussion Form Handler dialog box controls the page layout of discussion-group articles. This tab, shown in Figure 21-34, has the following properties.

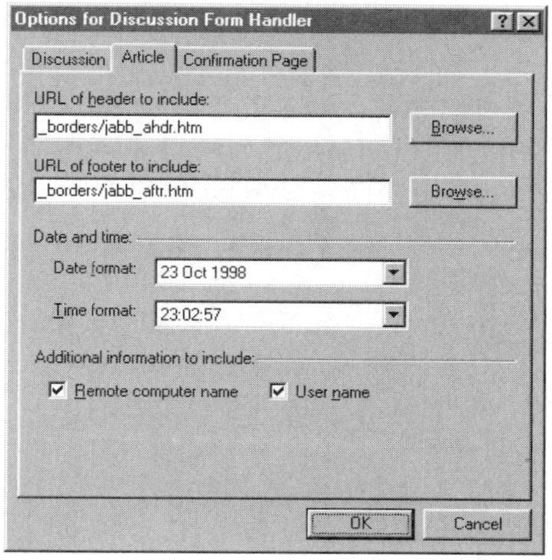

FIGURE 21-34.

The Article tab controls the format of pages the Discussion Form Handler creates.

- **URL Of Header To Include.** Specify the location of a page FrontPage will include as the header of each article, or click the Browse button to select the header page from the current Web.

- **URL Of Footer To Include.** Specify the location of a page FrontPage will include as the footer of each article, or click the Browse button to select the footer page from the current Web.

- **Date and Time.** Choose a format or (none).

    - **Date Format.** Choosing a date format will display the date the Web visitor submitted the article.

    - **Time Format.** Choosing a time format will display the time the Web visitor submitted the article.

- **Additional Information To Include.** Turn on any of the boxes in this group to include the corresponding information on each article page.

- **Remote Computer Name.** The name of the submitting user's computer.

- **User Name.** The name of the remote user who submitted the article.

? SEE ALSO

For advice in creating Confirmation pages, read, "Managing Confirmation Pages," below..

Confirmation Page is the final tab of the Discussion Form Handler dialog box. It specifies the location of a page that will provide feedback to Web visitors who post articles.

The Search facility is optional. If included, it uses the same Search facilities as any other FrontPage Web—those described earlier in this chapter.

Discussion Webs are an add-only facility. There's no mechanism to purge old articles or offensive postings; the Discussion Web simply grows forever. A Web administrator can replace the content of an article with *Expletive deleted* or some other phrase, but deleting an article results in broken links from the preceding and following articles.

FrontPage Discussion Webs can be useful and convenient tools, but their lack of a purge mechanism for old articles is a serious limitation. Discussion Webs are best suited to topics requiring permanent retention or topics where the entire Discussion Web can be deleted after some period.

Managing Confirmation Pages

Certain FrontPage components prompt your Web visitors for data, and then submit the data to a Web server for processing by the FrontPage Server Extensions. Three of these components—Save Results, Registration, and Discussion—confirm successful server-side processing by echoing the data back to the person who entered it. A Web page that echoes submitted data this way is called a *confirmation page*. The same three components also *support validation failure pages*—pages that report failures caused by invalid input.

If you don't specify a confirmation page or a validation failure page, the component's form handler will generate default pages as required.

Enabling Confirmation Prompts

The dialog boxes for the Save Results, Registration, and Discussion components each contain a Confirmation Page tab as shown in Figure 21-35. The tab has these properties:

- **URL Of Confirmation Page.** Supply the location of a page FrontPage will use as a template when it reports successful processing. If this field is left blank, the form handler generates a default format on the fly. You can click the Browse button to select a confirmation page from the current Web.

- **URL Of Validation Failure Page.** Specify the location of a page FrontPage will use to inform the user when it rejects input. This option is sometimes unavailable. If it's left blank, the form handler generates a default format on the fly. You can also use the Browse button to select a validation failure page from the current Web.

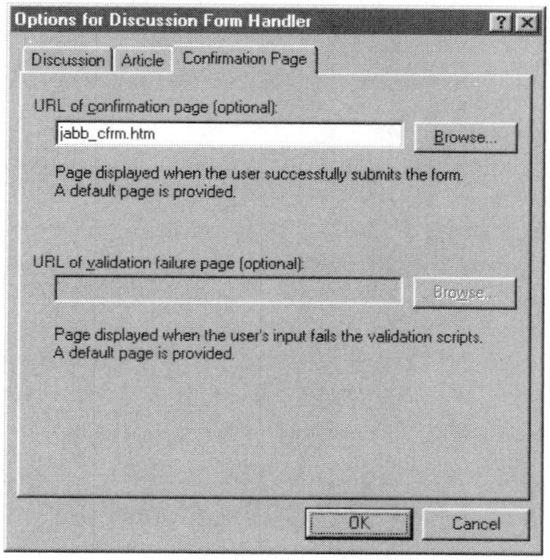

FIGURE 21-35.

The Confirmation Page tab controls feedback to Web visitors.

Using the Confirmation Field FrontPage Component

You can design a confirmation page like any other, but you need some means to tell the Server Extensions where to put the submitted data values. The Confirmation Field component provides this. Each such component contains the name of one data field. The Server Extensions replace each component with its named data value during transmission to the remote user.

Figure 21-36 shows a Confirmation page created for a FrontPage Discussion Web. The discussion form handler will send this form to the user whenever an article is submitted successfully. The visible text *[Subject]* is actually a FrontPage component that will, on output, be replaced by whatever the user typed in the form element named Subject.

FIGURE 21-36.

Confirmation pages generally contain confirmation field components the form handler replaces with user input values, such as *[Subject]* in this figure.

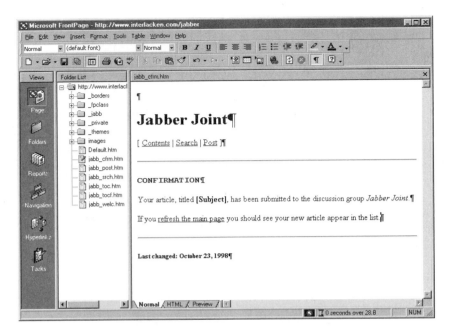

To help you get started with Confirmation pages, FrontPage provides a Confirmation Form template. There's nothing terribly unique about this template except that it contains some sample text and a few sample Confirmation Field components. If you find creating something from something easier than creating something from nothing, take the following approach:

1 Use FrontPage to open the Web where the Confirmation page will reside.

2 Choose New from the File menu, and then choose Page.

3 Choose Confirmation Form from the Page tab.

4 Click OK.

To add a Confirmation Field component—that is, an object the server will replace with a submitted data value—to any Web page, proceed as follows:

1 Set the insertion point where you want the component to appear.

2 Choose Component from the Insert menu, and then choose Confirmation Field.

3 When the dialog box shown in Figure 21-37 appears, enter the name of the input field and click OK.

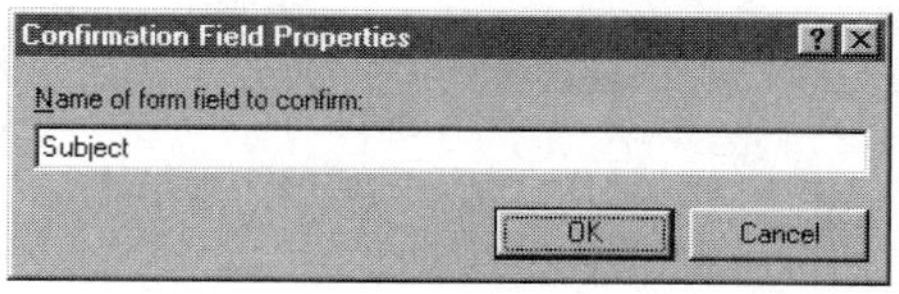

FIGURE 21-37.

Enter the name of the form element the Confirmation Field component should display.

Confirmation Field Properties   ? X

Name of form field to confirm:

Subject

OK   Cancel

> **TIP**
>
> To find the name of a submitted field, open the Web page containing the HTML form, and then double-click the form element. The Name field on the element's dialog box contains the name the Confirmation Field component expects.

Normally, the name you enter in the Confirmation Field Properties dialog box should be the name of an element on the form the user submits. However, for the registration component only, the following names are also valid:

- **Registration-Username.** The name of the remote user attempting to register.

- **Registration-Password.** The password the remote user requested.

- **Registration-Error.** A text explanation of a run-time error condition.

You can include any text, images, hyperlinks, or other Web page objects you want on a Confirmation page. Confirmation pages are normal Web pages in every way, except that a form handler will replace any Confirmation Field components you insert with user input data. You can format the page in any style and with any text or images you want.

In Summary...

This chapter has explained how to use FrontPage components that require presence of the FrontPage Server Extensions on the Web server your visitors access. Each of these components runs programs on the Web server at the time of the Web visit.

The next chapter explains how FrontPage works with databases.

CHAPTER 22

Accessing Databases with FrontPage

As the Web progresses from passive viewing to interaction between remote user and server, databases are critical and inevitable building blocks. If your applications involve remote users querying, entering, or updating persistent data, you need Web access to database services.

Microsoft FrontPage 2000 isn't a full-blown client-server database development system but it does provide a number of useful database features.

- **Save Results To Database** is an enhancement to the Save Results component described in Chapter 21. This feature appends form data directly to a database table rather than, as previously described, to Web pages or a text file.

- **One-Button Database Publishing** is an option within the Save Results To Database feature. It creates a database file, creates a new table named *Results* within that database, and creates columns within that table for each field in an HTML form.

- **Database Results Wizard** is a tool for creating Web-based database queries. The wizard prompts you for the name of the database, the name of a table or query, the columns you want to list, and formatting options, and then it creates Web pages that look up and display the requested data on demand.

- **Data Access Pages** are Web pages that, once displayed on the Web visitor's browser, open a connection to the Web server and update databases interactively. You need Microsoft Access to create a Data Access Page, but FrontPage can open them, edit them, and change their page layout.

Database systems are inherently complex, and a usual way of approaching complex topics is to start with fundamentals and proceed with rigorous, ever-increasing detail. This produces an incredibly boring chapter with no payoff until the end, so here we'll do it backwards: practical information up front, supporting details to follow.

Database Requirements and Restrictions

To create database Web pages requires that you work in a FrontPage 2000 Web. If it's a disk-based Web, the database must be accessible from your PC. If it's a server-based Web, the database must be accessible from the PC where the Web physically resides.

You need to use a FrontPage 2000 Web because FrontPage stores certain information about databases at the Web level, and not within each page. The database needs to be readable during authoring so that FrontPage can retrieve the table names and field names for various selection lists.

For database pages to actually run against the database—that is, to insert records, make queries, and display results—a disk-based Web won't suffice. Instead, you'll need a FrontPage 2000 server-based Web on a Web server that supports Active Server Pages and Active Data Objects. This includes the following:

- Internet Information Server 4.0 or above running on Windows NT Server 4.0 or above.

- Microsoft Personal Web Server 4.0 or above running on Windows NT Workstation 4.0 or above.

- Microsoft Personal Web Server 4.0 or above running on Windows 95 or Windows 98.

- FrontPage 2000 Server Extensions (required on all of the above).

SEE ALSO
For more information about ODBC Data Sources, see "Configuring ODBC Data Sources," page 761.

As to database types, FrontPage database pages can access:

■ File-oriented databases such as Microsoft Access, Paradox, and dBase located in the same Web.

■ Any database defined as an ODBC System Data Source on the Web server.

■ Other network databases such as Microsoft SQL Server and Oracle, provided they have drivers installed on the Web server.

If you don't have a database for data entry, FrontPage can create a Microsoft Access database for you. The next section explains how.

Although FrontPage can insert and display database records, it has no facilities for updating or deleting existing records. To accomplish those tasks, you'll have to develop Web pages in HTML view, in Microsoft Access, in Microsoft Visual InterDev, or in some other tool.

Saving Form Results to a Database

Chapter 21 discussed using the FrontPage Save Results component to save data from HTML forms as a text file on the server or transmit it as mail. This section explains how to save the same sort of data directly to a database.

SEE ALSO
For more information about creating HTML forms and naming form fields, see Chapter 10, "Creating and Using Forms."

Figure 22-1 shows a simple HTML form designed for a simple application: a guest book. A guest book provides Web visitors the opportunity to leave their names and comments. Here are the steps required to save this data directly to a database.

1 Design an HTML form, making sure to give each form field an intuitive name.

2 Save the page containing the HTML form with an ASP file name extension.

SEE ALSO
Active Server Pages contain program statements (scripts) that execute on the Web server whenever a Web visitor requests that page. For more information about Active Server Pages, see "Server-Side Scripting," page 432.

3 Right-click anywhere in the form area and choose Form Properties from the pop-up menu.

4 When the Form Properties dialog box appears, turn on the option titled Send To Database and then click the Options button. The dialog box shown in the foreground of Figure 22-2 will result. Note the four options under the Connection heading.

- **Database Connection To Use** selects an existing database connection to use for storing the collected data.

? SEE ALSO

A database connection is a pointer to a database—a pointer defined at the FrontPage Web level. For more information about database connections, see "Configuring a FrontPage Data Connection," page 756.

- **Add Connection** creates a new connection to an existing database. In essence, this is a shortcut to the Tools, Web Options, Database tab.

- **Create Database** creates a new database to store the form results. In that database, FrontPage creates a new table with a column for each element in the form. Finally, FrontPage creates a connection to the new database.

- **Update Database** revises the structure of an existing database to reflect the current collection of form fields.

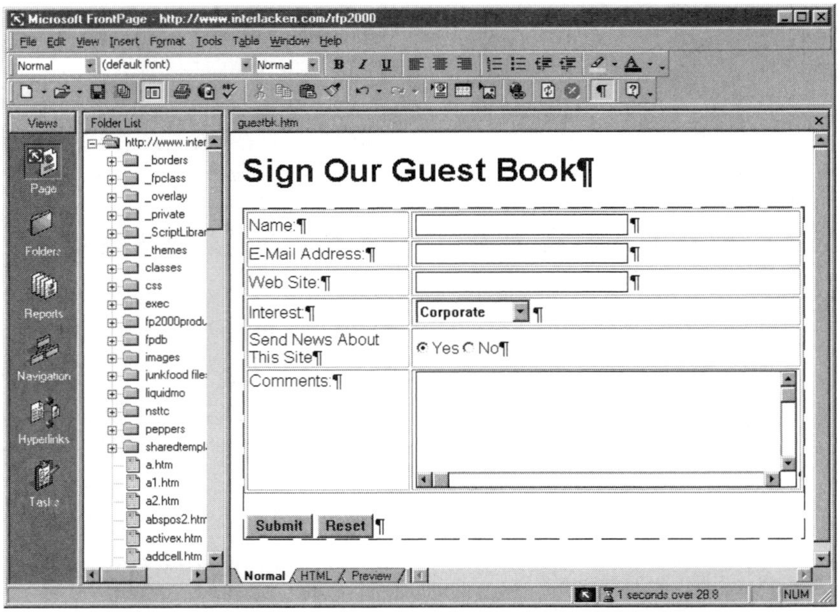

FIGURE 22-1.

This data collection form is a candidate for saving results directly to a database.

For the example, we'll click the Create Database button.

> NOTE

Clicking the Create Database button in step 4 constitutes the One Button Database Publishing feature promoted as part of FrontPage 2000. Although FrontPage provides additional features related to saving HTML form data to a database, they're all optional.

5 After you click Create Database, FrontPage creates a database named *guestbk.mdb* in the Web's /fpdb folder, and creates a database connection named *guestbk*. The string guestbk comes from the name of the Web page: guestbk.asp.

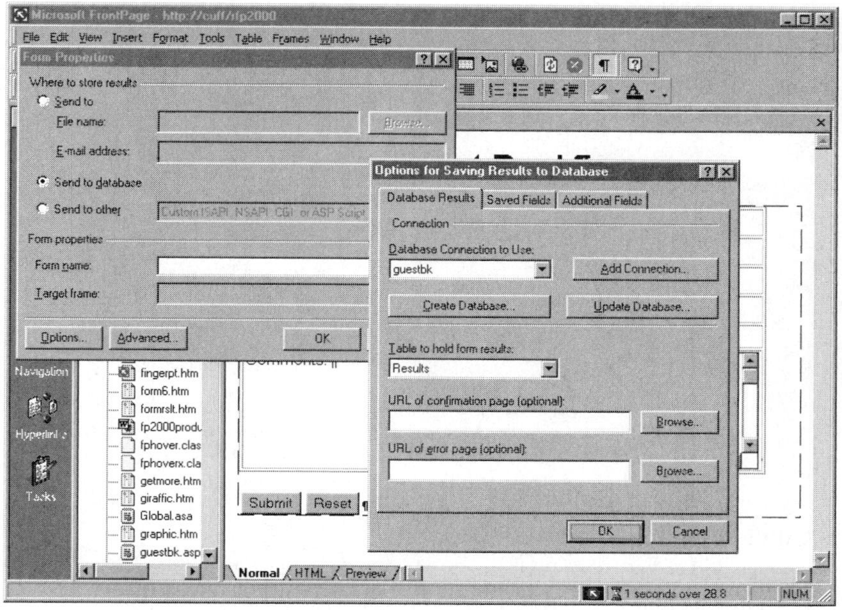

FIGURE 22-2.

The Database Results tab of this dialog box controls basic options for saving form data to a database.

6 Clicking the Saved Fields tab displays the dialog box pictured in Figure 22-3. The Form Fields To Save list itemizes which form fields will be saved in the database, and in what database fields. The four buttons along the right edge provide these functions.

- **All Fields** adds every field in the HTML form to the list.

- **Add** adds one field from the HTML form to the list. A dialog box prompts for the specific field.

TIP

Working with the list of form fields will be much easier if each form field has a concise, meaningful name. To rename a form field, double-click it in Page view and update the Name field.

- **Modify** changes the database field that receives data from the currently selected form field.

- **Remove** stops recording data from the currently selected field.

Update the Form Fields To Save list in any way you want.

7 The Additional Fields tab, shown in Figure 22-4, saves up to four additional fields in the database. The data for these fields isn't part of the HTML form; instead, the browser transmits it as HTTP headers along with the form data. Again, you can remove or re-insert these fields as you wish.

FIGURE 22-3.

The Saved Fields tab displays each field in the HTML form and the database field, if any, that will receive its values.

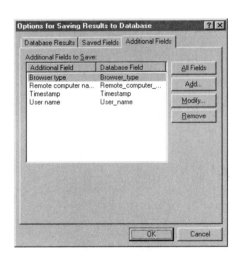

FIGURE 22-4.

The Additional Fields tab controls fields received not from the HTML form, but from the HTTP transaction that submits it.

8 Returning to Figure 22-2, note these additional fields:

- **Table To Hold Form Results** names the table that will receive the data from the HTML form you selected in the Database Connection To Use box. Clicking Create Database in step 3 creates a table called Results.

For more information about confirmation pages, see "Managing Confirmation Pages," page 726.

- **URL Of Confirmation Page** provides the URL of a page the Web visitor will receive if the server can successfully update the database. This field and the next are optional. If you leave them blank, Save Results will generate confirmation and error pages on the fly.

- **URL Of Error Page** provides the URL of a page the Web visitor will receive if the server fails to update the database.

9 When all three tabs are configured to your satisfaction, click the OK button.

SEE ALSO

For more information about installing and configuring a Web server as described in this paragraph, see Chapters 16, 17, and 18.

To actually run the page and add data to the database, both the Web page and the database need to be on a Web server running Microsoft Internet Information Server or Microsoft Personal Web server, plus the FrontPage 2000 Server Extensions. Furthermore, the Web page must be in a folder that can execute Active Server Page scripts.

Figure 22-5 shows data being entered in the Guest Book form, and Figure 22-6 shows the default confirmation page sent after FrontPage had added a new record to the database.

Figure 22-7 shows Microsoft Access 2000 displaying some data collected from the Guest Book form described in this section. To process the database with Access, you would either download the database to your PC, open it through a file-sharing connection to the Web server, or run Access directly on the server.

FIGURE 22-5.

This is the HTML form shown previously in Figure 22-1, this time displayed by a browser and filled out by a fictitious visitor.

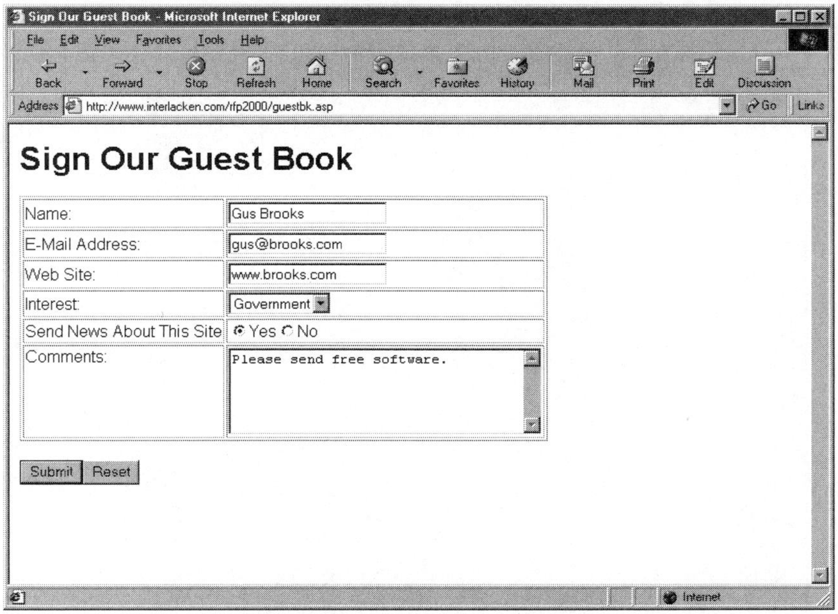

![Screenshot of Internet Explorer showing the "Sign Our Guest Book" form. Title bar reads "Sign Our Guest Book - Microsoft Internet Explorer". Address field shows http://www.interlacken.com/rfp2000/guestbk.asp. The form shows: Name: Gus Brooks; E-Mail Address: gus@brooks.com; Web Site: www.brooks.com; Interest: Government; Send News About This Site: Yes (selected) No; Comments: Please send free software. Submit and Reset buttons at the bottom.]

FIGURE 22-6.

Clicking Submit on the Guest Book page adds a record to the database and displays this confirmation page.

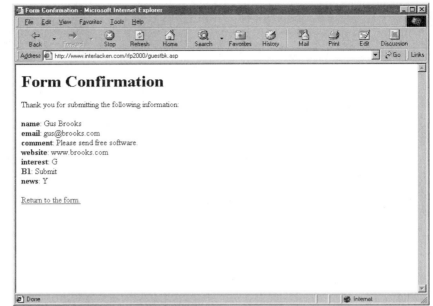

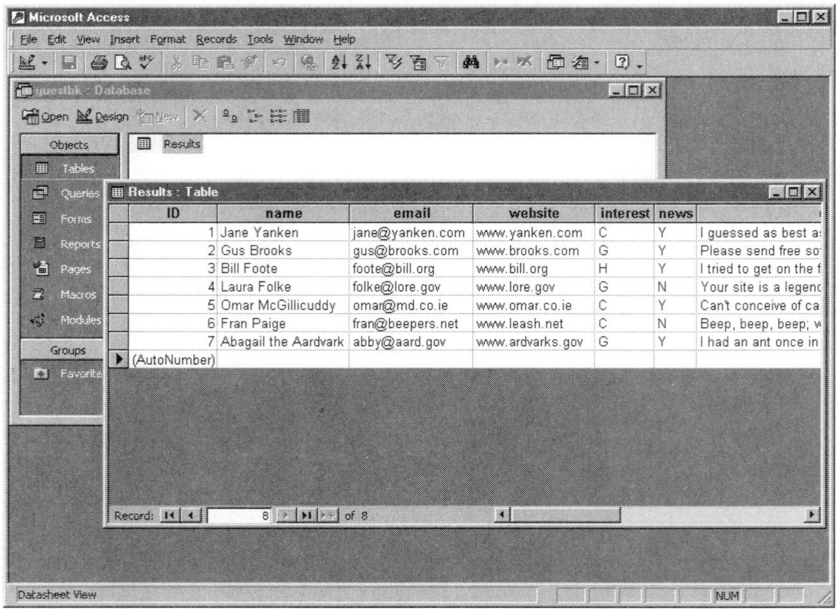

FIGURE 22-7.

Microsoft Access displays some data collected through the Guest Book form.

① SEE ALSO
For information on
configuring Web fold-
ers as executable,
see "Choosing and
Configuring Your Web
Server," page 502.

> **Executable Web Folders**
>
> Programs that run on Web servers present a significant security risk. Allowing
> Web authors (or Web visitors!) to store and execute programs on the server
> grants them capability to do *anything* a program can do. This could be useful
> work, certainly, but it could also interfere with normal server operation or in-
> vade the privacy of others. For this reason, most server administrators allow
> programs to execute only if they reside in certain folders that only a few trusted
> individuals can update.
>
> ASP files contain source code rather than executable programs but, because
> they trigger executable processes, they too must reside in an executable folder.
> For FrontPage database development, the executable folder can reside on any
> enterprise, workgroup, or personal Web server that has access to a test copy or
> production copy of the database.

Using the Database Results Wizard

The previous section showed how to use the database features of the
Save Results component for adding records to a database. This section
shows how to query and display database information, and for this we
need some new FrontPage components.

- The **Database Column Value** component is a placeholder that's
  replaced by the value of a database field when a Web visitor displays the page.

- The **Database Results Region** component contains one or more
  Database Column Value components, and repeats once for each
  record returned by a database query.

- The **Database Results Wizard** displays a series of five screens
  that configure a Database Results region and any Database Column Values the region contains.

Don't confuse the Database Results Wizard with the database features
of the Save Results component.

- The Database Results Wizard—described in this section—queries
  a database and formats the results.

- The Save Results component—described in the previous section—
  accepts and saves data from an HTML form, optionally in a database.

Displaying a Simple Query

To illustrate the Database Results Wizard, we'll create a Web page that displays data collected by the Guest Book page. To keep the example simple, it will display the entire contents of the table, using the table's default sort order. Figure 22-8 shows the finished product.

CAUTION

The Web page in Figure 22-8 uses default formatting from the Database Results Wizard. You can enhance such pages considerably using FrontPage's normal formatting commands.

Here's the step-by-step procedure to create this Web page.

1. Create a new blank Web page in FrontPage.
2. Choose Database from the Insert menu, and then choose Results. The dialog box shown in Figure 22-9 will offer these choices.
   - **Use A Sample Database Connection (Northwind)** adds a sample database to your Web, builds a connection to it, and selects that connection.
   - **Use An Existing Database Connection** selects a database connection already defined within this Web.

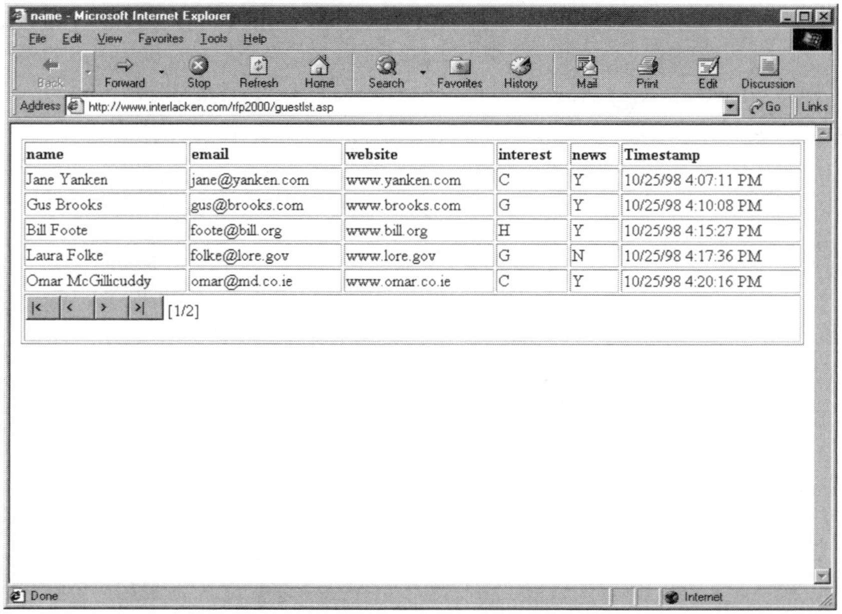

name	email	website	interest	news	Timestamp
Jane Yanken	jane@yanken.com	www.yanken.com	C	Y	10/25/98 4:07:11 PM
Gus Brooks	gus@brooks.com	www.brooks.com	G	Y	10/25/98 4:10:08 PM
Bill Foote	foote@bill.org	www.bill.org	H	Y	10/25/98 4:15:27 PM
Laura Folke	folke@lore.gov	www.lore.gov	G	N	10/25/98 4:17:36 PM
Omar McGillicuddy	omar@md.co.ie	www.omar.co.ie	C	Y	10/25/98 4:20:16 PM

FIGURE 22-8.
This Web page queries and displays the guest book database constructed in the previous section.

- **Use A New Database Connection** enables the Create button, which displays the Database Web Settings dialog box shown later in Figure 22-29.

For this example, we'll use the existing database connection *guestbk*, created in the previous section.

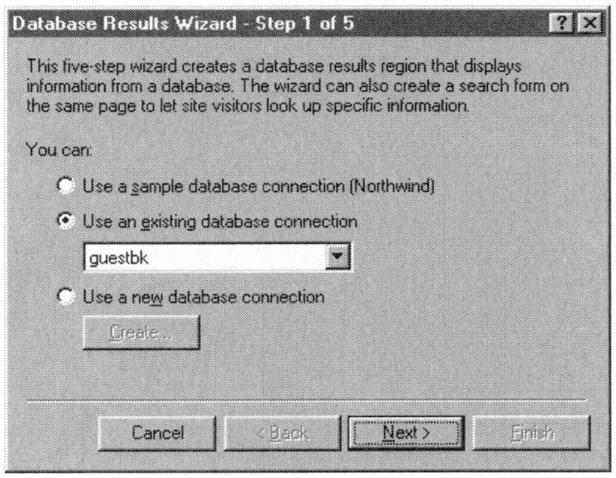

FIGURE 22-9.

The first dialog box in the Database Results Wizard selects the database connection that will provide the displayed data.

3 Click Next to display the second dialog box in the Database Results Wizard, shown in Figure 22-10.

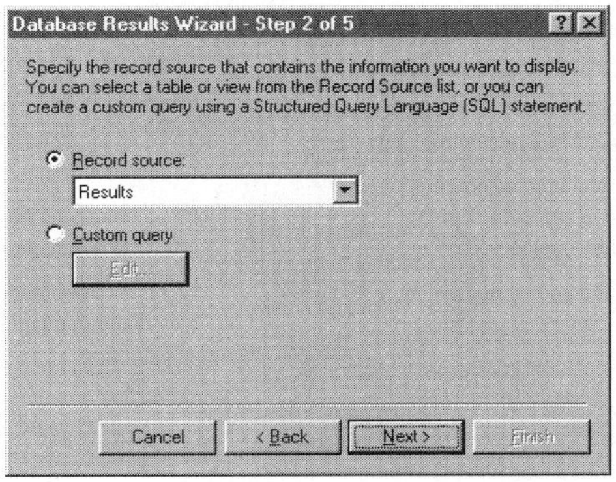

FIGURE 22-10.

The second database Results screen specifies the table or query that provides the displayed data.

- **Record Source** selects a table or query from the database connection you chose in the previous screen.

- **Custom Query** enables the Edit button, which displays a dialog box where you can enter a SQL statement. We'll examine this option later.

For the example, we'll choose the Results table as the record source for this query. This is the one and only table in the *guestbk* database.

4 Figure 22-11 shows the wizard's third dialog box. There are two options:

- **Edit List** controls which fields the Web page displays.

- **More Options** controls selection criteria, sequence, default criteria values, and some additional display options.

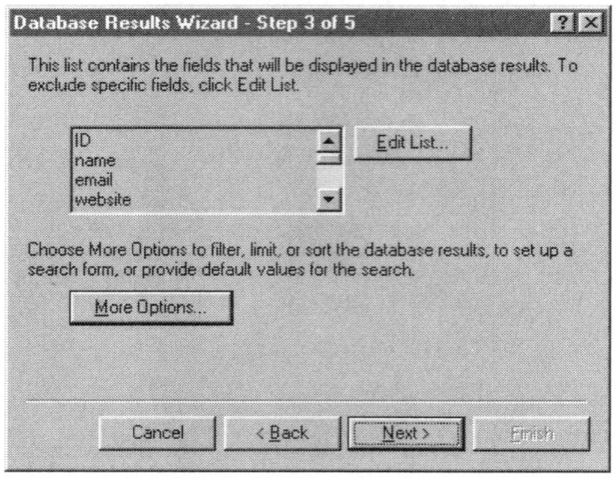

FIGURE 22-11.

The Edit List button controls which table fields the Web page will display. The More Options button controls selection criteria, reporting order, default criteria, and other display options.

5 Click the Edit List button to display the dialog box shown in Figure 22-12.

- **Available Fields** lists fields from the database table that don't currently appear on the Web page.

- **Displayed Fields** lists fields that do appear on the Web page, and specifies their order.

- **Add** moves any selected fields out of Available Fields and into Displayed Fields.

- **Remove** moves any selected fields out of Displayed Fields and into Available Fields.

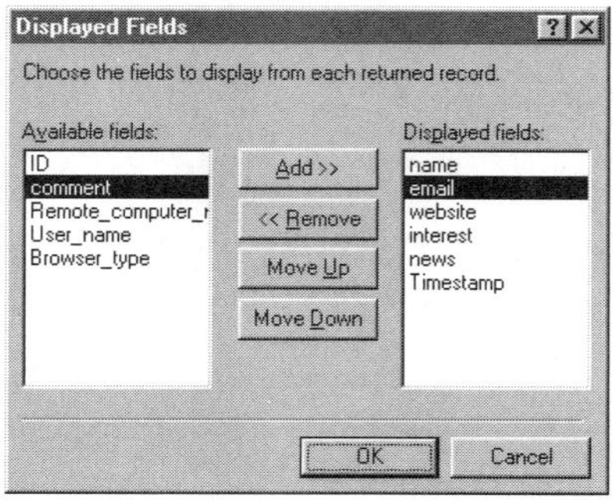

FIGURE 22-12.

Clicking the Edit List button in Figure 22-11 displays this dialog box, which selects and orders fields for appearance on the Web Page.

- **Move Up** moves any selected Displayed Fields one position higher in the list.

- **Move Down** moves any selected Displayed Fields one position lower in the list.

  For the example, we'll select and arrange the fields as shown in Figure 22-12.

6 Clicking the More Options button displays the dialog box shown in Figure 22-13.

- **Criteria** controls which records from the database table, based on their data values, are reported.

- **Ordering** controls the order in which records appear— from top to bottom—on the Web page.

- **Defaults** will be dimmed unless you've specified criteria. In the presence of criteria, it provides substitutes for criteria left blank.

- **Limit Number Of Returned Records To,** if turned on, limits the number of records displayed on one Web page. This option provides no way to view additional records that may have been suppressed.

- **Message To Display If No Records Are Returned** specifies the text FrontPage will display if there are no database records to display.

  For the example, we won't use any of these options. However, we'll review them in more detail later.

? SEE ALSO

For more information about using advanced query settings, see "Using Advanced Query Settings," page 750.

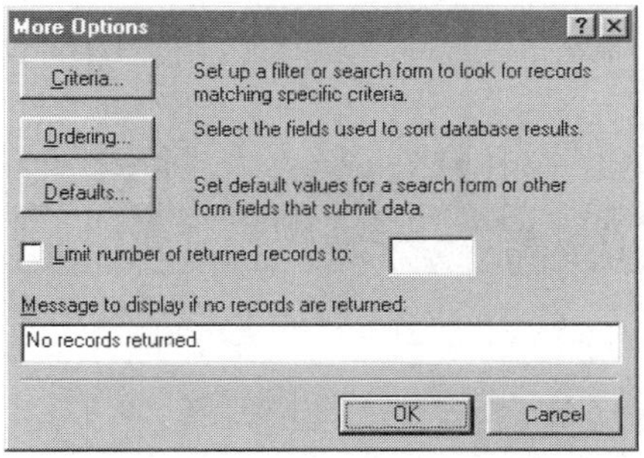

FIGURE 22-13.

Clicking the More Options button in Figure 22-13 displays this dialog box.

7 Figure 22-14 shows the fourth dialog box in the Database Results Wizard, which controls layout of the displayed data.

- **Choose Formatting Options For The Records Returned By The Query** determines how FrontPage will display each record returned by the query. There are two overall formats, each with variations.

  Table - One Record Per Row means FrontPage will create an HTML table where each column corresponds to a field in the database and each row contains these fields from a different record. Figure 22-14 shows this option selected. Table 22-1 lists additional options for this choice.

  List - One Record Per List means FrontPage will display each field on a separate line, with formatting breaks between records. To select this option, drop down the list box shown in Figure 22-14 and select it. Table 22-2 lists additional options.

FIGURE 22-14.

The fourth dialog box in the Database Results wizard controls arrangement of the displayed data.

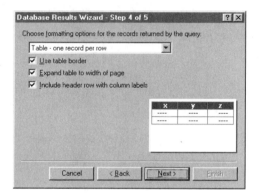

8 The Database Results Wizard's final dialog box provides another way of limiting the number of records displayed per page. It appears in Figure 22-15.

TABLE 22-1. Formatting Options for Table - One Record Per Row

Option	Effect (If Turned On)
User Table Border	Specifies that the table will have borders.
Expand Table To Width Of Page	Sets the table's width to 100%.
Include Header Row With Column Labels	Provides a row of column headings above the table. The captions are the field names.

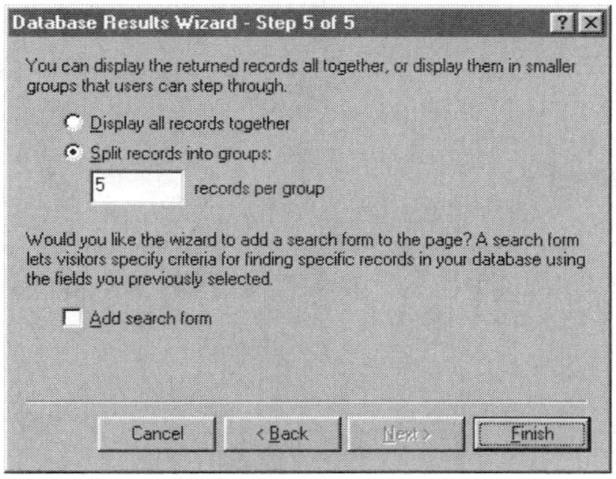

FIGURE 22-15.

The wizard's last dialog box displays either an unlimited number of records per Web page or a set number with forward and back buttons.

- **Display All Records Together** displays all selected records on one Web page.

- **Split Records Into Groups** displays a limited number of records per Web page. FrontPage creates first, last, forward, and back buttons so the Web visitor can move through the database. The Records Per Group text box specifies the number of records per page.

- **Add Search Form** appears only if you specified—via options in earlier panels—that values from HTML form fields should limit the query. The next section in this chapter describes how to do this.

For the example, we'll choose 5 records per page.

TABLE 22-2.   Formatting Options for List - One Record Per List

Option	Effect (If Turned On)
Add Labels For All Field Values	Precedes each field value with the corresponding field name.
Place Horizontal Separator Between Records	Displays a horizontal rule between each record.

List Options:
   Paragraphs
   Line Breaks
   Bullet List
   Numbered List
   Definition List
   Table
   Formatted
   Text Fields
   Scrolling Text Fields
	Determines the paragraph style used for fields within a record.

Clicking Finish on the final Database Results dialog box creates the Web page shown in Figure 22-16. The two shaded table rows are just for information and don't appear on the Web visitor's browser. The middle row is the Database Results region, which repeats once per record displayed.

FIGURE 22-16.

This is the Web page that results from the choices described in this section.

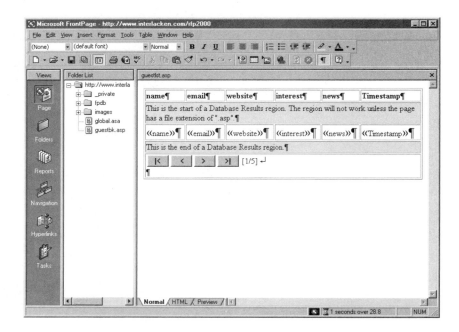

FrontPage Preview mode won't display data in pages containing Database Results regions; Preview mode actually displays Web pages temporarily saved to disk and doesn't have access to all the facilities of a Web server. To view the page in action, save it with an ASP file name extension in an executable folder in a server-based Web, and then choose the Preview In Browser command or toolbar button. Figure 22-8, on page 740, shows the Web page displayed after these actions are taken.

Refining Database Queries

? SEE ALSO

For more information about Structured Query Language (SQL), see "SQL," page 775.

Selecting Record Source in Figure 22-10 generates the simplest possible database query; it selects all fields from all records in the given table, and presents them in the table's default sequence. FrontPage provides two alternatives that query the database with more specific options.

■ Using the Custom Query option in Figure 22-10 (the second panel of the Database Results Wizard), you can query the database any way you want by writing your own SQL statement.

■ Using the Record Source option in Figure 22-10, you can still specify complex queries using the More Options option in Figure 22-11 (the third panel of the Database Results Wizard).

- The Criteria button in the resulting dialog box (Figure 22-13) can select records based on comparisons to either form fields or constants.

- The Ordering button in the same dialog box controls the sequence in which the records will appear.

Figure 22-17 shows the type of Web page these techniques can produce. Entering a Category ID in the text box and clicking Submit Query displays products in that category, in Product ID order. The next two sections will describe each alternative in detail.

> **NOTE**

The formatting in Figure 22-17 was applied manually, using a combination of table attributes and CSS properties. For clarity in the example, the column headings remain equal to the database column names. This is the default, but something you'd want to change in a real application. Changing the column headings is a simple matter of editing them as text in FrontPage.

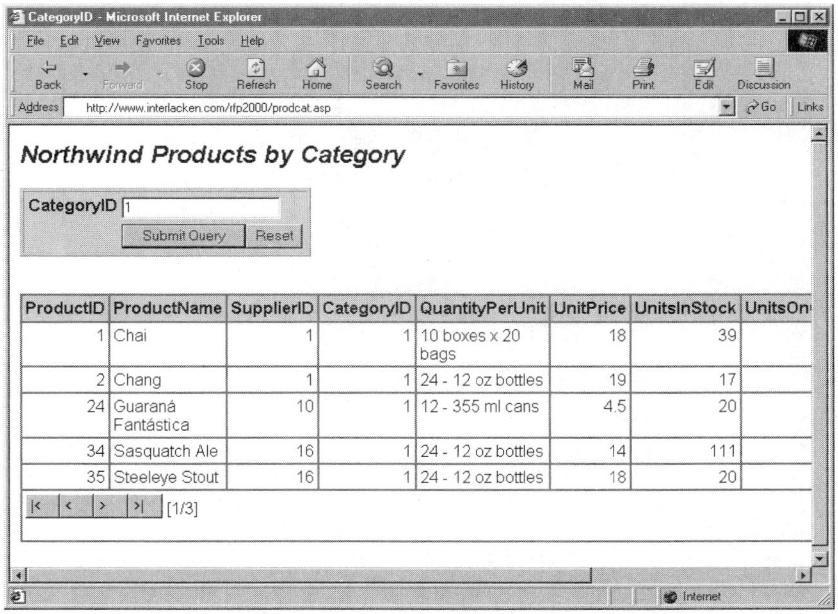

FIGURE 22-17.

Entering a Category ID and clicking Submit Query displays matching records in Product ID order.

Northwind Products by Category

CategoryID [1]

Submit Query   Reset

ProductID	ProductName	SupplierID	CategoryID	QuantityPerUnit	UnitPrice	UnitsInStock	UnitsOn
1	Chai	1	1	10 boxes x 20 bags	18	39	
2	Chang	1	1	24 - 12 oz bottles	19	17	
24	Guaraná Fantástica	10	1	12 - 355 ml cans	4.5	20	
34	Sasquatch Ale	16	1	24 - 12 oz bottles	14	111	
35	Steeleye Stout	16	1	24 - 12 oz bottles	18	20	

|< < > >| [1/3]

Using Custom Queries

Selecting Custom Query and clicking the Edit button in Figure 22-10 displays the dialog box pictured in Figure 22-18. This option provides great flexibility by accepting any SQL statement you wish to enter, but it requires knowledge of SQL.

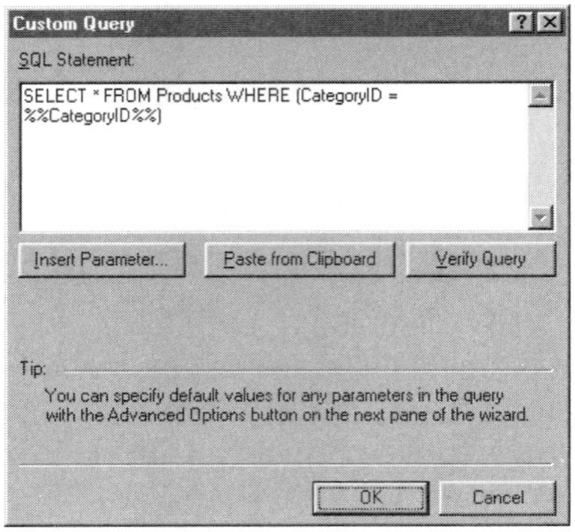

FIGURE 22-18.

The Custom Query function permits entering SQL statements either by hand or by pasting from the Clipboard.

- **SQL Statement** contains a Structured Query Language command. It tells the database software what data to retrieve.

- **Insert Parameter** displays the dialog box of Figure 22-19, where you can enter the name of an HTML form field.

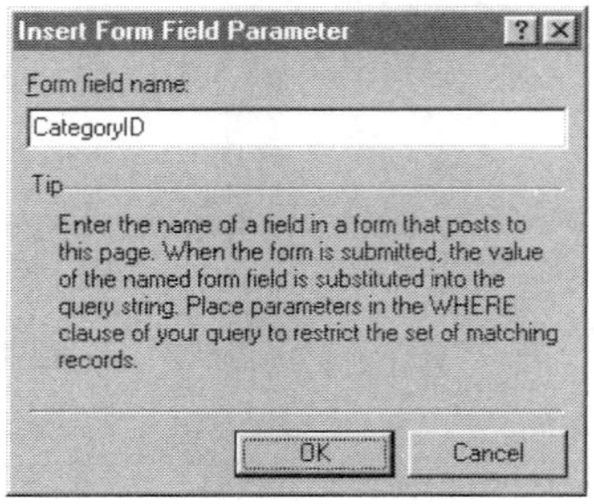

FIGURE 22-19.

This dialog box specifies the name of an HTML form field whose value will become part of the SQL statement.

- **Paste From Clipboard** copies any text currently in the Clipboard to the SQL Statement text box.

- **Verify Query** submits the current SQL statement to the database software and reports any errors. This permits testing the query before closing the dialog box.

Be sure to set the insertion point properly before clicking the Insert Parameter button—usually where a constant would appear in a HAVING

For more information about using form fields to supply query values, see "Using Form Fields to Supply Query Values," page 753.

or WHERE expression. FrontPage will insert the HTML form field name based on the insertion point's location before you click the Insert Parameter button.

If you wish, you can skip pressing the Insert Parameter button and just insert the form field code yourself. Just type two percent signs, the name of the form field, and two more percent signs wherever you want the form field's value to appear.

⭐ TIP

> Be sure to surround any form field parameters with the usual delimiters required by SQL. Values compared to character fields must be enclosed in parentheses, while values compared to numeric fields must not.

The Paste From Clipboard button permits creating and debugging queries in Microsoft Access, and then transferring them to FrontPage. Here's the procedure.

1 Open the database (or a copy of it) in Microsoft Access 2000.

2 Open or create a query that displays the data you want. Use constants in place of any form field values you plan to use.

3 Choose SQL View from the View menu or from the View button on the Query Design toolbar. Figure 22-20 shows this operation in progress.

FIGURE 22-20.

Once you get a query working in Microsoft Access, you can display the SQL code and copy it to the Clipboard for pasting into the Database Results Wizard.

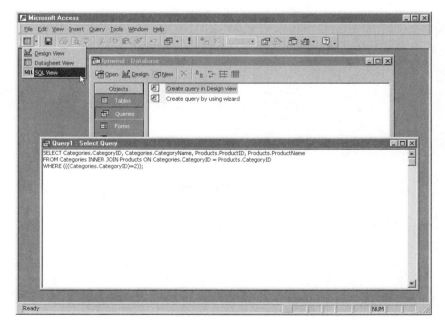

4 Select all the text in the SQL statement, and then copy it to the Clipboard by choosing Copy from the Edit menu, by pressing Ctrl+C, or by pressing Ctrl+Insert.

5 Switch to FrontPage and display the Custom Query dialog box (Figure 22-18).

6 Click the Paste From Clipboard button to insert the SQL statement.

Using Advanced Query Settings

Writing SQL statements provides total control over selection of records from a database table and the order in which they appear. The catch, of course, is that you have to know SQL. This section describes another way to control record selection and ordering—one slightly less flexible but requiring no SQL proficiency.

To use this method, advance to the third dialog box of the Database Results Wizard (Figure 22-10), and then click the More Options button. This displays the More Options dialog box shown in Figure 22-11.

NOTE

If you clicked the Custom Query button in Figure 22-11, the Advanced button in Figure 22-13 will be dimmed. This is because a SQL statement entered as a custom query might contain options the Advanced dialog box can't preserve.

Clicking the Criteria button in Figure 22-13 displays the Criteria dialog box shown in Figure 22-21. The list headed Select All Records Matching These Criteria lists criteria currently in effect. The buttons below it modify the list.

Criteria
Select all records matching these criteria:
Field
Comparison
Value
And/Or
CategoryID
Equals
[CategoryID]
And
Add...
Modify...
Remove...
OK
Cancel

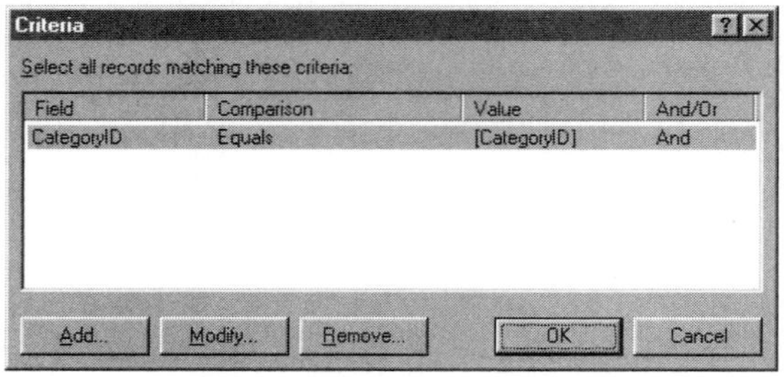

FIGURE 22-21.
Clicking the Criteria button in Figure 22-13 displays this dialog box, which controls selection of database records for display.

- The **Add** button displays the dialog box shown in Figure 22-22, which adds a new criterion to the list.
- The **Modify** button displays a dialog box very similar to Figure 22-22, where you can change the properties of an existing criterion.

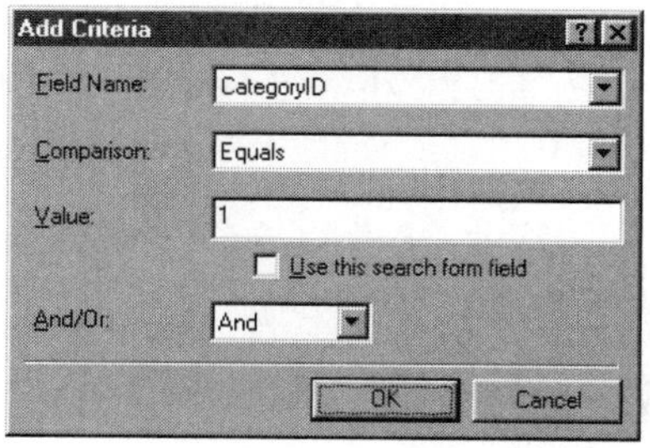

FIGURE 22-22.

This dialog box specifies selection criteria for database records.

- The **Remove** button deletes the currently selected criterion from the list.

Here are the fields that control selection of database records.

- **Field Name.** Select the field whose value you want to test.

- **Comparison.** Specify the operator for the comparison: Equals, Not Equal, Less Than, and so forth.

- **Value.** There are three ways to use this field.

  - If you wish to select records based on the value of an HTML form field, turn on the box titled Use This Search Form Field and enter the name of the form field in the box above.

  - If you wish to select records based on a fixed value, turn off the box titled Use This Search Form Field and enter the fixed value in the box above.

  - If you chose a Comparison operator of Is Null or Not Null, the Value field will be dimmed.

NOTE

A null value in a database field means the field currently has no value. This is different from a numeric field being zero, or a character field containing a zero-length string: in both those cases, the field *has* a value. A field whose value is null has no known value: not even zero or an empty string.

- **And/Or.** Choose And if other criteria, as well as this one, must be true for the record to be selected. Choose Or if this is one of several criteria, any one of which, if true, is sufficient to select the record.

The Ordering button in Figure 22-13 displays the dialog box pictured in Figure 22-23. Each field in the current database query initially appears in the Available Fields columns, and initially has no effect on sorting the results of the query. The Sort Order column lists fields that do affect the order of query results. Fields higher in the column have precedence over fields below, and an Up or Down arrow icon indicates ascending or descending sequence for each field.

- The **Add** button moves any selected fields out of the Available Fields column and into the Sort Order column.

- The **Remove** button moves any selected fields out of the Sort Order column and into the Available Fields column.

- The **Move Up** button moves one selected Sort Order field one position higher in the list. This and the next two buttons will be dimmed unless one and only one Sort Order field is selected.

- The **Move Down** button moves one selected Sort Order field one position lower in the list.

- The **Change Sort** button toggles one selected Sort Order field between ascending and descending sequence.

The Defaults button in the More Options dialog box (Figure 22-13 on page 743) specifies default values for criteria received from HTML forms. That is, if the HTML form value is blank or missing, the default supplied here takes effect. The dialog box in the background of Figure 22-24 results from clicking the Defaults button.

Initially, the Input Parameters list contains each field having a defined criteria (Figure 22-21) based on an HTML form value. To supply a default value for any field, either double-click it or select it and click Edit. The result will be the dialog box in the foreground of Figure 22-24. Enter the default value, and then click OK.

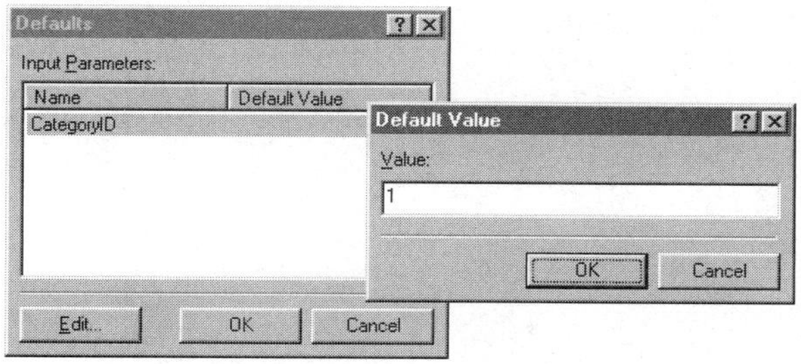

FIGURE 22-24.

The Defaults dialog box lists each database field.

Using Form Fields to Supply Query Values

If you specified database selection criteria based on HTML form fields— either by entering parameters in the Custom Query dialog box (Figure 22-18) or criteria in the Criteria dialog box (Figure 22-21)—the final dialog box in the Database Results Wizard (Figure 22-15) will contain a check box titled Add Search Form. Turning this check box on will create an HTML form like the one that appears near the top of Figure 22-25.

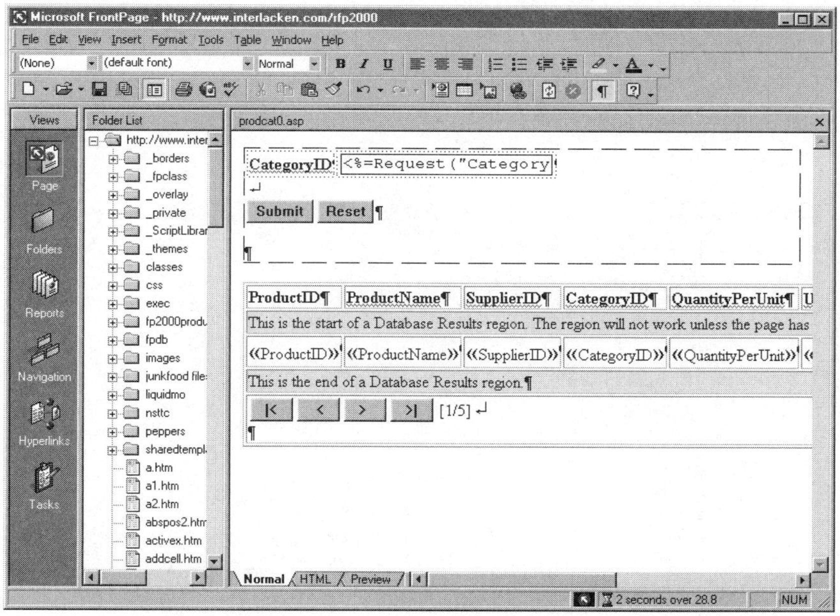

FIGURE 22-25.

The HTML form at the top of this page controls which records appear in the Database Results region below it.

This Web page handles both input and output of database queries. The Web visitor enters a CategoryID, clicks Submit, and, as seen in Figure 22-26, the form's Action property submits the form value to the same ASP page that contains the form.

FIGURE 22-26.

Pressing the Submit button on this Active Server Page re-executes the same page. The results will be different if either the form input or the database has changed.

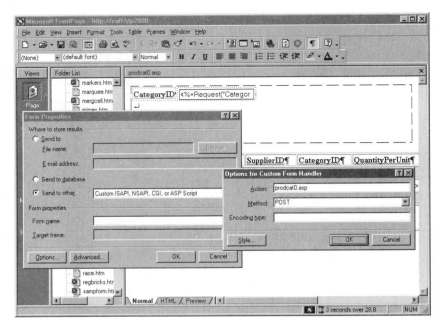

Figure 22-27 shows the properties of the text box from Figure 22-25. Its name is CategoryID, the same as the name of the database field it selects. The use of like names is a convention followed by the Database Results Wizard, and not a firm requirement.

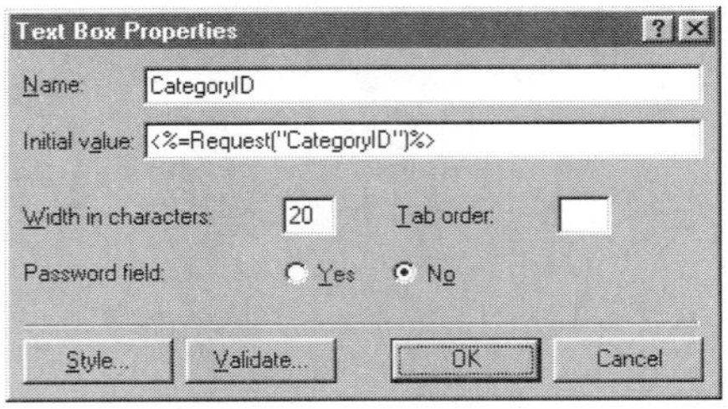

FIGURE 22-27.

The text box in Figure 22-26 has these properties.

The Initial Value field might look a bit peculiar until you realize it's a piece of Active Server Page code. When the Web server processes the ASP page, the expression <%=Request("CategoryID")%> obtains the form field value named CategoryID and writes it out as part of the Web page. Thus, the text box is always initialized to its previous value.

Nothing prevents having the HTML form and the Database Results region on different Web pages. To make them separate pages, just cut the HTML form out of the database results page and paste it wherever you want. Adjust the relative URL in the form's Action property if necessary.

If you keep the HTML form and the Database Results region on the same page, be sure to specify defaults for all input fields used in database queries. This is because the Web server will run the database query every time it transmits the ASP page—including the first time, before the Web visitor has entered any query fields. Without default field value, the page will display an error message rather than any sort of reasonable data.

Re-creating and Formatting Database Results Regions

You can rerun the Database Results Wizard at will simply by double-clicking any part of the Database Results region that isn't another Front-Page component or HTML element. You can also rerun the wizard by right-clicking the Database Results region and choosing Database Results Properties, or by selecting the region and choosing Properties from the Format menu.

Objects displayed as <<ProductID>>, <<ProductName>>, <<SupplierID>>, and so forth in Figure 22-25 are Database Column Value components. These components are valid only inside a Database Results region, and each one contains the name of a database field to display. Whenever the Database Results region has a record to display, it replaces each Database Column Value component with the value of its corresponding field.

Here are the steps to insert a new Database Column Value component.

1 Set the insertion point where you want the component to appear. However, it must be within a Database Results region.

2 Select Database from the Insert menu, and then select Column Value. The dialog box pictured in Figure 22-28 will appear.

3 Drop down the list titled Column To Display and select the field you want displayed.

4 If the database field contains HTML code, turn on the check box titled Common Value ContainsHTML..

5 Click OK.

FIGURE 22-28.

This dialog box configures the database field a Database Column Value component will display.

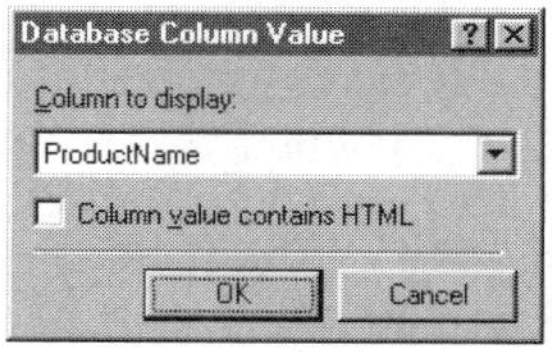

To modify a Database Column Value component, double-click it, right-click it and choose Database Column Value Properties from the pop-up menu, or select it and choose Properties from the Format menu. This again displays the dialog box of Figure 22-28, permitting modification.

You can format Database Results regions and their accompanying forms as much as you like, but keep in mind that rerunning the wizard may discard your formatting when it overwrites the Database Results region. You can never solve this problem completely, but here are some ways to minimize it.

- First get the Database Results region working as you want it, and then worry about formatting.

- As much as possible, format the Database Results region using CSS styles. Because CSS styles appear in the <HEAD> section and not intermixed with the HTML, overwriting the HTML won't overwrite the CSS styles.

- FrontPage uses a fake HTML attribute called BOTID to associate the HTML form with its Database Results region. Whenever called upon to generate an input form, the wizard inserts BOTID="X" into the <FORM> tag, where X is an arbitrary number. BOTID isn't a valid attribute for the <FORM> tag, so browsers and other programs will ignore it. However, the Database Results Wizard uses this attribute to locate and replace the correct HTML form.

  If you have trouble with the Database Results Wizard replacing the wrong form (or not replacing the correct one), view the page in HTML view and look for BOTID attributes.

Figure 22-17 shows a partially formatted version of the page appearing in Figure 22-25.

Configuring a FrontPage Data Connection

(2000) Unlike previous versions of FrontPage, FrontPage 2000 reads and writes database information through named *connections*. A database connection names a Microsoft Access database located in the current Web, an Open Database Connectivity (ODBC) Data Source on the Web server, or a direct connection to some other database. Connections may at first strike you as yet another abstract entity between you and your data, but they provide a number of advantages.

- You can define all the information about a database once, and then use that definition in multiple Web pages.

- You can create or upload databases to your FrontPage Web, and then access them with Web pages, without assistance from the server administrator. For example, you don't need the administrator to set up an ODBC Data Source.

IV

■ You can access databases in your Web, ODBC Data Sources on the Web server, and any other databases available to the Web server, all in a uniform way.

Whenever you drag and drop a Microsoft Access file into Folder List or view, FrontPage will offer to create a database connection.

If you're planning to use an Access database stored within the same FrontPage Web, first create it or upload it to the desired location—somewhere your Web visitors won't find it by accident. The /fpdb folder is a good choice. Then:

1 Choose Web Settings from the Tools menu.

2 Click the Database tab. This displays the dialog box shown in Figure 22-29.

FIGURE 22-29.
The Database Web Settings tab lists a Web's currently defined database connections.

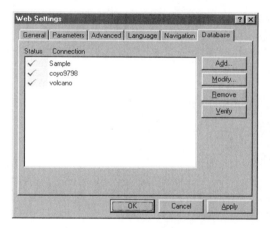

3 Click the Add button, displaying the dialog box shown in Figure 22-30.

FIGURE 22-30.
This dialog box adds a new database connection to a Web.

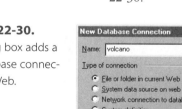

- **Name** is the identifier you plan to use when accessing the connection from a Web page. Simple names of 6 to 8 characters are best.

- **File Or Folder In Current Web** connects to a database in the current FrontPage Web.

- **Data Source On Web Server** connects to an ODBC System Data Source Name defined on the Web server.

- **Other Database Server On The Network** connects to another database driver installed on the Web server.

- **Custom Definition** connects to an ODBC data source using connection data you specify manually.

- **Browse** displays a dialog box for selecting the specific database.

4 Click OK.

The Browse button in Figure 22-30 displays a different dialog box, depending on the Type Of Connection selection. Clicking the Browse button after choosing File Or Folder In Current Web displays the dialog box shown in Figure 22-31.

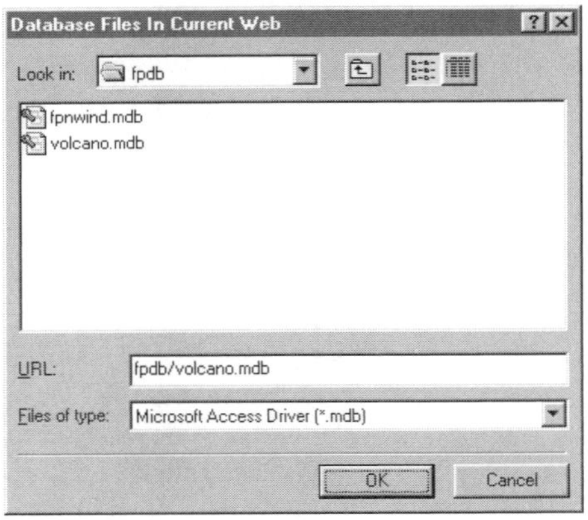

FIGURE 22-31.

This dialog box locates a database in the current FrontPage Web.

- **Look In** selects folders in the current Web.

- **URL** specifies the database for this connection. Clicking a file listed in the center of the dialog box updates this field.

- **Files Of Type** specifies the type of database. This can be Access, dBase, FoxPro, Paradox, or any file-oriented database with a driver installed on the Web server.

🛈 **SEE ALSO**

For more information about ODBC Data Sources, see "Configuring ODBC Data Sources," page 761.

If you click Browse after choosing Data Source On Web Server, FrontPage displays the dialog box of Figure 22-32. The listed items are ODBC System Data Source Names defined in the ODBC32 Control Panel applet on the computer where the FrontPage Web resides. Select the Data Source you want, then click OK.

Clicking Browse after choosing Other Database Server On The Network displays the dialog box pictured in Figure 22-33. Select the type of database system, specify the server where it runs, and enter the name of the database on that server.

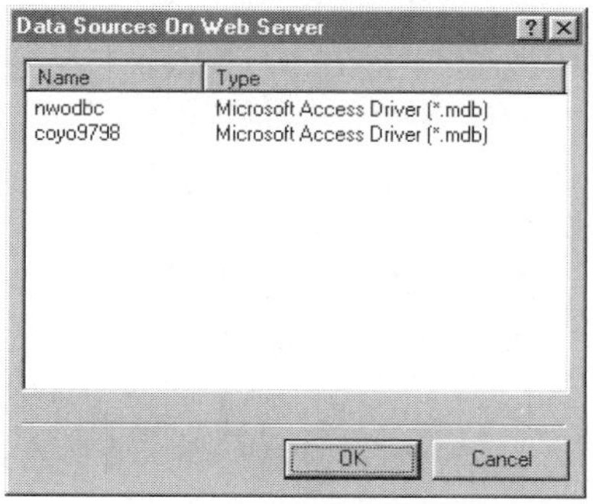

FIGURE 22-32.

This dialog box locates an ODBC System Data Source Name defined on the Web server.

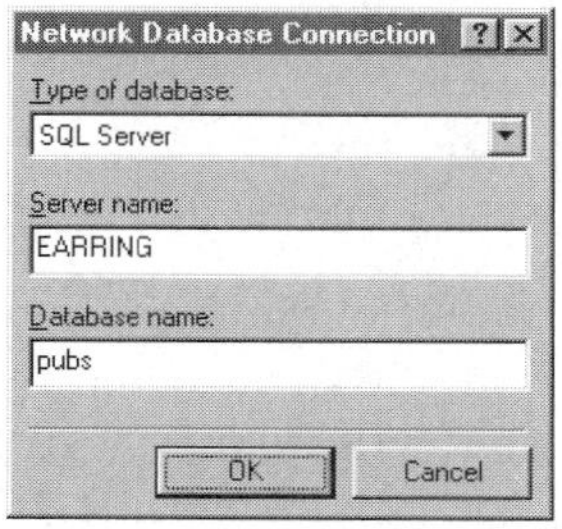

FIGURE 22-33.

This dialog box locates a database through client software installed on the Web server.

Clicking Browse after choosing Custom Definition displays a dialog box very similar to that of Figure 22-31, except that it searches for an ODBC File Data Source Name. Such files have a *dsn* file name extension.

Clicking the Advanced button on the New Database Connection dialog box (Figure 22-30) is seldom necessary, especially with file oriented databases, but it displays the dialog box shown in Figure 22-34. You can obtain this information from the creator of the database or, in enterprise environments, from the database administrator.

- **Authorization** specifies logon credentials needed to access the database.

- **Username** is a logon account permitted to use the database.

- **Password** is the authentication code assigned to the given account.

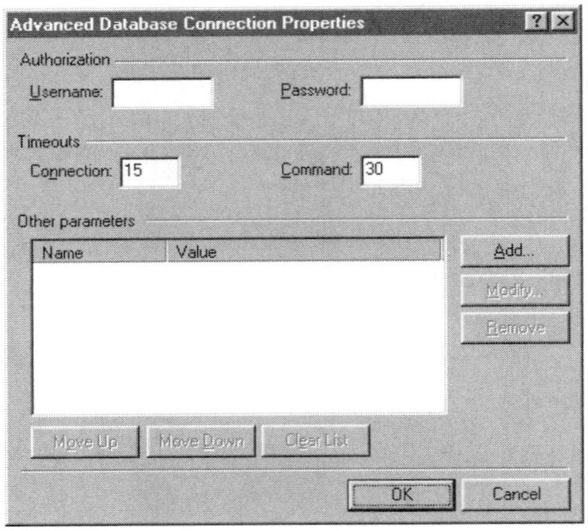

FIGURE 22-34.

Clicking the Advanced button in Figure 22-30 displays the additional options in this dialog box.

■ **Timeouts** specifies time limits that, if exceeded, will cancel a database operation.

- **Connection** specifies the number of seconds allowable for opening a connection to the database.

- **Command** specifies the number of seconds allowable for completing a database command—a query, for example.

■ **Other Parameters** is a list of named values required by the database driver. The Add, Modify, and Remove buttons control individual parameters. The Move Up and Move Down buttons reorder selected items in the list, and the Clear List button removes all entries.

The Other Parameters block will be differrent if you chose Custom Connection in the New Database Connection dialog box. Rather than a list of named values, the Other Parameters block will present a text box for entering the custom connection string, and a drop-down list box for specifying the cursor location: Client, Server, or None.

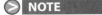 **NOTE**

In database terminology, the cursor is a pointer that keeps track of the current record position. It has nothing to do with the cursor on a computer screen.

The remaining buttons in the Database Web Settings tab (Figure 22-29) are Modify, Remove, and Verify.

- **Modify** displays a Database Connection Properties dialog box identical to Figure 22-30. This updates an existing database connection.

- **Remove** deletes the database connection.

- **Verify** attempts a connection to the database and reports the results. A check mark means the connection succeeded, while a broken link means the connection failed. Unverified connections have a question mark icon.

Configuring ODBC Data Sources

FrontPage database connectors define database settings once—at the Web level—for use by any page in the same Web. Likewise, an ODBC Data Source defines database settings once for use by any application on the entire server.

(X) CAUTION

> If all usage for a particular database occurs within a single Web, put the database inside that Web and provide access through a simple database connector. If multiple Webs—or a mixture of Web pages and background processes—need to use the database, it probably makes sense to define the database as an ODBC Data Source.

Think of ODBC (Open Database Connectivity) as a collection of definitions and software drivers that isolate applications from differences among database systems. An ODBC Data Source, using a single name, identifies the type, location, and operating parameters of any database supporting ODBC. The procedures and dialog boxes needed to define ODBC Data Sources vary, depending on the operating system, the type of database, and the version of ODBC itself.

There are two kinds of ODBC Data Source Names (DSN): User and System. User Data Source Names are in effect only when a certain user is logged in to the local system. System Data Source Names are in effect for all users and background processes, even when no one's logged in. Web page access requires System Data Source Names.

Opening the ODBC Data Source Administrator

The process for defining a System Data Source Name is very similar for Windows 95, Windows 98, and Windows NT. To start, open the Control Panel and double-click the 32-bit ODBC icon, as shown here.

The dialog box shown in Figure 22-35 will appear. Selecting the System DSN tab displays these options.

- **Add** creates a new System Data Source Name.

- **Remove** deletes an existing System DSN. First select the System DSN you want to delete, and then click the Remove button.

- **Configure** displays (and optionally modifies) an existing System DSN. Select the System DSN you desire, and then click the Configure button. Double-clicking a listed System DSN has the same effect.

In the procedures described below, you'll click the Add button and then select a driver you wish to configure.

Defining a Data Source Name for Microsoft Access

If the Data Source names a Microsoft Access database, proceed this way:

1 Click the Add button on the System DSN tab of the ODBC Data Source Administrator dialog box shown in Figure 22-35.

FIGURE 22-35.

This is the ODBC Data Source Administration dialog box.

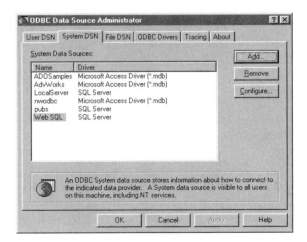

2 Select Microsoft Access Driver from the list of ODBC Drivers displayed in the dialog box shown in Figure 22-37, and then click the Finish button. (Alternatively, double-click the Microsoft Access Driver entry.)

3 The ODBC Microsoft Access Setup dialog box shown in Figure 22-36 will appear next.

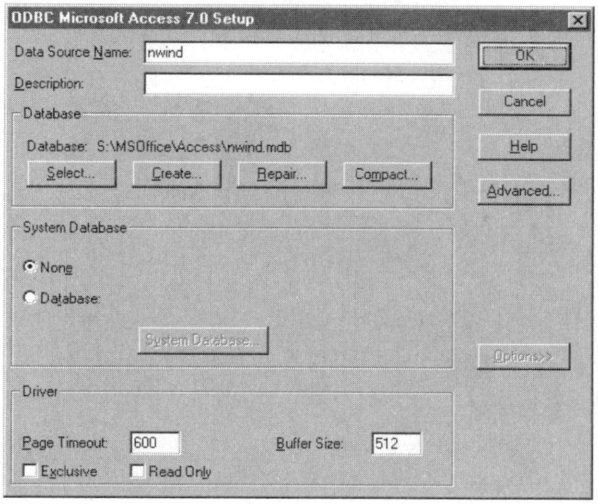

FIGURE 22-36.

This dialog box defines a Microsoft Access ODBC System Data Source Name.

This is the dialog box where you actually define the Microsoft Access System DSN. Enter the following options:

- **Data Source Name** supplies the name that Active Server Pages and other processes will specify to access the database. Short, meaningful names are best.

- **Description** provides a brief text description. This entry is optional.

- **Database** specifies the name of the Access database and provides certain management functions.

TIP

If an Access database isn't on the local system, specify a universal naming convention (UNC) name. Don't use mapped drive letters. Drive mappings change as different users log on and off the computer, and when no one's logged on there are no drive mappings in effect at all. UNC names have the form \\<computer name>\<share name>\<path>\<file name>.

Select browses the local or network file system to locate and select the target Access database. An Access database normally has an MDB file name extension.

Create creates a new, empty database containing no tables.

Repair performs consistency checks and attempts to repair structural problems in the database.

Compact recovers unused space from the database file.

System Database controls use of a system database in conjunction with the normal Access database. The system database stores security and option settings for Access databases.

None signifies that the Access database isn't controlled through a system database.

Database signifies that a system database controls the Access database. Click the System Database button to specify the system database's location.

4   Click the Options button to display the following data fields that control operating parameters specific to the Microsoft Access driver.

- **Page Timeout** specifies a time limit for completing ODBC operations. The default value is normally adequate.

- **Buffer Size** specifies the number of bytes available for ODBC buffering. The default value is normally adequate.

- **Exclusive,** if turned on, opens the database for exclusive use.

- **Read Only,** if turned on, opens the database for read-only use.

5   When done, click the OK button.

Defining a Data Source Name for SQL Server

To define a System DSN for a SQL Server database, proceed as follows:

1   Click the Add button on the System DSN tab of the ODBC Data Source Administrator dialog box shown in Figure 22-35.

2   The Create New Data Source dialog box shown in Figure 22-37 will appear next. Select the SQL Server entry from the list and then click the Finish button. (Alternatively, double-click the SQL Server entry.)

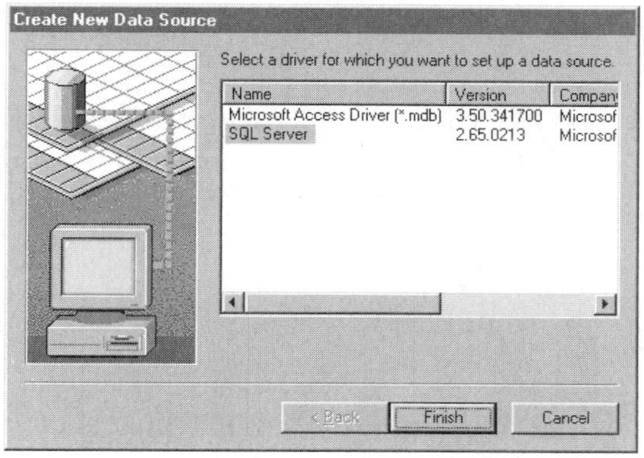

FIGURE 22-37.

This Windows NT dialog box specifies the driver for a new ODBC System DSN.

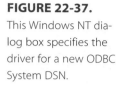

3 The ODBC SQL Server Setup dialog box shown in Figure 22-38 will appear next. This is the dialog box where you actually define the SQL Server System DSN.

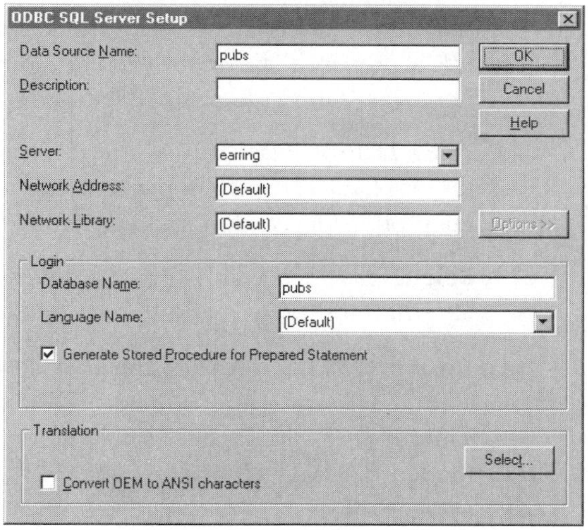

FIGURE 22-38.

This dialog box defines a SQL Server ODBC System Data Source Name.

Enter the following options:

- **Data Source Name** supplies the name that Active Server Pages and other processes will specify to access the database. Short, meaningful names are best.

- **Description** provides a brief text description. This entry is optional.

- **Server** identifies the name of the computer where SQL Server runs. Hand-type the computer name or select it from the drop-down list.

- **Network Address** gives the network location of the named SQL Server. Normally, this can be (Default).

- **Network Library** names the Net-Library DLL the SQL Server driver should use to communicate with the network software. Normally, this can be (Default).

  Click the Options button to display the following data fields.

- **Login.** This section specifies information required for connecting to the database.

  Database Name gives the name of the SQL Server database you wish to access.

  Language Name sets SQL Server to use English or another available language. Typically this can be (Default).

  Generate Stored Procedure For Prepared Statement, if turned on, creates stored procedure code for common functions, saves it on the server, and compiles it. If the box is off, a prepared statement is stored and executed at execution time. On is the normal setting.

- **Translation.** This section controls translation between different character sets. Translation can also perform tasks like encryption/decryption and compression/decompression.

  Select provides a list of installed translators. However, usually no translation is required.

  Convert OEM To ANSI Characters should be turned off. Turn it on only if the SQL Server client and server use the same non-ANSI character set. When on, this converts extended database characters to ANSI for use by Windows applications.

4 When done, click the OK button.

Resolving ODBC Issues

If the Data Source is intended for some other type of database, use the procedures above as a general guide. Also, consult the online help or documentation for the applicable ODBC driver.

Completing this process allows any ODBC application, including a Database Results region, to open and manipulate the database in a uniform way based on a single identity—the System Data Source Name you assigned. ODBC determines the correct driver type, physical location, and name of the database from the information you supplied.

Be aware that ODBC drivers are updated frequently, and new versions tend to appear whenever you install database-related software. This might result in minor changes in the dialog box options and settings described above.

The number one cause of ODBC driver failure is mismatched versions. If you run into system-related problems, click the About button in the ODBC Data Source Administrator dialog box shown in Figure 22-35. If all the listed modules aren't the same version, replace them with a set that are the same.

Creating Web Applications with Access 2000

Microsoft Access 2000 includes two features capable of creating Web pages having database capability.

- **Data Access Pages** provide a high-function development and run-time environment for Web pages with database capability. You can design custom forms, incorporate scripting, and perform any database operation, including querying, inserting, updating, and deleting.

  Data Access Pages have two significant limitations. First, they work only with Internet Explorer 5.0 and above. Second, they don't use standard Web protocols for communication with the database. Using an Access database requires that each Web visitor have file sharing access to the database. Using the SQL Server database requires that each Web visitor have network access to the SQL Server database. Because of these restrictions, Data Access Pages are best suited to intranet applications.

- **Export As HTML Document Or Active Server Page** provides a way to publish database content on the Web. Saving a table, query, or report as HTML creates a static Web page; saving the same object as an Active Server Page creates a page that queries and lists the database interactively.

The next two sections will briefly describe these features and how they relate to FrontPage.

Building Data Access Pages

To begin working with Data Access Pages, open a database in Access 2000 and then click the Pages icon in the Objects bar. This will list any existing Data Access Pages, plus options to create a new Data Access Page manually, create a new Data Access Page by wizard, and edit an existing Data Access Page.

Figure 22-39 shows the first step in creating a Data Access Page by wizard. The user double-clicked the option Create Data Access Page By Using Wizard, then chose the Categories table, and then clicked the >> button to move all the fields in the Categories table to the Selected Fields column.

FIGURE 22-39.

This is the first step in creating an Access 2000 Data Access Page by wizard.

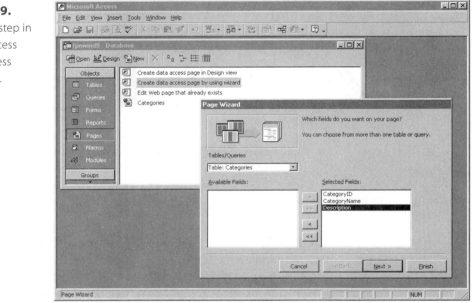

Taking all the defaults through the rest of the wizard produces the Data Access Page shown in Figure 22-40. The Toolbox toolbar, shown detached, contains a selection of objects you can add to the Data Access Page. The Alignment toolbar, also detached, aligns form elements relative to each other. The Field List window displays the objects in the current database.

When a Web visitor receives a Data Access Page, the form and each control will be ActiveX controls. Specifically, they will *not* be conventional HTML form fields. The ActiveX controls, plus code in Internet Explorer 5, will function not so much as a Web page, but more like a stand-alone Access 2000 application. Putting this functionality in a Web page avoids the problems in distributing stand-alone applications to large groups of PCs.

Unlike the FrontPage Save Results and Database Results components, Data Access Pages don't submit changes or commands to a Web server for processing. For Access 2000 databases, the Data Access Page opens the database as a file on the local PC or on a file server. Of these two options, most real-world applications will probably involve databases on a file server, and this makes drive-letter access to the Access database unreliable. The best approach is to put the database on a file server, open the database using a universal naming convention (UNC) file name, and then create the Data Access Page. Opening the database with a UNC in Access 2000 ensures that the Data Access Page, and therefore the eventual Web visitors, access the database using the same UNC name. A UNC file name like \\server1\myapp\mydatab1.mdb is independent of any drive mappings the Web visitor may have in effect.

FIGURE 22-40.
Access 2000 provides a rich development environment for Data Access Pages.

Aligns objects relative to each other

Itemizes objects in database

Provides ActiveX objects for insertion

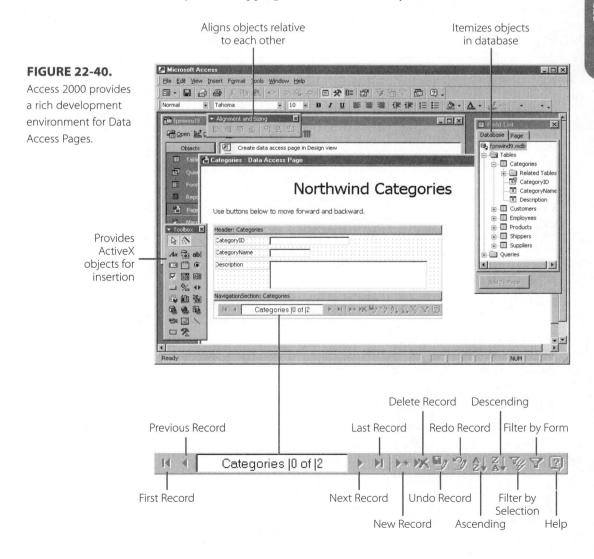

Delete Record

Descending

Previous Record

Last Record

Redo Record

Filter by Form

First Record

Next Record

Undo Record

Filter by Selection

Help

New Record

Ascending

TIP

> UNC provides a way for Windows computers to access files on a file server without mapping any drive letters. To open an Access database using UNC, first locate and double-click its file server in Network Neighborhood, then locate and double-click its sharename, and then locate and double-click the database file.

For SQL Server databases, each Web visitor will need the usual SQL-server-client software. For either type of database, normal client-server security applies.

Here's the procedure to transfer a Data Access Page into a FrontPage Web.

1 Test and debug the Data Access Page in Access 2000.

2 With the Data Access Page in the active window, choose Export from the File menu.

3 When the Export Data Access Page dialog box of Figure 22-41 appears:

    a Choose a temporary location on your PC.

    b Assign a file name.

    c Select Microsoft Access Data Access Page as the Save As Type.

    d Click the Save button.

4 Open the FrontPage Web.

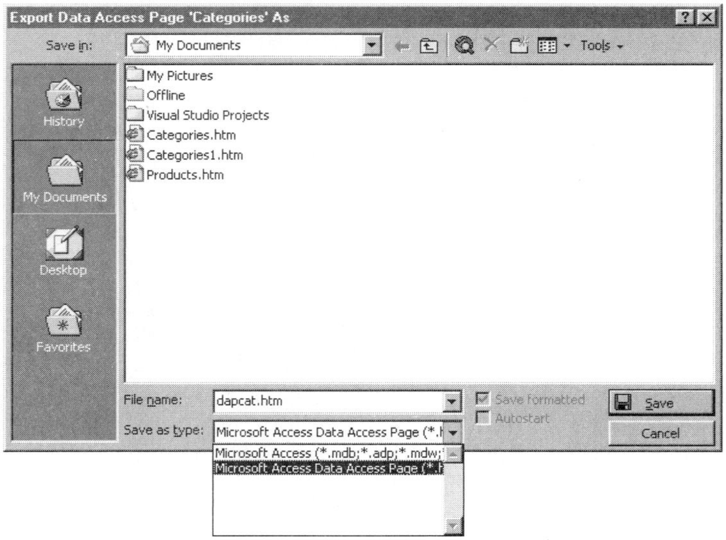

FIGURE 22-41.

To export a Data Access Page from Access 2000, choose Export from the File menu and then select Microsoft Access Data Access Page.

5   Import the Data Access Page by choosing Import from the File menu, or by dragging the file from Windows Explorer into the Folder List or view.

Figure 22-42 shows Internet Explorer displaying the Data Access Page developed in Figure 22-40. The Web author applied a theme, drew a table around the Data Access Page form, added the page to Navigation view, and inserted Page Banner and Navigation Bar components.

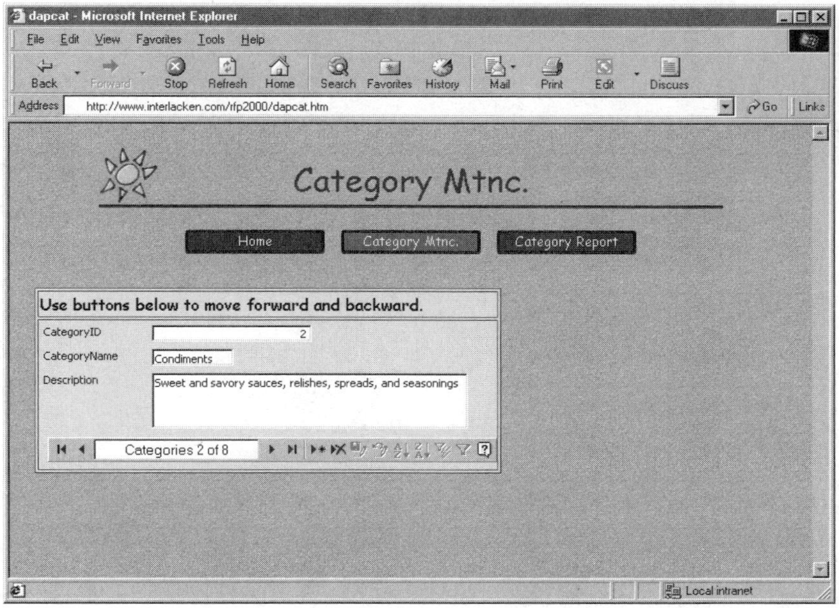

FIGURE 22-42.

Internet Explorer displays the Data Access Page previously shown in Figure 22-40. Note the many formatting enhancements made in FrontPage.

You can change the location of the Access database after transferring the Data Access Page to FrontPage, but only with difficulty. The database file location is stored within each Data Access Page as part of a long XML string that's a parameter to an ActiveX control in the <HEAD> section. The only way to modify this information involves switching to HTML view, searching for the database file name or .mdb extension, and then *carefully* changing the fully qualified name.

Exporting Data in Web Format

Compared to Data Access Pages, the second Access 2000 Web interface is much more limited in function but much more universal in audience. It saves any view of data as a listing on a Web page. The listing can either be *static*—meaning fixed values saved as a point in time—or *dynamic*—meaning the page queries the database and displays current data each time a visitor requests the page.

You can export many kinds of Access 2000 objects as Web pages—tables, queries, reports, and forms, for example—but what you get is always a simple listing resembling Access 2000's Datasheet view. Saving an Access form as HTML doesn't create an HTML form with similar update capabilities, for example. Likewise, saving an Access report doesn't re-create in HTML all the control breaks, totals, and formatting the Access report may have. Don't expect this facility to do more than it's capable of.

Figure 22-43 shows Access 2000 saving a table as an Active Server Page. The procedure is simple.

FIGURE 22-43.

To save the data in any table, query, or report as a Web page, export it as HTML or an Active Server Page.

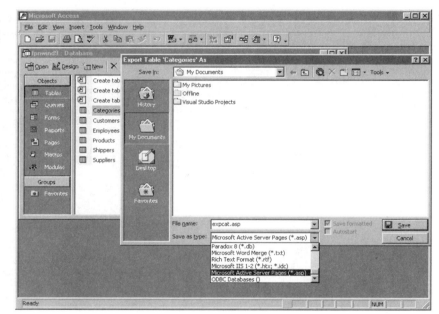

1 Select the table.

2 Choose Export from the File menu.

3 Specify a temporary storage area on your disk.

4 Adjust the suggested file name if necessary.

5 Choose HTML Documents or Microsoft Active Server Pages as the Save As Type.

6 Click the Save button.

If you chose Microsoft Active Server Pages in step 5, Access 2000 will display the Output Options dialog box shown in Figure 22-44.

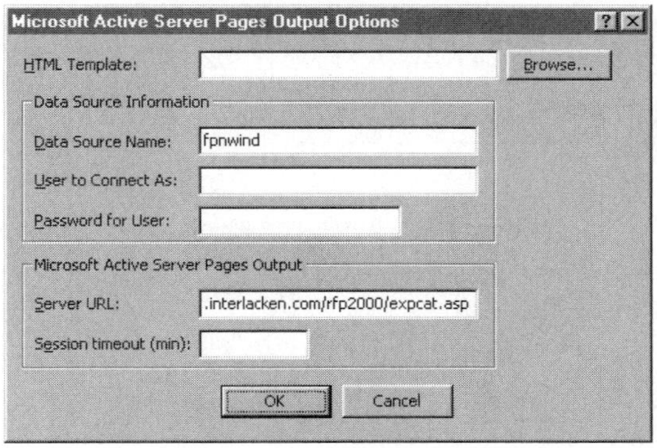

FIGURE 22-44.

With this dialog box Access 2000 prompts for the ODBC Data Source an Active Server Page will use.

SEE ALSO

For more information about ODBC Data Sources, see "Configuring ODBC Data Sources," page 761.

- **HTML Template,** if specified, provides the name of a sample Web page that provides formatting. These templates normally reside at C:\ProgramFiles\MicrosoftOffice\Office\Samples, and have nothing to do with FrontPage templates.

- **Data Source Name** is required. Specify the name of an ODBC System Data Source defined on the Web server.

- **User To Connect As,** if specified, provides a user name required to access the database.

- **Password For User,** if specified, specifies the authentication code for the specified user name.

- **Server URL** specifies the page's intended URL. This is optional.

- **Session Timeout** specifies how long the server will wait before abandoning a database query.

Figure 22-45 provides a brief review of what's required to set up an ODBC System Data Source Name. To display the dialog box shown in the background, the user opened the ODBC icon in Windows Control Panel. Choosing the System DSN tab and clicking Add displayed a list of available drivers, and double-clicking the Microsoft Access driver displayed the window shown in the foreground. The Data Source Name field supplies the name by which the exported ASP file will reference the database. Clicking the Select button locates the actual database file.

Getting ODBC System Data Source Names set up on a Web server can be a nuisance, because it's something only an administrator working at the server's keyboard can do. Access 2000, unfortunately, doesn't know how to use FrontPage Database Connections (which are user-defined).

FIGURE 22-45.

The Access database fpnwind.mdb is configured as System Data Source Name fpnwind.

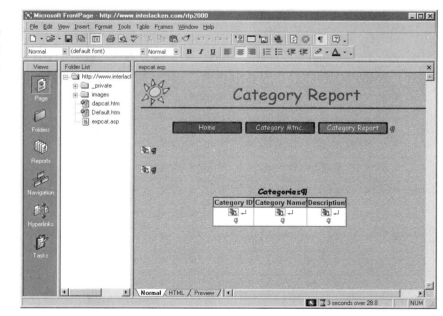

Once you've exported the Web page from Access 2000 to disk, you can add it to a FrontPage Web either by choosing Import from the File menu or by dragging the file from Windows Explorer into any Folder List or view. Figure 22-46 shows such a page open in FrontPage. As before, the Web author has applied a theme, added the page to Navigation view, and added Page Banner and Navigation Bar components.

FIGURE 22-46.

An Active Server Page exported from Access 2000 can be added to a FrontPage Web and formatted.

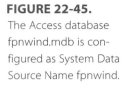

Note the script icons in Figure 22-46. These are places where Access 2000 has inserted code to query the database and display the results. Don't modify or delete them unless you're very sure of what you're doing, and unless you either have a good backup or don't mind restarting from scratch.

Figure 22-47 shows the same page displaying data in Internet Explorer. As usual, the ASP file must reside in an executable folder on the Web server. In addition, the ODBC System Data Source Name must be defined on the server that delivers the page.

FIGURE 22-47.

Internet Explorer displays the Web page saved in Figure 22-43 and formatted in Figure 22-46.

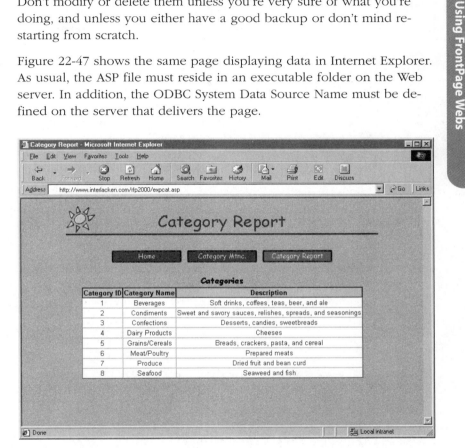

SQL

② SEE ALSO

For more information about SQL statements, see the documentation that came with your database application or one of the many books available on SQL.

Virtually all modern relational databases use SQL as the means for accepting database commands.

A typical SQL statement looks like this, with line numbers added to facilitate discussion. All fields named in the SQL statement must exist in the specified table.

```
1 SELECT <field>, <field>...
2  FROM <table>
3  GROUP BY <field>, <field>...
4  HAVING (<field><op><value>) AND/OR (<field><op>
     <value>)...
5  ORDER BY <field>, <field>...
```

1 The fields named after the SELECT keyword are the only fields returned. To return all fields in a table, specify an asterisk (*) rather than a field list.

2 The FROM clause specifies the table being queried.

3 The GROUP BY clause consolidates rows with equal values in the named fields.

4 The HAVING clause specifies one or more field comparisons that restrict the records returned.

5 The ORDER BY clause controls the order in which returned records appear.

Unfortunately, FrontPage provides only a simple point-and-click means for generating SQL statements or for looking up the properties of a database. One alternative is to get a listing of table names and field definitions from the owner or administrator of the database, and then to type the required SQL statement manually. Another is to create the query graphically in Microsoft Access, copy it to the Clipboard, and paste it into FrontPage using the Paste From Clipboard button. The section titled "Refining Database Queries," on page 746, describes this procedure in detail.

Databases on the Web—An Overview

Despite the widespread use of databases and the long efforts of many smart people, using databases remains somewhat complex. Multiple layers of software are required, each with its own eccentricities and configuration requirements. Web server interfaces add yet another layer of complexity.

This section will explain, as simply as possible, what you need to know about database technology and configuration to use the facilties in FrontPage for creating Web pages that access databases.

IV

Using FrontPage Webs

The FrontPage Database Environment

Figure 22-48 is a simple block diagram illustrating how database access on the Web typically occurs. The step-by-step process flow consists of this:

1 An ordinary HTML form, as described in Chapter 10, collects any required or optional input fields from the remote user. The form's Action property specifies the Web page or program containing the database code. For database applications created in FrontPage, this will be an Active Server Page (ASP) file residing on the Web server.

If database function requires no user input, no HTML form is required. Instead, the ASP file or program that contains the database code is simply the target of a hyperlink.

FIGURE 22-48.

This diagram illustrates the operation of an Internet Database Connector.

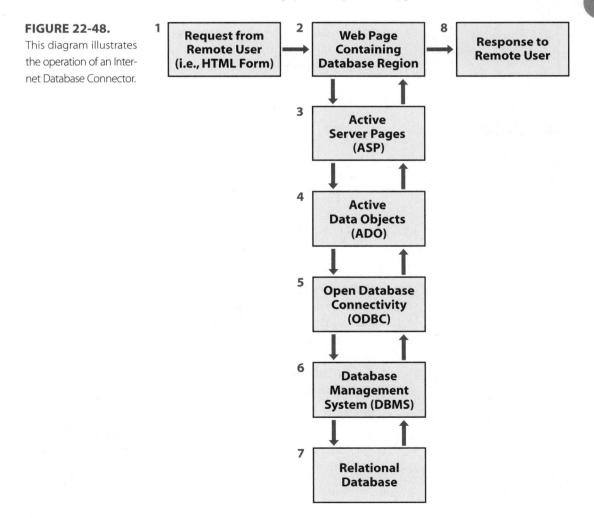

2 As it delivers the requested ASP file, the Web server calls the ASP script processor into play. The script processor executes VBScript code FrontPage has placed in the HTML. This code performs three key functions.

- It merges any variable data into a SQL (pronounced sequel, short for Structured Query Language) statement that specifies what data to retrieve.

- It opens a connection to the database and sends the SQL statement.

- When Active Data Objects returns the data, VBScript code in the HTML reads each record and replaces itself with HTML that displays the results.

3 Active Server Pages (ASP) is an interpreter that executes specially marked lines of VBScript, JavaScript, or other languages embedded within HTML. Server-side script code isn't transmitted to the remote user, but the remote user *does* receive any HTML such scripts generate.

> **NOTE**
>
> If you look at an ASP file on the server, you'll see any server-side script code it contains. If you browse the same file—using an *http://* URL—and choose your browser's View Source command, you'll see either generated HTML or nothing where the script code resided.

4 ActiveX Data Objects (ADO) provide database capability for server-side scripts. They are ActiveX objects without a user interface—they operate in background mode only.

5 Open Database Connectivity (ODBC) is a software component that provides a relatively standard interface for applications despite differences in database systems. It consists of general-purpose modules that make up ODBC itself, plus specific drivers for each database system. An initial set of ODBC drivers comes with the Windows operating system. Upgrades and additions typically come with various kinds of database software.

An ODBC Data Source is a definition, made through the ODBC Control Panel applet, that equates a Data Source Name (DSN) to a database driver, the name of a database, and other settings, depending on the database type.

FrontPage Database Connections are a type of ODBC Data Source created on the fly.

6 A database management system (DBMS) accepts high-level transaction commands—usually SQL statements—and manipulates the physical files that constitute databases. Microsoft SQL Server and the Jet database engine in Microsoft Access are examples.

7 A relational database consists of data arranged in rows and columns—that is, in tables. Each row is in essence a record, each column a field. All records in the same table contain the same fields (but not, of course, the same values). If two tables have identifying fields in common, the DBMS can match rows having like values and present the results as a joined table. The DBMS can present any desired combination of columns to the calling program, and can select records based on data values.

8 The response delivered to the remote user consists of ordinary HTML (plus, of course, any script or CSS code). Except for the ASP file name extension and the variability of output, the remote user won't be aware that a server-side script is involved.

Of the eight components shown in Figure 22-48, FrontPage can create and maintain items 1, 2, and 7: the submitted HTML form (if any), the Web page containing the Save Results coding or Database Results region, and in some cases the database itself. All these files must reside on the same Web server that accepts transactions from remote users, runs the database query, and returns the response. In addition, the page containing the Database Results region must reside in an executable folder on that Web server.

Design and configuration of the databases, the database management system, and the ODBC interface all occur completely outside FrontPage. If these resources don't already exist, use standard database development tools such as Microsoft SQL Server or Microsoft Access to develop and implement them. If they do exist, get the necessary file locations and record layouts from their owner or administrator.

Designing Active Pages in a Static Environment

The difference in mind-set between FrontPage components and Active Server Pages is a classic one: Active Server Pages are *procedural,* while the FrontPage WYSIWYG editor is *specification-oriented.*

■ The procedural approach requires lines of program code that describe, stepwise, how to produce the desired result. Its statements are imperative (that is, they're commands).

- The specification-oriented approach involves describing what you want rather than how to produce it. Its statements are declarative (that is, they're descriptions).

Specification-oriented approaches may be easier for nonprogrammers to learn and use, but only for relatively simple and well-known problems. The specification approach deals poorly with both complex logic and conditions that require change to the specified output. When the output is too variable, specifying it declaratively becomes very awkward.

It's worth noting that WYSIWYG editing of any kind is inherently specification-oriented. When you format content in any of the Microsoft Office applications, you specify what you want and *not* how to program the printer. When you write a SUM formula in Excel, you say what cells you want added and not how to loop through an array or increment an accumulator. Drawing Access forms, reports, and queries is specification-oriented as well.

True to its membership in the Microsoft Office family, FrontPage is also specification-oriented. You tell FrontPage what you want a Web page to look like, and FrontPage does the work of writing the HTML. This is probably, after all, why you bought FrontPage.

FrontPage is also a *static* environment. Animated GIF files don't play, nor do video clips. Scripts don't run. ActiveX controls and Java applets don't start. The reason is that FrontPage displays a point in time, not an active environment. Editing a document that constantly changes itself would be an exercise in reflexes—perhaps an exercise in futility. The experience of playing a video game comes to mind.

? SEE ALSO

For more information about writing Active Server Page scripts in FrontPage, see "Server-Side Scripting," page 432.

Although Active Server Pages and Active Data Objects undoubtedly provide a rich, full-function database environment, their procedural nature doesn't mesh as well with FrontPage. If your requirements go beyond simple queries, you'll have to create your own Active Server Page code, enter it, and debug it. FrontPage can insert such scripts, but it can't write them for you.

Locating a Web Database Facility

Running database applications on a Web server is more difficult than delivering simple Web pages for two reasons: complexity and resource consumption.

- Complexity issues arise because database management systems require much more effort to install, configure, and manage than ordinary Web servers. In addition, DBMSs are usually administered at the system rather than the user level. Not many system administrators are willing to turn over administration of a DBMS to end users; the potential problems and the difficulty in analyzing them are simply too extreme. However, these same administrators frequently lack the time to do database administration for a large base of diverse users.

■ Issues of resource consumption arise because a database transaction can consume far more processor time, memory, and disk activity than delivering any simple Web page.

These issues usually aren't serious obstacles on intranets and public Web sites having dedicated communication lines and servers. Intranets usually have plentiful bandwidth and server capacity, together with a more homogeneous community of developers and users than, say, a public Internet service provider. Most public Web sites belonging to corporations, government agencies, and other organizations also enjoy adequate bandwidth and dedicated servers.

If you have a typical dial-up ISP account, you may lack the capability to run ASP pages, to use databases, and thus to offer database services on your personal Web pages. Obtaining these capabilities may require paying additional service charges or changing ISPs.

In general, however, any service that provides Windows NT servers running the FrontPage 2000 Server Extensions will probably support use of FrontPage database connectors pointing to Microsoft Access databases within the same Web. After all, these capabilities are built into the Server Extensions and require no special configuration by the ISP.

Configuring a Web Database Environment

Table 22-3 lists the Web servers that support Active Server Pages, Active Data Objects, and Open Database Connectivity. You can use any database system that has thread-safe ODBC drivers, though the most common are Microsoft Access and Microsoft SQL Server.

TABLE 22-3.   Web Servers Supporting ASP, ADO, and ODBC

Web Server	Operating System
Microsoft Personal Web Server	Windows 95 and Windows 98
Microsoft Personal Web Server	Windows NT Workstation
Microsoft Internet Information Server	Windows NT Server

The issue with thread-safe ODBC drivers is this: the ADO facility pushes database requests into ODBC as fast as they arrive, rather than waiting for one request to be completed before submitting another. Some ODBC drivers can cope with this and some can't; the ones that can't malfunction or fail completely when two requests arrive too close together. The current drivers for Microsoft Access and SQL Server are thread-safe.

Microsoft's top-of-the-line, industrial-strength server components are Windows NT Server, Internet Information Server, and SQL Server. All three components are designed for high-volume use. Extensive multi-threading ensures optimal performance under heavy load. Their system management and administration are also enterprise-strength.

The combination of Windows 95, Microsoft Personal Web Server, and Microsoft Access consists entirely of tools designed for individual desktop use. This is both its greatest strength and greatest weakness. In terms of strength, the Windows 95/Microsoft Personal Web Server/Access combination is undoubtedly the easiest for new Web authors to learn and deal with. Its performance and stability as a production environment, however, are moderate at best.

Likewise, few production environments have such casual requirements that Windows 95 and Access can satisfy them. Windows NT Server and Access might be adequate for light database use, but Windows NT Server and SQL Server are clearly optimal in most cases.

The best production and development environments for your project will lie somewhere between Access on Windows 95 (at the low end) and SQL Server on Windows NT Server (at the high end).

Choosing a Web Database Development Environment

Running the combination of Windows NT Server, Internet Information Server (IIS), and a full-blown copy of SQL Server is probably overkill for any developer. Windows NT Workstation, Microsoft Personal Web Server, and a developer version of SQL Server provide essentially the same software at a much lower price (albeit with license restrictions that prevent use as a production server).

The degree of separation between your test and development environments depends on their natures. For informal intranet applications with no critical service requirements, the development and production environments may be one and the same. For mission-critical and highly secure applications, elaborate implementation and quality assurance procedures will generally be necessary, and these will involve development and production environments that are quite distinct.

The risk of problems moving from your development environment to production environment is least if you develop on Windows NT Workstation and run on Windows NT Server. Transitioning from Windows 95 and Microsoft Personal Web Server might involve additional problems because Windows 95 doesn't provide all of Windows NT Server's security features.

Moving from a Microsoft Access development environment over to the SQL Server production environment can also be difficult. These two database systems use different dialects of SQL, and at least some SQL statements will likely need adjustment. Copying database and table definitions from Access to SQL Server is more problematic than copying them between like systems. In short, whatever problems you sought to avoid by developing with Microsoft Access, you're likely to encounter anyway when you transfer the system to production.

If you decide on a development environment using SQL Server, remember that not every developer needs a private copy. In most cases, a single copy of SQL Server running on a local Windows NT server or workstation can easily support an entire workgroup of developers.

Don't overlook the attractive possibility of running FrontPage on Windows 95 or Windows 98 while locating your Web and database servers on Windows NT. Remember, FrontPage manages the files in your Web using HTTP and doesn't require local file access.

In Summary...

FrontPage has convenient, built-in features that can add and display database records without programming. In addition, it supports Web pages exported from Access 2000. Developing more complex applications, however, generally requires programming skills beyond the scope of FrontPage. Working with code in HTML view may provide a solution in some cases, but for maximum function you may need a hard-core programming tool like Microsoft Visual InterDev.

The next chapter reviews a variety of tools for general Web site upkeep.

Maintaining Your Site

CHAPTER 23

Keeping Your Site Up-to-Date

As time passes, your site will likely grow in size and complexity. Pages will evolve, gaining and losing both hyperlinks and images along the way. As this process continues, the difficulty of maintaining technical and visual continuity will grow as well. Microsoft FrontPage provides a number of features to assist in ongoing maintenance. These include:

- A way to update hyperlinks automatically when you move or rename a page.

- A way to find or replace text anywhere in your Web.

- A way to check the spelling of text throughout your Web.

- A command for updating all cross-references and indexes for your site.

Moving, Renaming, and Reorganizing Pages

As the number of files in your site grows, organizing them into folders and establishing naming conventions will become increasingly important. The need to reorganize or rename pages isn't necessarily a sign of poor planning; more often it's simply a sign that your site has grown. A topic that began as a single Web page may, over time, become a dozen pages and warrant its own folder. And a small collection of image files will likely become difficult to search after growing to a hundred or so images.

? SEE ALSO

For details of the mechanics of moving, copying, and deleting files in FrontPage, see "Working with Web Folder Lists," page 620.

If you have local or file-sharing access to your Web's file area, you can move, copy, rename, or delete files with Windows Explorer, the command prompt, or any number of utility programs. Even if you don't have such access, you can make such changes with an FTP program. Unfortunately, these approaches do nothing to adjust hyperlinks from other pages to the moved or renamed files. Unless you locate and correct these links manually, your Web won't function properly.

? SEE ALSO

Because it works through the FrontPage Server Extensions, the Web Folders feature in Office 2000 keeps FrontPage indexes properly updated. For more information about Web folders, see, "Built-In Upload/Download," page 32.

Changing file names and locations from within FrontPage avoids the problem of broken hyperlinks because FrontPage corrects links automatically. FrontPage maintains indexes of all links within a Web, and uses these to find and update the necessary Web pages. To keep these indexes accurate, it's best to always use FrontPage for organizing Web pages.

Here are several cautions:

- FrontPage corrects hyperlink and image references only within the current Web. When you reorganize pages or images, the maintainers of other Webs will need to correct their references manually.

- If you have reason to suspect FrontPage's indexes are out-of-date, re-create the indexes before reorganizing files. The procedure is described later in this chapter. FrontPage can't update your Web correctly if its indexes are incorrect.

- Changing a FrontPage Web by any means other than FrontPage is the number one cause of incorrect indexes.

? SEE ALSO

If you suspect that your site already has broken hyperlinks or image locations, see "Link Checking," page 798.

- FrontPage can't reliably identify image tags and hyperlinks coded as values within script code. Thus, FrontPage won't update hyperlinks and image references located within scripts.

- Close any Web pages open in FrontPage before reorganizing files. FrontPage doesn't update hyperlinks located within open pages.

Finding and Replacing Text

From time to time you'll no doubt find it valuable to search your FrontPage Web for all occurrences of a certain word or phrase. You may need to locate all occurrences of a person's name, a product name, an address, or some other text expression and check those pages for accuracy. The Cross File Find feature in FrontPage provides an excellent facility for such searches.

 **SEE ALSO**

For more information about the FrontPage Search component, see "Search Form," page 695.

Cross File Find differs from the FrontPage Search component in that:

- Cross File Find operates in the FrontPage environment. Once you find a matching page, a single mouse click will open it with FrontPage. Cross File Find is always available.

- The FrontPage Search component operates at run time, using a browser, and has no direct links to authoring tools. Also, it must be activated in advance as part of your Web.

Cross File Find differs from file system search utilities as well.

- Cross File Find offers one-click access to editing Web pages in FrontPage.

- A file system search will locate word or phrase occurrences in both FrontPage index and cross-reference files, as well as in Web pages.

- A file-system search will miss phrase occurrences that contain carriage returns, line feeds, tabs, or extra spaces.

Both cross-file operations—Find and Replace—are two-phase processes. Phase one creates a list of Web pages containing a specified string, and phase two opens each found page for editing. To run Cross File Find on your Web:

1 Open the Web in FrontPage.

2 To ensure accurate results, save any pages that are open for edit.

3 Choose Find from the Edit menu.

4 Configure the following settings when the dialog box shown in Figure 23-1 appears.

V

Maintaining Your Site

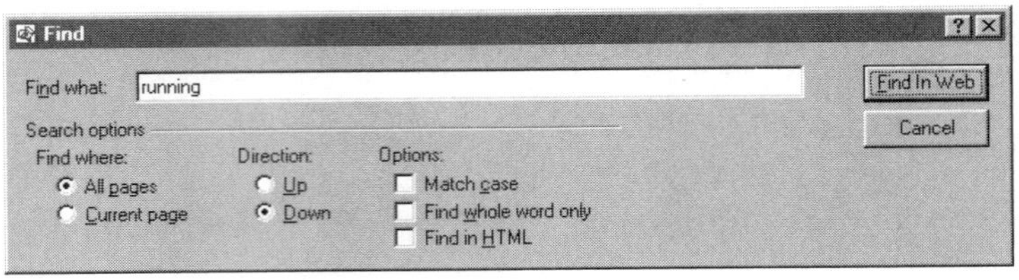

FIGURE 23-1.

This dialog box begins a Cross File Find operation in FrontPage.

- **Find What** specifies the word or phrase you want to find.

- **Find Where** controls the pages searched.

  All Pages searches the entire Web. Always choose this option for searching an entire Web.

  Current Page searches the active open document in Page view.

- **Direction** controls the order of searching within each Web page.

  Up means FrontPage will find and display the Find What text starting from the bottom of each page, and proceeding toward the top.

  Down means FrontPage will find and display the Find What text starting from the top of each page, and proceeding toward the bottom.

- **Options**

  Match Case, if turned on, indicates that matching terms must have exactly the same capitalization. If this option is turned off, capitalization doesn't matter.

  Find Whole Word Only, if turned on, specifies that Front-Page will match only complete words. The search term, *basket*, for example, would not find the word *basketball*. Clearing the box searches for words of any length that contain the search term.

  Find in HTML, if turned on, specifies that FrontPage should search each Web page's hidden HTML code as well as its visible text.

5 After completing the entries in Figure 23-1, click the Find In Web button. FrontPage will then display the dialog box pictured in Figure 23-2. The button in the upper-right corner will be captioned Stop, and the Cancel and Add Task buttons will be unavailable. Progress messages will appear across the bottom of the window. Click Stop to pause or abandon the search.

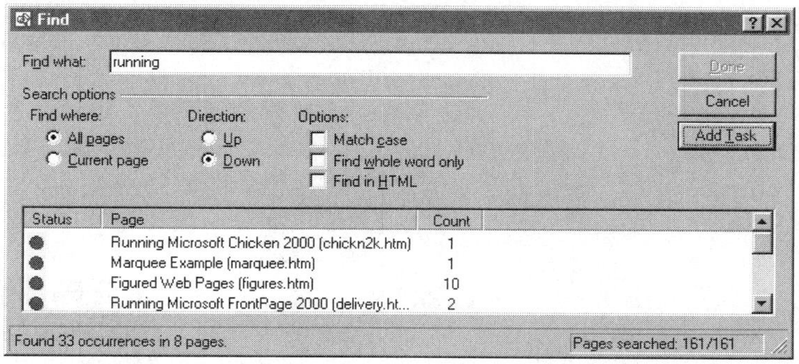

FIGURE 23-2.

This window displays Cross File Find progress and eventually search results.

6 When the search finishes, the caption on the Stop button changes to Done and the button becomes dimmed. The Cancel and Add Task buttons, by contrast, become available. The list box contains the following column entries for each page containing a match:

- **Status** initially displays a red circle, indicating that no action has yet been taken.

- **Page** displays the title and name of each page that contains the text you specified in the Find What field in step 4.

- **Count** reports the number of matches on each page.

7 To view or edit a found page, double-click its entry in the list box. As shown in Figure 23-3, FrontPage opens the page and finds the first occurrence of the Find What text.

The options in Figure 23-3 default to the values you assigned in Figure 23-1. Changes pertain to searching of the current page only. Repeatedly clicking the Find Next button will search the document from top to bottom or bottom to top, depending on the Direction setting.

8 Clicking the Back To Web button or searching past the last occurrence of the Find What text displays the dialog box shown in Figure 23-4.

- **Save And Close The Current Document,** if turned on, saves the current Web page and closes its editing window. If you turn this box off, FrontPage will keep the page open for further editing.

V

Maintaining Your Site

- **Next Document** opens the next document in the Cross File Find list (Figure 23-2).

- **Cancel** terminates the process of opening successive documents in the Cross File Find list. It also leaves the current page open for further editing.

FIGURE 23-3.

Double-clicking a page listed in Figure 23-2 opens it in FrontPage.

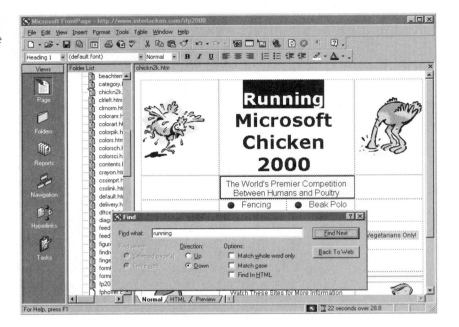

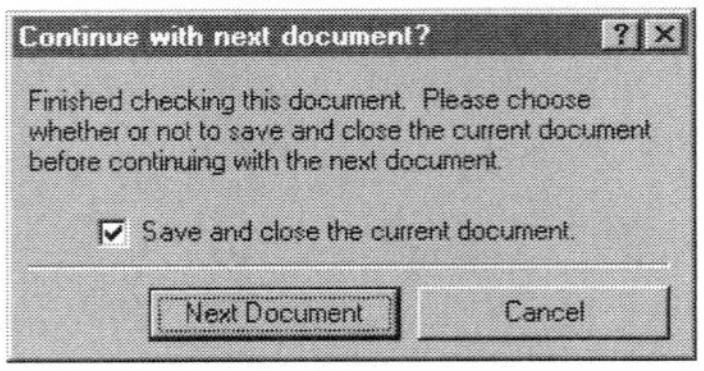

FIGURE 23-4.

This dialog box prompts for the disposition of Web pages found and opened by Cross File Find.

9 Opening a found page in FrontPage changes its Status icon (in Figure 23-2) from a red circle to a yellow circle followed by the word "Edited."

10 To create a Task list entry for a found page, select its entry in the list box, and then click the Add Task button.

- The Status entry will change from a red circle to a yellow circle and the words "Added Task" will appear.

- To view the task, in FrontPage choose Tasks from the View menu or click the Tasks icon. The list in Figure 23-5 shows the new task.

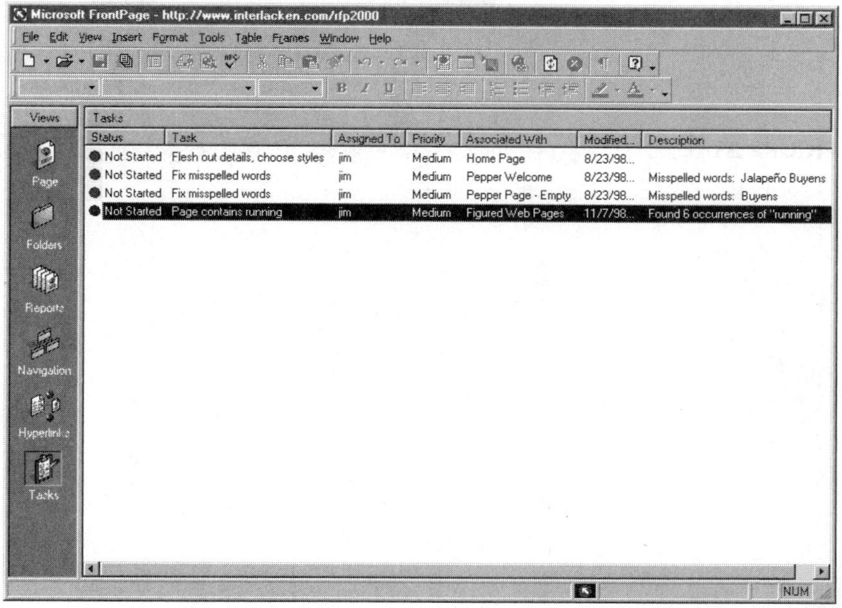

FIGURE 23-5.

The Add Task button in Figure 23-2 created the task highlighted in Tasks view.

As you might expect, the process of running a Cross File Replace greatly resembles that for Cross File Find. There are two major differences, however:

- When specifying the text to find, you must also specify the text to substitute.

- When you open a Web page from the Find Occurrences list, FrontPage displays its Find/Replace dialog box instead of its Find dialog box.

Cross File Replace has no unattended Replace All option. First it displays a list of pages, and then you must select and edit each found page. You can click the Replace All button when FrontPage opens a page and displays its Edit Replace dialog box, but this replaces all occurrences in the current page and not all occurrences in the current Web.

Here's the full procedure for performing a Cross File Replace.

1 Open the FrontPage Web in FrontPage.

2 Close any editing sessions.

3 Choose Replace from the Edit menu.

4 When the dialog box shown in Figure 23-6 appears, configure the settings as described in step 4 of the Cross File Find procedure. There is one additional field, namely:

- **Replace With,** which specifies the word or phrase that should replace the found text.

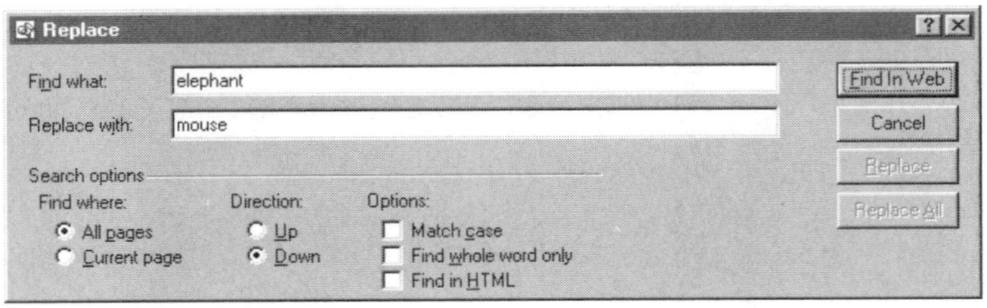

FIGURE 23-6.

Begin a Cross File Replace operation with this dialog box.

5 After you Click OK, FrontPage will run the Cross File Find process and display, as before, the dialog box shown in Figure 23-2.

6 At this point in the Cross File Replace process, no actual replacements will have occurred. To begin replacing text on a listed page, first double-click it. As shown in Figure 23-7, FrontPage will open the page for editing, find the first occurrence of the Find What text, and offer to replace it. To replace all occurrences on a page, click the Replace All button.

FIGURE 23-7.

To replace text on a given page, double-click its entry in Figure 23-3. FrontPage will display an Edit Replace dialog box.

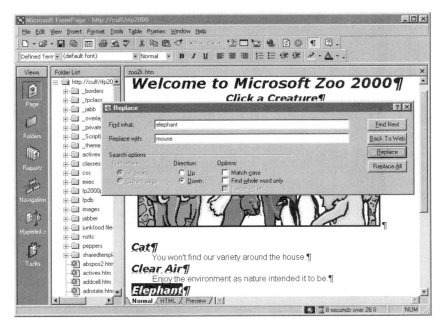

7 If you click Replace All or click either Find Next or Replace past the end of the page, FrontPage will offer to save the current page and open the next page containing found text, again using the dialog box in Figure 23-4.

8 You can add found pages to Tasks view using the same procedure as for Cross File Find—that is, by clicking the Add Task button.

Each page you examine will be marked Edited when you return to the list of matches, even if you don't make any changes.

Spell Checking Your Web

The procedure to check spelling throughout all or part of a FrontPage Web strongly resembles that for replacing text. Instead of replacing one word or phrase with another, however, spell checking replaces misspelled word with correct ones. Like Find and Replace, Spell checking multiple files first builds a list of pages containing misspelled words, then provides choices for editing pages or adding them to Task View. If you choose to edit a listed page, FrontPage steps through the misspelled words.

To check the spelling of all or part of a FrontPage Web:

1 Close any pages that are open for editing.

2 Switch to any view *other* than Page view.

3 If you plan to use the spelling checker on less than the entire Web, select the pages you want to check. This will probably be easiest in Folder view or Report view.

4 Choose Spelling from the Tools menu.

5 The dialog box in Figure 23-8 will appear. Configure the following settings.

   • **Check Spelling Of** specifies the range of pages to check for correct spelling.

   • **Selected Page(s)** checks only pages you highlighted in step 3.

   • **All Pages** checks all pages in the current Web.

   • **Add A Task For Each Page With Misspellings** indicates you want to bypass the list of pages containing misspelled words and instead add each page to Task View.

FIGURE 23-8.

Use this dialog box to initiate Cross File Spelling.

6 After you click Start, FrontPage will check the specified pages for spelling.

- If you chose Add A Task For Each Page With Misspellings, FrontPage will display a simple progress bar during the spell check, then close the spelling dialog box. This was the origin of the tasks titled Fix Misspelled Words in Figure 19-19.

- If you didn't choose Add Pages With Misspellings To Task View, FrontPage will display the dialog box of Figure 23-9, which lists all selected pages containing misspelled words. As with the Find and Replace functions, you can edit these pages in Page view or add them individually to Task view. Figure 23-10 shows FrontPage opening a page with the first misspelled word ready for correction.

FIGURE 23-9.

FrontPage displays this dialog box to identify pages with contain spelling errors.

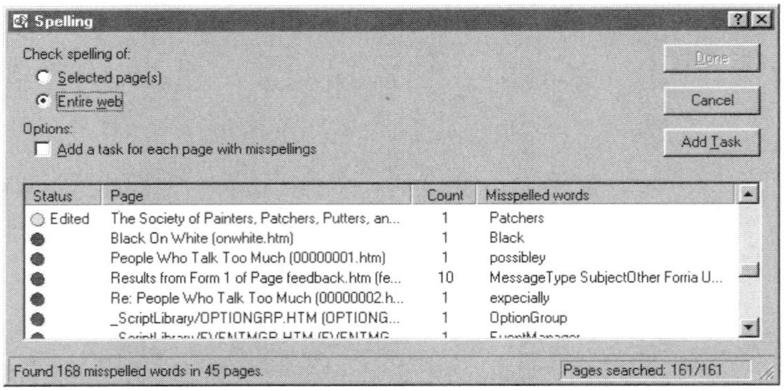

(?) SEE ALSO

For more information about spell checking individual Web pages, see "Checking Spelling," page 121.

You can also display the dialog box of Figure 23-10 yourself to check an individual page you've opened in FrontPage. Choose Spelling from the Tools menu, and then use the elements in this window as follows.

- **Not In Dictionary** displays the misspelled word.

- **Change To** supplies a corrected word. You can accept the word FrontPage suggests, type a word on the keyboard, or pick a word from the drop-down list of suggestions.

- **Suggestions** provides a list of possible corrections to the misspelling.

FIGURE 23-10.

FrontPage uses this dialog box to correct spelling of questionable words.

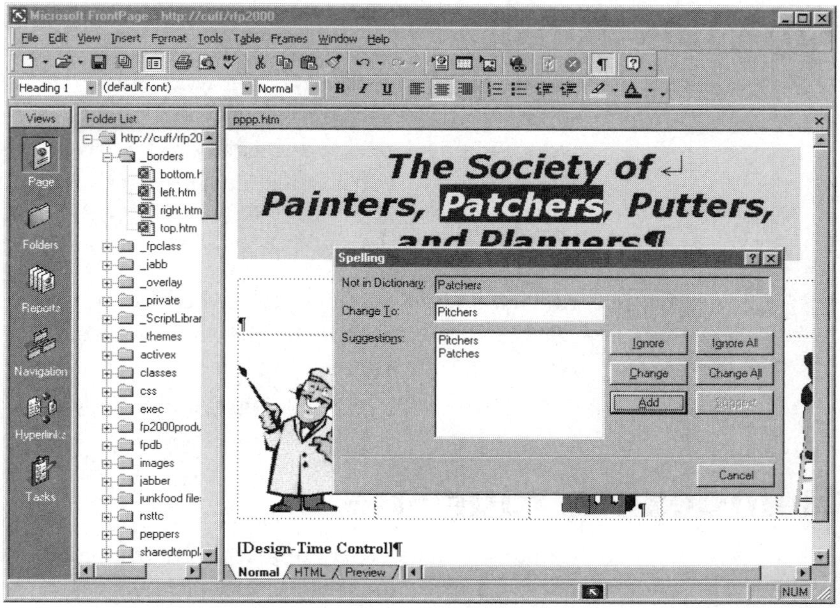

■ **Ignore** bypasses the current word.

■ **Ignore All** ignores the current word if it appears again in the same Web page.

■ **Change** replaces the misspelled word with the contents of the Change To field.

■ **Change All** replaces the current misspelled word with the contents of the Change To field everywhere on the page.

■ **Add** adds the current word to the custom dictionary. Future spelling checks will no longer report this word as an error.

■ **Suggest** checks the spelling of a word you typed by hand into the Change To box. This is useful when the correct word doesn't appear in the Suggestions list, you attempt a correction by hand, and you want to check your work before moving on.

> **NOTE**

FrontPage uses the custom dictionary at C:\Windows\Application Data\ Microsoft\Proof\custom.dic (where C:\Windows is the Windows install location). Because this file is on the FrontPage user's local machine, dictionary additions made by one user won't be available to others users on the same Web.

Link Checking

A widely accepted principle of physics is that, left to itself, order inevitably reverts to chaos. Hyperlinks provide a perfect example of such entropy at work. While FrontPage can greatly reduce instances of broken hyperlinks within your Web, still, typing errors and changes at remote sites inevitably break even the most carefully created hyperlinks. FrontPage provides the Broken Hyperlinks report to detect and correct such errors.

⊗ CAUTION

It's best to close any open files in your Web before recalculating hyperlinks.

All Web authors should check hyperlinks occasionally, because there's no reliable means to catch changes as they occur throughout the entire World Wide Web. The frequency of checking will vary, depending on the number of links, their volatility, and the level of service you wish to provide.

Reindexing Your Site

FrontPage maintains a number of databases and index files that cross-reference hyperlinks and other elements in your Web pages. If these files and your Web pages get out of sync, FrontPage may produce incorrect search results, incorrectly size images, or incompletely update hyperlinks.

FrontPage always updates the necessary indexes whenever it makes changes to a Web, but other programs and utilities don't. You should reindex your site every time you make changes with external tools, anytime you suspect indexes of being corrupted, or in general, anytime your Web seems to be acting strangely.

? SEE ALSO

For more information about the Broken Hyperlinks report, see "Using the Troubleshooting Reports," page 636.

To reindex a Web, open it in FrontPage and choose Recalculate Hyperlinks from the Tools menu. This accomplishes three things:

- It updates the display for all current views of the FrontPage Web.

- It regenerates all dependencies. If, for example, you use an external editor to modify an included page, any pages that include it will continue to display the old version. Recalculating hyperlinks refreshes the affected Include Page components.

- It rebuilds the text index used by the FrontPage Search feature. This can get out-of-date if you externally add, change, or delete files in your Web.

Recalculating hyperlinks can take several minutes for a large FrontPage Web. FrontPage warns you of this before starting the recalculation. Once recalculation starts, FrontPage will flash its logo at the right of the toolbar area until recalculation finishes, and only then can you do further work in FrontPage.

Testing Your Web

Utilities such as the Broken Hyperlinks report and Cross File Spelling provide excellent ways to check the content of your site, and using FrontPage produces error-free HTML. Nevertheless, there's no substitute for browsing your own Web and testing its functions online.

Two fundamental things to check are the correct operation of all hyperlinks and reasonable page transmission times under typical conditions. However, you should also do a test drive to confirm proper appearance and operation under the following conditions:

- **Different Browsers.** Test your pages with at least the current production versions of Internet Explorer, Netscape Navigator, and any other browser used by your audience, plus the previous production version and perhaps the current pre-release version of each.

- **Different Browser Settings.** Remember that users can turn some browser features on and off, such as the ability to run scripts, run Java applets, and load ActiveX controls. If you use these facilities, make sure your pages degrade gracefully, rather than crash and burn, if users turn them off.

- **Different Color Depths.** View your pages in 256 color mode as well as 24-bit true color. Depending on your user base, you might also wish to test at 16 colors and in 64K high-color mode.

- **Different Screen Sizes.** Make sure your pages are viewable on systems with 640x480 pixel displays.

- **Different Servers.** Don't assume that everything on multiple servers will work the same way (presuming your environment uses more than one, such as a Microsoft Personal Web Server for authoring and an ISP's Unix server for production). The more different the servers, the more that can go wrong. Test and debug each server environment thoroughly.

Scripts are probably the most sensitive components in your Web. Java-Script, in particular, hasn't benefited from a formal language specification, nor does it have a comprehensive test suite. Bugs and features seem to come and go with each browser version, so testing is an absolute necessity. Remember that browser-side VBScript isn't supported by Netscape browsers.

Test after each change to your Web—each set of page changes, each Copy Web, each server upgrade, each new version of FrontPage, each new browser version that appears. Even if nothing else changes, hyperlinks will; verify them periodically.

V

Maintaining Your Site

In Summary...

This chapter examined a number of useful techniques for keeping your Web page up-to-date, both technically and in terms of content. The next chapter will explain how to move FrontPage Webs from one location to another.

Publishing Your FrontPage Web

Once you've developed a Microsoft FrontPage Web, you'll almost certainly develop a need to copy it. The most common reason is to copy the Web from your development environment to a public Web server, making its content available to the intended audience. However, there are lots of other reasons for copying Webs from place to place, including delivery to a client, a change of working environment, and precautionary backups. Some people even copy Webs to compact discs for distribution with computer books!

Of course, FrontPage Webs are nothing more than sets of files, and copying files is hardly cutting-edge technology. You can do it with Windows Explorer, a tape-backup program, an FTP program, or the MS-DOS prompt, just to name a few. None of those approaches copies every aspect of a FrontPage Web, however, adjusting all the FrontPage indexes and pointers so they work properly in their new location. For that, you need to use the FrontPage Publish command.

This chapter will explain everything you need to know about publishing FrontPage Webs, even if the destination is a Web server not running the FrontPage Server Extensions or not running a Web server at all. What's more, one command does it all. What could be easier than that?

Web Publishing Fundamentals

Publishing is the only supported means of copying or transmitting a FrontPage Web from one location to another. Publishing transfers not only your content files—Web pages, pictures, programs, applets, and the like—but also unique FrontPage information such as Navigation view and database connections. And finally, Publishing *won't* transfer certain data—such as security settings and hit counts—that *ought* to be different in the two locations.

Publishing always begins with opening the FrontPage Web you want to transmit. This will be the *source* of the publishing operation. The *target* will be the location that receives the transmitted content. The target can be a server-based Web, a disk-based Web, or an FTP location anywhere your network can reach. Table 24-1 summarizes these points.

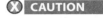

Because you can't open an FTP location as a FrontPage Web, FTP locations can't be the source of a publishing operation.

TABLE 24-1.   Acceptable Sources and Targets for Publishing

Type of Web	Source	Target
Disk-based	OK	OK
Server-based	OK	OK
FTP accessible	Not Supported	OK*

* Result is not a FrontPage Web.

You should think of publishing as a *push* operation, and not necessarily as an *upload* operation. Although the most common use of the Publish command is uploading Webs from your computer to a production Web server, publishing can also *download* Webs from the production server to your local machine. To do this, open the Web on the production server and specify your computer as the target.

To emphasize, these two operations *don't* produce the same results:

- Opening the target Web and importing the source Web (by choosing Import from the file menu). You might think of this as *pulling* the source Web into the target Web.

- Opening the source Web and publishing to the target Web. Think of this as *pushing* the source Web into the target Web.

Importing the source Web adds its home page, all hyperlinked pages in the same folder tree, and all ancillary files such as pictures and animations to the target Web. This may not include every file in the source Web, however. Importing an entire Web misses orphan pages, unused pictures, and other files with no hyperlinks in the current Web. In addition, importing an entire Web won't include Navigation view structure, the task list, Web settings, and other FrontPage data. To transfer all aspects of a Web from place to place, always open the source Web and use the Publish command.

Note that FrontPage Publishing transfers entire Webs. To publish only certain pages, open both Webs in FrontPage and drag the pages you want from one folder List or view to the other.

The next three sections will describe the process of publishing Webs to three different kinds of target:

- Publishing to a FrontPage Web Server.
- Publishing to a non-extended Web Server.
- Publishing to a disk-based Web.

Publishing to a FrontPage Web Server

The first step in publishing any FrontPage Web is to open it in FrontPage. The second step is to choose Publish Web from the File menu, which displays the dialog box shown in Figure 24-1.

⭐ TIP

The Publish Web button on the Standard toolbar and the Publish Web command on the File menu *don't* work alike.
- The File menu command always displays the dialog box shown in Figure 24-1.
- The toolbar button skips the dialog box and immediately begins publishing using the most recent settings. (Of course, if you've never published the current Web, there are no saved settings, and FrontPage displays the dialog box.)

- **Specify The Location To Publish Your Web To** determines where FrontPage will transfer the contents of the current Web. To specify a server-based FrontPage Web, use this format:

  http://<server name>/<web name>

where <server name> identifies the Web server and <web name> specifies the path to the Web's home folder.

■ **WPPs** starts your browser and displays the Web page at

http://www.microsoft.com/frontpage/wpp/list.htm

This page lists Web Presence Providers that sell Web space with the FrontPage 2000 Server Extensions installed.

NOTE

A Web Presence Provider (WPP) is an organization that provides Web servers and Internet connections for clients who want Web sites.

FIGURE 24-1.

To publish the current FrontPage Web to a server-based Web located elsewhere, specify the target location as an HTTP URL.

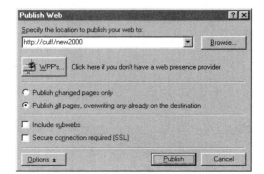

To display the following options, click the Options button. Figure 24-1 shows the dialog box after clicking this button.

■ **Publish Changed Pages Only** transfers only those pages whose version on the source Web is different from that on the target Web.

■ **Publish All Pages, Overwriting Any Already On The Destination** transfers every page in the source Web to the target Web.

SEE ALSO
For more information about setting up Web servers to require SSL, see "Using the MMC Server Extensions Tab," page 549.

■ **Include Subwebs,** if checked, transfers not only the current Web, but all Webs within it.

■ **Secure Connection Required (SSL),** if checked, sets up communication with the target Web server using Secure Sockets Layer encryption.

To create a new Web on the target server, specify the path you want it to have. However, as when creating any new Web, all path directories but the last must already exist. To create a Web at http://yourserver/veggies/green/broccoli/, for example, the path http://yourserver/veggies/green/ must already exist.

Click the Publish button when you're satisfied all entries are correct. If the target Web server has security controls in effect, FrontPage may prompt you for an authorized user name and password. For updating an existing Web, this must be a user name with authoring privileges. For creating a new Web, the user name must be an administrator of the new Web's parent.

Publishing to a Non-Extended Web Server

If your target Web server doesn't have the FrontPage Server Extensions installed, attempting to publish a Web as described in the previous section will produce the dialog box shown in Figure 24-2. Fear not, however; with minor changes in procedure, you can publish your Web using FTP, the Internet's File Transfer Protocol.

FIGURE 24-2.

If the target Web server doesn't have the Front-Page Server Extensions installed, publishing to an HTTP URL results in this error message.

Microsoft FrontPage

The web server at "http://www.primenet.com" does not appear to have the FrontPage server extensions installed.

OK

Providers who offer Web servers lacking the FrontPage Server Extensions almost always provide users with FTP access to their home directories. This involves four pieces of information:

- The name of the FTP server.

- A user name for logging on.

- A password for logging on.

- A directory path that accesses your HTTP home directory.

To upload files, users run command-line or graphical FTP programs. The start of a typical session appears below, with the four items listed above in bold. The *put* command uploads the file default.htm.

```
ftp earring.interlacken.com
Connected to earring.interlacken.com.
220 earring Microsoft FTP Service (Version 4.0).
User (earring.interlacken.com:(none)): jim
331 Password required for jim.
Password: xxxxxx
230 User jim logged in.
```

```
ftp> cd public_html
250 CWD command successful.
ftp> put default.htm default.htm
```

Fortunately, FrontPage can upload your entire Web without exposing you to any of this gibberish. The procedure for publishing by FTP is the same as that for publishing to a FrontPage-extended Web server, with three exceptions.

- In the box titled **Specify The Location To Publish Your Web To** enter an FTP URL like the example shown below.

  ftp://<server name>/<path>

  where <server name> identifies the FTP server, and <path> is the value required to access the Web's home folder. The URL corresponding to the character-mode FTP session above would be:

  ftp:// earring.interlacken.com/public_html

  Figure 24-3 shows the Publish Web dialog box with this URL entered.

FIGURE 24-3.
To publish the current Web via FTP, enter an FTP URL.

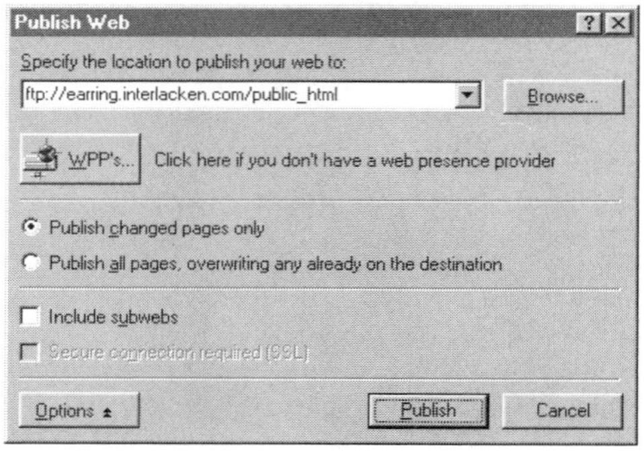

- The option Secure Connection Required (SSL) will be dimmed.
- After you click the Publish button, FrontPage will connect to the FTP server and then, with the dialog box shown in Figure 24-4, prompt you for a user name and password acceptable to the FTP server.

FIGURE 24-4.
This dialog box prompts for an FTP login username and password.

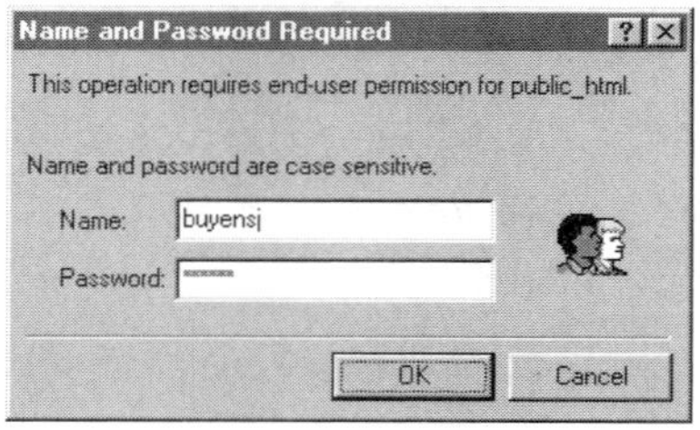

Uploading a Web via FTP doesn't create a FrontPage Web on the target server. Specifically, FrontPage doesn't upload all the private directories, indexes, and settings it would upload to a server running the FrontPage Server Extensions. This saves bandwidth and upload time, but the lack of Server Extensions means you won't have any FrontPage authoring or run-time services on the target server.

Publishing to a Disk-Based Web

The Publish command can also create disk-based copies of FrontPage Webs, regardless of whether the original Web was disk-based or server-based. This can be useful to create backup copies of a Web, to move your Web to a drive with more space, or to put it on a removable drive for portability (a ZIP or JAZ drive, for example).

 TIP

> To put a disk-based Web on a compact disc, first publish it to your hard disk and then use a CD creator program to copy the hard-disk version to the CD.

Publishing to a disk-based Web is just as easy as publishing to a server-based Web or FTP location. In the field titled Specify The Location To Publish Your Web To, simply enter the desired disk location. Figure 24-5 illustrates this. Click the Publish button and away you go.

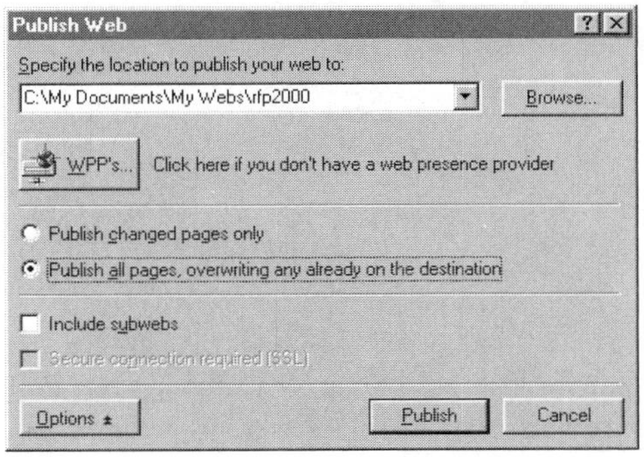

FIGURE 24-5.
To publish to a disk-based Web, enter a disk location as the target.

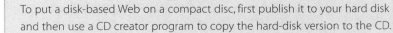

How Web Publishing Works

Regardless of the type of source Web and the type of target Web, Web publishing basically occurs in four phases:

1 Tabulate the names and versions of all the files in the source and target Webs.

2 Compare the source and target Web tabulations, creating, updating, or deleting files on the target as necessary.

3 Process all updates on the target Web server. This includes both normal file updates and recalculation of hyperlinks.

4 Report completion.

Figure 24-6 shows the status display for each of these steps. A Cancel button in the lower-right corner of the first three boxes is hidden, but they look much like Cancel buttons anywhere. Clicking Cancel terminates the publishing operation.

FIGURE 24-6.

These are the four status messages you'll receive during a successful FrontPage publishing operation.

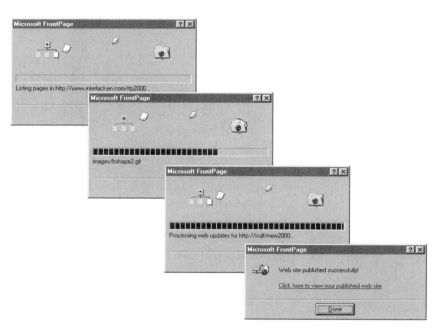

The dialog box shown in Figure 24-7 may appear when publishing to a disk-based Web. It warns you of any pages that won't work because the FrontPage Server Extensions won't be present. Despite the warning, FrontPage still copies the listed pages into the server-based Web. Those pages will start working, of course, if you later publish the disk-based Web to a server-based Web.

Figure 24-8 shows another dialog box that may appear during a Web-publishing operation. It appears when the publishing operation detects that any file version on the target server has changed since the current Web was last published to it. This usually involves the following chain of events:

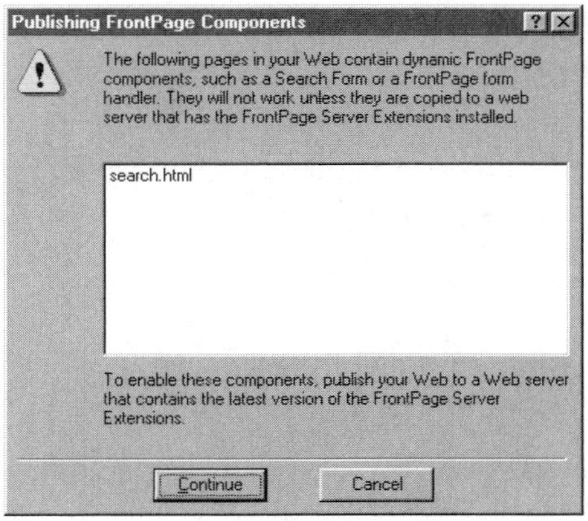

FIGURE 24-7.

This dialog box warns you of any pages that won't work properly after being published to a disk-based web.

1   Someone publishes Web A to Web B.

2   Someone updates a file in Web B by some means other than publishing Web A.

3   Someone publishes Web A to Web B, and this includes a change to the file updated in step 2.

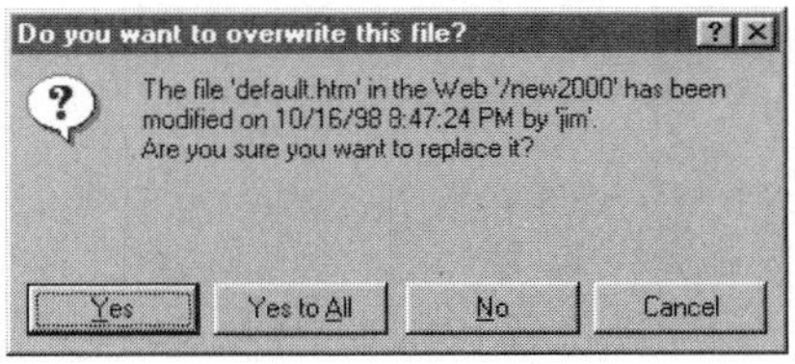

FIGURE 24-8.

This prompt occurs when corresponding files on the source and target Webs both get updated with no intervening synchronization.

The problem here is that the change in step 3 may or may not include the changes made in step 2, and FrontPage has no way of knowing which file to accept. You have four options.

■   **Yes** replaces the existing file on the target Web with the corresponding file in the source Web.

■   **Yes To All** works the same as Yes. Additionally, it applies the Yes answer to all future prompts of this type, for the duration of the current publishing operation.

■   **No** bypasses update of the questionable file, but continues the publishing operation.

■   **Cancel** bypasses update of the questionable file and terminates the publishing operation.

A similar message may appear if the target Web contains files not present in the source Web. FrontPage offers the choice of keeping or deleting such files.

If the prompt shown in Figure 24-9 appears during a publishing operation, it means there's a version conflict between the Navigation view structures of the source and target Webs. To understand how this can happen, consider the following series of events:

1 You create a new Web, enter a Navigation view structure, and publish the Web to your production server.

2 You create some new pages, enter them in Navigation view, and publish your Web once more to the same production server.

   No error or warning message occurs from this pattern of working, no matter how often you repeat step 2. Imagine, however, that events continue this way.

3 You publish the Web to the production server.

4 Someone else downloads the Web, changes its Navigation view structure, and then publishes it to the production server.

5 You update your copy of the Web, change its Navigation view structure, and then try publishing it to the production server.

Step 5 will produce the dialog box shown in Figure 24-9, because FrontPage knows the target Web contains Navigation view changes not reflected in your copy of the Web. Here are your choices:

■ **Do Not Replace The Navigation Structure Of The Destination Web.** This option publishes your revised content, but not the revised Navigation view.

   This is probably the safest choice because it leaves both versions of the Navigation view intact. After publishing completes, you can open both Webs, compare the two Navigation view structures, and decide what to do.

■ **Replace The Navigational Structure Of The Destination Web.** This choice replaces the target Web's Navigation view with the source Web's Navigation view, based on revision dates for each Navigation view entry. As to any other Navigation view changes made to the target Web, they'll be lost.

- **Let FrontPage Merge The Changes.** This option tells FrontPage to reconcile the two Navigation view structures. This is a somewhat risky choice, because the assumptions coded in FrontPage may be contrary to your wishes.

If you choose either the first or third options above, the two Navigation structures will still be different, after the publishing operation ends. To recover, correct the Navigation view in either the source or the target Web, and then publish that Web to the other location.

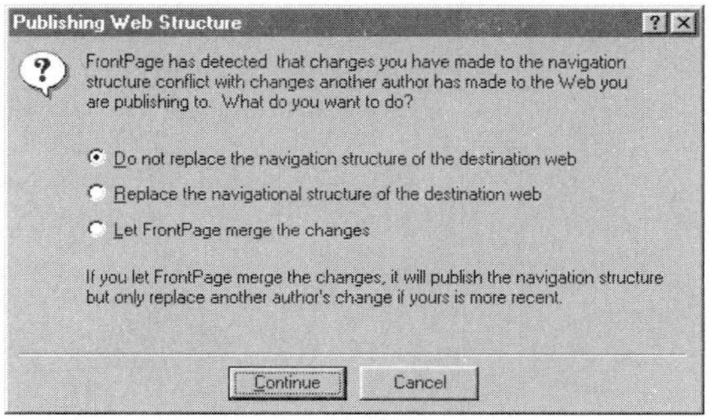

FIGURE 24-9.

This dialog box appears if the target Web's Navigation view changes between successive publications from the same source Web.

In Summary...

This chapter described the most common scenarios for moving FrontPage Webs from place to place, how to accomplish those scenarios in FrontPage, and some of the most common error messages and recoveries.

Afterword

Concepts, Ink, and Bits

The previous chapter concludes our travels through FrontPage, at least for this edition of the book and this version of the software. There are always more questions to be asked, and there is always more material to write about…but only so much time and paper and ink. I hope the book has answered at least most of your questions and given you some ideas and techniques you might not have encountered otherwise. In short, I hope the book was worth what you paid for it.

But even more, I hope that the combination of this book and the Front-Page software will expedite the flow of your thoughts and ideas from concept to expression. I hope you've learned to express yourself more completely, more powerfully, more effectively, and more eloquently than would otherwise have been possible—and thus more honestly as well.

The World Wide Web is the most democratic publishing medium yet created. No other medium allows so many people to present their ideas so rapidly, so cheaply, and so broadly to such an audience—both large and diverse. The result is the tumultuous chorus of ideas flowing today across the Web, educating the curious, opening vistas for the isolated, rousing the apathetic, and multiplying appreciation of the human condition. There's no more powerful force for peace, prosperity, and progress than diverse people discovering each other, communicating, and building understanding.

With this thought I repeat my hope that this book and FrontPage itself provide the means for you to express yourself, convey your message, and attract the attention of others in ways unparalleled. May it lead to relationships and experiences you never dreamed possible. Let's go to press…

Index

About the Author

Jim Buyens is the senior PC-LAN administrator for AG Communication Systems, a leading provider of telephone switching equipment and software. An early proponent of TCP/IP connectivity, he administers a worldwide corporate network that includes more than 50 Windows NT servers and more than 2,000 client personal computers. He was an early champion of World Wide Web applications for intranet use, and he administers a corporate Web site at *www.agcs.com*.

Jim received a Bachelor of Science degree in Computer Science from Purdue University in 1971 and a Master of Business Administration degree from Arizona State University in 1992. When not administering a network or writing books, he enjoys traveling and attending professional sports events—especially NHL hockey. He resides with his family in Phoenix.

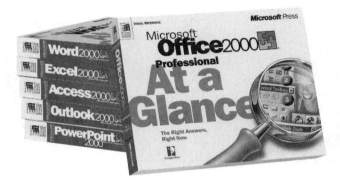

Microsoft Press offers *comprehensive* **learning solutions** to help new users, power users, and professionals get the most from *Microsoft technology.*

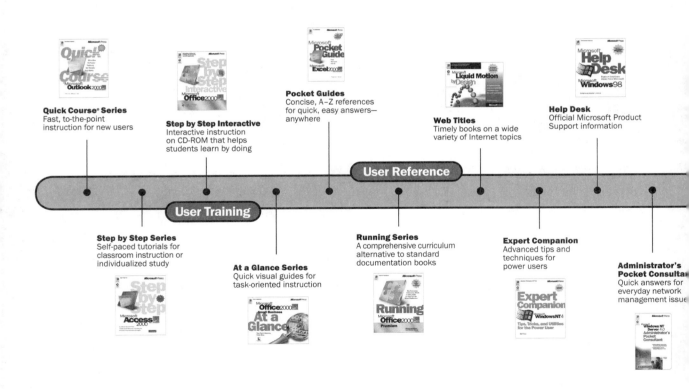

Quick Course® Series
Fast, to-the-point instruction for new users

Step by Step Interactive
Interactive instruction on CD-ROM that helps students learn by doing

Pocket Guides
Concise, A–Z references for quick, easy answers—anywhere

Web Titles
Timely books on a wide variety of Internet topics

Help Desk
Official Microsoft Product Support information

User Reference

User Training

Step by Step Series
Self-paced tutorials for classroom instruction or individualized study

At a Glance Series
Quick visual guides for task-oriented instruction

Running Series
A comprehensive curriculum alternative to standard documentation books

Expert Companion
Advanced tips and techniques for power users

Administrator's Pocket Consultant
Quick answers for everyday network management issues

Microsoft Press® products are available worldwide wherever quality computer books are sold. For more information, contact your book or computer retailer, software reseller, or local Microsoft Sales Office, or visit our Web site at mspress.microsoft.com. To locate your nearest source for Microsoft Press products, or to order directly, call 1-800-MSPRESS in the U.S. (in Canada, call 1-800-268-2222).

Prices and availability dates are subject to change.

With **over 200** *print,* *multimedia, and online resources—* whatever your information need or learning style, **we've got a solution** to help you *start faster and go farther.*

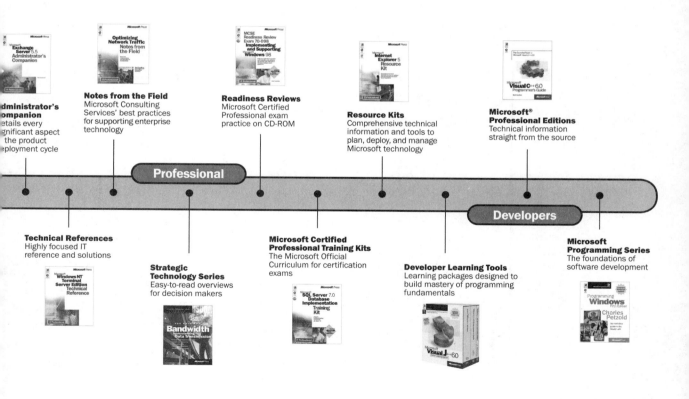

Exchange Server 5.5 Administrator's Companion

Administrator's Companion
Details every significant aspect of the product deployment cycle

Notes from the Field
Microsoft Consulting Services' best practices for supporting enterprise technology

Readiness Reviews
Microsoft Certified Professional exam practice on CD-ROM

Resource Kits
Comprehensive technical information and tools to plan, deploy, and manage Microsoft technology

Microsoft® Professional Editions
Technical information straight from the source

Professional

Developers

Technical References
Highly focused IT reference and solutions

Strategic Technology Series
Easy-to-read overviews for decision makers

Microsoft Certified Professional Training Kits
The Microsoft Official Curriculum for certification exams

Developer Learning Tools
Learning packages designed to build mastery of programming fundamentals

Microsoft Programming Series
The foundations of software development

Look for them at your bookstore or computer store today!

Microsoft®

mspress.microsoft.com

up! Step

STEP BY STEP books provide quick and easy self-training—to help you learn to use the powerful word processing, spreadsheet, database, presentation, communication, and Internet components of Microsoft® Office 2000—both individually and together. The easy-to-follow lessons present clear objectives and real-world business examples, with numerous screen shots and illustrations. Put Office 2000 to work today, with STEP BY STEP learning solutions, made by Microsoft.

- MICROSOFT OFFICE PROFESSONAL 8-IN-1 STEP BY STEP
- MICROSOFT WORD 2000 STEP BY STEP
- MICROSOFT EXCEL 2000 STEP BY STEP
- MICROSOFT POWERPOINT® 2000 STEP BY STEP
- MICROSOFT INTERNET EXPLORER 5 STEP BY STEP
- MICROSOFT PUBLISHER 2000 STEP BY STEP
- MICROSOFT ACCESS 2000 STEP BY STEP
- MICROSOFT FRONTPAGE 2000 STEP BY STEP
- MICROSOFT OUTLOOK 2000 STEP BY STEP

Microsoft Press® products are available worldwide wherever quality computer books are sold. For more information, contact your book or computer retailer, software reseller, or local Microsoft Sales Office, or visit our Web site at mspress.microsoft.com. To locate your nearest source for Microsoft Press products, or to order directly, call 1-800-MSPRESS in the U.S. (in Canada, call 1-800-268-2222).

Prices and availability dates are subject to change.

Microsoft®

mspress.microsoft.com

MICROSOFT LICENSE AGREEMENT
Book Companion CD

IMPORTANT—READ CAREFULLY: This Microsoft End-User License Agreement ("EULA") is a legal agreement between you (either an individual or an entity) and Microsoft Corporation for the Microsoft product identified above, which includes computer software and may include associated media, printed materials, and "on-line" or electronic documentation ("SOFTWARE PRODUCT"). Any component included within the SOFTWARE PRODUCT that is accompanied by a separate End-User License Agreement shall be governed by such agreement and not the terms set forth below. By installing, copying, or otherwise using the SOFTWARE PRODUCT, you agree to be bound by the terms of this EULA. If you do not agree to the terms of this EULA, you are not authorized to install, copy, or otherwise use the SOFTWARE PRODUCT; you may, however, return the SOFTWARE PRODUCT, along with all printed materials and other items that form a part of the Microsoft product that includes the SOFTWARE PRODUCT, to the place you obtained them for a full refund.

SOFTWARE PRODUCT LICENSE

The SOFTWARE PRODUCT is protected by United States copyright laws and international copyright treaties, as well as other intellectual property laws and treaties. The SOFTWARE PRODUCT is licensed, not sold.

1. GRANT OF LICENSE. This EULA grants you the following rights:

  a. Software Product. You may install and use one copy of the SOFTWARE PRODUCT on a single computer. The primary user of the computer on which the SOFTWARE PRODUCT is installed may make a second copy for his or her exclusive use on a portable computer.

  b. Storage/Network Use. You may also store or install a copy of the SOFTWARE PRODUCT on a storage device, such as a network server, used only to install or run the SOFTWARE PRODUCT on your other computers over an internal network; however, you must acquire and dedicate a license for each separate computer on which the SOFTWARE PRODUCT is installed or run from the storage device. A license for the SOFTWARE PRODUCT may not be shared or used concurrently on different computers.

  c. License Pak. If you have acquired this EULA in a Microsoft License Pak, you may make the number of additional copies of the computer software portion of the SOFTWARE PRODUCT authorized on the printed copy of this EULA, and you may use each copy in the manner specified above. You are also entitled to make a corresponding number of secondary copies for portable computer use as specified above.

  d. Sample Code. Solely with respect to portions, if any, of the SOFTWARE PRODUCT that are identified within the SOFTWARE PRODUCT as sample code (the "SAMPLE CODE"):

    i. Use and Modification. Microsoft grants you the right to use and modify the source code version of the SAMPLE CODE, *provided* you comply with subsection (d)(iii) below. You may not distribute the SAMPLE CODE, or any modified version of the SAMPLE CODE, in source code form.

    ii. Redistributable Files. Provided you comply with subsection (d)(iii) below, Microsoft grants you a nonexclusive, royalty-free right to reproduce and distribute the object code version of the SAMPLE CODE and of any modified SAMPLE CODE, other than SAMPLE CODE (or any modified version thereof) designated as not redistributable in the Readme file that forms a part of the SOFTWARE PRODUCT (the "Non-Redistributable Sample Code"). All SAMPLE CODE other than the Non-Redistributable Sample Code is collectively referred to as the "REDISTRIBUTABLES."

    iii. Redistribution Requirements. If you redistribute the REDISTRIBUTABLES, you agree to: (i) distribute the REDISTRIBUTABLES in object code form only in conjunction with and as a part of your software application product; (ii) not use Microsoft's name, logo, or trademarks to market your software application product; (iii) include a valid copyright notice on your software application product; (iv) indemnify, hold harmless, and defend Microsoft from and against any claims or lawsuits, including attorney's fees, that arise or result from the use or distribution of your software application product; and (v) not permit further distribution of the REDISTRIBUTABLES by your end user. Contact Microsoft for the applicable royalties due and other licensing terms for all other uses and/or distribution of the REDISTRIBUTABLES.

2. DESCRIPTION OF OTHER RIGHTS AND LIMITATIONS.

  • **Limitations on Reverse Engineering, Decompilation, and Disassembly.** You may not reverse engineer, decompile, or disassemble the SOFTWARE PRODUCT, except and only to the extent that such activity is expressly permitted by applicable law notwithstanding this limitation.

  • **Separation of Components.** The SOFTWARE PRODUCT is licensed as a single product. Its component parts may not be separated for use on more than one computer.

  • **Rental.** You may not rent, lease, or lend the SOFTWARE PRODUCT.

  • **Support Services.** Microsoft may, but is not obligated to, provide you with support services related to the SOFTWARE PRODUCT ("Support Services"). Use of Support Services is governed by the Microsoft policies and programs described in the user manual, in "on-line" documentation, and/or in other Microsoft-provided materials. Any supplemental software code provided to you as part of the Support Services shall be considered part of the SOFTWARE PRODUCT and subject to the terms and conditions of this EULA. With respect to technical information you provide to Microsoft as part of the Support Services, Microsoft may use such information for its business purposes, including for product support and development. Microsoft will not utilize such technical information in a form that personally identifies you.

- **Software Transfer.** You may permanently transfer all of your rights under this EULA, provided you retain no copies, you transfer all of the SOFTWARE PRODUCT (including all component parts, the media and printed materials, any upgrades, this EULA, and, if applicable, the Certificate of Authenticity), **and** the recipient agrees to the terms of this EULA.

- **Termination.** Without prejudice to any other rights, Microsoft may terminate this EULA if you fail to comply with the terms and conditions of this EULA. In such event, you must destroy all copies of the SOFTWARE PRODUCT and all of its component parts.

3. **COPYRIGHT.** All title and copyrights in and to the SOFTWARE PRODUCT (including but not limited to any images, photographs, animations, video, audio, music, text, SAMPLE CODE, REDISTRIBUTABLES, and "applets" incorporated into the SOFTWARE PRODUCT) and any copies of the SOFTWARE PRODUCT are owned by Microsoft or its suppliers. The SOFTWARE PRODUCT is protected by copyright laws and international treaty provisions. Therefore, you must treat the SOFTWARE PRODUCT like any other copyrighted material **except** that you may install the SOFTWARE PRODUCT on a single computer provided you keep the original solely for backup or archival purposes. You may not copy the printed materials accompanying the SOFTWARE PRODUCT.

4. **U.S. GOVERNMENT RESTRICTED RIGHTS.** The SOFTWARE PRODUCT and documentation are provided with RESTRICTED RIGHTS. Use, duplication, or disclosure by the Government is subject to restrictions as set forth in subparagraph (c)(1)(ii) of the Rights in Technical Data and Computer Software clause at DFARS 252.227-7013 or subparagraphs (c)(1) and (2) of the Commercial Computer Software—Restricted Rights at 48 CFR 52.227-19, as applicable. Manufacturer is Microsoft Corporation/One Microsoft Way/Redmond, WA 98052-6399.

5. **EXPORT RESTRICTIONS.** You agree that you will not export or re-export the SOFTWARE PRODUCT, any part thereof, or any process or service that is the direct product of the SOFTWARE PRODUCT (the foregoing collectively referred to as the "Restricted Components"), to any country, person, entity, or end user subject to U.S. export restrictions. You specifically agree not to export or re-export any of the Restricted Components (i) to any country to which the U.S. has embargoed or restricted the export of goods or services, which currently include, but are not necessarily limited to, Cuba, Iran, Iraq, Libya, North Korea, Sudan, and Syria, or to any national of any such country, wherever located, who intends to transmit or transport the Restricted Components back to such country; (ii) to any end user who you know or have reason to know will utilize the Restricted Components in the design, development, or production of nuclear, chemical, or biological weapons; or (iii) to any end user who has been prohibited from participating in U.S. export transactions by any federal agency of the U.S. government. You warrant and represent that neither the BXA nor any other U.S. federal agency has suspended, revoked, or denied your export privileges.

6. **NOTE ON JAVA SUPPORT.** THE SOFTWARE PRODUCT MAY CONTAIN SUPPORT FOR PROGRAMS WRITTEN IN JAVA. JAVA TECHNOLOGY IS NOT FAULT TOLERANT AND IS NOT DESIGNED, MANUFACTURED, OR INTENDED FOR USE OR RESALE AS ON-LINE CONTROL EQUIPMENT IN HAZARDOUS ENVIRONMENTS REQUIRING FAIL-SAFE PERFORMANCE, SUCH AS IN THE OPERATION OF NUCLEAR FACILITIES, AIRCRAFT NAVIGATION OR COMMUNICATION SYSTEMS, AIR TRAFFIC CONTROL, DIRECT LIFE SUPPORT MACHINES, OR WEAPONS SYSTEMS, IN WHICH THE FAILURE OF JAVA TECHNOLOGY COULD LEAD DIRECTLY TO DEATH, PERSONAL INJURY, OR SEVERE PHYSICAL OR ENVIRONMENTAL DAMAGE. SUN MICROSYSTEMS, INC. HAS CONTRACTUALLY OBLIGATED MICROSOFT TO MAKE THIS DISCLAIMER.

DISCLAIMER OF WARRANTY

NO WARRANTIES OR CONDITIONS. MICROSOFT EXPRESSLY DISCLAIMS ANY WARRANTY OR CONDITION FOR THE SOFTWARE PRODUCT. THE SOFTWARE PRODUCT AND ANY RELATED DOCUMENTATION IS PROVIDED "AS IS" WITHOUT WARRANTY OR CONDITION OF ANY KIND, EITHER EXPRESS OR IMPLIED, INCLUDING, WITHOUT LIMITATION, THE IMPLIED WARRANTIES OF MERCHANTABILITY, FITNESS FOR A PARTICULAR PURPOSE, OR NONINFRINGEMENT. THE ENTIRE RISK ARISING OUT OF USE OR PERFORMANCE OF THE SOFTWARE PRODUCT REMAINS WITH YOU.

LIMITATION OF LIABILITY. TO THE MAXIMUM EXTENT PERMITTED BY APPLICABLE LAW, IN NO EVENT SHALL MICROSOFT OR ITS SUPPLIERS BE LIABLE FOR ANY SPECIAL, INCIDENTAL, INDIRECT, OR CONSEQUENTIAL DAMAGES WHATSOEVER (INCLUDING, WITHOUT LIMITATION, DAMAGES FOR LOSS OF BUSINESS PROFITS, BUSINESS INTERRUPTION, LOSS OF BUSINESS INFORMATION, OR ANY OTHER PECUNIARY LOSS) ARISING OUT OF THE USE OF OR INABILITY TO USE THE SOFTWARE PRODUCT OR THE PROVISION OF OR FAILURE TO PROVIDE SUPPORT SERVICES, EVEN IF MICROSOFT HAS BEEN ADVISED OF THE POSSIBILITY OF SUCH DAMAGES. IN ANY CASE, MICROSOFT'S ENTIRE LIABILITY UNDER ANY PROVISION OF THIS EULA SHALL BE LIMITED TO THE GREATER OF THE AMOUNT ACTUALLY PAID BY YOU FOR THE SOFTWARE PRODUCT OR US$5.00; PROVIDED, HOWEVER, IF YOU HAVE ENTERED INTO A MICROSOFT SUPPORT SERVICES AGREEMENT, MICROSOFT'S ENTIRE LIABILITY REGARDING SUPPORT SERVICES SHALL BE GOVERNED BY THE TERMS OF THAT AGREEMENT. BECAUSE SOME STATES AND JURISDICTIONS DO NOT ALLOW THE EXCLUSION OR LIMITATION OF LIABILITY, THE ABOVE LIMITATION MAY NOT APPLY TO YOU.

MISCELLANEOUS

This EULA is governed by the laws of the State of Washington USA, except and only to the extent that applicable law mandates governing law of a different jurisdiction.

Should you have any questions concerning this EULA, or if you desire to contact Microsoft for any reason, please contact the Microsoft subsidiary serving your country, or write: Microsoft Sales Information Center/One Microsoft Way/Redmond, WA 98052-6399.

Register Today!

Return this
Running Microsoft® FrontPage® 2000
registration card today

mspress.microsoft.com

OWNER REGISTRATION CARD

1-57231-947-X

Running Microsoft® FrontPage® 2000

_____   _____   _____
FIRST NAME   MIDDLE INITIAL   LAST NAME

_____
INSTITUTION OR COMPANY NAME

_____
ADDRESS

_____

_____   _____   _____
CITY   STATE   ZIP

_____   ( ) _____
E-MAIL ADDRESS   PHONE NUMBER

U.S. and Canada addresses only. Fill in information above and mail postage-free.
Please mail only the bottom half of this page.

For information about Microsoft Press®
products, visit our Web site at
mspress.microsoft.com

Microsoft ·Press

||||

IIlıIıIılıIIIlıIııIıɪIııIIIlIıIıIıııIıIIIIıɪɪıIIlI